THE EARLY YEARS FOUNDATION STAGE

THEORY AND PRACTICE

EDITED BY

IOANNA PALAIOLOGOU

3RD EDITION

SAGE

Los Angeles | London | New Delhi
Singapore | Washington DC | Melbourne

Los Angeles | London | New Delhi
Singapore | Washington DC | Melbourne

SAGE Publications Ltd
1 Oliver's Yard
55 City Road
London EC1Y 1SP

SAGE Publications Inc.
2455 Teller Road
Thousand Oaks, California 91320

SAGE Publications India Pvt Ltd
B 1/I 1 Mohan Cooperative Industrial Area
Mathura Road
New Delhi 110 044

SAGE Publications Asia-Pacific Pte Ltd
3 Church Street
#10-04 Samsung Hub
Singapore 049483

Publisher: Jude Bowen
Assistant editor: George Knowles
Production editor: Nicola Marshall
Copyeditor: Elaine Leek
Proofreader: Emily Ayers
Indexer: Silvia Benvenuto
Marketing manager: Lorna Patkai
Cover design: Wendy Scott
Typeset by: C&M Digitals (P) Ltd, Chennai, India
Printed and bound in Great Britain by Ashford
Colour Press Ltd

First Edition Published 2010 (Reprinted 2011)
Second Edition Published 2013 (Reprinted 2014 & 2015)
Third Edition Published 2016

Library of Congress Control Number: 2015948412

British Library Cataloguing in Publication data

A catalogue record for this book is available from
the British Library

ISBN 978-1-47390-820-8 (pbk)
ISBN 978-1-47390-819-2

THE EARLY YEARS FOUNDATION STAGE

SAGE was founded in 1965 by Sara Miller McCune to support the dissemination of usable knowledge by publishing innovative and high-quality research and teaching content. Today, we publish over 900 journals, including those of more than 400 learned societies, more than 800 new books per year, and a growing range of library products including archives, data, case studies, reports, and video. SAGE remains majority-owned by our founder, and after Sara's lifetime will become owned by a charitable trust that secures our continued independence.

Los Angeles | London | New Delhi | Singapore | Washington DC | Melbourne

To my Dad

Contents

Contributors

About the Editor

Ioanna Palaiologou

 Ioanna Palaiologou is an Associate at the Institute of Education, University College London, Centre for Leadership in Learning. She is a Chartered Psychologist with the British Psychological Society, and works as an independent psychologist with a specialism in child development and learning theories. During her time in HE she has worked for five universities and among her main responsibilities have been supervision of postgraduate research students and mentoring early career researchers. Her research interests are focused on ethics in research, child development and implications for pedagogy and the epistemic nature of pedagogy.

About the Contributors

Babs Anderson

Babs Anderson is a Lecturer in Early Childhood at Liverpool Hope University. Her research interests include young children's collaborative learning, including when playing in continuous provision, the use of language as a cultural tool, young children's thinking skills, Education for Sustainable Development and the co-construction of knowledge and understanding, within adult–child dyads, child–child dyads and collaborative groups. Babs is a co-convenor of the EECERA Special Interest Group 'Holistic well-being'.

Lorna Arnott

Lorna Arnott is a Lecturer in the School of Education, University of Strathclyde. Lorna's main area of interest is in children's early experiences with technologies, particularly in relation to social and creative play. She also has a keen interest in research methodologies, with a specialist focus on consulting with children. Lorna is the convener for the Digital Childhoods Special Interest Group as part of the European Early Childhood Educational Research Association.

Gary Beauchamp

Gary Beauchamp is Professor of Education and Associate Dean (Research) in the School of Education at Cardiff Metropolitan University. He worked for many years as a primary school teacher, before moving into higher education where he has led undergraduate and postgraduate courses in education. His research interests focus on ICT in education, particularly the use of interactive technologies in learning and teaching. He has published widely in academic journals, books and research reports. In addition he is Additional Inspector for Estyn, Chair of Governor in a primary school and has served as external examiner for many universities.

John Bennett

John Bennett is a Lecturer in Education at the University of Hull. His PhD included a significant focus on the potential impact of the original National Curriculum on personal, social and moral education in primary schools, and his research interests have continued to be around those areas. Before moving into working in higher education, he was a primary school headteacher and in his twenty-five years working in primary schools he also acted as a curriculum support teacher, working with many different settings.

Elizabeth Dunphy

Liz Dunphy is Senior Lecturer in Early Childhood Education at St Patrick's College (Institute of Education, Dublin City University), Ireland. Her research interests include young children's mathematics, early childhood pedagogy and the assessment of early learning. She has recently been responsible for the development of the Institute's new Bachelor in Early Childhood Education (BECE) which welcomed its first cohort of students in September 2015. Recent publications include two research reports for the National Council for Curriculum and Assessment in Ireland (with colleagues Dr Therese Dooley and Dr Gerry Shiel). These are *Research Report No. 17: Mathematics in Early Childhood and Primary Education (3–8 years): Definitions, Theories, Development and Progressions*; and *Research Report No. 18: Mathematics in Early Childhood and Primary Education (3–8 years): Teaching and Learning* (see www.ncca.ie).

Cheryl Ellis

Cheryl Ellis is a Principal Lecturer on the Education Studies and Early Childhood Studies degrees at Cardiff Metropolitan University. She is a member of the university's outdoor learning team and regularly works with children and students within Forest School. Her key areas of research interest include outdoor learning and play, inclusion and additional learning needs. Having previously worked as a primary school teacher, Cheryl has experienced the 'practical realities' of classroom life.

Michiko Fujii

Michiko Fujii is an artist and creative practitioner based in the North West of England. She has worked on a number of creative learning projects in schools, centres and galleries since 2005. Her Masters research focused upon the role of the artist as both an outsider and collaborative educator within the early years. Michiko continues to fuse her practice as a visual artist with her ongoing work as a creative practitioner working with different learner groups.

Laura Grindley

Laura Grindley is a qualified early years professional with a BA Hons degree in Early Childhood Studies and has subsequently worked in nursery settings in Children's Centres in Merseyside. She has taken on many additional roles, including Early Years Professional Coordinator and Early Years Professional Mentor and has been published in *Nursery World* and *Impact* magazines.

Chantelle Haughton

Chantelle Haughton is a Senior Lecturer in Education Studies and Early Childhood Studies. In addition to her full-time lecturing role; Chantelle initiates and coordinates outdoor play and learning projects within campus-based woodlands in partnership with local primary schools and other external partners. Previously, Chantelle worked in a diverse range of roles and settings in education, community work and business. Her current research interests stem from connecting theoretical perspectives and real-life practice in outdoor play and learning through current active engagement with external stakeholders on a range of projects providing scope for strategic insight.

Claire Head

Claire Head is Lecturer in Primary English and Early Years Education on undergraduate and postgraduate degree programmes at the University of Hull, Scarborough Campus. Her research interests centre on dialogic teaching approaches to early reading, early literacy, the multi-lingual classroom, collaborative approaches to learning and early years pedagogy and practice. Claire formerly worked as a primary school teacher in Bradford, where she assumed leadership responsibility for English and assessment across the curriculum and was the coordinator for Special Educational Needs, Early Years and Key Stage 1.

Sally Howard

Sally Howard has been a teacher, headteacher, education consultant, Ofsted inspector, university lecturer and midwife. She is currently a researcher at Kings College London engaged in a large European Project exploring assessment and inquiry science (SAIlS). She is the co-author of the highly successful book 'Inside the Primary Black Box: Assessment for Learning in Primary and Early Years Classrooms' and has written a number of other publications and presented at conferences around the world relating to learning and assessment.

Angie Hutchinson

Angie Hutchinson is a Specialist Leader of Education (Early Years), where she enjoys supporting leaders in their settings; she also teaches in a Foundation Stage class. She has led a large Foundation Stage Unit and has been a Senior Leader in a primary school. Angie has also been the module leader for Early Child Development module on a BA (Hons) Education and Early Years course. She graduated with a First Class BA (Hons) in Educational Studies, specialising in early childhood, and more recently attained MEd with Distinction where the focus for the dissertation was UK educational policy versus the social and emotional learning in young children.

Anna Knowles

Anna Knowles has worked in early education for a number of years and currently works as a teacher at McMillan Nursery School in Hull. When working with families in a family support role, she developed a particular interest in effective engagement of parents. Working closely with parents and carers, to support the learning and development of the child, continues to be an area of research interest. She has lectured in the areas of child observation and working with young children at the University of Hull and worked as a placement mentor for degree students.

Paulette Luff

Paulette Luff is Senior Lecturer in the Department of Education at Anglia Ruskin University (in Chelmsford) where she leads the MA in Early Childhood Education and teaches on other early years degree courses. For the past ten years, much of Paulette's research has focused on the topic of child observation and its role in the planning, implementation and evaluation of early childhood curricula. Paulette has worked in the field of early childhood throughout her career, as a teacher, foster carer, school–home liaison worker, nursery practitioner and adviser, and as a lecturer in further and higher education.

Natalie Macdonald

Natalie Macdonald is a researcher with the Wales Centre for Equity in Education, looking at Policy, Practice and Research; with a focus on early years provision, pedagogy, additional needs, and the impact of poverty on attainment, qualifications and professional development for the childcare workforce in Wales. Natalie has over seven years' experience of working within Flying Start and primary school environments, particularly in areas of multiple deprivation.

Sarah MacQuarrie

Sarah MacQuarrie is a lecturer in Psychology of Education at the Manchester Institute of Education, University of Manchester. Her research is focused on the application of psychology in education and considers the relationship between theory and practice in education, in particular investigating ways to support the implementation of research-based practice. Sarah is a Chartered Psychologist and Associate Fellow of the British Psychological Society.

Trevor Male

Trevor Male is a Senior Lecturer at UCL Institute of Education, working in the London Centre for Leadership in Learning. He has worked in education for over forty years, including full-time employment in universities as a Senior Lecturer in

Education for the last half of his career. In 2014 he was admitted as a Fellow to the Royal Society of Arts and also appointed as a member of the Associate Analytic Pool to the UK Department for Education. His research now concentrates on the concepts of pedagogical leadership and the use of digital technologies in learning.

Estelle Martin

Estelle Martin is Senior Lecturer in Early Childhood and Education Studies at the University of East London, where she is Programme Leader for the MA in Early Childhood. Her research interests focus on emotional and social development and learning in childhood. Estelle's PhD research has included children's participation and the role of emotions and learning in early childhood.

David Needham

David Needham is Senior Lecturer in the School of Education at Nottingham Trent University. In his current role he supervises a number of research students. David's evolving research interests have focused upon and related to how young people learn within the business classroom, as well as enterprise education. His recent work has focused upon notions of art or science within education, the influence of reflexivity upon teacher trainees' experiences within the classroom, as well as those of staff new to higher education teaching.

Graham Needham

Graham Needham has been both a Sampford and Oldroyd mathematics prize winner from the University of Liverpool, and a former colleague of Dr Ian Porteous, whom he accompanied on many Fun Maths Roadshows. Graham graduated with First Class Honours in his MMath. Since then he has developed an eclectic range of interests, while teaching mathematics at Loughborough High School.

Nyree Nicholson

Nyree Nicholson is Senior Lecturer in Applied Studies at Bishop Grosseteste University in Lincoln. She worked for eleven years as a childminder and spent twenty years as a local authority foster carer, in addition to being a Programme Leader on an Early Years degree course. Nyree also sits on a steering committee for SEND (Special Educational

Needs and Disabilities) reforms in Hull. Nyree has an interest in young children's speech and language, and how this can be developed through an integrated approach from multi-agency working.

Zoi Nikiforidou

Zoi Nikiforidou is Lecturer in Early Childhood at Liverpool Hope University. She is teaching undergraduate and postgraduate courses, and has been a kindergarten teacher in Greece. Her research interests relate to both methodological and theoretical issues in teaching and learning, considering the role of technology, pedagogy and cognition. Her main focus is on aspects of cognitive development in early childhood, specifically, young children's reasoning, decision making, probabilistic thinking and risk taking. Zoi is a co-convenor of the EECERA Special Interest Group 'Holistic well-being'.

Clare Nugent

Clare Nugent is Lecturer at the University of Edinburgh. Following a PGCE in outdoor education, Clare taught in both the state and private sectors before a move to Scotland. She received her MEd in Early Childhood Education from the University of Edinburgh in 2007 and is now completing her PhD: a comparative account of three case studies of nature kindergartens in Denmark, Finland and Scotland. The aim of this research is to better understand nature-based practice as constructed in different socio-cultural contexts.

Alex Owen

Alex Owen is Head of Department: Early Childhood at Liverpool Hope University. Her research focuses on the impact of poverty upon young children's current life experiences and future life chances. Alex's research explores how engagement with informal social support networks has value in terms of a parent's mental well-being and a parent's peer education; both of which support a parent's ability to parent a young child appropriately within a context of poverty. She is a Senior Fellow of the HEA and a trustee for Oasis Community Learning, one of the largest multi-Academy sponsors in England.

Nick Owen

Nick Owen MBE is a producer, educator and writer who has spent over thirty years developing arts education practice in community and cultural contexts across the UK and internationally. He was the first Head of Community Arts at the Liverpool Institute of Performing Arts (LIPA) between 1994 and 2002. Here, he initiated and developed the UK's first full-time performing arts course in Higher Education for Disabled People. He was awarded Honorary Fellowships in Education at both the University of Hull, UK and University of Tasmania, Australia in 2012.

Theodora Papatheodorou

Theodora Papatheodorou, PhD; MBPsS, is Professorial Fellow in Early Childhood at Liverpool Hope University and an independent early childhood educator and researcher. Previously she worked at Save the Children, UK, as education adviser and in several higher education institutions holding different posts. She started her career as a preschool teacher and worked with young children in mainstream, bilingual and special education settings. Theodora has conducted extensive research on several topics in the field of early childhood, and disseminated results in different formats and for different audiences.

Donna Potts

Donna Potts' interest in early years began in 1987 when she became mother to her son, followed by her daughter in 1989. The raising of her children inspired a passion in the developmental early years and she volunteered to help in their classes when they started school. This led to the offer of a teaching assistant job and after ten fulfilling years she was encouraged to consider a career in teaching. She qualified as a teacher in 2006 and has recently retired from full-time teaching to spend more time with her family, teaching on a supply basis.

Carolyn Silberfeld

Carolyn Silberfeld spent twenty-one years developing and leading Early Childhood Studies degrees. She is Chair/Director of the ECS Degrees Network and has contributed to all aspects of the development of ECS degrees, including development of the QAA ECS Benchmark statements, and practitioners' options. During the last twenty years Carolyn coordinated several international projects, including student exchanges to Europe, Africa, Australia and North America. Her research interests include reflective learning in higher education; the influence of studying abroad; post course destinations and employment opportunities for ECS graduates; and the impact of the EYFS on professional practice and the subsequent effects on children's learning and development.

Glenda Walsh

Glenda Walsh is Head of Early Years Education at Stranmillis University College, a College of Queen's University Belfast. Her research interests focus on quality issues in Early Childhood Education, particularly in the field of pedagogy and curriculum. She played a significant role in the longitudinal evaluation of the Early Years Enriched Curriculum Project in Northern Ireland that has guided the course of the Foundation Stage of the revised Northern Ireland Primary Curriculum. Her interests in curriculum and pedagogy also involved her in heading a project on examining pedagogy in Early Childhood Education for the Department of Education in the Republic of Ireland.

Jane Waters

Jane Waters is Head of the South West Wales Centre of Teacher Education, based in the University of Wales Trinity Saint David. Jane's research interests lie in early childhood education, adult–child interaction in educative spaces, young children's agency and voice, and young children's experiences of outdoor spaces. Current research projects include working with national and international colleagues to consider pedagogy related to outdoor provision in early education contexts. This project further extends Jane's doctoral research that focused on adult–child interaction, sustained shared thinking and the affordance of different educative spaces.

Chris Williamson

Chris Williamson is an Assistant Head specialising in the EYFS and English as an additional language (EAL) at a primary school in the East Midlands. She draws on her depth of experience as a teacher within primary and EYFS settings to enhance children's learning through play, drama and storytelling. Her early background in drama shines through her ability to tell amazing stories and enhance and engage learners of all ages.

Mark Wilson

Mark Wilson Fellow of the Higher Education Academy, is a Lecturer in Childhood and Education Studies at the University of East London, and prior to that he used to be particularly engaged with the work of NGOs around the world. He now delivers lectures on the historic, contemporary and future issues relating to the debates and controversies surrounding globalisation – with an emphasis on the ongoing effects that globally-influential cultural, political and economic flows have on families, childhood and education.

Foreword

Early childhood education and care: enhancing effective practice

This new edition has been updated, shaped, and re-formed by an experienced editor who has drawn together highly skilled commentators who have produced chapters which are informative and thought provoking. The result is a book which is much more than a description of the Early Years Foundation Stage and involves a close examination of wider facets of early learning. A central theme within the book is a recognition of the way quality early education and care improves the life chances of children, which is important both economically and socially. It also recognises that quality early learning is influenced by a whole variety of factors as well as the design of the curriculum. Some are easily identified, such as the availability of Government finance, the ratio between children and adults, the requirements of inspection services or the physical resources a setting has available. Others are less visible and may be driven by policies which see quality early education and care as enhancing employment opportunities, or a means to lessen disadvantage or a way to prepare young children for school. However, one factor in particular will have a pronounced influence on the distinctiveness of provision, and that is the quality of interactions between educators and children and the influence of those leading practice. This is especially effective when the leader engages colleagues in a process that involves a close examination of the characteristics of effective learning. They are then in a position to consider what learning opportunities need to be refined and how best to monitor progress. It is an approach reliant on a clear understanding of curriculum requirements and this provides educators with an opportunity to come together and consciously consider how best to help children learn. A process which can be aided by reading the chapter provocations in this book because they consider the influence of the curriculum and wider features including the values and beliefs that underpin early learning. They are features which encompass quite complex issues such as the welfare of the child and the importance of seeing the child's parents and carers as first educators. They also encompass the importance of maintaining positive relationships with other professionals.

The focus on children's learning is clearly visible within the book as is the value of promoting children's interests and there are chapters which explain why these features are essential components of collective ongoing evaluation. A view which will help educators to look beyond curriculum outcomes and outputs and consider how best to refine and shape the learning environment children inhabit. An important aspect of promoting effective learning. It is therefore wise to see the chapters as providing an interrelationship between how children think and learn, the influence of national policies and how these impact upon day-to-day practice. This may well form the basis for new understandings and actions which can encourage innovative approaches. In particular, if these are seen as valuable to a local setting as well as meeting the requirements of the statutory curriculum.

It is a book which offers a close examination of early learning. It informs the reader and provokes questions. This is important because as soon as questions are asked they influence how the curriculum is seen in practice and its relationship with the learning environment. They also touch upon moral and social issues. The book therefore enhances effective practice, because developing a detailed knowledge of curriculum requirements and challenging assumptions ensures a deep consideration of what children should learn and how they learn.

Michael Reed, Senior Lecturer at the Centre for Early Childhood, within the Institute of Education at the University of Worcester.

Preface

The implementation of the Early Years Foundation Stage (EYFS) opened to public debate the issues of what constitutes effective practice, what should be done in the early years sector, and how the optimum programme should be delivered. The first edition of this book *Early Years Foundation Stage: Theory and Practice* (2010) was written when all of us working in the sector were learning to work with the EYFS. That first edition aimed to invite all readers to share a critical analysis of the EYFS by taking a journey into political, social and pedagogical analyses in order to search for an effective implementation of the EYFS and its impact on the sector.

In the light of the publication of the revised EYFS in March 2012, and thanks to your valuable feedback as users of the book, the book published in its second edition in 2013. This improved edition aimed to maintain the same ethos of balancing theory and practice, so that students would be able to develop a critical approach to key issues around the EYFS.

Since then the sector has seen more changes, so a third edition is considered timely and necessary. In order to develop a book that students will continue to find helpful, alongside the old elements such as reflective tasks, case studies and pedagogical features such as discussion points to encourage critical reflection, we expand further on theory, yet without losing the focus on practice, and we are including a new Companion Website where students can find additional materials and a number of examples.

In this new edition you will notice that there is a shift away from the term 'early years education and care' to '*early childhood education and care*'. These two terms have been used in the sector as synonymous, but we feel that in this book we try to bridge theory and practice and so we propose that the term *early childhood education and care* is appropriate. In the sector for many years there has been an increasing search for effective pedagogy, for common spaces where children and adults come together (workforce, parents, community), searching for in-depth understanding of early childhood education and care. There is much debate as to the extent to which Early Childhood Studies is an academic subject, or a discipline, in the field of education. In contributing to this discourse, this book has now shifted to using the term *early childhood education and care* as a way of adding to the creation of an epistemology of our study. We feel that a textbook has a duty to offer students a critical approach to key themes, but at the same time has an obligation and accountability to the field of early childhood to use a terminology that is meaningful. This book thus seeks to move away from a didactic approach and aims to enact the search for knowing in education in a way that means we all learn and develop knowledge together.

As demonstrated throughout this book, in an era where policy makers are driving a standardised agenda, we, as the people who are working, studying and researching the lives of young children, need to make a standpoint to unify terminology that will shape our provision on the ground and demonstrate scholarship in relation to theory and practice. In that sense, early childhood education and care should be acknowledged as a body of knowledge that is recognised as valid and important in its own right, in the hope that this will be transmitted to policy makers. Thus there is a deliberate intention in this book to go beyond the 'how to do' simplistic approach and focus on 'why we do'.

In previous editions this book tried to show how children can develop, learn and enjoy in early childhood education and care. Has anything been added to our knowledge, has anything been learned, can anything change? The best way to answer these questions is to listen to a student at the end of her degree:

> This year was for me a stream of knowledge [...] I cannot remember everything, but at least I think I know the way now. Theory can become practice, I just have to understand the theory, but I feel I need support. In our degree, we are always told what we have to do, but they never tell us why [...] It seemed so easy when you know the 'how', but I prefer to know the 'why'. This is the only way for me to be able to do what I have learnt. (Claudia, 2015)

Although the EYFS has been welcomed generally as an overarching framework of guidance for practice in early childhood education and care, there is still some scepticism around its implementation, especially with its inherent emphasis on 'school readiness'. Some contributors to this book draw attention to the statutory nature of the EYFS assessment profile, the inspection of settings, the emphasis on school readiness and argue this is not so much demonstrating a culture of framework and guidance as displaying characteristics of a central, prescribed and standardised curriculum. The EYFS, it is argued, thus continues to represent a totality and control of the learning and development assistance provided through education and care to support children from birth to 5 years of age and is underpinned by a raft of statutory and non-statutory guidance that forms the framework for inspection and accountability. In the light of these developments, this edition of the book aims to offer a critical examination of the EYFS through political, social and pedagogical lenses. Continuing with the tone of the first and second editions, this book does not aim to become a guide to implementing the EYFS; rather it aims to offer an in-depth understanding of key issues in early childhood education and care and consider how these can be applied. This edition is based, therefore, on the belief that practitioners need to develop a theoretical understanding and in-depth knowledge of key issues of pedagogy in order to be able to reflect and mirror these in their practice.

We consider the way forward in early childhood education and care is to raise the quality of provision, which may be achieved in a plethora of ways. Thus this book aims to bring a number of voices through the authors' chapters. It is essential that we 'listen' to pluralistic 'voices' in order to make informed decisions and not just simply accept practices that meet government requirements. Thus the tone of each author's 'voice' has not been changed. Consequently, the collective focus of the book suggests that in early childhood education and care, the EYFS should be implemented in an effective way in order to create a learning environment for young children where play is central, rather than as a preparation for school. While the current policy in which early childhood education and care is situated is both exciting and challenging, it remains imperative that we rise to the challenge of critically reflecting upon how we are positioned, and how we seek to construct an early childhood pedagogy.

This new third edition is divided into four parts:

Part 1 discusses the policy context from which the Early Years Foundation Stage emerged and offers an overview of the national picture. It also engages with the international perspectives and problematises the issue of professionalism in early childhood education and care. It comprises five chapters:

Chapter 1   Historical developments in policy for early childhood education and care

Chapter 2   Early Years Foundation Stage

Chapter 3   The national picture

Chapter 4   The international perspective on early childhood education and care

Chapter 5   The issue of professionalism

Part 2 deals with key issues on pedagogy. Chapter 6 discusses the essence of the concept of pedagogy, Chapter 7 explores the role of play in early childhood, Chapters 8 and 9 focus on the key aspects of pedagogical observation and assessment. Chapters 10, 11 and 12 explore key issues of early childhood practice around the use of documentation as an example of effective practice, effective transitions and, finally, the importance of the outdoor environments. This Part includes the following chapters:

Chapter 6   Pedagogy in practice

Chapter 7   Play

Chapter 8   Observations: recording and analysis

Chapter 9   Assessment

Chapter 10   Pedagogical documentation

Chapter 11   Effective transitions

Chapter 12   Using the outdoor environment in early childhood pedagogy

Part 3 focuses on key aspects of implementing the EYFS that are related to the multi/inter-agency ethos. It includes the following chapters:

Chapter 13   Working in partnership with parents

Chapter 14   Working together to safeguard children

Chapter 15   Children's health and well-being

Chapter 16   Inclusion

Chapter 17   Leadership

Chapter 18   The role of digital technologies

Finally, **Part 4** explores the prime and specific areas of the Early Learning Goals within the EYFS. All seven chapters offer a theoretical approach to these areas of development:

Chapter 19   Personal, social and emotional development

Chapter 20   Communication and language

Chapter 21   Literacy

Chapter 22   Mathematics

Chapter 23   Understanding the world

Chapter 24   Physical development

Chapter 25   Expressive arts and design

As an editor, I have been overwhelmed by how previous editions of the book have been received by academics, students and practitioners. As I said above, the aim of the book is to learn together so we as editor and contributing authors hope that our work on this third edition will continue to provide clear guidance for early childhood students. We have aimed to create a book offering students a knowledgeable, holistic understanding of early childhood education and care that they will be able to apply effectively within the EYFS, while also developing their critical skills.

Ioanna Palaiologou

Acknowledgements

This book could not have been completed without the help of the people who gave us permission to use observations of their children or material from their settings. We would like to thank the following people:

Anastasia, David, George and
Harry Hollings

Melvin King Childminders, Liverpool   Childhaven Nursery School, Scarborough

Aspire Trust, Merseyside   Ruth Spencer Nursery School, Hull

Creative Partnerships, Hull   The Lemon Tree Nursery at Bude

Croxteth Children's Centre, Liverpool   Children's Centre, Hull

Jude Bird   Childhaven Nursery School, Scarborough

Andrew Shimmin and the staff in
McMillan Nursery, Hull

I would also like to thank all the chapter authors for their contributions. Without them, this book would have not happened.

A great thank you as always to the team at SAGE for their support and help: Jude Bowen and George Knowles. But also to the people at SAGE whom I worked with on the previous editions: Robin Lupton and Amy Jarrold.

Last but not least, thank you to all lecturers and students in early childhood studies who have supported this book and continue to support it with their choice to use it as core or supplementary reading.

Reviews of previous editions

Praise for the First Edition ...

Essential book for every student interested in the Early Years. Up-to-date information and good examples of practices.

Paivi Valtonen, Education, Grimsby Institute of Further and Higher Education

A book that is very appropriate for students engaged in the study of early years policy and practice. Clear, well focused and enables students to reflect on practice.

Michael Reed, Institute of Education, Worcester University

An accessible and practical guide for students working in the Early Years. The layout ensures that the reader can access relevant material quickly. A very good resource book for practice.

Judy Gracey, Education, Canterbury Christ Church University

This book is an essential text for all students undertaking a degree or foundation degree in early childhood studies. It is informative, readable and undeniably the practitioner's bible to gaining insight into the theory, policy and application of this distinct phase of education. Excellent read.

Joanne Hall, Health, Care and Early Years, Blackpool and the Fylde College

The text encourages a critical approach to existing and new frameworks that is essential for current practitioners to extend their understanding and awareness of the influences at work within early years and education.

Chelle Davison, Education, Leeds Metropolitan University

Praise for the Second Edition ...

A brilliant overview of the EYFS, definitely recommended reading for a Level 3 in children and young people's workforce.

Mrs Liz Tomlin, Early years, Adult Education Centre

A fantastic resource to signpost students to help develop an enhanced understanding of the origins of the Early Years Foundation Stage along with how to develop their practice in line with current guidance. Very informative, great to challenge Level 3 students and consolidate knowledge for Level 4 and beyond.

Mrs Caroline Guard, School of Applied and Health Sciences,
Farnborough College of Technology

This really captures all the aspects required for my students – clearly formatted and easy to navigate. Explores contemporary issues – provides background. Excellent.

Mrs Sarah Barton, School of Education, Portsmouth University

The 2nd edition by Palaiologou (2013) is a must have. The *Early Years Foundation Stage: Theory and Practice* edition contains over 300 pages of policy, pedagogy, practice and the areas of learning and development in revised EYFS across an early years arena. The book links theory to practice impeccably through several hands on case studies and activities which makes the reading enjoyable and practical. Excellent resource for students studying for their foundation degree in Early Childhood Education.

Mrs Paivi Valtonen, Education, Grimsby Institute of
Further and Higher Education

Companion Website

This new edition of *The Early Years Foundation Stage* is supported by a wealth of online resources which you can access at https://study.sagepub.com/EYFS3e

Visit the website to:

- *Access* a selection of free SAGE journal articles supplementing each chapter. Ideal for your literature review!
- *Follow* web links which direct you to useful websites to further your study and support you in practice.
- *Check out* further readings to expand your knowledge.
- *Read* about some of the key contributors to the development of early years provision.
- *Explore* more examples of case studies and assessments.

PART 1
POLICY
CONTEXT

Historical Developments in Policy for Early Childhood Education and Care

Trevor Male and Ioanna Palaiologou

 Chapter overview

The Early Years Foundation Stage (EYFS), described by the Department for Children, Schools and Families (DCSF) as 'a comprehensive framework which sets the standards for learning, development and care of children from birth to five', was first introduced for early childhood providers and schools from September 2008, with revisions made in 2012 and updates in 2014. The introduction of the EYFS thus ended a history of nearly 200 years of discussion and debate surrounding the philosophy, purpose and provision for early childhood education and care in the UK, a period where policy had been advisory rather than statutory. The discussion regarding the appropriateness of the EYFS still continues (as will be seen elsewhere in this book), but finally government policy has been clarified and ratified.

There have been several key reports and Acts of Parliament through the last two centuries that have shaped the nature of provision for children up to the age of 5 years, with most of those elements still evident at the time this book is published. The 1870 (Forster) Education Act, the series of reports from the Hadow Committee between 1923 and 1933 and the Plowden Report of 1967 together constitute the main influences, but other legislation and reports have also contributed to the current situation.

(Continued)

(Continued)

This chapter aims to help you develop an understanding of:

- the three key issues that have emerged in the development of mass education in general and specifically in pre-school education:
  - education of the masses should be undertaken for the benefit of the national economy
  - education that liberated children or was child-centred was not always popular with those in privileged positions
  - educational settings should provide nurture and care for children in addition to that provided by the family and serve as a safety net for society
- the historical developments in policy in early childhood education and care
- the policy context in which early childhood education and care is based
- the antecedents that have led to the introduction of the EYFS.

In addition, vignettes of key contributors to the development of early childhood education and care and additional material will be provided on the companion website.

Policy context

The government of education and care in Great Britain and Northern Ireland is complicated, as four countries together form the United Kingdom (UK). As a consequence of the development of the Union, separate regulations apply to Scotland and Northern Ireland than to England and Wales, with further complications arising from devolution to national assemblies during the latter stages of the twentieth century. The commonalities and differences are explored in more detail in Chapter 3, whilst the discussion in this chapter will not seek to highlight differences between the countries. Instead, the exploration of policy conducted here will consider the UK as a single entity, particularly in regard to developments during the nineteenth century. It was during this century that the major elements of discourse emerged.

The EYFS, as will be explored more fully in Chapter 2, establishes a framework for children up to the age of 5 years, an age at which the UK required children to participate in compulsory education following the passing of the 1870 Education Act. Provision for younger children was thus non-compulsory, although there is ample evidence of education and care outside of the home and family environment since the first infant school was established by Robert Owen in New Lanark, Scotland, in 1816. In this instance children were admitted at the age of 2 and cared for while their parents were at work in the local cotton mills. As the century progressed the label attached to provision for children younger than 5 years changed, but was generally referred to as 'nursery schools or classes', albeit with some examples of 'kindergarten' and 'babies'. The key factor here was to distinguish between the provision offered for older children, for whom 'infant' (generally 5 to 7 years of age) and 'junior' (over the age of 7 years) schools were established as part of the drive to universal education that took place in the latter stages of the nineteenth century.

The driving forces for nursery provision were twofold: the desire for providing education appropriate to age and the desire to provide alternative care systems for young children than could be found in some social settings. These two driving forces subsequently have been features of state maintained provision and are ones that have also affected the private sector. Whilst at various times and in certain circumstances one or other of these driving forces has been uppermost in terms of policy determination, an examination of this history shows there to be consistent recognition of the centrality of the family (and mostly the mother) as being the most significant feature in the health, well-being and education of a young child. Early childhood education and care was considered supplemental to the family, therefore, and is probably best described by the joint circular on children under school age from the Ministry of Health and the Board of Education issued in 1929 to maternity and child welfare agencies and local education authorities:

> The purpose of a nursery school is to provide for the healthy physical and mental development of children over two and under five years of age.

The purpose was thus twofold: 'nurture' and education, and these two driving forces have seldom been separated subsequently.

Influences on 'pre-school' provision prior to the 1870 Education Act

As indicated above, the first recorded attempt to establish an early childhood education and care setting in Lanark was posited on the need to provide care whilst parents were at work. At this time the instruction of children under 6 years of age was to consist of 'whatever might be supposed useful that they could understand, and much attention was devoted to singing, dancing, and playing' (Hadow, 1931: 3). Such schools were thus at first partly 'minding schools' for young children (mostly) in industrial areas, but they also sought to promote the children's physical well-being, to offer opportunities for their moral and social training and to provide some elementary instruction in basic educational functions so that the children could make more rapid progress when they entered school.

At this time mainstream education was being geared to the needs of the industrial revolution, with schools for older children reflecting the immediate need of this rapidly growing economy. 'Schools of Industry' were established that focused on providing the poor with manual training and elementary instruction, soon to be rivalled by 'Monitorial Schools', which involved the use of monitors and standard repetitive exercises so that one teacher could teach hundreds of children at the same time in one location. In both types of school the curriculum comprised basic literacy and numeracy plus practical activities related to the occupations of the age. Provision for children too young to enter these elementary schools tended, however, to mirror this curriculum rather than offer something more appropriate to their age and capability. Owen's model of infant schools was copied, notably by Samuel Wilderspin (McCann 1966), although these schools were later criticised as having 'a mistaken zeal for the initiation of children at too early an age to formal instruction' (Hadow, 1931: 3).

By 1836 a child-centred approach to infant education, based on the work of Pestalozzi (the Swiss educational reformer), was being promoted through the newly initiated Home and Colonial Society. Here the curriculum specifically rejected rote-learning and was based on providing the child with a secure emotional environment and allowing their development through their senses.

Neither the utilitarian approach to schools, whereby children were trained for industry, nor the emancipatory approach envisaged within the child-centred approach was universally popular however, with key figures in society speaking out against the education of the 'poor'. Educating children, suggested one MP in 1807, would lead 'them to despise their lot in life, instead of making them good servants in agriculture and other laborious employments to which their rank in society had destined them and [...] would [eventually] render them insolent to their superiors'.

Nevertheless, calls for more and better education were increasing in number and volume and were endorsed by school inspectors (Hadow, 1926: 8). From around 1830, national funds began to be made available for school building and five Acts of Parliament were passed between 1841 and 1852 designed to facilitate the purchase of land for school buildings and to provide grants for the education of the poor, with the consequence that schools were being built and school attendance was rising.

Unfortunately, and as Gillard carefully documents, successive governments had allowed a divided school system to develop in line with its class structure, a situation further exacerbated by three national education commissions, whose reports – and the Acts which followed them – each related to provision for a particular social class (Gillard, 2011). Only one of these, the Newcastle report of 1861 (and the subsequent 1870 Elementary Education Act) made provision for schools for the masses, whilst the other two continued to support the more privileged middle and upper classes. It was not until well into the second half of the next century, following the 1944 Education Act and the move to comprehensive education in the 1960s, before universal education for the masses superseded the interests of the upper and middle classes (although even now there are still many who would disagree with that statement).

The Newcastle Commissioners commented, however, that infant schools for children up to the age of 7 were 'of great utility', providing places of security as well as of education, since 'they were the only means of keeping children of poor families off the streets in town, or out of the roads and fields in the country' (Gillard, 2011). They distinguished two types of infant schools: the public infant schools, which often formed a department of the ordinary day school; and the private or 'dame' schools, which were very common in both town and country, but were frequently little more than nurseries in which 'the nurse collected the children of many families into her own house instead of attending upon the children' (Hadow, 1933: 17). The subsequent Education Act of 1870 (the Forster Act) effectively saw the demise of Dame schools, however, as infant schools became a permanent part of the public elementary school system. The age of 5 years was established by the Act as the lower limit for obligatory attendance at public elementary schools, with separate provision to be made for infants within the school buildings.

Building regulations

Up to the 1860s, the main objective in separating the infants had been to ensure that the teaching of the older children should not be 'unduly disturbed' (Galton et al., 1980: 31). After 1870, building regulations required distinction between the infant school or department and the rest of the elementary school. Infants should always be on the ground floor, with a separate room for 'babies', and have their own outdoor playground (or exclusive use at certain times) which should have direct access to the playground and latrines without the necessity of passing through the schoolroom. Thus it was established that provision for nursery school or classes should recognise the distinctive needs of younger children and the need for play, features that can still be seen in the twenty-first century.

The rationale underpinning these regulations appears to stem from a growing knowledge of child development whereby formal 'lessons' should be short in length and be followed by intervals of rest, play and song. In Revised Instructions to School Inspectors issued in February 1891 it was advised that the 'subjects of lessons should be varied, beginning with familiar objects and animals, and interspersed with songs and stories appropriate to the lessons' (Revised Instructions to Inspectors, February 1891, cited in Hadow, 1933: 27). The guidance also noted that cooperation between the children was judged to be a key factor in their learning.

In a similar vein, the first London School Board appointed a committee chaired by Professor Huxley to review the system of school organisation (Hadow, 1931: 11). The Huxley Committee was convinced of the importance of infant schools, arguing that they protected children from evil and corrupt influences and disciplined them in proper habits, and recommended introducing Froebel's kindergarten methods into their infant schools. Two leading principles were to be regarded as a sound basis for the education of early childhood:

(1) The recognition of the child's spontaneous activity, and the stimulation of this activity in certain well-defined directions by the teachers.

(2) The harmonious and complete development of the whole of the child's faculties. The teacher should pay especial regard to the love of movement, which can alone secure healthy physical conditions; to the observant use of the organs of sense, especially those of sight and touch; and to that eager desire of questioning which intelligent children exhibit. All these should be encouraged under due limitations, and should be developed simultaneously, so that each stage of development may be complete in itself. (Hadow, 1933: 27)

Thus we can see the first emergence of the learning process in early childhood settings we are familiar with in the twenty-first century whereby young children intersperse formal lessons with play and other activities that sustain and stimulate their natural interest in the world around them.

Understanding child development into the twentieth century

By the early 1900s the environmental conditions needed for the proper physical and mental development of young children were better understood than before, and the training of children below the age of 5 was discussed by both educationalists and doctors. Educationalists argued that the elementary schools were not providing a suitable type of education for under-5s, while doctors suggested that attendance at school was actually prejudicial to health, since it deprived young children of sleep, fresh air, exercise and freedom of movement at a critical stage in their development (Hadow, 1933: 30–31). The newly formed Local Education Authorities (LEAs), formed as a consequence of the 1902 Education Act, sought guidance on the issue. Consequently, the national Board of Education asked five women inspectors to conduct an inquiry regarding the admission of infants to public elementary schools and the curriculum suitable for under-5s. The inspectors were agreed that children between the ages of 3 and 5 did not benefit intellectually from school instruction and that the mechanical teaching which they often received dulled their imagination and weakened their power of independent observation (Board of Education, 1905). Kindergarten teachers were praised, but kindergarten 'occupations' – when taught mechanically in large classes – were condemned as being contrary to the spirit of Froebel, the originator of the kindergarten system, which placed emphasis on play, play materials and activities.

The discourse thus continued on the purposes of schools for children under the age of 5 with some prominent campaigners promoting the benefits of formative education, whilst some sought closure of such provision as it damaged health and others suggesting that the nursery school was the best place to bring up young children as:

All observers agree that children attending school are better looked after than by their parents, kept cleaner and tidier, than they would be if they stayed at home. [...]

One capable, motherly, experienced woman, with a suitable number of trained assistants, can superintend the tending and training of a large number of infants; while one woman with a house to clean, a family to feed and clothe, and the washing to do, cannot properly care for one. (Townshend, 1909: 4–5)

Case study

Extracts from: Reports on Children under 5 Years of Age in Public Elementary Schools by Women Inspectors of the Board of Education (1905). London: HMSO.

Miss Munday's Report

In the schools visited for the purpose of this inquiry in London all except four have a separate room or in some cases two rooms for the use of the children under five. This is so far satisfactory, though in some cases the rooms are very small. In situation and aspect, however, they leave much to be desired. Many are due north, or north-east, thus practically sunless.

The furniture of our infant babies' room still chiefly consists of a huge gallery constructed to hold nominally forty to sixty children, but often containing as many as eighty at the end of the educational year, or if classes have to be put together owing to the lack of sufficiency of staff.

Arrangements for sleeping, either cots or frames, are provided in a few schools, but in some are never used owing to the danger of spreading dirt, infectious and contagious diseases through their use. Four head mistresses informed me that they used to have arrangements for sleeping in the baby rooms, but that they had to have them removed for sanitary reasons. One head mistress told me that she would like a cot in the baby room, but when I asked her if she would put her own little girl, present at school, to rest in it after certain other children had used it, she replied rather indignantly and inconsistently, 'most certainly not'.

Reflective task

- After you have studied Chapters 1 and 2 drawing on the key policies and reports that have led to the EYFS becoming statutory , reflect on how the political landscape has changed our views of childcare. Do you see any differences from the twenty-first century child and this case study?

Greater clarity on purpose was therefore sought throughout the following period, which included the Great War of 1914–18 and the economic depression of the 1930s, which caused immense poverty.

Shaping early childhood provision through the twentieth century

Through the 1921 Education Act LEAs were empowered to provide or aid nursery schools for 2–5-year-olds, although these schools were to attend to the 'health, nourishment, and physical welfare' of children attending such schools, including, in one memorable phrase, the 'cleansing of verminous children'. Even though the Board of Education would make grants for such schools provided they were inspected by the LEA, there was no obligation to do so and a survey undertaken by the Consultative Committee in 1908 showed that, from the 327 LEAs in England and Wales, 32 wholly excluded children under 5 from their elementary schools, 154 retained all children between 3 and 5, while the remaining 136 took a middle course, retaining some and excluding others (Board of Education, 1908). Thus the pattern was set for the next 100 years in that government seemed convinced of the need for nursery education, yet it was not until the twenty-first century that funding matched this desire, a situation perhaps best summed up in the Plowden Report, which noted 'Nursery education on a large scale remains an unfulfilled promise' (CACE, 1967: 116).

Whilst there was still an active debate at this time about the nature of primary education, there was growing interest in the works of John Dewey, Maria Montessori, Edmond Holmes, Margaret and Rachel McMillan and Susan Isaacs (see companion website for vignettes of their work). The Hadow committees of 1931 and 1933, which focused on the needs of young children, can be accredited with most successfully taking account of these influences, whilst still recognising the need for children's health and thus defining the purpose and desired processes of early childhood education and care (Hadow, 1931 and 1933). The reports made recommendations that would shape the national education system for the rest of the century, with Lady Plowden herself confirming that 'we did not invent anything new' (Plowden, 1987: 120). In its conclusion the Hadow Committee of 1933 urged the provision of early childhood education and care for children between the ages of 2 and 5 years, stating:

> … it is a desirable adjunct to the national system of education; and […] in districts where the housing and general economic conditions are seriously below the average, a nursery school should if possible be provided. (Hadow, 1933: 187–8)

The series of reports from the Hadow Committee between 1926 and 1933, together with the Spens Report from 1938, which focused on secondary schooling, formed the basis of the discussion around educational provision undertaken by the coalition government during the Second World War of 1939–45.

From war to prosperity: 1944–67

Planning for a post-war society began in 1940 and was based on the desire, stated by the war-time coalition leader Winston Churchill, of 'establishing a state of society where the advantages and privileges which hitherto have been enjoyed only by the few, shall be far more widely shared by the men and youth of the nation as a whole' (Taylor, 1977: 158). This was to lead to the provision of free universal education for all children and young people aged 5–18 through the 1944 Education Act. This was intended to be the establishment of a tri-partite educational system consisting of compulsory primary and secondary education, with further, non-compulsory education beyond the age of 15. Significantly, however, nothing was included about pre-schools provision, although in 1948 the Nurseries & Child-Minder Regulation Act was published, which required local health authorities to register and monitor premises where children under the age of 5 years were looked after for a substantial part of the day. Once again we can see, therefore, the continued engagement of the education and health authorities in the management of pre-school provision.

A Labour government was elected in 1945 and pursued a series of initiatives, including the establishment of the National Health Service, which together sought to create a welfare state to reduce poverty and the influence of social class. When a Conservative government under the leadership of Churchill came to power in 1951, however, it immediately cut spending on education. In the ensuing 13 years of Conservative government, however, they accepted the notion that increased investment in education led to national economic growth. Consequently, public expenditure on education rose from 3% of GDP (Gross Domestic Product) in 1953–4 to 4.3% in 1964–5, with a concomitant huge improvement in educational provision (Gillard, 2011).

This investment in education was not directed to the under-5s, however, despite a growth in demand that was driven both by greater numbers of women entering employment and increasing numbers of parents desiring some pre-school education for their children. In fact, nursery education during the 1950s faced a long period with no expansion even though this was a time of relative government prosperity. The answer to greater provision, the government signalled through Circular 8/60, lay in the private and voluntary sectors, as there was to be no expansion of local authority nursery school provision (Cleave et al., 1982). Day nurseries only provided a very small number of places, however, and in their absence the Playgroup Movement was started. In 1961 a young London mother, Belle Tutaev, wrote to the *Guardian* newspaper about how, in the absence of a state nursery place for her young daughter, she had set up a group of her own. The idea proved attractive and groups grew in number dramatically, not only providing necessary care for children but also becoming valuable places of nurture through the direct involvement of parents. By 1973 the Secretary of State, Sir Keith Joseph, described the family support they offered as 'an essential social service' (Pre-School Learning Alliance, 2012).

Belle Tutaev and the birth of playgroups

As a young mother and teacher living in London, Belle Tutaev started the Playgroup movement in 1961 by writing a letter to the *Guardian*. In the letter, published on 25 August 1961, she asked the Education Minister for more nursery schools and play facilities for children under 5 and encouraged mothers to start their own provision for under-5s.

What happened next?

The response was overwhelming, from people wanting to establish such groups and from some already running them. Belle borrowed a typewriter, set up a duplicator in her garage and started to put people in touch with one another. Within a year, 150 members attended the first AGM of the Pre-school Playgroups Association, which was to become a major educational charity.

By 1966 membership had increased to 1,300 and the new organisation opened its first office, with a staff of two. Within the next year membership almost doubled again, to 2,200, and the Department for Education and Science provided the charity with a grant to employ its first national adviser.

The Pre-school Learning Alliance continued to grow and now supports more than 800,000 children and their families in England through its membership network of more than 14,000 day nurseries, sessional pre-schools, and parent and toddler groups. It directly manages 493 early childhood settings, including 113 registered childcare and early childhood settings, predominantly in socially and economically disadvantaged areas.

Belle was awarded the OBE in the Queen's Birthday Honours in 2012 for services to children and families.

Plowden Report

Most commentators recognise the investigation carried out by the Central Advisory Council for Education (CACE: The Plowden Report) in 1967 as being the defining moment for child-centred primary education. Prior to this, and despite the intentions underpinning the 1944 Act, there had been little progress in changing the secondary selection system. Most primary education had been geared to the examination culture of the 11 Plus, the entrance test that determined whether children in the state-maintained sector went to grammar, technical or secondary modern schools, with selection all too often becoming the main determinant of life chances. The newly elected Labour government sought to change this inequity and published Circular 10/65, which began with the bold declaration that it intended 'to end selection at eleven plus and to eliminate separatism in secondary education' (DES, 1965: para.1). This was the first call for comprehensivisation of the secondary sector and it was in the spirit of the time that the Plowden Committee was established to review primary education and was described as 'a welcome push in the direction of solving the central problem of educational inequality through its concern with the mainstream of state-provided schools for the vast majority' (Halsey and Sylva, 1987).

The Plowden Report was the first thorough review of primary education since Hadow (1931) and was commissioned at a time of great change in educational policies. The essence of the findings from the inquiry document was that at 'the heart of the educational process lies the child' (CACE, 1967: 1: 7), a philosophy that:

> espoused child-centred approaches in general, the concept of 'informal' education, flexibility of internal organisation and non-streaming in a general humanist approach – stressing particularly the uniqueness of each individual and the paramount need for individualisation of the teaching and learning process. (Galton et al., 1980: 40)

Whilst not focusing specifically on the under-5s, the committee agreed that nursery provision on a substantial scale was desirable, not only on educational grounds but also for social, health and welfare considerations (1: 296). There should be a large expansion of nursery education which, however, they considered, should be part-time as young children should not be separated for long from their mothers. 'In the words of Susan Isaacs: the nursery school is not a substitute for a good home: its prime function […] is to supplement the normal services which the home renders to its children and to make a link between the natural and indispensable fostering of the child in the home and social life of the world at large' (1: 301). In a list of thirteen recommendations the committee determined that, in addition to sentiments already expressed, nurseries should be: for children aged 3–5, the responsibility of education rather than health authorities and under the ultimate supervision of qualified teachers. Such provision should be funded as non-profit-making nursery classes in primary schools or separate nursery centres and to be subject to inspection in a similar manner to all other educational provision (1: 343). The Plowden Committee thus set the standard for nursery provision for the next fifty years.

Austerity rules

The impetus provided by the Plowden Report led to plans for a ten-year expansion of facilities for the under-5s in the government White Paper that withdrew Circular 8/60 entitled: 'Education: A Framework for Expansion' (DES, 1972). Places were to be available for half of all 3-year-olds and 90% of all 4-year-olds by 1982 and investment was also to be made into playgroups and the training of specialist teachers and assistants, principally through the National Nursery Examination Board (NNEB). The 1970s were a period of economic depression, however, shaped by labour disputes and the oil crisis of 1971–3 which together saw the demise of the 'post-war [welfare] consensus' (Chitty, 2004: 31). In the absence of continued prosperity, further investment leading towards universal pre-school education was suspended.

The following years featured successive Conservative and Labour governments wrestling with difficult economic conditions that eventually led to application to the International Monetary Fund (IMF) for financial support and the 'Winter of Discontent' in 1978, both of which paved the way for the election of Margaret Thatcher as Prime Minister in 1979. The ensuing period was based on a market-driven policy whereby businesses and public services were to survive, thrive or die according to their use and popularity. The twin-track policy in education was to transfer power from local to central government and to transform schooling from a public service to a market economy. With a drive to reduce inflation proving unpopular and producing increasing social unrest over the ensuing years Thatcher eventually lost power in 1990, by which time investment in education had slumped dramatically in terms of proportion of GDP. In short, there had been no focus of attention on pre-school education with most effort, discourse, policy and legislation focusing on compulsory schooling.

Reflective task

- Reflect on the current economic situation and with reference to the above section, 'Austerity rules'. Can you identify any similarities and differences?

Resourcing issues

Seemingly the only emergent policy issue during the period of austerity described above that was relevant to children of pre-school age was the prospect of 'school vouchers'. The prominent Conservative politician Keith Joseph, also Secretary of State for Education from 1981 to 1986, was a champion of the market place philosophy based on the belief that more provision by the independent sector would increase competition and provide more choice for parents. During the 1990s a number of government policies were introduced that encouraged the use of formal childcare, based on the notion of attracting people to work rather than remaining on social welfare. Tax relief for employer-provided workplace childcare was introduced in 1990, for example, followed by the reform of the Family Credit programme for working parents in 1994, which allowed some to claim deduction of childcare costs in income assessment. When vouchers for all parents of 4-year-olds to buy part-time nursery school or playgroup places were introduced in 1996 it was on the back of a long debate relating to the marketisation of education.

The incoming Labour government of 1997 brought radical changes to the field of early childhood education and care. In a similar manner to the previous government, it was high on the Labour government's agenda to minimise poverty and increase quality in early childhood education and care by modernising the services. They demonstrated the commitment of the new government to raising quality in early childhood education and care by investing money in the sector, as well as in research. The voucher scheme was replaced in 1997 with a Nursery Education Grant (NEG) which was paid to providers rather than parents. This was followed by the launch of the National Childcare Strategy in 1998, based on the notion of a mixed economy under the banner of 'partnership'. This was the first time in British history the government recognized the need for a national childcare policy (Lewis and Lee, 2002). Childcare provision became the responsibility of the Department for Education and Employment, who introduced the first Childcare Unit in 1998.

Consequently the administrative boundary between childcare and early childhood education has been eroded through the funding mechanisms provided by government. Funding channelled through local government, the *supply* side of funding, has often been allied to funding received by parents, the *demand* side, that has led to most working parents in the UK constructing 'packages' of childcare by using both (Lewis and Lee, 2002). For pre-school providers, and notably playgroups, it created a radical shift as many state-maintained schools were attracted by additional funds and either lowered admission ages for Reception classes or opened new nursery units. By 2001, parents in the UK were spending over £3 billion on childcare, including £1.33 billion on day nurseries – 15% more than in 2000. This was an increase fuelled by a steady rise in employment rates of women with pre-school children, an increasing preference for nursery provision over other forms of childcare and increasing government support to help parents meet the costs (DfES, 2001).

Into the new millennium

At the beginning of the new millennium, childcare categorised as *education* could take place in: nursery schools (public or private), nursery classes in schools, reception classes in schools, playgroups and pre-schools, and occasionally with suitably qualified and registered childminders in private homes. Childcare categorised as *care* could take place in playgroups and pre-schools (in the voluntary sector); out-of-school clubs on school sites, day nurseries, family centres and Early Excellence Centres (in the state sector); day nurseries and community day nurseries, out-of-school clubs (in the independent sector); with childminders, nannies and au pairs (in the private sector). Childcare provision designated as education must meet different standards, and is differently regulated from childcare provision that is designated as care. Thus, provision for the education of 3- and 4-year-olds could be offered by childcare centres that registered as education providers (Lewis and Lee, 2002).

By this time government policy intentions had shifted to aiming to provide a better start in life for deprived children, using education as a tool. Pre-school education was seen as a key aspect of helping children to break the 'cycle of deprivation' (Baldock et al., 2009). This did not translate, however, into a long-term 'coherent policy except in so far as practitioners and local politicians made something of any opportunities they offered' (Baldock et al., 2009: 20). The government's commitment to improving early childhood education and care was shown by the launch of the Excellence in Schools programme (DfEE, 1997). In this White Paper the targets within early childhood education and care for the year 2002 were set out. There was an emphasis on improving quality in early childhood for all children from the age of 4 years, to meet the local needs of childcare and education, and to improve good practice in early childhood. Cohen et al. (2004), in their studies of early childhood education and care systems of national governments in three countries – England, Scotland and Sweden – and on the types of children's services found there, summarised the key features of the post-1997 period regarding children's services as:

> Split departmental responsibility between welfare (DoH), responsible for day-care/childcare services, and education (DfEE) responsible for nursery and compulsory schooling. (Cohen et al., 2004: 55)

This dichotomy of responsibilities between childcare services and formal schooling had an impact on funding, the structuring of provisions and, of course, upon different levels of the workforce. As a result this led to a 'fragmented body of services [...] low levels of publicly funded childcare and early education [...] a growing marketisation of all services [...] and an increasing role for central [...] controlling government' (Cohen et al., 2004: 55–6).

It was evident by this stage that the government was seeking to decentralise children's services by delegating the concomitant responsibilities and implementation to local authorities. The government intended to remain in control, however, by setting targets with specific measurements, with the focal point for measurement to be the assessment of all children. Subsequently the decentralisation of early childhood education and care began with the requirement of all local authorities to set up an Early Years Development and Childcare Partnership (EYDCP) with responsibility for delivering the National Childcare Strategy (DfES, 2001). The aim of EYDCP was to operate independently of local authorities to expand childcare provision. This service was later replaced by Children's Trusts in 2004.

Towards integrated provision

The Early Excellence Centres programme had been set up in 1997 to develop models of good practice in integrating early education, care and family support services. The government's aim was to establish a network of holistic, one-stop services for children and parents that were to be run under local control and in the context of local need. The commitment to 'lift families out of poverty' and improve educational outcomes for all children was translated into an ambitious and well-funded intervention programme, Sure Start, which commenced in 1998. Sure Start was designed to be a ten-year programme for children under 4 years of age and for families living in deprived and disadvantaged conditions. Glass (1999), influenced by the Head Start intervention programme in the USA, founded Sure Start as an intervention programme to help tackle poverty and offer a good start in life to disadvantaged and deprived children.

Sure Start local programmes were transferred into Children's Centres in 2006, a somewhat precipitate move as the action was taken before the evaluation of Sure Start was complete (as will be discussed further in Chapter 2). It appeared that the government was determined to implement changes and sometimes these changes were probably too hasty. Local authorities felt they were unable to apply these in practice and early childhood practitioners were left with uncertainty as to how best to proceed. As part of the continued process of devolution, however, local authorities were given the responsibility to develop the Children and Young People's Plan by 2006, establish the Children's Trust, and appoint Directors of Children's Services. They were also responsible for the unification of inspection systems across all children's services. A ten-year strategy for childcare (DfES, 2004) was developed which aimed to provide out-of-school childcare for all children aged between 3 and 14 years. In consequence, by the end of the first decade of the new millennium expectations and minimum standards for provision of early childhood education and care had been established and consolidated through the statutory framework of the EYFS, with appropriate advice available through the accompanying non-statutory guidance. The evolution and effectiveness of the EYFS, including the revised version of 2012, will be reported and evaluated in the next chapter.

Reflective task

- Study the chapter and with the help of Table 1.1 below reflect on the ideology of each government. Can you identify whether their policies reflect their ideology?

Summary

The policy context explored in this chapter has focused on the legislation and administrative arrangements framing provision over the last 200 years for pre-school children in the UK, and specifically in England and Wales. This process of policy evolution has consistently featured the dichotomy of provision for education and care, with evidence of government intent often matched by a failure to provide adequate funding. By the beginning of the new millennium, however, there were clear indications (by successive governments) that the policy intention was to break the cycle of deprivation and provide a better start in life by using early childhood education and care as a tool. Despite the introduction of a national childcare strategy, however, this has not yet developed into a wholly coherent policy, although the discussion emanating from recent research has informed the development and amendment to the EYFS which will be explored in greater depth in the next chapter.

Key points to remember

Table 1.1   Historical developments in policy in early childhood education and care

Date	Policy	Key changes
1816	First infant school established in Scotland	Children aged 2 years and above cared for whilst parent(s) worked in local cotton mill
1836	Home and Colonial Society promotes Pestalozzi approach to child-centred education	Early childhood curriculum rejects rote-learning and promotes learning through use of senses
1841–52	Five Acts of Parliament related to building of schools	Provision and standardisation of school buildings for 'education of the poor'
1861	Newcastle Report	Provision of schools for the masses with infant schools up to age of 7 years 'of great utility [...] to keep children of poor families off the streets'
1870	(Forster) Education Act	Education for under-5s was non-compulsory, but where provided was to have separate building requirements
1890s	Kindergarten movement	Based on Froebel's theory and practice
1891	Revised Instructions to Inspectors	Formal 'lessons' should be short in length and be followed by intervals of rest, play and song
1900s	Work of Dr Maria Montessori	Emphasis on structured learning, sense training and individualisation
1902	Board of Education appoints five Women Inspectors to conduct an inquiry regarding the admission of infants to public elementary schools and the curriculum suitable for under-5s	1905 Report indicates children between the ages of 3 and 5 did not benefit intellectually from school instruction and that the mechanical teaching which they often received dulled their imagination and weakened their power of independent observation

Date	Policy	Key changes
1921	Education Act	LEAs were empowered to provide or aid nursery schools for 2–5-year-olds
1923–3	Series of reports from Hadow Committee(s)	Defining the purpose and desired processes of early childhood education and care
1929	Ministry of Health and the Board of Education issues Joint Circular on maternity and child welfare to local authorities	Care and education were the two driving forces
1930/33	Work of Susan Isaacs	Two influential books on the intellectual and social development of children
1944	Education Act	Expansion of education to the masses, but still not early childhood provision
1948	Nurseries & Child-Minder Regulation Act	Local health authorities to register and monitor premises for children under the age of 5 years
1960	Government Circular 8/60	Greater nursery school provision to be in the private and voluntary sectors
1961	Bella Tutaev letter to the *Guardian* newspaper	First playgroup established
1967	The 'Plowden Report'	Part-time nursery provision confirmed desirable on both educational grounds and for social, health and welfare considerations
1989	The United Nations Convention on the Rights of Child	The Convention (discussed in Chapters 4 and 14) acknowledged that: • Children are seen as full individual human beings • Children are active members of their societies • Parents/family are primary cares and protectors • Society has obligation to children The key contribution of the CRC in early childhood education is that governments start thinking of children's participation in policy making
1990s	Government policies on tax relief for employers and Family Credit programme for working parents	Principle of educational vouchers established
	19 April 1990 the UK signed the convention	This meant that the UK had to produce a report on how they meet children's rights and what they plan to do at a policy level to implement all children's rights
1991	UNCRC confirmed 16 December 1991 and came into force on 15 January 1992	With the final ratification of the UNCRC, the UK government was committed to make all laws, policy and practice compatible (although it registered some reservations which have since been removed). As a result of the rights being embedded in the law and policies, UNCRC should be followed and referred to by courts, tribunals and other administrative processes when making decisions that affect children
1997	New Labour government	Introduction of Nursery Education Grant

(Continued)

(Continued)

Date	Policy	Key changes
1998	National Childcare Strategy	Notion of a mixed economy under the banner of 'partnership' (i.e. integrated services)
2001	Establishment of Early Years Development and Childcare Partnerships (EYDCP)	Decentralisation of early childhood education and care
2003	Every Child Matters (ECM)	One of the most important policy initiatives and development programmes in response to UNCRC. It aimed to reform services and covered children and young adults up to the age of 19, or 24 for those with disabilities
		Its main aims were for every child, whatever their background or circumstances, to have the support needed to:
		• stay safe • be healthy • enjoy and achieve • make a positive contribution • achieve economic well-being
2004	Children Act 2004	Its primary purpose was to help local authorities and/or other entities to better regulate official intervention in the interests of children
2006	Children and Young People's Plan	Establishment of the Children's Trust and appointment of Directors of Children's Services
2008	Early Years Foundation Stage (EYFS) introduced	Framework of standards for learning, development and care of children from birth to 5 years of age
2010	Conservative and Liberal Democrat Coalition government	The UK government began a series of reductions in public spending, intended to reduce the budget deficit. The cuts affected the National Health Service, welfare, education and other public institutions
		Policy paper 2010 to 2015 on childcare and early education published (updated 8 May 2015 – see below)
2011	Tickell Review	Reviewed the implementation of the EYFS and recommended changes and revisions in the EYFS with emphasis on safeguarding children and fewer bureaucratic processes
2012	Revised version of the EYFS	Introduced to ensure less bureaucracy and to increase the role of parents and carers in their children's learning, reduce the learning and development areas and give added emphasis on the welfare and safeguarding of children; introduction of Age Two check
	June: Nutbrown Report published: an independent review of early education and childcare qualifications	The report recommended a clear, rigorous system of qualifications be set in place to ensure a competent and confident workforce as the existing system was confusing, with many practitioners not holding any qualifications

Date	Policy	Key changes
2014	Introduction of Early Years Educators	Specialist educators from September with a Level 3 qualification approved by NCTL. The ambition was for the majority of staff working in the early childhood to be Early Years Educators
2014	Further revisions to EYFS	Stronger emphasis on safeguarding children and readiness for school. Implemented in September 2014
	Early Intervention Foundation published	The Early Intervention Foundation (EIF) was established to support local agencies and national policy makers to tackle the root causes of problems for children and young people, rather than waiting to address issues once they are embedded
2015	2010–2015 government policy: Childcare and Early Education (revised 8 May 2015)	Aims to: • extend early learning places to around 40% of all 2-year-olds from September 2014 • help parents arrange more informal childcare by allowing them to pay a neighbour or relative not registered with Ofsted for up to 3 hours of childcare a day • introduce new childminder agencies that will provide rigorous training and match childminders with parents • encourage more schools to offer nursery provision and extend provision from 8am to 6pm • help schools to offer affordable after-school and holiday care, either alone or working with private or voluntary providers • reduce unnecessary regulations to help good nurseries expand their business
	Introduction of Baseline Assessment	From September 2014 children entering Reception will be assessed face-to-face individually to identify the level of their development
2015	Clear funding stream identified for supporting early childhood education and care	• Progress Check at Age Two and EYFS Profile become the Integrated Review at Age Two • Early Years Pupil Premium – March • Dedicated Schools Grant (DSG) – May • 2-year-old early education entitlement – May • Childcare Bill – July • Introduction of the Baseline Assessment – September (For more information and updates visit www.gov.uk/topic/schools-colleges-childrens-services/early-years/latest)

> ### Points for discussion
>
> - With reference to the key historical developments summarised in Table 1.1, what similarities and differences in the policy changes can you identify among them?
>
> - Key to recent government policies is the integration of services, the development of a skilful early childhood workforce, and parental involvement. How have these changes affected your practice?
>
> - Discuss the role of the economy in policy formation and the implications for early childhood education and care.

Further reading

Fitzgerald, D. and Kay, J. (eds) (2016) *Understanding Early Years Policy*, 4th edn. London: Sage.
Miller, L. and Hevey, D. (eds) (2012) *Policy Issues in the Early Years*. London: Sage.
Pugh, G. and Duffy, B. (eds) (2013) *Contemporary Issues in the Early Years*, 6th edn. London: Sage.

For an overview of the social constructions of childhood and education:
Blundell, D. (2012) *Education and Constructions of Childhood*. London: Continuum.

For an overview of the key influential philosophers in education:
Nutbrown, C. and Clough, P. (2014) *Early Childhood Education*, 2nd edn. London: Sage.

Useful websites

For more information on government policies and documents:
www.education.gov.uk/publications

References

Baldock, P., Fitzgerald, D. and Kay, J. (eds) (2009) *Understanding Early Years Policy*, 2nd edn. London: Sage.
Board of Education (1905) *Reports on Children under Five Years of Age in Public Elementary Schools, by Women Inspectors*. Cd 2726. London: HMSO.
Board of Education (1908) *Report of the Consultative Committee upon the School Attendance of Children under Five*. Cd 4259. London: HMSO.
CACE (Central Advisory Council for Education) (1967) *The Plowden Report: Children and Their Primary Schools*. London: HMSO.

Chitty, C. (2004) *Education Policy in Britain*. Basingstoke: Palgrave Macmillan.

Cleave, S., Jowett, S. and Bate, M. (1982) *And So to School: A Study of Continuity from Pre-school to Infant School*. Windsor: NFER–Nelson.

Cohen, B., Moss, B., Petrie, P. and Wallace, J. (2004) *A New Deal for Children? Reforming Education and Care in England, Scotland and Sweden*. London: Policy Press.

DES (Department of Education and Science) (1965) *Circular 10/65: The Organisation of Secondary Education*. London: DES.

DES (Department of Education and Science) (1972) *Education: A Framework for Expansion*. Cmnd 5174. London: HMSO.

DfEE (Department for Education and Employment) (1997) *Tomorrow's Future: Building a Strategy for Children and Young People*. London: DfEE.

DfES (Department for Education and Skills) (2001) *Neighbourhood Nurseries Initiative (NNI): Prospectus*. London: DfES.

DfES (Department for Education and Skills) (2004) *Choice for Parents, The Best Start for Children: A Ten Year Strategy for Childcare*. London: TSO.

Galton, M., Simon, B. and Croll, S. (1980) *Inside the Primary School*. London Routledge & Kegan Paul.

Gillard, D. (2011) *Education in England: A Brief History.* Available at: educationengland.org.uk/history (accessed 13 July 2015).

Glass, N. (1999) 'Sure Start: The development of an early intervention programme for young children in the United Kingdom', *Children and Society*, 13: 257–264.

Hadow (1926). *The Education of the Adolescent*. Report of the Consultative Committee. London: HMSO.

Hadow (1931) *The Primary School*. Report of the Consultative Committee. London: HMSO.

Hadow (1933) *Infant and Nursery Schools*. Report of the Consultative Committee. London: HMSO.

Halsey, A. and Sylva, K. (1987) 'Introduction to the special "Plowden Twenty Years On" edition', *Oxford Review of Education*, 13 (1).

Lewis, J. and Lee, C. (2002) *Changing Family Structures and Social Policy: Child Care Services in Europe and Social Cohesion*. TSFEPS Project: National Report (UK): European Research Network.

McCann, W. (1966) 'Wilderspin and the early infant schools', *British Journal of Educational Studies*, 14 (2): 188–204.

Plowden, B. (1987) *'Plowden' Twenty Years On*. London: Carfax Publishing.

Pre-School Learning Alliance (2012) *A History of the Pre-School Learning Alliance*. Available at: www.pre-school.org.uk/ (accessed 13 July 2015).

Taylor (1977) *A New Partnership for Our Schools*. Report of the Committee of Inquiry. London: HMSO.

Townshend, Mrs (1909). *The Case for School Nurseries: School Attendance of Children Below the Age of Five*. London: The Fabian Society.

Want to learn more about this chapter? Visit the companion website at https://study.sagepub.com/EYFS3e for access to free SAGE journal articles and book chapters, weblinks, annotated further readings and more.

2

The Early Years Foundation Stage

Ioanna Palaiologou and Trevor Male

👍 **Chapter overview**

The field of early childhood education and care has been transformed over the last two decades and is still witnessing a number of changes. As of September 2008, the Early Years Foundation Stage (EYFS) was implemented for all children aged 0–5 years in England. It was recognised 'that a child's experience in the early years has a major impact on their future life chances' (DCSF, 2008: 7). It was also recognised that 'families [of children] will be at the centre', in terms of helping them to meet their responsibilities and support them in their involvement in their children's education and care, emphasising the important role of families within early childhood (DCSF, 2007). In March 2012 the government published the revised version of the EYFS which was implemented later that year, with the statutory framework being updated in 2014 (DfE, 2014a). The field of early childhood has welcomed these developments as the recognition of the significance of early childhood education and care. As was demonstrated in Chapter 1, at the policy level the field is now receiving positive attention and the government's commitment to making early childhood education and care a policy priority is appreciated after many years' experience of either low status care for young children or a lack of coherent policies and legislation.

This chapter aims to help you to develop an understanding of:

- the development of the Early Years Foundation Stage in England
- the impact of contemporary research in the developments of the early childhood curriculum
- the main principles and learning goals of the EYFS
- issues relating to the children's workforce, how roles and responsibilities have been changed and what challenges are now faced by practitioners.

Curriculum historical developments

As was demonstrated in Chapter 1, the field of early childhood education and care has not always received an appropriate degree of attention. The study by Bertman and Pascal (2002), for example, revealed that early childhood education and care policies in England were dominated by the short-term priorities of government and local authorities, outcomes that were also demonstrated in the previous chapter. It has taken many years to reach this level of recognition of the importance of early childhood education and care.

Earlier research had emphasised the key influence of early childhood in children's and their families' lives, yet a successful synergy between policy developments and research findings was not then established and it was only in the 1990s that the situation began to change. The introduction of Early Childhood Studies or Early Years Education degrees as university subjects in their own right led to the qualification of graduates outside traditional teacher training. Students on these courses found themselves studying a number of child-related subjects, such as psychology, the history of childhood, sociology and pedagogy while their career intentions remained unclear. At the same time there was a boost in academic research within the field of early childhood education and care. A number of academics started looking at the early childhood provision and services of other countries (Hennessy et al., 1992; David, 1993; Goldschmied and Jackson, 1994; Smith and Vernon, 1994; Pugh, 1996; Penn, 1997; Anning, 2009). This was in addition to looking at the international context of the United Nations Convention on the Rights of the Child of 1989 (United Nations, 1989; Nutbrown, 1999) and comparing early childhood education and care in England with that of other European countries. There was an attempt to compare systems and services then to reflect on the current practices in this country (Penn, 1997, 2000; Moss, 2000, 2001; Moss and Pence, 1994).

There was also much research on the impact of early childhood education and care on children's development and learning (Moyles, 1989, 2007; Athey, 1990; Alexander et al.,

1992; Nutbrown, 1999; Moyles et al., 2001; Sylva et al., 2001; Devereux and Miller, 2003; Penn, 2008). All of these findings strongly argued in favour of improvement in the sector, raising the need for further policy and curriculum development.

As reported in Chapter 1, policy in the field was often designed as a way to reduce levels of poverty and to help children to have better prospects in life. The impact of the research by Mortimore et al. (1998) showed that the quality of teaching and management of schools play a central role in children's quality of learning; it was not, as then thought, the socio-economic and educational background of children that brought about changes. The government of the time took on board the findings of this research and introduced the notion of Effective Schools and School Improvement. A number of developments followed within the school context, including curriculum changes, as well as alterations regarding inspections. These changes were not implemented, however, in early childhood provision.

It was the attempt to analyse poverty and deprivation that motivated the government to turn its attention to early childhood education and care. It was high on the agenda of the incoming Labour government in 1997 to minimise poverty and increase quality by modernising services. The commitment of the new government to raising quality was demonstrated by financial investment in the sector, including research and the evaluation of its projects. This can be seen as a positive attempt to bring synergy between research and policy developments and occurred at a time when there was an urgent need for the government not only to improve practice, but also to investigate in depth, through research findings, the effectiveness of its initiatives and policies.

The impact of research

The most influential study during this period was the Effective Provision of Pre-School Education (EPPE) Project (Sylva et al., 2001). This government-funded research programme, which lasted for nearly seven years (1997–2003), was further extended until 2008 and followed these children into secondary school, looking at what effect early childhood education and care had on young children's lives. The project had some interesting findings in terms of the quality of training of people in the early childhood sector, as it was clear from the results that adult and child interactions had a decisive impact on children's development and learning. Also, there was an emphasis on creating relationships with parents and the key role that parent involvement can play within early childhood. It was encouraging that it seemed, at the time, that the government was taking into account research findings in the context of policy. Research, however, continued to raise issues about the quality of provision and training.

Alongside the EPPE project, research by Anning and Edwards (2006) into what constitutes quality in pre-school education offered important evidence regarding the quality of experiences for young children before they start school. They added to the EPPE project and emphasised the effectiveness of early childhood provision. They found that to raise quality required a partnership between parents and staff in educational settings. They also proposed an expansion of services for young children to meet the changing needs and lifestyles of modern families and employers. One of the key findings in their research was that pre-school children's experiences are determined by the commitment demonstrated by practitioners. These, in turn, determine the quality of the relationships and interactions with children and parents. The research by Anning and Edwards further showed that children attending pre-school education benefited in many ways, most importantly in their cognitive, social and emotional development, and were thus better prepared for the demands of formal schooling. They also argued, however, that their findings demonstrated that poor quality of day care could result in high levels of aggression and poorer social skills when children come to enter formal schooling. Finally, and equally importantly, they found that children from less privileged backgrounds achieve better results during formal schooling if the pre-school education they have experienced is of a high standard and is delivered by well-trained day carers. Key findings to both research projects and additional independent research strongly suggested that, to improve quality in early childhood education and care, a careful consideration of policy, funding, structuring, staffing and delivering services for young children – and the inclusion of parents – were integral.

The reforms that followed these findings appeared to have been embraced to a certain degree by new government policy and there was a commitment to translating this into practice. In their first term of office the incoming Labour government of 1997 demonstrated a positive attitude towards improving quality in early childhood provision. Policy and implementation in this first term of power, however, was characterised by haste. For example, the government, despite funding the EPPE project, did not wait for the full report of the Sure Start evaluation, and moved into creating Children's Centres, leaving Sure Start staff uncertain of what was to follow and the new roles and responsibilities that would subsequently emerge. To some extent this haste continued in their second term, after 2001. It appeared that the government was determined to implement changes and this was translated into the creation of policies, and in changes to services and structures for children and young people. A number of reforms followed and sometimes these changes were deemed to be too hasty. Local authorities felt they were unable to apply these in practice, as it left professionals with an uncertainty as to how best to proceed. This period can be characterised as a time when early childhood practitioners, as well as local authorities, were trying to incorporate these restructuring and reshaping issues within Children's Services.

Integrated services and The Children's Plan: Building Brighter Futures

Central to all these changes to improve quality of life for children and families, and to promote a welfare concept, was the creation of the 'joined-up' thinking of the integration of services. In a commitment to modernise public services, the government aimed to restructure and reshape services so that they would become flexible, immediate and proactive in their responses and would meet local needs. With the UK government having signed the United Nations Convention on the Rights of the Child (UNCRC) they had to demonstrate that the rights of children were embedded as part of the legislation, with policy to reflect on all aspects of the daily life of children.

At the time when the government was advocating these changes and supporting the ways in which the new integrating services would improve the life of children, a young girl – Victoria Climbié – was killed by her carers in 2000. This was a shocking case as the child had been abused over a period of time and it seemed that all children's services had an awareness that this was happening, but had failed to communicate information effectively, with none of the services wanting to take the necessary responsibility to act. The inquiry led by Lord Laming that followed revealed problems regarding the structure and management of these services (Laming, 2003). The government then acted decisively and the principles of joined-up thinking and working in a multi-agency, multi-professional and multi-departmental mentality were reflected by two Green Papers: *Every Child Matters* (DfES, 2003) and *Every Child Matters: Change for Children* (DfES, 2004a). These led to the Children Act of 2004 and it is interesting to note here that the government sought to map the UNCRC with the initiatives that they were planning to introduce at the time.

Reflective task

- After studying Chapters 1 and 2 and reflecting on your own experience of early childhood education and care provision, discuss the impact of UNCRC in policy making for early childhood and in every day lives of children.

Children's services then had to respond to five outcomes of the Every Child Matters (ECM) agenda for all children from birth to 18 years of age: being healthy, being protected from harm and neglect, being enabled to enjoy and achieve, making a positive contribution to society, and contributing to economic well-being (DfES, 2004a). Central to ECM is the protection of children's well-being.

ECM was followed by *Choice for Parents, The Best Start for Children: A Ten Year Strategy for Childcare* (DfES, 2004b) and the Childcare Act of 2006, which identified the need for high-quality, well-trained and educated professionals to work with the youngest child groups.

In December 2007 *The Children's Plan: Building Brighter Futures* (DCSF, 2007) was published. The document emerged in response to the urgent need of the government to demonstrate that it planned for children and families and that its plans were long term in order to produce effective outcomes. The Children's Plan strategy suggested that it 'strengthen support for all children and for all families during the formative early childhood' (DCSF, 2007). The government's visions to create world class schools, an excellent education for every child, to create partnerships with parents, help young people to enhance their interests, find interesting activities outside the school and to create safe areas for children to play were all incorporated.

There was a clear emphasis on the role of integrated services as facilitators for families and children's needs, and it is suggested that 'traditional institutional and professional structures' would be challenged and reshaped to accommodate these needs. One of the first targets was the creation of new leadership roles for the Children's Trust in every area; in new roles for schools as part of communities and effective links between schools, the National Health Service (NHS) and other children's services, to achieve the engagement of parents in order to tackle problems with children's learning and the health and happiness of every child. Such a method of services working together is viewed as the beginning of integration, not only to meet government targets, but also to demonstrate to the world how England is meeting the UNCRC (DCSF, 2007: 159–61).

The Children's Plan was a principled approach to children's services. There are five key principles:

- supporting parents to bring up their children;
- all children to have the potential to achieve and succeed in life if they are given the right opportunities;
- children and young people need to enjoy their childhood whilst at the same time becoming prepared for adult life;
- services need to be shared and responsive to children;
- professional boundaries have to become flexible and adopt a proactive and preventative role. (DCSF, 2007)

Within this document the new targets for 'lifting children and families from poverty' were announced:

> Poverty blights children's lives, which is why we have committed to halve child poverty by 2010 and eradicate it by 2020. (DCSF, 2007)

A new joint Department for Children, Schools and Families (DCSF), and the Department for Work and Pensions Child Poverty Unit was created and were expected to coordinate work across government to break the cycle of poverty from generation to generation. The government also went ahead with the commitment to children's safety by introducing the Staying Safe Action Plan, 2008, and the Staying Safe consultation. As part of this plan the government intended to continue the flow of money to improve services for children. The government announced that £225m – with a potential increase to £235m – would be invested in creating playgrounds nationally and making accessible play areas for children with disabilities. In July 2008 a national

Play Strategy was published: 'Fair Play'. It stated that research findings had been taken on board, as well as consultation with parents, play experts and children, for transforming the quality of children's play.

After the general election of 2010 there was a change in government. The Conservative and Liberal Democrat Coalition government announced budget cuts in order to achieve a balanced budget as the country was entering a financial recession. This was a five-year plan which started in June 2010 and the end of the forecast period was 2015–16. In 2014, however, the Treasury extended the proposed austerity period until at least 2018, which meant that there were serious budget cuts in sectors such as National Health and Education. The early childhood sector was affected equally by these cuts despite the government's reassurance and commitment to high-quality childcare provision.

The impact of austerity on schooling and children's education soon began to appear (e.g. Lupton and Thomson, 2015). Children's services were affected by the budget cuts and it was clear to people involved with inclusion and child protection in education that cutbacks in government-sponsored services, falling real wages and changes in housing and income support were impacting on the lives of children and creating major challenges. Key areas causing concerns were:

- an increase in poverty, with nearly 13 million people in the UK affected (MacInnes et al., 2013)
- a 24% rise in 2008 to 27% in 2012/13 of children living in poverty, with this proportion estimated to increase. According to the Child Poverty Action Group the 3.5 million children living in poverty in 2012/13 will be joined by another 600,000 by 2016, with the total rising to 4.7 million by 2020 (Hirsch, 2014)
- an increase in the gap between rich and poor. Although the economy grew by around 40% during the 1990s and 2000s, this would have been almost 50% had inequality not risen (OECD, 2014).

(See Chapter 15 for more information on the impact of poverty in young children.)

In 2015 a Conservative government was elected and in the budget that followed it was announced that the emphasis will be on reducing child poverty by increasing the hours children will spend in early childhood settings in order for parents to be able to gain employment.

Curriculum context in England

These wide changes to policy had an impact in terms of quality in provision and were reflected in the shape of alterations to the curriculum. In September 2000 the Qualifications and Curriculum Authority (QCA) introduced the Foundation Phase, which aimed to become the 'recognised stage of education relating to children from three years old to the end of reception year in primary school'. The Desirable Learning Outcomes introduced by the Conservative government in the 1990s were replaced with the Early Learning Goals and all providers of early childhood education and care followed the Curriculum Guidance for the Foundation Stage (QCA/DfEE, 2000). In 2002, in an attempt to include provision for children under the age of 3 years, the *Birth to Three Matters* paper was published by the DfES (Sure Start Unit, 2002). Concerns were raised, however, as to how these connected with the Foundation Phase and the transition to the National Curriculum. Young children attending informal (Birth to Three Matters) and formal (Foundation Phase) education were progressing to formal schooling at the age of 5 years and were working under the National Curriculum. This presented transitional problems, as well as problems in the continuity of assessment. The continuity desired appeared not to be implemented. Moreover, in 2003, there was the publication of the National Standards for Under Eights Day care and Childminding which set out requirements for all children attending sessional childcare, and formed part of the Ofsted inspection.

As mentioned earlier, ECM was implemented as a law, and consequently all children's services and settings – including early childhood settings – had to demonstrate that they met the five outcomes of the ECM agenda. In Birth to Three Matters, as well as in the Foundation Phase, it was not clear how the early childhood workforce could meet the ECM outcomes. Moreover, the Children's Plan was setting new targets and principles for children's services.

At a time when practitioners in early childhood education and care were trying to adapt to these changes and translate policy into practice, the government moved by introducing the Early Years Foundation Stage (EYFS) in 2007, to be implemented in all early childhood settings from September 2008. The statutory document aimed to ensure a 'coherent and flexible approach to care and learning so that whatever setting parents choose, they can be confident that they will receive a quality experience that supports their development and learning' (DfES, 2007: 7). Since the first introduction of the EYFS in September 2008 a revised, slimmed down version was introduced in 2012 which was designed to strengthen key aspects and reduce bureaucracy. The accompanying statutory framework has been further updated and implemented in 2014 (DfE, 2014a).

The EYFS – aims, principles and learning requirements

The EYFS was introduced to bring together and replace the existing documents *Every Child Matters, Curriculum Guidance for the Foundation Stage* and the *Full Day Care National Standards for Under 8s Day Care and Child Minders* and provided a cohesive, statutory framework for early childhood education and care. This means that from September 2008 the implementation of the EYFS was a legal requirement for all early childhood settings for children from birth to 5 years of age. The current version of the EYFS is fully described in the *Statutory Framework for the Early Years Foundation Stage* (DfE, 2014a), which explains aims, principles, learning requirements and required assessment processes.

Aims of the EYFS

The central aim of the EYFS is to help all in the early childhood sector to meet the outcomes of the ECM imperative. The EYFS seeks to set the standards for children's learning and development, show a commitment to cultural diversity and anti-discriminatory practice, bridge the gap between parents and childhood settings, ensure there would not be a distinction between 'care' and 'education' and assess children effectively throughout their early childhood.

The EYFS specifies requirements for learning and development and for safeguarding children and promoting their welfare. The learning and development requirements cover:

- the areas of learning and development that must shape activities and experiences (educational programmes) for children in all early childhood settings;
- the early learning goals that providers must help children work towards (the knowledge, skills and understanding children should have at the end of the academic year in which they turn 5); and
- assessment arrangements for measuring progress (and requirements for reporting to parents and/or carers).

The safeguarding and welfare requirements cover the steps that providers must take to keep children safe and promote their welfare (DfE, 2014a: 5).

Principles of the EYFS

Similarly to the Children's Plan (published in 2007), the EYFS is a principled approach to young children's care and education. The four key principles of the unique child, positive relationships, enabling environments and learning and development illustrate the commitment to the government's emphasis on integration and parental involvement:

- every child is a unique child, who is constantly learning and can be resilient, capable, confident and self-assured;
- children learn to be strong and independent through positive relationships;
- children learn and develop well in enabling environments, in which their experiences respond to their individual needs and there is a strong partnership between practitioners and parents and/or carers; and

- children develop and learn in different ways and at different rates. The framework covers the education and care of all children in early childhood provision, including children with special educational needs and disabilities. (DfE, 2014a: 6)

These principles thus reflect the commitment of the government to viewing early childhood education and care as an important part of the community; it recognises the individuality of each child, the diversity of learning and the importance of partnerships with parents and other services for better provision. Care is emphasised and providers are required to take all necessary steps to keep children safe and well.

Learning and Development

The EYFS learning and development requirements comprise:

- seven areas of learning and development;
- the early learning goals, which summarise the knowledge, skills and understanding that all young children should have gained by the end of the Reception year; and
- the assessment requirements (when and how practitioners must assess children's achievements, and when and how they should discuss children's progress with parents and/or carers).

The seven areas of learning and development identified are inter-connected and must shape educational programmes in early childhood settings, of which three areas are deemed to be particularly crucial for igniting children's curiosity and enthusiasm for learning and for building their capacity to learn, form relationships and thrive. These three areas are:

- communication and language;
- physical development; and
- personal, social and emotional development.

Providers must also support children in four specific areas, through which the three prime areas are strengthened and applied. The specific areas are:

- literacy;
- mathematics;
- understanding the world; and
- expressive arts and design.

These requirements are supplemented by guidance on how to structure and implement educational programmes through planned, purposeful play and through a mix of adult-led and child-initiated activity.

The role of assessment in the EYFS

Central within the EYFS are the assessment processes. Considerable emphasis is placed upon the ongoing assessment of children, and this is viewed as an integral part of the learning and development process.

The key assessment procedures are the Integrated Baseline Assessment and the EYFS Profile, although providers must ensure that at all stages practitioners are observing children and responding appropriately to help them to make progress from birth towards the early learning goals. It is expected that all adults who interact with the child should contribute to that process, thus information provided from parents would be taken into account.

- *Integrated Review at Age Two*: From September 2015 the Integrated Review at Age Two (a merger of the Progress Check at Age Two and the Healthy Child Programme health and development review) came into use. For children between 2 and 3 years of age practitioners must review individual progress and provide parents and/or carers with a short written summary of their child's health and development in the prime areas. This integrated review must identify the child's strengths and any areas where the child's development or progress is less than expected.
- *Baseline assessment*: From September 2015 the government introduced an assessment at the start of Reception year in order to collect a score for each child. This baseline assessment for each pupil is to provide a means by which it can be calculated how much progress children have made when they reach the end of Key Stage 2 compared to others with the same starting point. It is intended that the baseline assessment will be part of teachers' broader assessments of children's development, which will be wider than any single baseline assessment can accurately capture. Early childhood settings must choose one of six government-approved providers for the assessment tool they are to use.
- *EYFS Profile*: In the final term of the year in which the child reaches age 5 the EYFS Profile must be completed for each child. The profile provides parents and carers, practitioners and teachers with a well-rounded picture of a child's knowledge, understanding and abilities, their progress against expected levels and their readiness for Year 1. The Profile must reflect: ongoing observation; all relevant records held by the setting; discussions with parents and carers, and any other adults whom the teacher, parent or carer judges can offer a useful contribution.

Inspection in the EYFS

EYFS providers are inspected by the Office for Standards in Education (Ofsted). There are four aspects to Ofsted's regulation of early childhood providers (Ofsted, 2008a). These are:

- registration of applicants;
- inspection of registered providers;
- checking that providers, including those who are not registered with us but may need to be, meet legal requirements for registration;
- taking enforcement action where the requirements of registration are not met.

August 2008 saw the publication of *Early Years Leading to Excellence*, a two-part report on how providers should promote the ECM outcomes for children (Ofsted, 2008b). Although the EYFS is a detailed and descriptive practical guide to play-based activities for young children, the government originally did not want it to be seen as part of the National Curriculum (DCSF, 2007), but current statutory guidance is largely prescriptive and provides a robust framework for implementation (DfE, 2014a), with Ofsted now the sole arbiter of provider quality (DfE, 2014b).

The role of local authorities and childminding agencies

Crucial to the implementation of the EYFS in the early days was the role and responsibilities of local authorities, although these have now been degraded with the new regulations pertaining to childminding agencies introduced in 2014. The original intention in 2008 within the EYFS Statutory Framework, as demonstrated in Chapter 1, was a clear attempt by the government to delegate the responsibilities of the implementation of early childhood provision to local authorities whilst maintaining overall central government through Ofsted inspection reports serving as a measurement tool for effective practice. As a result of measures in the Children and Families Act 2014, however, the government is seeking to encourage the development of childminding agencies, ostensibly to give parents more choice and help with securing childcare that meets their needs. These are intended to be 'one-stop' shops that will help childminders with training, business support, advice and finding parents seeking childcare (DfE, 2014b). Whilst this proposal is not offered as a mode of removing individual childminders, it is a measure designed to amalgamate provision, thus making parents less vulnerable to providers who have no ancillary resources. Once registered with Ofsted, childminder agencies will – in turn – be able to register and quality-assure childminders, help new people take up childminder roles and enable parents to have a greater choice over the early education and childcare they want for their children.

The proposals from government, implemented from September 2014, thus identify a number of changes to the role and responsibilities for local authorities who will no longer, for example, undertake their own assessment of a provider's quality before funding them to deliver early childhood education and care. Instead Ofsted will apply national criteria and be solely responsible for assessing the quality of provider. Local authorities are now required by legislation to secure and fund early education places of appropriate quality for eligible 2-year-olds and all 3–4-year-old children in their area, offering 570 hours a year over no fewer than 38 weeks of the year. Additionally they are to provide information, advice and assistance to parents and prospective parents on the provision of childcare in their area (DfE, 2014b). They are also required to provide information, advice and training to childcare providers, although this responsibility is somewhat diluted by the introduction of childminding agencies each of whom have a requirement to provide adequate continuous professional development (CPD) to practitioners they represent or employ.

This is a significant reduction in the power and authority of local authorities who, in the early stages of EYFS introduction in 2008, were given responsibilities for assessment, training, staff support and collecting the documentation from all early childhood providers. At that stage they were also required to play a key role in meeting the needs of EYFS, as well as the individual needs of each child, in a proactive and protective way, so that cases such as that of Victoria Climbié should be prevented in the future.

Practitioners – expectations and qualifications

A review of early childhood practitioners' qualifications was undertaken by Professor Cathy Nutbrown (2012), which suggests that the biggest factor in determining quality and delivering an effective curriculum in early childhood education and care lies with the qualifications of the workforce. The review demonstrated that 'the current early childhood qualifications system was not systematically equipping practitioners with the knowledge, skills and understanding they need to give babies and young children high quality experiences' (2012: 5). Whilst the report recommended management of early childhood group settings should be undertaken by a practitioner with at least a Level 3 qualification, with a majority of employed staff to be Level 2, it also expressed concern that many qualifications currently were insufficient in content and standard. The conclusion was that the skills, knowledge and understanding of those who work with young children needed to be improved if the sector wished to develop a positive early education and care experience enabling children to have the best start in life (see Chapter 5 for more information).

Research has shown that graduate status of practitioners can have a huge impact on areas of child development such as early literacy and social development, so efforts were made by government to develop such capability. In 2007 the Children's Workforce Development Council (CWDC) introduced the Early Years Professional Status (EYPS), a graduate level qualification, which was intended to be broadly equivalent to Qualified Teacher Status (QTS) in mainstream schools. The intention was that by 2012 there be an Early Years Professional (EYP) in all early childhood children's centres in England, and by 2015 all full day care settings would be required to have at least one. There were problems with this strategy, however, in that the notion of equivalence was not achieved, particularly because the salary level for an EYP was typically less than half of that received by those with QTS. Nevertheless by 2009 there were more than 2,500 graduate EYPs and a further 2,900 in training, which suggested the government was likely to reach its target figures.

Following the election of the Coalition government in 2010, however, new investigations were made into the nature of early childhood provision in the search for enhanced quality. The government commissioned a number of reviews to be undertaken in the policies related to early childhood education and care. This resulted in the publication of: Frank Field's review *The Foundation Years: Preventing Poor Children Becoming Poor Adults* (2010), which examined poverty in England and ways to support poor families to get out of a cycle of social deprivation; Graham Allen's *Early Intervention: The Next Steps* (2011); Michael Marmot's review *Fair Society, Healthy Lives* (2010) and the final report of the *Munro Review of Child Protection* (2011). All these reports aimed to bring changes in the sector and to investigate ways to protect children and address issues of child poverty and safeguarding.

One of the most important reviews in the field was the Tickell Review, *The Early Years: Foundations for Life, Health and Learning*, which examined the implementation of the EYFS. The key points were that there is a need to continue providing good-quality care and support for early learning as a key to later success of children and a way of helping them to overcome disadvantage. Tickell (2011) suggested a clear, accessible, flexible and less bureaucratic EYFS, the government to increase the emphasis on the role of parents and carers in their children's learning, and to reduce the learning and development areas with an increased emphasis on the welfare and safeguarding of children.

Just before the release of the Tickell Review, Ofsted published, in February 2011, a report on *The Impact of the Early Years Foundation Stage* (Ofsted, 2011). This survey aimed to evaluate the EYFS in the embryonic stages and investigate whether in the first stages of the implementation of the EYFS outcomes for children have been improved. The key findings demonstrated that there was an improvement in the children's outcomes on the key learning and development areas, but what is interesting in the report is that Ofsted emphasised that in settings where early childhood practitioners had achieved qualifications above the minimum requirement, the outcomes were better.

Subsequently, therefore, the emphasis shifted toward enhancing the expectations of qualifications in the sector. A new qualification – Early Years Teacher Status (EYTS) – has been introduced as has the concept of Early Years Educator. EYTS is an initial teacher training route allowing for both graduate and undergraduate entry, for which applicants must have GCSE Grade C in English, Mathematics and Science and pass Literacy and Numeracy tests. Bursaries are available to suitably qualified participants who will be awarded EYTS after completion of early years initial teacher training (ITT) which is based on Teacher Standards (Early Years). These operate in parallel with the current Teachers' Standards, and have been designed specifically for early childhood teachers to ensure that training and assessment is appropriate for children from birth to age 5. The concept of Early Years Educator has similarly been developed, with criteria now published (NCTL, 2013). Legislation now expects that in group settings, the manager (i.e. the formal leader of the setting) and at least half of all other staff must hold full and relevant qualifications, in other words to be Early Years Educators (DfE, 2014a). The policy direction now, therefore, is for a professionalised workforce (see Chapters 5 and 17 for further discussion on this issue).

Discussion

To conclude, as was demonstrated in Chapter 1, after two centuries where the early childhood sector was left with no coherent policy, practices or legislation and there were boundaries between childcare and education, the situation has, since 2008, moved to the implementation of EYFS which is focusing on children's development, with clear age ranges, stages and goals 'in an attempt to make clear that there are no clear boundaries, and to value the unique progress made by every child' (Devereux and Miller, 2003: 2). These standards reflect the government's urgent attempt to raise quality in the early childhood sector, as does its interest in ensuring a professionalised workforce is created through initial entry qualifications and sustained through CPD.

The sceptics in early childhood education and care, however, have been concerned that raising the standards can be achieved in a plethora of ways – other than investing much of our efforts into meeting the outcomes and outputs targets in a bureaucratic way such as underpinned the EYFS. The limitation on fixed standards around development and learning allows no space for autonomous, creative and constructive early childhood practice. There is also concern about government intentions that frequently refer to the concept of 'school readiness', as if the only purpose of early childhood education and care is to prepare young children for entry into the formalised learning environment of mainstream schools at age 5. The term is highlighted by Ofsted, who describe the notion as an indicator of the effectiveness of early childhood group settings and provide guidance of how it can be achieved (Ofsted, 2014). The statement offered by Children's Minister Sarah Teather in March 2012, when introducing the revised version of the EYFS, reinforces that view:

> What really matters is making sure a child is able to start school ready to learn, able to make friends and play, ready to ask for what they need and say what they think. These are critical foundations for really getting the best out of school. It is vital we have the right framework to support high quality early years education. Our changes, including the progress check at age two, will support early years professionals and families to give children the best possible start in life.

It is the latter part of the statement that allows critics to voice their concerns whereby child development in the early childhood stage should be seen in its own light and not as a preparation for school. Consequently, overall the EYFS in all its manifestations has been welcomed with mixed feelings. On the one hand the emphasis on play-based learning, inclusion and safeguarding children has been welcomed by practitioners, academics and researchers, but on the other hand the emphasis through-out for readiness for formal education and learning contradicts an ethos that 'all children, at all ages, are ready to learn' (Whitebread and Bingham, 2011: 1). It appears in the approach to the child in the EYFS:

> [the EYFS] places value on children in terms of their meeting future goals and standards and their learning outcomes. It assumes that children need to progress to the next stage of development, from lesser child to better child. The terms 'development', 'developmental goals' or 'learning goals' invoke a sense that children are not yet developed (whole/holistic) and thus need developing ('improving'), or that there is an existing, pre-determined place at which a child may arrive (presumably school). (Palaiologou, 2012: 137)

One final thought in this discussion is with the concern that although government policy intends to extend universal (and free) pre-school education there are potential problems with funding. The intention to double the number of hours per week to 30 for working families, where all parents in the household work even if part-time (from eight hours a week), is not underpinned by ring-fenced funding, which suggests this policy intention could be vulnerable at a time when public spending is to be reduced as a part of overall economic strategy. If it does proceed, however, the new offer would come into effect from 2017 as would additional capital spending to increase pre-school provision. At this stage, therefore, this policy intention should be seen as aspirational and one that needs to be monitored in the next few years to see if it becomes reality.

Reflective tasks

- Reflect on the changes that the revised EYFS have brought and discuss what implications these changes will have in your practice regarding its effective implementation, how local needs are met, or how a common understanding of the principles of the EYFS are achieved.

- In your view what socio-constructions of childhood emerge from the EYFS? How are children viewed? How does the EYFS consider children's participation?

- Reflect on government policy and perspectives on 'school readiness' and what this term means. How and why should a child should be 'ready' for school? Is this the role of an early childhood curriculum?

Summary

Chapters 1 and 2 seek to demonstrate the historical policy developments in early childhood education and care that led to the introduction of the EYFS in September 2008. Alongside the changes in policy, research in the field was trying to establish an ethos whereby all children, families and early childhood practitioners were valued. As has been shown, early childhood education and care was not given its due weight until the twenty-first century. The introduction of the EYFS and the standards that were set within it reflect the government's urgent attempt to raise quality in the sector. Consequently, there has been public discussion about the meaning of quality in early childhood education and care and this is a growing theme. To conclude, an examination of the EYFS has revealed that, on the positive side, there is much-needed regulation; it seems that there is a positive move towards increasing early childhood workforce qualifications and a significant amount of money had been invested towards that direction. Owing to economic difficulties, however, this investment has now been withdrawn and additionally the revised EYFS seems to place emphasis on children's readiness for school. On one hand a major change brought by the EYFS is that the welfare of children is seen to be 'nested' within the wider social context of the family and community. On the other hand, however, it seems that children are perceived as needing socialisation in preparation for their future role as adults, given that emphasis is placed on what the child will become, rather than the child's current state of being.

Key points to remember

- The field of early childhood education and care has experienced radical changes since the Labour government came to power in 1997. The most important policies have been *Every Child Matters*, the *Children's Plan* and the *Early Years Foundation Stage*.

- Key to all government policies is the integration of services, the development of a skilful early childhood workforce, parental involvement and excellence in provision.

- All early childhood settings were required to implement the EYFS from September 2008.

- The early childhood workforce is changing since new roles and responsibilities – as well as new standards – have been introduced by the government. This professionalisation process includes the introduction of Early Years Teacher Status (EYTS) and the publication of criteria for Early Years Educator (Level 3 qualification).

- In March 2012 the Coalition government published the revised EYFS, which keeps the original principles of the first version of EYFS and places emphasis on children's learning, development, well-being and safeguarding. The statutory framework was updated in 2014.

Points for discussion

- Discuss what, in your view, a curriculum for young children should be. Should it be appropriate to their stage of learning or should it be outcomes driven?

- What are your views on the learning and development requirements in the EYFS?

- In your view what should be the purpose of early childhood education and care?

Further reading

Clark, M. and Waller, T. (2007) *Early Childhood Education and Care: Policy and Practice*. London: Sage.

Dahlberg, G. and Moss, P. (2012) *Contesting Early Childhood and Opening for Change*. London: Routledge.

National Children's Bureau Early Childhood Unit (2015) *The Integrated Review*. London: NCB. Available at: www.ncb.org.uk/media/1201160/ncb_integrated_review_supporting_materials_for_practitioners_march_2015.pdf.

Parker-Rees, R. and Leeson, C. (eds) (2015) *Early Childhood Studies*, 4th edn. London: Sage.

For a historical review on early childhood:

Cohen, B., Moss, P., Petrie, P. and Wallace, J. (2004) *A New Deal for Children? Re-forming Education and Care in England, Scotland and Sweden*. Bristol: The Policy Press.

Useful websites

The relevant documentation on EYFS and other information can be accessed at:

www.education.gov.uk/schools/teachingandlearning/curriculum/a0068102/early-years-foundation-stage-eyfs

www.foundationyears.org.uk

For the final report *Foundation for Quality: Review of Early Education and Childcare Qualifications (the Nutbrown Review)*:

www.education.gov.uk/nutbrownreview

References

Alexander, R., Rose, J. and Woodhead, C. (eds) (1992) *Curriculum Organization and Classroom Practice in Primary Schools: A Discussion Paper*. London: DES.

Allen, G. (2011) *Early Intervention: The Next Steps*. An Independent Report to Her Majesty's Government. London: Cabinet Office.

Anning, A. (2009) 'The co-construction of an early childhood curriculum', in A. Anning, J. Cullen and M. Fleer (eds), *Early Childhood Education: Society and Culture*. London: Sage. pp. 67–79.

Anning, A. and Edwards, A. (eds) (2006) *Promoting Children's Learning from Birth to Five: Developing the New Early Years Professional*. Milton Keynes: Open University Press.

Athey, C. (1990) *Extending Thought in Young Children*. London: Paul Chapman Publishing.

Baldock, P., Fitzgerald, D. and Kay, J. (2009) *Understanding Early Years Policy*, 2nd edn. London: Paul Chapman Publishing.

Bertman, P. and Pascal, C. (2002) *Early Years Education: An International Perspective*. Available at: www.inca.org.uk (accessed September 2008).

CWDC (Children's Workforce Development Council) (2007) *Guidance to the Standards for the Award of Early Professional Status*. Leeds: CWDC.

David, T. (1993) 'Educating children under 5 in the U.K.', in T. David (ed.), *Educational Provision for Our Youngest Children, European Perspectives*. London: Paul Chapman Publishing.

DCSF (Department for Children, Schools and Families) (2007) *The Children's Plan: Building Brighter Futures*. London: HMSO.

DCSF (Department for Children, Schools and Families) (2008) *The Early Years Foundation Stage: Setting the Standards for Learning, Development and Care for Children from Birth to Five*. Nottingham: DCSF Publications. (Comprises the *Statutory Framework, Practice Guidance*, Cards and other resources.)

Devereux, J. and Miller, L. (eds) (2003) *Working with Children in the Early Years*. London: David Fulton.

DfE (Department for Education) (2014a) *Statutory Framework for the Early Years Foundation Stage: Setting the Standards for Learning, Development and Care for Children from Birth to Five*. Available at: www.foundationyears.org.uk/files/2014/07/EYFS_framework_from_1_September_2014__with_clarification_note.pdf (accessed 21 September 2015).

DfE (Department for Education) (2014b) *Early Education and Childcare: Statutory Guidance for Local Authorities*. London: DfE.

DfES (Department for Education and Skills) (2003) *Every Child Matters*. Nottingham: DfES Publications.

DfES (Department for Education and Skills) (2004a) *Every Child Matters: Change for Children*, Nottingham: DfES Publications.

DfES (Department for Education and Skills) (2004b) *Choice for Parents, The Best Start for Children: A Ten Year Strategy for Childcare*. London: HMSO.

DfES (Department for Education and Skills) (2007) *Practice Guidance for the Early Years Foundation Stage: Setting the Standards for Learning, Development, and Care for Children from Birth to Five*. Nottingham: DfES Publications.

Field, F. (2010) *The Foundation Years: Preventing Poor Children Becoming Poor Adults*. Report of the Independent Review on Poverty and Life Chances. London: Cabinet Office.

Goldschmied, E. and Jackson, S. (1994) *People Under Three: Young Children in Day Care*. London: Routledge.

Hennessy, E., Martin, S., Moss, P. and Melhuish, P. (1992) *Children and Day Care: Lessons from Research*. London: Paul Chapman Publishing.

Hirsch, D. (2014) *The Cost of Child 2014*. London: Child Poverty Action Group.

Laming, Lord (2003) *The Victoria Climbié Inquiry*. London: HMSO.

Lupton, R. and Thomson, S. (2015) The Coalition's Record on Schools, Spending and Outcomes. SPCC WP14. Social Policy in a Cold Climate: London.

MacInnes, T., Aldridge, H., Bushe, S., Kenway, P. and Tinson, A. (2013) *Monitoring Poverty and Social Exclusion 2013*. York: Joseph Rowntree Foundation.

Marmot Review (2010) *Fair Society, Healthy Lives: Strategic Review of Health Inequalities in England Post-2010*. London: The Marmot Review.

Mortimore, P., Sammons, P., Stoll, L., Lewis, D. and Ecob, R. (eds) (1998) *School Matters*. London: Open Books.

Moss, P. (2000) 'Foreign services', *Nursery World*, 3733: 10–13.

Moss, P. (2001) 'Britain in Europe: finger or heart?', in G. Pugh (ed.), *Contemporary Issues in the Early Years*, 3rd edn. London: Paul Chapman Publishing. pp. 25–39.

Moss, P. and Pence, A. (eds) (1994) *Valuing Quality in Early Childhood Services: New Approaches to Defining Quality*. London: Paul Chapman Publishing.

Moyles, J.R. (1989) *Just Playing? The Role and Status of Play in Early Childhood Education*. Milton Keynes: Open University Press.

Moyles, J. (ed.) (2007) *Early Years Foundations: Meeting the Challenge*. Maidenhead: Open University Press.

Moyles, J., Adams, S. and Musgrove, A. (2001) *The Study of Pedagogical Effectiveness: A Confidential Report to the DfES*. Chelmsford: Anglia Polytechnic University.

Munro, E. (2011) *The Munro Review of Child Protection: Final Report: A Child-Centred System*. London: TSO.

NCTL (National College for Teaching and Leadership) (2013) *Early Years Educator (Level 3): Qualifications Criteria*. Nottingham: NCTL.

Nutbrown, C. (1999) *Threads of Thinking*. London: Paul Chapman Publishing.

Nutbrown, C. (2012) *Foundations for Quality: The Independent Review of Early Education and Childcare Qualifications. Final Report. Runcorn:* Department for Education. Available at: www.gov.uk/government/uploads/system/uploads/attachment_data/file/175463/Nutbrown-Review.pdf.

OECD (2014) *Education at a Glance 2014: OECD Indicators*. Paris: OECD Publishing.

Ofsted (2008a) Early Years Foundation Stage (EYFS). www.ofsted.gov.uk (accessed September 2008).

Ofsted (2008b) *Early Years: Leading to Excellence*. Available at: http://webarchive.national archives.gov.uk/20130401151715/http://www.education.gov.uk/publications/standard/publicationdetail/page1/HMI-080044 (accessed 29 January 2016).

Ofsted (2011) *The Impact of the Early Years Foundation Stage*. London: Ofsted.

Oftsed (2014) *Are You Ready? Good Practice in School Readiness*. London: Ofsted.

Palaiologou, I. (2012) *Child Observation for the Early Years*, 2nd edn. London: Sage.

Penn, H. (1997) *Comparing Nurseries: Staff and Children in Italy, Spain and the UK*. London: Paul Chapman Publishing.

Penn, H. (2000) *Early Childhood Services: Theory, Policy and Practice*. Oxford: Oxford University Press.

Penn, H. (2008) *Understanding Early Childhood: Issues and Controversies*. Maidenhead: Open University Press.

Pugh, G. (ed.) (1996) *Contemporary Issues in the Early Years: Working Collaboratively for Children*, 2nd edn. London: Paul Chapman Publishing.

QCA/DfEE (Qualifications and Curriculum Authority/Department for Education and Employment) (2000) *Curriculum Guidance for the Foundation Stage*. London: QCA.

Smith, C. and Vernon, J. (1994) *Day Nurseries at the Crossroads: Meeting the Childcare Challenges*. London: National Children's Bureau.

Sure Start Unit (2002) *Birth to Three Matters: A Framework to Support Children in Their Earliest Years*. Nottingham: DfES Publications.

Sylva, K., Melhuish, E., Sammons, P. and Siraj-Blatchford, I. (2001) *The Effective Provision of Pre-School Education (EPPE) Project*. The EPPE Symposium at the British Educational Research Association Annual Conference, University of Leeds, September 2001.

Tickell, C. (2011) *The Early Years: Foundations for Life, Health and Learning*. An Independent Report on the Early Years Foundation Stage to Her Majesty's Government. London: Crown. Available at: www.education.gov.uk/tickellreview (accessed July 2012).

United Nations (1989) *Convention on the Rights of the Child*. Geneva: Defence International and the United Nations Children's Fund. Available at: www.ohchr.org/en/professionalinterest/pages/crc.aspx.

Whitebread, D and Bingham, S. (2011) *School Readiness: A Critical Review of Perspectives and Evidence*. Birmingham: TACTYC.

Want to learn more about this chapter? Visit the companion website at https://study.sagepub.com/EYFS3e for access to free SAGE journal articles and book chapters, weblinks, annotated further readings and more.

3

The National Picture

Ioanna Palaiologou, Glenda Walsh, Sarah MacQuarrie, Jane Waters, Natalie Macdonald and Elizabeth Dunphy

 Chapter overview

As mentioned in Chapter 1, the education and care of young children in Great Britain and Northern Ireland is complex, as four countries together form the United Kingdom (UK). As a result of the Union, separate regulations apply to Northern Ireland, Scotland and Wales. This book aims to discuss the Early Years Foundation Stage as it is applied in England. After reviewing the historical developments in early childhood policy in England and the implementation of the EYFS, however, it is important to consider the bigger picture as a way to investigate what happens, not only in the constituent parts of the UK, but also within the entire British Isles (which also include the Republic of Ireland). Thus this chapter examines early childhood education and care in the British Isles and aims to help you:

- have an overview of early childhood education and care in the British Isles
- develop an understanding of the implementation of different curricula
- develop an understanding of the role of policy in curricula implementation
- make comparisons via your own reflections through the case studies from each country.

Early childhood education and care in Northern Ireland

Glenda Walsh

Historical perspective

Northern Ireland, the smallest of the four devolved nations within the UK, with a population of approximately 1.5 million, is a country slowly emerging from a troubled past, when from the late 1960s to the mid-1990s it was fraught with political and sectarian violence. Peace was finally restored as a result of the paramilitary ceasefires in 1994 and subsequently the Belfast Agreement of 1998, which provided Northern Ireland with its own devolved government and enabled it to start on a journey towards a peaceful society and a better future for its children and young people (Walsh and McMillan, 2010).

Pre-school developments

3–4-year-olds

Pre-school education still remains a non-compulsory phase of education, but since the publication of the Learning to Learn Framework (DENI, 2013), it is now deemed to be part of the Foundation Stage in an effort to ensure smoother transitions for young children. The government in Northern Ireland is still committed to making available at least one year of pre-school education to every family that wants it, reiterating the requirements of the Pre-School Education Expansion Programme – PSEEP (DENI and DHSSPS, 1998) – designed as a partnership between the statutory and voluntary/ private sectors. The PSEEP incorporated a number of features such as the adherence to a common curriculum in all settings in line with the Curricular Guidance for Pre-School Education (CCEA, DENI, DHSSPS, 2006)[1] and a quality assurance mechanism whereby all funded settings are inspected by the Education and Training Inspectorate (ETI), features that are still being practised today. It is important to note that voluntary and private providers who wish to offer funded pre-school places must also be registered with a Health and Social Care Trust (HSCT). As a result they are also subject to inspection by HSCT inspectors in addition to the ETI.

---

[1] The Curricular Guidance for Pre-School Provision embraces a child-centred and play-based pedagogy, premised on six discrete themes, namely the arts; language development; early mathematical experiences; personal, social and emotional development; physical development; and exploration of both the indoor and outdoor worlds. While the guidance recognises that children learn and develop in different ways, it emphasises the need for a programme where children get the opportunity to progress their learning and reach their full potential.

A statistical review conducted by the Department of Education Northern Ireland suggests that in February 2015 there were almost 24,000 pupils (equating to 91% of all 3-year-olds in the population) in funded pre-school education in Northern Ireland, the highest figure on record, and the number of schools with Reception classes (considered to be a less suitable form of pre-school provision) had substantially decreased to 70 (DENI, 2015).[2] With regard to the quality of pre-school provision, the Chief Inspector's Report for 2012–2014 (ETI, 2014) indicated that the overall effectiveness of 83% of the pre-school settings inspected was evaluated as good or better (an improvement of seven percentage points in comparison with the settings inspected during the last reporting period). Despite this favourable result, however, fewer settings in general were evaluated as very good or outstanding, indicating that there is still some work to be done. To ensure improvement, the Department (DENI, 2013: 27) intends to 'establish appropriate support mechanisms to achieve the highest standards for pre-school provision through collaboration and dissemination of best practice'. For example, the Department anticipates 'creating a number of pilot Early Years Education Support Clusters to raise standards by making greater use of the teaching expertise in nursery schools and units, special schools, expertise across other relevant providers and early years specialists' (DENI, 2013: 27).

Within the pre-school sector, there is still the on-going debate about who is best placed to 'teach' young children in pre-school. Much has been written about the link between a graduate workforce and quality (see McMillan, 2008; Nutbrown, 2012) and according to McMillan and McConnell (in press) the language within recent policy in Northern Ireland (in particular the Learning to Learn framework, DENI, 2013) implicitly acknowledges the argument for graduate leadership in early years childhood and care, but fails to make any explicit move to actually achieving it in practice. ETI (2014) has emphasized the variation that presently exists particularly in the private/voluntary sector in the quantity and quality of support available to promote improvement, which might be overcome, it could be argued, if a graduate leader/teacher were in place. However the conundrum of whether a trained teacher is best has yet to be unraveled.

0–3-year-olds

The government in Northern Ireland has also committed an annual budget of approximately £3 million to a Sure Start developmental programme for 2–3-year-old children from socio-economically deprived backgrounds. This initiative began in March 2006 as part of the Children and Young People's Package and was developed in February 2007 when *Early Years: The Organisation for Young Children* won DENI's tender to develop a suitable programme for 2-year-olds and accompanying training for Sure Start practitioners to deliver the programme, commencing in 2008. According to

---

[2]As part of the Learning to Learn Framework (DENI, 2013), the Department is legislating to remove the ability of primary schools to admit underage children to Reception.

DENI (2013), there are currently 142 programmes in place, offering a service for approximately 12 children per programme.

The Programme for 2 Year Olds aims to 'enhance the child's social and emotional development, build on their communication and language skills, and encourage their imagination through play' DENI (2013: 4). Although evidence from an ETI evaluation showed that satisfactory-to-good progress has been made in the early development of the Programme for 2 Year Olds, there is still much work to be done in terms of strategic planning, better training, higher levels of qualifications, appropriate accommodation and resources, effective support and access to specialist support when required and more developed collaborative working practices (ETI, 2010). In an effort to respond to such requirements, the Department initially intends to lead a review of the programme to assess the extent to which the investment is helping to secure improved well-being and development outcomes for children and families in the most disadvantaged areas (DENI, 2013). Then, in light of the findings, the Department will develop potential options for the expansion of the programme and in turn will ensure that all settings delivering it are subjected to an area-based inspection process.

School developments

It is in the area of school developments that early childhood education and care in Northern Ireland has seen the most significant change over recent years, with the compulsory implementation of the Foundation Stage Curriculum for all 4–6-year-old children in Years 1 and 2 of primary school from September 2007 and September 2008, respectively (CCEA, 2007). Northern Ireland has the youngest statutory school starting age of all the devolved nations[3] and concerns about the inappropriateness of a formal curriculum for young children led to a pilot study being conducted that espoused a child-centred and play-based approach known as the Early Years Enriched Curriculum. The findings from the Early Years Enriched Curriculum project were principally positive where the learning experience on offer in the play-based classrooms was much superior in terms of children's learning dispositions, social development and emotional well-being (Walsh et al., 2010). To ensure effective challenge and progression for young children, however, a more balanced and integrated pedagogy known as playful structure has been recommended where adults initiate and maintain a degree of 'playfulness' in the child's learning experience, while at the same time maintaining adequate structure to ensure that effective learning takes place (Walsh et al., 2010; Walsh et al., 2011).

These findings were pivotal in the subsequent and recent introduction of the Foundation Stage (FS) curriculum (CCEA, 2007), where children in their first two years of schooling should 'experience much of their learning through well-planned and

---

[3]Children in Northern Ireland who have attained the age of 4 on or before 1st July will start primary school at the beginning of the September of that year.

challenging play' (CCEA, 2007: 9) and their learning should be supported by early childhood practitioners who are 'committed, sensitive, enthusiastic and interact effectively to challenge children's thinking and learning' (CCEA, 2007: 16).

The shift towards play as pedagogy in practice has been problematical, it seems, where according to Hunter and Walsh (2014), despite the political endorsement of play as pedagogy in the new NI FS curriculum, the complexities involved in implementing high-quality challenging play in practice do not appear to have been fully resolved. Comments from the Chief Inspectors Report (ETI, 2014: 43) reiterate such findings, highlighting that teachers in Years 1 and 2 'need to build upon children's pre-school learning, set higher expectations for all children to write independently and to develop their thinking skills through numeracy, literacy and play-based activities'.

Indeed Hunter and Walsh (2014: 15) call for an upskilling on the part of practitioners in Northern Ireland to ensure that 'they have a more nuanced and sophisticated understanding of the meaning of play as pedagogy in EY classes, necessitating a high level of expertise on the part of the professionals'. To this end, the Department (DENI, 2013) also acknowledges this need and has committed to creating a programme of continuous professional development for early childhood practitioners, teachers, principals and staff with a focus on the pedagogy of play.

Next steps

The way forward for early childhood education in the context of Northern Ireland certainly looks promising in light of the Department's recent publication of the Learning to Learn Framework (DENI, 2013), which clearly articulates the political vision for early childhood education and care (0–6 years) in Northern Ireland over a coming number of years. The overarching aims of such a Framework are reflective of the overall DENI vision that 'every young person achieves to his or her full potential at each stage of his or her development' (DENI, 2013: 16), focusing in particular on:

raising standards for all; and

closing the performance gap, increasing access and equality.

However, against this backdrop of progress and development is a seriously constrained economic climate[4] which will have, it appears, a detrimental impact on the strategic planning and delivery of education across the entire community, including early childhood education and care. Although, it is claimed by the Department that the Minister aims to protect frontline services as far as possible, 'maintaining all core

---

[4]The Department for Education faces a 4.9% resource reduction and 19.7% capital reduction in the budget for 2015–2016 on top of a 2011–2015 budget which incurred a Resource reduction of 13.6% (see DENI, 2014).

services at current levels will simply not be deliverable' (DENI, 2014: 4). In this way, the policy rhetoric may never be fully realised in our Northern Ireland early childhood settings and classrooms.

Case study

The story of Ethan

Ethan was born on 29 July 2009. Both his parents work full-time – his mother is a secondary school teacher and his father is a joiner. Ethan spent the first year of his life at home with his mother and then he was cared for full-time by a registered childminder until he turned 3 and was able to attend the local playgroup on a part-time facility from September to June, from 9am to 11:15am, three days per week. In the September after his fourth birthday, he began the local full-time nursery school, where he was taught by a trained Early Years Teacher. His parents were nervous that he might not get a place in the chosen nursery school as the admissions criteria had just changed that year, no longer favouring July/August-born babies. They were so delighted that he received a place and he attended on a full-time basis (9am to 1:15pm), being able to have his lunch on the premises – something that is becoming more rare in nursery education in Northern Ireland. Ethan really enjoyed his pre-school experience and learned greatly from it in terms of learning to socialise with children of his own age, having been used to playing with two older brothers. His parents also were very pleased with Ethan's progress, particularly as he was one of the oldest children in his class, but they felt on occasions that their own needs as parents could be better catered for. Any training opportunities or indeed appointments to learn of Ethan's progress tended to take place during the day, which made it extremely difficult for both of his parents to attend as they were working. Ethan started primary school on 1 September 2014, the oldest child in his class, having turned 5 earlier that year on 29 July. He settled extremely well, probably due to the more play-based curriculum that was being practised. However his parents were a little concerned with the lack of challenge that he was experiencing. They were certainly not against the new ideas of the Foundation Stage curriculum, but as Ethan was one of the older children, they felt that, at times, the teacher was not building on the profitable experience he had received during pre-school and extending his learning in playful ways. As the school year drew to a close, however, they certainly had seen progress on Ethan's part, particularly in terms of how learning disposed he was. They felt that more training should be offered to parents, however, to enable them to be more fully equipped to support their children in the home, using more playful and age-appropriate methods.

Reflective task

- Reflect on the areas of learning and development of the EYFS in England and compare this with the curriculum approach in Northern Ireland. If Ethan lived in England, how would he have been treated within the EYFS?

Early childhood education and care in Scotland

Sarah MacQuarrie

Historical perspective

Since devolution in 1999, education in Scotland is a devolved matter governed solely by the Scottish Parliament, meaning that the UK Parliament at Westminster has no direct jurisdiction. The introduction of the Standards in Scotland's Schools Act set out the guidelines for the free and compulsory schooling of all children between 5 and 16 years of age (Scottish Executive, 2000). Younger children were at that time covered in an earlier separate publication, *Education of Children under Five in Scotland* (SOED, 1994).

The philosophy of comprehensive education embedded in Scottish policy has long been recognised as a distinctive feature of provision in Scotland (Humes and Bryce, 2003). Scottish schools are holistic in their approach to pupils' learning and development, exemplified by the revision and updating of inclusion policies (HM Inspectorate of Education, 2002, 2005a) and mirrored in the role and approach undertaken by the HMI (HM Inspectorate of Education, 2009). Decision making in Scotland is less centralised, as schools and stakeholders play a major role in their own organisation and management. The comprehensive philosophy is most evident in the creation of a single body, 'Education Scotland', that brought together Learning and Teaching Scotland (which provided advice, practical materials and resources to enhance the quality of learning and teaching) and Her Majesty's Inspectorate of Education.

A further distinctive feature relates to the provision of Gaelic Medium Education (GME), which spans pre-school, primary and secondary education where the Scottish curriculum is delivered through the medium of Gaelic. An encouraging picture is evident, as the 2014 annual census showed there were more than 2,500 children enrolled in GME in 60 primary schools across Scotland (Summary Statistics for Schools in Scotland, 2014). Considering that GME was only formally introduced in 1986, these figures can be taken as an indicator of the demand (HM Inspectorate of Education, 2005b, 2011). A commitment to the provision of Gaelic within Scotland is noted by the publication of the first Gaelic Language (Scotland) Act in 2005, followed in 2007 by the National Plan for Gaelic[5] and the subsequent Gaelic plans of a wide range of local and national organisations.

A key strength of Scottish education is collaboration between practitioners, evident in the development of inclusion-orientated strategies. The New Community Schools Initiative (later Integrated Community Schools) began in 1998 as a component of the Scottish social inclusion strategy (HM Inspectors of Schools, 1999). Schools were obliged to introduce the child-centred strategy by 2007. It recommended that schools adopt an integrated approach, increase inter-agency working and take advantage of resources available in their communities, and this is visible as a central tenet within the Scottish Curriculum.

Curriculum and policy

Curriculum guidelines in Scotland support teaching with examples of good practice, with teachers in Scotland having considerable autonomy (Leat et al., 2013). In 1991 the Scottish Office Education Department (SOED, later the Scottish Executive Education Department, SEED) developed a series of curriculum and assessment national guidelines covering the 5–14 curriculum, from the first year of primary school to the second year of secondary school. In Scotland these requirements and relevant support materials constituted a broadly agreed agenda for over a decade.

A curriculum review group was established in 2003, based on the findings of a national consultation on education, where the consensus was that a more engaging curriculum was needed (Education Scotland, n.d.). An extended period of development ensued (2005–2009), involving a wide variety of practitioners and research processes. Revised curriculum guidelines were published in 2009 ready for implementation. Scotland now has a single curriculum for ages 3–18 known as 'A Curriculum for Excellence'. Further developments (largely pertaining to qualifications) are ongoing. The purpose of the curriculum is represented within 'Four capacities' and through the curriculum each child should be a successful learner, a confident individual, an effective contributor and a responsible citizen. Attributes and capabilities that underpin each of the four capacities are clearly signalled and provide a straightforward resource for educators, allowing them to make provisions for learners' progression. 'Experiences and outcomes' are used within the Curriculum for Excellence to describe the nature of learning (experiences) and how they ought to be recognised (outcomes). 'Experiences and outcomes' are referred to in four of the five levels of learning;[6] of particular relevance is the 'early' level that encompasses both pre-school and Primary 1.

---

[5]In accordance with the 2005 Act, National Plans are to be released every five years. Bòrd na Gàidhlig (2007) The National Plan for Gaelic 2007–2012. Inverness: Bòrd na Gàidhlig.

[6]The fifth level refers to qualifications (Scottish Executive, 2010). Scottish Government (2010) Building the Curriculum 5: A Framework for Assessment. Edinburgh: Scottish Government.

Educational settings are provided with guidance on how to ensure that all children in pre-school and primary school settings experience stimulating, effective learning in ways that are appropriate to their needs (example documents are Scottish Executive, 2007; Scottish Government, 2008a). Scottish schools and local authorities are encouraged to design a customised curriculum using input from stakeholders, teachers and parents as well as drawing on National Guidelines and support materials. Their aim is to meet the schools' and local communities' expectations and to ensure each child acquires the four capacities of Curriculum for Excellence.

Children younger than 3 are covered separately within the publication *Pre-birth to Three: Positive Outcomes for Scotland's Children and Families* (Learning and Teaching Scotland, 2010). This national guidance is in line with the principles and philosophy that underpin the Curriculum for Excellence and is supported by the Early Years framework (Scottish Government, 2008b). The framework presents a ten-year strategy that aims to enable those caring for children younger than 3 to develop a child's social and interactive skills, so that a child is supported and able to achieve its full potential. The framework spans the interests of children from pre-birth to the age of 8 and proposes ten elements of transformational change, each supported by examples of good practice. These examples (taken from actual practice within Scotland) reflect key elements of the framework, including a focus on children's play, experiential and holistic approaches to learning and supporting children's progression and transition. The Early Years Collaborative signals an interesting approach. This inter-agency collaboration was launched in October 2012 aiming to support implementation of policy and encourage practice to develop across Scotland .This approach to developing and leading change Scotland-wide is a hallmark of the early childhood framework and it is encouraging to see that the commitment to such collaboration has been extended beyond its initial two years of activity (Scottish Government, 2015).

A strength of the framework is its commitment to the promoting and upholding of children's rights as defined by the UN Convention on the Rights of the Child (UNCRC) (UN General Assembly, 1989). A series of vision statements refer regularly to UNCRC articles in order to illustrate the aims of the framework. Of particular relevance is the emphasis given to valuing the child's voice – 'Children and families are valued and respected at all levels in our society and have the right to have their voices sought, heard and acted upon by all those who support them and who provide services to help them' (Article 12 of UNCRC) – and the provision of a range of learning opportunities indoors and out – 'Children are entitled to take part in physical activities and to play, including outdoors, and have an opportunity to experience and judge and manage risk (Article 31)' (Scottish Government, 2008a: 11). These values were condensed and included within the Children and Young People (Scotland) Act 2014, which includes noteworthy items such as increasing funded pre-school provision for children (including specific measures for vulnerable children) and establishing free school meals for children in Primary 1–3 (ages 5–7, respectively) across Scotland. Such developments mean it continues to be an exciting time for early childhood in Scotland.

Moving from England to Scotland: the voice of a mother

When my husband changed jobs and we decided to move from the Midlands to Scotland I had concerns about our children's education. I have a daughter who was 4 years old at the time and she would have attended the Reception class in England, but when we moved to Scotland she spent another year in nursery and she only moved to what they call in Scotland P1 (equivalent to English Key Stage 1).

When we first moved to Scotland she used to spend two and half hours daily in the nursery. Now she attends P1 and I have found that it has been extremely helpful. What they do in her school is to mix children from different classes and they do a lot of shared activities and lessons. I found that very helpful as it has helped her social skills. I was concerned when we moved that my daughter would have been held back in not starting school as it would have happened if we had stayed in England, but I am so pleased about this now. She had an extra year of playing with no 'structured' learning [*laughter*] although her teacher said to me that they do have structured learning although it does not seem that they learn letters, reading and writing as in the Reception class in England. When she moved to P1 she did not have any problems to do the Jolly Phonics, read and write and I feel lucky that she had the extra year of play in nursery.

My son was 2 years old when we moved. He was assessed in Scotland with Complex and Severe Disabilities and required additional support needs. I am not sure what support I would have had in England, but I am grateful to the Scottish system. He attends a nursery for only children with Complex and Severe Disabilities where he is in a class with only four children, one teacher and two learning support assistants and has one-to-one support. In this school there are also occupational health professionals, psychotherapists and any other services that we might need. As a parent of a child with severe disabilities I was worried, but his nursery had offered us a lot of support, communicates with us regularly and I feel it has helped my son and us as parents. I feel as a parent that I am listened to and valued. Now my son's speech has improved, he has better interactions with others and I am very pleased with his progress. I am not sure I would also have this support in England, but I am pleased he goes to this nursery as I do not think he could have coped in a mainstream school. I have a friend in England that also has a child with disability and when we talk about what is offered to us it seems it is a struggle for her when I feel I am very lucky to have these services for my children.

Early childhood education and care in Wales

Jane Waters and Natalie Macdonald

Historical perspective and context

Wales has a population of just over 3 million people (WG, 2014a) and, of these, 18% are children aged 0–15 years. In the 2011 census, 19% of the Welsh population reported being able to speak Welsh (WG, 2012a), a drop of 2% from the 2001 census. The development of Wales as a bilingual nation is a central Welsh Government policy focus (e.g. WG, 2011) and the study of Welsh is compulsory in all maintained educational settings until learners are 16 years of age.

The Welsh Government (WG)[7] came into being after the first Welsh general election on 6 May 1999, following a referendum on 19 September 1997 in which there was a narrow majority in favour of the devolution of Wales from the UK central government. This signified the devolution of responsibility for education within Wales from the national government at Westminster to the Welsh Government in Cardiff. Now administered by the Department for Education and Skills (DES),[8] education policy for the first decade of devolution was informed by the vision document *The Learning Country* (NAfW, 2001a), which set out the intention to 'build stronger foundations for learning in primary schools with a radical improvement for early years provision' (p. 12). The subsequent consultation document, *The Learning Country: Foundation Phase 3–7 Years* (NAfW, 2003), set out the proposals for a Foundation Phase curriculum framework for children aged 3–7 years to 'create a rich curriculum under seven Areas of Learning for children in the Foundation Phase' (WAG, 2008a: 3). This radical overhaul of early childhood education and care in Wales signalled a shift away from UK central government education policy. It was also predicated upon a concern, supported by

[7]Previously the National Assembly for Wales (NAfW) then the Welsh Assembly Government (WAG).

[8]Previously ACCAC (Awdurdod Cymwysterau Cwricwlwm ac Asesu Cymru: the Welsh Assembly Government Department for Curriculum and Qualifications) and Department for Children, Education and Lifelong Learning and Skills (DCELLS).

research literature, about the 'detrimental' (NAfW, 2001b: 8) effect of an overly formal approach to early childhood education and care for children below 6 years of age.

The Foundation Phase Framework for Children's Learning for 3–7-Year-Olds in Wales

Following an evaluation of the two-year pilot period (Siraj-Blatchford et al., 2005), the Foundation Phase Framework (WAG, 2008b) was introduced for school children aged 3–7 years (Nursery, Reception, Year 1 and Year 2 classes) and those children aged 3 and over in maintained and non-maintained settings, in an annual roll-out over the period from 2008 to 2011. The statutory curriculum document advocates the adoption of a play-based approach to early childhood education within the context of a balance of adult-directed and child-directed activity. Educational settings are required to provide children with access to 'indoor and outdoor environments that are fun, exciting, stimulating and safe' and to 'promote children's development and natural curiosity to explore and learn through first-hand experiences' (WAG, 2008a: 4). In addition, children are to interact with adults with whom they should share episodes of sustained and shared thinking and adults are to 'build on what they [children] already know and can do, their interests and what they understand' (WAG, 2008b: 6). The Foundation Phase Framework requires, therefore, that practitioners, in part at least, engage flexibly and contingently with child-initiated activity in order to support learning indoors and outdoors. This requirement is situated within the broader context of the Welsh Government's overall vision for children and young people which is based around seven core aims developed from the United Nations Convention on the Rights of the Child (see WAG, 2006, 2008a: 3). The Foundation Phase sits within this overarching and emancipatory vision for children with an emphasis on the personal development and well-being of the child:

> Children learn through first-hand experiential activities with the serious business of 'play' providing the vehicle. Through their play, children practice and consolidate their learning, play with ideas, experiment, take risks, solve problems, and make decisions individually, in small and in large groups. First-hand experiences allow children to develop an understanding of themselves and the world in which they live. The development of children's self-image and feelings of self-worth and self-esteem are at the core of this phase. (WAG, 2008b: 6)

Seven areas of learning are identified, the first of which is situated 'at the heart of the Foundation Phase' (WAG, 2008b: 16):

- Personal and social development, well-being and cultural diversity
- Language, literacy and communication skills
- Mathematical development
- Welsh-language development

- Knowledge and understanding of the world
- Physical development
- Creative development

There is a specific directive for 'a greater emphasis on using the outdoor environment as a resource for children's learning' (WAG, 2008b: 4). During the pilot stages, research indicated that some schools may have missed the opportunities for children's learning that the policy initiative offered (Maynard and Waters, 2007), though recent evaluation indicates positive development in the use of the outdoors (WG, 2014b). The implicit emphasis in the Foundation Phase documentation on 'proactive and intentional pedagogy' (Wood, 2007b: 127) has been recognised as providing the potential for Welsh practitioners to 'develop the integrated approaches that are advocated in contemporary play research' (Wood, 2007a: 313). However, two sets of disappointing PISA scores for Wales (OECD, 2010; WG, 2010; Wheater et al., 2013) have heralded an intense focus on pupils' development in literacy and numeracy throughout the Welsh education system. A national literacy and numeracy framework was made statutory in September 2012, and is now incorporated into revised curriculum orders for September 2015. The associated imposition of national tests in literacy and numeracy for 7-year-olds may pose a threat to the play-based, child-initiated aspects of the Foundation Phase initiative despite continued ministerial support for the initiative (WG, 2013).

Looking to the future

Since the introduction of the Foundation Phase, the Welsh Government has re-emphasised its education priorities; breaking the link between poverty and attainment is now central to policy development (WG, 2012b, 2013). There have been two evaluations of the Foundation Phase curriculum initiative. The first to report was a review of progress or 'stocktake', undertaken by Siraj and Kingston (2014) at the request of Welsh Government. The stocktake highlighted that where the Foundation Phase was working well the outcomes for children appeared to be good (Siraj and Kingston, 2014: 18–19). However, the report emphasised that there was significant variation in the experiences of children in Foundation Phase within and across the maintained and non-maintained sectors.

The Welsh Government also instigated a three-year evaluation of the Foundation Phase which reports in more detail, though with similar headline findings (WG, 2015). This evaluation highlights the warm support that the Foundation Phase receives from stakeholders and that children experiencing Foundation Phase pedagogy are engaged and achieving well. The variation in provision across Wales remains a significant issue, however. Maynard et al. (2013) undertook a review of the curriculum documentation as a part of the three-year evaluation and highlighted possible tensions within the Foundation Phase framework, for example, tension between the play-based pedagogy, underpinned by a developmental approach, and detailed statutory curriculum expectations, especially for Years 1 and 2. Such tensions have been recognised within Wales and a review of the curriculum and assessment in Wales has been undertaken and has recently reported. The Donaldson review, 'Successful futures', suggests a radical overhaul of the Welsh curriculum for 3–16-year-olds (Donaldson, 2015). The implications of the review for the Foundation Phase remain unclear at the time of writing though it would be fair to say that the proposals would support the ongoing development of the Foundation Phase in line with recommendations from the recent evaluations.

Importantly, the evaluation reported that 'The Foundation Phase is associated with improved attainment for pupils eligible for free school meals, but the evaluation has found no evidence to suggest it has made any observable impact so far on reducing inequalities in attainment at the end of Key Stage 2' (WG, 2015: 3). The Welsh Government is seeking to respond to research that suggests that improvements to the Home Learning Environment and positive transition experiences to the early years in school are critical to making an impact on the attainment of children who live in poverty (e.g. see the Effective Provision of Pre-School Education [EPPSE] study findings: EPPSE, n.d.). The Welsh Government recently published its ten-year plan for the future of Early Years and Childcare (WG, 2013), acknowledging that provision for the sector, particularly for children aged 0–3 years, is variable and currently lacks coherence. The plan includes five key themes:

- children's health and well-being
- supporting families and parents
- high-quality early education and childcare
- effective primary education
- raising standards.

The aim of the plan is for 'all of our children to have a flying start in life; be well-educated; enjoy the best possible health; live in a decent home; have access to an enriched environment including play, leisure, sporting and cultural activities; be listened to, treated with respect and feel safe' (WG, 2013: 2).

Case study

Going to 'big school' in Wales

The Welsh Government Flying Start initiative was set up in 2007. It aimed at reducing the impact of poverty on educational achievement, targeting families with children below 4 years of age, giving children a flying start in life and providing early intervention. It includes an enhanced health visiting programme, parenting support programmes, early language development and free high-quality childcare.

Dafydd is now 3 years and 2 months old; he lives at home with his mother in a low Super Output[9] area of Wales. His mother is a single parent and they live in a Flying Start catchment area. They have been in receipt of an enhanced health visiting service through Flying Start since birth and Dafydd attended a Flying Start childcare setting based in a purpose-built centre within the catchment primary school, attending for 2.5 hours per day, five days a week.

Transition and parental engagement into school in Wales begins when a child reaches age 2, when they become eligible for Flying Start childcare. Dafydd's mother was contacted by the childcare setting and a home visit was arranged. During a home visit both the child and the parent(s) have the opportunity to meet the childcare manager and the child's key worker at the setting, to complete all necessary paperwork and to ask any questions they may have.

During Dafydd's time in Flying Start he was immersed in the Foundation Phase environment; within the classroom the areas of learning, planning, enhanced provision and development trackers all follow the Foundation Phase ethos. His mother attended regular parent meetings, parent events, language and play groups and open days throughout Dafydd's time in Flying Start, building good relationships with Flying Start staff.

Dafydd's Flying Start class was involved in all the elements of school life, including joint events such as sports day, concerts and school trips. His mother was able to meet the staff, parents and children in the nursery class long before the formal transition process began, and felt that she and Dafydd were very much part of the school before moving on to the Foundation Phase at age 3.

In the term before turning 3 and moving up to nursery Dafydd began weekly visits to 'big school' where he enjoyed playing in the new environment, building new relationships and friendships with the nursery teacher and children, and getting to know the routine.

Dafydd began to love the trips to 'big school' and would proudly tell his mother 'I've been to big school' at the end of the sessions. She felt these visits lessened her anxiety about the move up to nursery as she could see his excitement grow. She also attended the school readiness program run by Flying Start in conjunction with the nursery teacher. These sessions allowed her to meet the new staff, encounter the environment, new routines and times, and discuss any concerns. She was able to visit the nursery with Dafydd and see for herself how relaxed and confident Dafydd was in the new environment.

(Continued)

[9]Super Output areas are a geography for the collection and publication of small area statistics. They are used on the Neighbourhood Statistics site and across National Statistics.

(Continued)

Dafydd's mother didn't have to worry about Foundation Phase staff having to learn all about her son; all of his progress, development tracker and information had already been shared with the teacher by the Flying Start Childcare manager before he moved up. The new teacher knew his strengths, the things he enjoyed and even how to comfort Dafydd when he was upset.

On his first day in nursery Dafydd's Flying Start key worker was there as a friendly face and he walked confidently in and over to his favourite area. His mother was able to walk off confident that Dafydd would enjoy the first day in 'big school'.

Reflective task

- After you have studied Chapter 11, reflect on this case study and compare this experience with the EYFS. Do you identify any similarities or differences? After studying Chapter 13, discuss how the team can work to support both children and parents.

Early childhood education and care in the Republic of Ireland

Elizabeth Dunphy

Ireland, one of the smallest countries in Europe, has a population of about four and a half million, with a large and growing population of young children under 6 years of age. There are now approximately half a million children in this age cohort.

Current provision of early childhood education and care

Birth to age 3

There is at present no state provision for children under 3 years of age and, except for some voluntary and community provision, it is largely provided by commercial interests and paid for by parents. Data about mothers' return to work and childcare choices for infants from the *Growing up in Ireland Survey* (McGinnity et al., 2013) reveal that at

9 months, just under 40% of infants were in regular non-parental childcare. Of children in non-parental childcare, 42% were cared for by relatives (mostly grandparents); 31% by non-relatives (mostly childminders) and 27% were in centre-based care. As in many other countries (e.g., Dalli et al., 2011), the quality of care for infants in group-based early childhood services is an issue of public concern. Indeed the last few years have seen some worrying media features exposing undesirable and potentially harmful practices in some settings providing early childhood education and care.

Children aged 3 to 4

Since 2010, the Irish government provides what is referred to as a *free pre-school year* for all children in the year prior to enrolment in primary school (3 hours a day, 36 weeks of the year). The objective of the programme, provided by a range of service providers (community, voluntary and commercial), is to benefit children in the key developmental period prior to starting school. The OECD Ireland Survey Report (2011) recommended that budget funds be reallocated to lengthen the duration of the day in pre-school. An increase in the provision of pre-primary education to children under the age of 3 was also recommended, with a lowering of the entry age to primary also envisaged. The government has indicated, however, that any increase in universal pre-school provision is contingent on achieving significantly higher quality standards in care, in pedagogy and in curriculum. The preparation and training of the workforce is generally seen as a key factor in achieving higher quality (e.g., Start Strong, 2014). Within the primary school system, the Department of Education and Skills (DES) provides targeted provision (*Early Start*) for some (1,600) 3-year-old children identified as at risk because of economic and social disadvantage.

School-aged children

Statutory school starting age in Ireland is 6 years, though in practice traditionally about half of all 4-year-old children and almost all 5-year-old children have attended infant classes (Junior and Senior) in primary school. There is poor structural support for early childhood education in primary schools. Changes in the pupil–teacher ratio in primary schools have resulted in increased numbers of children in infant classes, some with in excess of 30 children. Cuts to additional support for young children with special educational needs have also impacted on provision. There is some relief for schools in areas of economic and social disadvantage where the *Delivering Equality of Opportunity in Schools* (DEIS) programme extends additional support to teachers and schools.

Affordability

The issue of affordability has arisen as a key issue for both parents and providers in recent years. Indeed the European Commission, in its 2014 recommendations for Ireland, strongly advised that the Irish Government tackle this issue. In January 2015 the government agreed to set up an inter-departmental committee (comprising of representatives of seven different departments) to bring forward proposals for developing more affordable 'childcare'.

National Frameworks

Síolta: The National Quality Framework for Early Childhood Education

Síolta is the Irish word for 'seed'. Síolta: The National Quality Framework for Early Childhood Education (Centre for Early Childhood Development and Education, 2006) presents 12 principles related to quality (see www.siolta.ie.)

Aistear: The Early Childhood Curriculum Framework

Aistear is the Irish word for 'journey'. Aistear: The Early Childhood Curriculum Framework (NCCA, 2009) is a curriculum framework for children from birth to 6 years of age. It supports educators, including parents, in planning learning experiences for young children. It describes the learning that takes place in early childhood education and care in terms of the development of dispositions, knowledge, skills, values and attitudes. Importantly, it provides guidelines in four key areas: play, assessment, interactions and partnerships with parents. The framework presents learning and development using four themes: well-being; identity and belonging; communicating; and exploring and thinking (see: www.ncca.ie). There is no requirement for any specific content, programme or philosophy with the framework, rather the intention is that practitioners judge how best to work with the themes to enable the children they work with to reach the goals of the curriculum.

Improving quality of services

Issues related to quality are the responsibility of the Department for Children and Youth Affairs (DCYA). In recent years the improvement of quality has been the major concern for all involved with the provision of early childhood education and care in Ireland. Research has shown the quality to be variable with many services below standard on a number of measures (Hanafin, 2014). The following areas have been targeted by government as a means of promoting and enhancing the quality of education and care for children aged birth to 6 years.

Inspection of pre-schools

There is now a dedicated team of inspectors who will work to improve and enhance educational standards in the free pre-school year. Their work, overseen by the DES, complements inspections undertaken by Tusla, The Child and Family Agency. This agency is responsible for inspecting pre-schools, play groups, nurseries, crèches, daycare and similar services that cater for children aged 0–6, under the Child Care (Pre-School Services) Regulations 2006. This two-pronged approach to inspection has met considerable initial resistance within the sector, where the demand seems to be for an integrated inspection system.

Development of the workforce

The Early Years Education Policy Unit, which is co-located with the DCYA and DES, was responsible for the development of what was termed 'a childcare training strategy' (www.dcya.gov.ie). This was deemed important in order to meet the target of providing 17,000 childcare training places by 2010. The workforce development plan for the early childhood education and care sector in Ireland identified a range of flexible education and training opportunities for the development of the current workforce (DES, 2010).

Support of educators

At present there is a programme of support for teachers using *Aistear*, working with 4–6-year-old children in primary schools. This is delivered by specially trained Aistear tutors through the network of Teachers' Centres. Educators can access resources to support their pedagogy, including examples of Aistear in practice, on the NCCA website (www.ncca.ie). A major thrust of the support programme has been towards promoting an increase in play and playful learning in infant classes.

In 2014, Better Start: A National Early Years Quality Support Service was established. The aim of the service is to enhance the quality of practice in settings. The support service works in partnership with practitioners in implementing the guidance contained in the Síolta and Aistear frameworks.

Review of qualifications

Qualification levels of those working in settings remain low by international standards. Only about 15% of practitioners working in services have degree-level qualifications or equivalent and most have much lower levels of qualifications. Research demonstrates the marked impact that quality environments and attuned adults have on the development and learning of children in the first years of life (National Research Council and Institute of Medicine, 2000). The first major review of education and training programmes that lead to qualifications in the early childhood education and care sector is now much under way by the DCYA.

An integrated, high-quality system of early childhood education and care

Late in 2012 an Expert Advisory Group was established to advise on the preparation of Ireland's first Early Years Strategy. The advisory group addressed the needs and opportunities for children from birth to 6 years. Their report, published in September

2013, set out a vision for an integrated, high-quality system of early childhood educa-tion and care addressing all aspects of children's experiences, including health, family support, care and education. In December 2014 a new Early Years Advisory Group was formed. This group is a formal structure to provide advice to the Minister on education issues in the early childhood sector (0–6). The Group will help to develop policy in the sector in the coming years and is inclusive of the range of experience and expertise across the sector.

Summary

The early childhood education and care sector in Ireland is an increasingly complex and challenging environment that is constantly evolving. The sector is marked by great diversity in relation to quality of provision, underpinning philosophies and levels of qualifications. Recent concerns have focused on the issue of quality. The lack of accountability regarding the quality of the provision for children under 3 years 3 months is of serious concern. The prohibitive cost of provision for this age cohort is an enormous burden and concern for parents who need to make use of it. The old divide between education and care appears still to persist in the minds of policy mak-ers at least. The development of separate inspection systems related to education of children and to childcare is testimony to the fact that these are seen as separate under-takings and, as such, can be examined separately even within the same provision.

However, the good news is that the Irish government now appears to be address-ing in a systematic and focused way the issue of how best to invest in childcare in Ireland. In July 2015 the government published proposals for strategic investment to improve affordability, quality and accessibility in relation to early childhood care and education. The report presents options to enhance affordability for parents, improve the quality of services and outcomes for children, and promote greater accessibility in the sector. Policy objectives for future investment include: supporting parental choice and removing barriers to work; making services affordable and responsive to the needs of parents; and building parents' understanding of and demand for quality (DCYA, 2015). The report is seen as a discussion document and it remains to be seen what aspects of it will have an impact on future developments.

Case study

Sam's early childhood education and care in Ireland (2010–2015)

Sam is 4 years 6 months old. He is an only child and his mother works full time and his father is now a part-time/shift worker and looks after Sam the rest of the time.

Sam was in a crèche (8am to 6pm) for about 18 months when he was a baby, but his mother described this time as *not a happy experience* for either Sam or his parents. They were not confident that it was the best arrangement for Sam, who seemed to his parents to be a happier, more outgoing baby at the weekends. Also, the cost of the care was very high and when they did the sums it seemed that the best arrangement for all was for Sam's father to avail of the opportunity to do shift work on a part-time basis. Sam was cared for at home by his father full-time for about a year and then when he was 4 he started to attend a local pre-school which offers the Free-Preschool Year. Sam's mother brings him to pre-school for 9am and his father collects him at 1pm, five days a week. Since the scheme covers only three hours a day, Sam's parents pay the additional 125 Euro necessary each month. The pre-school closes during official school breaks (e.g. Christmas, Easter, Mid-term breaks) so for each of those weeks there is an additional cost of 64 Euro. Sam will start primary school in September so his parents will pay for the additional weeks that exceed the 36 allowed under the scheme because they believe that it is best for Sam, as an only child, to be with other children on a daily basis.

Sam loves his time at the pre-school and gets on very well there. His parents really value what it offers him in terms of social skills, routine and opportunities to play with other children. On the other hand, Sam's mother commented on her disappointment at the lack of opportunities offered for interactions with the environment (trips to the playground, walks and so on). She wondered if this was to do with issues such as adult–child ratios or perhaps regulations or even curriculum. She compares the provision unfavourably with her expectations of what pre-school would entail and what she knows of the experiences of her nieces and nephews attending pre-school in another country. She would love Sam to have more experiences outside, more visits, more exciting opportunities to learn. She also commented on the fact that they have only ever been invited into the pre-school on one occasion, at Christmas.

Reflective task

Reflect on the areas of learning and development of the EYFS in England and compare it with the curricula approaches in Northern Ireland, Scotland, Wales and the Republic of Ireland. Is there a dichotomy between officially, centralised, pre-described concepts of what quality is, on the one hand, and of what quality is at a local level on the other, based on discussions between practitioners, parents or guardians and the child?

Summary

Examining the early childhood education and care provision in Northern Ireland, Scotland, Wales and the Republic of Ireland helps to put into perspective the developments in the sector. As can be seen in all four countries, there are attempts to develop a coherent policy and curriculum framework in an effort to improve quality. Quality as portrayed in the government policies, however, is 'fixed' and 'limited' to standardised outcomes and outputs. A common theme is that policies attempt to improve quality by placing emphasis on assessed standards. These standards appear to be the 'official approach' to quality, characterised by an objective reality that can be defined, measured, evaluated, assured and inspected (Moss and Pence, 1994; Dahlberg et al., 2007). A key common element in curricula approaches is that these standards of quality are related to children's development. There is now a shift of concern onto what is learned in terms of children's interests, as these will be translated into the child's assessment and children's performativity, outcomes or outputs in order that we can ensure that quality in early childhood education and care is achieved. On a positive note, all the countries examined here reflect the idea that there is now discourse taking place as to what constitutes good, effective practice.

Key points to remember

- Attitudes towards improving early childhood education and care can be identified in all countries of the British Isles. A common element is that these changes have resulted from political changes and, in the current era of economic instability, we can see a cut in funding across the sector.

- Key themes to all the curricular approaches are an emphasis on play and play-based activities, bridging the gap between parents and settings, with observations as a tool to inform planning, inform assessment and to open communication with families and other services. Integration is the concept that all curricula seek to embody.

- Integration hides its problems, however, as there are complex issues to be overcome, such as the professional and financial boundaries, variations in training, the creation of a common work culture, and a lack of clarity in roles and responsibilities. Practitioners are asked to overcome these problems in order to meet the individual children's needs and to promote children's development and learning.

- The emerging role of the early childhood workforce across all curricula appears to be more complex than ever. Meeting standards or competences is not the only challenge they face. The role of practitioners in curricular implementation is becoming multi-dimensional, requiring a good understanding of the theoretical aspects of children's development, as well as its pedagogical aspects. It is also necessary to develop a good understanding of the curriculum.

- It is argued that it is equally important for practitioners to voice their own opinions about curricular implementation. These voices need to be informed not only by a knowledgeable, theoretically grounded workforce, but also by effective practice. Practitioners are required to develop a range of skills in order to be able to promote a pedagogy based on flexible planning, driven by children's interests, and informed by on-going observation of children and evaluation of practice. Dialogue requiring listening to children's interests and needs will become the starting point, in order to communicate with parents, staff and other necessary, related services.

- Another important aspect is recognition that in early childhood education and care effective practice cannot be seen in isolation from the community and the family environment. Considerable emphasis is placed on the role of parents in children's activities, assessment and observation.

 Points for discussion

- Compare the early childhood education and care among these countries and try to identify the similarities and differences in their curriculum practices.

- What are your personal thoughts on curriculum developments in early childhood in the region in which you are studying/working?

- What do you think about the role of play in curriculum implementation in early childhood education and care?

Further reading

Books

Campbell-Bar, V. and Leeson, C. (2016) *Quality and Leadership in the Early Years*. London: Sage.
Fitzgerald, D. and Kay, J. (2016) 'Early years policy in Wales, Scotland and Northern Ireland: the impact of devolution', in *Understanding Early Years Policy*, 4th edn. London: Sage.

Nutbrown, C. (2011) *Key Concepts in Early Childhood Education and Care*, 2nd edn. London: Sage.

Papatheodorou, T. and Moyles, J. (eds) (2012) *Cross-Cultural Perspectives on Early Childhood*. London: Sage.

Reed, M. and Canning N. (eds) (2011) *Implementing Quality Improvement and Change in the Early Years*. London: Sage.

Taylor, C., Joshi, H. and Wright, C. (2014) 'Evaluating the impact of Early Years educational reform in Wales to age seven: the potential use of the UK Millennium Cohort Study', *Journal of Education Policy*, 30 (5): 688–712.

Useful websites

Northern Ireland early childhood provision:
www.deni.gov.uk

Scotland early childhood provision:
www.educationscotland.gov.uk

Wales early childhood provision:
www.gov.wales

Republic of Ireland early childhood provision:
www.siolta.ie
www.ncca.ie

References

CCEA (Council for Examinations and Assessment in Northern Ireland) (2007) *The Northern Ireland Curriculum: Primary*. Belfast: CCEA.

CCEA, DENI, DHSSPS (2006) *Curricular Guidance for Pre-school Education*. Belfast: CCEA.

Centre for Early Childhood Development and Education (2006) *Síolta: The National Quality Framework for Early Childhood Education*. Dublin: CECDE.

Dahlberg, G., Moss, P. and Pence, A. (2007) *Beyond Quality in Early Childhood Education and Care: Languages of Evaluation*, 2nd edn. London: Routledge.

Dalli, C., White, E.J., Rockel, J., Duhn, I., with Buchanan, E., Davidson, S., Ganly, S., Kus, L. and Wang, B. (2011) *Quality Early Childhood Education for Under-Two-Year-Olds: What Should It Look Like? A Literature Review*. Auckland, NZ: Ministry of Education.

DCYA (Department for Children and Youth Affairs) (2015) Early Years (Pre-school) Regulations and DCYA Childcare Programmes Qualification Requirements. [Online] http://dcya.gov.ie/viewdoc. asp?fn=%2Fdocuments%2Fchildcare%2Fqualifications.htm (accessed 24th November 2015)

DCYA (Department for Children and Youth Affairs) (2015) 'Minister Reilly publishes major new childcare report: Proposals for strategic investment to improve affordability, quality and accessibility'. [Online] www.dcya.gov.ie/viewdoc.asp?DocID=3487.

DENI (Department for Education in Northern Ireland) (2013) *Learning to Learn: A Framework for Early Years Education in Northern Ireland*. Bangor: DENI. Available at: www.deni.gov. uk/publications/framework-early-years-education-and-learning-october-2013 (accessed 29 January 2016).

DENI (Department for Education in Northern Ireland) (2014) Draft Budget for 2015–2016. Bangor: DENI. Available at: www.deni.gov.uk/articles/draft-early-years-0-6-strategy-consultation (accessed 29 January 2016).

DENI (Department for Education in Northern Ireland) (2015) Enrolments at school and in funded pre-school education in Northern Ireland: Statistical Bulletin 3/2015. Bangor: DENI. Available at: www.deni.gov.uk/articles/statistical-assessments (accessed 29 January 2016).

DENI (Department for Education in Northern Ireland) and DHSSPS (Department of Health, Social Services and Public Safety) (1998) *Investing in Early Learning: Pre-School Education in Northern Ireland*. Belfast: The Stationery Office.

DES (Department of Education and Skills) (2010) *A Workforce Development Plan for the Early Childhood Care and Education Sector in Ireland*. Dublin: DES. Available at: www.education.ie/en/Schools-Colleges/Information/Early-Years/eye_workforce_dev_plan.pdf (accessed September 2015).

Donaldson, G. (2015) *Successful Futures: An Independent Review of Curriculum and Assessment Arrangements in Wales*. Cardiff: Welsh Government.

Education Scotland (n.d.) 'What is the Curriculum for Excellence? Process of change'. [Online] www.educationscotland.gov.uk/learningandteaching/the curriculum/whatiscurriculumfor excellence/ (accessed 29 January 2016).

EPPSE (Effective Provision of Pre-School Education) (n.d.) [Online] www.ioe.ac.uk/research/4586.html.

ETI (2010) *An Evaluation of the SureStart Programme for 2 Year Olds*. Bangor: ETI. Available at: www.etini.gov.uk/index/surveys-evaluations/surveys-evaluations-pre-school-centre-and-nursery-school/surveys-evaluations-pre-school-centre-and-nursery-school-2010/an-evaluation-of-the-surestart-programme-for-2–year-olds.pdf (accessed 17 May 2014).

ETI (Education and Training Inspectorate) (2014) *The Chief Inspector's Report 2012–2014*. Bangor: ETI. Available at: www.etini.gov.uk/index/inspection-reports/the-chief-inspectors-report/ci-report-2012–2014.pdf (accessed 15 May 2015).

Expert Advisory Group on the Early Years Strategy (2103) *Right From the Start*. Dublin: DCYA.

Hanafin, S. (2014) *Report on the Quality of Pre-school Services: Analysis of Pre-school Inspection Reports*. Dublin: Tusla, Child and Family Agency. Available at: www.tusla.ie/uploads/content/Report_on_the_Quality_of_Pre-school_services.pdf (accessed September 2015).

HM Inspectorate of Education (2002) *Count Us In: Achieving Inclusion in Scottish Schools*. Edinburgh: Her Majesty's Inspectorate of Education.

HM Inspectorate of Education (2005a) *A Climate for Learning. A Review of the Implementation of the 'Better Behaviour – Better Learning' Report*. Edinburgh: Her Majesty's Inspectorate of Education.

HM Inspectorate of Education (2005b) *Improving Achievement in Gaelic*. Her Majesty's Inspectorate of Education.

HM Inspectorate of Education (2009) About us. [Online] www.educationscotland.gov.uk/Images/ise09_tcm4-712882.pdf (accessed 29 January 2016).

HM Inspectorate of Education (2011) *Gaelic Education: Building on the Successes, Addressing the Barriers*. Edinburgh: Her Majesty's Inspectorate of Education.

HM Inspectors of Schools (1999) *Improving Science Education 5–14: A Report*. Edinburgh: Scottish Executive Education Department.

Humes, W.M. and Bryce, T.G.K. (2003) 'The distinctiveness of Scottish education', in T.G.K. Bryce and W.M. Humes (eds), *Scottish Education: Post Devolution*. Edinburgh: Edinburgh University Press.

Hunter, T and Walsh, G. (2014) 'From policy to practice? The reality of play in primary school classes in Northern Ireland', *International Journal of Early Years Education*, 22 (1): 19–36.

Learning and Teaching Scotland (2010) *Pre-Birth to Three: Positive Outcomes for Scotland's Children and Families*. Edinburgh: Scottish Government.

Leat, D., Livingston, K. and Priestley, M. (2013) 'Curriculum deregulation in England and Scotland – different directions of travel?', in W. Kuiper and J. Berkvens (eds), *Balancing Curriculum Regulation and Freedom across Europe*. CIDREE Yearbook. Enschede, The Netherlands: SLO Netherlands Institute for Curriculum Development. pp. 229–248.

Maynard, T. and Waters, J. (2007) 'Learning in the outdoor environment: a missed opportunity?', *Early Years*, 27 (3): 255-265.

Maynard, T., Taylor, C., Waldron, S., Rhys, M., Smith, R., Power, S. and Clement, J. (2013) *Evaluating the Foundation Phase: Policy Logic Model and Programme Theory*. Cardiff: Welsh Government Social Research.

McGinnity, F., Murray, A. and McNally, S. (2013) *Growing Up in Ireland – National Longitudinal Study of Children: Mothers' Return to Work and Childcare Choices for Infants in Ireland*. Dublin: The Stationery Office.

McMillan, D. (2008) 'Education and Care: Implications for Educare Training in Northern Ireland'. Unpublished PhD thesis, Queen's University, Belfast.

McMillan, D. and McConnell, B. (in press) 'Strategies, systems and services: Northern Ireland early years policy perspective', *International Journal of Early Years Education* (Special Edition).

Moss, P. and Pence, A. (eds) (1994) *Valuing Quality in Early Childhood Services: New Approaches to Defining Quality*. London: Paul Chapman Publishing.

NAfW (2001a) *The Learning Country: A Paving Document*. Cardiff: National Assembly for Wales.

NAfW (2001b) *Laying the Foundations: Early Years Provision for Three Year Olds*. Cardiff: National Assembly for Wales.

NAfW (2003) *The Learning Country: The Foundation Phase – 3–7 Years*. Cardiff: National Assembly for Wales.

National Research Council and Institute of Medicine (2000) *From Neurons to Neighborhoods: The Science of Early Childhood Development. Committee on Integrating the Science of Early Childhood Development* (Jack P. Shonkoff and Deborah A. Phillips, eds, Board on Children, Youth, and Families, Commission on Behavioral and Social Sciences and Education). Washington, DC: National Academy Press.

NCCA (National Council for Curriculum and Assessment) (2009) *Aistear: The Early Childhood Curriculum Framework*. Dublin: NCCA.

Nutbrown, C. (2012) *Foundations for Quality: The Independent Review of Early Education and Childcare Qualifications. Final Report*. Runcorn: Department for Education. Available at: www.gov.uk/government/uploads/system/uploads/attachment_data/file/175463/Nutbrown-Review.pdf.

OECD (Organisation for Economic Cooperation and Development) (2010) *PISA 2009 Results: What Students Know and Can Do*. Paris: OECD. Available at: www.oecd.org/pisa/pisa products/pisa2009results/whatstudentsknowandcandostudentsperformanceinreading mathematicsandsciencevolumei.htm (accessed 29 January 2016).

OECD (Organisation for Economic Cooperation and Development) (2011) *Economic Survey of Ireland*. Paris: OECD. Available at: www.finance.gov.ie/what-we-do/economic-policy/ publications/reports-research/oecd-economic-survey-ireland (accessed 29 January 2016).

Scottish Executive (2000) Standards in Scotland's Schools Act. Edinburgh: HMSO.

Scottish Executive (2007) *Building the Curriculum 2: Active Learning in the Early Years*. Edinburgh: Scottish Executive.

Scottish Government (2008a) *Building the Curriculum 3: A Framework for Learning and Teaching*. Edinburgh: Scottish Government.

Scottish Government (2008b) *Early Years Framework*. Edinburgh: Scottish Government.

Scottish Government (2015) Early Years Collaborative. [Online] www.gov.scot/Topics/People/Young-People/early-years/early-years-collaborative (accessed 5 April 2015).

SOED (The Scottish Office Education Department) (1994) *Education of Children Under Five in Scotland*, The HMI report. SOED.

SOED (Scottish Office Education Department) (1994) *5–14 Practice Guide*. Edinburgh: SOED.

Siraj, I. and Kingston, D. (2014) *An Independent Stocktake of the Foundation Phase in Wales: Final Report*. Cardiff: Welsh Assembly Government.

Siraj-Blatchford, I., Sylva, K., Laugharne, J., Milton, E. and Charles, F. (2005) *Monitoring and Evaluation of the Effective Implementation of the Foundation Phase (MEEIFP) Project Across Wales*. Final Report of Year 1 Pilot – Roll Out Age 3–5 Years November 2005. An Evaluation Funded by the Welsh Assembly Government 2004–2005. Cardiff: Welsh Assembly Government.

Start Strong (2014) *Childcare: Business or Profession*. Dublin: Start Strong.

Summary Statistics for Schools in Scotland (2014) *A National Statistics Publication for Scotland, Statistical Bulletin*. Education Series. No. 5 2014 Edition.

United Nations (1989) *Convention on the Rights of the Child*. Geneva: Defence International and the United Nations Children's Fund. Available at: www.ohchr.org/en/professionalinterest/pages/crc.aspx.

WAG (2006) *The Learning Country 2: Delivering the Promise*. Cardiff: Welsh Assembly Government.

WAG (2008a) *Foundation Phase Framework for Children's Learning for 3–7 Year Olds in Wales*. Cardiff: Welsh Assembly Government.

WAG (2008b) *Learning and Teaching Pedagogy: Foundation Phase Guidance Material*. Cardiff: Welsh Assembly Government.

Walsh, G. and McMillan, D. (2010) 'War and peace in Northern Ireland: childhood in transition', in M. Clark and S. Tucker (eds), *Early Childhoods in a Changing World*. Stoke-on-Trent: Trentham.

Walsh, G., McGuinness, C., Sproule, L. and Trew, K. (2010) 'Implementing a play-based and developmentally appropriate curriculum in NI primary schools: what lessons have we learned?', *Early Years: An International Journal of Research and Development*, 30 (1): 53–66.

Walsh, G., Sproule, L., McGuinness, C. and Trew, K. (2011) 'Playful structure: a novel image of early years pedagogy for primary school classrooms', *Early Years: An International Journal of Research and Development*, 31 (2): 107–19.

WG (2010) 'Minister responds to PISA results'. [Online] http://gov.wales/newsroom/educationandskills/?lang=en (accessed 29 January 2016).

WG (2011) Our Welsh language scheme. [Online] http://gov.wales/topics/welshlanguage/policy/wls/?lang=en (accessed 11 May 2015).

WG (2012a) Census 2011: Number of Welsh speakers falling. [Online] www.bbc.co.uk/news/uk-wales-20677528 (accessed 11 May 2015).

WG (2012b) *Improving Schools*. Cardiff: Welsh Government.

WG (2013) *Building a Brighter Future: Early Years and Childcare Plan*. Cardiff: Welsh Government.

WG (2014a) Mid-year population estimates June 2013. [Online] http://gov.wales/statistics-and-research/mid-year-estimates-population/?lang=en (accessed 11 May 2015).

WG (2014b) *Evaluating the Foundation Phase: Key findings on the Environment (Indoor/Outdoor)*. Research Summary Number: 53/2014. Cardiff: Welsh Government. Available at http://gov.wales/statistics-and-research/evaluation-foundation-phase/?lang=en (accessed 11 May 2015).

WG (2015) *Evaluating the Foundation Phase: Final Report*. Cardiff. Welsh Government.

Wheater, R., Ager, R., Burge, B. and Sizmur, J. (2013) *Achievement of 15-Year-Olds in Wales: PISA 2012 National Report (OECD Programme for International Student Assessment)*. Slough: NFER. Available at: www.nfer.ac.uk/publications/PQUK02.

Wood, E. (2007a) 'New directions in play: consensus or collision?', *Education 3–13*, 35 (4): 309–20.

Wood, E. (2007b) 'Reconceptualising child-centred education: contemporary directions in policy, theory and practice in early childhood', *FORUM*, 49 (1&2): 119–33.

Want to learn more about this chapter? Visit the companion website at https://study.sagepub.com/EYFS3e for access to free SAGE journal articles and book chapters, weblinks, annotated further readings and more.

4

The International Perspective on Early Childhood Education and Care

Theodora Papatheodorou and Mark Wilson

 Chapter overview

The aim of this chapter is to stimulate thinking about international research and policy developments in early childhood education and care (ECEC) and their influence on a country's policy, provision and practice. For this, we present a brief overview of key international research evidence and policy developments in order to provide a framework for understanding current national policies and practice.

This chapter aims to:

- discuss why it is important to think about international perspectives
- offer an overview of international research evidence
- provide a case study for reflection
- consider where international research and policy signpost us.

Introduction: why international perspectives matter

Traditionally, as discussed in Chapter 1, early childhood education and care was seen as being the responsibility of the family. When out-of-home care was available this was offered on welfare grounds to enable parental employment, while its focus was on children's development through playful occupation. During the last 25 years, the landscape has changed. Enabling parental employment, especially for women, continues to under-pin such changes, but the introduction of the United Nations Convention on the Rights of the Child (UNCRC) (United Nations, 1989) – ratified by all but one country (United States) – has formed the basis for advocating early childhood education and care as a means of fulfilling children's rights to education, health and protection from birth. At the same time an increased body of evidence, from many fields of study, about the immedi-ate and long-term impact of early childhood education and care on children, families and communities has been instrumental in achieving the greater attention paid to the sector, and the investment made by governments in promoting it as a foundation for a nation's economic prosperity and well-being. Such evidence has now become the cor-nerstone for introducing relevant policies at supranational level and for informing national policies, government spending, programme development and practices.

It is important that early childhood practitioners are aware of such research and policy initiatives, in order to appreciate their influence on national policy and practices. Being informed about research evidence and the context in which it has been produced enables practitioners to respond to policy changes in a balanced and constructive way. Practitioners are enabled to take a critical stance on new early childhood education and care policies and initiatives, consider their influence on practice and, ultimately, examine their impact on children's experiences, their learning and development. Most impor-tantly, learning about global and international approaches gives practitioners and those studying early childhood a much broader view of the landscape helping them realise that early childhood education and care is a product of ideological (both epistemologi-cal and political), historical, cultural and socio-economic influences (Jackson, 2014).

With this in mind, in the following sections we provide a brief overview of key interna-tional research evidence about the impact of early childhood education and care and outline a policy case study (in the English context) for reflection. Next, we look at some of the policies introduced at supranational and national level and discuss how research evi-dence and policy imperatives have shaped and continue to shape provision and practice.

International research evidence and policy[1] – an overview

Currently, there is indisputable evidence about the impact of early childhood education and care on children's education, health and protection as well as on nations' social capital and economic prosperity. The majority of evidence comes from high income countries, but gradually an increased body of evidence is emerging from low and middle income coun-tries showing similar trends. A brief overview of research evidence is where we begin.

---

[1]The international research and policy review is based on an extensive literature review that was first conducted for the purpose of the mid-term and final evaluation of an Early Childhood Care and Development (ECCD) programme in Rwanda (Papatheodorou, 2012/3). This was consequently updated for drafting the Save the Children UK position paper for Early Childhood Care and Development (Papatheodorou, 2014) and for the purpose of this chapter.

Educational outcomes

The High/Scope Perry Preschool Project was a high-quality pre-school programme, established in the USA, to support children of 3 and 4 years at risk of school failure, and the first longitudinal study that followed participants to the age of 41 to evaluate its impact (Schweinhart, 2003). Key findings of this programme showed that, at the age of 27, programme participants compared with those in the control group did better academically, especially in literacy, language, reading and arithmetic, and achieved better grades and graduation rates, while they had fewer placements in special education; they demonstrated more positive attitudes toward school and their parents had higher aspirations for their children. Later in adulthood, programme participants also showed higher social responsibility, as measured by lower incidence of misconduct, fighting, violent behaviour, property damage, drug dealing and fewer contacts with police; they were more successful socio-economically by being employed, self-supporting and less dependent on welfare. A cost–benefit analysis showed savings more than seven times of the initial investment made per child ($7.16:1). These were savings in welfare assistance, special education, criminal justice system and crime victim support, and from increased tax revenue from higher earnings (Parks, 2000; Schweinhart, 2003). These findings have been further supported by a comparative analysis of several other pre-school programmes, implemented in the USA (see Heckman, 2000; Belfield and Schwartz, 2006).

In the UK, the Effective Provision for Pre-School Education (EPPE) longitudinal study also demonstrated the positive effects of high-quality pre-school provision on children's learning and behaviour, especially for children who experienced social disadvantage and/or had special educational needs (Sylva et al., 2004a, 2004b). The researchers concluded that high-quality pre-school enabled children to reach their potential and acquire skills necessary for school readiness.

In low and middle income countries equally promising findings were revealed in the evaluation of a pre-school intervention in rural Mozambique, where the findings showed that children attending pre-schools had higher scores in literacy, vocabulary, mathematics and reasoning than children in the control group (Martinez et al., 2012). In a review of 42 early childhood education and care efficacy and effectiveness studies, conducted by Engle and colleagues (2011), it was found that higher test scores were achieved by children attending pre-schools for longer periods (over fifteen weeks) than children of the same age who attended for shorter periods (less than two weeks). Greater benefits were revealed for higher-risk or more disadvantaged children compared with lower-risk or less disadvantaged children. The effects of formal pre-schools were stronger than the effects of non-formal pre-schools, although some of the latter resulted in better child outcomes compared with children who had no access to early childhood education and care at all. Better outcomes were associated with higher-quality programmes compared with standard programmes. Parent education was also a significant component of early childhood education and care programmes as they equipped them with knowledge and skills about child upbringing, promoted positive interaction with children, increased attachment and encouraged learning, shared book reading and play activities. In addition, it enabled them to become better at problem solving related to their children's development and their own situations and challenges (Engle et al., 2011).

Such research evidence is now frequently quoted and used by policy makers to promote high-quality early childhood education and care for enabling children to reach their potential, especially in terms of academic outcomes, and for closing the achievement gap later in their schooling.

Health outcomes

Early childhood education and care that integrates nutrition and health services (alongside parenting education) has wider impact, beyond educational outcomes, especially on child and maternal health and child protection. Integrated early childhood education and care decreases child morbidity and mortality, reduces malnutrition and stunting, and improves overall health, care and hygiene. These findings are particularly relevant to low and middle income countries, where a range of risk factors such as child and maternal malnutrition, iodine and iron-deficiency, malaria, diarrhoea, HIV/ AIDS and other preventable infections and diseases, maternal depression, exposure to violence, and lack of early stimulation and learning opportunities impact negatively on children's development, and contribute to child mortality (Walker et al., 2011).

Child undernutrition, especially during the first 1,000 days from conception, is the major contributory factor to children's stunting, wasting and being underweight. Children affected by malnutrition are prone to many infections and many preventable diseases, especially during this critical period of life (Bryce et al., 2008). As adults, these children are more likely to have lower levels of education and employment opportunities, earn less, have larger families and provide poor care for their children. Evidently, the compound and accumulative long-term effects of malnutrition perpetuate inter-generational poverty, resulting in immeasurable human and economic cost (Bhutta et al., 2008).

Prevention programmes are key to reducing stunting and decreasing disability and mortality rates related to malnutrition. Several studies have shown that preventative programmes that run for a longer duration, aimed at children from 6 to 36 months, targeting children and communities experiencing social and economic disadvantage and delivered by trained workers, have greater effects (Bhutta et al., 2008; Ruel et al., 2008; UNESCO, 2010a; Engle et al., 2011).

Social and child protection outcomes

So far, brain development research has provided the most compelling evidence of the impact of lack of stimulation and persistent stress on children's development. The multiple risks which children experience early in their lives undermine substantially their development and ability to reach their full potential (National Scientific Council on the Developing Child, 2010). Children who are unstimulated and exposed to adverse conditions, especially during the first three years of life, have underdeveloped neural connections that affect their cognitive functioning and behaviours with lifelong consequences (Fox and Shonkoff, 2011). In addition, the more adverse the children's experiences, the greater the likelihood of showing developmental delays (IN BRIEF, n/d). Corporal punishment in particular has been closely associated with lower IQ measurements, while boys' exposure to violence in childhood is likely to lead to violence in adulthood and mental health problems (Straus, 2009; Corteras et al., 2011).

By offering early stimulation and learning experiences and promoting adult–child interactions and attachment, early childhood education and care is seen as a child protection service. High quality early childhood education and care, especially during the first two years of a child's life, influences positively brain development and enhances cognitive and social functioning. The impact of pre-school is on children's attachment, emotional and social skills and parents' improved interactions with their children through early stimulation and learning experiences (Heckman, 2000; Siraj-Blatchford et al., 2002; Papatheodorou, 2013). These outcomes appear to be maintained longer than any cognitive gains, as demonstrated in reading and writing test scores (US Department of Health and Human Services, Administration for Children and Families, 2010). In the long run, these skills benefit adults' functioning in society, and their parenting of the next generation (Martorell et al., 1994; Young and Richardson, 2007).

Women's employment

In addition to these benefits, the impact and benefits of early childhood provision on women's employment and the improvement of their family income cannot be underestimated. Since the last part of the twentieth century, childcare availability has increased women's participation in employment and provided employment opportunities. Many women who secured childcare were able to take up employment and others joined the early childhood workforce itself. Both the availability and demand of early childhood services increased women's personal financial status (Papatheodorou, 2013) and their employment in the early childhood sector contributed to local economies (Brown et al., 2008; OECD, 2011). Education and training opportunities, offered through engagement and employment in early childhood, have also been a catalyst for women's empowerment and exercise of choice in their lives.

Returns on investment made for early childhood education and care

In high income countries, economists have calculated the returns of investments made for early childhood education and care provision. For example, the returns of the High/Scope Perry pre-school programme is estimated to be $17.07 for every dollar invested per participant (Schweinhart, 2007), while the potential annual return from other focused high-quality early childhood education and care programmes has been as high as 16% (Grunewald and Rolnick, 2003). Furthermore, the return for every dollar invested in pre-school is much greater (8:1) for the individual and society than is an investment in school-based programs (3:1) (Heckman, 2000). In addition, each dollar invested creates a return of around $2–3 in earnings to the state (in low and middle income countries, a systematic simulation economic analysis of existing programmes has revealed that the potential long-term economic effects of increasing pre-school enrolment to 25% or 50% in these countries has a potential benefit-to-cost ratio ranging from 6.4 to 17.6) (Engle et al., 2011).

Who has access to early childhood education and care?

International evidence in high income countries has shown that the children that are in most need of early education and care services continue to be less likely to attend high-quality programmes (The Sutton Trust, 2012). Similarly, in low and middle income countries, children in the poorest households are less likely to access early childhood education and care programmes. These children are also more likely to be left alone at home, or in the care of another young child, and to experience a home environment that is not conducive to their optimal development and learning by not receiving adequate stimulation and early learning experiences, by being exposed to authoritarian and harsh forms of discipline and by experiencing stress and common precipitants of stress such as neglect, abuse, parental distress, mental illness, domestic violence and substance abuse (UNICEF, 2012). Adverse home conditions not only affect children directly, but they also diminish parents' capacity to offer their children appropriate care and protection.

Case study

Early childhood education and care policy in England

Current policy in England mandates that all 3- and 4-year-olds are entitled to 15 hours of free early education a week, for 38 weeks of the year. From April 2015, settings will have access to the Early Years Pupil Premium (EYPP) to support disadvantaged 3- and 4-year-olds. Settings are required to demonstrate that they use the EYPP to close the attainment gap between the most disadvantaged children and their peers.

Some eligible 2-year-olds are also entitled to the same amount of free early education as 3- and 4-year-olds. Their eligibility is determined by using similar criteria to those children who qualify for free school meals. It was expected that, by 2014–15, this provision will be extended to 40% of 2-year-olds.

The EYFS 2014 also requires that settings complete the Profile to summarise and describe children's attainment in 17 early learning goals at the end of the EYFS. Settings are also required to report to parents on the progress of their 2-year-old child in the prime areas of learning.

(Source: EYFS and EYFS Profile)

Reflective tasks

Considering the case study, you may reflect on:

- the influences of international research evidence on current early childhood education and care policy in England

- the arguments that have shifted attention from universal to targeted provision, especially, for the youngest children and children experiencing disadvantage

- how the expectation that early childhood education and care provision closes the attainment gap between children experiencing disadvantage and their peers may shape early childhood practice

- the possible advantages and potential challenges and unintended effects of the requirement that early childhood settings (i) complete the EYFS Profile at the end of EYFS and (ii) report to parents on the learning of their 2-year-olds.

Early childhood education and care provision: child rights and economic arguments

The findings of international research (summarised in Table 4.1) have shown that the earlier children are exposed to stimulation and learning opportunities, and receive appropriate health, nutrition, care and protection, the better their development and learning outcomes and their function in society later in life. High-quality early childhood education and care plays a pivotal role in enhancing the educational

Table 4.1   **Summary of accrued benefits of early childhood education and care**

Benefits For attending ECEC	Education (academic and social competence)	Health and welfare	Economy (family/society)
Children	Higher IQ, reading, literacy and math scores	Less malnutrition and stunting	Investment returns to society: $17.07 per dollar invested in early childhood development (High/Scope Perry study)
	Lower rates of grade repetition	Less child and maternal morbidity and mortality	
	Reduced placement in special education	Less child abuse	Investment return: at least 8:1 (investment in education in general is at 3:1)
	More years of higher and tertiary education	Better hygiene and health care	
	Understanding of their role in the educational process and their success	Better pre-natal and post-natal care	Returns as high as 16% for high quality early childhood development, of which public return is 12%
	Increased social competence and attachment skills		In low/middle income countries returns are from 6·4% to 17·6%
	Early identification of and support for special needs		
Children as adults	Further education and training	Lower rates of early teen pregnancy, smoking and drug use	Greater likelihood of full-time and higher status employment
	Positive parenting	Less single parenthood	Property/house ownership
	Better child/parent interaction	Brought up their own children	Better salaries and payment of higher taxes
		Less antisocial and criminal activity	Reduced judicial, court and welfare costs
		Less dependency on welfare	

Source: Papatheodorou, 2014

attainment and health outcomes of young children. It safeguards children's rights and, in adulthood, reduces their dependency on welfare, minimises costs incurred because of potential anti-social and criminal activity and contributes to better and higher status jobs with good payment rewards. It is a protective factor against social and economic disadvantage by enabling parental employment, increasing household income and reducing poverty and, in the long run, equipping children to be productive citizens.

These arguments have shifted attention from 'child development' to 'human development' and from focusing on the child's 'being' here-and-now to the child's 'becoming' a productive adult; from an ideological position of early childhood education and care as a playful endeavour to socio-economic arguments for intentional learning and for bridging the achievement gap; from being a service to the child to becoming a service to the child and family; from being a fragmented service, offered by different government departments (e.g. health, education, welfare), to being conceptualised as an integrated and multi-sectoral component. Figure 4.1 presents a framework for multi-component integrated early childhood education and care provision and quality parameters that determine its impact.

As a result, early childhood education and care is now seen as an interventionist service, especially for the youngest children and children at risk due to the adverse and disadvantaged conditions of their life and has gained prominence among policy makers who are called to integrate it into social and economic development policies (UNESCO, 2010b). The arguments are that well-targeted, planned and implemented early childhood education and care programmes are initiators of human development (van der Gaag, 2002). Thus, investments in such programmes, especially for the most disadvantaged children, is good economics and good public policy (Heckman, 2007).

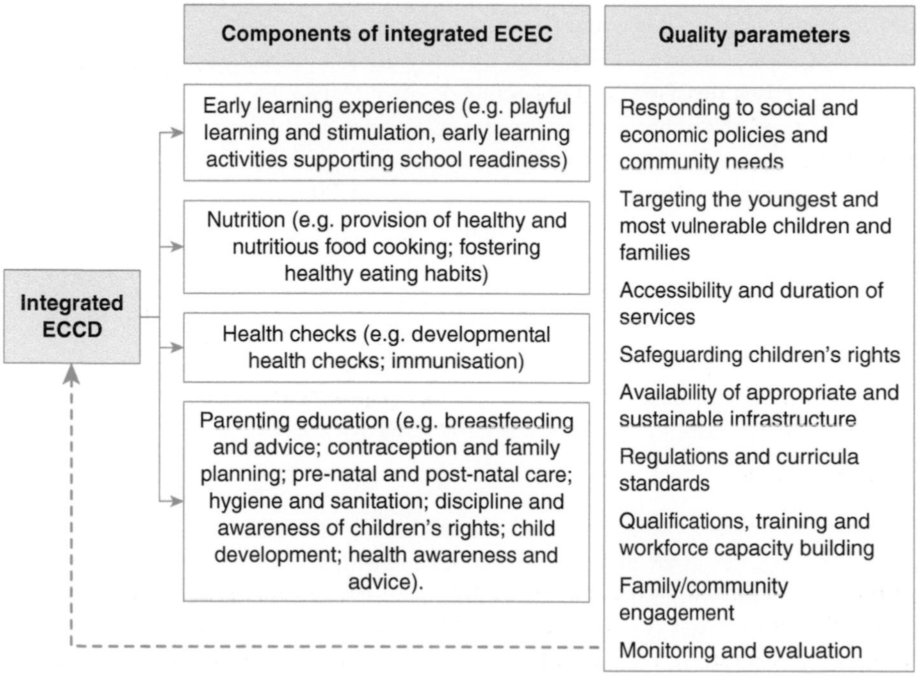

Components of integrated ECEC	Quality parameters
Early learning experiences (e.g. playful learning and stimulation, early learning activities supporting school readiness)	Responding to social and economic policies and community needs
Nutrition (e.g. provision of healthy and nutritious food cooking; fostering healthy eating habits)	Targeting the youngest and most vulnerable children and families
Health checks (e.g. developmental health checks; immunisation)	Accessibility and duration of services
Parenting education (e.g. breastfeeding and advice; contraception and family planning; pre-natal and post-natal care; hygiene and sanitation; discipline and awareness of children's rights; child development; health awareness and advice).	Safeguarding children's rights
	Availability of appropriate and sustainable infrastructure
	Regulations and curricula standards
	Qualifications, training and workforce capacity building
	Family/community engagement
	Monitoring and evaluation

Integrated ECCD

Figure 4.1 *A framework for integrated early childhood education and care and quality parameters (source: Papatheodorou, 2013)*

Early childhood education and care: a global policy agenda

Given the research evidence, it is not surprising that early childhood education and care has gained a central place in international policies that mandate the expansion and improvement of provision, especially for the most vulnerable and disadvantaged children, with calls for this to be prioritised within the wider post-2015 development agenda. In 1989, the UNCRC set out universal values and aspirations for children's development and well-being, education, protection and participation (United Nations, 1989). It later asserted that these rights apply to young children (up to the age of 5 years) too and mandated that children's services should be assessed on the extent to which the children's rights are observed (UNICEF, 2006: 1). The UNCRC was followed by the Jomtien Declaration on 'Education for All' (EFA), which affirmed that learning starts at birth (UNESCO, 1990), while the subsequent 'Dakar Framework for Action' identified the expansion and improvement of early childhood care and education by 2015 as its first EFA goal (UNESCO, 2000). Considering the available research evidence, early childhood education and care was seen as impacting, directly and indirectly, on the Millennium Development Goals, set out by the United Nations Development Programme (UNDP, 2000), that is, achieving universal primary education (MDG2), promoting gender equality and empowering women (MDG3), reducing child mortality (MDG4), improving maternal health (MDG5), combating HIV/AIDS, malaria and other diseases (MDG6), and reducing poverty (MDG 1).

Most countries are signatories of these declarations and have committed to observe them by introducing and/or aligning their policies with the values, aspirations and intended outcomes underpinning the declarations and increasing investment, although this is not nearly enough to cover demand for early childhood education and care services. Introduced policies focus mainly on quality improvement by setting out standards and regulations for designing and implementing curricula; improving qualifications, training and working conditions for practitioners; engaging families and communities; and advancing data collection, research and monitoring (OECD, 2012).

The demand for evidence has led to the development of a global tool, the Holistic Early Childhood Development Index (HECDI) (UNESCO, 2014), which provides a framework for assessing children's:

- survival and age-appropriate development and learning;
- home experiences that are cognitively stimulating and emotionally supportive;
- access to quality programmes and services addressing health care, good nutrition, education and social protection; and that their
- rights are protected and upheld through the implementation of policies and programmes to support children and families.

Early childhood education and care in the EU

In Europe, a review of early childhood education and care policies among member-states echoes the same aims, goals and aspirations of global policies about children and quality early childhood provision, although each country may seek different ways of achieving them. In England and the UK in general, policy priorities increasingly focus on the integration of education, health and social care services; development and professionalisation of the workforce (discussed in Chapter 5); early childhood curricula, children's assessment and evaluation of provision (discussed in Chapters 2 and 9); engaging families and communities (discussed in Chapter 13); children's voice and participation; and economic conditions.

The government's commitment to integrated early childhood education and care and the engagement of families and communities are clearly articulated in the publication 'Supporting Families in the Foundation Years' (DfE and DH, 2011), while the publication 'Improving the quality and range of education and childcare from birth to 5 years' has set the agenda for building a 'stronger and better-qualified' early childhood workforce (DfE and HM Treasury, 2014). The EYFS framework has been repeatedly reviewed and revised, with the latest version explicitly focusing on 'school readiness' and mandating providers to prepare young children for the compulsory school system (DfE, 2014). This suggests a shift away 'from a broader developmental focus on the outcomes of the Every Child Matters agenda' (Bertram and Pascal, 2014: 13) towards achieving academic outcomes and filling in the gaps later in schooling. The academic outcomes and focus of early childhood education and care experience is further reinforced by the requirement that children are assessed at the end of the EYFS and parents receive reports for their 2-year-old children. At the same time, evaluation of early childhood education and care services (e.g. Ofsted inspection and the self-evaluation of settings) has long been established to demonstrate their impact.

In championing the UNCRC and upholding the rights of all children, the child's voice remains embedded in policy making (HM Government, 2006), with attempts made, at varying levels and to varying extents, to involve young children in decision making that affects their lives (NCB, 2010). This focus on the participation and engagement of young children in policy and decision making has become an important tenet of the early childhood education and care discourse that has gradually informed practices within the UK and internationally.

Economic conditions have increasingly influenced policy development which has gradually focused on targeted provision, especially for children and families experiencing poverty and disadvantage. There are increased concerns about the 'extent of poverty, inequality and social disadvantage' in European societies, including England, and the impact of this on 'the educational attainment, life chances, health and social contribution of many of our children' (Bertram and Pascal, 2014: 14). In the UK, successive governments have set an ambitious target to eliminate child poverty by 2020, and early childhood education and care provision is seen as one way of doing so. However, for early childhood education and care to contribute to poverty reduction and, consequently, inequality among young children and families, it requires long-term, ring-fenced and sustained public funding. In an era of 'deficit reduction' it is difficult to see how such a target could be achieved, especially when by 2013 the number of Children's Centres had been reduced (House of Commons Education Committee, 2013). In England and the UK more widely, early childhood education and care operates mostly on a model of 'mixed economy' provided by a mix of public, private and non-profit providers, with many charging fees for the services. For many families these charges are a significant expenditure, and for the poorest, are often unaffordable (Lloyd and Penn, 2014). Inevitably, children and families that most need early childhood education and care are excluded from such services.

Summary

To sum up, in this chapter we briefly reviewed some of the key evidence from international research that is used for arguing for early childhood education and care as a means of safeguarding children's rights and for making the case for increased investment. We also discussed how such evidence has influenced the discourse in the field of early childhood, shaped international and national policies and informed practices. Whilst as practitioners the focus remains on the direct contact and practices with and for children, awareness of the wider research and policy landscape enables a better understanding of policy implications for practice.

Key points to remember

- An increased body of evidence has formed the basis for advocating early childhood education and care as a means of fulfilling children's rights and promoting it as a foundation for a nation's social capital and economic prosperity.

- Early childhood education and care has gradually been seen as an interventionist service, especially for combating early disadvantage, experienced by children and families, and filling the achievement gap later in schooling.

- The UNCRC has been instrumental in the increased interest paid to early childhood education and care, but the economic argument has been instrumental in the increased investment in the sector.

- Early childhood education and care practices are influenced by a combination of prevailing theories, political, economic, socio-historical and cultural factors.

Points for discussion

- Central to international and national policies is early childhood education and care as an interventionist service for children and families. What kind of evidence is informing this trend, and why?

- How does international and national research and policy developments on early childhood education and care inform your own practice? What are the advantages and possible challenges?

- In your view, what are the potential unintended adverse consequences of the argument 'the earlier the better' that is the prevailing current thinking in early childhood education and care?

Further reading

Gupta, A. (2008) 'Tracing Global-Local Transitions within Early Childhood Curriculum and Practice in India', *Research in Comparative and International Education*, September, *3* (3): 266–80.

Katz, L. (2015) *Lively Minds: Distinctions Between Academic Versus Intellectual Goals For Young Children*. Available at: https://deyproject.files.wordpress.com/2015/04/dey-lively-minds-4-8-15.pdf (accessed 30 May 2015).

National Scientific Council on the Developing Child (2010) *Early Experiences Can Alter Gene Expression and Affect Long-Term Development*. Working paper No. 10. Available at: http://developingchild.harvard.edu/index.php/resources/reports_and_working_papers/working_papers/wp10 (accessed on 31 August 2011).

Park, E., Lee, J. and Jun, H-J. (2013) 'Making use of Old and New: Korean early childhood education in the global context', *Global Studies of Childhood, Special Issue 2013; 3* (1): 40–52.

Simpson, D. and Envy, R. (2015) 'Subsidizing early childhood education and care or parents on low income: Moving beyond the individualized economic rationale of neoliberalism, *Contemporary Issues in Early Childhood, June 2015,* 16 (2): 166–178.

Walker, S.P., Wachs, T.D., Grantham-McGregor, S., Black, M.M., Nelson, C.A., Huffman, S.L., Baker-Henningham, H., Chang, S.M., Hamadani, J.D., Lozoff, B., Meeks Gardner, J.M., Powell, C.A., Rahman, A. and Richter, L. (2011) 'Inequality in early childhood: risk and protective factors for early child development', *The Lancet*, 378: 1325–1338.

Useful websites

Association for Childhood Education International – promotes and supports optimal education, development, and well-being for children worldwide:
http://acei.org/

World Organisation for Early Childhood Education – an international organisation that aims to promote the rights of the child to education and care worldwide:
www.worldomep.org/en/

Center on the Developing Child, Harvard University:
http://developingchild.harvard.edu/

which has a Global Children's Initiative section at:
http://developingchild.harvard.edu/activities/global_initiative/.

References

Belfield, C.R. and Schwartz, H. (2006) *The Economic Consequences of Early Childhood Education on the School System*. Research prepared for the National Institute of Early Education Research Rutgers University. Available at: http://nieer.org/publications/nieer-working-papers/economic-consequences-early-childhood-education-school-system (accessed 21 May 2015).

Bertram, T. and Pascal, C. (2014) *Early Years Literature Review*. Birmingham: The Centre for Research in Early Childhood. Available at: www.early-education.org.uk/early-years-literature-review (accessed 21 May 2015).

Bhutta, Z.A., Ahmed, T., Black, R.E., Cousens, S., Dewey, K., Giugliani, E., Haider, B.A., Kirkwood, B., Morris, S.S., Sachdev, H.P.S. and Shekar, M., for the Maternal and Child Undernutrition Study Group (2008) 'What works? Interventions for maternal and child under-nutrition and survival', *The Lancet*, 371 (9610): 417–440.

Brown, B., Ramos, M. and Traill, S. (2008) *The Economic Impact of the Early Care and Education Industry in Los Angeles County*, Los Angeles: The Insight, Centre for Community Economic Development. Available at: http://ceo.lacounty.gov/ccp/pdf/LA Economic Impact Report-Jan08.pdf (accessed 21 May 2015).

Bryce, J., Coitinho, D., Darnton-Hill, I., Pellerier, D., Pinstru Andersen, P. and the Maternal and Child Undernutrition Study Group (2008) 'Maternal and child undernutrition: effective action at national level', *The Lancet*, 371 (9611): 510–526.

Corteras, M., Singh, A., Heilman, B., Barker, G. and Verma, R. (2011) 'Analysing data from the International Men and Gender Equality Survey (IMAGES). Connections between early childhood experience of violence and intimate partner violence', in Bernard van Leer Foundation (ed.), *Early Childhood Matters. Hidden Violence: Protecting Young Children at* Home. 116: 26–31. Available at: http://resourcecentre.savethechildren.se/library/hidden-violence-protecting-young-children-home-early-childhood-matters (accessed 29 January 2016).

DfE (Department for Education) (2014) *Statutory Framework for the Early Years Foundation Stage: Setting the Standards for Learning, Development and Care for Children Birth to Five*. Available at: www.foundationyears.org.uk/files/2014/07/EYFS_framework_from_1_September_2014__with_clarification_note.pdf (accessed 31 May 2014).

DfE (Department for Education) and DH (Department of Health) (2011) *Supporting Families in the Foundation Year*. Nottingham: DfE Publications.

DfE (Department for Education) and HM Treasury (2014) *Improving the Quality and Range of Education and Childcare from Birth to 5 years*. London: DfE.

Engle, P.L., Fernald, L.C.H., Alderman, H., Behrman, J., O'Gara, C., Yousafzai, A., Cabral de Mello, M., Hidrobo, M., Ulkuer, N., Ertem, I., Iltus, S., and the Global Child Development Steering Group (2011) 'Strategies for reducing inequalities and improving developmental outcomes for young children in low-income and middle-income countries', *The Lancet*, 378: 1339–53.

Fox, N.A. and Shonkoff, J.P. (2011) 'Violence and development: how persistent fear and anxiety can affect young children's learning and behaviour and health', in Bernard van Leer Foundation (ed.), *Early Childhood Matters, Hidden Violence: Protecting Young Children at Home*, 116: 8–14. Available at: http://resourcecentre.savethechildren.se/library/hidden-violence-protecting-young-children-home-early-childhood-matters (accessed 29 January 2016).

Grunewald, R. and Rolnick, A. (2003) 'Early childhood development: economic development with a high public return', *The Region*, 17, No. 4: 6–12.

Heckman, J.J. (2000) *Policies to Foster Human Capital.* Joint Center for Poverty Research Working Papers 154. Chicago: Northwestern University/University of Chicago.

Heckman, J. (2007) *Investing in Disadvantaged Young Children Is Good Economics and Good Public Policy.* Presentation at Culture, Investments, and Human Development, New York University, 5 October.

HM Government (2006) *Raising Standards – Improving Outcomes Statutory Guidance. Early Years Outcomes Duty, Childcare Act 2006.* Available at: http://dera.ioe.ac.uk/6889/5/Raising%20 Standards%20-%20Improving%20Outcomes%20-%2003%20Dec.pdf (accessed 22 September 2015).

House of Commons Education Committee (2013) *Foundation Years: Sure Start Children's Centres.* Fifth Report of Session 2013–14. London: HMSO. Available at at: www.publications. parliament.uk/pa/cm201314/cmselect/cmeduc/364/364.pdf (accessed 25 May 2015).

IN BRIEF (n.d.) *The Impact of Early Adversity on Children's Development.* Available at: http:// developingchild.harvard.edu/index.php/resources/briefs/inbrief_series/inbrief_the_impact_ of_early_adversity/ (accessed 21 May 2015).

Jackson, S. (2014) 'Early childhood policy and services', in T. Maynard and S. Powell (eds), *An Introduction to Early Childhood Studies.* London: Sage.

Lloyd, E. and Penn, H. (2014) 'Childcare markets in an age of austerity', *European Early Childhood Education Research Journal,* 22 (3): 386–396.

Martinez, A., Naudeau, S. and Pereira, V. (2012) *The Promise of Preschool in Africa: A Randomized Impact Evaluation of Early Childhood Development in Rural Mozambique.* The World Bank Group and Save the Children. Available at: www.savethechildren.org/atf/ cf/%7B9def2ebe-10ae-432c-9bd0–df91d2eba74a%7D/MARTINEZ_NAUDEAU_PEREIRA. MOZ_ECD_REPORT-FEB_7_2012.PDF (accessed 21 May 2015).

Martorell, R., Khan, L.K. and Schroeder, D.G. (1994) 'Reversibility of stunting: epidemiological findings in children from developing countries', *European Journal of Clinical Nutrition,* 48 (1): 45–57.

National Scientific Council on the Developing Child (2010) *Early Experiences Can Alter Gene Expression and Affect Long-Term Development,* Working paper No. 10. Available at: http:// developingchild.harvard.edu/index.php/resources/reports_and_working_papers/working_ papers/wp10 (accessed 21 May 2015).

NCB (2010) *Let's Listen: Young Children's Voices – Profiling and Planning to Enable Their Participation in Children's Services.* London: NCB. Available at: www.participationworks.org. uk/resources/lets-listen-young-childrens-voices-profiling-and-planning-to-enable-their- participation-in (accessed 29 January 2016).

OECD (2011) *How Can We Do Better for Our Families? Issues, Outcomes, Policy Objectives and Recommendations.* Paris: OECD. Available at: www.oecd.org/edu/school/startingstrongiii- aqualitytoolboxorearlychildhoodeducationandcare.htm (accessed 29 January 2016).

OECD (2012) *Starting Strong III: A Quality Toolbox for Early Childhood Education and Care.* Executive Summary. Available at: www.oecd.org/edu/school/startingstrongiii-aqualitytool boxorearlychildhoodeducationandcare.htm (accessed 21 May 2015).

Papatheodorou, T. (2012) *Review of International Research on ECD.* Advocacy papers on Education, Health, Child Protection, Social Protection and Finance, submitted to Save the Children International Rwanda.

Papatheodorou, T. (2013) *Enhancing Early Childhood and Development Opportunities in Rwanda.* Final Monitoring and Evaluation Report, submitted to Save the Children International Rwanda.

Papatheodorou, T. (2014) *Early Childhood Care and Development (ECCD).* Position Paper, SCUK Education Team.

Parks, G. (2000) 'The High/Scope Perry Preschool Project', Juvenile Justice Bulletin (US Department of Justice, Office of Justice Programs, Office of Juvenile Justice and Delinquency Prevention). Available at: www.ncjrs.gov/pdffiles1/ojjdp/181725.pdf (accessed 21 May 2015).

Ruel, M.T., Menon, P., Habicht, J-P., Loechl, C., Bergeron, G., Pelto, G., Arimond, M., Maluccio, J., Michaud, L. and Hankebo, B. (2008) 'Age-based preventive targeting of food assistance and behaviour change and communication for reduction of childhood undernutrition in Haiti: a cluster randomised trial', *The Lancet*, 371 (9612): 588–595.

Schweinhart, L.J. (2003) 'Benefits, costs, and explanation of the High/Scope Perry Preschool Program'. Paper presented at the Meeting of the Society for Research in Child Development Tampa, Florida, April 26. Available at: www.highscope.org/file/Research/PerryProject/Perry-SRCD_2003.pdf (accessed 21 May 2015).

Schweinhart, L.J. (2007) 'Outcomes of the High/Scope Perry Preschool Study and Michigan School Readiness Program', in E.M. Young, and L.M. Richardson (eds), *Early Child Development: From Measurement to Action, A Priority for Growth and Equity*. Washington, DC: The International Bank for Reconstruction and Development. Available at: https://open knowledge.worldbank.org/handle/10986/6837 (accessed 21 May 2015).

Siraj-Blatchford, I., Sylva, K., Muttock, S., Gilden, R. and Bell, D. (2002) *Researching Effective Pedagogy in the Early Years*, Research Report 356. Norwich: DfES.

Straus, M.A. (2009) 'Differences in corporal punishment by parents in 32 nations and its relation to national differences in IQ'. Paper presented at the 14th International Conference on Violence, Abuse and Trauma, San Diego, California, 25 September. Available at: http://pubpages.unh. edu/~mas2/Cp98D%20CP%20%20IQ%20world-wide.pdf (accessed 21 May 2015).

Sutton Trust (2012) *Social Mobility and Education Gaps in the Four Major Anglophone Countries: Research Findings for the Social Mobility Summit*. Available at: www.suttontrust. com/wp-content/uploads/2012/05/social-mobility-summit2012.pdf (accessed 21 May 2015).

Sylva, K., Melhuish, E.C., Sammons, P., Siraj-Blatchford, I. and Taggart, B. (2004a) *The Effective Provision of Pre-School Education (EPPE) Project*. Technical Paper No. 12. London: DfES/ Institute Education, University of London.

Sylva, K., Melhuish, E., Sammons, P., Siraj-Blatchford, I. and Taggart, B. (eds) (2004b) *The Effective Provision of Pre-School Education [EPPE] Project: Final Report*. London: Institute of Education, University of London.

UNDP (United Nations Development Programme) (2000) Millennium Development Goals. Available at: www.undp.org/content/undp/en/home/mdgoverview/mdg_goals.html (accessed 31 May 2015).

UNESCO (1990) *Meeting Basic Learning Needs: A Vision for the 1990s. Background Document*. World Conference on Education for All, 5–8 March, Jomptien Thailand.

UNESCO (2000) *The Dakar Framework for Action. Education for All: Meeting Our Collective Commitments*. Adopted by the World Education Forum, Dakar Senegal, 26–28 April.

UNESCO (2010a) *EFA Global Monitoring Report 2010: Reaching the Marginalized*. Paris: UNESCO and Oxford University Press.

UNESCO (2010b) 'Moscow Framework for Action and Cooperation: Harnessing the Wealth of Nations'. World Conference on Early Childhood Care and Education (ECCE) Building the Wealth of Nations 27–29 September 2010, Moscow. Available at: http://unesdoc.unesco.org/ images/0018/001898/189882e.pdf (accessed 21 May 2015).

UNESCO (2014) *Holistic Early Childhood Development Index (HECDI) Framework: A Technical Guide*. Paris: UNESCO. Available at: http://unesdoc.unesco.org/images/0022/002291/229188e. pdf (accessed 21 May 2015).

UNICEF (United Nations Children's Fund) (2012) *Inequalities in Early Childhood Development. What the Data Say. Evidence from Multiple Indicator Cluster Survey.* New York: UNICEF.

UNICEF (United Nations Children's Fund) (2006) General Comment No. 7 (2005), Implementing child rights in early childhood. Committee on the Rights of the Child, Fortieth Session, Geneva, 12–30 September 2005. Available at: http://www2.ohchr.org/english/bodies/crc/docs/Advance Versions/GeneralComment7Rev1.pdf (accessed 21 May 2015).

United Nations (1989) *United Nations Convention on the Rights of the Child.* Geneva: Defence International and United Nations Children's Fund. Available at: www.ohchr.org/en/professionalinterest/pages/crc.aspx.

US Department of Health and Human Services, Administration for Children and Families (2010) *Head Start Impact Study, Final Report.* Washington, DC: US Department of Health and Human Services, Administration for Children and Families. Available at: www.acf.hhs.gov/programs/opre/hs/impact_study/reports/impact_study/executive_summary_final.pdf (accessed 21 May 2015).

van der Gaag, J. (2002) 'From child development to human development', in E.M. Young (ed.), *From Early Child Development to Human Development: Investing in Our Children's Future.* Washington, DC: The International Bank for Reconstruction and Development. Available at: www.sck.gov.tr/oecd/From%20Early%20Child%20Development%20to%20Human%20Development.pdf (accessed 21 May 2015).

Walker, S.P., Wachs, T.D., Grantham-McGregor, S., Black, M.M., Nelson, C.A., Huffman, S.L., Baker-Henningham, H., Chang, S.M., Hamadani, J.D., Lozoff, B., Meeks Gardner, J.M., Powell, C.A., Rahman, A. and Richter, L. (2011) 'Inequality in early childhood: risk and protective factors for early child development', *The Lancet*, 378: 1325–1338.

Young, E.M. and Richardson, L.M. (eds) (2007) *Early Child Development: From Measurement to Action, A Priority for Growth and Equity.* Washington, DC: The International Bank for Reconstruction and Development. Available at: https://openknowledge.worldbank.org/handle/10986/6837 (accessed 21 May 2015).

Want to learn more about this chapter? Visit the companion website at https://study.sagepub.com/EYFS3e for access to free SAGE journal articles and book chapters, weblinks, annotated further readings and more.

5

The Issue of Professionalism

Nyree Nicholson

👍 **Chapter overview**

In the last decade the field of early childhood education and care has seen a number of changes with the introduction of new qualifications alongside the revision of existing qualifications. As has been demonstrated in Chapters 1 and 2, a national framework for the sector – The Early Years Foundation Stage – was implemented in September 2008 and since then it has been revised twice, in 2012 and in 2014. Similarly, the workforce in early childhood education and care has seen changes with the aims of raising quality and training among people working in the sector. The introduction of the Early Years Professional Status (a status, not qualification) was initially seen as the way to raise standards in workforce training, in an attempt to meet the quality requirements of the EYFS (CWDC, 2006). As was shown in Chapters 1 and 2, the Conservative and Liberal Democrat Coalition government commissioned Professor Nutbrown to undertake an in-depth investigation of the qualifications in the early childhood workforce. This report was published in June 2012 and concluded that early childhood education and care needed a highly qualified and professional workforce. As a result, the government withdrew the EYPS award and replaced it with the Early Years Educator and Early Years Teacher qualifications.

Historically, the term 'professional' was reserved for specific occupations such as doctor or lawyer (Runte, 1995). The concept of a 'professional', however, is expanding to incorporate a diverse range of differing occupations (Western et al., 2006). This diversity has aided ambiguity in the concept of 'the professional' on an international scale, particularly so within occupations in the sphere of early childhood education and care (Bankovic, 2014). This chapter will explore the concept of what it means to be 'professional' in an early childhood occupation.

In writing about roles, responsibilities and professionalism it is difficult to keep up to date because changes are rapid, but it is important to state that the role of the early childhood workforce as educators is not isolated or distinct from the role in the context of policy. These are inter-linked roles, thus this chapter aims to discuss the theoretical aspects of a early childhood workforce rather than describe the qualifications themselves.

This chapter aims to help you to:

- understand theoretical concepts about professionalism and consider what it means to the concepts of 'professional' and 'professionalism' in early childhood education and care

- discuss elements of what constitutes a professional in early childhood education and care

- understand concepts about the skills and the roles required of an early childhood workforce.

Towards a definition of professionalism

Runte (1995) suggests that professionalism holds particular 'traits', including knowledge, competency and levels of qualification, whereas Dalli and Urban (2013) suggest professionalism is a shared ideology; it is a set of agreed rules that professionals agree to act purposefully within when conducting their professional lives. Runte (1995) argues that in today's society professionalism does not exist in the traditional sense of the word. Many professions attempt to align themselves with some sort of professional status, in an effort to legitimise their working lives (Broadbridge and Parsons, 2003; Simpson, 2010; Thomas and Thomas, 2014). Professionalism in this respect is constructed and shaped by society, therefore, and as society adapts and evolves, so too does the professional discourse aligned to particular occupations. Fox (1992) suggests, therefore, that the interpretation of professionalism is in the individual's understanding of the term based on their own experiences of what it means to be a professional. For example, a doctor might say professionalism relates to their occupational Code of Ethics, the Hippocratic Oath, whilst other occupations might require a distinct qualification, or to be a member of a relevant professional body. Alternatively, an early childhood practitioner might argue a professional is a person who uses experience, knowledge of individual children, to lead children to learning through their pedagogy.

Professionalism in early childhood education and care

The early childhood sector has seen dramatic changes over the past few decades (Adams, 2008; Male and Palaiologou, 2013; Pugh, 2014), including inspections of settings from social services and Ofsted (Owen, 2003), the introduction of the first curriculum for 3- to 5-year-olds in 2000 (QCA/DfEE, 2000) and the implementation of the Early Years Foundation Stage (DCSF, 2008). Woodrow (2007), however, argues that there has been increasing attention to the pedagogic teaching discourse within early childhood education and care, which appears to have confused the issue of professionalism within the sector.

Historically early childhood providers have not been seen as teachers and have struggled to identify themselves within the educational community. Under the educational umbrella, a multitude of discourses exists, each sitting within their own historical, cultural context and helping to form professional identity. Primary and secondary schools, and further and higher education organisations, for example, are all accepted unquestioningly as educational establishments, whilst early childhood settings have not been viewed in the same way. Originally they have been considered as being within the caring sector, and perceived as coming under the jurisdiction of health and then social care (Owen, 2003; Chalke, 2013). Early childhood settings have been evolving within the current era, however, and are now considered as institutions with responsibility for education and care for children in their early years (Male and Palaiologou, 2013; Jones, 2014). The starting point for this change was in 2001 when the early childhood provision in the UK began to be inspected by Ofsted (Owen, 2003) and the Curriculum Guidance for the Foundation Stage (QCA/DfEE, 2000) was introduced. This move suggested a change in the way the early childhood sector was perceived by social policy and as an educational discourse in its own right (Wright, 2014). This shift in focus is proving difficult, however, in terms of how early childhood practitioners are seen by others in the educational community, by parents and by other practitioners (Brock, 2012; Chalke, 2013). The essence of 'childcare' is discussed by Taggart (2011), who suggests that the very nature of 'caring' is in conflict with how professional identity is conceptualised. Taggart suggests that as childhood is seen as a predominately female domain, in which the workforce is cast as caring and loving, this is a sharp contrast to how society perceives professionalism. Taggart argues that merely associating with babies and young children forces the concept that professionalism does not and cannot co-exist. This form of stereotyping has consequently delayed the progression in terms of how professionalism is viewed by many. This perception of the caring element of the role has caused difficulties with other educationalists, parents and the general public, who struggle to see that practitioners who offer both care and education to young children can be deemed to be professional.

This struggle with professional identity within early childhood education and care has been echoed globally (Brock, 2012; Bankovic, 2014), with discussion as to whether early childhood practitioners are teachers, pedagogues or carers. It could be argued they are all of these and this ambiguity of what it means to be an early childhood practitioner has been highlighted in the different titles attributed to early childhood practitioners: pedagogue, practitioner, early years professional, early years teacher and nursery nurse to name a few (Osgood, 2004; Adams, 2008; Chalke, 2013). The ambiguity of the many different names causes difficulties for practitioners in terms of positioning themselves within their own professional identity, in addition to *dispersing the focus for professionalism*' (Adams, 2008: 200).

Bankovic (2014) discusses the notion that professional within the sector is constantly changing and going through stages of modernisation, based on societal and political influences of the country that the early childhood education and care setting is based within. For example, in Serbia, early childhood education and care professionals are known as 'pre-school teachers' (Bankovic, 2014), whereas in New Zealand children are taught by 'teachers' (Oberhuemer, 2005), and in many European countries early childhood education and care professionals are known as 'pedagogues', taking on the role of supporting children's learning and development (Hallet, 2013). This could potentially be the source of the ambiguity around the ideology of professionalism in early childhood. If you are a doctor, you are called a doctor in all countries. Similarly the occupations of engineering and plumbing are recognised professions globally. The differences in the early childhood dynamic, depending on where a practitioner works and in what country, will depend on the name to which they align themselves (Brock, 2012). These differences have created a divide within the workforce in terms of status and ambiguous job descriptions (Brock, 2012). Professionalism in early childhood is difficult to define, therefore, and professional identity problematic.

Simpson (2010) argues this is due to the sector not fully evolving from a stage of professionalisation and suggests that until the early childhood sector has gone through a change as a whole its members (practitioners) are unable to attain professionalism or the utopian vision of it. Simpson (2010) argues that professionalisation is shaped within a political context and that this creates friction as the ideologies of government and the sector differ. For example, the UK government has been constructing the idealism of professionalism for the early childhood sector through proposing minimum levels of qualifications for practitioners without further investing in supporting the sector to become professional (Stewart and Obolenskaya, 2015). Moreover, the UK government is pushing the agenda, that to be professional, a practitioner must be qualified to a certain level (Tickell, 2011; Nutbrown, 2012). Processes were in place to aid the sector to achieve this ideal, through the Graduate Leader Fund where practitioners were able to apply for financial support for course fees, and settings were able to apply for funding to employ cover for the studying practitioner. The Graduate Leader Fund was abolished, however, making it difficult for practitioners to access training (Stewart and Obolenskaya, 2015). Many practitioners are working for minimum wage and cannot afford the high university fees to gain a degree, particularly as there is often little or no reward in terms of remuneration or status (Osgood, 2004; Eisenstadt et al., 2013; Moss, 2014). It has been argued in light of these factors the aim of minimum levels of qualifications is unlikely (Waniganayake, 2002).

What does it mean to be professional?

The challenge then becomes, what does it mean to be an early childhood professional? One suggestion is that it is based on qualifications (Osgood, 2004, 2006; Cable and Goodliff, 2011; Tickell, 2011; Nutbrown, 2012; Bankovic, 2014; Davis, 2014; Moss, 2014; Urban, 2014). The current UK government appears to support the notion that a higher qualified workforce increases outcomes for children (Hallet, 2013; Moss, 2014). This is echoed by international governments, such as New Zealand, Serbia and Australia, which endorse the view that qualifications and training are key to a professional provision (Miller and Dalli, 2014). Nutbrown (2012) points out, however, that qualifications have historically not been a prerequisite of the English early childhood profession, suggesting the sector itself has a responsibility for raising expectations.

Cable and Goodliff (2011: 182) argue that being an early childhood professional means more than acquiring qualifications; professional identity is the skills, the beliefs and '*tools and notions of professional expertise*'. Osgood (2004) suggests, however, that raising qualifications of the workforce is one way to raise the professional status of early childhood practitioners. Lyons (1996) highlights this point from an international perspective, explaining that care and education in Australia are separated by the qualifications of the professionals that work there. If the person has basic qualifications they are able to care for the child and if they have a degree they are able to educate the child, thereby suggesting that education can only be facilitated by those qualified to degree level.

Professionalising early childhood

The Early Years Professional Status (EYPS) was introduced in 2006 in an attempt to address the issues of both professional identity and qualifications. The EYPS was designed to acknowledge the skills and qualifications of practitioners, providing both an identity and a parallel discourse with qualified teacher status (QTS). Although EYPS was not recognised as a qualification in its own right (CWDC, 2006), the intention was to create recognition of 'graduate leaders' within the workforce (Lloyd and Hallet, 2010; Davis, 2014). Critics argued, however, that the EYPS was not seen as equivalent to the QTS in terms of pay or professional recognition (Nutbrown, 2012). The Nutbrown Review (2012) suggested a new qualification – the Early Years Teacher (EYT) – to replace the EYPS in order to address these issues. The entry requirements for the course would be the same as for the QTS and it was hoped the new qualification would rectify, at least partially, the lack of parity between the two qualifications.

Recent research suggests that although individual practitioners felt gaining the EYPS aided their own professional development, it was not recognised by others (Davis, 2014). I would conclude, therefore, that professionalism is a personal reflection of self rather than a trait or skill recognised by others. This takes the discussion back to the point that the concept of professionalism is difficult to define.

Osgood (2009) argues that it can be damaging to define the early childhood profession based on the skills and knowledge of a graduate workforce. Davis (2014) illustrates that as a large portion of the workforce are not trained to graduate level, defining professionalism in this way could be demoralising and demotivating. Recent changes in the UK, following the Nutbrown Review (2012), have meant that practitioners will now need to have appropriate qualifications in mathematics and English at the end of compulsory schooling in order to become part of the workforce. In the UK this means practitioners will need GCSEs in both mathematics and English to achieve a place on a post-compulsory school course, identified as a Level 3 course in the UK (Faux, 2014). A Level 3 qualification in the UK is a one- or two-year college course covering child development and play, but there are vast differences in the Level 3 qualifications offered in terms of 'content and standard' (Nutbrown, 2012: 6). The Nutbrown Review (2012) advised changes to the qualification system to ensure that practitioners held full and current qualification, with a Level 3 course taking two years to complete. As a consequence the government has now brought in a new qualification – the Early Years Educator (EYE).

The key problem with this change is that this has also led to a decrease in the numbers of students applying for the Level 3 course (Crown, 2015). It could be suggested that in trying to increase entry requirements the courses are now becoming inaccessible to those practitioners without those basic qualifications. To achieve a GCSE in mathematics and English could take practitioners an additional two years (if not achieved at the end of compulsory schooling), in addition to two years for the Level 3 and an additional three years for a degree. Thus it could take some practitioners up to seven years to achieve graduate status. This also takes the discussion back to the issue of low pay and the difficulty early childhood practitioners may have in funding their studies. The government announced in July 2015 that practitioners can work towards these GCSEs whilst studying, but they must have them by the end of their course in order to be given the Level 3 qualification, so they have become an exit rather than an entry requirement.

One question that needs to be asked, however, is what is more important, a basic level of English and mathematics, or an evolved understanding of child development? This debate is causing a split in what is considered important within the sector. While recognising the importance of mathematics and English in professionalising the sector, the argument is that the vehicle chosen to steer this agenda is also causing a barrier to those practitioners wanting to enlarge their child development knowledge and skills (Faux, 2014). This potentially means that the sector could see a decrease in the number of people achieving appropriate qualifications, the opposite of what is trying to be achieved. Local authorities used to be able to offer a quality supplement, in terms of additional payments for the percentage of staff qualified to a particular level, to encourage providers to skill the workforce, but this too has now also been abolished (Gaunt, 2013). It is also important to note that although students have to have maths and English GCSE qualifications at Level 3 they do not need this to gain entry onto many higher education courses, such as foundation or first degrees.

Nutbrown (2012) highlights that although there has been investment in the early childhood sector in terms of raising qualifications, the Private, Voluntary and Independent (PVI) sector still retains an overall low level of qualification as was echoed more recently by Moss (2014). The PVI sector is the term reserved for all childcare provision that operates outside of state-maintained childcare provision (Gambaro et al., 2014). A potential reason for this could be that even with a degree, practitioner professional roles do not appear to be recognised as such within the wider community (Adams, 2008). The pay scales reflect this, with many early childhood practitioners achieving minimum wage despite having gained a professional qualification. Again this anomaly is reflected internationally (Lyons, 1996; Waniganayake, 2002; Ackerman 2005; Osgood; 2004; Findlay et al., 2009; Douglass and Gitell, 2012; Hordern, 2012). A key feature of the Nutbrown Review (2012) was to identify the lack of pay and recognition as a contributing factor for those practitioners who were considering progressing beyond a Level 3 qualification.

Shared body of knowledge

As has been discussed above, defining professionalism can be difficult, yet many agree a common factor is a shared body of knowledge (Hegarty, 2000; Kinchloe, 2004; Coleman et al., 2012). Cruess and Cruess (1997: 1675) propose that to understand professionalism you must look at the word itself. They argue the significant section of the word is 'profess', as this is how a practitioner dedicates themselves to an occupation. Cruess and Cruess (1997) suggest that to dedicate oneself to a profession, one must first have a body of knowledge on the service or provision. This emphasises the need to have a good body of knowledge and 'a commitment to service' (Cruess and Cruess, 1997: 1675).

Knowledge is accrued and shared, evolving to create new understanding through reflection and interaction with principles and experiences (Kinchloe, 2004). According to

Coleman et al. (2012), knowledge is two-pronged: professionals need both subject and professional knowledge. Subject knowledge can be defined as knowledge of all aspects of child development and pedagogy, with professional knowledge as the environmental systems defined by Bronfenbrenner's (1979) Ecological Model. In this way, professionals operate in different dimensions to meet the needs of each individual child. This suggests that practitioners have to share values and ideologies in addition to the shared body of knowledge.

Coleman et al. (2012: 29) hold the view that 'the knowledge base of practitioners is not static', suggesting that practitioners should be in a perpetual state of adding to and taking from the shared body of knowledge of the profession. There is some evidence, however, to suggest that the accumulation of knowledge is not always shared to underpin practice by practitioners (Hiebert et al., 2002). Brock (2012) argues there is complexity surrounding the relationships of professionals, suggesting that professionalism does not occur in a vacuum (Coleman et al., 2012). Defining professionalism, Brock (2012) asserts there needs to be recognition in the shared cultural and situational context, allowing an exploration of shared values and understanding.

According to Rodd (2012), the early childhood sector is currently operating in a disjointed way, with conflicting ideologies and no real understanding of a way to unite the sector and move forward, thus making practitioners ineffective in supporting and promoting children's rights. Adler et al. (2008: 371) proposes that real collaboration involves 'professional communities and non-professionals as sources of learning and support'; in this way, the body of knowledge is distributed and added to by all participants, including parents. This argument appears to support the notion that knowledge is not created in a vacuum, but is socially constructed by all contributors in a 'shared' approach.

'Educare'

As discussed above, childcare in the UK was historically under the jurisdiction of Social Services (Owen, 2003). Childcare was seen as a caring occupation rather than an educative one. Conversely, schools were seen as places for education rather than any caring-type role, suggesting care and education happened in isolation, rather than in tandem with the other. There has been a shift over the past few decades to integrate education and care across childcare provisions and schools alike (Sylva et al., 2004; Male and Palaiologou, 2013). This began with the move of childcare services from Social Services, where the concentration was on the care provided by settings, to Ofsted, which provided the inspection process and, thereby, the measure by which provision would be judged. The actual service is provided through a combination of private and publicly funded settings, all of whom attract a combination of funds from government and parents. Moreover, the introduction of the EYFS (DfE, 2012) heralded changes in the provision of education and care in the UK, unifying the early childhood sector under one child-focused curriculum, as discussed in detail in Chapter 1.

Ofsted inspects settings based on the education offered (in terms of the EYFS) and the welfare provided by settings to children. This move was seen as an integration of separate ideologies, into a shared philosophy of Educare, first introduced by Nordic countries (Eydal and Rostgaard, 2011). This move mirrors international perspectives which argued that care and education were synonymous and could not be split (Van Laere et al., 2012; Happo et al., 2013). There is inconsistency with this argument, however, as Urban (2014) points out that there appears to have been a shift in recent years towards education rather than care. The 'schoolification' of early childhood provision in the UK has seen an increase in demands to ensure children are 'school ready' (Van Laere et al., 2012; Male and Palaiologou, 2013; Cowley, 2014; Duffy, 2014), with this concept being echoed globally (Alcock and Haggarty, 2013; Gunnarsdottir, 2014). Gammage (2006) suggests this comes from a culture of accountability, driven both from governments and parents alike, that places emphasis on children's performance in terms of assessment. This shift in school readiness has highly significant implications for the Early Years Foundation Stage (EYFS) in terms of organisation and delivery. The EYFS is currently situated in an educational paradigm, based on learning through play (Haughton and Ellis, 2013). The direction of school readiness could move the focus towards education attainment, however, rather than in the holistic sense of child development. Research by the Professional Association for Childcare and Early Years (PACEY) (2013), suggests that the term 'school readiness' is lost in translation between policy makers in government and in how that translation is perceived by the sector. This ambiguity is causing tension for professionals within the sector and how this is translated into practice. An overarching argument within the sector is the notion that the shift involves the EYFS becoming about preparing children for school and formal learning (Langston, 2014), rather than valuing it as a phase in its own right (DfE, 2011: 31). Whitebread and Bingham (2014: 187) propose that the term 'school ready' indicates a child, upon leaving the EYFS, will have reached a predetermined level of skills and be ready to fit into the 'set' National Curriculum of Key Stage 1. One potential way around this is in the development of pedagogical leadership skills of the workforce. Male and Palaiologou (2012) suggest that pedagogic leadership enables environments to be created to enable practitioners to facilitate meaningful interactions with children in which to learn. Through pedagogic leadership and leading children to learning, it could be possible to help children to build skills to help them prepare for the next transition in their development.

The focus on school readiness has wider implications in the light of the move towards school-based environments and providing provision for 2-year-old children (Cowley, 2014; Swinford, 2014). Cowley (2014) highlights that there is a discrepancy in how the early childhood sector and the government understand the term 'school ready', further illustrating the divide between the two concepts. Sargent (2004) argues that this divide exists in terms of the PVI sector, both in the UK and the USA.

The term 'childcare' is still used by parents reflecting the emphasis on the caring aspect of the profession. Lyons (1996) argues historically that the main skills needed to be a practitioner were seen to be 'innate maternal qualities'. This is reflected in the early childhood dynamic where men are under-represented in a predominantly female-dominated workforce (Ackerman, 2005; Dunlop, 2008; Tickell, 2011; Douglass and Gitell, 2012), with only some 2% being male (Baker, 2012). Peeters (2013) argues that men in childcare globally struggle with professional identity due to the stereo-typical vision of how childcare should look. Men were traditionally seen as breadwinners taking on the role of disciplinarian whilst mothers took on the 'mater-nal caring' role (Rolfe, 2006; Department for Economic and Social Affairs, 2011; Cronin, 2014). Recent research has demonstrated that this gender stereotyping is a barrier to more men choosing early childhood education and care as a career option (Cronin, 2014).

This view appears to be slowly changing, at least in the home, with more fathers providing primary care for their own children (Cronin, 2014). In an economy that dictates that both parents should work where possible, or the parent with the greater job opportunities should work, less frequently the role of primary carer is expected of women. This has meant that the stereotype of men within the family is starting to change (Department for Economic and Social Affairs, 2011). Gender stereotypes are situated in the socio-demographic of the era they began in, so this is not a new phe-nomenon. For a man to choose nursing at one point was unusual and socially unacceptable, for example, where now it is common to see male nurses and the stigma appears to have been removed.

The key words to consider in this examination are 'education' and 'care'. The current shift in focus within the sector towards school readiness would imply that education is the most important element according to current policy. I argue that teaching and learning are not gender-specific roles, however, so both men and women can work with children in their learning journey. Cronin's (2014) research demonstrated that men who are working with children were motivated into the career by a desire to make a lasting impact. Care is not and should not be gender-specific as this alone does not guarantee a quality caring experience (Holloway, 2006).

Professional as leader

Although leadership in the early childhood sector is explored in detail in Chapter 17, this chapter explores the perception that to be a professional implies that you are also a leader. It is a widely held view that professionalism is related to leadership (Rodd, 1997; Muijs et al., 2004; Dunlop, 2008; Tickell, 2011; Heikka et al., 2012; Nutbrown, 2012; Male and Palaiologou, 2013a and b; Hallet, 2013; Bankovic, 2014). This is an interesting perspective that all professionals are leaders and all leaders are profession-als. This implies that leadership is a prerequisite of professionalism and vice versa, assuming the two concepts are mutually inclusive or exclusive. Both terms are problematic within early childhood. Professionalism is a goal to be strived for and achieved within practice, yet there is some evidence to suggest that early childhood practitioners do not perceive themselves as leaders (Muijs et al., 2004; Rodd, 2012; Pound, 2011; Taggart, 2011; Jones, 2014).

Hallet (2013) highlights there is an understanding for graduates to lead practice in settings, however Cooke and Henehan (2012) suggest there should be 'a focus on improving the knowledge and capabilities of leaders and practitioners', implying this is a work in progress and a continuous reflective process. According to Dunlop (2008), leadership is integral for increasing professionalism and accountability throughout the sector. Rodd (2012) asserts that leadership is not and should not be a module that sits within a degree programme, dusted off when needed. Leadership, Rodd (2012) argues, should be ingrained throughout practice and education. In this respect leadership can be seen as a distributed process, with all practitioners regardless of level of qualification or status capable of being leaders. Heikka et al. (2012) suggest distributed leadership is a process of building relationships, empowering individuals and utilising their professional strengths. Male and Palaiologou (2013) agrees that different leadership styles are required throughout early childhood practice (as will be demonstrated in Chapter 17).

Case study

Leanne's story

Leanne is currently employed as a manager in a private day care setting, on the outskirts of a busy city centre. The setting is relatively large, with the capacity to provide day care for eighty children from 6 weeks to 5 years old. Leanne started in the setting as a school leaver and is currently in her final year of a Foundation Degree in Early Childhood Studies.

I began by gaining my Level 3 in Child Development through the local college, studying during the evenings, before starting my Foundation Degree two years ago. I intend to complete a full Honours Degree. I have been asked why I want to do a Degree as my wages will not reflect the level of qualification I have achieved. For me, it is not just about the money, although I can see why that is a problem for some practitioners, I feel that I owe it to the children, families and myself to be the most professional practitioner I can be, and for me personally that involves gaining qualifications. Although, I do not believe professionalism is just about qualifications. It is also about the experience a person has and the way a practitioner works to ensure the child is at the centre of every decision that is made within the setting.

Case study

John's story

John has been registered as a childminder for eleven years, within a busy city classified as deprived by the local authority. When John first became registered there was only one other male childminder registered within the city; the number has now risen to around five, with the majority of male childminders in the city working in partnership with their wives/partners.

I love being a childminder and being involved in children's learning and development. To see a child arrive as a baby and follow their development all the way through to school gives me amazing job satisfaction. I get to know my families and work closely with them on a daily basis; I am able to see and help with the challenges and celebrate the achievements. However, there are challenges to being a male childminder. The difficulties I have faced is that some parents don't see me as a professional; they see me as a babysitter. There are some parents who are put off by the fact that I am a man, mostly if the child is still in nappies, and particularly when I first became registered. Parents appear to divide into two camps: those that have a liberal view and like the idea of a male childminder, and those who view male childminders with some suspicion. Parents who do choose to employ me to care for their children say that their children are gaining a valuable male perspective that they may not receive from a woman, but I think the quality of education and care should be the same regardless of the gender of the person delivering it. Perceptions have slowly changed over the years, however I am still struggling to gain the parent enquiries that other female childminders receive. This could be for a number of reasons, however conversations with parents have demonstrated that some parents view childminding as a job for a woman and struggle to identify me within a caring role, until they come to meet me.

Reflective tasks

After studying this chapter, reflect on the case studies and consider:

- what the concepts of 'professional' and 'professionalism' in early childhood mean to you and your group

- what it means to be a professional

- whether there is a division between 'care' and 'education' in early childhood.

Summary

As mentioned at the beginning of this chapter, the aim was to discuss issues of professionalism and address the fact that, in early childhood education and care, the term professionalism is still used in a loose way. It has been demonstrated that in order to have a professional body the following elements are a requirement:

- shared body of knowledge
- shared values
- shared ideology
- shared practice
- reflection 'in' action (Schön, 1983)
- reflection 'on' action (Tabachnick and Zeichner, 2002)
- course of study
- code of practice/ethics
- experience
- peer observations of the practice
- continuous assessment against standards
- continuous development.

In that sense the closing conclusion in this chapter echoes Eraut (1994: 1), who defines 'professionalism' as an ideology, rather than an accepted state, and 'professionalisation' as the process by which occupations seek to gain status and privilege in accord with that ideology. Professionalism defined as an ideology means that no agreed criteria exist that allow for the classification of an occupation as a profession. Consequently 'professionalism' is a state of mind, rather than a classified occupation, characterised by the behaviours of those who occupy the job (Male, 2004).

Key points to remember

- The issue of professionalism in early childhood education and care is problematic and complex and the term is still to be clarified.

- The field of early childhood needs clear ideology and agreed criteria that allow for the classification of the early years workforce as a profession. Consequently 'professionalism' is still a debatable issue and one can only discuss characteristics and behaviours that exist in the field.

- Although the early childhood sector has seen improvements (as has been addressed in Chapters 1 and 2), there is still a need for high-quality qualifications that will help towards the construction of a professional identity in the field.

Points for discussion

- Based on what has been discussed in this chapter, write down the key elements that you would include in the early childhood professional body of knowledge and practice.

- Discuss the code of practice in an early childhood setting that you are familiar with or you are working in. Consider what a code of practice for early childhood should include.

- Discuss the shared body of knowledge in the field of early childhood and consider the current qualifications that exist in the sector. In your view, does the field of early childhood education and care share a body of knowledge and an ideology? If yes, what is this?

Further reading

Book

Miller, L. and Cable, C. (eds) (2008) *Professionalism in the Early Years*. London: Hodder/Arnold.

Articles

Evans, L. (2008) 'Professionalism, professionality and the development of education professionals', *British Journal of Educational Studies*, 56 (1): 20–38.
Miller, L. and Dalli, C. (2014) 'Early years professionalism: reflections', *International Journal of Early Years*, 22 (3): 239–241.
Osgood, J. (2009) 'Childcare workforce reform in England and "the early years professional": a critical discourse analysis', *Journal of Education Policy*, 24 (6): 733–751.

Useful websites

To keep up to date with the developments of qualifications in the sector visit: www.gov.uk/government/publications/

To read more about the Nutbrown Review visit: www.gov.uk/government/collections/nutbrown-review

References

Ackerman, D.J. (2005) 'Getting teachers from here to there: Examining issues related to an early care and education teacher policy'. *Early Childhood Research and Practice*, 7 (1): 1–17. Available at: http://ecrp.uiuc.edu/v7n1/Ackerman.html (Accessed February 15, 2015).

Adams, K. (2008) 'What's in a name? Seeking professional status through degree studies within the Scottish early years context', *European Early Childhood Education Research Journal*, 16 (2): 196–209.

Adler, P.S., Kwon, S-W. and Heckscher, C. (2008) 'Perspective-professional work: the emergence of collaborative community', *Organization Science*, 19 (2): 359–376. Available at: http://pubsonline.informs.org/doi/abs/10.1287/orsc.1070.0293 (accessed 27 March 2015).

Alcock, S. and Haggarty, M. (2013) 'Recent policy developments and the "schoolification" of early childhood care and education in Aotearoa New Zealand', *Signs*, 26: 27. Available at: www.nzcer.org.nz/system/files/ECF2013_2_021_0.pdf (accessed 27 March 2015).

Baker, R. (2012) '"Childcare is not just a woman's job" – why only two per cent of the day nurseries and childcare workforce is male'. [Online] www.daynurseries.co.uk/news/article.cfm/id/1557858/childcare-is-not-just-a-womans-job-why-only-two-per-cent-of-the-day-nurseries-and-childcare-workforce-is-male (accessed 27 March 2015).

Bankovic, I. (2014) 'Early childhood professionalism in Serbia: current issues and developments', *International Journal of Early Years Education*, 22 (3): 251–62.

Broadbridge, A. and Parsons, E. (2003) 'UK charity retailing: managing in a newly professionalised sector', *Journal of Marketing Management*, 19 (7/8): 729–48.

Brock, A. (2012) 'Building a model of early years professionalism from practitioners' perspectives', *Journal of Early Childhood Research*, 11 (1): 27–44. Available at: http://ecr.sagepub.com/content/11/1/27.short (accessed 13 February 2015).

Brock, A. and Ranklin, C. (2011) 'Perspectives on professionalism'. In A. Brock, (ed.) Professionalism in the Interdisciplinary Early Years Team: Supporting Young Children and their Families. London: Continuum International Publishing Group.

Bronfenbrenner, U. (1979) *The Ecology of Human Development: Experiments by Nature and Design*. Cambridge, MA: Harvard University Press.

Cable, C. and Goodliff, G. (2011) 'Transitions in professional identity: women in the early years workforce', in *Gendered Choices: Learning, Work, Identities in Lifelong Learning*. London: Springer.

Chalke, J. (2013) 'Will the early years professional please stand up? Professionalism in the early childhood workforce in England', *Contemporary Issues in Early Childhood*, 14 (3): 212–22.

Coleman, M.R., Gallagher, J.J. and Job, J. (2012) 'Developing and sustaining professionalism within gifted education', *Gifted Child Today*, 35 (1): 27–37.

Cooke, G. and Henehan, K. (2012) *Double Dutch: The Case Against Deregulation and Demand-Led Funding in Childcare*. London: Institute for Public Policy Research. Available at: www.ippr.org/files/images/media/files/publication/2012/10/double-dutch-childcare_Oct2012_9763.pdf?noredirect=1 (accessed 22 September 2015).

Cowley, S. (2014) 'Does two into school really go?', *Forum*, 56 (2): 235–43.

Cronin, M. (2014) 'Men in early childhood: a moral panic? A research report from a UK university', *Social Change Review*, 12 (1): 3–24.

Crown, H. (2015) 'Huge slump in student numbers for EYE Level 3 courses', *Nursery World*. Available at: www.nurseryworld.co.uk/nursery-world/news/1148717/huge-slump-student-eye-level-courses (accessed 22 September 2015).

Cruess, S.R. and Cruess, R.L. (1997) 'Professionalism must be taught', *BMJ*, 315: 1674–7.

CWDC (Children's Workforce Development Council) (2006) *The Early Years Professional Prospectus*. London: CWDC.

Dalli, C. and Urban, M. (2013) *Professionalism in Early Childhood Education and Care: International Perspectives*. Abingdon: Routledge.

Davis, G. (2014) 'Graduate leaders in early childhood education and care settings: the practitioner perspective', *Management in Education*, 28 (4): 156–60.

DCSF (Department for Children, Schools and Families) (2008) *The Early Years Foundation Stage: Setting the Standards for Learning, Development and Care for Children from Birth to Five.* Nottingham: DCSF Publications.

Department for Economic and Social Affairs (2011) *Men in Families and Family Policy in a Changing World,* New York: United Nations Publication.

DfE (Department for Education) (2011) *Reforming the Early Years Foundation Stage. The EYFS: Government Response to Consultation.* London: DfE.

DfE (Department for Education) (2012) *Statutory Framework for the Early Years Foundation Stage. Setting the Standards for Learning, Development and Care for Children from Birth to Five.* Runcorn: DfE Publications.

Douglass, A. and Gitell, J.H. (2012) 'Transforming professionalism: relational bureaucracy and parent teacher partnerships in child care settings', *Journal of Early Childhood Research,* 10 (3): 267–81.

Duffy, B. (2014) 'The Early Years Curriculum', in G. Pugh and B. Duffy (eds), *Contemporary Issues in the Early Years.* London: Sage.

Dunlop, A.W. (2008) *A Literature Review on Leadership in The Early Years.* Glasgow: Learning and Teaching Scotland (LTS).

Eisenstadt, N., Sylva, K., Mathers, S. and Taggart, B. (2013) *More Great Childcare: Research Evidence.* London: Institute of Education, University of London.

Eraut, M. (1994) *Developing Professional Knowledge and Competence.* London: Falmer Press.

Evans, L. (2008) 'Professionalism, professionality and the development of education professionals', *British Journal of Educational Studies,* 56 (1): 20–38.

Eydal, G.B. and Rostgaard, T. (2011) 'Day-care schemes and cash-for-care at home', in I.V. Gislason and G.B. Eydal (eds). Copenhagen: Nordic Council of Ministers.

Faux, K. (2014) 'DfE confirms grade C English and Mathematics GCSE required for Early Years Educator', *Nursery World.* Available at: www.nurseryworld.co.uk/nursery-world/news/1142389/dfe-confirms-grade-english-Mathematics-gcse-required-educator (Accessed 27 March 2015).

Findlay, P., Findlay, J. and Stewart, R. (2009) 'The consequences of caring: skills, regulation and reward among early years workers', *Work, Employment & Society,* 2 (3): 422–41. Available at: http://wes.sagepub.com/content/23/3/422.short (accessed 13 February 2015).

Fox, C.J. (1992) 'What do we mean when we say "professionalism?": A language usage analysis for public administration', *The American Review of Public Administration,* 22 (1): 1–17. Available at: http://arp.sagepub.com/content/22/1/1.short (accessed 2 March 2015).

Gambaro, L., Stewart, K. and Waldfogel, J. (2014) 'Equal access to early childhood education and care', in L. Gambaro, K. Stewart and J. Waldfogel (eds), *An Equal Start? Providing Quality Early Education and Care for Disadvantaged Children.* Bristol: Policy Press.

Gammage, P. (2006) Early Childhood Education and Care: Politics, Policies and Possibilities. *Early Years: An International Research Journal ,* 26(3), pp.235–248.

Gaunt, C. (2013) 'Consultation opens on changes to way LAs fund providers', *Nursery World.* [Online] www.nurseryworld.co.uk/nursery-world/news/1097707/consultation-changes-las-fund-providers (accessed 2 March 2015).

Gunnarsdottir, B. (2014) 'From play to school: are core values of ECEC in Iceland being undermined by "schoolification"?' *International Journal of Early Years Education,* 22 (3): 242–50.

Hallet, E. (2013) 'We all share a common vision and passion: early years professionals reflect upon their leadership of practice role', *Journal of Early Childhood Research,* 11 (3): 312–25.

Happo, I., Määttä, K. and Uusiautti, S., (2012) 'Experts or good educators–or both? The development of early childhood educators' expertise in Finland'. *Early Child Development and Care,*

182(3–4): 487–504. Available at: http://www.tandfonline.com/doi/abs/10.1080/03004430.201
1.646719 (Accessed February 15, 2015).

Haughton, C. and Ellis, C. (2013) 'Play in the Early Years Foundation Stage', in *The Early Years Foundation Stage: Theory and Practice*. London: Sage.

Hegarty, S. (2000) 'Teaching as a knowledge-based activity', *Oxford Review of Education*, 26 (3&4): 451–65.

Heikka, J., Waniganayaka, M. and Hujala, E. (2012) 'Contextualising Distributed Leadership Within Early Childhood Education: Current Understandings, Research Evidence and Future Challenges', *Educational Management Administration and Leadership*, 41 (1): 30–44.

Hiebert, J., Gallimore, R. and Stigler, J.W. (2002) 'A knowledge base for the teaching profession: what would it look like and how can we get one?', *Educational Researcher*, 31 (5): 3–15.

Holloway, W. (2006) *The Capacity to Care: Gender and Ethical Subjectivity*. Hove: Routledge.

Hordern, J. (2012) 'A productive system of early years professional development', *Early Years*, 33 (2): 106–18. Available at: http://dx.doi.org/10.1080/09575146.2012.744958 (accessed 13 February 2015).

Jones, P. (2014) 'Training and Workforce Issues in the Early Years'. In: G. Pugh and B. Duffy (eds), *Contemporary Issues in the Early Years* (6th ed.). London: Sage, pp. 255–272.

Kincheloe, J. (2004) 'The knowledge of teacher education: developing a critical complex epistemology', *Teaching Education Quarterly*, pp. 49–66.

Langston, A. (2014) *Facilitating Children's Learning in the EYFS*. Maidenhead: Open University Press.

Lloyd, E. and Hallet, E. (2010) Professionalising the early childhood workforce in England: work in progress or missed opportunity? *Contemporary Issues in Early Childhood*, 11(1), p.75. Available at: www.wwwords.co.uk/rss/abstract.asp?j=ciec&aid=3962&doi=1 (accessed 13 February 2015).

Lyons, M. (1996) 'Who cares? Child-care, trade unions and staff turnover', *Journal of Industrial Relations*, 38(4): 629–647. Available at: http://jir.sagepub.com/content/38/4/629.short (Accessed February 15, 2015).

Male, T. (2004) 'Preparing for and entering headship in England: a study of career transition'. University of Lincoln, unpublished PhD thesis.

Male, T. and Palaiologou, I. (2012) 'Learning-centred leadership or pedagogical leadership? An alternative approach to leadership in education contexts'. *International Journal of Leadership in Education*, 15(1): 107–118. Available at: http://www.tandfonline.com/doi/full/10.1080/13 603124.2011.617839 (Accessed October 29, 2015).

Male, T. and Palaiologou, I. (2013a) 'Historical developments in policy for early years education and care', in I. Palaiologou (ed.), *The Early Years Foundation Stage: Theory and Practice*. London: Sage.

Male, T. and Palaiologou, I. (2013b) 'Pedagogical leadership in the 21st century: evidence from the field'. *Educational Management Administration & Leadership*, 1–18. Available at: http://ema.sagepub.com/content/early/2013/09/20/1741143213494889.abstract (Accessed October 29, 2015).

Miller, L. and Dalli, C. (2014) 'Early years professionalism: reflections', *International Journal of Early Years*, 22 (3): 239–41.

Moss, P. (2014) 'Early childhood policy in England 1997–2013: anatomy of a missed opportunity', *International Journal of Early Years Education*, 22 (4): 346–58.

Muijs, D., Aubrey, C., Harris, A. and Briggs, M. (2004) 'How do they manage? A review of the research in early childhood', *Journal of Childhood Research*, 2 (2): 157–69.

Nutbrown, C. (2012) *Foundations for Quality: The Independent Review of Early Education and Childcare Qualifications. Final Report*. Runcorn: Department for Education. Available at: www.gov.uk/government/uploads/system/uploads/attachment_data/file/175463/Nutbrown-Review.pdf.

Oberhuemer, P. (2005) 'Conceptualising the early childhood pedagogue: policy approaches and issues of professionalism', *European Early Childhood Education Research Journal*, 13 (1): 5–16.

Osgood, J. (2004) 'Time to get down to business? The responses of early years practitioners to entrepreneurial approaches to professionalism', *Journal of Early Childhood Research*, 2 (1): 5–24.

Osgood, J. (2006) 'Deconstructing professionalism in early childhood education: resisting the regulatory gaze', *Contemporary Issues in Early Childhood*, 7 (1): 5–14.

Osgood, J. (2009) 'Childcare workforce reform in England and "the early years professional": a critical discourse analysis', *Journal of Education Policy*, 24 (6): 733–51.

Owen, S. (2003) 'The development of childminding networks in Britain: sharing the caring', in A. Mooney and J. Statham (eds), *Family Day care: International Perspectives on Policy, Practice and Quality*. London: Jessica Kingsley Publishers.

PACEY (2013) 'What does "school ready" really mean? A Research Report from the Professional Association for Childcare and Early Years'. [Online] www.pacey.org.uk/news-and-views/news/archive/2013-news/september-2013/school-ready-research-launched/ (accessed 29 January 2016).

Peeters, J. (2013) 'Towards a gender neutral interpretation of professionalism in early childhood education and care (ECEC)', *Revista Española de Educación Comparada*, (21): 119–44.

Pound, L. (2011) 'Exploring leadership: roles and responsibilities of the early years professional', in *Developing Reflective Practice in the Early Years*. Maidenhead: Open University Press.

Pugh, G. (2014) 'The policy agenda for early childhood services', in G. Pugh and B. Duffy (eds), *Contemporary Issues in the Early Years*. London: Sage.

QCA/DfEE (Qualifications and Curriculum Authority/Department for Education and Employment) (2000) *Curriculum Guidance for the Foundation Stage*. London: QCA.

Rodd, J. (1997) 'Learning to be leaders: perceptions of early childhood professionals about leadership roles and responsibilities', *Early Years*, 18 (1): 40–4.

Rodd, J. (2012) *Leadership in Early Childhood*, 4th edn. Maidenhead: McGraw–Hill International.

Rolfe, H. (2006) 'Where are the men? Gender segregation in the childcare and early years sector', *National Institute Economic Review*, 195: 103–17.

Runte, G. (1995) 'Is teaching a profession?', in *Thinking About Teaching: An Introduction*. Toronto: Harcourt Brace.

Sargent, P. (2004) 'Between and rock and a hard place: men caught in the gender bind of early childhood education', *Journal of Men's Studies*, 12 (3): 179–92.

Schön, D. (1983) *The Reflective Practitioner: How Professionals Think in Action*. New York: Basic Books.

Simpson, D. (2010) 'Becoming professional? Exploring early years professional status and its implications for workforce reform in England', *Journal of Early Childhood Research*, 8 (3): 269–81.

Stewart, K. and Obolenskaya, P. (2015) 'The Coalition's record on the under fives: policy, spending and outcomes 2010–2015', in *Social Policy in a Cold Climate*, Working Paper WP12. London: Centre for Analysis of Social Exclusion, LSE.

Swinford, S. (2014) 'Schools encouraged to take 2-year-olds to tackle childcare crisis', *Daily Telegraph*. [Online] www.telegraph.co.uk/education/educationnews/10615824/Schools-encouraged-to-take-2–year-olds-to-tackle-childcare-crisis.html (accessed 27 March 2015).

Sylva, K., Mehuish, E., Sammons, P., Siraj-Blatchford, I. and Taggart, B. (2004) *The Effective Provision of Pre-School Education (EPPE) Project: Findings From Pre-School to end of Key Stage 1*. Nottingham: DfES Publications.

Tabachnick, R. and Zeichner, K. (2002) 'Reading 1.4: reflection on reflective reading', in A. Pollard (ed.), *Reading for Reflective Teaching*. London: Continuum.

Taggart, G. (2011) 'Don't we care? The ethics and emotional labour of early years professionalism', *Early Years*, 31 (1): 85–95.

Thomas, R. and Thomas, H. (2014) 'Professional Associations and the professionalisation of tourism', *The Service Industries Journal*, 34 (1): 38–55.

Tickell, C. (2011) *The Early Years: Foundations for Life, Health and Learning*. An Independent Report on the Early Years Foundation Stage to Her Majesty's Government. London: Crown. Available at: www3.hants.gov.uk/the_tickell_review_the_early_years_-_foundations_for_life__health_and_learning.pdf (accessed 13 February 2015).

Urban, M. (2014) 'Not solving problems, managing messes: competent systems in early childhood education and care', *Management in Education*, 28 (4): 125–9.

van Laere, K., Peeters, J. and Vandenbroeck, M. (2012) 'The education and care divide: the role of the early childhood workforce in 15 European countries', *European Journal of Education*, 47 (4): 527–41.

Waniganayake, M. (2002) 'Growth of leadership: with training, can anyone become a leader?', in V. Nivala and E. Hujala (eds), *Leadership in Early Childhood Education*. Oulu: University of Oulu.

Western, J., Haynes, M., Durrington, D.A. and Dwan, K. (2006) 'Characteristics and benefits of professional work assessment of their importance over a 30-year career', *Journal of Sociology*, 42 (2): 165–88.

Whitebread, D. and Bingham, S. (2014) 'School readiness: starting age, cohorts, and transitions in the early years', in J. Moyles, J. Payler and J. Georgeson (eds), *Early Years Foundation Stage: Critical Issues*. Maidenhead: Open University Press.

Woodrow, C. (2007) 'Whither the early childhood teacher?: Tensions for early childhood professional identity between the policy landscape and the politics of teacher regulation', *Contemporary Issues in Early Childhood*, 8 (3): 233–43.

Wright, H.R., (2014) *The Child in Society*. London: Sage.

Want to learn more about this chapter? Visit the companion website at https://study.sagepub.com/EYFS3e for access to free SAGE journal articles and book chapters, weblinks, annotated further readings and more.

PART 2
PEDAGOGY

6

Pedagogy in Practice

Theodora Papatheodorou and Donna Potts

 Chapter overview

The aim of this chapter is to develop an understanding of pedagogy as a theoretical and applied concept. For this, we will first explore the concept of pedagogy in the light of different theories and policy requirements that, over time, have informed and shaped pedagogical practice. Drawing upon a case study, we will then illustrate the conscious and unconscious complex processes that take place during practice to reach a pedagogical approach that responds to and addresses children's individual needs and potential. We will conclude the chapter arguing that in early childhood practice there is a need to espouse a pedagogy that is purposeful and intentional, appropriate and relevant to children's interest and potential, is transformative and empowering and fosters resilience.

This chapter aims to:

- develop a theoretical understanding of the concept of pedagogy
- understand key ideas that impact on pedagogy
- explore the impact of policy (nationally and internationally) on pedagogy
- link current thinking and theory of pedagogy with practice in early childhood education and care.

Towards a definition of pedagogy

In the English context, pedagogy is often understood as simply being the act of teaching or the performance of curricula delivery. Pedagogy, however, is more than teaching; it encompasses the act of teaching together with the theories, beliefs, policies and challenges that underline and shape it (Alexander, 2000). Pedagogy is what 'practitioners actually DO and THINK' (Moyles et al., 2002: 5; original emphasis). These definitions acknowledge *teaching* as being part of pedagogy, but highlight that it is the *thinking* behind teaching that is at the heart of pedagogy.

Drawing upon Woodhead's (2006) work, the next section will explore four major perspectives of child development and learning that have influenced pedagogical thinking and practice, that is, developmental perspectives; socio-cultural perspectives; policy perspectives; and the child rights perspective.

Developmental perspectives

The image of the developmental child has emerged mainly from biological and child development theories which understood development as a maturational process, taking place in different stages and ages. Notably, Piaget viewed children as progressing through a series of development stages with recognisable cognitive attributes. Through his studies Piaget demonstrated that young children are curious and intrinsically motivated to explore their environment and, through their doings, to work out the principles underpinning phenomena. Given suitable resources and an appropriate level of challenge, children are able to construct their own ideas and knowledge. Piaget's ideas have been particularly influential in creating learning environments that provide appropriate stimuli for investigation, experimentation and hands-on activities (Piaget, 1952).

In contrast to the Piagetian view, behaviourists saw learning as being the direct outcome of responses to environmental stimuli through a process of (positive and/or negative) reinforcement. According to this stimulus–response model, the child makes an association between a stimulus and the consequences that follow the triggered behaviour; a rewarding consequence is likely to increase the occurrence of the exhibited behaviour, while a punishing consequence would minimise it. The belief in the power and impact of behaviourism is better expressed in John Watson's (1930: 104) quotation below:

> Give me a dozen healthy infants, well-formed, and my own specified world to bring them up in and I'll guarantee to take any one at random and train him to become any type of specialist I might select – doctor, lawyer, artist, merchant-chief and, yes, even beggar-man and thief, regardless of his talents, penchants, tendencies, abilities, vocations, and race of his ancestors.

The unidirectional influence of the environment on individuals has been criticised from within behaviourism. Social learning behaviourists argued that environmental, biological, cognitive and other personal factors influence each other bidirectionally. Children are not passive in the learning process; instead their learning takes place within the social context and through observation, imitation, association and generalisation processes (Bandura, 1977).

Today the importance of the environment in which children live, and especially the early experiences they have there, cannot be disputed. Research in the field of neuroscience demonstrates that early stimulation and experiences shape the architecture of the brain and determine future development (National Scientific Council on the Developing Child, 2010). Lack of appropriate nutrition, health and care undermine children's survival, while adverse life experiences (such as care deprivation, chronic fear and anxiety, harsh punishment and mistreatment, and inadequate stimulation) affect negatively children's psycho-social and cognitive development. In contrast, early stimulation and positive experiences increase resilience and ameliorate negative effects (Shonkoff and Phillips, 2000; Fox and Shonkoff, 2011). The evidence from psychoanalytical theory, and mainly the work of Freud, as well as attachment theory (which will be discussed in Chapters 11 and 19), has been further supported by neuroscience, which recognises the significance of early experiences with regard to children's attachment, emotional security and mental health in later life.

Child development theories raise awareness of early childhood as a discrete period of life that is characterised by certain needs and requires certain conditions for children to flourish. In many ways, these theories echo and further support the ideas of early pioneers, who had long before argued for age-appropriate resources to enable children's exploration through hands-on activities (e.g. Froebel's occupations and Montessori's learning resources) and the impact of environmental stimuli (e.g. John Locke, who claimed that children are *tabulae rasae* [blank slates] where environmental stimuli leave their imprint).

Some well-known ideas in the field of early childhood derive from developmental theories. For example:

- development takes place at certain stages and ages, determined by maturational processes;
- children are viewed as being curious and intrinsically motivated and having enquiring minds;
- children need access to resources that enable exploration, active experimentation, hands-on activities;
- children thrive in stimulating, supportive and positively reinforcing environments;
- early childhood is valued as a discrete period in life, where children's *being* itself is valued.

These ideas made a significant contribution to pedagogical practice by:

- contesting traditional adult/teacher-centred pedagogical practice, which focuses on knowledge transmission;
- introducing notions of child-centred, play-based, experiential and hands-on learning;
- influencing the way learning environments are organised to offer rewarding and positive experiences;
- contributing to the introduction of developmentally appropriate practice.

Socio-cultural perspectives

Socio-cultural theories have furthered our understanding of child development and learning as a social process. Vygotsky (2002) argued that development and learning take place within the social and cultural milieu: children are neither the lone scientists, isolated from their social environment (assumed in Piaget's theory), nor the product of direct stimuli of the environment and the process of positive or negative reinforcement (argued by behaviourists). Children are the product of their socio-cultural milieu, its beliefs and values, and its customs and practices.

Socio-cultural theorists emphasise interdependence and relationships with others: how children learn to negotiate, problem solve and make meaning out of their experiences through the facilitation of knowledgeable others, be it parents, teachers or other children. Malaguzzi (1993: 10), the founder of Reggio Emilia pre-schools, saw children as being 'rich in potential, strong, powerful, competent and most of all, connected to adults and other children', and Bruner and Haste (1987) referred to children as *meaning makers*. Children reach their potential through adult *scaffolding* (Bruner, 2006), *guided participation* (Rogoff et al., 1993) and *sustained shared thinking* with knowledgeable others (Siraj-Blatchford et al., 2002), as they work within their *zone of proximal development* (Vygotsky, 1978).

Bronfenbrenner's (1979) Ecological Theory attempted to provide a broader framework for understanding children's development and learning. He highlighted the influence of dynamic interactions of many factors within and between different systems in which the children find themselves. It is not any single factor that is more important than others; instead, it is the cumulative effect of the complex interactions of many factors, taking place over time, that influence and determine child development and learning.

Many contemporary theorists have also challenged the image of the *developmental* child in the light of the widespread diversity encountered in today's societies (e.g. of ethnicity, religion, social class, disability, linguistic) and the unspoken power of dominant ideologies and institutions. They have argued that notions such as stages and ages (the developmental child) assume distinct universal features that are applicable to all children, at all times and in all societies, and ignore social and cultural influences (Cannella, 2005; Dahlberg et al., 2007; Moss, 2008). Developmentally Appropriate Practice, in particular, was contested and became Developmentally and Culturally (or Contextually) Appropriate Practice (DCAP) to highlight that *what we learn* and *how we learn* are informed and influenced by the cultures of particular communities (NAEYC, 1996; Hyun, 1998).

These theories have furthered understanding of:

- the influences of the social and cultural milieu on child development and learning;
- the significant role of cultural values and practices;
- the role of knowledgeable adults/others in children's learning through processes of scaffolding, guided participation and sustained shared thinking;
- the influence and power of dominant ideologies embraced by particular groups and institutions, and/or policies;
- the importance of children's sense of *belonging* in the context and place, where they find themselves.

These ideas have extended pedagogical thinking and practice to include:

- greater emphasis on social and contextual factors;
- collaborative learning and group work, where children work together, support each other, encounter challenges, problem solve, cooperate, negotiate and arrive at shared meaning and action;
- scaffolding, guided participation and sustained shared thinking to facilitate children's learning;
- greater emphasis on the processes of learning (i.e. how and why we learn);
- acknowledgement of diversity and creation of cultures of inclusion and celebration of diversity;
- forging relationships and a sense of belonging;
- development of assessment and evaluation strategies that reflect diversity and capture contextual influences (e.g. introduction of documentation and learning journeys/ stories; self-evaluation of early childhood settings).

Policy perspectives

As discussed in Chapter 4, the accrued impact of early childhood provision on children, their families and societies, and the economic returns on investment for early childhood education and care became the cornerstone of international and national policies. As a result, during the last two decades we saw a plethora of international policies that legally bind governments to make appropriate provisions for children to enjoy a certain level of living standards. The government commitments were followed by increased investment for early childhood provision, an emphasis on the professionalisation of the workforce and the introduction of focused curricula, child assessment and evaluation of provision.

As the investment for early childhood provision increased, so did the demands for evidence about its returns. The *developmental* child, portrayed especially in ages and stages developmental theories, became the gold standard to measuring the development of all children, independently of their cultural and contextual milieu. Standards, associated with and deriving from the *universal developmental* child, have been extensively used for programme evaluation to demonstrate their impact (see, for example, longitudinal studies such as EPPE in the UK – Sylva et al., 2004; High/Scope and Head Start in the USA –Schweinhart, 1994; US Department of Health and Human Services, 2010).

Child development theories have provided an understanding of development and raised awareness of the importance of children's experiences and their being, but their underpinning ideas also became a double-edged sword. They provided a framework for defining and quantifying terms such as developmental standards, desirable learning outcomes, quality indicators and benchmarking. Although highly contested by many contemporary schools, these terms remain the yardstick for child assessment and programme evaluation (Cannella, 2005; Dahlberg et al., 2007; Moss, 2008).

In the UK context (as discussed in Chapters 1, 2 and 3), the Early Years Foundation Stage curriculum was introduced in the mid-1990s and since then it has been reviewed and revised several times. Child assessment and increased external inspections and programme evaluation followed (e.g. Ofsted inspections; National Evaluation of Sure Start). Despite its attempts to incorporate and negotiate different theoretical perspective, the latest version of the EYFS curriculum is informed by developmental perspectives and places particular emphasis on academic and cognitive development and especially on school readiness (DfE, 2014).

Policy has influenced thinking in:

- seeing the child *in the making, in becoming* tomorrow's productive citizen, by emphasising development and the acquisition of certain valued skills;
- assessing and evaluating children's progress against identified learning outcomes;
- viewing early childhood education and care as interventionist, especially for children and families experiencing disadvantage;
- evaluating provision to measure its accrued impact;
- seeing early childhood provision as interventionist aiming to ameliorate and combat disadvantage experienced by children and families.

The impact of policy on pedagogical practice is evident in:

- curricula frameworks that are learning outcomes-based/oriented;
- child assessment and profiling;

- use of developmental checklists for assessing children;
- increased external evaluation of early childhood provision;
- emphasis on acquisition of skills for later schooling and especially school readiness.

The child rights perspective

The United Nations Convention on the Rights of the Child (UNCRC) has made an important contribution to understanding of young children as citizens of today rather than as individuals in the making (United Nations, 1989). The UNCRC starts from the principle of acting in the best interest of the child and articulates specific rights that children are entitled to enjoy, including: adequate living standards (article 25), education (article 28), health (article 24), rest and recreational activities and enjoyment (article 31), social security (article 26), and participation in decision making for matters that affect them (article 12).

The UNCRC, in its fortieth session in 2005, reiterated and affirmed that children are 'rights holders' from birth. More importantly, it mandated that the quality of services for children should be evaluated to the extent that children's rights are observed (UNCRC, 2006). The UNCRC places the responsibility for observing children's rights with parents and/or carers, but holds governments accountable in supporting parents for doing so.

The UNCRC has changed the landscape for early childhood education and care in many ways. At policy level, governments are expected to align aims, targets and priorities that meet children's rights. In the English context, for example, children's rights are reflected in the five outcomes of Every Child Matters, that is: being healthy; staying safe; enjoying and achieving; making a positive contribution; and achieving economic well-being (DfES, 2004). The EYFS 2014 is also positioned within a rights perspective by stating that children deserve 'the best possible start in life' and need support 'to fulfil their potential'. It acknowledges that: 'A secure, safe and happy childhood is important in its own right' (DfE, 2014: 5), ensured by adhering to four overarching principles: the unique child, positive relationships, enabling environments and that children develop and learn in different ways and at different rates (DfE, 2014: 6).

In terms of pedagogical practices, awareness of children's rights, and especially their participation in decisions that affect them, has raised awareness about listening to young children's voices. A growing body of research has enriched our understanding of the many ways that children can express their views and the attentive listening of adults that is required (see for example, Malaguzzi's (1993) idea of children's *hundred languages* and Rinaldi's (2001) concept of a *pedagogy of listening*). Children are natural communicators from birth, but adults need to invest in relational inter-subjectivity in order to capture and give meaning to children's many communicative signs (Trevarthen, 2011).

The UNCRC has:

- enriched our understanding of the child as a unique and potent individual, who is able to express her/his views and influence the care and education received;
- recognised the importance of maturational factors (e.g. right to health and nutrition) and acknowledged the significance of the social and cultural context (e.g. right to education, leisure and enjoyment) for child development and learning;
- explicitly articulated the obligations of families, communities and the state towards children.

As a result, pedagogical practices are explicitly aligned with the UNCRC principles, by enabling children's voices to be heard and listened to.

Pedagogy: a framework for practice

It is evident that the field of early childhood education and care draws upon a range of ideas from different theoretical perspectives and policy requirements to understand development and learning and to inform pedagogical practice. In the next section this will be illustrated with reference to a case study.

Case study

Ben's story (through the voice of the teacher)

Ben spent two years in nursery and a full year in a Reception class. At the age of 6 years, he was admitted in Year 1. Due to his low Foundation Stage Profile score he was kept in a Year 1 class where he would continue the EYFS for the first two terms. There was concern for his low achievements in reading and writing and he was highlighted as a potential candidate for the Reading Recovery programme ... an expensive and intensive intervention programme for which Ben was assessed and qualified ...

Further assessment showed that Ben had very weak pencil control and was unable to form letters to write his name correctly. He was still undecided about his hand preference for writing. When he did attempt to put pen to paper he kept swapping hands, questioning the strength of his fine motor control. During initial assessments, Ben said, 'I can't read, I can't write.' 'I don't want to do it.' He had very low self-esteem and a poor concept of himself as a reader and writer and a negative disposition towards learning in general.

From discussions with his previous teachers and parents, in the Reception year Ben would mostly 'choose' either the computer or to be outside on the bikes; at home, he spends his time playing on the computer.

I [the Reading Recovery teacher] called upon all of my known strategies trying to get Ben enthusiastic to articulate a sentence for writing. I tried to focus on his own experiences, but he just shrugged. I tried using playdough and paint to try to engage him in talking while developing his fine motor skills. Very, very slowly he began to gain trust in me and respond. I knew I needed to break through his attitude first and to get him to see what learning looked like. Finally, I found a picture of a boy sitting on the ground with a bleeding knee.

Me:	What has happened to this boy?
Ben:	[*Shrug*]
Me:	Look at the picture and tell me what you see.
Ben:	[*Silent*]
Me:	I think he has fallen over and cut his knee. I bet you have fallen over and cut your knee before haven't you?
Ben:	Yeah, but I ain't gonna write about it!

Teacher's reflection

I had a response and could see from it that he was sharp to be on to me so fast. It took 9 weeks – 22.5 hours – of hard work and effort to build a relationship with Ben and get him to see that with my support he could begin to read and write and maybe even enjoy it. He suddenly started to see that he could do it for himself. I withdrew my support slowly as he gained in confidence. His attitude has turned around and he now sees himself more positively. When asked what he needs to do when he gets stuck he reels off the strategies he has learned (and has been taught!) in order to solve his problems more independently rather than wait and expect to be told.

Reflective tasks

Considering the case study, you may reflect on the following:

- how formative assessment (e.g. the EYFS Profile score) can become a tool for observing children's rights to receive an education that enables them to reach their potential (please read also Chapters 8 and 9 to assist you in this reflective task);

(Continued)

> *(Continued)*
>
> • the theoretical perspectives that the teacher has called upon to inform her pedagogical approach with Ben;
>
> • the ways and methods the teacher used to listen to and capture Ben's voices and, consequently, inform her pedagogical practice.

Emerging issues

The case study above exemplifies what pedagogy looks like in practice. It raises awareness of the potential of child profiling scores, when used in an informative and systematic way for appropriate provision, and highlights the importance of reflection during the pedagogical process. It demonstrates the importance of building relationships, fostering self-esteem and self-worth, so that children acquire positive dispositions to learning and become resilient and self-reliant learners. The teacher's response to Ben's needs and potential illustrate that pedagogy is not only a matter of skill development and knowledge acquisition; it is a relational and ethical stance.

Enacting pedagogy

The case study exemplifies the definition of pedagogy as being both the act of teaching and the thinking behind it. Drawing upon 'known' strategies, the teacher started working with Ben in order to support his fine motor skills (concrete teaching strategy) required for pencil control and writing (rationale). The teacher called upon ideas and notions from different theoretical and policy frameworks to inform her pedagogy. She employed a number of child-appropriate activities and materials such as playing with playdough and painting, drawing upon her knowledge from child development theories. She drew upon Ben's possible experiences, such as falling from the bike and/or hurting his knee, adhering to principles of contextually relevant practice. She tried to enthuse and enable Ben to enjoy learning, and to build up his confidence, self-esteem and self-worth, acknowledging developmental and rights perspectives, and she aimed at improving Ben's reading and writing skills (policy requirements). This, however, does not mean that the teacher's pedagogy was either arbitrary or selective. Instead, as is discussed in the following sections, this was a dynamic and ever-evolving process that was well reasoned against certain principles and substantiated with evidence and through reflection.

Reflection

Confronted with Ben's refusal to engage with the tasks and his overall negative disposition to learning, the teacher embarked on a process of continuous reflection *in action* and *on action* (Schön, 1983). She became more aware of what she was doing when working with Ben (reflection in action) and stood back and looked at the whole experience to gain deeper insights (reflection on action) to inform her pedagogy. The teacher engaged in a process of what we might call *investigative* reflection, aiming at *seeing* the child behind the mask of observable behaviour and understanding the unspoken messages conveyed by such behaviour. This involved attentive listening and interpretation of Ben's overt messages (e.g. 'I can't read, I can't write', 'I don't want to do it.') and the effect of her strategies on him. Ben's refusal and avoidance techniques were interpreted in terms of his potential, not in the light of what he was lacking. She concluded that, while the concerns were about Ben's 'low achievement in reading and writing', the actual barrier was his 'low self-esteem and self-worth' and 'negative dispositions to learning in general'.

Reciprocal relationships

The teacher recognised that Ben's 'response' to and 'trust' in her and a 'relationship' with him were a prerequisite in order to engage him with reading and writing activities. This required the teacher's attentive listening to Ben's explicit messages (e.g. I can't) and subtle cues (e.g. lack of confidence and self-esteem). The teacher took the time to watch Ben's responses and, in turn, modified her responses too. She waited and took the cues from Ben rather than applying her knowledge of what children need in general.

It necessitated reflection on the impact of the teacher's planned learning activities on Ben and the subtle negotiation and renegotiation of activities that provided meaningful experience to both of them. Building a relationship with Ben meant that the teacher was in tune with him; she was able to think with him, not for him. Such a reciprocal relationship made the teacher and the child co-travellers in the learning journey rather than the teacher trying to determine the learning journey and mould the child in dominant images.

Self-esteem, self-worth and resilience

Building relationships is not an end in itself, it is the building block for the child's self-awareness, self-worth and self-esteem, for these are attributes that derive from the ways others relate to the child and the acknowledgement of her/his efforts (Papatheodorou, 2006, 2009). The teacher saw Ben as a potent learner who was 'sharp' and able to exercise his agency; she respected him as a knower and provided him with learning experience that emphasised meaning makings (Brownlee, 2004). This enabled Ben to become aware of what he was able to do and this, in turn, increased his self-worth and self-esteem and gave him the confidence to engage with tasks that he previously thought as being beyond his skills or too challenging to attempt.

The teacher drew upon a range of strategies, informed by concepts such as scaffolding, guided participation, sustained thinking and the Zone of Proximal Development, to support a confident and resilient learner. She noted that 'with my support he [Ben] could begin to read and write', 'started to see that he could do it for himself'. By appropriating her pedagogical approach, the teacher enabled Ben to evolve as a resilient learner who was able 'to solve his problems', to be 'independent' and 'reel off the strategies he had learned', to 'see what learning is like', 'not to expect to be told'. The teacher withdrew her support slowly as 'he [Ben] gained confidence' and noted that his 'attitude has turned around and he now sees himself more positively'.

Positive dispositions and development of skill

Development of positive dispositions such as curiosity, creativity, independence, cooperativeness and persistence are at the heart of early childhood education and care. Dispositions are conscious and deliberate or habitual/automatic acts that seem to be intuitive and spontaneous; they are goal-orientated and exhibited frequently, and in the absence of coercion (Katz, 1993). The development of dispositions is supported by valuing and modelling them, orchestrating interactions that support them, teaching them and providing support and affirmation to children (Carr, 1995).

Working with Ben, the teacher herself demonstrated positive dispositions and modelled them (e.g. relating, trusting, showing perseverance and confidence in herself and Ben). She created an environment where relationships and positive interactions were created; offered support and taught Ben skills and tools to use. The teacher noted that 'when he gets stuck he reels off the strategies he has learned (and has been taught!) in order to solve his problems'.

While skill training *per se* is questionable, provision of appropriate support and at the right time is necessary for the child to cross the threshold of challenge, gain confidence and persevere with the task at hand (Papatheodorou and Loader, 2009). Positive dispositions enable children to develop skills and competences, but supporting skills and competences can forge positive dispositions too. There is a dialectical and interactive relationship between the two, but it requires an insightful teacher with positive dispositions to learning to provide the right balance.

School readiness

School readiness is a contested notion, much debated and challenged in terms of its definition (e.g. certain level of cognitive skills) and as to whether the child or the school should be ready (Pre-school Learning Alliance, 2011). Children's assessment in early childhood is an equally contested notion, for it may indicate the child's challenges, but it says nothing about why these challenges exist. Whilst caution may be exercised on how school readiness and assessment are understood and utilised in early childhood, to ignore them may mean that a potent child, like Ben, may be left behind his peers (e.g. to continue with the EYFS for the first two terms on transition to Year 1 class), placed in an intensive and expensive intervention programme (Reading Recovery) with the danger not to fulfil his potential and ultimately his self-esteem and self-worth may be lowered further.

To act in the best interest of the child and serve her/him well entails careful considerations of how policy requirements are utilised to inform pedagogical options and to guide appropriate choices. In Ben's case, his low EYFS Profile was the starting point for further assessment using the Reading Recovery initial assessments (Clay 2005a). Because of his low scores, Ben was place in the Reading Recovery programme for 20 weeks. Discussions with his nursery teacher, his parents and the teacher's own observations confirmed Ben's preference and insistence to be involved with a limited range of activities and situations, where he felt comfortable.

Two weeks before the implementation of the Reading Recovery programme, Ben engaged with 'roaming around the known' (RAK) activities, where he worked purely on what he could already do to increase his confidence, create a secure environment and build a relationship with the teacher (Clay, 2005b). Although reading and writing were seen as Ben's main difficulties, the teacher soon realised that there was a web of complex dynamics between lack of skill and positive dispositions, low self-esteem and confidence that acted in a vicious cycle. Therefore, building Ben's self-esteem and confidence became the starting point for improving his reading and writing.

Playful learning

Working with Ben, the teacher employed a playful learning pedagogy that, initially, was mostly adult-led, aiming at the particular objective of improving skills and competences necessary for reading and writing skills. The teacher appreciated that Ben's previous play was mainly static and around solitary activities (e.g. spending time on the bike or the computer), so she invested in joined and interactive playful activities (e.g. playing with playdough, sharing reading). She provided space and made time for both of them to find common ground of understanding in order to develop purposeful and playful learning that would be owned by Ben. This was a flexible, playful approach that gave Ben (and the teacher) the opportunity to draw upon his experiences and interests and exercise his agency.

Play is enshrined in the consciousness and practices of early childhood practitioners for its impact on all areas of development (e.g. physical, cognitive, emotional and social), positive dispositions and skill development (for more on play see Chapter 7). Play and the pedagogy of play are not without challenges, however. In a culture and context of outcomes-based curricula and children's profiling, even the discourse of play has changed. This has shifted from play to playful learning; from child-initiated play to balanced child-led and adult-led play (for an extensive overview of play, see Moyles, 2010). Practices – as the case study illustrates – are also variable. In some cases play may become so open-ended as to allow children to engage with limited preferred choices and refuse to extend their play repertoire. In other instances, play may be narrowed down to the extent that it is mostly, if not exclusively, adult-led.

Considering Ben's challenges, it is important to remember that whatever play or playful approach to learning is chosen, this should:

- contribute to children's positive dispositions to learning;
- develop an appropriate level of skill and competences that enable children to engage with challenging tasks and enjoy them;
- enable children to interact, collaborate and work with others and to problem solve;
- instil a sense of self-esteem and self-worth and confidence;
- lead to independence and self-reliance.

Relational pedagogy

The case study illustrates that adoption of well-known and good practices need to be framed against an appropriate pedagogy that leads to a meaningful experience for both the child and the teacher. This requires, to recall Dahlberg and Moss (2005: 1), investment in 'a relation, a network of obligation' and 'infinite attention to the other'. By investing in relational inter-subjectivity – to recall Trevarthen (2011) – pedagogy bridges dichotomies and polarised discourses such as child-centred/led/initiated versus adult-centred/led learning; learning processes versus outcomes/competences-based education; or children's *being* versus children's *becoming*. In doing so it necessitates continuous negotiation of different, and often conflicting, influences and ongoing reflection for developing meaningful and worthwhile practices. Such reciprocal relational inter-subjectivity informs and enables a pedagogy that is respectful and relevant to the child's potential and interests, is purposeful and intentional and is transformative and empowering. It fosters resilience through a dynamic interaction of caring relationships, a supportive and affirming environment and the child's increased belief in her/his capacity to overcome challenges (National Scientific Council on the Developing Child, 2015).

Summary

In conclusion, pedagogy offers a broad framework that informs the ways in which early childhood practitioners engage with children and plan learning activities. It is the

springboard for conscious and unconscious reflections and forms the basis for e____
ing whether these actions are responsive to children's interests and/or brough___
by intended outcomes. It offers the lenses and filters by which theoretical perspectives,
policy requirements and established good practices are critiqued and questioned in
order to act in the best interest of children and in safeguarding best outcomes for them.
It is neither the child's being here-and-now (developmental perspectives), nor her/his
becoming in some distant future (policy perspectives) that is more important than the
other. There is a moral and ethical obligation to observe children's being and becoming and instil a sense of belonging through an appropriate pedagogy (Papatheodorou,
2010). For this, engagement is needed in a dialectical manner with theoretical perspectives and policy requirements, as both inform and shape each other
(Papatheodorou, 2012). The ability to critique and negotiate different and often conflicting and polarised discourses can only enable creativity and flexibility of thinking
and thus advance practice.

Key points to remember

- Pedagogy is more than teaching. It encompasses both the act of teaching and the thinking that lies behind teaching.

- Pedagogy is influenced and shaped by ideas and concepts from different fields of study, policy imperatives, research findings and the debates in the profession.

- Pedagogy in practice should build upon the notion of the potent child; invest in reciprocal relationships; enhance self-esteem, self-worth and foster resilience; cultivate positive dispositions and develop appropriate skills; con-sider policy imperatives, whilst it remains rooted in a philosophy of playful learning.

Points for discussion

- To what extent do the concepts of scaffolding, guided participation and sustained shared thinking reflect similar ideas, and how might they be different?

- What are the characteristics, similarities and differences between play, playful learning, child-initiated and adult-led learning?

- What does it mean to 'act in the best interest of children' and 'safeguard children's rights'?

Further reading

Allen, S. and Whalley, M.E (2010) *Supporting Pedagogy and Practice in Early Years Settings.* London: Sage.

DECD (2013) Early Years Learning Framework. Perspectives on Pedagogy. Government of South Australia. Available at: www.decd.sa.gov.au/docs/documents/1/perspectivesonpedagogybro. pdf (accessed 5 March 2015).

Gupta, A. (2015) 'Pedagogy of third space: A multidimensional early childhood curriculum', *Policy Futures in Education*, February 2015, 13 (2): 260–72.

Moyles, J. (2014) *The Excellence of Play*, 4th edn. Maidenhead: Open University Press.

Useful websites

Foundation Years: Great Early Years and Childcare:
www.foundationyears.org.uk/pedagogy-early-learning

TACTYC Reflections:
http://tactyc.org.uk/reflections/

References

Alexander, R. (2000) *Culture and Pedagogy. International Comparisons in Primary Education.* Malden, MA: Blackwell.

Bandura, A. (1977) *Social Learning: Theory.* New York: General Learning Press.

Bronfenbrenner, U. (1979) *The Ecology of Human Development.* Cambridge, MA: Harvard University Press.

Brownlee, J. (2004) 'Teacher education students' epistemological beliefs: developing a relational model of teaching', *Research in Education*, 72: 1–17.

Bruner, J.S. (2006) *In Search of Pedagogy*, Volume II: *The Selected Works of Jerome S. Bruner.* Oxford: Routledge.

Bruner, J.S. and Haste, H. (1987) 'Introduction', in J.S. Bruner and H. Haste (eds), *Making Sense: The Child's Construction of the World.* London: Methuen.

Cannella, G.S. (2005) 'Reconceptualizing the field (of early care and education): if "Western" child development is a problem, then what do we do?', in N. Yelland (ed.), *Critical Issues in Early Childhood Education.* Maidenhead: Open University Press.

Carr, M. (1995) 'Dispositions as an outcome for early childhood curriculum', paper presented at the 5th European Conference on Quality of Early Childhood Education, La Sorbonne, Paris (7–9 September), available at: http://eric.ed.gov/ERICWebPortal/recordDetail?accno=ED407055 (accessed 5 March 2015).

Clay, M. (2005a) *An Observation Survey of Early Literacy Achievement.* Portsmouth, NH: Heinemann.

Clay, M. (2005b) *Literacy Lessons Designed For Individuals, Why? When? And How?* Part One. New Zealand: Reed Publishing.

Dahlberg, G. and Moss, P. (2005) *Ethics and Politics in Early Childhood Education.* London: RoutledgeFalmer.

Dahlberg, G., Moss, P. and Pence, A. (2007) *Beyond Quality in Early Childhood Education and Care: Languages of Evaluation*. London: Routledge.

DfE (Department for Education) (2012) *Statutory Framework for the Early Years Foundation Stage: Setting the Standards for Learning, Development and Care for Children from Birth to Five*. Runcorn: DfE Publications. Available at: http://www.foundationyears.org.uk/eyfs-statutory-framework (accessed 29 January 2016).

DfE (Department for Education) (2014) *Statutory Framework for the Early Years Foundation Stage: Setting the Standards for Learning, Development and Care for Children from Birth to Five*. Available at: www.foundationyears.org.uk/files/2014/07/EYFS_framework_from_1_September_2014__with_clarification_note.pdf (accessed 21 September 2015).

DfES (Department for Education and Skills) (2004) *Every Child Matters: Change for Children in Schools*. Nottingham: DfES Publications.

Fox, N.A and Shonkoff, J.P. (2011) 'Violence and development: how persistent fear and anxiety can affect young children's learning and behaviour and health', in Bernard van Leer Foundation (ed.), *Hidden Violence: Protecting Young Children at Home*. Early Childhood Matters No. 116. The Hague: Bernard van Leer Foundation.

Hyun, E. (1998) *Making Sense of Developmentally and Culturally Appropriate Practice (DCAP) in Early Childhood Education*. New York: Peter Lang.

Katz, L. (1993) *Dispositions: Definitions and Implications for Early Childhood Practice*. Champaign, Il: Clearing House of Early Childhood and Parenting (CEEP). Available at: http://eric.ed.gov/?id=ED363454 (accessed 5 March 2015).

Malaguzzi, L. (1993) 'History, ideas and basic philosophy', in C. Edwards, L. Gandini and G. Forman (eds), *The Hundred Languages of Children*. Norwood, NJ: Ablex.

Moss, P. (2008) 'Meeting across the paradigmatic divide', in S. Farquhar and P. Fitzsimons (eds), *Philosophy of Early Childhood Education: Transforming Narratives*. Malden, MA: Blackwell.

Moyles, J. (2010) *The Excellence of Play*, 3rd edn. Maidenhead: Open University Press.

Moyles, J., Adams, S. and Musgrove, A. (2002) *SPEEL: Study of Pedagogical Effectiveness in Early Learning*. London: Department for Education and Skills. Report No. 363.

NAEYC (1996) Developmentally Appropriate Practice in Early Childhood Programs Serving Children from Birth through Age 8. Position Statement. Available at: www.naeyc.org/files/naeyc/file/positions/position%20statement%20Web.pdf (accessed 5 March 2015).

National Scientific Council on the Developing Child (2010) *Early Experiences Can Alter Gene Expression and Affect Long-Term Development*. Working Paper No. 10. Available at: http://developingchild.harvard.edu/index.php/resources/reports_and_working_papers/working_papers/wp10/ (accessed 5 March 2015).

National Scientific Council on the Developing Child (2015) *Supportive Relationships and Active Skill-Building Strengthen the Foundations of Resilience*: Working Paper No. 13. Available at www.developingchild.harvard.edu (accessed 5 March 2015).

Papatheodorou, T. (2006) *Seeing the Wider Picture: Reflections on the Reggio Emilia Approach*. Available at: http://tactyc.org.uk/pdfs/Reflection-Papatheodorou.pdf (accessed 5 March 2015).

Papatheodorou, T. (2009) 'Exploring relational pedagogy', in T. Papatheodorou and J. Moyles (eds), *Learning Together in the Early Years: Exploring Relational Pedagogy*. London: Routledge.

Papatheodorou, T. (2010) 'Being, belonging and becoming: some world views of early childhood in contemporary curricula', *Forum on Public Policy Online*, Vol. 2. Available at: http://forumonpublicpolicy.com/spring2010.vol2010/spring2010archive/papatheodorou.pdf (accessed 5 March 2015).

Papatheodorou, T. (2012) 'Introduction: early childhood policies and practices', in T. Papatheodorou (ed.), *Debates on Early Childhood Policies and Practices: Global Snapshots of Pedagogical Thinking and Encounters*. London: Routledge.

Papatheodorou, T. and Loader, P. (2009) 'The Reggio Emilia Artists' Project: changing culture – changing pedagogy'. Paper presented at the 19th EECERA conference, Strasbourg France.

Piaget, J. (1952) *The Origins of Intelligence in Children* (trans. M. Cook). New York: International Universities Press.

Pre-School Learning Alliance (2011) 'Alliance voices concerns about meaning of "school readiness" as Government unveils its early years reforms'. Available at: www.pre-school.org.uk/media/press-releases/245/alliance-voices-concerns-about-meaning-of-school-readiness-as-government-unveils-its-early-years-reforms (accessed 5 March 2015).

Rinaldi, C. (2001) 'The pedagogy of listening: the listening perspective from Reggio Emilia', *Innovations in Early Education: The International Reggio Exchange*, Vol. 8, No. 4. Available at: http://academic.udayton.edu/JamesBiddle/Pedagogy%20of%20Listening.pdf (accessed 5 March 2015).

Rogoff, B., Mosier, C., Mistry, J. and Goncu, A. (1993) 'Toddlers' guided participation with their caregivers in cultural activity', in E.A. Forman, N. Mimick and C. Addison Stone (eds), *Contexts for Learning: Socio-Cultural Dynamics in Children's Development*. New York: Oxford University Press.

Schön, D. (1983) *The Reflective Practitioner: How Professionals Think in Action*. London: Temple Smith.

Schweinhart, L.J. (1994) 'Lasting benefits of preschool programs', *ERIC Digest* (ERIC Clearinghouse on Elementary and Early Childhood Education, ERIC Identifier: ED 365478). Available at: www.ericdigests.org/1994/lasting.htm (accessed 5 March 2015).

Shonkoff, J.P. and Phillips, D. (eds) (2000) *From Neurons to Neighborhoods: The Science of Early Child Development*. Washington, DC: National Academy Press.

Siraj-Blatchford, I., Sylva, K., Muttock, S., Gilden, R. and Bell, D. (2002) *Researching Effective Pedagogy in the Early Years*, Research Report 356. London: Department for Education and Skills.

Sylva, K., Melhuish, E.C., Sammons, P., Siraj-Blatchford, I. and Taggart, B. (2004) *The Effective Provision of Pre-school Education (EPPE) Project*. Technical Paper No. 12. London: DfES/Institute of Education, University of London.

Trevarthen, C. (2011) 'How is meaning made before words – and why does it matter so much?'. Lecture at Anglia Ruskin University, 28 March.

United Nations (1989) *United Nations Convention on the Rights of the Child*. Geneva: Defence International and United Nations Children's Fund. Available at: www.ohchr.org/en/professionalinterest/pages/crc.aspx.

UNCRC (2006) *Convention on the Rights of the Child, General Comment No. 7 [2005]*, Implementing Child Rights in Early Childhood, fortieth session, Geneva, 20 September. Available at: http://www2.ohchr.org/english/bodies/crc/docs/AdvanceVersions/GeneralComment7Rev1.pdf (accessed 5 March 2015).

US Department of Health and Human Services (2010) *Head Start Impact Study, Final Report*. Washington, DC: US Department of Health and Human Services, Administration for Children and Families. Available at: www.acf.hhs.gov/programs/opre/resource/head-start-impact-study-final-report-executive-summary (accessed 5 March 2015).

Vygotsky, L.S. (1978) *Mind in Society: The Development of Higher Psychological Processes.* London: Harvard University Press.

Vygotsky, L. (2002) *Language and Thought* (ed. and rev. A. Kozulin). Cambridge, MA: MIT Press.

Watson, J.B. (1930) *Behaviorism,* rev. edn. Chicago, IL: University of Chicago Press.

Woodhead, M. (2006) 'Changing perspectives on early childhood: theory, research and policy', *International Journal of Equity and Innovation in Early Childhood*, 4 (2): 1–43. Available at: http://oro.open.ac.uk/6778/1/Woodhead_paper_for_UNESCO_EFA_2007.pdf (accessed 5 March 2015).

Want to learn more about this chapter? Visit the companion website at https://study.sagepub.com/EYFS3e for access to free SAGE journal articles and book chapters, weblinks, annotated further readings and more.

7

Play

Chantelle Haughton and Cheryl Ellis

 Chapter overview

Play is integral to early childhood. As has been explored throughout this book, play is central to children's development, and early childhood education and care is concerned with how a play-based curriculum can be implemented in order to enhance children's experiences and development. Issues around children's play and the purposes of play have a profound impact on children's lives . Thus this chapter will highlight key features of play, acknowledging different forms of play, including child-initiated and adult-led play. It will identify how play experiences may impact on holistic child development. Recommendations for good practice will be explored, including the identification of some benefits and challenges for both adults and children which can result from a play-based pedagogy. Issues relating to the use of indoor and outdoor play spaces will also be reflected upon.

This chapter aims to help you to:

- define play and its various forms
- identify and reflect upon elements of good practice in play provision, establishing links with the Early Years Foundation Stage
- develop an element of criticality by thinking about issues related to working within a play environment.

Theoretical perspectives on play

Chapter 6 discussed the notion of pedagogy in early childhood education and care and suggested 'playful learning' as a key element that allows children to engage in meaningful sense-making of the world. Wood and Bennett (1997) acknowledge that support for the importance of play is based on a number of psychological theories, philosophies and educational principles from different eras and cultures. They suggest that there is broad agreement that young children need to play in order to find out more about themselves, their culture, roles and relationships. There is no unified theoretical or pedagogical base to guide practice in relation to play, however, which has resulted in 'conceptual confusion' regarding the role of play within an educational setting (McAuley and Jackson, 1992 cited in Wood and Bennett, 1997). Indeed, a review of literature by the BERA Early Years Special Interest Group (2003: 14) identified that:

> Whilst play forms the bedrock of early learning, an agreed pedagogy of play is less well articulated, and play in practice is deeply problematic. The dominant ideology is not underpinned by systematic empirical research, and key studies both in preschool and statutory school settings have identified significant gaps between the rhetoric and the reality of practice.

BERA (2003: 13) identify four key areas of concern:

- There is little understanding of how play progresses in early childhood, and how progression can be supported.
- Practitioners tend to espouse an ideological adherence to the efficacy of free play, even though there is little empirical evidence to support this.
- Practitioners make assumptions about the competence and ability of young learners to benefit from a predominantly *laissez-faire* environment, in which they are expected to choose from a wide range of activities and experiences.
- Not all young children know how to play.

Many argue, however, that true play encourages children to engage in active discovery that is fluid and spontaneous. Bruner (2006: 91) acknowledges the creative freedom of children's play:

> It is not that children don't pursue ends and employ means to get them in their play, but that they often change their goals en route to suit new means or change the means to suit new goals. Nor is it that they do so only because they have run into blocks, but out of sheer jubilation of good spirits. It provides not only medium for exploration, but also for invention.

Case study

Pirates

Within a Reception class, a group of children aged 4–5 years move from bridge builders to pirates. (Creative freedom – changing goals in the course of play.)

Story time has just ended. A small group of children feel inspired to work at the craft table to build a bridge, 'just like the one the troll lives under'. The teacher agrees this would be a fantastic idea and the children quickly start searching through the 'crafty chest' for building materials. They come across a number of boxes and kitchen roll tubes which they think they could use. Katy suggests they use glue; in response Bessy says that 'glue takes too long'. Bessy works with the sticky tape to join two tubes together and Katy assists by holding them. Khalid and Tom work alongside them, building 'the tall bits'. Khalid takes the lead on building the bridge tower as Tom sits holding another tube. Tom peeps through the tube and says, 'This can be a troll telescope. Look.' All four of the children take turns to look through it as Tom holds the 'troll telescope'. Bessy says, 'We can use it to be troll pirates. We can be pirates and find the trolls and their treasure.' Tom jumps up and moves away from the table. 'Come on,' he says, skipping towards the role-play corner. Katy, Bessy and Khalid drop what they are doing at the craft table and follow excitedly. A game of 'troll-seeking pirates' begins, using the telescopes. The children select items from the costume box to dress as pirates and Katy runs back to the craft table to get herself a telescope. Soon, all four of the children have a telescope and others join in the search for trolls and treasure.

As the above case study demonstrates, within the first few years of life play develops from the 'physical' play of a small baby into more complex play that involves many sophisticated mental processes. Children use all of their senses during play. From a Piagetian perspective, this enables children to assimilate new information. This information is stored with existing ideas until something happens, i.e. until new information is assimilated that contradicts or questions this existing knowledge. This discomfort or disequilibrium of thought causes children to rethink the idea that they had assimilated (Pound, 2005). This re-thinking, known as accommodation, enables them to adjust or adapt their thinking to restore equilibrium. Pound (2005: 37) refers to the outcome of equilibrium as 'feeling comfortable with our own thinking'. Stephen (2010) identifies that Piaget's focus on the child's active exploration and movement through the processes of assimilation and accommodation can be seen in the emphasis that practitioners place on providing resource-rich play environments and ample opportunities for children to explore as they choose. These provide opportunities for children to experience novel situations and experiences that can trigger assimilation and accommodation (Pound, 2005). This can be viewed as a two-way relationship, whereby more complex forms of play can aid cognitive development and whereby cognitive development aids more complex forms of play.

Socially, play develops from the solitary play of a young child, to parallel play (where children play side by side but function separately; for more on the types of play see Chapter 19) and then to socially interactive play where much of the play relies on the interactions with others. Avgitidou (1997) suggests that play with friends is characterised by specific qualities that encourage children's social, cognitive and affective development and that 'these qualities reflect patterns of interaction among friends which are duration, intensity, coordination and continuity of interaction, interdependence and the development of a shared knowledge of the relationship' (Avgitidou, 1997: 6). Play that facilitates the development of these qualities helps children to form positive attitudes towards others as they assist each other, share and exchange information. Play can therefore involve high levels of intellectual demand and creativity, particularly within reciprocal play as children sustain cooperative endeavour, a key feature of which is joint problem solving in a variety of forms (BERA, 2003).

While play may well be a powerful aid to learning within the EYFS, it also has a crucial part to play in the wider, holistic development of individuals. As Walker (2005) acknowledges, the aim of education should be to equip individuals with self-determination and the development of a sense of self which enables active involvement in emotional, intellectual and professional relationships with others. Play within trusting and caring environments can help to foster this positive sense of self.

The meaningful business of play: what is it all about?

As we have seen, play has been studied from different theoretical approaches, but a common element to all studies about play is that it is an activity that children undertake for pleasure and is one of children's primary needs in their development. The Early Years Foundation Stage (DfE, 2014) promotes the use of play to help children develop a broad range of knowledge and skills that provide the right foundation for future progress through school and throughout life. There is, however, no concise or agreed definition of 'play'. Santer et al. (2007: xviii) acknowledge that 'Play is perhaps too profound and intangible a concept to neatly define in a way that brooks no argument.' Lindon (2001: 2) does suggest, however, that 'play includes a range of activities, undertaken for their own interest, enjoyment or the satisfaction that results'. Similarly, the Department for Culture, Media and Sport highlights that 'Play is what children and young people do when they follow their own ideas in their own way and for their own reasons' (DCMS, 2004: 8). A powerful element of this is that children have ownership of their play. From a child's perspective, play can be a satisfying and enjoyable occupation that can promote feelings of inner well-being.

The importance of the pleasure gained from play should not be underestimated both for psychological and physiological development. Children play because it is fun. From a child's perspective, any learning that arises from play is likely to be incidental as it is often the process of play that is most satisfying. When choosing to bake a cake, for example, the business of mixing flour and eggs can be pleasurable and rewarding in itself. In some instances the actual finished product, the cake, may be of far less interest.

Where children choose and have control over their play, this can be viewed as 'free-play'. The Early Years Foundation Stage (DCSF, 2008) has embedded into its framework the twelve features of free-play identified by Bruce and since updated (Bruce, 2005, cited in Bruce and Ockelford, 2010: 113), which are summarised below. These features embrace a diverse approach to play cross-culturally and in relation to children with disabilities and learning difficulties and are considered to provide a 'birth throughout life' approach (Bruce and Ockelford, 2010: 113).

1   Children draw upon the first-hand experiences they have had in their play. The richer and deeper the experiences, in the way they bring into action all the senses as well as movement and the kinaesthetic feedback that accompanies it, the more the child's possibilities for rich play develop.
2   In play children make up their own rules.
3   Children make play props from found materials and sometimes from toys. Home-made play props are often thought to be most loved by children in their play rather than expensive toys, as they are more open-ended and flexible to use, offering more play opportunities (see Bruce and Ockelford, 2010, for further detail).
4   One of the most crucial features of play is that children must choose to do it. They cannot be made to play. Children have to move into play in their own way, at their own pace.
5   Children rehearse future possibilities when they play (for example in role-play).
6   Play opens up opportunities to pretend.
7   Sometimes children play alone. This is in no way inferior to playing alongside or with others.
8   When children are playing with others they might play in companionship, which means they play in parallel, enjoying each other's company, but not wishing to interact directly, or they may play cooperatively with others.
9   It is easier to play in a larger group cooperatively if everyone is clear what the play theme is and has realistic props to use.
10 Quality free-flowing play means that children become deeply involved in their play.
11 When children are involved in their play, they often demonstrate their recent learning.
12 Free-flow play helps children to coordinate and bring together their learning.

It is important to acknowledge that play can be a highly personal and rewarding experience for all children. The BERA Early Years Special Interest Group (2003) question the efficacy of 'free play', however, and describe how play can be stereotypical and lacking in challenge. It is suggested here that this is more likely to be the case where the principles detailed above are not present. If we accept that 'free play' is socially and culturally constructed, however, we do need to consider the level of 'freedom' for each individual within it. As Wood and Bennett (1997) highlight, children's skills and competences as 'players' vary considerably.

Play as a platform for learning

It is crucial that adults appreciate the importance of play as a process and do not become overly focused on end results. While any learning that may result from free-play is likely to be incidental, practitioners are also encouraged to develop 'purposeful play' with the aim of promoting learning. This can create a dilemma for practitioners as they endeavour to find a balance between child-initiated free-play and adult-led play. Gaining a balance between free-play and adult-led play can be a complex process that may be compounded by a need to meet explicit learning goals. One suggestion is that free-play can be enriched when a more knowledgeable or experienced individual extends or enriches the play. From a Vygotskian perspective this refers to the difference between what a child can do on his/her own and what they can do when guided by someone else (either an adult or a more able child) (Vygotsky, 1978). The Effective Provision of Pre-school Education Project (EPPE, 1997–2004) identified 'sustained shared thinking' within adult–child interactions as a necessary prerequisite for excellent early years practice. They describe this as an episode in which two or more individuals 'work together' in an intellectual way to solve a problem, clarify a concept, evaluate activities and extend a narrative (Sylva et al., 2004). Both parties must contribute to the thinking in order to develop and extend thinking. More challenging forms of sustained shared thinking can be encouraged by using increasingly more sophisticated and abstract scaffolding props (Siraj-Blatchford, 2009).

Supporting learning through play: 'sensitive intervention'

One form of scaffolding can be provided by 'sensitive intervention' which is necessary to enable the child to maintain control of play while providing opportunities and ideas to develop it further. By scaffolding children's play experiences, young children can develop the skills they need to become successful learners – for example, building their confidence, developing their flexibility of thought and seeing problems from different perspectives (Tickell, 2011). This supports the use of play-based approaches for learning that combine instructional and playful teaching. It highlights the importance of techniques such as modelling, demonstrating and questioning while engaging in fun and active experiences. The EPPE Project (Sylva et al., 2004) identified that adult 'modelling' is often combined with longer periods of more focused thinking and that open-ended questioning is also associated with improved cognitive development. The Project identified that even in settings classed as 'excellent', however, the frequency of use of these approaches was very low.

Sensitive intervention may involve initiating particular activities with specific children: individually, in small groups or as a whole class or it may entail observing the activities chosen by children and then scaffolding their learning via prompts to extend the opportunities for learning. A key element of this may be to encourage children to verbalise what they are doing, to help develop linguistic and cognitive skills and confidence in their own abilities. Freely chosen play activities often provide the best opportunities for adults to extend children's thinking. Adults need, therefore, to create opportunities to extend child-initiated play as well as teacher-initiated group work, as both have been found to be important vehicles for promoting learning (Sylva et al., 2004). The skill of the practitioner may, therefore, be viewed as the ability to know how and when to intervene and collaborate within the play experience to nurture 'sustained shared thinking'. Moyles (2010) describes this process as a spiral that begins with free-play, continues with adult-directed play and then extends to enriched free-play as knowledge and abilities are acquired and consolidated.

The key element identified here is the use of a flexible approach to play-based learning, based on the level of development, needs and interest of the individual child. While in theory this may seem quite straightforward, in reality it may be difficult to judge when to intervene within a play scenario to further extend learning. Practitioners need to be aware of the possible detrimental impact of 'interrupting' young children who are involved and enthused within play. Indeed, Wood and Bennett (1997) identified a common concern among practitioners that they may 'spoil' or 'intrude upon' children's play. As Lindon (2001) suggests, there may be a difference in perceptions between practitioners and children regarding the quality of play whereby some activities, games and play resources, important to children, may be misinterpreted and/or undervalued by practitioners. As a result, it is important to pause, observe and reflect before stepping into a play interaction. Practitioners need to become 'play partners', who participate within children's play with sincerity and enthusiasm. Some practitioners can do this with ease whilst others may find it more difficult to achieve (Smidt, 2010).

Case study

Play partnership and 'sensitive intervention' episode

Cassie is 2 years of age and attends full-time day care five days per week. Amina has been her key worker for over a year now and so Amina feels very in tune with Cassie's developmental progress. Generally, Cassie plays confidently on her own and alongside others. Across the week it has been noticed that Cassie usually chooses a variety of activities from those on offer, but often seems to prefer to join in with activities that involve the use of gross motor movements and she is particularly drawn to play in the garden when the doors are open during the free-play period. Amina has reflected upon her observations and decided to focus on developing Cassie's thinking skills and fine motor skills. Amina will engage in 'sensitive intervention' by working as a 'play partner'. The focus will be on explicitly extending Cassie's involvement in some of the play activities that focus on development of thinking skills and also hand–eye coordination. Amina has set these areas of development as specific targets for intervention and observation in play over the next few weeks.

On top of the grass mound Amina has positioned a play activity and herself, with the hope that Cassie will be enticed to join her. Amina sits on a blanket on the grass. A pile of small items are in one basket (such as pebbles, corks, acorns). Another basket holds a variety of containers (including small boxes, bottles with different-sized openings and jars).

The doors into the garden are opened by Sally, another childcare assistant, and the children are encouraged to look out to see what there is to play with in the garden today. Amina is already positioned sitting on the grass mound and can be seen by the eight children as they enter the garden.

Cassie hurries towards the small red tricycle and gets on. After a few minutes of using the tricycle, Cassie moves on to the grass area, climbs over the tyres and spends a moment lying quietly on her tummy on the grass. Before long, Cassie notices Amina playing. Playfully, Amina talks through her play actions. Picking up a pebble she says, 'Mmmm, I think I'll put this in here,' and tries to put it into the neck of a bottle. 'Oh no, that won't fit!' Amina uses a pole-bridging technique by reporting out loud to herself her every move and thought. Amina works through different items and containers. 'Ahh, this fits. What else can I put in here?' Cassie followed by Jak comes and stands alongside Amina. Amina welcomes the children

(Continued)

(Continued)

and continues to play. Cassie is tempted to join in the game and starts by selecting a jam jar. Smiling to herself, after a little persistence, Cassie is able to remove the loose lid and picks pebbles to place in the jar. She smiles maybe at the sound of the small pebbles dropping into the glass jar. Amina continues to talk through her thoughts and actions. 'Ooh, that won't fit. Maybe it will if I try and move it this way? No, maybe I need to try something different. In it goes ... and in goes another.' Cassie puts down the jar, moves to sit down and shifts a little closer to Amina. Cassie picks up a different jar, but she has trouble opening it and holds it out to Amina. She encourages Cassie to twist the lid instead of pulling; Cassie is delighted when she succeeds. The side-by-side playing continues for some time and Cassie starts to join in talking through her actions: 'In ... No, too big ... In this one.'

Through reflection, simple planning and playful partnership, valuable and sensitive intervention can be achieved. In this episode, Cassie was encouraged subtly to choose to participate and continue with involvement in a play activity that had a specific link to identified developmental targets.

Reflective task

- Reflect on the case study above and consider the scenarios below and identify possible positive and negative consequences of each. Try to reflect on both viewpoints and fill in a grid, like the one below:

Table 7.1

Scenario	Practitioner perspective (positives and negatives)	Child perspective (positives and negatives)
Withdrawal of a young child from a free-play situation to complete an adult-initiated activity		
Long periods of time devoted to free-play without adult intervention		
During free-play, a child chooses to remain in one area of the setting, e.g. the sand play area (for an extended period of time)		
During free-play a child chooses to repeat the same activity consecutively over a number of sessions		

- Scenario: A group of children aged 3–4 years are playing in a wooded spot at the end of the playing field. Shannon and Malik are busy giggling and running along the uneven pathway. The practitioner calls out a warning to the children to 'Take care and walk, not run.' A positive outcome of the warning may be to prevent the children from falling and hurting themselves. A possible negative outcome may be that they miss out on the chance to take a calculated risk of running on uneven ground which may help them to refine their gross motor skills. Reflect on the EYFS Section 3: Safeguarding and Welfare Requirements. Can you identify other possible consequences for their development?

Early Years Foundation Stage and play

A key emphasis within the EYFS (and in other educational systems, such as the Foundation Phase in Wales) is the use of play as a vehicle for learning. In this context, play may be viewed as a platform for desirable forms of learning rather than play for its own sake.

The EYFS (DfE, 2014) identifies three main characteristics of effective learning: *Playing and exploring*, which may include the children:

- investigating
- experiencing
- being willing to 'have a go'.

Active learning, which may include the children:

- being involved and concentrating
- keeping on trying (even when encountering difficulties)
- experiencing achievement in what they set out to do.

Creating and thinking critically, which may include the children:

- developing their own ideas
- making links between ideas, knowledge and experiences
- developing a range of strategies for doing things.

An engaging and stimulating play environment provides opportunities for these characteristics to be experienced and crafted. This can impact positively on holistic child development, enabling progress across the seven areas of learning and development.

Possible benefits for learning and development within the EYFS as highlighted by Moyles (2010) include the following.

- Children have confidence in play activities and this has a positive effect on motivation, concentration and self-image.
- Play involves children in using imagination and creativity.
- Play requires experimentation and exploration.
- Children enjoy cooperating and collaborating with their peers in play activities.
- Children learn to make decisions and organise their own time and activities.
- Play exercises the mind and the body and aids motor and perceptual development.

As well as the importance of the play environment, it is also crucial to acknowledge that each child is unique and so practitioners will need to spend time to get to know each individual child. In addition, to facilitate learning and development through play, positive relationships and a sense of belonging within the setting will need to be nurtured and maintained. This interconnection is illustrated in Figure 7.1.

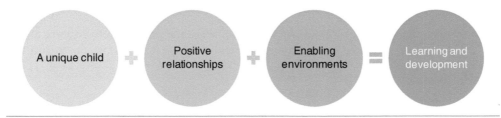

Figure 7.1 *The four themes of EYFS (DfE, 2014)*

While play can help children to learn and develop, some practitioners question whether approaching their interactions with children from the perspective of supporting learning and development conflicts with what they see as their overarching caring role. For example, many playwork providers view it as against core principles to observe children with the intention of guiding them to their next level of development. Likewise, some childminders argue that they are there to provide a home-from-home environment, in line with parents' and carers' wishes, and feel they are not 'educators' (Tickell, 2011). Some practitioners consider their role to be more focused on caring for the child, which includes nurturing and developing individual play choices.

While this view may be more prevalent with carers or practitioners of very young children, it does highlight possible tensions between the 'process' of play (i.e. inner well-being of the individual) versus the 'product' (i.e. to meet specific learning outcomes).

Outdoor play

One area of play that is growing in popularity in early childhood settings is outdoor play, which can provide a rich setting for children's imagination and fantasy (see Chapter 12 on more on the use of outdoor environments). Indeed, Dowdell et al. (2011) found that exploration and discovery of nature were a significant part of children's play within an outdoor setting. For outdoor play to be at its most effective it should not be seen as an opportunity to take indoor activities outside. Rather it should be viewed as an opportunity for children to play in a context that allows them to combine play with sensorial experiences, talk and movement.

Opportunities to play with natural resources can stimulate children's natural curiosity and their intrinsic motivation, enabling them to develop a range of skills such as problem solving, negotiation and cooperation. Open access between the indoor and outdoor play spaces can empower young children to make choices about where, what and how to play. Equipping children and practitioners with appropriate clothing and footwear for all weathers can extend the use of the outdoor play environment across all seasons (Knight, 2009). Nevertheless, a challenge for practitioners is to identify opportunities for outdoor play in natural environments (Waller et al., 2010). This may require creative use of existing outdoor space or the use of community areas such as local parks. While the environment must be assessed to ensure that it is a safe place to play, it is also beneficial for young children's development to engage in 'risky' play as many children have an appetite for risk-taking (Gill, 2007; Little et al., 2011). If we are empowering children, this may entail children taking risks they consider acceptable. This can be a difficult and contentious issue for many practitioners, as their level of tolerance to risk within play can limit the opportunities for such play. Practitioners may also have fears of legal action if a child is injured while in their care (Waller et al., 2010). Ideally, children need to be supported to assess their own capabilities and regulate their own behaviours within a safe environment. This requires an underlying view of the child as competent rather than one of the child as vulnerable and in need of adult protection (Sandseter, 2009).

Observation and reflective practice

This move to child-led play in a variety of settings makes assessment more challenging and, therefore, observational assessment is a key aspect of effective early childhood education and care (discussed further in Chapters 8, 9 and 10). Practitioners can observe children while they act and interact in their play, everyday activities and planned activities. This can provide a valuable insight into individual children's achievements, interests and progress. As Chapter 8 will demonstrate, reflection on these observations can help practitioners to tailor their provision to support the emerging needs of each individual. It is essential that adequate time is taken to undertake and reflect upon these observations, both as individual practitioners and, wherever possible, as a whole team.

Observations of play can provide:

- a comprehensive picture of each individual child in relation to knowledge and understanding, skills and attitudes;
- opportunities for the progression of play via the varied use of strategies, resources and changes to the learning environment.

Planning for quality play experiences

It is important to note, however, that even apparently 'free' play requires careful planning and skilled practitioners will keep children at the heart of the planning process. They will actively seek and engage with the interests, needs and ideas of children so that play can be fun, enticing and yet instructional. When play is a vehicle for learning, practitioners' knowledge and expertise combined with the creative thoughts of children can shape the planning process.

Some key aspects of good practice in this process to consider are:

- Each child is unique and will have his/her own individual interests, needs and ideas.
- Prior learning can be used to inform the 'next steps' for the enrichment of play.
- A responsive approach towards 'golden moments' (unanticipated learning opportunities) can lead to a spontaneous change in emphasis.

The role of the practitioner is central, therefore, to providing a supportive and stimulating environment with opportunities for free-play and more structured play. The practitioner is pivotal in providing themes for play and a range of resources, but should not be afraid to let children transform, extend or adapt play. Above all, although play can provide a valuable platform for learning, practitioners should not lose sight of the fact that play should be a valuable and enjoyable activity in its own right.

Tension between pedagogy of play and accountability

Practitioners have an obligation to fulfil statutory requirements within curriculum frameworks whilst at the same time providing authentic, playful experiences that appeal to young children. For many, the challenge is to implement curricular targets whilst attempting to maintain an environment that allows for child-centred activity. As Ranz-Smith (2007: 272) highlights, practitioners are 'engaged in a precarious balancing act as they strive to meet increasing curriculum requirements while remaining responsive to children and their play'. Whilst policy recommendations acknowledge the value of children's freedom, choice and autonomy within play, tensions can often arise between the ideology of playful pedagogy and play focused upon specific learning outcomes in light of curriculum demands.

Case study

Mr Smith, classroom teacher, is conscious that it is nearly lunch time and he needs to fit in his teacher-directed literacy session (which is part of a whole-school approach to literacy development) before then. As he looks around the room, he notices that a number of children are engaged in directing their own play, fully immersed in their activities. This creates a dilemma: should he observe the children and make relevant field-notes or should he signal the start of the more formal part of the morning? Mr Smith feels an obligation to complete the literacy session in line with the whole-school approach, something Ofsted has identified as a strength of the school's provision. However, he also is aware of the benefits of enabling the children to extend and transform their self-development by continuing their play uninterrupted.

Reflective task

- Good practice requires listening to children's own ideas as part of the planning process. Reflect on how the voice of individual children can be captured for the purpose of planning the play curriculum across different age ranges. Are there any restrictions from the EYFS?

Wood (2007) argues that practitioners need to respond creatively to policy frameworks to develop integrated curriculum and pedagogical approaches that value child and adult-led activities. However, how this can be done in practice remains unclear. With an ever-increasing focus on educational standards, practitioners face increasing levels of accountability within their day-to-day roles. This may reduce the level of freedom to develop creative and innovative approaches as the demand for evidence-based records pressurises practitioners to provide records/evidence of how learning outcomes are being addressed within pedagogical approaches and how these are being met by individual children.

Summary

This chapter has discussed the role of play in early childhood education and care. It is encouraging to see that within the EYFS the role of play is emphasised, both indoors and outdoors, and that the importance of the practitioner in facilitating children's play is acknowledged. Children need play opportunities to initiate their own learning, to develop social interactions, negotiate relationships with their peers and pursue their own interests. Theoretical perspectives on play conclude that children develop and learn through play both in an enjoyable, pleasurable way and at the same time in a challenging way. This learning can be both planned and unplanned and practitioners play a central role in facilitating opportunities to play, but also in providing the freedom for children to explore their own ideas. In doing so, play provides an opportunity for children to build communication skills, social and emotional skills, physical skills and creativity.

Key points to remember

- The EYFS promotes the use of play as a vehicle for learning for holistic child development.

- Each child is unique and will have his/her own individual interests, needs and ideas in relation to play.

- Play is a valuable activity in its own right.

- Sensorial experiences, talk and movement can be woven together through play.

- 'Free-play' enables children to make choices and experience ownership.

- It is the process of play and not necessarily the product that is important.

- Sustained shared thinking provides opportunities to extend the learning that can result from play.

- Techniques such as modelling, scaffolding and open-ended questioning within play can result in enriched and extended play.

- Sensitive intervention requires practitioners to think carefully about how and when to intervene in child's play.

- Observation is a valuable tool for creating a comprehensive picture of each individual child in relation to knowledge and understanding, skills and attitudes.

- It can be a challenge for practitioners to sustain a balance between evidencing achieved learning outcomes and facilitating child-centred play provision.

Points for discussion

- Drawing upon the work of Bruce and Moyles, which is explored in the chapter, consider how you could improve play provision for a group of young children. Discuss how the use of play activities and resources could be enhanced within an early years setting.

- Discuss your own experiences of supporting 'sustained shared thinking' episodes within play.

- Undertake observations of children during play and try to analyse your observations of play focusing on the role of the adult, the play environment and the resources children used, together with the aspects of development that children demonstrated during their play.

Further reading

Books

Brock, A., Dodds, S., Jarvis, P. and Olusoga, Y. (2009) *Perspective on Play: Learning for Life*. London: Pearson Education.
Smidt, S. (2010) *Playing to Learn: The Role of Play in the Early Years*. London: Routledge.
Wood, E. (2013) *Play, Learning and the Early Childhood Curriculum*. London: Sage.

Articles

Avgitidou, S. (1997) 'Children's play: an investigation of children's co-construction of their world within early school settings', *Early Years: An International Journal of Research and Development*, 17 (2): 6–10.
Dowdell, K., Graya, T. and Maloneb, K. (2011) 'Nature and its influence on children's outdoor play', *Australian Journal of Outdoor Education*, 15 (2): 24–35.

Useful websites

www.playwales.org/eng
www.estyn.gov.uk
www.ofsted.gov.uk

References

Avgitidou, S. (1997) 'Children's play: an investigation of children's co-construction of their world within early school settings', *Early Years: An International Journal of Research and Development*, 17 (2): 6–10.

BERA Early Years Special Interest Group (2003) *Early Years Research: Pedagogy, Curriculum and Adult Roles, Training and Professionalism.* Southwell: BERA.

Bruce, T. and Ockelford, A. (2010) 'Understanding symbolic development', in T. Bruce (ed.), *Early Childhood: A Guide for Students*, 2nd edn. London: Sage.

Bruner, J.S. (2006) *In Search of Pedagogy.* Volume II: *The Selected Works of Jerome S. Bruner, 1979–2006.* Oxford: Routledge.

DCMS (Department for Culture, Media and Sport) (2004) *Getting Serious About Play – A Review of Children's Play.* London: DCMS.

DCSF (Department for Children, School and Families) (2008) *The Early Years Foundation Stage.* Nottingham: DCSF Publications.

DfE (Department for Education) (2014) *Statutory Framework for the Early Years Foundation Stage. Setting the Standards for Learning, Development and Care for Children from Birth to Five.* London: DfE. Available at: www.foundationyears.org.uk/files/2014/07/EYFS_framework_from_1_September_2014__with_clarification_note.pdf (accessed 21 September 2015).

Dowdell, K., Graya, T. and Maloneb, K. (2011) 'Nature and its influence on children's outdoor play', *Australian Journal of Outdoor Education*, 15 (2): 24–35.

Gill, T. (2007) *No Fear: Growing Up in a Risk Averse Society.* London: Calouste Gulbenkian Foundation.

Knight, S. (2009) *Forest Schools and Outdoor Learning in the Early Years.* London: Sage.

Lindon, J. (2001) *Understanding Children's Play.* Cheltenham: Nelson Thornes.

Little, H., Wyver, S. and Gibson, F. (2011) 'The influence of play context and adult attitudes on young children's physical risk-taking during outdoor play', *European Early Childhood Education Research Journal*, 19 (1): 113–31.

Moyles, J. (2010) *Just Playing?* Milton Keynes: Open University Press.

Pound, L. (2005) *How Children Learn: From Montessori to Vygotsky.* London: Step Forward Publishing.

Ranz-Smith, D. (2007) 'Teachers' perception of play: in leaving no child behind are teachers leaving childhood behind?', *Early Education and Development*, 18 (2), 271–303.

Sandseter, E. (2009) 'Affordances for risky play in preschool: the importance of features in the play environment', *Early Childhood Education Journal*, 36 (5): 439–46.

Santer, J. and Griffiths, G. with Goodall, D. (2007) *Free Play in Early Childhood: A Literature Review.* London: National Children's Bureau.

Siraj-Blatchford, I. (2009) 'Conceptualising progression in the pedagogy of play and sustained shared thinking in early childhood education: a Vygotskian perspective', *Educational and Child Psychology*, 26 (2): 77–89.

Smidt, S. (2010) *Playing to Learn: The Role of Play in the Early Years.* London: Routledge.

Stephen, C. (2010) 'Pedagogy: the silent partner in early years learning', *Early Years: Journal of International Research and Development*, 30 (1): 15–28.

Sylva, K., Melhuish, E., Sammons, P., Siraj-Blatchford, I. and Taggart, B. (2004) *The Effective Provision of Pre-School Education (EPPE) Project: Final Report: a Longitudinal Study (1997–2004).* London: Department for Education and Skills.

Tickell, C. (2011) *The Early Years: Foundations for Life, Health and Learning*. An Independent Report on the Early Years Foundation Stage to Her Majesty's Government. London: Crown. Available at: www.education.gov.uk/tickellreview (accessed July 2012).

Vygotsky, L.S. (1978) *Mind in Society: The Development of Higher Psychological Processes*. London: Harvard University Press.

Walker, J.C. (2005) 'Self-determination as an educational aim', in W. Carr (ed.), *The Routledge Reader in Philosophy of Education*. Oxford: Routledge.

Waller, T., Sandseter, E., Wyver, S., Arlemalm-Hagser, E. and Maynard, T. (2010) 'The dynamics of early childhood spaces: opportunities for outdoor play?', *European Early Childhood Education Research Journal*, 18 (4): 437–43.

Wood, L. and Bennett, N. (1997) 'The rhetoric and reality of play: teachers' thinking and class-room practice', *Early Years: An International Journal of Research and Development*, 17 (2): 22–7.

Wood, E. (2007) 'Reconceptualising child-centred education: contemporary directions in policy, theory and practice in early childhood', *Forum*, 49 (1&2): 119–134. Available at: http://dx.doi.org/10.2304/forum.2007.49.1.119 (accessed 24th November 2015).

Want to learn more about this chapter? Visit the companion website at https://study.sagepub.com/EYFS3e for access to free SAGE journal articles and book chapters, weblinks, annotated further readings and more.

8

Observations: Recording and Analysis

Paulette Luff

👍 Chapter overview

Observation is of great importance within early childhood education and care, including the Early Years Foundation Stage in England. Through using observations, present-day early childhood practitioners are following in the footsteps of pioneers such as John Dewey, Maria Montessori and Susan Isaacs. While these traditions continue to inspire our current practice, ideas are emerging about new ways to observe. There are differences between narrative observations, which are undertaken in order to get to know children and foster their development, and more objective, scientific approaches employed in making summative assessments. Whatever types of observations are used in early childhood education and care, it is important to record, analyse and interpret these carefully in order to appreciate children's capabilities and to support and enrich meaningful learning.

The aims of this chapter are to:

- note the history of observation and its importance in early childhood education and care
- emphasise the place of observation within EYFS
- consider some ways of understanding and knowing young children through observations.

Observation in early childhood education practice and care – some historical influences

Observation has a long-held and important place in early childhood education and care. This is because the discoveries that arise from careful observation are well recognised as central to learning. In Maria Montessori's (1912) pedagogical method, for example, the child is encouraged to observe, and his/her senses are trained to enable perception of geometric forms, colours and the features of the natural environment. Similarly for John Dewey (1933/1998), thoughtful observations provide a basis for the reflective enquiries that promote learning at every age.

Dewey and Montessori both stress that observations of children should form the basis of pedagogy. In his *Pedagogic Creed*, Dewey stated:

> I believe that … the constant and careful observation of interests is of the utmost importance for the educator … only through the continual and sympathetic observation of childhood's interests can the adult enter into the child's life and see what it is ready for and upon what material it could work most readily and fruitfully. (1897/1974: 436)

Montessori, similarly, explained that she developed and trialled her methods on the basis of numerous exact observations and advocated that teaching should stem from systematic observations of children acting freely in natural contexts. She stressed that observational study of children, within learning environments free from negative constraints, can yield 'great surprises and unexpected possibilities' (1912: 30).

As a scientist, Montessori emphasised the close observation of the external and visible world, highlighting the relationship between objective observation and logical thought. Yet observation, for Montessori, also went beyond scientific interest to the close relationships that can exist between the observer and the observed. She draws interesting parallels between the observant child and watchful adults:

> He stands with respect to the plants and animals in relations analogous to those in which the observing teacher stands towards him. Little by little, as interest and observation grow, his zealous care for the living creatures grows also and, in this way, the child can logically be brought to appreciate the care which the mother and the teacher take of him. (1912: 157)

Thus Montessori recognised that the attention and love of one human being for another can make observant teaching a deeply caring act.

As a trained psychoanalyst, Susan Isaacs also recognised the significance of undertaking and analysing observations for seeing, knowing and empathising with young children:

> by patient listening to the talk of even little children, and watching what they do, with the one purpose of understanding them, we can imaginatively feel their fears and angers, their bewilderments and triumphs; we can wish their wishes, see their pictures and think their thoughts. (Isaacs, 1929: 165)

Like Dewey and Montessori, Isaacs promoted an approach to learning based upon observing children in order to understand and meet their needs. From 1924 to 1927 she was headteacher at the Malting House experimental school in Cambridge, where children were offered a range of real-world experiences in order to stimulate their natural curiosity. Narrative observations of children engaged in these experiences formed a basis for provision of rich opportunities for learning. Isaacs' (1930, 1933) books about children's development were based upon her observations, and those who studied with her while she was head of the first Department of Child Development at the Institute of Education in London were encouraged to engage actively with observational enquiries (Podmore and Luff, 2012).

The place of observation within the EYFS

As proposed by Montessori and Dewey (see above), the Early Years Foundation Stage includes a requirement for children to observe and to become observant. In the understanding the world area of learning, for example, it is noted: 'They make observations of animals and plants and explain why some things occur, and talk about changes'. In the associated *Development Matters* document (Early Education/DfE, 2012) adults are advised to provide opportunities and materials to encourage close observation, to support children to discuss their observations, introducing relevant vocabulary, and to offer resources to enable children to represent what they have observed. For babies and toddlers, 'treasure baskets' and 'heuristic play' (Goldschmeid and Jackson, 2004; Jackson and Forbes, 2015) offer possibilities for observing objects with all the senses as adults watch; older children can engage with more structured explorations and observant adults may guide these early scientific investigations through a 'spiral of discovery' (Brunton and Thornton, 2010).

In order to support each 'unique child' practitioners are advised to 'understand and observe each child's development and learning, assess progress, plan for next steps' (Early Education/DfE, 2012: 2). Observation, of children's play and other activities, forms the basis for a cycle of formative assessment and curriculum planning. Being observant is crucial to the formation of 'positive relationships', in which the practitioner understands the child and sees and supports his or her interests. It also plays a part in the provision of 'enabling environments' where adults notice what resources and opportunities they could provide.

Practitioners are advised to look, listen and note what children are doing, when they play and interact and then analyse what they have observed to use their findings as the basis for planning. Once experiences and opportunities have been planned and implemented observation is used as a basis for evaluating the activity, taking note of children's progress and considering possibilities for enrichment and extension. Thus the cycle continues as a constant process designed to stimulate and support learning.

Observation is also central to the partnership working between parents and practitioners that is valued in the EYFS (as discussed in Chapter 13). Sharing observations between home and early childhood settings offers opportunities for dialogue about the child in order to identify the progress he or she is making and create plans for further supporting and promoting learning and development. These shared observations may be informal anecdotes, photographs capturing particular moments, or more structured records. It is stated in the EYFS statutory framework document that 'Paperwork should be limited to that which is absolutely necessary to promote children's successful learning and development' (DfE, 2014: 13), so it is important that whatever is documented is necessary and meaningful.

There are two points within the EYFS when summative assessments are made and recorded. The first is for 2-year-olds, reviewing their progress in the prime areas of learning (i.e. communication and language (see Chapter 20); physical development (see Chapter 24); and personal, social and emotional development (see Chapter 19). The second is the Early Years Profile, completed during the Reception year at the end of the EYFS (see Chapter 9). In order for robust, accurate judgements to be made these assessments of children have to be underpinned by precise, systematic observations. The most common of these are brief notes taken during children's naturally occurring play activities, often jotted on labels or stick-it notes. The observations of 2-year-old Ola, shown in the reflective task for this chapter, offer good examples. In order for these to show a fair representation of a child's achievements, they must be collected carefully over a period of time, at different points during the day and week. Practitioners should ensure that they are providing rich opportunities and a supportive context so that all children can show their abilities to the fullest extent and reveal their potential (Dubiel, 2014).

Approaches to seeing and knowing young children

For implementation of a key person approach, and for formative assessment and curriculum planning in early childhood education, methods of observation are needed that will enable the observer to get close to and understand children. For this purpose narrative methods of observation are useful. These can be traditional written narratives, but may also involve photograph sequences and/or audio and video recordings to capture learning. The three approaches to observation and analysis suggested below are drawn from different theoretical perspectives and are, therefore, undertaken and evaluated in different ways. What they have in common is their basis in narrative, recognising the importance of stories in human lives and harnessing this for educative purposes (e.g. Carr, 2001; Goodson et al., 2010; Carr and Lee, 2012). The chapters that follow in this book about assessment (Chapter 9) and the use of pedagogical documentation (Chapter 10) provide further strong examples of approaches to observation that can be used to foster learning. There are also many excellent books devoted to the topic of observation in early childhood that explain and showcase different methods (see the Further Reading section of this chapter). Observing the youngest children and making sense of their body language and emotional expression is particularly important and sometimes challenging.

Close observation: the Tavistock approach

The Tavistock approach to close observation of babies and young children is named after the London clinic where it was developed. The method was pioneered by Esther Bick (1964) for use in the training of psychotherapists. As originally conceived, the approach involves weekly, hour-long visits to a family home in order to follow the development of a baby or very young child throughout a year of their life (Miller et al., 1989). The observer aims to be neutral and non-participant, yet fully tuned in to the inner thoughts and feelings of the child. No notes are taken during the hour, but very close attention is paid to non-verbal signals and the features of any interaction between the child and parents and particularly the mother. A detailed account of the session is later written up in which, as far as possible, the complete sequence of events is recalled and described. The observation accounts are interpreted using psychodynamic theory and pay particular attention to the emotional responses of the observer.

Elfer (2005) suggests that a modified version of this close observation technique can be used in early childhood settings to foster relationships and understanding of emotions. The time and frequency of the observations may be reduced, for example, to recording just 10–20 minutes of interaction. The method is retained: paying close attention while observing and then producing a written record from memory in as much detail as possible and acknowledging feelings and subjectivities.

Case study

Feeding Jake

This observation is of a 7-month-old baby, Jake, who has recently begun to attend part-time at a day nursery, being fed fruit purée by his key person, Jenny.
    Jake is seated in the low high chair, wedged securely with a small cushion. He is awake and wide-eyed. He raises and lowers his arms in front of him and clasps and unclasps his hands. Jenny brings the small bowl of apple purée and places it on the tray of the high chair, in front of him. Jake smiles widely and opens his mouth. Jenny smiles in response, but Jake is looking at the food bowl and not back at her. He watches as Jenny dips the tip of the spoon in the purée, opens his

mouth even more widely and wriggles his whole body in anticipation. Jenny places the spoon in his mouth, quite slowly and gently. Jake closes his mouth around the spoon, momentarily, and then opens it again and turns his head away. He waves his arms and moves his mouth, as though sucking the food. Jenny scoops a little more apple onto the spoon, then watches him and waits. Jake opens his mouth widely and Jenny feeds him another spoonful. They continue in this pattern for several more mouthfuls. Jake continues to move his arms, but does not reach for the spoon or the bowl. When Jake closes his mouth, and grips the side edges of the high chair with both hands, Jenny offers his trainer cup with some water and he drinks.

Watching, I like the way that even during the busy nursery lunchtime Jenny is not rushing to feed Jake, but seems tuned in to his body language and she is prepared to go at his preferred pace. In interpreting the observation, I can detail aspects of his personal, social and emotional development and recognise his progress with weaning onto solid foods. I am also aware of the positive emotions that are aroused in me, when observing Jenny carefully and responsively feeding Jake, and from this I sense that the mealtime is pleasurable for both of them.

Reflective tasks

- Reflect on this case study and using as an example Chloe's case study (see below) try to analyse the observation in relation to learning areas of the EYFS.

- Reflect on your own experience of the use of observation in early childhood education and care, and think: How do you make meaningful use of observation and how important do you consider observation to be as a strategy for learning?

Observing in this way, even for a short time, is a valuable way of getting to know the child, understand the developing relationship with his or her key person and appreciating the quality of the care provided. Practitioners who have observed children using close observation techniques report increased feelings of empathy towards the children and an ability to recognise their own emotions. The EYFS includes a requirement for providers to make arrangements for supervision of staff who have contact with children and families. Close observations could be a useful tool for supportive discussion of the well-being of children and of a key person's caring responses towards their key children (Elfer, 2005; Elfer et al., 2011).

Possible lines of direction

Planning the curriculum on the basis of information about children's interests and abilities, gleaned from observations, is central within the EYFS. It is, however, not always a simple process. Many educators have drawn inspiration from the work at the Pen Green Centre, including the use of Possible Lines of Direction (PLOD) charts (Whalley et al., 2007). Staff in other early childhood settings have adapted this idea and created their own forms of PLOD chart. This method works by selecting different children from a class or group each week and concentrating upon those children when making observations. In a nursery group with 24 children attending each morning, for example, a focus upon four children each week will mean that every child will be targeted once each half-term throughout the year. Narrative observations will be made of the focus children, typically, two or three sustained ten-minute observations during the week. The following case study is an extract from one such narrative observation.

Case study

Observation of Chloe painting

Chloe, who is 3 years 5 months old, is in her first term in the nursery class of a village primary school.

Chloe walks over to the painting area. She takes an apron off the peg, without being reminded, and manages to put it on without any assistance. Chloe picks up a sheet of light-purple sugar paper from the centre of the painting table and places it in front of her. Tracy [teacher], who is sitting at the painting table, offers to write Chloe's name on the paper. Chloe nods and Tracy prints 'C-h-l-o-e', sounding each letter. Chloe is looking at the trays of red and yellow paint. She stretches out her right hand and puts it into the tray of yellow paint. She spreads her fingers and moves her hand backwards and forwards. Chloe then lifts her hand and places it down firmly on the piece of paper and raises it again. She looks at the clear hand print and smiles and then puts her hand back into the tray of paint. She then makes two more firm and clear prints on the paper. Tracy speaks to her, asking if she likes the colour yellow and how many fingers on her hand, but Chloe just nods and does not answer. Chloe reaches to put her right hand in the red paint, but then changes her mind and reaches out her left hand instead. She presses her hand into the paint tray and then onto the paper, applying less pressure than when using her right hand. Chloe then rubs her hands together, looking quite intently at the red and yellow colours merging together. She then puts her right hand down on her paper again, choosing the remaining empty space on the page to place the print.

Table 8.1 Initial interpretation of observation of Chloe painting

Observation	Interpretation: observer's initial notes
Chloe walks over to the painting area. She takes an apron off the peg, without being reminded, and manages to put it on without any assistance.	Showing initiative and independence
Chloe picks up a sheet of light-purple sugar paper from the centre of the painting table and places it in front of her.	Chooses between purple and green
Tracy [teacher], who is sitting at the painting table, offers to write Chloe's name on the paper. Chloe nods and Tracy prints 'C-h-l-o-e', sounding each letter.	Doesn't take much notice of the teacher writing her name – is focused upon starting painting
Chloe is looking at the trays of red and yellow paint. She stretches out her right hand and puts it into the tray of yellow paint. She spreads her fingers and moves her hand backwards and forwards.	Seems to enjoy the sensation of the paint beneath her hand
Chloe then lifts her hand and places it down firmly on the piece of paper and raises it again. She looks at the clear hand print and smiles and then puts her hand back into the tray of paint. She then makes two more firm and clear prints on the paper.	Strong and definite movements, appears to gain satisfaction from this mark making Is concentrating on what she is doing
Tracy speaks to her, asking if she likes the colour yellow and how many fingers on her hand, but Chloe just nods and does not answer.	Seems more interested in her hand painting than the questions
Chloe reaches to put her right hand in the red paint but then changes her mind and reaches out her left hand instead. She presses her hand into the paint tray and then onto the paper, applying less pressure than when using her right hand.	Realises here that she still has yellow paint on her right hand and solves the problem by using her other hand Right hand is dominant
Chloe then rubs her hands together, looking quite intently at the red and yellow colours merging together. She then puts her right hand down on her paper again, choosing the remaining empty space on the page to place the print.	She seems quite absorbed watching the colours mix to form orange Seems to be experimenting with the effect of the new colour

Table 8.2   Analysis of observation of Chloe painting in relation to areas of learning

Observation	Analysis: links to areas of learning
Chloe walks over to the painting area. She takes an apron off the peg, without being reminded, and manages to put it on without any assistance.	PSED
Chloe picks up a sheet of light-purple sugar paper from the centre of the painting table and places it in front of her.	PSED
Tracy [teacher], who is sitting at the painting table, offers to write Chloe's name on the paper. Chloe nods and Tracy prints 'C-h-l-o-e', sounding each letter.	Literacy
Chloe is looking at the trays of red and yellow paint. She stretches out her right hand and puts it into the tray of yellow paint. She spreads her fingers and moves her hand backwards and forwards. Chloe then lifts her hand and places it down firmly on the piece of paper and raises it again. She looks at the clear hand print and smiles and then puts her hand back into the tray of paint. She then makes two more firm and clear prints on the paper.	Physical development Expressive arts and design
Tracy speaks to her, asking if she likes the colour yellow and how many fingers on her hand, but Chloe just nods and does not answer.	Mathematics
Chloe reaches to put her right hand in the red paint but then changes her mind and reaches out her left hand instead. She presses her hand into the paint tray and then onto the paper, applying less pressure than when using her right hand.	Physical development
Chloe then rubs her hands together, looking quite intently at the red and yellow colours merging together. She then puts her right hand down on her paper again, choosing the remaining empty space on the page to place the print.	Understanding the world Expressive arts and design

---

Reflective task

Using the above case study as an example, reflect on the following:

Ola is 2 years and 4 months old. The objectives of the observation are to investigate how Ola is behaving during storytelling time. Reflect on the following observations and try to use the three planes of analysis:

Observation 1:   *4 March*

Is beginning to join in (sit down) with the group story time (picks up and opens a flap in a book and joins in the group)

Observation 2:   *10 March*

Ola sat on Janet's [the teacher] knee during story time with four other children. Janet read 'Jack and Stack' and Ola was looking at the pictures and was repeating words from the story all the way through. She joined in lifting the flaps and accepted other children taking turns.

Observation 3:   *14 March*

Ola points to pictures in the book with Janet:

'Cat,' she says, turns page.

'Dog,' turns page, 'kangaroo'.

Observation 4:   *17 March*

After the story time with Teddy story, Ola is playing with Teddy's suitcase (that has books and toys from the story book). She is repeating the words from the book, she uses comb to brush Teddy, dresses Teddy.

- Can you create Possible Lines of Direction for Ola?

Analysis and interpretation of observations

The next step is to analyse and interpret the narrative observations. The person who recorded the observation, typically the key person, will read through and annotate the observations (see the example in Table 8.1) and make initial interpretations of the observation.

The main questions, at this stage, will relate to what the observation is telling us about the child:

- What personality traits are revealed?
- What skills and abilities is the child showing?
- What is the child interested in?
- What is the child learning?
- What does this observation reveal that I didn't know before?
- Are there patterns of behaviour that can be seen in all the observations?

There is rarely one answer to any of these questions. In order to analyse the child's skills, in relation to the areas of learning in the EYFS, the observer can also annotate the observation to highlight which areas were covered during the activity seen in the observation (see the example in Table 8.2) and how the child responded.

It is helpful for staff teams to work in pairs or small groups to discuss all the observations of the child and compare their interpretations. Following from discussions of the child's learning it is possible to move on and to identify possibilities for development and ideas for activities. These can be recorded on a PLOD chart, with a learning target, and one or more ideas for activities for each of the areas of learning. PLOD charts vary in format from linear tables, to charts resembling mind maps and circular or spiral designs that show a starting point with new ideas and experiences constantly added. Curriculum in early childhood is not only planned and implemented in settings, such as pre-school playgroups and Foundation Stage classes, but also in children's homes and communities. It is important, therefore, to share the observations and interpretations with parents in order to ensure that experiences are planned that the child will benefit from. Parents will be able to confirm whether what is seen from the child's play at nursery is similar to, or different from, their perceptions of the child in the home environment. They will also be able to comment on the ideas for activities and perhaps add some useful suggestions that can be incorporated on the PLOD chart.

Three planes of analysis

When we observe, we do not observe the child in isolation, but also see the child's interactions with others and the environment. This is recognised in the work of Barbara Rogoff (1995, 2003), who writes of the significance of three planes of analysis: personal, interpersonal and community. *Development Matters*, the non-statutory EYFS guidance (Early Education/DfE, 2012), echoes this in organising the characteristics of effective learning and the areas of learning and development under three headings. A *unique child* involves observing what the child is learning and can be equated with a personal or individual plane of analysis. *Positive relationships* concerns what adults could do to support development, linking with an interpersonal plane, while *enabling environments* consists of planning and provision within the institution and wider community.

Observations using three planes of analysis focus not only upon the individual child, but also upon the social and cultural context in which he or she is being observed. Fleer and Richardson (2009) have described how practitioners in Canberra, Australia, changed their approaches to observation and began using personal, interpersonal and community planes of analysis as lenses. A particular advantage of this approach is that, rather than just noting the actual level of development that a child has reached, it is possible to record what a child can achieve with assistance. This enables the observer to see the child's potential and to plan activities and experiences that will be stimulating and challenging.

The observation of Chloe and the interpretations shown above (in Tables 8.1. and 8.2) centre upon her as an individual, the traditional focus for child observations, and thus correspond with a personal plane of analysis. It is possible to view this observation through an interpersonal lens and analyse the interaction between Chloe and the teacher (see Table 8.3). This raises questions about the nature of the teacher's communication: on the one hand, we can see that she is supportive, but not intrusive, available to give help when needed (such as writing names on paint-ings), whilst on the other hand it is possible to critique her responses. Why did she ask closed questions about colours and numbers? How else could she have responded to Chloe's handprinting? Similarly, the third lens is brought to bear on the context and questions can be asked about the institution and learning community. Why is this type of activity valued?

Table 8.3   Observation of the interaction between Chloe and her teacher

Observation – interpersonal lens	Environment – institutional lens	Interpretation and analysis – supporting Chloe's learning
Tracy is sitting in the painting area. She smiles as Chloe walks over to the painting area. Chloe takes an apron off the peg, without being reminded, and manages to put it on without any assistance.	The painting area is set up with space for an adult and up to four children, with aprons that are hung close by at child height and easy for children to put on (velcro fastenings).	Having an adult based in the painting area is supportive. It is good that Tracy allowed Chloe's independence. Should Tracy have commented or praised Chloe here?
Chloe picks up a sheet of light-purple sugar paper from the centre of the painting table and places it in front of her. Tracy watches whilst assisting another child with his painting apron.	The activity is set out in a simple, orderly way with two choices of paper and paint all within reach of the children.	It was good to offer easy choices here. Could more independence be fostered if children had to collect paper and paint? Could Tracy have asked Chloe why she chose purple?
Tracy offers to write Chloe's name on the paper. Chloe nods and Tracy prints 'C-h-l-o-e', sounding each letter.	Pencils are available and names are written on paintings for easy identification at the end of the day when children take them home.	Good to encourage name recognition. Would pre-printed labels enable children to add their own names quite quickly?
Tracy watches as Chloe looks at the trays of paint then stretches out her right hand and puts it into the tray of yellow paint.	The paint is bright and mixed to a very suitable, quite thick consistency for hand-printing.	Are bright contrasting colours always best? Could the children have mixed the paint? Could Tracy have commented on what Chloe was doing?

Observation as a way to develop practice

Observations using planes of analysis can provide a means of reflecting upon and developing positive relationships and enabling learning environments for children. Similarly, observant leaders can use their observation skills to notice what is going on around them and then to model good practice that encourages both practitioners and children to observe more closely.

Observing hands

This account of using observation as a means of supervision is written by Jane Gibbs, an Early Years Professional in Essex, who describes her approach to supporting and coaching staff whilst also fostering children's observant learning and holistic development

I had observed practitioners putting aprons on the children, talking to them about the changing colours of the paint as the children mixed them on their hands and then proceeded to place their hands carefully on the paper. Some children were being very particular to lift their hand and study the marks that they had left behind in an array of colours. They were commenting and discussing what they saw with their peers and practitioners alike. This continued for over 15 minutes and had altered as the children were now wiping their hands across the paper and not making any attempt to look at it and the team members were now putting their work on the drying rack with interaction being limited.

I was sitting at the mark making table and continued to observe. I realised that a couple of the children were opening and closing their hands with the paint on it and examining their hands closely. I mimicked their actions and then drew around my hands and began to examine my hands again. A couple of the children noticed this and hurried to wash the paint off their hands and came over to see what I was doing, with one of the older ones asking me if I would draw around their hands too. I said that I could but maybe they would like to try to do it, which they did and were very proud. I gave plenty of praise. After we counted the fingers, I began having a closer look at my hands to see what was on them and started vocalising what I could see and drawing it on the correct position on my picture, referring to patterns and shapes. Before I knew it, the table was full of children and we were all conversing about what we could see. The children had noticed how I had more lines on my hands and how big and prominent my veins were in comparison to theirs; this provided opportunities to discuss how we change as we get older. We also looked at the colours of our skin and found our matching colours. I explained that we all have melanin in us which gives us colour. I explained that as I have got older my skin has got darker and that I have more melanin in my skin than they have. They all began to explore and say who had more melanin. When we had finished I explained to some members of the team how the activity had met many areas of learning and development for the children (see Table 8.4).

Table 8.4 Mapping of outcomes of an activity to areas of development

PSE	Communication & Language	Physical	Literacy	Maths	Understanding the World	Expressive Arts & Design
Children play cooperatively, taking turns with others.	Children listen attentively in a range of situations.	Children show good control and coordination in large and small movements.	Children understand simple sentences.	Children count reliably.	They know about similarities and differences between themselves and others.	They represent their own ideas, thoughts and feelings through design
They show sensitivity to others' needs and feelings, and form positive relationships with adults and other children.		They handle equipment and tools effectively, including pencils for writing.		They recognise, create and describe patterns. They explore characteristics of everyday objects and shapes and use mathematical language to describe them.	They make observations of animals and plants and explain why some things occur, and talk about changes.	

In this example the skilled leader evaluates and responds to the situation that she observes and, with care and sensitivity, models a balance between child- and adult-led activities. She is also able to analyse and explain how the simple activity maps onto all the areas of learning in the EYFS curriculum.

Summary

In stressing that paperwork should be kept to a minimum, and yet retaining the emphasis upon planning that is based upon children's interests, the EYFS guidance provides practitioners with opportunities to think critically and creatively about the methods of observation that they choose. The methods described above have value for getting to know and appreciate children and are useful for formative assessment and curriculum planning. For summative assessments, at age 2 years and at the end of the Foundation Stage, it is important to conduct observations accurately and systematically in order to base decisions upon objective evidence of what each child knows and can do.

Whatever methods of observation are used, the role of adults is to look and listen actively and make sense of what children are doing and saying. The purpose of all analysis and interpretation of observations should be to open up possibilities for the children. If this is done well, practitioners will promote children's competence in making and expressing meanings and thus stimulate their learning. Importantly, the practitioner should also gain interest and satisfaction from observations of children as Dewey (1933/1998: 256) noted: 'the persons who enjoy seeing will be the best observers'.

Key points to remember

- Observations are central to early childhood education and care. They were introduced mainly by Maria Montessori and Susan Isaacs and they are now widely used as a way of collecting information about children and consequently assessing children.

- Within EYFS, observations keep a central role and it is now a requirement that early childhood practitioners use observations to support children's learning, plan their daily activities and communicate effectively with parents.

- There is a plethora of ways to observe children, interpret and analyse observations. A common approach in the early childhood sector is the Possible Lines of Direction (PLOD), introduced by Pen Green Centre.

- This chapter suggests the three planes of analysis approach to observations as this takes into consideration children as individuals as well as children's social and cultural context. It goes beyond what children can do, to what children can achieve with support in a stimulating environment.

Points for discussion

- In your opinion, how do key historical figures such as John Dewey, Maria Montessori and Susan Isaacs influence your current practice in early childhood education and care?

- In your experience what types of observations work best for getting to know children?

- How can we ensure that our summative assessments of children are rigorous and made on the basis of sound evidence?

Further reading

Dubiel, J. (2015) *Effective Assessment in the Early Years*, 2nd edn. London: Sage.

Elfer, P. (2005) 'Observation matters', in L. Abbott and A. Langston (eds), *Birth to Three Matters*. Maidenhead: Open University Press.

Fleer, M. and Richardson, C. (2009) 'Cultural-historical assessment: mapping the transformation of understanding', in A. Anning, J. Cullen and M. Fleer (eds), *Early Childhood Education*, 2nd edn. London: Sage.

Palaiologou, I. (2012) *Child Observation for the Early Years*, 2nd edn. London: Sage.

Useful websites

For more information on Pen Green Centre approach to observation and documentation: www.pengreen.org/

References

Bick, E. (1964) 'Notes on infant observation in psychoanalytic training', *International Journal of Psychoanalysis*, 45: 558–66.

Brunton, P. and Thornton, L. (2010) *Science in the Early Years*. London: Sage.

Carr, M. (2001) *Assessment in Early Childhood Settings: Learning Stories*. London: Paul Chapman Publishing.

Carr, M. and Lee, W. (2012) *Learning Stories: Constructing Learner Identities in Early Education*. London: Sage.

DfE (Department for Education) (2014) *Statutory Framework for the Early Years Foundation Stage. Setting the Standards for Learning: Development and Case for Children from Birth to Five*. London: DfE. Available at: www.foundationyears.org.uk/files/2014/07/EYFS_framework_ from_1_September_2014__with_clarification_note.pdf (accessed 21 September 2015).

Dewey, J. (1897/1974) 'My pedagogic creed', in R.D. Archambault (ed.), *John Dewey on Education: Selected Writings*. Chicago and London: University of Chicago Press.

Dewey, J. (1933/1998) *How We Think*. Boston, MA: Houghton Mifflin.

Dubiel, J. (2014) *Effective Assessment in the Early Years Foundation Stage*. London: Sage.

Early Education/DfE (Department for Education) (2012) *Development Matters in the Early Years Foundation Stage (EYFS)*. London: Early Education. Available at: www.education.gov.uk/ childrenandyoungpeople/earlylearningandchildcare/delivery/education/a0068102/early-years-foundation-stage-eyfs (accessed 4 April 2012).

Elfer, P. (2005) 'Observation matters', in L. Abbott and A. Langston (eds), *Birth to Three Matters*. Maidenhead: Open University Press.

Elfer, P., Goldschmied, E. and Selleck, D. (2011) *Key Persons in the Nursery and Reception Classes: Building Relationships for Quality Provision*, 3rd edn. London: David Fulton.

Fleer, M. and Richardson, C. (2009) 'Cultural-historical assessment: mapping the transformation of understanding', in A. Anning, J. Cullen and M. Fleer (eds), *Early Childhood Education*, 2nd edn. London: Sage.

Goldschmeid, E. and Jackson, S. (2004) *People Under Three: Young Children in Day care*, 2nd edn. London: Routledge.

Goodson, I.F., Biesta, G.J.J., Tedder, M. and Adair, M. (2010) *Narrative Learning*. London: Routledge.

Isaacs, S. (1929) *The Nursery Years*. London: Routledge & Kegan Paul.

Isaacs, S. (1930) *Intellectual Growth in Young Children*. London: Routledge & Kegan Paul.

Isaacs, S. (1933) *Social Development in Young Children*. London: Routledge & Kegan Paul.

Jackson, S. and Forbes, R. (2015) *People Under Three: Play, Work and Learning in a Childcare Setting*. London: Routledge.

Miller, L., Rustin, M., Rustin, M. and Shuttleworth, J. (1989) *Closely Observed Infants*. London: Duckworth.

Montessori, M. (1912) *The Montessori Method* (trans. A.E. George). New York: Frederick A. Stokes Company. Available at: http://web.archive.org/web/20050207205651/www.moteaco. com/method/method.html (accessed 4 April 2012).

Podmore, V. and Luff, P. (2012) *Observation: Origins and Approaches in Early Childhood*. Maidenhead: Open University Press.

Rogoff, B. (1995) 'Observing sociocultural activity on three planes: participatory appropriation, guided participation and apprenticeship', in J.V. Wertsch, P. del Rio and A. Alvarez (eds), *Sociocultural Studies of Mind*. Cambridge: Cambridge University Press.

Rogoff, B. (2003) *The Cultural Nature of Human Development*. New York: Oxford University Press.

Whalley, M. and the Pen Green Centre Team (2007) *Involving Parents in Their Children's Learning*, 2nd edn. London: Paul Chapman Publishing.

Want to learn more about this chapter? Visit the companion website at https://study.sagepub.com/EYFS3e for access to free SAGE journal articles and book chapters, weblinks, annotated further readings and more.

9

Assessment

Sally Howard, Nyree Nicholson and
Chris Williamson

 Chapter overview

Assessment is a crucial aspect of teaching and learning, yet often it is seen as a challenge when trying to align external pressures such as government standards with a practitioner's internal values and belief about how learners learn best. The EYFS states that every child deserves the best possible start in life so that they can fulfil their potential and recognises that the experiences children have before the age of 5 have an impact on their future life chances (Sammons et al., 2007; Sylva et al., 2012; DfE, 2014). However, an ambition to achieve what is best for the child can be problematic when different early childhood settings have to grapple with how the impact of learning experiences can be assessed and monitored in a manner that does not undermine effective pedagogy and play-based learning (Sylva et al., 2004), while at the same time attempting to provide continuity between providers through reporting mechanisms and being seen to be accountable. As a result, assessment can take centre stage instead of the child. In this chapter we discuss assessment that takes place in all early childhood contexts, such as childminders, crèche, nursery, preschool or school, as they all can provide quality provision and will use assessment to support and monitor learning. Good assessment practice also recognises the valuable role that parents and carers have in support of their

(Continued)

(Continued)

child's development, and their contribution to their learning and assessment is a crucial part of understanding the individual child's achievements.

Although in this chapter we explore some of the challenges associated with assessment and record keeping and share examples of effective practice from a number of different perspectives in England, it is important to say that the principles are equally applicable within other countries and can be translated for different ages as well as different settings.

This chapter aims to help you understand:

- the principles of key assessment types
- the challenges between a mechanistic approach to assessment and good practice
- the role of ongoing informed observation in gathering valid assessment evidence.

Assessment types

It is well documented that the experience a young child has during early childhood has a long-term impact on their future success (Save the Children Fund, 2013) and that through quality pre-school experiences, these benefits remain with the child past the age of 11 years thus demonstrating that quality early childhood provision, where teaching, learning, and assessment are used to enable a child to succeed, is highly influential in a child's continuing progress and success, especially for those from disadvantaged backgrounds (Sylva, 2008, Sylva et al., 2010).

Assessment in early childhood education and care is the gathering of a range of evidence about children's learning and behaviours so that judgements can be made about their progress. These judgements can fall into two broad categories:

- judgements about how to design and implement the next steps for further development in learning; and
- judgements on what has been learned and achieved.

Assessment can be divided into two main categories: assessment that is primarily about *learning* and assessment that is primarily about *accountability* (Black and Wiliam, 1998). Across all stages of education, assessment is growing in importance for the learner's perspective and for accountability purposes. There is a range of different ways in which assessment information is gathered and used, although not all of them place the child at the centre of the process and this can cause great pressure for practitioners and in some instances a cause of stress for the learner and their family (Ward, 2009).

The main types of assessment are:

- diagnostic
- formative
- authentic
- summative
- accountability.

Diagnostic assessment is usually undertaken when an issue is suspected. Its intention is to identify limiting factors that may impede a child's development in order to do something about it and also gives specific measurable knowledge about the current situation through specific tests or standardised activities. It includes specially designed optional tests within the first ten days of life to screen for issues such as hearing loss. Another example of diagnostic assessment occurs around the age of eighteen months for the checking for autism (CHAT). This screening assessment is undertaken by a primary healthcare worker and is usually conducted in the child's home. It includes discussions with the parent(s) as well as first-hand observation by the specially trained professional. These types of assessments tend to be undertaken by other professionals, such as healthcare workers, rather than early childhood practitioners, and the role of associated professionals will be explored in Chapter 15.

Assessment for learning (AFL) forms part of what is termed 'formative practice' and focuses on assessment that has at its core the child's learning and underpins effective pedagogy across all phases of education. Through a series of observations, listening, discussion and reflection, information about the child's learning and development is gathered – information about what the child currently knows and can do and what they still need to know or achieve. This results in the practitioner and learner taking the necessary action to promote further understanding and development (Harrison and Howard, 2009). This assessment process informs the practitioner, the parents and the child about the child's attainment and interests, which then informs the daily planning of experiences and scaffolds the child's learning to further support the successful development of the whole child. This 'taking action' ultimately needs to be done by the learner but scaffolded by the practitioner, and is crucial to the success of AFL. In this ongoing process of 'feedback-for-feedforward' the curriculum is a resource for learning rather than a limiting structure to meet external assessment requirements, and it is this that makes AFL an effective and efficient means of assessment.

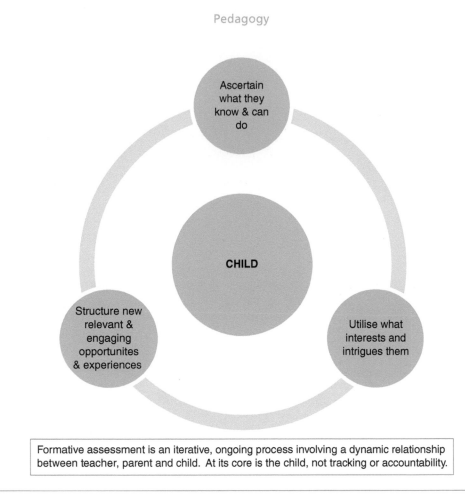

Ascertain what they know & can do

CHILD

Structure new relevant & engaging opportunites & experiences

Utilise what interests and intrigues them

Formative assessment is an iterative, ongoing process involving a dynamic relationship between teacher, parent and child. At its core is the child, not tracking or accountability.

Figure 9.1 *The circle of formative assessment*

Dubiel (2014) comments on the skill and apparent ease that an experienced practitioner has in finding 'invisible moments of possibility' because of their ability to communicate with children, observe with purpose and be prepared to expect the unexpected. In this way they are able to gather evidence of learning (assessment) to inform their practice and scaffold progress. Information gleaned through this ongoing assessment approach is then used to shape the curriculum by considering the child's personality, their cognitive and physical developmental needs and natural opportunities that may arise within the setting. Any planned scheme of work can then be adapted in response to this process of ongoing formative assessment and can focus on developing a particular skill, deepening cognitive understanding or enhancing a child's socialisation capabilities within the group.

Case study

Examples of formative assessment

The early childhood practitioners were using observation sheets to gather information and these were the steps that they followed:

1 On each play area there was a packet of blank observation forms stuck to the wall.
2 If a member of staff suddenly observed something relevant about a child (opportunistic assessment) they would complete a form and then put it in the child's folder (note the example in Figure 9.2 is observing four children).
3 At the end-of-the-day briefing, this information would be used to structure the next day's activities or groups (or influence the planning for the following weeks).
4 Where there was appropriate learning goals evidence, this was also recorded on the child's profile.

Observation sheet for 4 EY Formative Assessment	Adult Jane B.	Date	Time 2.10

The scene Brio Train Set

1 Adam	2 Sam	3 Harry	4 Ben	Setting
I'm going under the tunnel. The snow man's coming! Shu, shu, shu I've got an electric train at home. (leaves the area).	Watch out, here comes the carriage two' tututut Oh, we've stuck Excuse me (to Ben) I've got a train now. Somebody has left this. (makes "train" sound effects). Sam left area.	the train's crashed! 'Oops!'- knocks blocks over. Starts to build them up again. Oops a daisy! You've blocking the tunnel Sir! (to Ben). I haven't got a track at home this is best! Hey - you've broke the track (goes to hit Sam) "Crash" "Stop" Help! Help the train's crashed.	I need that (takes an engine). Begins to join carriages Ben put on hard hat & reflective jacket. Left area.	Train - carpet area

Any surprises	Involvement/interest.	What next
Worked well together - little disagreement & managed observed activity	Adam left - Sam Harry Ben very absorbed.	- encourage extension of this activity next session - use of maps? plans?

Ben played independently - made no sound effects no running commentary.
Emily arrived - "this train is going to the zoo" (she'd previously played here).

(Continued)

(Continued)

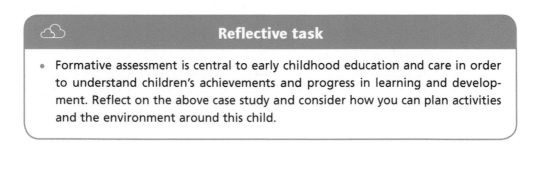

Observation sheet for 2	Adult	Date	Time
EY Formative Assessment.	J. ~~[redacted]~~	~~[redacted]~~	9.55 – 10.10

The scene Wet sand.

1 Ben	2 Stephen	Setting
"I know lets make a sandcastle. Well, we could pretend ←——→ "Sheee, shee sheeee" ——— Began shindurnig sand, patting + smoothing. "Look, I've found a flag." "I need people too". Right, we're looking for a flag. Look it becomes a sandcastle. (I asked Ben if he would like to make some flags – offered a range of materials /stickers – Ben stuck a label around a cardboard stick) "One for me, one for Stephen. D'you want one Max?"	O.K but we haven't got a flag Look, the snowball has broken "cree creeee" (lifting sand) Began to walk away, Ben called him back. Stephen copied Ben's actions Stephen distracted by other children playing dominoes. "We need a big castle like that" Kate arrived "that's our sandcastle. Shall we get some sand Kate? Went to get people figures. "Snowballs are coming down from the sky".	☐ St. X X Ben

Any surprises	Involvement/interest	What next
Stephen was very animated + lots of conversation.	Instigated by Ben	Record – draw?

Figure 9.2   *Example from formative assessment*

This seems a very 'manageable' process to give good formative information, which practitioners and other adults in the setting used well. It resulted in excellent assessment and was not onerous as it was often (but not solely) opportunistic. The reason it was good assessment for learning was because it informed next steps, and either activities were restructured to build on the learning or particular children were 'targeted' for specific activities and focused development.

Reflective task

- Formative assessment is central to early childhood education and care in order to understand children's achievements and progress in learning and development. Reflect on the above case study and consider how you can plan activities and the environment around this child.

Authentic assessment is ongoing observation of the child engaged in typical activities and routines in its environment. It is similar to formative assessment, but the information that is gathered with authentic assessment can be used immediately from the practitioners and others such as parents or children as they target learning goals and are personalised to children's skills and abilities.

Bagnato (2007) and Bagnato et al. (2010) describe eight standards for authentic assessment:

1   acceptability – focusing on what is desired behaviour;
2   authenticity – the use of natural observation methods and contexts;
3   collaboration – parent–professional teamwork;
4   evidence – evidence base;
5   multifactors – synthesis of the gathered information;
6   sensitivity – 'listening to the child' rather than the standards the child has to meet;
7   universality – individual focus on a child;
8   utility – usefulness for understanding the child's behaviour.

It can be described as an opportunistic assessment as it is often achieved 'on the fly' or 'on the spot', especially by experienced qualified practitioners as they are attuned to what is significant. These authentic assessments can be documented using a simple system of 'sticky-notes' written by the observer and placed in the child's individual folder or 'box' or for consideration by the key worker. By having a realistic period of time elapse before reviewing the evidence the key worker is also able to select the best evidence for record keeping purposes. This approach does not interfere with the learning, but runs seamlessly within the normal routine of the setting and capitalises on the moment as described in the following case study.

Case study

Authentic assessment

Previously an individual activity had taken place with the volunteer 'granny' who was a regular visitor to the setting and knew the children well. With her guidance each child had carefully planted bulbs for 'Mother's Day' and watered them. On a subsequent day the children were left to their own devices to plant sunflower seeds to grow in school, before taking them home. This was part of their topic on 'pets and plants'.

It was noticed by the teacher that a small group of children decided they were going to water the seedlings by themselves. One 4-year-old girl found using the

(Continued)

(Continued)

small watering can difficult to manipulate. This was noticed by a young 4-year-old boy who was engaged in a different task nearby. Unexpectedly, he got up and carefully helped to tip the watering can from the base, ensuring the young girl was still 'in charge' of the watering process.

The practitioner who noticed this recognised it as demonstrating a high level of problem solving, and care and consideration for others. This forms part of the English learning goals for 'personal, social and emotional development' and was considered significant as the practitioner recognised that most children of this age would have taken over and watered the seed for the girl, instead of scaffolding her success as he had.

Summative assessment refers to the final outcome and focus on what has been learnt and achieved at the conclusion of a defined period. The main purposes are:

- for accountability
- for tracking purposes
- evaluative
- and form part of the child's permanent assessment record.

It tends to focus on what has been learned when mapped against agreed benchmarks. This type of assessment summarises what the child can demonstrate at a particular point in time and can often be given a numerical value. Statutory national testing is an example where summative assessment data have become a principal means of measuring performance through which settings, schools and specific practitioners can be held accountable. This has led to certain aspects of the curriculum being given prominence over others, including an overemphasis on subject-specific assessments, such as phonological awareness or knowledge of numbers, compared to a more holistic assessment that includes important aspects of learning such as self-concepts and creativity (Dunphy, 2010). There are also summative assessment systems that give a measure of a child's engagement and emotional well-being, such as the Leuven Scales of Involvement and Well-Being (Laevers, 2005), which, in conjunction with other means of assessment, help not just to track development and characteristics of effective learning, but help to shape a more effective learning environment, particularly for those children who might be at risk.

Assessment for accountability: This accountability aspect of assessment is an important part of early childhood education and care. While recognised as necessary, one of the challenges that practitioners have to face is addressing statutory requirements without compromising the learning and well-being of the child. In recent times there has been a greater tendency for practitioners to limit their assessment evidence to the final products and outcomes (summative assessment) that a child produces with less value being placed on the evidence of the process. This seems to be in response to pressure from statutory assessment requirements, such as required for the EYFS framework in England or the Curriculum for Excellence in Scotland, and has led to a narrowing of the curriculum (NCSL, 2010), leading to an increase in adult-dominated activities so the necessary evidence can be observed and 'the list ticked'. As shown in Chapter 3, Northern Ireland has stipulated that assessment for accountability is most effective when it includes moderation of practice and the sharing of meaningful information about children's learning. This may include 'moderation' meetings within 'families' of providers to share effective practice and 'tease-out' specific concerns about the validity or reliability of the collated evidence. Accountability is also likely to include comparing assessment data across similar groups and this usually forms part of a statutory inspection process within a national framework such as Ofsted in England and Eystyn in Wales.

The specifics of this process of accountability vary across the four nations of the UK (see Chapter 3), although they all share the same principles in terms of providing a robust system that gives confidence in the decisions made by the professionals. The inspection process also draws on the summative assessment data to provide professional challenge in terms of ensuring all children are supported in the process of achieving their full potential.

Why assess?

The EPPE findings clearly state the importance of quality experiences within the pre-school period to enhance children's academic and socio-behavioural development (Sylva et al., 2004). This extensive piece of research identified specific factors that do, and do not, seem instrumental in good development for all children, and particularly in addressing the needs of disadvantaged children. Boys were found to gain significant benefit from quality pre-school experiences in relation to girls, although both boys and girls benefit regardless of part-time or full-time experiences. It seems to be in relation to long-term duration, such as three years of quality experience as opposed to just one year.

Bailey and Drummond's (2006: 149–70) small-scale research on assessing who is at risk and why in early literacy found that while early childhood practitioners are generally good at recognising which children are struggling with literacy skills development, they are less skilled at pinpointing the cause or how to intervene effectively. They suggest that in order to implement an effective assessment process that informs pedagogy the early childhood team should have continuous professional development.

It is well recognised that better-quality provision has been associated with more staff being qualified and guided by qualified teachers, which is where the current guidance in the EYFS documentation can contribute to addressing the professional development needs of all persons involved in early childhood provision (Nutbrown, 2012).

The work undertaken by Siraj-Blatchford et al. (2002) found that when educational and social development were seen as complementary and equally important, children made all-round good progress. She identified such things as structured interventions between adults and small groups of children and sustained shared thinking opportunities to extend children's learning as beneficial because they require a deep understanding of child development. The Tickell Review (2011) draws on a wealth of evidence to state that the experiences children have in their early lives have a profound impact on their cognitive, personal and social well-being, not just while in formal education, but throughout their life. She found that those children in the lowest 20% in terms of academic achievement and social well-being at the end of the Early Years Foundation Stage were six times more likely to be in the lowest 20% at the end of Key Stage 1.

Central to effective learning and development is an agreed understanding that communication and language, personal, social, emotional and physical development are not just related, but interconnected. It is because of this interconnection that early childhood providers, be they within a home setting or specialist environment, recognise that early experiences matter in terms of achieving an individual's lifelong potential (DfE, 2011: 9).

While there is still a debate about the distinct nature of development and learning, Davis et al. (2003) suggest that development is the outcome of experiences on an individual's genetic make-up and learning is an outcome of these experiences. It is the depth and breadth of understanding about how children learn, and how subject pedagogy can be structured, that underpins formative assessment. It is the means by which effective assessment can be embedded into daily practice so that a range of strategies and approaches are adapted to enable the child, and children, to become more effective and independent learners, rather than adopting an assessment approach that is bolted on as an additional activity.

The statutory requirements for assessment in the EYFS

Within the EYFS, formal reporting is required at two key points: first between 24 and 36 months of age (initially this was the Progress Check at Age Two, but from September 2015 this became the Integrated Review at Age Two) and then at the end of the Foundation Stage in the EYFS Profile (EYFSP), which is the transition point between Early Years and Year 1 . There is also a statutory requirement to have a written overview of a child's progress at least once a year.

Integrated Review at Age Two

The Integrated Review at Age Two was introduced in September 2015 and aimed to combine the Health Check and the Progress Check at Age Two. This review at the age of two attempts to become a supportive mechanism to share understanding of the child with the parents and others involved in the care of the child. However, the quality of the report varied from extremely detailed, which meant it was time-consuming to create, to something that was barely more than a line or two and gave very little insight in terms of understanding the individual and their achievements or their needs, yet both met the statutory requirement and form part of the local authority's data collection.

The example below shows aspects of an effective age 2 review based on the English system. It shows a well-articulated report that explains the areas being commented on and allows the practitioner to explain with short descriptions how the child is achieving. The parent has understood what is being said and has clearly articulated her relief that their child's needs have been understood and her own concerns recognised.

Case study

Callum's review

Full Name: Callum Knowel

Age: 35 months

Room: Nursery education children

Completed: N/A

Parent's Comments and Feedback:

I agree with the report that has been written, I have had concerns about Callum's development and I am relieved something is being done about it.

Next Steps:

To begin a new setting, work on transferring existing skills to other settings

Listening and Attention:

Through positive relationships children respond to eye contact, verbal and non-verbal interaction; they anticipate and initiate communication with others, learning

(Continued)

(Continued)

to respond in many ways. Children do this through listening to others, watching and imitating them and through joining in with rhymes, stories and games using sounds and words. In this way they learn to attend to important features of communication and to respond, eventually being able to divide their attention between what is being said and what they are doing.

Practitioner's remarks:

Callum struggles to maintain concentration in group and one-to-one situations. Bending down to his level and signing that he needs to be looking and listening, helps to focus his attention, but this may need to be done several times. Experience has shown that although Callum doesn't appear to be listening he is often taking in what is happening. This is demonstrated later by something Callum says or does that confirms his understanding, however usually comes at random and unrelated times. This can make it difficult to understand what Callum is trying to tell you. Callum has particular problems during group activities and he can become frustrated and demonstrate fidgety or disruptive behaviour. We have found that if you are at all able to use digital technology such as an ipad/laptop or story and singing, Callum's well-being and involvement increases dramatically.

Speaking:

Understanding what has been said to them, saying things to others, being treated as a communicator and sharing in talk with others is all part of the communication process. In this aspect of communication and language children will show understanding in many ways including by responding appropriately to what somebody has said, following instructions and responding to and asking questions to check out meaning. Their understanding of what is being said to them far outweighs what they can say. Every experience a child has will extend their understanding if adults are there sharing the experience and helping them.

Practitioner's remarks:

Callum often understands everything that is said to him and around him, he unfortunately cannot always demonstrate his understanding. If asked a question Callum will not be able to give an answer unless it requires a yes or no response. To gain clarity on his understanding other measures have to be taken. For example, if you line up coloured cars and ask Callum to pick out the yellow car, he can do this, if however you pick up the yellow car and ask Callum what colour it is he will become echolaliac and respond 'colour' (see observation).

> ### Reflective tasks
>
> - This is an effective review. Consider what the requirements are for the practitioner in order to complete the review. What are possible ways of communicating the information gathered with parents, other professionals? What skills do you think are required?
>
> Go to the companion website for an example of the Integrated Review at Age Two.

Early Years Foundation Stage Profile

The EYFSP must be completed by all providers in England, including those registered with childminding agencies as well as maintained school, non-maintained schools and

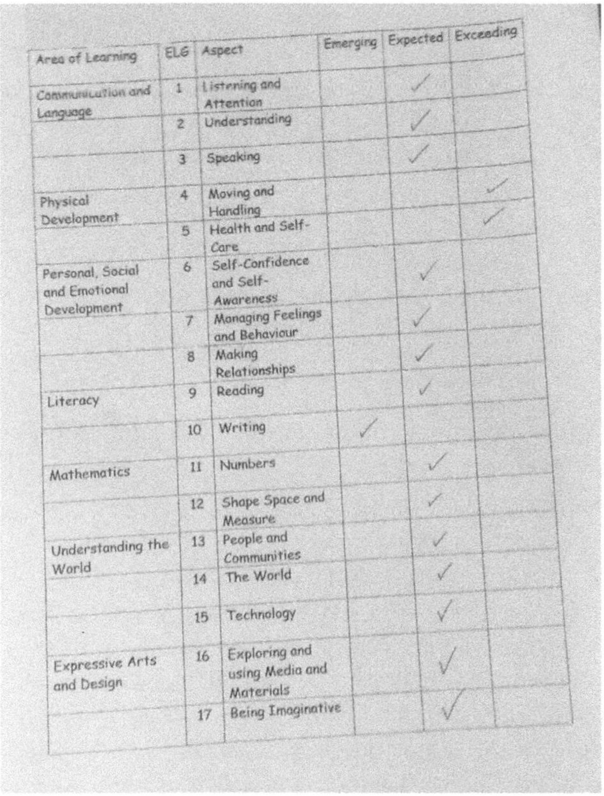

Area of Learning	ELG	Aspect	Emerging	Expected	Exceeding
Communication and Language	1	Listening and Attention		✓	
	2	Understanding		✓	
	3	Speaking		✓	
Physical Development	4	Moving and Handling			✓
	5	Health and Self-Care			✓
Personal, Social and Emotional Development	6	Self-Confidence and Self-Awareness		✓	
	7	Managing Feelings and Behaviour		✓	
	8	Making Relationships		✓	
Literacy	9	Reading		✓	
	10	Writing	✓		
Mathematics	11	Numbers		✓	
	12	Shape Space and Measure		✓	
Understanding the World	13	People and Communities		✓	
	14	The World		✓	
	15	Technology		✓	
Expressive Arts and Design	16	Exploring and using Media and Materials		✓	
	17	Being Imaginative		✓	

Figure 9.3 *Example of summative assessment within the EYFS*

independent schools. This profile is undertaken during the final term of the year in which the child turns 5 and no later than 30 June. It must be completed for every child using the same criteria for making judgement, including those with special educational needs, known disabilities and those for whom English is not their first language. The practitioner must draw on their observations and records of attainment gathered over a sustained period of time to make their final judgement. In this way it is hoped that they can form a rounded judgement of the child's knowledge, understanding and ability against the stated levels of attainment. The intention is to inform the Year 1 teacher on how 'school ready' the child is and provide a seamless transition between early childhood provision and formal education.

Each child's level of development is based on the early learning goals for England (DfE EYFS handbook, 2015) and a judgement must be made in terms of them exceeding expected levels, meeting the expected levels or not yet meeting these levels (emerging). The statutory reporting requirement can be met using a simple form (as the example in Figure 9.3) as there is no requirement to add any additional commentary, although there has to be an opportunity for the parent to meet and discuss the profile.

Reflective task

As the practices around the completion of the EYFSP vary among settings, reflect on the assessment process:

- Are there any tensions between what is best practice and what is statutory request in the EYFS?

- Rate the child's participation in their own assessment process.

- Consider whether the impetus of the assessment is for developing the individual child or a record keeping system.

While EYFSP data are not publically published, local authorities are monitored and judged by the aggregated EYFSP scores without due consideration to the rate of progress of individuals or their specific contexts that might impact on their attainment rather than their ability. For example, this might include a child having only recently arrived in England and for whom English is an additional language. This aggregation of scores might lead to undue pressure being put on practitioners to adopt approaches that overemphasise a narrow range of attainment in order to achieve their local authority target.

An over focus on summative assessment and testing may also have had a detrimental effect on teacher's confidence in terms of their own knowledge and understanding of a child's attainment and achievements. This lack of confidence appears to stem from policy makers' general distrust of teachers' ability to assess in a reliable and valid manner (Black et al., 2013) and has been attributed to causing a 'tick box' mentality in some settings, including schools.

Summative judgements in the early childhood setting should be underpinned by ongoing observations and ongoing record keeping which might be done by hand, using an individual child's progress book such as shown in Figure 9.4.

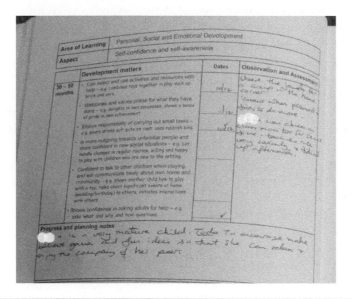

Figure 9.4 *Example of summative assessment for PSED*

Reflective task

- All of this recording of information takes a considerable amount of time, which some have argued is time that could be better spent with the child (Dubiel, 2014). Reflect on what the role of the assessment is and consider whether in the EYFS the priority should be to assess for the child or practitioners' time spent with the child.

A similar approach to ongoing assessment is used in Scotland and Northern Ireland, and, from September 2015, Wales (see Chapter 3) will be using the Early Years Development Assessment Framework (EYDAF) to develop a single overarching framework for a Foundation Phase Profile (FPP). This will include a range of assessment tools that will help chart a child's progress across early childhood. The aim is to create an effective system that has consistency and is manageable.

Challenges associated with summative testing

The issue for many practitioners, regardless of setting, is the overemphasis that is placed on summative assessment and achieving certain predetermined goals, especially when these are used in high stakes scenarios. The EYFSP is meant to focus on opportunities for next step development and provide a holistic summative assessment before a child reaches statutory school age. However, it is increasingly common that data collected from these individual assessments are also being used for high-stakes judgements about the quality of the practitioner and the settings.

A recent issue being faced by practitioners in England is the introduction of 'optional' baseline assessment of 4-year-olds from September 2016. It is the intention of the Department for Education to dispense with the EYFS Profile (which was an attempt to capture what a child can do spontaneously, independently and consistently over a range of contexts) and replace this with specific tests from authorised providers. These standardised tests will draw on the manipulation of virtual toys or real objects in order to provide correct or incorrect answers which will then translate into a score. Currently the DfE (2014) states that where English settings chose not to 'opt-in' they will be judged purely on attainment 'floor standards' (these are targets set by the local authority based on their centrally set targets). It is highly likely that settings will consider they are duty bound to undertake these 'optional' tests as there appear to be various other criteria for them to meet which will be extremely hard to achieve unless these are undertaken.

The prime purpose of these new baseline tests is focusing on effectiveness and accountability, rather than a child's learning or development needs, and this focus has been heavily criticised, not least because it seems to move the focus away from reporting to parents on the progress of their child to monitoring provision and managing performance of settings (Early Education, 2015). The emphasis for these baseline tests is supposed to be to provide information on the progress of a cohort of children throughout their primary school years. However, it currently fails to recognise that the individuals within the original cohort are unlikely to be the same children at future reporting points, which will invalidate the integrity of the data.

These baseline tests have been a controversial idea from the outset and many experts, including Professor Cathy Nutbrown and Dr Jane Payler (cited in Early Education, 2015), have argued that these tests are not in the best interest of the child and will take practitioners away from their prime role of educating, and place testing and preparation for testing at the core of the curriculum. Their argument draws attention to the recent experience of baseline tests when first introduced in Wales in 2011, which were then later withdrawn in 2012 because they were time-consuming and distracted from essential teaching time. They also argue that baseline assessments, such as the ones proposed, lack validity and reliability and are likely to narrow the curriculum offered to young children and undermine effective pedagogy.

Assessment and children with English as an additional language

For children whose home language is not English, providers must take reasonable steps to provide opportunities for children to develop and use their home language in play and learning, supporting their language development at home. Providers must also ensure that children have sufficient opportunities to learn and reach a good standard in English language during early childhood while ensuring children are ready to benefit from the opportunities available to them when they begin formal education in Year 1. A similar emphasis is placed on English and Welsh in Wales. In England, when assessing communication, language and literacy skills, practitioners must assess children's skills in English. If a child does not have a strong grasp of English language, practitioners must explore the child's skills in the home language with parents and/or carers, to establish whether there is cause for concern about language delay. Capturing evidence of attainment during meaningful episodes of learning needs to be done in time-efficient ways. When done within a formative practice approach such as 'assessment for learning', the information gleaned is more valid and more enjoyable for the child than withdrawing them from their chosen activity to sit at a table with an adult and being asked to write specific letters or saying the sounds to match a picture in order to demonstrate their attainment of phonemes and graphemes. Here are some strategies that can assist when working with children with English as an additional language:

- Create an engaging and rich role-play area (for an example see the companion website)
- A summary of a child's attainment entered into an electronic record of attainment for that individual and in this way their progress is tracked over time
- Personalised learning activities

Assessment and children at risk

Throughout this book it is emphasised that in an early childhood education and care environment it is essential to plan appropriate learning and monitor over time for children's effective learning and development. This process is a complex matter, however, as learning does not conform to a recipe and tangible progress can be made in very tiny steps. This is also the case for children identified as having special educational needs or those eligible for additional funding such as the English Pupil Premium Grant (PPG), where small steps might indicate significant progress for that child, and children who are struggling with emotional engagement (see Chapter 16).

The role of partnership in assessment

Throughout this chapter an emphasis is placed on the key role of practitioner support in assessing and structuring a child's learning and development. Working with the family and seeking the child's views, valuing their opinions and valuing the observations of practitioners is an important part of creating a rich picture of the child's capabilities. It is through observation of the child at play in isolation or interacting with their peers, and their engagement and response to adults' questions, that future learning opportunities can be structured. It is in collaboration with parents and carers that individual needs can be understood, such as identifying what the child likes doing and what they do not like doing. By asking about the sort of things that engage the child for sustained periods of time it is possible to understand and then build on the child's thinking and behaviours and attitudes in a constructive and beneficial way. This valuable information and engagement with parents, carers and others, including specialists such as health visitors, educational psychologists and social workers, is the collaborative assessment process that helps with the early identification of additional needs. For this information to be effective it has to be acted upon, otherwise it is just a summative measure at a certain point in time. This 'action' and 'partnership' is the fundamental difference between formative and summative assessment. In the case of the Early Learning Goals this is an opportunity for formative observations to be used as evidence to make a summative statement. It is also a means of tracking the rate of progress over time and in this way informing practice as part of the process.

The role of observation in assessment

As has been demonstrated above, the variation of different approaches to children's assessment can create anxiety due to ever-increasing pressures to collect data for accountability and this has driven some settings to adopt a mechanistic approach to assessment and a culture of 'testing' where assessment becomes a stand-alone activity (Dubiel, 2014). When assessment practice and practitioners' beliefs about theories of learning are conflicting, the focus shifts away from the child onto the assessment process. It is sometimes thought by policy makers and some teachers, that to make an 'accurate' summative assessment judgement there has to be a specific directed activity or 1:1 'test' rather than recognising the validity of 'on the fly' formative judgements, which can come about through unexpected authentic assessment opportunities as part of the normal day-to-day experiences of these children. For these unexpected authentic assessments (see the companion website for examples from a pre-school setting serving a mixed socio-economic area) observations are central. The role of observation is discussed in detail in Chapter 8, thus this chapter only emphasises the importance of observation in assessment as a valid tool for systemic collection of information about children's learning and development in formative and summative ways, as it helps practitioners to:

- collect and gather evidence that can offer an accurate picture of children, their learning and development;
- understand the reasons behind children's behaviour in certain situations;
- recognise stages in child development;
- inform planning and assessment;
- provide opportunities for collaboration with parents and other services;
- find out about children as individuals;
- monitor progress;
- inform curriculum planning;
- enable practitioners to evaluate their practice;
- provide a focus for discussion and improvement. (Palaiologou, 2012)

Reflective tasks

- Study Chapter 8 and with the help of the examples on the companion website reflect on the value of observations to formative and summative assessment.

The role of digital technologies in assessment

Dubiel (2014) suggests that practitioners have become absorbed with paperwork that seeks to 'tick a box', rather than to support a child's learning. Other chapters in this book explore the role of digital technologies in early childhood in relation to support for children's learning and development (Chapters 18, 20, 21, 22 and 23) as well as partnerships with parents (Chapter 13). However, digital technologies can become a useful tool in the assessment process. They can assist practitioners in the assessment and recording process, and this use of online technology to assess children's learning could potentially have a significant impact on the amount of time taken to complete children's record of assessments (Dubiel, 2014; Bruce et al., 2015).

A number of digital systems have already been created that are capable of capturing a child's learning journey as it occurs and these can be easily shared with parents and carers through a secure site, as is demonstrated in Chapter 13.

Case study

The use of digital assessment in a childminder setting to support children's learning

Working as part of a childminding partnership, I wanted an effective way to observe and assess children that fitted into my day, that I could also do while I was out on visits with children. I discovered an online interactive system which enables me to log on through my phone, tablet device or laptop. This flexibility has meant that I am able to observe children in situ, wherever I am.

For example, observations are linked to the Characteristics of Effective Learning, with the opportunity to link the observation to as many different learning outcomes as required. Photos can also be easily uploaded and again linked to the learning outcomes. This enables me to easily track a child's development in all areas of development or to search under an area of learning for all the successes the child has achieved within specified times. Reports can be instantly designed, including termly reports. The review at age 2 can also be completed with ease, as the system takes the information from the child's uploaded photos and observations, creating an annotated profile.

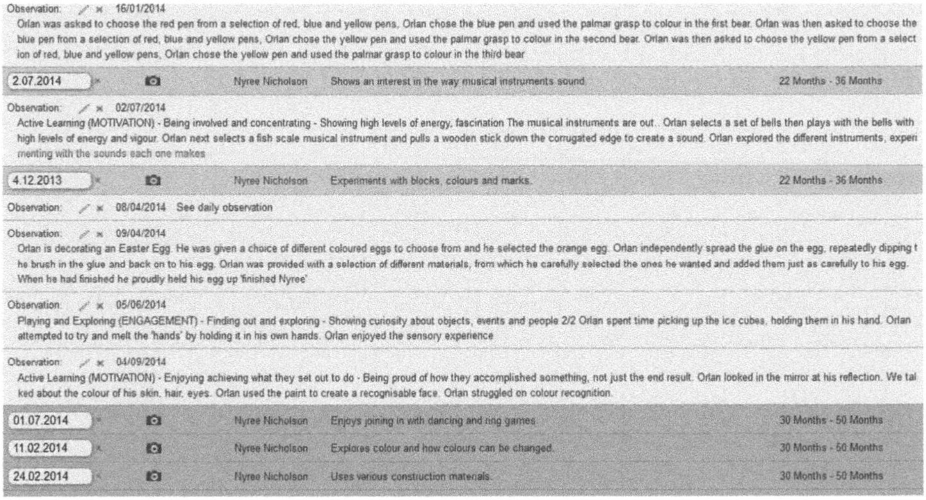
Observation: 16/01/2014
Orlan was asked to choose the red pen from a selection of red, blue and yellow pens, Orlan chose the blue pen and used the palmar grasp to colour in the first bear. Orlan was then asked to choose the blue pen from a selection of red, blue and yellow pens, Orlan chose the yellow pen and used the palmar grasp to colour in the second bear. Orlan was then asked to choose the yellow pen from a select ion of red, blue and yellow pens, Orlan chose the yellow pen and used the palmar grasp to colour in the third bear

2.07.2014	Nyree Nicholson	Shows an interest in the way musical instruments sound	22 Months - 36 Months

Observation: 02/07/2014
Active Learning (MOTIVATION) - Being involved and concentrating - Showing high levels of energy, fascination The musical instruments are out.. Orlan selects a set of bells then plays with the bells with high levels of energy and vigour. Orlan next selects a fish scale musical instrument and pulls a wooden stick down the corrugated edge to create a sound. Orlan explored the different instruments, experi menting with the sounds each one makes

4.12.2013	Nyree Nicholson	Experiments with blocks, colours and marks.	22 Months - 36 Months

Observation: 08/04/2014 See daily observation

Observation: 09/04/2014
Orlan is decorating an Easter Egg. He was given a choice of different coloured eggs to choose from and he selected the orange egg. Orlan independently spread the glue on the egg, repeatedly dipping t he brush in the glue and back on to his egg. Orlan was provided with a selection of different materials, from which he carefully selected the ones he wanted and added them just as carefully to his egg. When he had finished he proudly held his egg up 'finished Nyree'

Observation: 05/06/2014
Playing and Exploring (ENGAGEMENT) - Finding out and exploring - Showing curiosity about objects, events and people 2/2 Orlan spent time picking up the ice cubes, holding them in his hand. Orlan attempted to try and melt the 'hands' by holding it in his own hands. Orlan enjoyed the sensory experience

Observation: 04/09/2014
Active Learning (MOTIVATION) - Enjoying achieving what they set out to do - Being proud of how they accomplished something, not just the end result. Orlan looked in the mirror at his reflection. We tal ked about the colour of his skin, hair, eyes. Orlan used the paint to create a recognisable face. Orlan struggled on colour recognition.

01.07.2014	Nyree Nicholson	Enjoys joining in with dancing and ring games.	30 Months - 50 Months
11.02.2014	Nyree Nicholson	Explores colour and how colours can be changed.	30 Months - 50 Months
24.02.2014	Nyree Nicholson	Uses various construction materials.	30 Months - 50 Months

Figure 9.5 *Example of a child's learning journey in expressive arts and design*

This technology is also useful when children are attending more than one setting, as the setting (with parent permission) can also have access to the child's learning journey with another provider and add their own observations or photos, or comment on those that are already added. It is opening up the way for providers to truly work in a multi-agency way, ensuring that valuable learning experiences are shared and developed. Children's interests can fully be explored, enabling practitioners from a variety of settings and parents to get to know the many different facets of a child's learning. I have a child who attends a school nursery setting. The nursery observes the child through a different online tool that the school and parents have given me access to, and as a result I can see what she is doing in school and they have access to the software I use, enabling us both to plan around the child's interests displayed in both settings.

Moving forwards I can envisage options for this digital account of a child's learning journey to potentially move from setting to setting, if settings have the same online program, enabling children's learning journeys to be seamless, a continuous learning journey from the first day of a setting to the last.

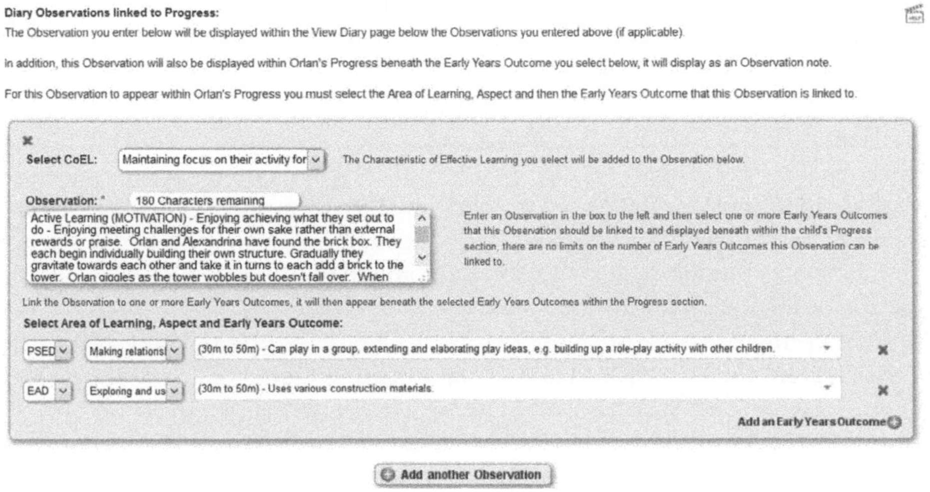

Figure 9.6 *Example of an observation linked to characteristics of effective learning and outcomes*

(Continued)

(Continued)

I am also able to upload photos and YouTube clips and link these to outcomes. This enables a learning journey to emerge of the child, through their own interests and achievements, in real time.

I like the fact that parents are also able to add their comments, photos or observations, which enables the practitioner to link these contributions to the Early Years Foundation Stage where approriate.

The role of record keeping and testing

Assessment reporting needs to be shared with parents and professionals in language that can be understood and not full of jargon or acronyms that might be misunderstood. Thus it is very important that records are kept in a format that can be communitated with all involved in children's progress.

As was shown in Chapter 5, the role of the practitioner is a complex mix of meeting the needs and interests of the individual child, working with their family, and respecting their perspectives while also being held accountable by external bodies. The effective practitioner will use assessment evidence to reshape and mediate opportunities for the individual to thrive and develop. This ongoing assessment is achieved through frequent observations of the child during their play and thoughtful moments. It includes interactions with the child to understand what they are doing, what they like and discussions with the parents so that a fuller picture of attainment and achievements can be gleaned. Key evidence of learning can then form part of a record keeping process. Record keeping is a necessary and a valuable part of the assessment process, but if it becomes burdensome it will distract from the teaching and learning and push the needs of the child into the background.

Tension clearly exists between teacher assessment based on ongoing observations and interactions with a child as part of their normal experiences, and those that are test-based assessments which usually require a more formal organisation and often involve the withdrawal of the child from their choice of play.

Unfortunately some assessment practice has led to unnecessary bureaucratic record keeping and the keeping of vast numbers of photographs, sticky-notes, pieces of work and even making the child do specific 'tests' through prescribed activities or questioning in order to measure their attainment. This approach seems to be based on a belief that 'measuring' a child's learning using fixed criteria for success, which can then be translated into a numerical formulae, is an accurate indicator of the child's ability and progress and can then be tracked and monitored through graphs and spreadsheets.

This accent on what can be measured easily can lead to negative labelling of a child as the emphasis is often on what the child can't do rather than what they can achieve or enjoy doing. This focus is often led by the criteria stated within the statutory assessment process and can result in a distorted view of the child's development characteristics which then leads to a restricted curriculum in a drive to achieve higher assessment outcomes within these narrow criteria.

Effective record keeping

Making a record of a child's achievement and attainment is an important part of the assessment process; however, there is a danger that the record keeping process becomes more important than the learning process. This can place unreasonable pressures on the practitioner and child. Sometimes these pressures are perceived rather than actual, especially when it comes to evidence gathering for a formal inspection, where practitioner anxiety leads them to undertake extra record keeping in the mistaken belief that this is what is required. There is also a significant amount of evidence collection using pre-structured forms, however, that distracts from good play-based learning and has been associated with testing situations such as 'baseline' data collection and phonics screening tests.

Useful record keeping needs to hold close the principles of early childhood education and care, and can be achieved in partnership with the parent and professionals involved in the care of the child. The child's development is a complex interaction between them, their environment and other people and it is through relevant record keeping that continuity and progression can be achieved within the setting and beyond.

Characteristics of useful records are that they:

- encompass and build on the principles of good early childhood pedagogy;
- help maintain a partnership between parent, child, teacher (and other relevant professionals where necessary);
- are user-friendly, time-efficient and effective;
- use a range of techniques to gather a range of valid evidence such as written, photography, video and audio recording;
- link assessment of a child's progress within a context and point in time;
- comment on the progress made and the next necessary steps to take for individuals (and or groups of children);
- are linked to the statutory requirements of the day in a purposeful way;
- are easy to review and summarise. (Adapted from Bruce et al. 2015: 20)

Chapter 10 provides guidance on some very interesting and helpful ways of record keeping.

Summary

This chapter focused on assessment in early childhood education and care with a focus on the requirements of EYFS. Assessment is important in order to understand children's learning and development. Although it is welcomed, the two-stage assessment process within EYFS, which includes the Integrated Review at Age Two and the EYFS Profile at the end of the Foundation Stage year, do raise some concerns. The focus of these assessments appears to be on 'school readiness' as an overall aim of early childhood education and care rather than what is the best development progress for that individual child. A concern has been that this assessment information should support learning, not drive a narrow curriculum by being limited to 'school readiness'. The EYFS Profile is intended to bring together a holistic picture of children's interests, ways of learning and their development. This collated information is very important in relation to effective transitions and enhancing learning potential through planned experiences (as discussed in Chapter 11). It can be a tool for all those involved in a child's education and care to discuss and celebrate a child's achievements, their rate of progress and their enjoyment and engagement in their learning and socialisation with their peers as well as adults.

Key points to remember

- There are two key types of assessment – summative and formative – and both need to take place in early childhood settings as they serve different purposes.

- Formative and summative assessment is a necessary and valuable aspect of effective teaching and learning. It is through a systematic approach to gathering a range of evidence of children's learning and development through authentic assessment opportunities that a practitioner is able to:
  - find out about children as individuals;
  - provide opportunities for meaningful collaboration with parents and other services;
  - create a holistic picture of children's learning, development and interest;
  - understand the reasons behind children's behaviour in certain situations;
  - recognise stages in children's development;
  - monitor progress and help identify areas for intervention;
  - inform curriculum planning;
  - evaluate their practice in terms of effectiveness and efficiency;
  - provide data for monitoring and accountability.

- The child should be at the centre of all assessment practice, with the curriculum providing the context for learning.

- Assessment of children should include parents' 'perspectives' of their children through a partnership approach.

- Assessment practice and record keeping need to be time-efficient and effective.

Points for discussion

- What do you consider that the appropriate balance of assessment approaches through practitioner-led, practitioner-initiated and child-initiated activities would look like to assist the assessment process for differently aged children?

- When you are in practice or work placement try to create an open-ended problem solving opportunity to assess through 'watching' and 'listening' for a specific age of child, rather than specific assessment task. After you have experimented a few times doing this, what are your thoughts about this approach? What possibilities can you find to use this alongside EYFS assessment requirements?

- Think of a recent situation where through an 'on the fly' observation you gained significant information about a child. How was this evidence 'captured' and then used?

Further reading

Books

Bruce, T., Louise, S. and MCall, G. (2015) *Observing Young Children*. London: Sage.

Dubiel, J. (2016) 'What are the purposes of assessment?', in *Effective Assessment in the Early Years Foundation Stage*, 2nd edn. London: Sage. ch. 3.

Formosinho, J. and Pascal, C. (eds) (2016) *Assessment and Evaluation for Transformation in Early Childhood*. London: Routledge.

Articles

Dunphy, E. (2010) 'Assessing early learning through formative assessment: key issues and considerations', *Irish Educational Studies*, 29 (1): 41–56.

National Children's Bureau Early Childhood Unit (2015) *The Integrated Review* London: NCB. Available at: www.ncb.org.uk/media/1201160/ncb_integrated_review_supporting_materials_for_practitioners_march_2015.pdf.

Report

NUT (National Union of Teachers) (2015) 'Exam factories?' [Online] www.teachers.org.uk/files/exam-factories.pdf (accessed 22 July 2015).

Useful websites

The Association for Achievement and Improvement through Assessment offers a useful way to keep up to date with assessment matters across all ages:
www.aaia.org.uk/category/aol/statutory/

Early Education: The British Association for Early Childhood Education:
www.early-education.org.uk/press-release/sector-unites-call-oppose-introduction-baseline-assessment

National curriculum and assessment guidance for Scotland, Northern Ireland, Wales and England:
www.educationscotland.gov.uk/learningandteaching/earlylearningandchildcare/curriculum/supportingearlylevel/implementation/assessment.asp
www.nicurriculum.org.uk/foundation_stage/assessment/index.asp
http://gov.wales/topics/educationandskills/earlyyearshome/?lang=en
www.lbhf.gov.uk/Directory/Education_and_Learning/Schools_and_Colleges/School_Staff_Zone/EYFSP%20Handbook%202015.pdf

References

Bagnato, S.J. (2007) *Authentic Assessment for Early Childhood Intervention: Best Practices*. New York, NY: Guilford.

Bagnato, S.J., Neisworth, J.T. and Pretti-Frontczak, K.L. (2010) *Linking Authentic Assessment and Early Childhood Intervention: Best Measures for Best Practices*, 4th edn. Baltimore, MD: Brookes.

Bailey, A. and Drummond, V. (2006) 'Who is at risk and why? Teachers' reasons for concern and their understanding and assessment of early literacy', *Educational Assessment*, 11 (3–4): 149–78.

Black, P., Harrison, C., Hodgen, J., Marshall, B. and Serret, N. (2013) *Inside the Black Box of Assessment: Assessment of Learning by Teachers and Schools*. London: GL Assessment.

Black, P.J. and Wiliam, D. (1998) 'Inside the black box: raising standards through classroom assessment', *Phi Delta Kappan*, 80 (2): 139–48.

Bruce, T., Louise, S. and McCall, G. (2015) *Observing Young Children*. London: Sage.

Davis, D., Evans, M., Jadad, A., Perrier, L., Rath, D. and Zwarenstain, M. (2003) 'The case for knowledge translation: shortening the journey from evidence to effect', *BMJ*, 327 (7405): 33–5.

DfE (Department for Education) (2011) Early Years Evidence Pack, available at www.education.gov.uk/publications/standard/Earlyyearsandchildcareworkforce/Page1/DFE-00274-2011 (accessed 19 July 2012).

DfE (Department for Education) (2014) *Statutory Framework for the Early Years Foundation Stage: Setting the Standards for Learning, Development and Care for Children Birth to Five*. Available at: www.foundationyears.org.uk/files/2014/07/EYFS_framework_from_1_September_2014_with_clarification_note.pdf (accessed 21 September 2015).

Dubiel, J. (2014) *Effective Assessment in the Early Years Foundation Stage*. London: Sage.

Dunphy, E. (2010) 'Assessing early learning through formative assessment: key issues and considerations', *Irish Educational Studies*, 29 (1): 41–56.

Early Education: British Association for Early Childhood Education (2015) 'Sector unites in call to oppose introduction of baseline assessment'. [Online] www.early-education.org.uk/press-release/sector-unites-call-oppose-introduction-baseline-assessment (accessed 16 May 2015).

Harrison, C. and Howard, S. (2009) *Inside the Primary Black Box: Assessment for Learning in Primary and Early Years Classrooms*. London: GL Assessment

Laevers, F. (ed.) (2005) *Well-Being and Involvement in Care Settings: A Process-Oriented Education Instrument*. Brussels: Kind and Gezint/Research Centre for Experiential Education.

NCSL (National College for Leadership of Schools and Children's Services) (2010) 'Leading curriculum innovation in primary schools'. Professor Mark Brundrett and Dr Diane Duncan, Liverpool John Moores University, September 2010.

Nutbrown, C. (2012) *Foundations for Quality: The Independent Review of Early Education and Childcare Qualifications. Final Report. Runcorn: Department for Education. Available at:* www.gov.uk/government/uploads/system/uploads/attachment_data/file/175463/Nutbrown-Review.pdf *(accessed September 2015)*.

Palaiologou, I. (2012) *Child Observation for the Early Years*. London: Learning Matters.

Sammons, P., Sylva, K., Melhuish, E., Siraj-Blatchford, I., Taggart, B., Grabbe, B. and Barreau, S. (2007) 'The Effective Pre-School and Primary Education 3–11 Project'. *Summary Report: Influences on Children's Attainment and Progress in Key Stage 2: Cognitive Outcomes in Year 5*. Report No. RR828. London: Institute of Education, University of London.

Save the Children Fund (2013) 'Too young to fail: giving all children a fair start to life'. [Online] www.savethechildren.org.uk/sites/default/files/docs/Too_Young_to_Fail_0.pdf (accessed 15 May 2015).

Siraj-Blatchford, I., Sylva K., Muttock, S. and Gilden, R. (2002) *Effective Pedagogy in the Early Years*, Research Report 356. London: Department for Education and Skills.

Sylva, K., Melhuish, E., Sammons, P., Siraj-Blatchford, I. and Taggart, B. (2004) *The Effective Provision of Pre-School Education Project*. Technical Paper No. 12 – The Final Report. London: Department for Education and Skills/Institute of Education, University of London.

Sylva, K. (2008) 'Final Report from the Primary Phase: Pre-school, School and Family Influences on Children's Development during Key Stage 2 (Age 7–11)'. Department for Children, Schools and Families Research Report No. DCSF-RR061.

Sylva, K., Melhuish, E., Sammons, P., Siraj-Blatchford, I. and Taggart, B. (Eds) (2010), *Early Childhood Matters: Evidence from the Effective Pre-school and Primary Education Project*. London: Routledge.

Sylva, K., Melhuish, E., Sammons, P., Siraj-Blatchford, I., Taggart, B. with Toth, K., Smees, R., Draghici, D., Mayo, A. and Welcomme, W. (2012) Effective Pre-School, Primary and Secondary Education 3–14 Project (EPPSE 3–14). *Final Report from the Key Stage 3 Phase: Influences on Students' Development from Age 11–14*. Ref No. DFE-RR202 ISBN: 978-1–78105–078–1. London: Institute of Education, University of London.

Tickell, C. (2011) *The Early Years: Foundations for Life, Health and Learning*. An Independent Report on the Early Years Foundation Stage to Her Majesty's Government. London: Crown. Available at: www.education.gov.uk/tickellreview (accessed September 2015).

Ward, H. (2009) 'Patterns of instability: Moves within the English care system, their reasons, contexts and consequences', *Child and Youth Services Review*, 31: 1113–1118.

Want to learn more about this chapter? Visit the companion website at **https://study.sagepub.com/EYFS3e** for access to free SAGE journal articles and book chapters, weblinks, annotated further readings and more.

Pedagogical Documentation

Estelle Martin

 Chapter overview

As discussed in Chapter 9, assessment is central to the EYFS. The Integrated Review (2015) that has been introduced by the current UK government incorporates the existing Early Years Foundation Stage progress check and the Health and Development Review at age 2 carried out by health visitors under the Healthy Child Programme. The policy is to promote early intervention for children to reduce and prevent health and social problems developing. The Integrated Review aims to give a holistic picture of the child, drawing on knowledge from a variety of sources such as health visitors, social care and early childhood practitioners. The sharing of information between agencies and parents is a designated area for improvement and an opportunity to establish trust and enhanced ways of communicating with parents and other professionals who are working with children and families as it refers to the EYFS Profile (EYFSP). As Chapter 9 concluded, in order for this communication to be achieved there is a need for effective recording so all interested in the child can understand the outcomes of the assessment.

This chapter aims to examine curricula practices to see how documentation can be used to enhance pedagogy in early childhood education and care. In Chapter 9 the purpose of the assessment and the EYFS requirements were discussed, but the approaches discussed here, such as Reggio Emilia and Te Whāriki, use effective record keeping to improve assessment that focuses on the child rather than just the legal requirements. Although there is a rich bibliography (see Further Reading) which offers a number of other examples, this chapter aims to provide an overview of a few different ways of using documentation to enhance children's learning. This chapter discusses, therefore, ways of effectively recording children's progress and development by focusing on pedagogical documentation (the Reggio Emilia approach), learning stories (Te Whāriki), the mosaic approach and the use of Ferre Laevers' scales.

This chapter aims to help you:

- understand the theory underpinning pedagogical documentation, learning stories, the mosaic approach and Laevers' Scales of Involvement and Well-being
- see how these types of documentation can be used as effective tools in early childhood education and care
- investigate how these can be linked and applied in daily practice.

Theoretical underpinnings of pedagogical documentation

Rinaldi (2006) promotes the value of documentation as a process, thus meaning it is part of the learning and teaching process. This approach recognises the value of documentation as a tool that is not only for assessment and evaluation of children's experience, but also for self-assessment and evaluation of educators and researchers in the process of dialogue, thus emphasising this as an opportunity for reflection in practice and research in early childhood education and care. Seen from a socio-cultural theory perspective, interactions with adults are a key ingredient in the learning and teaching process.

Scaffolding and guided interaction requires practitioners to be able to diagnose the child's current understanding and what could be achieved with specific kinds of adult and peer support in the zone of proximal development (Vygotsky, 1978: 86). The role of the interested adult, such as parents, carers and practitioners, provides a way to navigate across the concepts the child is exploring through 'scaffolding' by knowing the child and their next possible steps in their understanding, through dialogue and co-constructing narratives that represent the child's thinking and interests (Bruner, 1986).

Socio-cultural theory challenges practitioners and researchers to consider what early childhood settings can include from the ways in which children learn at home and in their community. Working in the socio-cultural tradition, Rogoff (2003) draws attention to the ways in which learning is supported in different communities and to the two forms of guided participation which she identifies as central to learning: mutual bridging of meaning and mutual structuring of opportunities. Rogoff (2003) further argues that these two processes are both fundamental to learning and development and are universal. This echoes the Vygotskian approach, although the observation of children in early childhood settings and at home can be vital for practitioners to understand the culture of the child's home and community as it refers to parents involved in their education and care. In this way a shared understanding can evolve between the parents and practitioners about the child's learning and development in the EYFS.

This sharing of observations and experiences of the children between parents and practitioners is fundamental to understanding the child's developmental process. The EYFS is connected to the wider National Curriculum framework and so the process that begins in early childhood does influence how parents may continue to be involved in their child's education.

The process of pedagogical documentation is a valuable part of the continuing discussion between parents, early childhood practitioners and teachers in schools. For Rinaldi (2006), the search for meaning in children and adults is a shared encounter where the Reggio pre-schools create a pedagogy of listening in order to support teaching and learning relationships. In other words, listening with respect, but taking an interest and being responsive to children's multi-modal learning and their representations. Malaguzzi (1993: 10) saw children as being 'rich in potential and a strong, powerful, component connected to adults and other children' (see section in Chapter 20 on Creating connections for communication). This has implications for constructing how we see the child influence the ways we treat, teach or plan for learning and so curriculum frameworks may be more or less open-ended according to their aims.

Malaguzzi's underpinning philosophy

Loris Malaguzzi (Correggio 1920 – Reggio Emilia 1994) was the founder of an educational philosophy for educating young children which now is represented in the Reggio Emilia early childhood education. He was the main driving force in rebuilding education in the Reggio Emilia area and established a network of municipal pre-schools (3–6) and infant–toddler centres (0–3). He promoted the idea of listening to children with his *theory of the hundred languages*, which emphasised the value of the potential, the resources and many intelligences of all children.

Fundamental to the Reggio philosophy is the construct of the child as rich in potential, strong, powerful and competent. Loris Malaguzzi's vision of a child was as an active, strong and powerful human being. Both Malaguzzi (1994) and his co-worker Rinaldi (1995) based their pedagogy on cognitive ideas of child development. As mentioned above, they placed particular emphasis on Vygotsky's ideas, that knowledge is not *adopted* by the child, but is *constructed* by the child through interaction with a more mature or experienced peer or adult as well as the community around them as part of the learning process.

Crucial elements in Malaguzzi's pedagogical approach are:

- the philosophy of the work of the Reggio Emilia's Pre-schools: the experience rather than the contents of learning where both children and educators are engaged with the search for knowledge;
- cooperation with families and community;
- community and citizenship;
- the physical environment as a motivating force and space for learning; use of light, mirrors and artistic artefacts;
- creative celebration of children's work;
- importance of relationship, curiosity and communication;
- importance of socio-cultural context for learning to take place;
- influential theorists were Dewey, Bronfenbrenner and Vygotsky;
- influential research and pedagogical partners were Bruner and Gardner.

The role of pedagogical documentation

Pedagogical documentation makes children's learning 'visible' through recording the experiences and learning activities children are involved in and contributing to that record of their lived experiences. The documentation process also enables evidence to be revealed that is meaningful for the child, practitioner and parents that may be discussed and developed as part of a series of dialogues between colleagues and external professionals who may contribute to the child's development and assessment of needs. This could be a health visitor, speech and language therapist, physiotherapist or language support teacher, for example.

Pedagogical documentation can underpin our understanding of individual children in their holistic development and learning; so pedagogical documentation is both a process and representation of experiences that are a range of activities, artefacts and projects which are displayed and accompanied by dialogue, description and sequences of actions that may be visualised.

There is an opportunity for practitioners and researchers to reflect and assess pedagogical practice as promoted by this chapter through consideration of some socio-cultural ideas underpinning pedagogical practice. The self-assessment and reflective practice can be strengthened by understanding the use of documentation with the children, and through the dialogues between adults, creating the conditions of a listening culture that overarches all the experiences in the early childhood setting.

This can be an aspect of professional development for practitioners in early childhood and care that can be supported through use of pedagogical documentation as a tool for learning and reflection on practice in addition to reflecting on children's learning. The importance of practitioners being able to express their own philosophy and pedagogical approach is essential, not just for accountability, but also for children's well-being and holistic development. It will enable practitioners to represent their own understandings of teaching and learning relationships to others and so enhance the quality and experiences of the dynamics in practice. For example, research relating to pedagogy of play with young children found practitioners were not always confident about expressing their philosophy and theories of play (Goouch, 2008). Thus it is important that practitioners be well informed and develop their practice by using reflection.

Carr (2001) refers to the concept of *affordance* to describe the relationship between learners and the early childhood setting. Affordance refers to:

- perceived and actual properties of resources in the environment (people, objects, artefacts and tools);
- how these are used;
- how these might be used;
- how these may help or hinder learning.

Thornton and Brunton (2007) interpret the Reggio Emilia approach as having as fundamental to its philosophy that children should have access to 'high affordance', intelligent resources to provoke learning.

Case study

My visit to Reggio Emilia

My own visit to Reggio Emilia pre-schools in 2004 did reveal the high quality of the materials and resources available for the children to use and the environment was indeed very aesthetically pleasing. There was strong evidence of pedagogical documentation in all areas, such as the baby and toddler rooms, which had their age ranges represented. For example, there were friezes on the walls positioned at eye level for the younger children and the children who were mobile. These friezes were documenting the process and sequence of a particular series of activities through photographs and some scribing through written text (and dialogues) to describe the sequence of events, such as exploring, responding and constructing with some blocks from beginning to the end of play. Another example was the babies playing with the equivalent of 'treasure baskets', although these had compartments for added curiosity for the babies to discover and manipulate. To some extent these friezes helped me to see the way tools and materials can be used and how the children could see the possibilities for their own use and learning and memory as they could revisit the images.

Documentation can provide children with memories of their activities and can build a portfolio of their achievements during a particular sequence of time.

Reflective task

- Reflect on your own early childhood setting or your placement and try to compare a Reggio Emilia classroom with the EYFS. Any similarities? Can you identify any influences of the Reggio Emilia in your setting?

The voice of the child: the contextual picture

The importance of drawing in young children's development has been acknowledged for several decades across professional disciplines in early childhood. A more socio-cultural orientated approach is documented by recent research studies; (Coates, 2002; Arizpe and Styles, 2003; Anning and Ring, 2004). Such literature reiterates the power of drawing as a significant mode of expression and construction of meaning. The contribution of the child participants in this case demonstrates the multi-layered nature of narratives and self-expression through their experiences of drawing (see Figure 10.1).

The participatory approach used in this case study is reflected in the conversational style of talking between the practitioner and the child participants, whilst encouraging the children to draw what is of interest to them and to talk about how they feel about those interests or people. This can provide an opportunity for child and adult to communicate through visual images as opposed to words alone, moving away from just a question and answer style. These two aspects of participation enable the children to have agency and more freedom to explore and express their thoughts, ideas and feelings.

Children's expression of self includes their internal world and responses to their environments, experiences and people. The following individual profiles of the children will illustrate their unique interpretations of their world and matters of interest to them, including their visual literacy. Children may express and work through some aspects of their lived and imagined experiences as part of sharing feelings and identifying with characters in stories. This can be through talk, but also through their drawings and mark making, helping the child to externalise their thoughts. Drawing is a first step in creating symbols to represent real objects, a form of communicative composition (Pahl, 1999). Social semiotic theory, argued by Kress (1997), underpins the interpretation process. Writing, he asserts, is a sign system that is interpreted visually and young children will observe there are multiple forms in which graphic representation takes place. Although this is associated with literacy, it is essentially linked to learning and construction of meaning that involves the abilities of the whole child in their understanding and use of texts, signs, symbols and scripts for the narratives of experience and communication in the wider world.

The recent recognition emerging from research studies and observation of current culture is that babies and children live with and will actively use a range of modes of communication, i.e. television, computers, mobile phones, electronic games and so on (Palaiologou, 2014). This multi-modality enables children more opportunities to represent their experience, which supports their agency, expression of self, imagination and understanding. This gives rise to the consideration of the generally held distinction between what is known and what is felt, i.e. cognition and affect, as if the two were independent processes. Eisner (1982) argues that the two interact and both are essential constituents of any successful education system. The creative media advocated so strongly by the Reggio Emilia pre-schools in Northern Italy support this, for example, in their pedagogy of listening and relationships that is documented thoroughly in order 'to make learning visible'. The Project Zero (2001), a research collaboration between Harvard Graduate School of Education and Reggio Emilia infant–toddler centres and pre-schools, explores this pedagogical approach across cultures. The children and the documentation that 'makes learning visible' demonstrate their active learning through a series of multimodal media of children's narrative expression with creative project work and interaction with peers.

Case study

Children's voices

Based on this pedagogical philosophy and using documentation that makes learning visible, in this case study I focused on a small group of children, consisting of two boys and two girls all aged 5 years, in Year 1 of an infants' school. The children and I were located in an empty classroom seated together facing each other at the tables. The focus of this activity was to find out about their thoughts and especially their feelings in relation to what has helped them to be happy in their new class (Year 1). I was interested in their views on the contemporary nature of their experience as I had observed and spent a whole term with these children in their Reception class during the previous year. Inviting the children to draw as we developed conversations was something with which the children were familiar as part of their everyday experiences. Some of the group had participated with me before in the research process, drawing and narrating their experience, thoughts and feelings, when they were in the Reception class.

The following extracts provide a flavour of the narratives throughout the drawing process, from a selection of transcriptions. The children are not required to describe what they are drawing as the focus is on the conversation whilst they are involved in their drawing. The children demonstrate real concentration and respond to each other's statements as well as answering my questions:

EM: I have come to ask you how you feel about your new class.

Bill: I feel happy, I like it because I can do more things. In the B class we didn't write and things. We can do more things and we like it.

Jay: Things like writing, add up numbers and stories.

EM: Shall we ask Lee and Lilly why they like it? Why are you happy in your new class?

Lee: We can make more pictures. We can learn things and have homework.

Lilly: It is getting harder but we can still do it, so I can be happy.

Figure 10.1   *'Perceptions of place'*

Lilly has drawn a traditional English house with a roof with what may be a mark for a chimney. The house may not be a realistic representation of Lilly's actual home, but we can interpret her intentions in noticing where she positions herself as central in the house. The house looks slightly off centre and is located in the lawn of a garden containing one flower. The lack of perspective is denoted with the flower alongside the house not in proportion or scale. This would be developmentally consistent for most 5-year-olds (Matthews, 1999). The house has two doors and numbers, or door furniture. There are four windows with

(Continued)

(Continued)

old-fashioned glazing bars, which are traditional in style, although still used in building new houses. There are seven rooms marked out in black as distinct from the windows. The house contains a person who is in the centre of the house. It is Lilly, situated above the door and has a smiling face and head on one side with distinctive long straight hair. The sun in the left of the drawing has a smiley face. In addition, there are brown-coloured trails or rays coming from the sun. The black cloud in the sky above the flower also has tails of black indicating movement down from the sky. A view may be that it may be about to rain even when the sun is out.

The six colours used in this drawing are strong and offer clarity of form and enhance the design. Lilly is a competent and skilled composer of her drawing with a sense of place identified within her home, by her choice of being positioned at the centre of the house. The geographies of children involve their developing sense of identity as part of an ongoing process which emerges, rather than being a static developmental outcome. Children's drawings can be seen as similar to freeze-frames; each one presents a slightly different aspect of the child who makes them (Malchiodi, 1998). I was able to witness Lilly's drawings and descriptions of her views in real time, which offered me a fuller representation of Lilly. During her drawing, Lilly gave me eye contact as she looked up from her paper. Lilly spoke about her views to the group and was able to concentrate on her composition and to engage and interact with ease.

I then began asking an open-ended question to explore the children's perceptions and feelings about the transition to their new class:

EM: What helped you to feel happy in your new class?

Lee: All of our Mummies stayed for a little while, so we could get used to it.

Jay: We could play with all the stuff.

Lilly: The teachers and our Mums showed us where the toilets were.

Bill: When I was in the B class we didn't know where it was, so our Mum showed us, so we are fine now.

EM: Was there anything else that helped you feel happy when you started your new class?

Lilly: I liked it because I could stay with my friend.

Jay: We looked around and saw what there was to play with.

EM: Who do you talk to if you are not sure about being happy?

Lee: We talk to teachers and our friends. We look after each other. I liked it when they were kind to me.

Lilly: Playing with each other helps.

EM: You can draw your own picture about feelings.

The voice of the child can thus be represented in different ways as shown and discussed in this case study. The parallel is that dialogue is a central part of the learning and teaching and principles of pedagogical documentation. The child's voice is interconnected to the voices of others and so adults and children are engaging in mutual and authentic listening and learning through reflections on their experiences and learning as part of a high-quality early childhood setting.

Reflective task

Reflect on the case study and on the definition below of 'sustained shared thinking' that is promoted as an indicator of good quality early childhood education and care and has been included in the Teacher Standards (Early Years) (NCTL, 2013).

Sustained shared thinking occurs when two or more individuals work together in an intellectual way to solve a problem, clarify a concept, evaluate an activity or extend a narrative. Both parties must contribute to the thinking and it must develop and extend the understanding. The Effective Provision of Pre-School Education (EPPE) Project (Sylva et al., 2004) demonstrated this was more likely to occur when children were interacting 1:1 with an adult, or with a single peer partner and during focused group work.

- Consider whether any sustained shared thinking takes place in the case study.

- Can you design and carry out an activity that promotes the philosophy of pedagogical documentation and evaluate whether any sustained shared thinking was promoted during the activity?

Learning stories

Te Whāriki is the New Zealand curriculum that places the emphasis on children's freedom to choose materials, activities and take ownership of their own learning. Within Te Whāriki children are viewed as being encouraged:

> To grow up as competent and confident learners and communicators, healthy in mind, body, and spirit, secure in their sense of belonging and in the knowledge that they make a valued contribution to society. (Te Whāriki, 1996).

The framework of this curriculum is based on children's interests and aspirations (Tyler, 2002). Similarly to the EYFS, there are some principles to guide the early childhood team:

- Empowerment (*Whakamana*) is central to the curriculum in that the child takes ownership of the development and learning.
- Holistic development (*Kotahitanga*) where the child is viewed as a 'whole'. It is emphasised that the child learns in a holistic way taking into consideration not only the child's physical, social, emotional and cognitive development, but also the cultural context and the spiritual aspects of children's environment.
- Family and Community (*Whanau Tangata*) – similarly to the EYFS partnership with the wider world of family and community this is an integral part of early childhood curriculum.
- Relationships (*Nga Hononga*) – children's interactions with peers, adults and real life objects enhance children's learning. (Palaiologou, 2012)

Similar to Reggio Emilia, Te Whāriki has a project approach where activities are documented at all stages (see case study in Chapter 24). This includes the voice of the children and segments of dialogues which are like a patchwork of concepts and knowledge the children are creating and revealing. Carr et al. (2009) explains that documentation in the Te Whāriki curriculum model provides evidence of learning in the making, not just the outcomes.

Carr (1999, 2001) and Carr and Lee (2012) created a model of assessment in the curriculum which is a bi-cultural example that underpins sensitivity to and recognition of diversity. There are four assessment methods that contribute to the 'Learning Stories' model for monitoring children's learning and holistic development. The four Ds are:

- Describing
- Documenting
- Discussing
- Deciding.

The emphasis on learning stories is not on what a child has achieved, or where the child is in relation to his/her development as in the EYFS, but on key dispositions, and the documentation is focusing on whether children are:

- Taking an interest;
- Coping with change and difference;
- Connecting places and experiences together;

- Finding out new things;
- Practising old things;
- Tackling difficulty;
- Developing relationships with adults;
- Developing relationships with peers;
- Taking responsibility. (Carr, 1999: 15)

Not all assessments will be documented and practitioners will develop their process of recording and collaborate on what should be included and why. One of the most important factors is that the child and the parents actively contribute to the learning story through dialogues with practitioners so there is a connectedness, where the child experiences others respecting and listening to their voice. The child being facilitated to express their voice and thoughts and ideas is also promoted by the multi-modal approach.

Case study

A learning story in EYFS: working in partnership with parents

By Sally Howard, Nyree Nicholson and Chris Williamson

In one pre-school setting the practitioner and her colleagues create a 'memory' book with each child where they can select from a range of evidence gathered over time and decide on a few examples of which the child is most proud. The opportunity to discuss learning and their interests with the child helps them to really know and understand things through the child's perspective and this information can then 'feed-forward' into adjusting the learning experiences to meet their needs within the group. This one-to-one opportunity provides an insight into their home environment as the child is able to chat about things that interest him or her and it provides the opportunity for the child to share particular worries they might be harbouring.

Together the child and teacher cut and stick in a sample of memories and leave room for the parents to add their voice using the 'proud cloud' system. This is a communication tool to supplement casual conversations when the parent or carer collects the child. A large sheet of paper with a cloud drawn on with the prompt 'I am proud of my child ...' is sent home every few weeks and the parent is asked to reflect on their child's progress (and let them know), while at the same time capturing this specific praise in a form that can contribute to the termly

(Continued)

(Continued)

memory book. These memories might include photographs or pieces of work created in the setting or at home and also include the child's voice through teacher annotation.

While these books take time to construct they are about the child and require them to use scissors and glue and justify their choices for selection in the book. It provides an opportunity to share their learning journey with them and their family as a celebration of achievement rather than focus on assessment as a product.

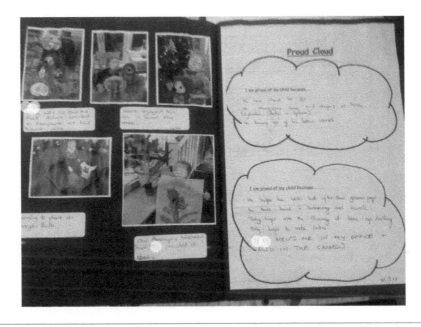

Figure 10.2 *Proud clouds*

In the example in Figure 10.2 the parent has made a contribution through the 'proud cloud' stating:

I am proud of my child ...

- He can count to 20
- He recognizes some 3-D shapes (cylinder, cube and sphere)
- He knows all of his letter sounds

I am proud of my child ....

- He helps his sister look after their guinea pigs
- He tries hard in swimming and karate
- He helps with the cleaning at home, especially the dusting
- He helps to make cakes
- He helps me in my office and also in the garden

Listening to children: the mosaic approach

Inspired by the learning stories, Clark and Moss (2001) introduced a culturally appropriate approach in England called the 'mosaic approach' to be used in assessment and research with children and also as a participatory approach for children and young people to have their voices heard. This could be through voice, spoken, visual and symbolic representation such as drawings and photographs. The Mosaic model utilizes two aspects of collecting and interpreting information. Firstly children and adults collect the examples of documents and, secondly, piece together the information for dialogue and interpretation and reflection. This provides agency for the child as they are involved in a continuous process of making the mosaic and in dialogues with adults about how the mosaic enables their representation of themselves.

Laevers' Scales of Involvement and Well-being

Ferre Laevers at the University of Leuven introduced the Scales of Involvement and Well-being in 1976. The instrument was developed at the Research Centre for Experiential Education (Leuven University, Belgium). The aim is that these scales will measure and monitor children's involvement and engagement in activities as well as their well-being. Such an approach relies on the constant monitoring of children and helps practitioners to identify children who need extra care. As the EYFS aims to help children to achieve the five outcomes of the Every Child Matters policy, the scales are becoming popular as they focus on children's well-being and involvement, and of course help to identify any additional needs for an early intervention. The scales aim to:

1   serve as a tool for self-assessment by early childhood settings;
2   focus on quality, taking into consideration the child and its experience of the care environment;
3   achieve appropriateness for the wide range of early childhood education and care. (Laevers, 2005)

After the scales have collected information about children through observations, practitioners can identify strengths and weaknesses. The results from the scales will enable them to create the best possible conditions for children to develop. There are three steps in the process:

- Step 1 – assessment of the actual levels of well-being and involvement
- Step 2 – analysis of observations
- Step 3 – selection and implementation of actions to improve quality of practice in the early childhood setting.

Laevers claims that this approach to the assessment of children can lead to significant changes in the setting as well as in the professional development of practitioners:

> Through the process [the practitioners] learn to take the perspective of the child in their approach and because of this to create optimal conditions for the social, emotional and cognitive development of the children. (Laevers, 2005: 5)

As the EYFS suggests, assessment scales are provided for each area of development, thus the reasons for the popularity of the Laevers scales can be understood.

Case study

Practitioner observation using well-being scales

This case study reflects the importance of emotional and social development given by practitioners, and the use of particular measures identified to support their identification of learning outcomes for the children was included. The Leuven Well-being Scale (Laevers, 2005) is used in the Reception class alongside the statutory Foundation Stage Early Learning Goals and Profiles (DfE, 2014; Early Education, 2012). The following example demonstrates what practitioners were looking for in their observation using the Leuven Well-being Scale at a children's centre in the daycare and baby unit.

George is a 2-year-old child who is attending the day care setting full time and is familiar with the geography of the nursery design, which is a large open space, partitioned areas for particular play or interest; children can move around freely.

The practitioner Mary interprets and says:

> The image demonstrates George's level of involvement which is focused and concentrated. George is interested and motivated and appears fascinated with the choice of book, which clearly he is enjoying exploring.

George spends a long time (approximately seven minutes) turning the pages of the book and repeats this more than once looking closely at the pictures. I have not noticed him concentrating for so long before! George is at ease and able to make choices for himself and persevere with his page turning and appears to have a sense of well-being.

Figure 10.3 *Levels of involvement: George*

This concurs with Laevers' argument that well-being and involvement are process variables:

> Both are process variables in that they inform us about what is going on in the child while present in the setting [...] involvement refers to another quality of the process in the child: the involved person finds himself or herself in a particular state characterised by concentration, intense experience, intrinsic motivation, flow of energy and a high level of satisfaction connected with the fulfilment of the exploratory drive. (Laevers, 2005: 6)

Mary, the observer, recognised the overall sense of well-being that George was experiencing in the process of self-initiated play. These data support the argument

(Continued)

(Continued)

that when children show signs of intense involvement in their play their learning will be at a high level (Howard, 2010).

The city nursery school used the ongoing responsive curriculum planning through observations of the children and reflecting on practice alongside the Early Learning Goals and Ofsted criteria met through inspection. The differences are relevant to highlight as the city nursery school appears more flexible and less bound by 'rating scales' or 'measurements' to assess and evaluate children's developmental outcomes. Culturally this is important to consider as the diversity of individual children requires practitioners to respond sensitively and plan a learning environment that includes relationships with adults to meet those unique needs. Albeit one can argue this is fundamental for all learning at any phase of education a child may be journeying, but it is particularly important in early childhood.

Reflective task

- After studying this chapter, reflect on the similarities in the approaches discussed and consider how, although there are differences, these can help us to move towards a more complete understanding about how to apply effective record keeping to support children's holistic development and learning in sensitive and culturally relevant ways.

Summary

This chapter aimed to discuss some effective ways of recording children's observations and documenting children's progress in early childhood education and care. In the EYFS, assessment (as has been mentioned at the beginning of this chapter and also in Chapter 9) is statutory and happens in two stages. The main focus of recording assessment in the EYFS is formal. This chapter showed some other ways of documenting children's assessments, however, which focus on more formative ways and with emphasis on the child's holistic development. The chapter discussed the key theoretical underpinnings of Reggio Emilia pedagogical documentation, Te Whāriki learning stories that inspired the mosaic approach introduced by Clark and Moss and, finally, the Laevers' Scales of Involvement and Well-being. Although these approaches are effective in the cultural context in which they have been implemented, it is important to say that in early child-hood education and care not only can we draw upon practices and examples from other cultures, but as practitioners we also need to develop a culturally appropriate practice that serves the purposes of our community and children. It is important when studying other approaches to assessment and documentation that we reflect on our practice and consider the purpose of our documentation, the degree to which a child's representation is contained in this process, that we allow space/s to enable the children to contribute to the review process and provide opportunities to create time for dia-logue with colleagues about how we interpret the material. Finally, we need to reflect on our own assessment processes to see to what extent they are inclusive of the range of voices and to create the possibilities for more of a listening culture.

Key points to remember

Pedagogical documentation can help early childhood practitioners to:

- include children in the documentation process and participation;

- facilitate the voice of the child through meaningful dialogues;

- create the conditions for children's symbolic representations and expression (Reggio Emilia);

- create the conditions for a listening culture (Hundred Languages).

Learning stories can help practitioners to:

- identify what the child already knows and their interests;

- engage with children to co-construct their learning intentions and experiences;

- enable the child's participation in documenting their own learning and holistic development.

Evaluation of levels of involvement and well-being can help practitioners to:

- consider the Laevers Scales of Well-being in children and levels of involvement as they refer to learning and development in children;

- evaluate the enabling environment, the quality and the process of experiential learning.

Points for discussion

- How would you discuss your 'scaffolding' of children's conversations with you?

- Why would you decide to implement a 'documentation system' in your setting? (and how might this improve your understanding of children's symbolic representation and their knowledge?)

- What technologies would you choose to represent the documentation to a wider audience, such as other colleagues and parents?

Further reading

Books

Carr, M. and Lee, W. (2012) *Learning Stories: Constructing Learner Identities in Early Education*. London: Sage.

Clark, A. and Moss, P. (2001) *Listening to Young Children: The Mosaic Approach*. London: National Children's Bureau.

Clark, A., Moss, P. and Kjorholt, A.T. (eds) (2005) *Beyond Listening to Children: Children's Perspectives on Early Childhood Services*. Bristol: The Policy Press.

Edwards, C., Gandini, L. and Forman, G. (eds) *The Hundred Languages of Children : The Reggio Emilia Experience in Transformation*, 3rd edn. California: Praeger.

Articles

Coates, E. (2002 '"I Forgot the Sky!" Children's stories contained within their drawings', *International Journal of Early Years Education*, 10 (1): 21–35.

Soler, J. and Miller, L. (2003) 'The struggle for early childhood curricula: a comparison of the English Foundation Stage curriculum, Te Whāriki and Reggio Emilia', *International Journal of Early Years Education*, 14 (2): 127–40.

Useful websites

Reggio Children – provides news, activities, professional development and case studies as well as promoting international recognition for the Reggio Emilia approach: www.reggiochildren. it/?lang=en

New Zealand Ministry of Education – Te Whāriki is the Ministry of Education's early childhood curriculum policy statement: www.educate.ece.govt.nz/learning/curriculumAndLearning/TeWhariki.aspx

References

Anning, A. and Ring, K. (2004) *Making Sense of Children's Drawings*. Maidenhead: McGraw–Hill: Open University Press.

Arizpe, E. and Styles, M. (2003) *Children Reading Pictures Interpreting Visual Texts*. London. Routledge Falmer.

Bruner, J. (1986) *Actual Minds, Possible Worlds*. Cambridge, MA: Harvard University Press.

Carr, M. (1999) *Learning and Teaching Stories: New Approaches to Assessment and Evaluation*. www.aare.edu.au/99pap/pod99298.htm (accessed December 2007).

Carr, M. (2001) *Assessment in Early Childhood Settings: Learning Stories*. London: Paul Chapman Publishing.

Carr, M., Smith, A.B., Duncan, J., Jones, C., Lee, W. and Marshall, K. (2010) *Learning in the Making: Disposition and Design in Early Education*. Sense Publishers: Rotterdam and New York.

Carr, M. and Lee, W. (2012) *Learning Stories: Constructing Learner Identities in Early Education*. London: Sage.

Clark, A. and Moss, P. (2001) *Listening to Young Children: The Mosaic Approach*. London: National Children's Bureau.

Coates, E. (2002 '"I Forgot the Sky!" Children's stories contained within their drawings', *International Journal of Early Years Education*,10 (1): 21–35.

DfE (Department for Education) (2014) *Statutory Framework for the Early Years Foundation Stage: Setting the Standards for Learning, Development and Care for Children from Birth to Five*. Available at: www.foundationyears.org.uk/files/2014/07/EYFS_framework_from_1_September_2014__with_clarification_note.pdf (accessed 21 September 2015).

Early Education (2012) *Development Matters in the Early Years Foundation* Stage (EYFS). London: Early Education.

Eisner, E.W. (1982) *Cognition and the Curriculum*. New York. London Longman.

Goouch, K. (2008) 'Understanding playful pedagogies, play narratives and play spaces', *Early Years*, 28 (1): 93–102.

Howard, J. (2010) 'Making the most of play in the early years: understanding and building on children's perceptions', In P. Broadhead, J. Howard and E. Wood (eds) *Play and Learning in Early Childhood: Research into Practice*. London: Sage.

Kress, G. (1997) *Before Writing: Rethinking Pathways to Literacy*. London: Routledge.

Laevers, F. (ed.) (2005) *Well-being and Involvement in Care Settings: A Process-Oriented Education Instrument*. Brussels: Kind and Gezint/Research Centre for Experiential Education.

Malaguzzi, L. (1993) 'For an education based on relationship', *Young Children*, 11: 9–13.

Malaguzzi, L. (1994) 'Your image of the child: Where teaching begins'. *Early Childhood Educational Exchange*, 96, 52–61.

Malchiodi, C.A. (1998) *Understanding Children's Drawings*. New York: Guilford Press.

Matthews. J. (1999) *The Art of Childhood and Adolescence. The Construction of Meaning*. London: Routledge Falmer.

NCTL (National College for Teaching and Leadership) (2013) *Teacher's Standards (Early Years)*. Available from: www.gov.uk/government/publications.

Pahl, K. (1999) *Transformations: Meaning Making in Nursery Education*. Stoke: Trentham Books.

Palaiologou, I. (ed) (2012) *Ethical Practice in Early Childhood*. London: Sage.

Palaiologou, I. (2014) 'Children under five and digital technologies: implications for Early Years Pedagogy', *European Early Childhood Education Research Journal*, DOI:10.1080/1350293X.2014.929876.

Project Zero (2001) Available at: http://www.pz.harvard.edu/ (accessed 29 January 2016).

Rinaldi, C. (1995) 'The emergent curriculum and the social constructivism: an interview with Lella Candini', in C. Edwards, L. Cangini and G. Forman (Eds) *The Hundred Languages of Children: the Reggio Emilia Approach to Early Childhood Education*. Norwood NJ: Ablex Publishing, pp. 233–46.

Rinaldi, C. (2006) *In Dialogue with Reggio Emilia: Listening, Researching and Learning*. Abingdon: Routledge.

Rogoff, B. (2003) *The Cultural Nature of Human Development*. New York: Oxford University Press.

Sylva, K., Melhuish, E., Sammons, P., Siraj-Blatchford, I. and Taggart, B. (2004) *The Effective Provision of Pre-School Education (EPPE) Project. Effective Pre-School Education: A Longitudinal Study funded by the DfES 1997–2004*. London: Department for Education and Skills.

Te Whāriki (1996) 'Early Childhood Curriculum'. New Zealand Ministry of Education. Wellington. New Zealand. Learning Media Ltd.

Thornton, L. and Brunton, P. (2007) *Bringing the Reggio Approach to Your Early Years Practice*. Abingdon: Routledge.

Tyler, J. (2002) *Te Whāriki: The New Zealand Curriculum Framework*. Available at: http://www.worldforumfoundation.org/wf/presentations/index.php?p=2002_tyler (accessed 5 July 2015).

Vygotsky, L. (1978) *Mind in Society: The Development of Higher Psychological Processes*. Cambridge, MA: Harvard University Press.

Want to learn more about this chapter? Visit the companion website at https://study.sagepub.com/EYFS3e for access to free SAGE journal articles and book chapters, weblinks, annotated further readings and more.

11

Effective Transitions

Angie Hutchinson and Ioanna Palaiologou

 Chapter overview

Children's experiences when they are growing up are full of changes, such as changes in their own bodies, in family circumstances, moving house, the possible break-up of the family or loss of a family member, going from home to a playgroup or nursery and then from nursery to school. All of these changes in a child's life can be regarded as transitions. The EPPE project (Sylva et al., 2003) revealed that children do actually experience a number of these transitions during the first years of their lives, describing two types of transitions: the 'horizontal' and the 'vertical'. Traditionally, moving from home to school (a horizontal displacement) was considered as the most important transition in children's lives. It is now recognised, however, that children move vertically in their lives, for example, from home to playgroup with a member of the family; also, as it is increasingly common for both parents to work, they move from their home to that of grandparents, or to half-day nursery and half-day playgroup, or childminder care.

The statutory framework for the EYFS is concerned with school readiness. It should be rather that early childhood settings and schools should be ready for the children by offering them rich experiences and stimulating learning environments.

(Continued)

(Continued)

Within the EYFS there is now an expectation that children are ready for entry to school in the key three prime areas: personal, social and emotional development, communication and language, and physical development. An integrated review at the age of 2 years has also been introduced, an assessment undertaken by practitioners to ensure that children's learning and development needs are identified early. The summary of the integrated review will be communicated if the child moves settings. There is also the EYFS Profile (EYFSP) report that aims to 'inform a dialogue between Reception and Year 1 teachers about each child's stage of development and learning needs and assist with the planning activities in Year 1' (DfE, 2014: 14).

In order to build effective and strong foundations in children's lives, however, it is important for practitioners to understand the importance of transitions in children's lives and try to accommodate these transitions. Early childhood settings and schools maintain a critical role in delivering a coherent approach both to the continuation of EYFS and when children are moving to Key Stage 1. The smooth transitions into and out of EYFS are important for children's well-being and, therefore, for their development. This chapter deals with the key issues around transitions and discusses theoretical perspectives in trying to understand transition and its implications for practice.

This chapter aims to help you to:

- understand the theoretical aspects of transitions
- understand the impact of transitions upon children's well-being and development
- examine how effective transitions can be implemented into and out of EYFS.

Understanding transitions: theoretical perspectives

In their lives children go through several transitions, such as: external transitions from home to the early childhood setting, from the setting to school, from school to childminders; or inner transitions such as their developmental growth and the changes that happen in their bodies. Transition is a complex concept as it is not only limited to changes in physical locations. Gorgorio et al. define transitions as:

> [n]ot as a moment of change, but as the experience of changing, of living the discontinuities between the different contexts … the construct 'transition' is, in our understanding a plural one. Transitions arise from the individual's need to live, cope and participate in

different contexts, to face different challenges, to take profit from the advantages of the new situation arising from the changes. Transitions include the process of adapting to new social and cultural experiences. (2002: 24)

A number of theorists have examined the concept of transitions and their impact on children's lives. James (1980), for example, discussed transitions in relation to self and self-identity (inner transitions as psychological and developmental changes that happen in individuals), whereas Erikson (1975) discussed transitions in relation to physical moves from one place to another (external transition). Piaget (1976) linked transitions with cognitive development and claimed that transitions bring children in a disequilibrium situation that can have an impact on their development. Vygotsky (1978) suggested that children try to construct knowledge through interacting with their social environment and are influenced by the culture, beliefs and values of this environment. In that sense, transitions can be viewed as a process where children try to make sense of the world and the communities to which they belong.

Bronfenbrenner (1979) approaches transitions from an ecological perspective and defines transitions as an alteration to a person's ecological environment that brings changes in a person's self or social identity, changes in physical spaces, or both. He identified 'systems' – layers that we move into and out of throughout our lives. He claims, for example, that the microsystem (of home, playgroup, or childminder) of a child's life is rich in transitions, and these have an effect on a child's well-being. Bronfenbrenner emphasised, for the child's well-being, the need for links in between the systems:

> The developmental potential of a setting is increased as a function of the number of supportive links existing between the setting and other settings (such as the home and the family). Thus, the least favourable condition for development is one in which supplementary links are either non-supportive or completely absent, when the mesosystem is weakly linked. (1979: 215)

Consequently, for Bronfenbrenner, when a child is moving from home to an early childhood setting or a Reception class it represents not only a change in the layers of his/her environment, but equally a change in this child's identity from 'child' to 'pupil'. In that sense, practitioners should understand that in order to effectively accommodate young children they need to ensure that they provide an environment where there is emphasis on the inner changes that happen to children as well as the external changes.

Brooker (2002) extended the work of Bronfenbrenner and examined the role of culture in transitions. She researched children's, parents' and teachers' experiences in relation to social class, culture, religion, linguistics and other macro systemic factors. She found that children had to adjust to school life, classroom rituals, rules, codes of communication and interaction, but at the same time recognised that an imbalance between home and classroom life could emerge. A classic example she offers is that some parents might advise their children to do what the teacher tells them to do in the classroom, yet this can be in direct conflict with what the teacher is trying to achieve with the pupils when promoting independent and autonomous learning.

In an earlier study, Beach (1999) tried to investigate how people transfer knowledge and skills successfully from one context to another: for example, if a child is using strategies to cope with literacy skills such as synthetic phonics at school, whether this child uses the same strategies to effectively read at home or in real life situations. He argues that transitions are consequential in the sense that they have an impact on the person and his/her social context and claims that transition 'is the conscious reflective struggle to reconstruct knowledge, skills, and identity in ways that are consequential to the individual becoming someone or something new' (Beach, 1999: 30). He suggests a typology in an attempt to understand the inner and external conflicts of transitions:

- *Lateral transitions* which involve the moves between two activities (such as moving from an early childhood setting to Reception class). In lateral transitions the person is replacing one activity (the early childhood setting) with another activity (Reception class) and this move is involving progression.
- *Collateral transitions* where an individual is involved in two or more related activities and they move simultaneously to both; for example, the move from home to early childhood setting where children are asked to move to different activities in the setting. This type of transition does not have the element of progression.
- *Encompassing transitions* which take place within the boundaries of an activity that is itself changing and the individual has to adjust in order to participate in the activity. For example, children during role-play decide to change the play so individual children either have to adapt to the change or otherwise they will not be able to participate in the new activity that has emerged.
- *Mediational transitions* which are mainly related to educational activities. For example, we create an activity where children are playing post office and exchange money when they are not old enough to have their own money. In early childhood settings we can see mediational transitions with boys, for example pretending they hold guns and play war when in real life they are not allowed to have guns (especially common in Greek early childhood education where military service is compulsory for all young men at the age of 18), or girls where they pretend to wear shoes with high heels or to use make-up.

Beach's research on consequential transitions has a number of implications for early childhood education and care. Practitioners should create a learning environment where children effectively are prepared to move from home to the setting and vice versa, but at the same time effectively be prepared to move in between activities. The concept of meditational transitions also enables children to experience real-life situations in a safe and secure environment.

Beach's work demonstrated that transitions are a 'struggle', but at the same time he found that transitions have the potential to 'alter one's sense of self' (1999: 114). Evangelou et al. (2008) add that successful transitions can change children's sense of self through improved confidence and self-esteem. The uncertainty and anxiety that occurs from changes in one's life can be problematic, however, with Zittoun (2006) referring to problems that might occur in transitions as 'rupture'. He has described three types of rupture that can occur as a result of transitions:

- Change in cultural context that can be a result of a war, natural catastrophe such as an earthquake or flood, or a technological change that brings radical change in one's life. This can be seen in children who have experienced war or the violent death of a parent.
- Change to a person's 'sphere of experience', such as moving countries, houses or schools.
- Changes in relationships or interaction, for example a new key person, a teacher or a friend is moving to another city and leaves the nursery; or there is a divorce in the family or a bereavement with loss of a loved one.

Zittoun's idea of rupture in transitions has implication in early childhood settings as it can be seen that children's lives can be complex and changes do occur consequently that have an impact on their lives. The importance of understanding the theoretical perspectives of transitions helps us to understand the role of the social environment and the cultural environment, and invest in implementing 'personalised, flexible, comprehensive, multi-faceted and prolonged approaches to transition support which accommodate individual variability' (Crafter and Maunder, 2012: 16).

Case study

Saffinatu moves to England from Sierra Leone

Saffinatu is 4 years old and she has moved with her mother from Sierra Leone. Her father died from malaria and her mother then moved to England where she is now staying with extended family. Saffinatu's mother works for a domestic cleaning company so Saffinatu attends an early childhood setting every day from 8:00am to 3:30pm. When she first arrived in the setting she could not speak English and lacked confidence to interact with other children. Her key person observed that she was demonstrating distress in the presence of other adults, such as parents of other children, and anxiety every time she was spoken to by a member of staff.

(Continued)

(Continued)

The practitioners in the setting worked with the Integrated Child Support Service 0–5 (ICSS) to implement a transition plan for Saffinatu. (For more information visit: www.south wark.gov.uk/info/200071/information_for_parents/2154/child_support_services/1).

The practitioners created a plan to support Saffinatu to achieve good levels in the EYFS Profile. The ICSS Transition Protocol was implemented and the Southwark Transition and Assessment Record (STAR) was developed.

Summary of Saffinatu's Transition Plan

Target 1:   Encourage functional communication system with the mother and the extended family and the Team Around the Child (TAC) to reflect on what is best for Saffinatu in terms of promoting all prime areas: PSED, communication and language, and physical development;

Target 2:   Create familiarity in terms of her culture, language, physical environment. Priority on building relationships with the mother and the extended family so they can be actively involved. Home visits to be encouraged;

Target 3:   TAC to provide psychological support to Saffinatu and her family. Practitioners to create an environment where Saffinatu has a sense of belonging, with familiar items, such as toys, food and photos;

Target 4:   Encourage Saffinatu to engage with activities and play indoors and outdoors.

The practitioners in the setting also used the Ecological and Dynamic Model *Ready Schools* framework (for more see the work of Pianta and Walsh, 1996; Pianta et al., 1999) and they developed steps of action:

Step 1:   Encourage strong links with the family and the nursery with visits to home.

Step 2:   Make connections with familiar contexts and if possible establish a continuation and connections in activities and other aspects of home and early childhood setting life.

Step 3:   To give adequate time to adjust to the new environment.

The practitioners decided to use the Ecological and Dynamic Model of Transitions as it provides a framework that allows multi-agency collaboration, with a number of external agencies such as psychologists, social workers and health visitors working at a number of levels in the transition process.

Reflective task

- Reflect on Saffinatu's case study. Using Bronfenbrenner's explanation of the ecological approach to transition discuss what inner and external changes Saffinatu is experiencing. Reflecting on Zittoun's types of rupture, what types can you identify in Saffinatu's life?

Attachment and transitions

As will also be seen in Chapter 19, Attachment Theory, as introduced by Bowlby (1969), has an impact on early childhood education and care. Attachment is the process where babies and parents or carers form a relationship and this leads to emotional bonds. Bowlby (1969) suggested that babies show stranger anxiety, a fear of unfamiliar persons or unfamiliar contexts, and this often causes stress to babies and young children. They also show separation anxiety at about the age of 6 months. This is a fear of being separated from care-givers (Vondra and Barnett, 1999). Babies appear to be upset when their parents or carers are leaving them and this can again cause distress. Early childhood practitioners who work with babies and toddlers are familiar with the signs of a child being distressed when the child initially arrives in the unfamiliar early childhood setting. Practitioners typically find the first few weeks in the setting the most difficult and challenging for children, who are anxious, distressed and disturbed until they settle down.

The dominant theory in the emotional development of children is that proposed by Bowlby (1951a, 1960, 1969, 1973, 1980, 1999, 2005) and Ainsworth (Ainsworth, 1969, 1979, 1985, 1989; Ainsworth and Bell, 1970; Ainsworth and Bowlby, 1991; Ainsworth et al., 1971a, 1971b, 1978) regarding 'attachment'. All these studies proposed that when babies are born they are 'pre-programmed' to form close relationships with the mother/carer. This bond is attachment. The ideas of Bowlby and Ainsworth have influenced the way mother–child and carer–child relationships are perceived. Bowlby and Ainsworth have each described in detail the stages of attachment and how the formation of the relationship between the mother (or carer) and the baby takes place. They have also discussed the consequences of the separation of the child from the mother/carer.

Bowlby (1969) proposed four main stages in the development of attachment. First, he claims that when babies are born and at about the age of 2 months they are in an 'orientation' stage, where the infant shows orientation to social stimuli such as grasping, smiling and babbling. The babies will stop crying when they are picked up or when they see a face or hear a familiar voice. These behaviours increase when the baby is in proximity to a companion or another person, mainly the parent or the carer, although the baby cannot distinguish one person from another; for example, they cannot yet distinguish the mother from the father. Evidence of discrimination begins at about 4 weeks, when the baby is listening to sounds such as the mother's voice, and at about the age of 10 weeks the orientation becomes visual: the baby tends to recognise the face of the mother and smile towards her.

Second, when babies grow to about the age of 3–6 months, their orientation to signals is directed towards one or more discriminated figures. It has been observed that slightly older babies direct their orientation to the primary care-giver.

Third, when babies are 6–30 months old, their repertoire of responses to people increases to include visually following a departing mother, greeting her on return and using her as a base for explorations. It is at that age when babies treat strangers with caution and may evidence alarm or withdrawal expressed through intense crying.

At the final stage, and at about the age of 24–48 months, the child begins to acquire insight into the mother's feelings and goals, which leads to cooperative interaction and partnership (Bowlby, 1969).

What is important with regards attachment theory is that:

> the infant and young children should experience a warm, intimate and continuous relationship with his mother (or permanent mother substitute), in which both find satisfaction and enjoyment. (Bowlby, 1951b: 13)

Attachment theory has demonstrated that the transition from home to school and the separation from the mother/carer is an emotional journey for children, thus early childhood education and care needs to create an environment where the 'loss' of attachment to mother/carer is acknowledged and children are given time to adjust to the change from home to the setting. The setting should create an environment that reflects warmth and enables children to have a sense of belonging. Activities such as encouraging children to bring photographs of their families or a display with photographs of children's family lives can become a comfort point for children. Prior to children's transition from home to a Foundation Stage, some settings hand an 'All About Me' booklet to the parents for them to complete with their child at home and bring into the setting on their first day. This involves parents in the transition (which will be discussed further momentarily), and gives the practitioners information about the children which help them to feel welcome. For example, a practitioner may use the information in the booklet to initiate a conversation around special people in the child's life, their pets or their likes and dislikes. Forming positive relationships early in the transition is important so the child feels secure and valued.

Reflective task

- Reflect on Beach's consequential transitions and discuss what types of transitions take place in early childhood education and care, and think how you can engage the families, other services and the children to overcome complexities of the transitions.

Transitional objects

Winnicott (1986, 1987, 1995, 2005) started his career as a paediatrician and sought to understand how children develop the concept of self into the context of the bonds they have with their parents. He investigated how children develop a healthy 'genuine self', as opposed to a 'false self', by looking closely at the relationships parents form with their children.

Winnicott uses the term 'self' to describe both 'ego' and self-as-object. He describes the self in terms of 'genuine' or 'true self', and 'false self'. For Winnicott, the 'genuine' or 'true self' is developed when the babies form their personalities by developing the capacity to recognise their needs and to express these. When babies are able genuinely to express their needs and their emotions, they are in the state of genuine or true self. For example, when a baby is hungry he or she usually cries. The mother responds to the crying by feeding the baby. Upon repetition of this behaviour the babies will realise that when they are hungry, they cry; the mother will feed them, thus their need will be met. A stable, consistent response or reaction by the mother to the baby's needs will help the baby to develop the genuine self. True self develops successfully only when the mother responds to the baby's spontaneous expressions and needs.

If the babies are growing up in an environment where their needs are not covered, however, they will build a 'false self'. Their real needs will not be expressed, which is a kind of mechanism for defending their 'true self' and is an unconscious process. Through the interactions with the mother or primary carer the babies are learning through experience and they begin to make sense of the world or, as Winnicott called it, acquire 'object reality'. The baby and carer enter what feels like a place of their own. Winnicott named that space a 'holding environment', which includes language and psychological and physical interactions between a mother and an infant. Thus, a holding environment is a space that is emotional and physical where the babies are protected without knowing they are protected. He claimed that for a child to form a healthy sense of self it is important for the child to know that the mother will be there when she is needed. Such a relationship with the mother makes the infant feel secure and protected; the child will then be well equipped to form a healthy self-concept.

The study of the 'holding environment' led Winnicott to develop his influential idea of the 'transitional experience'. He suggested that when children start becoming independent, for example when moving from the home to the outside world (such as to a nursery or a school), they need to represent their mothers when they are absent in order to feel secure. Children use objects such as teddy bears, blankets and dolls as transitional objects through which they facilitate a symbolic representation of the mother. In this way children can start enjoying the new environment into which they are moving (e.g. the nursery or the school) and become creative and independent; at the same time, the comfort provided by the transitional objects makes them feel protected.

The importance of transition objects has implications for children's transitions into and out of the EYFS. This also raises the issue of respecting the objects brought with them from home by the children when they come to the nursery.

Steps towards effective transitions: early childhood settings' readiness versus child's readiness

Develop a transition action plan

Although the EYFS argues that early childhood education and care should prepare children to be 'ready' for school, what will be argued here is that for effective transitions it is essential to prepare to receive children rather than to prepare children to 'fit' into the early childhood environment.

Practitioners have realised the significance of transitions in children's well-being and development. Thus, many settings and schools have developed 'transition programmes' consisting of a range of activities occurring throughout the year and constituting a process for preparing the children to accommodate 'horizontal' transitions. It is important, however, that early childhood settings develop action plans or transition programmes to also prepare children for 'vertical' transitions.

Many settings have adopted the Southwark Transition and Assessment Record (STAR) and the Integrated Child Support Service 0–5 component Transitions Protocol. STAR can become a useful tool for gathering information about individual children and it can provide the setting with necessary information to support transitions and aid the sharing of information with schools in order to meet the requirements of the EYFS.

An action plan is essential to make sure that the process of transition is implemented; it must not be forgotten or left too late in the hurry of the daily routine of the setting. All members of staff should participate in this action plan as each has an important role to play. Within this action plan practicalities need to be considered, such as completing the Integrated Review at Age Two in order for it to arrive at the new setting in time, determining who is going to work with the child (i.e. the key worker) and how many hours during the first couple of weeks a child will stay in the setting (see Chapter 9).

This action plan needs to involve the staff, children and parents. Brooker (2008) stresses the importance of this relationship and she describes it as 'a caring triangle'. She identifies three key processes for effective planning:

- understanding routines in the setting and at home, such as sleeping habits, feeding habits (for younger children) or children's interests (for example, whether they like to play outdoors or with construction materials);

- enjoying relationships and having pleasurable interaction with other children: friendships in the setting should be encouraged amongst children;
- making links with the outside world: 'Enabling Environments' is a principle within the EYFS, and the outside-of-the-class life of children is important; for example, little items such as a photograph of parents or a little toy help children to 'transfer' their own environment into the setting, as will be explained later in this chapter.

Involve the children

During transitions it is important for children to be actively involved in the process. Throughout the EYFS one of the key issues is to listen to the children, to ascertain how they feel about the setting, which activities they like to participate in and in which area in the setting they prefer to be. Observations are important in listening to children and involving them in the transitions. As was explained in Chapter 6, observations are a useful tool for assessment, while they also enable practitioners to listen to the children and understand their needs. Observations help recognise what the children like or dislike, especially where younger children (0–2) are concerned, as with their limited spoken language repertoire they cannot always effectively express what they want.

Case study

From home to nursery

Harry is 18 months old. He is starting private nursery care for three days a week for not more than three hours per session. The parents have decided to send him to the nursery as he is the only child in the family and they have noticed that he is not interacting with other children of his own age. His mother is not working so she can be reached any time. Prior to the official starting date, there were a few visits to the setting so that Harry could familiarise himself with the place.

During the first 'official' day at nursery Harry and his mother enter through the main door and Harry immediately runs to the outdoor area. He takes out his little red car and starts playing with it. The practitioner invites him into the class, but he declines to enter. His mother says goodbye and she leaves. Harry seems fine when his mother has left, but he still does not want to go inside. He enjoys playing in the outdoors area on his own.

(Continued)

(Continued)

The practitioner leaves the door open in case he wants to come inside and join the other children. Harry is observing what happens in the classroom area, yet he does not want to come indoors.

Harry spent the first month in the outdoors area observing what was happening indoors, sometimes joining in with a nursery rhyme and making moves to accompany them, although still on his own outside. It took him a month to come inside the class, and the first activity he joined in with was singing.

Reflective task

As the EYFS emphasises, and as High (2008: 1008) stresses, 'school readiness includes … the "readiness" of the individual child, the school's readiness for children and the ability of the family to communicate and support optimal child development'. In that sense transitions are complex, influenced by a number of factors and reflect interactions and relationships among the child, nursery, school, family and community factors such as culture, religion and language.

- Consider what implications this might have for the experiences of children's transitions in relation to the EYFS and how this impacts on your practice. What implications might this have for Harry's transition to the setting?

In this case the practitioners did not force Harry to come indoors and they were 'listening' to Harry's needs. He was ready to be in the nursery, although he was not ready to be indoors with others. When he was indeed ready, he moved of his own volition. During this transition from home to the setting Harry was listened to and involved in the transition – he was not forced to be indoors, but was given appropriate time in which to feel comfortable to join in with indoor activities at the moment of his choosing.

Another key issue for effective transitions is to understand and respect the objects brought by children into the class from home. These objects, as Winnicott's theory on transitional objects has demonstrated (the little toys that children carry with them), offer emotional comfort to young children, who carry and regard them as symbols: the items symbolise the continuation from home to the setting. Examining the theory of attachment, and focusing on the work of Bowlby and Ainsworth, the importance of these objects carried by children during transitions is that they are essential for the children's well-being. In the above case study of Harry, he had a little red car with him for two months. For the first month it never left his hands. During the second month, when he was coming into the setting, he wanted the toy for a while, and then, at the practitioner's suggestion, he left the car with the practitioner to 'sleep'. He always remembered to take it away with him, however, when he left the setting. Harry was observed again after seven months. He was still bringing in his little red car, but as soon as he arrived in the nursery he immediately gave it into the safekeeping of the practitioner.

It is very important that practitioners make every effort to ensure that children feel both confident and supported when they are still new to the environment, making sure the vocabulary is appropriate and that the children understand what it means. Each setting uses different terms to describe certain items or activities; for example, in a setting the staff may call the construction area something different from the term used in the Foundation Stage. So it is important to find out and clarify that everyone knows what items and locations are going to be called and therefore prevent confusion.

It is essential to explain what words mean – 'assembly', for instance, and 'corridor': words and concepts that adults use unconsciously yet that may not be familiar to children. Another example is the instruction 'Sit in a circle': 'But what is a circle?', 'How can I sit in a circle if there isn't one?'

As soon as children establish a relationship in the setting or school then they are ready to leave behind the objects they carry. Still, however, many children might feel the need to have them in their bags, such is the emotional attachment to these objects. Working in early childhood education and care, it is important to respect the children's need to bring little objects from home and what these objects mean for them. It is also essential to allow them to choose the materials they want to play with, to respect a child's daily routines and not to discourage constant links with home.

Involve the parents

Throughout the EYFS, the role of parents is highly emphasised. It is suggested that parents should be part of children's education and care and be encouraged to remain actively involved in all processes. The 'curriculum' of family life is vitally important because this is where young children spend much of their time. It is essential that we engage the parents so that there is a 'joined-up' aspect to the child's experiences.

What is important to understand when practitioners involve parents is that they themselves are also going through transitions. For example, they move between home and work and back again, changing 'hats' from parent to teacher, from daughter to mother, from son to father, and so on. As with early childhood practitioners, parents are as strongly influenced by the 'transition effect' as are their children. It also needs to be acknowledged that parents feel anxiety about their children's transitions. This is where the importance of taster sessions or a period of phased transition comes into play. Some settings may invite the child and the parent in prior to the child's official start date.

This is an excellent opportunity not only to build early relationships with the parents and the child, but it also has another important factor. When the children attend these taster sessions they are becoming familiar with the layout of the setting, they will develop an awareness of the activities available, they will remember other children who will become their peers and they will also develop a familiarity with the adults based there. The benefits of such taster sessions are two-fold. First, they will alleviate first-day anxiety for the child as they will be entering a setting with which they are familiar and, second, they alleviate first-day anxiety for the parent whose emotions may sometimes be overlooked. They will already have a good rapport with staff and know that their child will be safe and happy at the setting. Of course, they see the effect of the stress in the children at home in ways that may not be reported to the setting or the school, especially if the relationship with staff has not been established. Perhaps a child has started bed-wetting, or using 'baby talk'; perhaps a child is misbehaving, unusually, or perhaps they spend a lot of time hiding under their bed. All these may be signs that a child is stressed and the cause of this could be their transition. It is imperative that the parents are involved in the process of preparing the child to 'go up'. As mentioned above, Bronfenbrenner (1979) has shown that the more practitioners can combine the interactions of settings that the child has in his life (i.e. not just 'him-and-school' or 'him-and-parents', but 'him-*and*-school-*and*-parents') the more effective the child's development will be. Since the child's family home is the most important setting (because this is where he/she spends most of his/her time and is most strongly emotionally influenced) it is important that the setting communicates with the parents in a practical and positive way.

Building positive relationships with the parents helps effective transitions (for more on working with parents see Chapter 13). It is important to involve parents directly by making them feel really welcome in the setting by inviting them into the room to sit with their children and getting to know them (i.e. involving them not only in times of a crisis or trouble). The earlier the positive relationship is built with parents the better, and recognising this, some Foundation Stages offer the taster sessions previously mentioned prior to the child's first day where parents can stay with their child for part of a session. Once the child's start date arrives, it continues to be important for the setting to be welcoming to the parents. Some settings may encourage parents to stay a while at the beginning of the session where they can support their child with a short activity (name recognition or mark making for example). The parent leaves when they feel their child is settled. It is worth noting that the focus here is not on academic progress, but rather on welcoming the parent into the setting to enjoy these first few minutes of each session together. Furthermore, some settings hold special days for parents to stay and be involved for a part or a full session. Practitioners may use these event days to showcase teaching and learning in the EYFS, the teaching of phonics for example, so that parents may take new knowledge home with them so they feel confident in supporting their child. Furthermore, they provide a way to keep an open dialogue with the parents; a way of ensuring the home–school relationship is maintained.

Parents may also be kept informed of activities at the setting through the use of social media and many settings have accounts where they post photographs, statements and videos of the activities (see Chapter 13 on the use of digital media in building relationships with the parents for more ideas). This can be used as a conversation starter with young children once at home and an experience that parent and child can share. Newsletters too are often handed to parents, which draw attention not only to past activities but to future plans and important forthcoming events. All of this helps to keep parents informed and included in their child's care and education.

Documenting children's activities and sharing them with the parents helps to involve them indirectly (as has been shown in Chapters 8, 9 and 13).

Familiar staff – the key person

As has been shown above, for young children attachment is important to their emotional and social development. The EYFS has addressed this by identifying a key person for each child (see Chapter 19 for the role of the key person). For example, there may be three or four adults in Foundation Stage 1 and the children are divided equally between the adults and placed into groups. In every session there will be a 'Keyworker Group' session during which there will be similar activities. The children will quickly become familiar with this group and with their peers as well as with the practitioner who leads the group. Every day, the children will know that when this session happens, they will talk about the day of the week, the weather, count the number of children in the group, watch as writing is modelled and they will engage in frequently repeated songs. The children are thus given structure and consistency and opportunities to develop not only speaking and listening skills, but also their confidence and self-esteem in a small group. Some children can find large, whole-class activities and even free-play quite daunting, so this quiet time can help them to find their voice and to find comfort as this activity becomes routine.

The children may be able to discuss with their key person fears and concerns they are experiencing, as they will know this person well and they will have started establishing a relationship with them. Children are sometimes happier talking to a toy or a puppet, however, than to an adult – and if the Foundation Stage practitioners and Year 1 teachers use this knowledge to bring questions and concerns out into the open, this will lead to conversations and discussions through which fears can be expressed.

Visits and cross-phase activities

One of the strategies that can be developed to smooth transitions is to set up a series of visits in either direction for specific age groups: for example, younger children might go to visit their future class, and the Year 1 children might visit the Foundation Stage settings. These visits can lead to a project such as a 'post office' area, where there are exchanges of letters between Foundation Stages 1 and 2, or between Foundation Stage and Key Stage 1. Visits and cross-phase activities are a helpful technique, not only to ease the transition process, but also to provide enabling environments effectively.

Some settings may have completely separate Foundation Stage 1 (F1) and Foundation Stage 2 (F2) classes and other settings may operate as a Foundation Unit where there are mixed F1 and F2 with children sharing the same space. Some may even have a separate F1 and F2, but at certain times of the day open their doors, allowing the children to mix. This can help the F1 children to transition to F2. It can sometimes be tricky to allow the same transition opportunities to F2 children in readiness for Year 1 due to the logistics in a primary school setting, but nevertheless although these children may not get the opportunity throughout the year, they are often offered a transition stage during their last week in F2 to spend a whole week in their new classroom with their new teacher.

Quite often, the children have friends or siblings in the adjoining class so there can be benefits in a joined-up approach between the Foundation Stages. The older F2 children can use this time to scaffold their talents to the younger children and quite often the F2 children enjoy visiting their 'old' class and reminiscing about their time there. This being said, there can also be instances to be aware of as a practitioner. Those quiet, less confident children who are new to F1 may feel intimidated by a swell of children into their class. These children entering their 'safe' environment (their classroom) are much bigger, much louder and much quicker on their feet and this can make their classroom or their outdoor play area a scary place to be. There could be, for example, a sudden influx of a two-form entry F2 class of 60 children coming into F1 and care should be taken by the adults in the setting to ensure the emotional development of the younger F1 children does not become hindered. So, indeed there are advantages of joining F1 and F2 in relation to social and emotional learning, but practitioners should also be mindful of the disadvantages of this approach.

Case study

'Our post office': an opportunity to visit a KS1 class

After a visit to a local post office, the children created a post office area in a Foundation Stage class. In this area there were stamps, pens, envelopes, a set of scales and other material that one can find in a post office.

The children started writing letters and cards they wanted to post. The Foundation Stage teacher suggested posting letters to KS1 children. In this way they began a long and complex project where the two groups of children communicated with each other and provided a real opportunity for cross-phase working, which could be built upon during transition discussions.

Transitioning between activities

Transitioning between activities should be as well thought out as the activities them-selves. In some settings, the adults will begin a series of claps to signal to the children that it is time to stop and listen. Others may sound a musical instrument to gain the children's attention. Others may play a 'tidy-up' song as an auditory marker for the chil-dren. There are many ways to transition between activities and even the youngest of children newly entering F1 will quickly become familiar with the routine of stop, listen and tidy if done regularly enough. Even with no clapping or instrument to attract atten-tion, just the playing of a familiar tidy up tune will often trigger the children to tidy as they can associate a certain noise from a musical instrument with the routine of tidying up. As well as ensuring children are where they need to be, when they need to be, this transitioning routine in between activities helps to support the children. It is important for them to understand that there is going to be a change, and for them to be prepared for this change. A visual countdown on a computer or whiteboard can also be helpful for the children as they can see how long they have left to complete the transition.

Reflective task

- Reflect on the following scenario: There are 43 F1 children all engaged in free-choice play. The children are spread in equal proportion around the setting, the noise level is moderate and you need to begin a 'tidy-up' session so that you can begin your routine 'Keyworker Group'. How do you make them stop? Consider and plan how you support children through transitions between activities.

Use the outdoors

Many Foundation Stage classrooms and early childhood settings have their own out-side space so that there can be freedom to move between the indoor and outdoor areas. The outside is vital for children, so every effort should be made by KS1 regularly to go outside for work to take place there. (see Chapter 12 for more information and examples of the use of outdoors).

Staff liaison and transfer of records

Transfer of records such as the Integrated Review at Age Two is an important aspect of the EYFS (see Chapter 11). Transferring children's official records helps staff to familiarise themselves with the children's needs and the ethos of the EYFS, and to see how it can be transferred over to the National Curriculum.

Certain skills and abilities are to be expected after transition. If there is a lack of understanding, however, about a child's previous experience of learning – and, therefore, a lack of transition of methods – then the skills and abilities acquired by the child during EYFS might not be taken into consideration, with the result that learning opportunities are subsequently lost. Foundation Stage staff need to ensure that KS1 staff have attained the required understanding, in order to ensure that the delivery is appropriate until the children are settled. Otherwise, there is a clear danger that the children may become de-motivated because everything is so different. It is also important that the Foundation Stage staff have an understanding of the National Curriculum requirements in KS1 and can play their part in preparing children for the transition.

Summary

This chapter discussed the complex nature of transitions experienced by young children when leaving home for early childhood education and care. Transitions are changes that take place in individuals' lives and these may be not only inner psychological transitions such as developmental growth or constructions of self-identity, but also external transitions such as moving physical spaces or moving countries and cultures. All these changes have an impact on children's social, emotional, personal and cognitive development. It is important that policy makers take on board the impact transitions can have in children's lives. It is also necessary to create environments in settings that take into consideration the impact of transitions on children's learning and development and ensure that the environment offers smooth transitions and facilitates effective functioning of various contexts, cultures, religions and languages in which children live, learn and develop. Effective transitions in early childhood education and care should focus on supporting parents, children, practitioners and other key staff in creating effective environments to facilitate the transitions of children and not changing the child to 'fit' in the environment.

> ### Key points to remember
>
> - This chapter discussed the important role of transitions in children's lives. Transitions can become stressful for children and subsequently have an impact on children's well-being. Transitions cannot be avoided, but they can be effectively planned and organised so that the social and emotional effects of transition will not have a negative impact on children's well-being.

- This chapter offered some steps that can help children to experience effective transitions into and out of the EYFS. There is great emphasis on involving the children themselves in the process, as well as involving the parents. Early childhood practitioners should become facilitators in the transition processes of children, involving all staff in the environment, and creating creative and stimulating activities for children.

Points for discussion

- Imagine that a child in your setting is going away for a month. Can you create an action plan to smooth the transition for when he or she returns? How can you prepare the parents and the child before their departure and how can you welcome the child back?

- Study the EYFS and the KS1 curriculum and try to identify the differences (and similarities) between these two curricula. How can you prepare children for KS1?

- What are the main challenges faced by practitioners when they try to implement an 'enabling environment', organising visits and shared play, and liaising with other staff?

Further reading

Books

Brooker, L. (2008) *Supporting Transitions in the Early Years*. Maidenhead: Open University Press.

Dunlop, A.W. and Fabian, H. (eds) (2007) *Informing Transitions in the Early Years: Research, Policy and Practice*. Maidenhead: Open University Press.

Articles

Ainsworth, M.D.S. (1989) 'Attachment beyond infancy', *American Psychologist*, 44: 709–16.

Crafter, S. and Maunder, R. (2012) 'Understanding transitions using a sociocultural framework', *Educational and Child Psychology*, 29 (1): 10–18.

Useful websites

Southwark Integrated Child Support Service 0–5:
www.southwark.gov.uk/info/200335/pupil_health_and_wellbeing/956/educational_psychology/5

Early interventions support children and families:
www.corechildrensservices.co.uk/what-we-do/early-interventions

Early Intervention: the next steps (Allen, 2011):
www.preventionaction.org/prevention-news/allens-early-intervention-next-steps/5476

C4EO is a partner with NCB in a programme funded by the DfE, aiming to:

- identify and work towards direct outcomes for children and families;
- improve leadership and performance;
- embed peer-to-peer support and challenge;
- understand the requirements of a revised EYFS.

www.c4eo.org.uk

References

Ainsworth, M.D.S. (1969) 'Object relations, dependency, and attachment: a theoretical review of the infant–mother relationship', *Child Development*, 40: 969–1025.

Ainsworth, M.D.S. (1979) 'Attachment as related to mother–infant interaction', *Advances in the Study of Behaviour*, 9: 2–52.

Ainsworth, M.D.S. (1985) 'Attachments across the life span', *Bulletin of the New York Academy of Medicine*, 61: 792–812.

Ainsworth, M.D.S. (1989) 'Attachment beyond infancy', *American Psychologist*, 44: 709–16.

Ainsworth, M.D.S. and Bell, S.M. (1970) 'Attachment, exploration, and separation: illustrated by the behaviour of one-year-olds in a strange situation', *Child Development*, 41: 49–67.

Ainsworth, M.D.S. and Bowlby, J. (1991) 'An ethological approach to personality development', *American Psychologist*, 46: 333–41.

Ainsworth, M.D.S., Bell, S.M. and Stayton, D.J. (1971a) 'Individual differences in the strange situation behaviour of one-year-olds', in H.R. Schaffer (ed.), *The Origins of Human Social Relations*. New York: Academic Press. pp. 15–71.

Ainsworth, M.D.S., Bell, S.M., Blehar, M.C. and Main, M. (1971b) 'Physical contact: a study of infant responsiveness and its relation to maternal handling'. Paper presented at the biennial meeting of the Society for Research in Child Development, Minneapolis, MN.

Ainsworth, M.D.S., Blehar, M.C., Waters, E. and Wall, S. (1978) *Patterns of Attachment: A Study of the Strange Situation*. Hillsdale, NJ: Erlbaum Associates.

Beach, K.D. (1999) 'Consequential transitions: a sociocultural expedition beyond transfer in education', *Review of Research in Education*, 24: 101–39.

Bowlby, J. (1951a) *Maternal Care and Mental Health*. Geneva: World Health Organisation Monograph (Serial No. 2).

Bowlby, J. (1951b) *Child Care and the Growth of Love*. Harmondsworth: Penguin.

Bowlby, J. (1960) 'Grief and mourning in infancy and early childhood', *The Psychoanalytic Study of the Child*, 15: 9–52.

Bowlby, J. (1969) *Attachment and Loss, Volume 2. Separation: Anxiety and Anger*. New York: Basic Books.

Bowlby, J. (1973) *Attachment and Loss, Volume 2. Separation: Anxiety and Anger*. (International Psycho-analytical Library No. 95). London: Hogarth Press.

Bowlby, J. (1980) *Attachment and Loss, Volume 3. Loss: Sadness and Depression*. (International Psycho-analytical Library No. 109). London: Hogarth Press.

Bowlby, J. (1999) *Attachment and Loss*, Volume 1, 2nd edn. New York. Basic Books.

Bowlby, J. (2005) *The Making and Breaking of Affectional Bonds*. London: Routledge Classics.

Bronfenbrenner, U. (1979) *The Ecology of Human Development*. Cambridge, MA: Harvard University Press.

Brooker, L. (2002) *Starting School: Young Children Learning Cultures*. Buckingham: Open University Press.

Brooker, L. (2008) *Supporting Transitions in the Early Years*. Maidenhead: Open University Press.

Crafter, S. and Maunder, R. (2012) 'Understanding transitions using a sociocultural framework', *Educational and Child Psychology*, 29 (1): 10–18.

DfE (Department for Education) (2014) *Statutory Framework for the Early Years Foundation Stage: Setting the Standards for Learning, Development and Care for Children from Birth to Five*. Available at: www.foundationyears.org.uk/files/2014/07/EYFS_framework_from_1_September_2014__with_clarification_note.pdf (accessed 21 September 2015).

Erikson, E.H. (1975) *Life History and the Historical Moments*. London: WW Norton.

Evangelou, M., Taggart, B., Sylva, K., Melhuish, E., Sammons, P. and Siraj-Blatchford, I. (2008) 'What makes a successful transition from primary to secondary school?', Secondary Education 3–14 Project (EPPSE 3–14). Department for Children Schools and Families Research Report No. DCSF-RR 019. London: DCSF.

Gorgorio, N., Planas, N. and Vilella, X. (2002) 'Immigrant children learning mathematics in mainstream schools', in G. de Abreu, A. Bishop and N.C. Preseh (ed.), *Transitions between Contexts of Mathematical Practice*. Dordrecht: Kluwer Academic Press. pp. 23–52.

High, P.H. (2008) 'School readiness', *Pediatrics*, 123(e): 1008–15.

James, W. (1980) *The Principles of Psychology*: Volume 1. Mineola, NY: Dover Publications.

Piaget, J.J. (1976) *The Grasp of Consciousness: Action and Concept in the Young Child*. London: Routledge and Kegan Paul.

Pianta, R.C. and Walsh, D.J. (1996) *High Risk Children in Schools: Constructing Sustaining Relationships*. New York: Routledge.

Pianta, R.C., Cox, M.J., Taylor, L. and Early, D. (1999) 'Kindergarten teacher's practices related to transition to schools', *Elementary School Journal*, 100: 71–89.

Sylva, K., Melhuish, E., Sammons, P., Siraj-Blatchford, I., Taggart, B. and Elliot, K. (2003) *The Effective Provision of Pre-school Education (EPPE) Project: Findings from the Pre-school Period: Summary of Findings*. London: Institute of Education/Sure Start.

Vondra, J.I. and Barnett, D. (1999) 'Atypical attachment in infancy and early childhood among children at developmental risk', *Monographs of the Society for Research in Child Development*, 64 (Series No. 258).

Vygotsky, L. (1978) *Mind in Society: The Development of Higher Psychological Processes*. Cambridge, MA: Harvard University Press.

Winnicott, D.W. (1986) *Holding and Interpretation: Fragment of an Analysis*. New York: Hogarth Press.

Winnicott, D.W. (1987) *The Child, the Family, and the Outside World*. New York: Addison–Wesley.

Winnicott, D.W. (1995) *Maturational Processes and the Facilitating Environment: Studies in the Theory of Emotional Development*. New York: Stylus.

Winnicot, D.W. (2005) *Playing and Reality*. London: Routledge.

Zittoun, T. (2006) *Transitions: Development through Symbolic Resources*. Greenwich, CT: Information Age Publishing.

Want to learn more about this chapter? Visit the companion website at https://study.sagepub.com/EYFS3e for access to free SAGE journal articles and book chapters, weblinks, annotated further readings and more.

12

Using the Outdoor Environment in Early Childhood Pedagogy

Clare Nugent

 Chapter overview

Outdoor learning is a broad ideology. This chapter highlights common facets of the field, as appropriate to early childhood, and acknowledges several ways of using outdoor environments pedagogically. The use of outdoor environments is influenced by local as well as socio-cultural factors and, to this end, the case studies take a situated view, looking at outdoor learning in relation to the contexts in which it is occurring. We need to approach the outdoor classroom in a way that specifically suits each and every space while acknowledging that children's experiences will be subject to the attitudes and dispositions of the adults involved in each situation. It is important for early childhood practitioners to see opportunities within their own settings. As this chapter will show, children's learning and development are best supported when each context is rich and varied, safe and secure yet challenging. A spotlight is focused on the Forest School approach that has increased in popularity in recent years as through such practice the benefits and barriers of using outdoor environments can be investigated.

(Continued)

(Continued)

This chapter aims to help you to:

- appreciate that there are different ways of using the outdoor environment
- deepen your understanding of why the outdoor environment can be a beneficial asset to your daily practice
- consider the crucial role of the adult in emergent relationships that children have with nature and outdoor spaces
- see why fostering positive attitudes towards the 'great outdoors', and nature environments in particular, can be of lifelong benefit.

Policy and the outdoor classroom

The Council for Learning Outside the Classroom (LoTC) pledged in their manifesto to:

> Make a strong case for learning outside the classroom, so there is widespread appreciation of the unique contribution these experiences make to young people's lives. (LoTC, 2006)

Yet, five years on Parliament reported 'no clear picture of progression' in the use of the outdoor classroom across age ranges (House of Commons, 2010). That said, if we break down the evidence to look specifically at early childhood, the picture is brighter. Indeed, since the introduction of the EYFS in 2008 (see Chapter 2) outdoor learning has enjoyed a heightened emphasis in early childhood pedagogy that signifies positive attitudes towards outdoor environments. Additionally, recent policy acknowledges practitioners as imperative to advancing the use of the outdoors, saying that, 'Teachers need to be exposed to learning outside the curriculum from early on in their career, and this should not be left to chance' (House of Commons, 2010).

For children, there are notable physiological and psychological benefits in undirected exploration and unrestricted utility of resources outdoors. Research underpins policy and studies have time and again reported that children interacting with an outdoor space can engage in different behaviours, including risk-taking, messiness and exuberance. The literature reveals that there are positive benefits to childhood of spending time outdoors by virtue of its restorative qualities (Kaplan, 1995), capacity for the development of creativity (Wilson, 2012), well-being and physical activity (Kernan and Devine, 2010; Bruce, 2012). This chapter is timely as the benefits of the outdoors and practices advocated within it are the focus of a campaign by the RSPB and the Wildlife Trusts to see natural environments across the UK recognized through the 'Nature and Wellbeing Act' Green Paper.

The great outdoors: how did we get here?

The great outdoors and its incorporation within children's formative years has a long-standing legacy. Since Froebel's *kindergartens* or 'children's gardens' at the turn of the eighteenth century and McMillan's classroom 'roofed only by the sky' (Bruce, 2012), these learning environments have centred around outdoor spaces that are beneficial to the developing child. Numerous texts describe the roots of outdoor learning and interested readers may find some examples in the Further Reading. While it may be said that these are romantic views of childhoods past, there is inspiration in the work of these pioneers that stands out and is still relevant today. McMillan and others spoke out about accepted norms of her time to champion the needs of children. She recognized how children were healthier through being active, outdoors.

Examples across northern Europe that relate to this early work include the *waldkindergartens* of Germany and Switzerland as well as the *Ur och Skur* (Rain or Shine preschools) in Sweden that epitomize the *friluftsliv* (which roughly translates as 'fresh air life') ethos that pervades Nordic nations. This contrasts with modern UK society where outdoor play and close relationships with nature are not as easily identified as in some other cultures and steps to establish outdoor play are, by comparison, in their infancy. Our Forest School approach, for example, was only established in the UK in the late 1990s and examples of full-time provisions including nature kindergartens remain in the minority. The advent of Forest School, however, provided an opportunity for UK practitioners to achieve a relevant curriculum in the outdoor environment for all young children and now with free-flow access earnestly encouraged, our use of outdoor environments may not be the norm, but they are becoming more widely seen as places to be valued.

What is meant by 'outdoors'?

One key point we must take from this chapter is to question what is meant by 'outdoors'? It is difficult to answer this question, as no two outdoor environments are the same and they likely change on a daily basis – remember, these are unpredictable spaces. A clear, dry morning, for example, may change into a wet afternoon, and for me, this is what makes the outdoors exciting. If reaching a definition is difficult, we can use the common facets of outdoor environments to scrutinise the role of the outdoors in the way skills, understanding and knowledge develops.

The Chapter overview recommends that an outdoor environment should be *rich* and *varied*, *secure* yet *challenging*, and such facets are commonly noted in the literature (see Waite, 2011; White, 2011). In order to facilitate learning in these spaces, we need to understand what is meant by these adjectives. Rich environments offer excitement and interest for children. They enthuse via first-hand experience and allow children to structure their play to reflect their own inspiration. Stimuli are real and direct – hands, soiled and grainy with sticky mud, for example, can be a key component in the learning process and these places become sufficiently powerful so as to shape subsequent life choices (Wells and Lekies, 2006). Rich means teeming with variety and in turn, richness brings a diverse medley of choices. Diversity may stem, for example, from the weather and the unpredictability it brings or non-prescribed resources that offer endless possibilities to all the different children that use them in their myriad of ways. Practitioners should be adept in their planning to cope with such contingencies. Broadhead and Burt (2012) coined the term 'whatever you want it to be place[s]', following their work on sociable and cooperative play between peers, and is an apt depiction of the richness and diversity intrinsic to outdoor environments.

DfE (2014) states that children must be kept safe and secure yet outdoor play can routinely include risk-taking behaviours (Sandester, 2009) – risk ought to be seen as challenge and challenge is different from safety. There are valid reasons and restrictions as to *why* we *don't* go outdoors. Topics now ubiquitous within the field include urban lifestyles, curriculum, funding and time demands as well as practitioners' concerns over expertise and litigation. Such concerns may fuel the fear and limit outdoor learning (see Gill, 2007). In her blog, Ryder Richardson notes that the risk of 'unsafe weather' remains in the revised EYFS. In forest and woodland environments, trees in high winds (gale force 4 and above) or thunderstorms are a hazardous mix. Falling debris or the dangers from lightning are real and must be respected. It is, however, difficult to perceive extreme cold as 'unsafe' if those who intend to play in it are well prepared.

Outdoors, simply put, is an environment that is different from indoors. While there may be characteristics common to both spaces (the practitioners, the children, time, resources) there are features of the outdoors that set it apart. In essence, 'outdoors' can take a breadth of forms and approaches, just like the learning that takes place in it. The LoTC Manifesto recognises, alongside other documents, a wide range of possible routes and means to access the outdoors (Ofsted, 2008; LTS, 2010) and the next section, which looks at different examples of outdoor environments, is a good route to affirming a definition.

Examples of outdoor environments and how to use them

Gibsonian affordances are frequently used in the outdoor learning literature to frame an understanding of what an environment offers to humans who use it (Gibson, 1979). Each and every outdoor environment needs to be seen as a unique resource for practitioners to make the most of what a particular setting affords. The messages from practice are clear – experiences not equipment, process not product and simple resources are routinely effective.

Practitioners must see the potential benefits of their own school or nursery *grounds and gardens* and maximise the opportunities of this resource as part of their daily routine (DfES, 2006; Greater London Authority, 2011). The space outside the nursery door may be the first step, it may be the only step – either way, it is a worthwhile step and there are organisations that specialise in guiding and inspiring practitioners to help embed the EYFS through gardening (see the Useful websites and resources section of this chapter, below). Learning through Landscapes, for example, recognises that one size does not fit all and delivers training specific to the requirements of each setting or local authority.

Nature play is one form of outdoor learning that has a long history. Ghafouri neatly explains the breadth of modern day examples where 'children's encounters[s] and interaction[s] with nature exist on a continuum from wilderness to more humanly organized natural environments' (2014: 55). Children who play routinely learn through sensorial interaction and 'are natural fiddlers' (Andrews, 2012), hence, the first-hand interaction that is intrinsic to nature play is to be valued. Authors conclude that unless engaging *with* nature, any users' environmental interests may not wholly develop (Vadala et al., 2007). Richard Louv devised the term 'Nature Deficit Disorder' (Louv, 2005) to describe human alienation from nature and has written further on how childhood interactions with nature environments form an important contribution to pro-environmental attitudes in adulthood (Louv, 2011). Others have noted the correlation between childhood experiences and choices made in later life (Kopczak et al., 2013) and an overriding premise to this stance is the forming of a relatedness or connection with nature (Cheng and Monroe, 2012). In EYFS terms, therefore, regular access to outdoor environments can contribute to each child's development of such a connection.

Forest School has much to offer early childhood practice. Links have been drawn between the approach and improved outcomes for children's learning, development and well-being (Ridgers et al., 2012; Knight, 2013). Below, two case studies have been chosen as illustrations of the different interpretations of the Forest School approach. By focusing in more detail on this form of outdoor learning, we can use it to reflect on how we can garner meaningful contact with outdoor environments as well as seeing how to make provision an integral part of early childhood pedagogy.

Case study

Nature to Nurture – Julie White

There is season-round utility to be found in local parks, nature reserves, botanic gardens and other urban green spaces. On Merseyside, there is an outdoor nursery, established as a social enterprise, which is successfully combining EYFS requirements with the Forest School approach. 'Nature to Nurture' grew out of a pilot project in 2011–12 delivered by the group's founder, Julie White. Trained as a Level 3 Forest School Leader, Julie's palpable belief in the value of nature-based learning is clear and the group's tagline, 'Allowing nature to nurture our well-being', percolates

(Continued)

(Continued)

throughout practice. The group puts this ethos into action in the grounds of Croxteth Hall – a large, parkland space managed by Liverpool City Council.

Nature to Nurture has developed from facilitating woodland birthday parties to offer parent and toddler sessions as well as nursery sessions. Numerous local nurseries attend the 2½ hour sessions once a week.

Partnership with parents is highly valued and of particular note. During parent and toddler sessions, parental understanding of what a session involves can begin. Relations are further cultivated and strengthened by the use of technology as parents engage with sessions via a secret Facebook page or via footage from Go Pro cameras worn by the children. Such a community pays dividend when seeking consent for activities – albeit they are risky, dirty or otherwise.

Issues are presented by using this public space. The group uses pop-up toilet tents, for example, and all human waste is taken off site daily. Julie makes mention of vandalism; however, no buildings or in situ equipment, and a supportive landlord, have helped the group to overcome such barriers to provision.

Through its ability to adapt and change, the group has gained ground and Julie estimates that since its inception, Nature to Nurture has involved 2,000 local people in nature-based practice. This social impact is heightened at the individual child's level by evidence of increased confidence, resilience and recognition that their 'school ready' skills are transferred to other situations.

Reflective tasks

- Think about the practicalities presented by this case study and reflect on how these context-specific issues are tackled.

- How would you encourage the parents and carers to further embed the principles contributed by this group's ethos and its approach to the outdoor environment?

The second case study describes a Forest School delivered by practitioners within their own school grounds and helps confirm how this is an *approach* or a delivery mechanism rather than a prescribed model to be replicated.

Case study

Forest School

A new member of staff, Andy, started working in the Early Childhood department of a 3–11 years primary school. Before coming into childcare, Andy had studied environmental sciences and loved the outdoors. The school, located on the edge of a large city, had a hectare of grassy playing fields with a small stand of mature trees and shrubbery to its south-east corner. While the fields were routinely used for outdoor play, the woodland space was not utilised – until Andy recognized an opportunity. On an *ad hoc* basis, groups started to venture out and across the playing fields from the nursery building on 'nature walks' and 'bug hunts'. The children were keen to join these 'expeditions' and, back at nursery, contributed to displays as celebrations of their experiences.

Another colleague had heard of Forest School, but was initially reluctant to venture further. On making enquiries, however, team members decided that the Forest School approach offered a positive way forward. There was a training budget and Andy applied to use this funding to complete a Level 3 Forest School Leader Award while the other two practitioners opted for the Level 1 Basic Skills Award. The training comprised on-site observation, risk assessment, communicating with parents and diary keeping combined with off-site practical sessions and study. All three practitioners achieved their qualifications and the school community adopted Forest School wholeheartedly.

Now, all forty-eight 3½- to 4½-year-olds on roll use their Forest School site once a week. This cohort is divided into four groups of twelve and each group uses the woodland on different days to alleviate staffing and other demands.

Reflective tasks

- Thinking about your own context, and within the statutory framework for the EYFS, critically examine how Forest School could operate at your workplace.

- With regard to children who are new to Forest School, Knight (2012: 148) recognises how 'pupils usually have to grow into the "child-led" idea'. Try to think about how you might plan and manage for such a scenario.

What can we take from these case studies?

Forest School is a flexible approach that meets the requirements of statutory frameworks by virtue of its inclusive, respectful and supportive ethos. While the approach is adaptable and encourages process rather than outcome-led practices, the attitudes and dispositions of the practitioners are vital. Both studies tell about how the motivations of one adult encouraged others to take steps towards a mode of learning with which they were typically unfamiliar (see Waite, 2011). Allowing time to implement and adapt to the approach is important – for both children and adults. There are likely to be time, curriculum and training demands and the location of the site may introduce transport and safety considerations. There will be risk assessments and other paperwork to complete for the site, content of sessions and the group members.

Outdoors, what should adults aim to implement?

This last section of the chapter brings together links between the outdoor learning environment and the framework of the EYFS. Clearly, national policy has an impact upon the decisions that practitioners take and the way a curriculum is delivered; however, the adults themselves are another vital part of the learning environment. In early childhood, adults are omnipresent and have significant influence over children's experiences. Waller notes relationships and interaction between children and adults to be '*the* most important aspect of promoting effective outdoor play' (2011: 39; emphasis added). The case studies report interpretations of Forest School to suggest that the adults involved had a supportive attitude towards the outdoors although more broadly in early childhood practice, this may not be so. In considering the role of the adult, we must take account of differing attitudes, values and dispositions that are based on each adult's particular beliefs and backgrounds as these subjective facets steer our work. Wherever our differences are rooted (personal inhibitions, recollections, preferences and motivations relating to the physical design or layout of a setting), remember an adult's 'hostile attitudes towards [...] playing outdoors can have damaging implications for children's health and happiness' (Gleave and Cole-Hamilton, 2012: 2).

The EYFS speaks of Characteristics of Effective Learning (CoEL) and these are useful as a lens by which to look at adult roles in the outdoor classroom. The first characteristic is *playing and exploring*. Practitioners must reflect not only on the different ways that children investigate, explore and experiment in their outdoor play but also on their own supportive role in nurturing such interaction. At the adult level, 'confidence and expertise is only built through active engagement with outdoor contexts' (Passy and Waite, 2011: 174). While first-hand learning that is 'more vivid and interesting' for children can 'enhance their understanding' (Ofsted, 2008: 7), we must be mindful that children's behaviour is guided by those they observe, including the adults around them. We too may feel the dryness of soil and how sticky it turns when mixed with water. We may encourage others to taste snowflakes on the tongue by doing so ourselves in unison with the playing child.

The second characteristic asks for *active learning*. McMillan (1919) identified 'inert' children who needed to 'run and shout in the open'. Today's *active* learners go beyond the freedom to move and be more physical. We must understand that active participation during early childhood has lifelong benefit and can be habit forming. Adults can support active experiences by allowing opportunities away from 'an adult's gaze' (Waller, 2011: 38) and learning can be further enriched with provision for quieter spaces that foster calm reflection away from adult control (LoTC, 2009).

Finally, effective teaching and learning is evidenced by *creative and critical thinking*. When children apply independent and often original thought, they are being creative. As children develop their own ideas, adults may make links and help develop strategies to complete tasks or, as Wilson (2012: 2) aptly states, children will learn 'a lot by just "messing around" with simple materials'. Perceptive practitioners will know when to stand back and allow a stick to be a sword, wand, scaffold pole or microphone.

Summary

The EYFS framework sets standards to ensure children learn and develop in three prime and four specific areas. This chapter has reasoned *why* we ought to go outdoors and illustrated a few examples of *how* such practice may look. There is scrutiny of how we might think about outdoor learning from the facilitator's perspective and why practitioners may do what they do. We are working with children at a stage of development where memories and experiences can last a lifetime. We have teased out the contribution of childhood experiences to one's attitudes and beliefs later in adulthood and evidence from environmental education and psychologists affirm this. The message is to encourage practitioners to look beyond the label and see situated interpretations and possibilities – the 'use what you've got' argument. If we see potential in all outdoor spaces, then an urban green space with planted tubs, or a vegetable patch, need be no less enabling than a setting afforded a large area of 'wildness' or stands of mature trees.

In sum, therefore, when children engage in the outdoors in a supportive context and similarly motivated adults encourage meaningful interactions, they are likely to better placed to make sense of environmental challenges, live healthily and develop a lasting appreciation of outdoor environments.

Key points to remember

- Outdoor environments take many forms, like the learning opportunities that exist within them.

- Values that form within childhood can be habit forming and last a lifetime. Indeed, such values comprise our adult dispositions and attitudes.

- Children can be helped to value 'the great outdoors' with the goal of a lifelong respect of nature born of first-hand experience of habitats in direct ways.

- Requirements set out within the EYFS statutory framework can be creatively integrated into the use of any outdoor environment and whatever it has to offer.

Points for discussion

- Practitioners must consider their own attitudes, dispositions, motivations and those of the various adults who surround the child because they can, in turn, affect the opportunities provided and thus the relationships that children develop with the outdoors. In any setting, practitioners who differently value the outdoor environment may work alongside one another – how would you navigate such a scenario?

- In what ways would you say the outdoor space at your setting is viewed as an enabling environment?

- Outdoor environments are inherently flexible. If practitioners are to respond to each child's individual needs (DfE, 2014), as well as the unpredictability of the learning environment, then adaptability and preparation are key. Discuss how you will plan for this.

Further reading

Books

Knight, S. (2013) *Forest School and Outdoor Learning in the Early Years*, 2nd edn. London: Sage.

White, J. (ed.) (2011) *Outdoor Provision in the Early Years*. London: Sage.

Articles

Ridgers, N.D., Knowles, Z.R. and Sayers, J. (2012) 'Encouraging play in the natural environment: a child-focused case study of Forest School'. *Children's Geographies*, 10 (1): 49–65.

Sandester, E.B.H. (2009) 'Affordances for risky play in preschool: the importance of features in the play environment', *Early Childhood Education Journal*, 36 (5): 439–46.

Useful websites and resources

For interesting examples of good practice that illustrate the breadth of approaches to outdoor learning, readers are recommended to look at one example of Forest School established within school grounds:

www.ofsted.gov.uk/resources/good-practice-resource-developing-childrens-learning-through-work-natural-environment-preesall-fleet

The team at Norcot Early Years Centre have called their approach 'learning through nature' and it is based on practice their staff observed in Norway:

www.ofsted.gov.uk/resources/good-practice-resource-letting-children-make-decisions-natural-environment-norcot-early-years-centre

A fascinating new report from Scotland is:

Mannion, G., Mattu, L. and Wilson, M. (2015) Teaching, learning, and play in the outdoors: a survey of school and pre-school provision in Scotland. *Scottish Natural Heritage Commissioned Report No. 779* available at www.snh.org.uk/pdfs/publications/commissioned_reports/779.pdf

Learning through Landscapes have produced a short video entitled *Conserving Wonder* that helps justify the use of schools' outdoor environments. It is accessible at:

www.youtube.com/watch?v=ImZhcNIL07s

In relation to Forest School, there are several inspiring case studies from Wales, including:

www.naturalresourceswales.go.uk/about-us/media-and-news-centre/press-release/Welsh-in-the-woodland-as-children-take-their-classroom-outdoors

A useful education resource is:

www.forestsforthefuture.co.uk

A lovely international perspective can be found at:

http://blogs.kqed.org/mindshift/2014/07/let-em-out-the-many-benefits-of-outdoor-play-in-kindergarten/

'Nature and Wellbeing Act' Green Paper:

http://www.ywt.org.uk/nature-and-wellbeing-act

For organisations who specialise in guiding and inspiring practitioners to help embed EYFS through gardening:

www.rhs.org.uk/schoolgardening and www.growwilduk.com

References

Andrews, M. (2012) *Exploring Play for Early Childhood Studies.* London: Sage.

Broadhead, P. and Burt, A. (2012) *Learning through Play: Building Playful Pedagogies,* New York: Routledge.

Bruce, T. (2012) *Early Childhood Practice: Froebel Today.* London: Sage.

Cheng, J.C-H and Monroe, M.C. (2012) 'Connection to Nature: children's affective attitude toward nature', *Environment and Behavior,* 44, 31–49.

DfE (Department for Education) (2014) Statutory Framework for the Early Years Foundation Stage: Setting the Standards for Learning, Development and Care for Children from Birth to Five. Available at: www.foundationyears.org.uk/files/2014/07/EYFS_framework_from_1_September_2014__with_clarification_note.pdf (accessed 25 November 2015)

DfES (Department for Education and Skills) (2006) *Schools for the Future: Designing School Grounds.* Norwich: TSO. Available at: www.gov.uk/government/uploads/system/uploads/attachment_data/file/276691/schools_for_the_future_-_designing_school_grounds.pdf.

Ghafouri, F. (2014) 'Close encounters with nature in an urban kindergarten: a study of learners' inquiry and experience', *Education 3–13: International Journal of Primary, Elementary and Early Years Education,* 42 (1): 54–76.

Gill, T. (2007) *No Fear.* London: Calouste Gulbenkian Foundation.

Gibson, J.J. (1979) *The Ecological Approach to Visual Perception.* Hillsdale, NJ: Lawrence Erlbaum Associates.

Gleave, J. and Cole-Hamilton, I. (2012). *'A World Without Play' – A Literature Review.* London: Play England. Available at: www.playengland.org.uk/media/371031/a-world-without-play-literature-review-2012.pdf (accessed 14 July 2015).

Greater London Authority (2011) Sowing the seeds – reconnecting London's children with nature. Available at: www.londonsdc.org/documents/SowingtheSeeds–FullReport.pdf (accessed 14 July, 2015).

Kaplan, S. (1995) 'The restorative benefits of nature: Toward an integrative nature', *Journal of Environmental Psychology,* 15 (3): 169–182.

Kernan, M. and Devine, D. (2010) 'Being confined within? Constructions of the good childhood and outdoor play in early childhood education and care settings in Ireland', *Children and Society,* 24 (5): 371–85.

Knight, S. (2012) *Forest School for All.* London: Sage.

Knight, S. (2013) *Forest School and Outdoor Learning in the Early Years,* 2nd edn. London: Sage.

Kopczak, C., Kisiel, J.F. and Rowe, S. (2013) 'Families talking about ecology at touch tanks', *Environmental Education Research,* DOI: 10:1080/13504622.2013.860429

House of Commons (2010) *Transforming Education Outside the Classroom.* Available at: www.publications.parliament.uk/pa/cm200910/cmselect/cmchilsch/418/41806.htm (accessed 22 November 2014).

LTS (Learning and Teaching Scotland) (2010) *Curriculum for Excellence through Outdoor Learning.* Available at: www.educationscotland.gov.uk/Images/cfeOutdoorLearningfinal_tcm4–596061.pdf (accessed 2 November 2014).

Learning Outside the Classroom (2006) *Learning Outside the Classroom Manifesto.* Available at: www.lotc.org.uk/wp-content/uploads/2011/03/G1.-LOtC-Manifesto.pdf (accessed 21 September 2015).

Learning Outside the Classroom (2009) *Early Years Settings' Grounds.* Available at: www.lotc.org.uk/wp-content/uploads/2011/03/Early-Years-Settings-Grounds.pdf (accessed 14 July 2015).

Louv, R. (2005) *Last Child in the Woods*. Chapel Hill, NC: Algonquin Books of Chapel Hill.

Louv, R. (2011) *The Nature Principle: Human Restoration and the End of Nature-Deficit Disorder*. Chapel Hill, NC: Algonquin Books of Chapel Hill.

McMillan, M. (1919) *The Nursery School*. London: J.M. Dent and Sons Ltd.

Ofsted (2008) *Learning outside the classroom – how far should you go?* Available at: http://www. lotc.org.uk/why/ofsteds-view-of-lotc/ (accessed 25 November 2015)

Passy, R. and Waite, S. (2011) 'School gardens and Forest Schools', in S. Waite (ed.), *Children Learning Outside the Classroom: From Birth to Eleven*. London: Sage.

Ridgers, N.D., Knowles, Z.R. and Sayers, J. (2012) 'Encouraging play in the natural environment: a child-focused case study of Forest School', *Children's Geographies*, 10 (1): 49–65.

Sandester, E.B.H. (2009) 'Affordances for risky play in preschool: the importance of features in the play environment', *Early Childhood Education Journal*, 36 (5): 439–46.

Vadala, C.E., Bixler, R.D. and James, J. (2007) 'Childhood play and environmental interests: panacea or snake oil?', *Journal of Environmental Education*, 39 (1): 3–18.

Waite, S. (ed.) (2011) *Children Learning Outside the Classroom: From Birth to Eleven*. London: Sage.

Waller, T. (2011) 'Adults are essential', in J. White (ed.), *Outdoor Provision in the Early Years*. London: Sage.

Wells, N.N. and Lekies, K.S. (2006) 'Nature and the life course: pathways from childhood nature experiences to adult environmentalism', *Children, Youth and Environments*, 16 (1): 1–24.

White, J. (ed.) (2011) *Outdoor Provision in the Early Years*. London: Sage.

Wilson, R.A. (2012) *Nature and Young Children: Encouraging Creative Play and Learning in Natural Environments*. London: Routledge.

 Want to learn more about this chapter? Visit the companion website at **https://study.sagepub.com/EYFS3e** for access to free SAGE journal articles and book chapters, weblinks, annotated further readings and more.

PART 3
KEY ISSUES IN PRACTICE

13
Working in Partnership with Parents

Anna Knowles

 Chapter overview

The Statutory Framework for the Early Years Foundation Stage identifies the need for 'partnership working between practitioners and/or carers' (DfE, 2014a: 5). The building of a mutually responsive relationship with parents is central in supporting the well-being and development of the child. The need to work in collaboration with parents and carers was considered as a part of the government's *Choice for Parents, the Best Start for Children* strategy (HM Treasury, 2004). Prior to this, work with parents had lacked coherence and regularity. The strategy, which provided a foundation for EYFS, emphasised the need for partnership between practitioners and parents. This chapter will examine the challenges faced in engaging parents and the benefits of successful engagement. The term 'parent' will be used throughout the chapter to refer to any person who takes on a parental role, regardless of the biology of parenthood.

This chapter aims to help you to:

- understand the purpose and significance of working with parents and carers
- consider the ways in which we engage with parents to support children in early childhood education and care
- examine and reflect on the role of the early childhood practitioner in developing effective relationships with parents.

Building effective partnerships – a rationale

Building and maintaining effective partnerships with parents is essential in developing an awareness of the needs of the child. Jackson and Needham (2014: 8) emphasise that positive parent relationships are central to children's well-being. Parents are experts on their child and should be regarded as such; they have an astute awareness of the specific behaviours and unique habits exhibited by the child. The sharing of parental expertise enables the practitioner to gain a solid understanding of the child, which can then be shared with staff across the setting. Prior to a child entering into early childhood education and care the parent builds the primary learning experience. Practitioners need an understanding of the content of this experience to enable a starting point for working with the child.

The combination of parental perceptions and the knowledge of the early childhood practitioner assists in ensuring positive outcomes for the child. The Reggio Emilia approach, as discussed by Thornton and Brunton (2007), emphasises the parent, practitioner and child relationship as a three-way process (Figure 13.1). The practitioner gains knowledge from the expertise of the parent and the parent learns from someone experienced in the practice of early childhood education and care. The child participates in interactions with both adults and is recognised as 'rich in potential, strong, powerful and competent' (Malaguzzi, 2001: 5). All individuals have equal importance in shared communications that embrace respect, listening and cooperation. Active participation is essential to the success of the relationships.

The established three-way relationship provides the parent with an opportunity to develop an understanding of what is happening in the early childhood setting and why. Consider how often you have seen a child race to the door to share a picture they have produced in nursery, to be greeted by statements and questions from a parent that attempt to enforce meaning or suppress creativity. Such responses derive from a lack of understanding of the unique ways in which children learn and develop. Practitioners have the potential to support the parent in developing a new understanding for the way in which their child learns and the creative and imaginative processes involved.

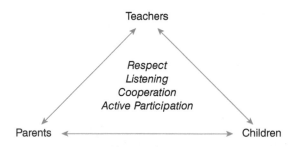

Figure 13.1 *The triangle of relationships (adapted from Thornton and Brunton, 2007)*

The Department for Children, Schools and Families highlighted how parental involvement in children's education from an early age significantly affects educational achievements (DCSF, 2008). Outcomes in cognitive development are better when parents are involved in learning. Feiler notes the development of children as stemming from 'guided participation' of adults in the home and school environment, who work together (Feiler, 2010: 14). Providing parents with an understanding of early childhood education and care assists them in effectively supporting and extending their child's learning in the home environment. It should not be assumed that parents are unwilling to learn more about the ways in which their children learn. Whalley emphasises parental enthusiasm in her discussions of research conducted around parental partnerships at the Pen Green Centre:

> We realised we had underestimated the enthusiasm which parents demonstrated for a deeper and more extended dialogue about their children's learning. We began to see that teaching and learning and curriculum issues, which had previously been the fairly uncontested domain of professional staff, needed to be opened up for wider discussion with parents in the early childhood community. (2007: 9)

Collaborative working with parents aims to promote the enthusiasm of parents. Effective partnerships stimulate shared verbal exchanges which derive from a reciprocal understanding of the child. Parent and practitioner should be attuned to the child's needs as this enables free and open discussion through mutually understandable communications.

Effective initial interactions

Initial interactions commence when a parent registers interest in a setting. It is important to reflect on the ways in which parents are engaged at this stage as early interactions form a basis for the partnership process. Practitioners should consider parental feelings about the process and allow time for partnerships to evolve.

The first face-to-face liaison with the parent is crucial in securing a successful future relationship. The practitioner's behaviour towards the parent should 'be a model of courtesy and respect' (Thornton and Brunton, 2007: 14). It is essential to adopt a sensitive, friendly and professional approach which takes account of the needs of the parent and, if present, the child. Affording time to initial meetings with parents undoubtedly presents implications to practice, but it is critical in ensuring the parent has confidence in their relationship with the early childhood setting. Time also provides the practitioner with the opportunity to gain preliminary knowledge of the parent and this knowledge positively benefits future interactions.

The context of the initial liaison will vary; first meetings will generally either take place in the early childhood setting or the family home. When discussing the use of narrative therapy in working towards a genuine partnership with parents,

McQueen and Hobbs (2014: 17) advise initial conversations should focus on asking parents about what is important to the family. If we consider this in the context of a child moving into an early childhood setting, we may focus on what is important to the family throughout the transition period and points they consider to be important in enhancing their child's experience within the setting.

Goodman and Greg (2010: 5) evidence that poorer children experience 'much less advantageous' environments than children from better off backgrounds. These environments are strongly associated with a child's cognitive development in early childhood. Visiting a parent and child in the home assists practitioners in building a picture of the child's primary environment. It also offers the family the opportunity to liaise with practitioners in a setting that is comfortable and familiar to them. It is advisable the visit be conducted by the child's potential key person along with another practitioner. One practitioner is able to spend time engaging the child while the other dedicates their time to listening and responding to the parent. Brief and objective observations of the child in their home environment may be noted down during or immediately following the visit. It is important not to spend too much time writing; a stronger foundation for future work is established when both the parent and the child feel sufficiently engaged during the visit. Some parents may not feel comfortable with a visit in their own home. This feeling must be respected and an alternative venue should be offered.

The practitioner is not provided with a second chance to make a good first impression so it is crucial to examine practices for the initial engagement of parents. MacNaughton emphasises reflective practice as a skill that can be identified in quality practitioners. She advises 'looking back' at practices and 'rethinking them' (MacNaughton, 2005: 6). It is essential to reflect on our behaviour in initial meetings with parents. It is not possible for every early interaction to be a success, but reflecting on our conduct assists in finding ways forward for future work with parents.

Sustaining parental involvement and the sharing of practice

Effective sustained relationships continue throughout the child's time in an early childhood setting and enable practitioner and parent to work together to highlight a child's achievements, extend learning opportunities and exchange anecdotes in a relaxed manner. Practitioners should develop opportunities to engage parents in their practices and share experiences of the child. Rouse (2012: 15) discusses a 'family centred' model of practice; the model is sustained by the belief that parents should be empowered to make decisions for their children. Practice highlights that when parents are regularly engaged in shared experiences with the setting, they are more likely to feel empowered to talk to staff about their child's learning.

The accessibility of the early childhood setting should be emphasised. Parents should be aware that they are able to stay to settle their child and join in with play. Open-door policies, if implemented, should be clearly explained. The EYFS highlights that information should be made available for parents as to the 'range and type of activities and experiences' provided, along with how parents can share learning at home (DfE, 2014a: 30). Organised 'stay and play' sessions provide an excellent opportunity for the sharing of activity through planned collaboration. The format for sessions will differ, but regularity and convenience are vital elements in securing attendance. Stay and play sessions can be particularly challenging for day care settings where a high proportion of the parents drop their children off to attend work. Close liaison with parents is necessary to inform decisions around effective times for inviting parents in, as it may be appropriate to consider a Saturday session. Alternatively, parents may have the time to stay and play for just five or ten minutes at the end of each day.

Reflective task

- You are working with a father who finds collaboration with practitioners a challenge. He tells you he had negative personal experiences of school and does not know how best to support his child in learning. List all the ways you will attempt to build the confidence of this father. How could you involve him in the day-to-day running of the nursery?

Collaboration in assessment

The EYFS Integrated Review at Age Two stipulates that practitioners should review a child's development in each of the prime areas and ensure parents have a 'clear picture' of their child's development (DfE, 2014a: 3). The suggested model for building a clear picture of the child includes using practitioner knowledge and assessment alongside information gathered from parents and other professionals. Messenger and Malloy (2014: 9) advise that when such collaborations occur, positive effects include improved parenting and cognitive performance in children.

Written summaries of development are an important means of sharing information about a child; a summary should provide the opportunity for parental feedback. In the statutory framework for the EYFS, the DfE (2014a: 13) advise that practitioners can decide on the format of the written summary for the two year integrated review, but they must discuss with parents and carers how the summary of development can be 'used to support learning at home'.

In addition to written methods it is important that parents are able to come in to the setting to discuss their child's development. Consultation meetings between key workers and parents offer the opportunity for this. In addition to more formal consultations, parents should feel enabled to talk to practitioners about their child's development at any time. This can present a challenge in busy settings and when parents have concerns, it may involve mutual agreement of an appropriate time for the discussion.

The DfE (2014b: 6–7) have outlined plans for the introduction of baseline assessments in the foundation year. In their accountability reform, the DfE advises that the baseline should be carefully communicated with parents and 'contextualised' by a teacher's range of assessments. Communication around the results of the baseline will be supported by building good relationships with parents in the transition to school phase.

Sharing everyday practice

Smidt discusses the involvement of parents in the day-to-day running of the early childhood setting, advising this as 'one of the best ways of genuinely involving parents in the life of the nursery' (Smidt, 2007: 176). She suggests that parents should be clear as to their role. In providing clarity, the practitioner emphasises what is happening and why. This enables the parent a greater understanding of the aims and ethos of the setting and ultimately impacts on how a child's learning is extended in the home environment. Day-to-day activities may include assisting during sessions, visits or fundraising events, interviewing potential practitioners, supporting baking or sharing stories.

The sharing of practice specific to a child provides parents with the motivation to become involved in beneficial and meaningful collaborations with practitioners. Athey highlights that '[n]othing gets under a parent's skin more quickly and more permanently than the illumination of his or her own child's behaviour' (2007: 209). There are a number of ways in which settings can gather information from parents, including the noting down of conversations and collaborative learning journeys and diaries. ICT also provides a powerful tool for communication with parents and carers, the use of email and shared assessment apps can be really beneficial for parents who cannot regularly come in to the setting due to work or other commitments. Collaborations involving reading and writing should be sensitively approached. They involve knowledge of the capabilities of the parent, and competence in reading and writing should never be assumed.

Digital photography and hand-held recording equipment have modified the ability to effectively share practice with parents. Annotated photographs and snippets of video supported by practitioner observation provide meaningful ways of sharing experiences of the child. O'Hara (2011: 229) found that parents make a big impact on children's learning with ICT through activities such as playing with children using programmable toys and using audio and visual recording. Sending cameras home for parents and children to document their weekend allows the practitioner the opportunity for extending a child's interests and pursuits through sharing and discussion of the resulting photographs.

Using display space effectively can positively enhance partnerships as parents will frequently stop to discuss a photograph of their child that has been placed on the wall. A parent's information board serves as a tool for sharing information about the setting and should be placed on a display board directly visible to parents. Waiting areas, corridors and cloakrooms are all areas that are frequently accessed by parents. If you have children with English as an additional language, ensure your parent display offers information in both English and children's home languages.

Using ICT and social media to engage with parents in a maintained nursery school

As a staff team, we noticed that many of the parents who came in to the setting owned a smart phone and home visits also identified that many had tablets in the home environment. The proficiency of many of the children in ICT on entry evidenced that they were well used to using mobile technology. We began to think about this technology as a tool for sharing practice and ideas. We introduced class email addresses that the parents can use to email pictures and tell us about what they have been doing at home. This has been a popular way to engage with our parents – it is simple for them to share pictures from a smart phone and we have a regular flow of information. The pictures provide an excellent opportunity to encourage verbal language within the nursery, they are added to learning journey folders and we talk about them with the children.

Stepping into the use of social media was a little more daunting. Controversy continues to surround the use of social media applications such as Twitter and Facebook. As a team we evaluated our opinions around social media and began to think about using it to positively support our families. We decided we did not feel comfortable in sharing images of children through social media and as yet we have not progressed to this. The nursery now has a Facebook page and a Twitter feed. We use these pages to support our nursery website and to inform the parents about what we've been doing. We find that social media is very much a tool of modern society, our parents engage with it, and it has enabled us an outlet for a flow of information. We set challenges via our social media pages, for example: 'Can you be listening detectives?', i.e. encouraging parents and children to go for listening walks and talk about what they can hear. It is important to mention that engagement of ICT has not replaced our more traditional methods of communication; rather we seek to enhance these methods. In cases where we communicate via social media, we will generally always support this through written letters as we cannot assume that all parents favour this method of communicating.

So what's next?

We feel we have released the positive potential of social media and intend to continue on our journey in using it to benefit our practice. We are also fortunate to be working alongside an ICT consultancy in piloting an app which focuses on using ICT as a means for enhancing language and communication. We will continue to strive to use ICT and evaluate its position as a tool for enhancing the lives of our families.

Reflective task

- Reflect on all of the benefits and disadvantages for using social media to engage with parents and to support information sharing. Consider social media as a tool for modern interaction as well as safety implications around information sharing on the internet.

When parents disengage

When parents disengage it is necessary to consider the reasons for this. Friendly verbal communications are often useful in ascertaining why a parent, who has previously engaged successfully, ceases interacting with the setting. Factors such as alterations to work commitments or changes in the home or setting environment impact on engagement. Changes to a setting should be introduced sensitively in collaboration with the parents and new staff should be personally introduced.

Ward (2013: 111) advises use of evaluation methods such as comments boxes, sticky-notes and focus groups to assist in re-engaging families. Questionnaires can also serve as a tool in establishing effective ways to re-engage parents as they enable honest feedback. Comments boxes are quick and easy ways to gain the views of parents and, as with questionnaires, they can allow anonymity. Practitioners should be assertive in instigating conversations to ascertain why parents may be choosing not to engage with the setting, especially when engagement was once evident.

Disengagement is particularly concerning when it is associated with concerns around a child's welfare. Contact with external agencies, such as social services, may be necessary in such cases. It is beneficial to adopt a reflective approach in all instances of disengagement. The study of recent actions and events can enlighten the practitioner as to the reasons for a parent's sudden reluctance to interact and assist in re-establishing relationships.

Considering the individual needs of parents

It is important to remember that not all parents will engage with a setting with confidence. In the same way that we consider the needs of the child, we also need to think about the needs of the parent. Parents who do not speak English may feel embarrassed or nervous about interactions. Parents who have negative experiences of education may be reluctant to engage. Remember, if this is their first child, you are potentially the first educational setting they have entered since they left school themselves. Arnold (2003) explored personal and interpersonal barriers to involvement. She identified the following feelings that prevented parents from feeling at ease in an education environment:

- anger, fear and anxiety
- not fitting in
- feeling undervalued
- feeling numb
- isolation
- tendency to run away/avoid authority
- inadequacy (2003: 99)

Feiler emphasises that aspects preventing engagement are both 'diverse and complex' and advises that they include 'social deprivation, poverty, ethnicity and the experience of disability' (Feiler, 2010: 53). It is vital that practitioners are mindful as to the experiences and feelings that may prevent parents from becoming involved with the setting. Knowledge of such experiences allows practitioners to contemplate and plan appropriate opportunities for collaboration. It is essential to retain an approach that is sensitive, non-judgemental and structured around awareness of the family.

We can support parents who do not speak English by ensuring we offer them information in their own language. We may also use interpreters to assist during home visits or consultations. Encouraging the sharing of home photographs can be beneficial for families with English as an additional language; it is important to offer them the opportunity to talk about their home environment, special occasions and celebrations.

The following case study examines how the staff at McMillan Nursery School worked to form partnerships with parents who had traditionally found collaborations a challenge. This is a large nursery school, built in 1939 at the same time as the large council housing estate which it serves. It has established relationships with families in the area, with some children having siblings, parents and grandparents who have all attended the school. Demographically the locality is one of the most deprived in the UK, with families facing a wide range of difficulties, including drug and alcohol abuse, domestic violence, unemployment, family breakdown, social isolation and mental health issues. A high proportion of the children have special educational needs and many families are involved with external agencies such as social services. In addition, many parents have had negative experiences of school as teenagers, and qualifications in the area are low. Despite such challenges, the children are described as 'happy, clever, enthusiastic, independent, resourceful, imaginative, friendly, lively, active and energetic, and creative'. Parents are described by staff as 'passively supportive' of the school and demonstrate a reluctance to collaborate with the setting. Practitioners have explored a range of traditional methods to try to engage parents positively in their children's learning.

Case study

McMillan Nursery School: Encouraging parental involvement through the 'In the Woods' Forest Project

With Andrew Shimmin

Consideration of the approach

The McMillan Nursery has been a Creative Partnerships 'School of Creativity' since 2008. Through this project members of staff were able to train as Forest School practitioners, qualified to lead activities in a woodland environment. The team decided that parental involvement would be a central feature of planned Forest Projects in an attempt to engage parents in children's learning. Staff hypothesised that for various reasons parents might be more inclined to become more deeply involved:

Parents are historically enthusiastic about offsite visits, therefore might be more inclined to take part.

Focusing on 'forest' activities might be less threatening to less confident parents than more traditional 'curriculum'-orientated activities.

Structuring a programme over six weeks would allow opportunities for longer-term engagement between parents, children and practitioners.

As a result, a regular programme is planned which involves a series of visits by the same small group of children and parents; the group includes children from our 2-year-old provision as well as our 3- and 4-year-olds. Sessions are led by trained

Forest School practitioners and run on a regular basis throughout the year. Parents are asked to commit to attending all sessions and are invited to a parents-only pre-session. Staff explain and introduce Forest Practice, as well as safety and practical arrangements. A range of parents continue to express interest in attending, including a significant number of fathers (traditionally a group less likely to become involved in nursery activities).

Initial visits focused on setting safety boundaries, introductions and establishing a group. Sessions consisted of a mix of practitioner-led activities and games and structured free exploration. Staff facilitated group reflection and planning from week to week and promoted group bonding. Parents were encouraged to express views and ideas; their contributions were valued and respected. Practitioners took early childhood practice models as a basis for a participant-led approach within Forest School structures. Foundation Stage practice was used to build confidence and self-esteem among both the children and their parents. Sessions have also explored transition relationships through the participation of local foundation stage teachers and groups of children.

Outcomes of our projects

Some parents, fathers in particular, seemed confident outdoors. Other parents gave feedback on feeling nervous, worried or lacking in confidence initially. As sessions developed they described the development of confidence and group responsibility along with increased relaxation and enjoyment. Evident new friendships developed between both the parents and the children. These friendships support transition in to the primary school setting. Parents engaged with the experiences and feelings of their children, with one parent commenting: 'I've learned that going to the forest makes you more calm and carefree and I thought a lot of the children liked that feeling.'

Fun, enjoyment and time are crucial elements in the success of the project. Parents have commented that they appreciated the time for them and their children to 'explore and spend quality time together'. The approaches explored in the forest are developed back at the nursery school and early childhood practitioners have set up and modelled shared explorations to support parents in their interactions with children. After the project a number of parents who had taken part volunteered to become governors and also signed up for further education childcare courses through the adult training provision at the Children's Centre.

Reflective tasks

Reflecting on the above case study, consider that you are visiting a family in the home environment for an initial home visit. How will you ensure that you effectively engage with both the parent and the child? Think about the information you will need from the visit. Consider:

- How do I attempt to engage the parent and the child in the first meeting?

- Do I have knowledge of the family's home language? If they do not speak English how will I communicate?

- How will I ensure both parent and child leave the meeting feeling they have received my attention?

- How do I emphasise a three-way process?

- Is the setting appropriate?

Summary

It is essential to work progressively with parents who find collaboration a challenge; emphasising their valuable contributions develops confidence in their opinions and ideas. The case studies demonstrate how sensitive and well-considered interventions can encourage effective partnerships that positively benefit children, practitioners and parents.

Key points to remember

- This chapter examined the principles for engaging with parents and the creation and continuation of successful partnerships. Collaboration with parents has a positive impact on the achievements of children.

- Quality first interactions with parents and children provide a greater opportunity for sustained collaborations.

- Collaboration should be viewed as a three-way process between practitioner, parent and child.

Points for discussion

- Consider the messages parents receive from your early childhood setting in initial interactions. How do you ensure they are given time to discuss their concerns? How do you welcome and value their contributions?

- How can you encourage the parents of children in your setting to share a skill or talent with the children?

- How could you use ICT and social media creatively to engage with parents?

Further reading

Books

Feiler, A. (2010) *Engaging 'Hard to Reach' Parents*. Chichester: Wiley–Blackwell.
Jackson, D. and Needham, M. (2014) *Engaging with Parents in Early Years Settings*. London: Sage.
Whalley, M. (2007) *Involving Parents in Their Children's Learning*, 2nd edn. London: Paul Chapman Publishing.

Article

McQueen, C. and Hobbs, C. (2014) 'Working with parents: using narrative therapy to work towards greater partnership', *Educational and Child* Psychology, 31 (4): 9–17.

Useful websites

www.forestschools.com
www.foundationyears.org.uk
www.pengreen.org

References

Arnold, C. (2003) *Observing Harry: Child Development and Learning 0–5*. Maidenhead: Open University Press.
Athey, C. (2007) *Extending Thought in Young Children: A Parent–Teacher Partnership*. London: Sage.

DCSF (Department for Children, Schools and Families) (2008) *The Impact of Parental Involvement on Children's Education*. Nottingham: DCSF Publications.

DfE (Department for Education) (2012) *The EYFS Progress Check at 2: A Know How Guide*. Available at: www.gov.uk/government/uploads/system/uploads/attachment_data/file/175311/EYFS_-_know_how_materials.pdf (accessed 28 September 2015).

DfE (Department for Education) (2014a) *Statutory Framework for the Early Years Foundation Stage: Setting the Standards for Learning, Development and Care for Children from Birth to Five*. Available at: www.foundationyears.org.uk/files/2014/07/EYFS_framework_from_1_September_2014__with_clarification_note.pdf (accessed 28 September 2015).

DfE (Department for Education) (2014b) *Reforming Assessment and Accountability for Primary Schools*. Available at: www.gov.uk/government/uploads/system/uploads/attachment_data/file/297595/Primary_Accountability_and_Assessment_Consultation_Response.pdf (accessed 28 September 2015).

Feiler, A. (2010) *Engaging 'Hard to Reach' Parents*. Chichester: Wiley–Blackwell.

Goodman, A. and Greg, P. (2010) *Poorer Children's Education Achievement: How Important Are Attitudes and Behaviour?* York: Joseph Rowntree Foundation.

HM Treasury (2004) *Choice for Parents, the Best Start for Children: A Ten-Year Strategy for Childcare*. London: TSO.

Jackson, D. and Needham, M. (2014) *Engaging with Parents in Early Years Settings*. London: Sage.

MacNaughton, G. (2005) *Doing Foucault in Early Childhood Studies*. Oxford: Routledge.

Malaguzzi, L., quoted in L. Abbot and C. Nutbrown (2001) *Experiencing Reggio Emilia – Implications for Pre-school Provision*. Maidenhead: Open University Press.

McQueen, C. and Hobbs, C. (2014) 'Working with parents: using narrative therapy to work towards greater partnership', *Educational and Child Psychology*, 31 (4): 9–17.

Messenger, C. and Malloy, D. (2014) *Getting It Right for Families: A Review of Integrated Systems and Promising Practice in the Early Years*. London: LGA.

O'Hara, M. (2011) 'Young children's ICT experiences', *Journal of Early Childhood Research*, 9 (3): 220–31.

Rouse, E. (2012) *Global Studies of Childhood*, 2 (1): 14–25.

Smidt, S. (2007) *A Guide to Early Years Practice*, 3rd edn. London: Routledge.

Thornton, L. and Brunton, P. (2007) *Bringing the Reggio Approach to Your Early Years Practice*. Abingdon: Routledge.

Ward, U. (2013) *Working with Parents in Early Years* (2nd Edn), London: SAGE.

Whalley, M. (2007) *Involving Parents in their Children's Learning,* 2nd edn. London: Paul Chapman Publishing.

Want to learn more about this chapter? Visit the companion website at https://study.sagepub.com/EYFS3e for access to free SAGE journal articles and book chapters, weblinks, annotated further readings and more.

14

Working Together to Safeguard Children

Zoi Nikiforidou and Babs Anderson

 Chapter overview

Safeguarding and promoting the welfare of children is fundamental to children's well-being. As such, this is integral to the intentions of the EYFS (DfE, 2014) in illustrating that everyone who works with children has a responsibility for safeguarding. In this, practitioners need to be proactive in matters of child protection but also in ensuring safe and secure environments in order for every child to thrive.

This chapter aims to:

- explore the concepts of safeguarding and child protection and highlight the applications to practice
- examine the legislative requirements and expectations on safeguarding and welfare within early childhood services
- reflect on implications of a child-centred and coordinated approach to safeguarding.

The importance of safeguarding children

Child protection and welfare service systems are structured and function differently around the world as they are 'social configurations rooted in specific visions for children, families, communities and societies' (Cameron and Freymond, 2006: 3). In every case, it is undeniable that children thrive and develop socially, mentally, physically, emotionally and personally when they interact and grow up in safe and secure environments in their homes, classrooms, neighbourhoods and communities. Maslow (1943) emphasizes within his motivation theory how hierarchically after the satisfaction of the physiological needs, the safety needs are significant, and subsequently the love needs, the esteem needs and finally the self-actualisation needs. He mentions that precisely in cases of threat or pain, infants understand that: 'the whole world suddenly changes from sunniness to darkness' (1943: 377) and need 'all-powerful parents who protect and shield him from harm' (p. 378).

Child safeguarding refers to the responsibility, the activities and the functioning that civil society has through parents, professionals, operations and programmes, in ensuring that children are not exposed to any risk, harm and/or abuse (Sloth-Nielsen, 2014). Child safeguarding is rooted in recognising the risks and/or possible maltreatment children may face and, in turn, in assessing, addressing and intervening in a timely manner with measures and actions that create child- and family-centred safe or safer environments. Identifying these risk factors and intervening early provides a major strategy for overcoming possible social exclusion and wider problems in later life (Parton, 2011). '*Guarding*' children's safety and welfare aims to ensure the holistic well-being of children and young people and implies a proactive, rather than reactive, approach, attitude and action in supporting every child to reach their full potential. In doing so, children's voices, views and own perceptions can play a significant role and should be appreciated.

Safeguarding children means far more than child protection and regards children in need, children at risk and vulnerable children as well as every single child. A child is 'everyone under the age of 18' (DfE, 2015a; United Nations, 1989). Any child, at any point in their life, can be seen as vulnerable to some form of risk and might require support, guidance and protection. In this direction, the object of concern is primarily children who are likely to experience abuse and 'significant harm'. Moreover, all children are vulnerable to some extent by virtue of their age, immaturity and dependence on adults (Munro, 2011). However, effective safeguarding promotes children's and families' welfare through the wider range of support systems and services provided to meet their needs and interests. As Parton (2011) states, the role of prevention and protection is not only to combat the negatives involved, but also to enhance the positive opportunities for child development via maximising protective factors and processes.

There are different types of harm and four main categories of child abuse and neglect: physical, emotional, sexual abuse and neglect (DfE, 2015a). *Physical abuse* may involve hitting, shaking, throwing, poisoning, burning or scalding, drowning, suffocating or otherwise causing physical harm to a child. Physical harm may also be caused when a parent or carer fabricates the symptoms of, or deliberately induces, illness in a child.

Emotional abuse occurs through the persistent emotional maltreatment of a child so as to cause severe and persistent adverse effects on the child's emotional development. It may involve conveying to a child that they are worthless or unloved, inadequate, or valued only insofar as they meet the needs of another person. It may include not giving the child opportunities to express their views, deliberately silencing them or 'making fun' of what they say or how they communicate. It may feature age or developmentally inappropriate expectations being imposed on children. These may include interactions that are beyond a child's developmental capability as well as overprotection and limitation of exploration and learning, or preventing the child participating in normal social interaction. It may involve seeing or hearing the ill-treatment of another. It may involve serious bullying (including cyberbullying), causing children frequently to feel frightened or in danger, or the exploitation or corruption of children. Some level of emotional abuse is involved in all types of maltreatment of a child, although it may occur alone.

Sexual abuse involves forcing or enticing a child or young person to take part in sexual activities, including prostitution, whether or not the child is aware of what is happening. The activities may involve physical contact, including assault by penetration (rape, buggery or oral sex) or non-penetrative acts. They may include non-contact activities such as involving children in looking at, or in the production of, sexual online images, watching sexual activities, or encouraging children to behave in sexually inappropriate ways, or grooming a child in preparation for abuse (including via the internet). Sexual abuse is not solely perpetrated by adult males. Women also commit acts of sexual abuse, as can other children.

Neglect occurs through the persistent failure to meet a child's basic physical and/or psychological needs likely to result in the serious impairment of the child's health or development. Neglect may occur during pregnancy as a result of maternal substance abuse. Once a child is born, neglect may involve a parent or carer failing to provide adequate food, clothing and shelter (including exclusion from home or abandonment), protect a child from physical and emotional harm or danger, ensure adequate supervision (including the use of inadequate care-givers), or ensure access to appropriate medical care or treatment. It may also include neglect of, or unresponsiveness to, a child's basic emotional needs.

In addition, the significance of children's and young people's safety and welfare, is manifested in the United Nations Convention on the Rights of the Child (UNCRC) (United Nations, 1989) that underlines children's 'right to survival; to develop to the fullest; to protection from harmful influences, abuse and exploitation; and to participate fully in family, cultural and social life'. Article 19 states that:

> Parties shall take all appropriate legislative, administrative, social and educational measures to protect the child from all forms of physical or mental violence, injury or abuse, neglect or negligent treatment, maltreatment or exploitation, including sexual abuse, while in the care of parent(s), legal guardian(s) or any other person who has the care of the child.

In the UK it has been suggested that the Every Child Matters (ECM) (DfES, 2003) agenda marks the most significant change in the philosophy and delivery of children's services in England since 1948 (Hudson, 2005). Regarding child safeguarding, ECM and the legal framework, the Children Act 2004, focus on improving children's well-being by promoting better outcomes in five aspects of their lives: being healthy, staying safe, enjoying and achieving, making a positive contribution and achieving economic well-being through the integrated services of health, social care, education and criminal justice. Today, in the UK there are three core statutory frameworks in relation to education in place concerning safeguarding and promoting the welfare of young children aiming at a child-centred and coordinated approach:

- The revised EYFS statutory framework (2014) stresses a greater emphasis in detailing the safeguarding and welfare requirements in section 3.
- The 'Working Together to Safeguard Children' (DfE, 2015b) guidance covers the legislative requirements and expectations of individual services and the framework for the Local Safeguarding Children Boards (LSCBs) to monitor the effectiveness of local services;
- The 'Keeping Children Safe in Education' (DfE, 2015a) statutory guidance for schools and colleges, excluding maintained nursery schools, sets out the legal duties to be met.

These statutory frameworks define safeguarding and promoting the welfare of children under four key principles: protecting children from maltreatment; preventing impairment of children's health or development; ensuring that children grow up in circumstances consistent with the provision of safe and effective care; taking action to enable all children to have the best outcomes (DfE, 2015a: 6; DfE, 2015b: 5).

The legislative requirements and expectations on early childhood services

The Children Act (1989, amended in 2004) provides the legislative context for early childhood services, such as childminding and day care for children under the statutory school starting age of 5 years old in England. The Act requires local authorities (LAs) to provide services for children in need for the purposes of safeguarding and promoting their welfare. It also reflects the intention underpinning the UNCRC, ratified by the UK Government in 1991, for a child-centred approach to children's services. More recently, the Equality Act 2010 lays a particular duty on LAs to eliminate discrimination and promote equality of opportunity, so that all children have equal access to provision, which meets their needs. These responsibilities are enshrined in the two key principles of a child-centred and coordinated approach to safeguarding as advocated by the UK Government in the 'Working Together to Safeguard Children' guidance (DfE, 2015b).

The first key principle is that safeguarding is everyone's responsibility as a professional member of an organisation or agency, and that sole devolution of this responsibility to a named role is not sufficient. The second principle relates to a child-centred approach, such that children have said they need:

- Vigilance: to have adults notice when things are troubling them;
- Understanding and action: to understand what is happening; to be heard and understood; and to have that understanding acted upon;
- Stability: to be able to develop an on-going stable relationship of trust with those helping them;
- Respect: to be treated with the expectation that they are competent rather than not;
- Information and engagement: to be informed about and involved in procedures, decisions, concerns and plans;
- Explanation: to be informed of the outcomes of assessments and decisions and reasons when their views have not met with a positive response;
- Support: to be provided with support in their own right as well as a member of their family;
- Advocacy: to be provided with advocacy to assist them in putting forward their views. (DfE, 2015b: 11)

Safeguarding requires a clear understanding, therefore, on the part of professionals in early childhood services of the needs and views of children and how they can best support them. This is also incumbent at LA level for the collective needs of children within the locality. The identification of emerging problems and unmet needs for individual children and their families is part of the professional duties of the early childhood education and care practitioner within universal services, as well as other more specialist targeted agencies. This proposes an ongoing continuing professional development requirement for the practitioner to know how to identify and respond effectively to the symptoms and triggers of abuse and neglect, particularly where these concern vulnerable children, whilst being aware of what types of interventions may be appropriate.

Case study

Rob, age 3

Rob is 3 years old, with two older siblings. He has chronic ear problems. His family situation is that he lives in a detached house in a high socio-economic status (SES) area. His mother has recently died from cancer and his father is determined to

(Continued)

(Continued)

maintain the family unit, including their affluent lifestyle. Rob has been really quiet and reserved in the nursery and practitioners are concerned about his lack of engagement. They are also concerned that Rob has missed a number of medical appointments to do with his hearing.

The father denies any health or behaviour issues regarding Rob, saying that he is well and being cared for by his elder brother Ken, who is 12 years old. One day Rob was really hyperactive at home and would not eat his dinner. His father was away on business and had laid the responsibility on Ken to feed Rob and get him ready for bed. However, Ken got frustrated and responded to Rob's behaviour by hitting him.

The next day after this incident Rob's key person notices the bruise and informs the safeguarding lead of the nursery. They both discuss their next steps.

Reflective task

Taking into account that children have the right (Article 19) to be safe from violence, abuse and neglect by their parents, or anyone else who looks after them (United Nations, 1989):

- How would you support young children's understanding of this right?
- What activities would you plan?
- How would you involve parents and local authorities/communities?

Early help services form a continuum of support depending on the identified need of individual children and families. Where there is a low level of support required, this may be possible for individual or universal services to take definitive action, for example signposting a parent to a positive parenting support network. For other needs a coordinated approach exists through the Common Assessment Framework (CAF), where a nominated lead professional coordinates the inter-agency assessment, acting to synthesise information and knowledge from a range of agencies. The intention is to provide relevant and appropriate support through an intermediary as the lead professional to the family rather than overwhelming children and their families with a wide range of professional input. Where there are more complex needs or child protection concerns, the Children Act 1989, sections 17 and 47, provides the rationale for support for children in need or LA social care services action.

Serious case reviews (SCRs) are undertaken when there has been a breakdown in safeguarding, resulting in the death or serious injury of a child, where abuse or neglect are known or suspected. Brandon et al. (2012) detail the potentials for learning from the examination of such cases, where new insights are generated, which may then positively impact on practice. However, Rawlings et al. (2014) offer an identification of emerging themes that indicate why lessons learnt from SCRs have not been embedded in policy and practice. One of these themes, classified as barriers to learning from SCRs, includes the recognition that the large numbers of recommendations from diverse SCRs to generate new policies and procedures is overwhelming and can act to reduce efficiency rather than supporting it. A second theme, learning culture and training, indicates that there is a lack of consistent relevant training that is accessible for practitioners, and the third theme, policy and procedures, details '[r]apid policy and procedural change and implementation impacts significantly on frontline staff creating confusion and tensions relating to workload, roles and responsibilities and accountability' (Rawlings et al., 2014: 7). All of these findings indicate that the well-intentioned public examination of SCRs requires a more coordinated approach, when safeguarding fails, in order to support wider, more embedded change in policy and practice.

The safeguarding and welfare requirements of the Early Years Foundation Stage

The safeguarding and welfare requirements of the EYFS (DfE, 2014) make it abundantly clear as to the public accountability (Ball, 2013) of providers of early childhood education and care. The requirements are framed in such a manner as to ensure compliance, using such terms as 'must' throughout the documentation to emphasise the importance of meeting each requirement.

Providers of settings have a number of key responsibilities, which are designed to enable the creation of 'high quality settings, which are welcoming, safe and stimulating, and where children are able to enjoy learning and grow in confidence' (DfE, 2014: 16). In these settings, children are kept safe and well, yet there is also an obligation on practitioners to be alert to issues of concern in the child's wider experiences, at home as well as elsewhere. From 1 July 2015, for example, all public bodies are subject to a duty under the Counter-Terrorism and Security Act 2015 to have 'due regard to the need to prevent people from being drawn into terrorism'. This duty is known as the Prevent Duty to which early childhood care providers must have regard to the statutory guidance. In fulfilling this duty staff are expected to be able to identify children who may be vulnerable to radicalization and Ofsted's inspection framework now makes specific reference to this need. The demands on practitioners for a duty of care for the young children attending their setting thus extends beyond the workplace into the community and this raises its own challenges.

The requirements fall into a number of categories, such as policy and procedures, characteristics of practitioners, relationships, the environment and information sharing. The provider must ensure that they have a policy for safeguarding that meets the guidance of the Local Safeguarding Children Board (LSCB), including procedures for mobile telephones in the setting. This must also reflect the guidance given in Working Together to Safeguard Children (DfE, 2015b). A lead practitioner for safeguarding in each setting should be identified, who undertakes the necessary child protection training, acts as liaison contact with the LSCB and who can support their colleagues in all matters of safeguarding. This does not replace, however, the requirement for all staff members to be fully cognisant of safeguarding issues, so that they are able to identify and respond to incidents when they arise. Other key policies and procedures are health-related, such as administering medication to children, control of infection and its spread, accidental injury and a healthy food policy. This reflects the government's aim to reduce levels of childhood obesity (Public Health England, 2014).

The characteristics of practitioners include suitability, which is supported by a criminal records check and staff qualifications, training, support and skills. The latter includes knowledge about procedures for safeguarding, emergency evacuation of the premises and health and safety issues. It also covers knowledge and understanding of young children's learning and development as well as the setting's equality policy, so that welfare or well-being is considered from a more holistic viewpoint, including social and emotional aspects of health in addition to physical aspects. Members of staff are entitled to regular support sessions, such as coaching in order to continually improve their practice. They must also have the ability to communicate effectively in English, both orally and in writing. Other requirements are for at least one member of staff to have a paediatric first aid certificate, when children are on the premises or on outings and for one member of staff to act as the Special Educational Needs Coordinator (SENCO).

Relationships form the basis of the key person role, with each child having a key person as their immediate point of contact. The practitioner needs to tune into the individual child in order to understand their needs (Elfer, 2012) and to support the child, whilst in the setting. They must also be able to build a reciprocal relationship with the child's parents through effective communication. Managing behaviour is also foregrounded implicitly that the practitioner is required to use appropriate methods of managing behaviour, with corporal punishment or 'smacking' clearly prohibited.

Case study

Nia, practitioner at a nursery

Laura is 4 years old and lives with her mother. Her mother's sister, Laura's aunt, brings her to nursery every day. Recently Laura's behaviour has changed, she has become aggressive and antagonistic, initiating conflicts with her peers constantly. She also looks tired and her clothes are not clean. As a result, her classmates do not want to play and spend time with her, and this is leading her to become even more hostile.

Her key person, Nia, has recorded some incidents, whilst encouraging conflict resolution; however, the evidence for the reasons in this change of behaviour is limited. Nia decides not to inform the safeguarding lead of the nursery yet. She tries to approach Laura's aunt, who claims no responsibility and avoids any conversation. As Nia has a close relationship with Laura, she chats with her. After this conversation, Nia finds out barely any information that could give her indications of potential risks and causes for these behavioural changes.

Later that week, Nia uses in class the 'three houses' tool (Weld, 2008) as part of the PSED curriculum. This tool focuses on interviewing children through their own drawings and own oral interpretations focusing on a 'house of worries', 'house of good things' and 'house of dreams'. Based on Laura's drawings, Nia realizes that there are issues going on at home and makes the decision to arrange a meeting with her mother to discuss these. As Laura's mother doesn't show up to the meeting, Nia informs the safeguarding lead of the nursery. In turn, they make a formal report.

Reflective task

There is a debate on how to achieve a balance between health and safety issues within settings and the management of children's reasonable risk-taking.

- Which aspects of health and safety issues would you take into consideration based on the EYFS (DfE, 2014)?

- Why would you be interested in promoting children's own risk competence?

The environment of settings plays a key role in supporting children's welfare. This includes organisation of the available space, both inside and outside, with the express stipulation that provision must include outdoor availability at least once per day, unless extreme weather conditions prevail. The requirement for regular risk assessments is evident, including when outings from the setting occur. There should also be a space available for confidential meetings between staff and parents, in order to support respectful relationships when discussing potentially difficult issues.

Information sharing and record-keeping are integral to the efficient working of the setting, where confidential records are maintained for each individual child, in collaboration with the parents. These records are also available for sharing where the child attends other settings, such as a childminder's home setting or a breakfast/after-school club. Other cases, where information may be shared, involves the child's best interests, so that this includes information sharing with other agencies, such as children's social care, the police or other professional bodies, such as speech and language therapists.

Child-centred and coordinated approach to safeguarding

Safeguarding is everyone's responsibility. Everyone involved in child protection should pursue child-centred inter-agency working by playing their full part effectively and by recognising children's views and needs as the centre of the system. Children and young people are individuals with rights, including their right to participation in decisions about them in line with their age and maturity (Munro, 2011). Moreover, children and young people are a key source of information about their lives and the impact any problem has on them in the specific culture of their family (Willow, 2009), and if allowing children's voices to be heard is undertaken well this participation can be empowering. In addition, coordination, cooperation, assessment, working together and taking respective action falls within the responsibility of everyone who works with children and their families, namely: teachers, GPs, nurses, midwives, health visitors, early childhood professionals, youth workers, police, accident and emergency staff, paediatricians, voluntary and community workers and social workers (DfE, 2015b).

Everyone who comes into contact with children and families has a role to play in safeguarding and promoting the welfare of children; in identifying concerns, sharing information and taking prompt action in collaboration with other professionals and agencies. Where a child is suffering significant harm, or is likely to do so, action should be taken to protect that child. Action should also be taken to promote the welfare of a child in need of additional support, even if they are not suffering from harm or are at immediate risk (DfE, 2015a). Professionals and practitioners play a particularly important role as they are in a position to identify concerns early and provide help and support to prevent the escalation of these concerns, as every day matters. If intervention takes place at an early stage in children's lives then there is likelihood to prevent a range of problems in later life in relation to educational attainment, unemployment, crime and anti-social behaviour (Parton, 2011).

No system can fully eliminate risk, and according to Adams (2006), everyone is a risk 'expert' in the sense of being trained by practice and experience on the management of risk and risky situations. Risks and dangers are part of our lives and are dynamic and transformative; they have diverse forms, causes, impacts, degrees, layers, complexities, constructs. Understanding risk involves judgement and balance. To manage risks related to children, professionals should make decisions having in mind the best interests of the child, informed by evidence available and underpinned by knowledge of child development. Safeguarding and promoting the welfare of children can be achieved through critical reflection, high-quality assessments, decision and review points with a clear analysis, timeliness and systematic investigation of the child's developmental needs, parents' or carers' capacity to respond to those needs, and the broader impact of the family, community and environmental circumstances. The interaction of these domains

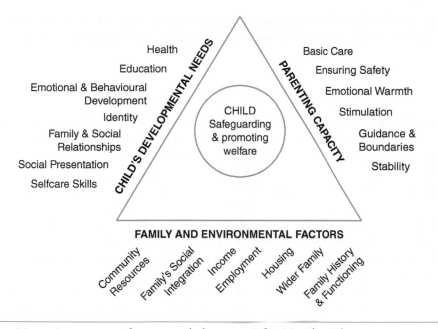

Figure 14.1 *Assessment framework (source: DfE, 2015b: 22)*

requires careful investigation and the aim is to reach a judgement about the nature and level of needs and/or risks that the child may be facing within their family (Figure 14.1).

However, safeguarding is much more complex than child protection, important as this may be. It may be viewed as enabling the child to reach their full potential rather than insisting on an overprotective stance that hinders children's independence, self-esteem and risk-taking. Adults cannot be always there for children. Safeguarding is not only about the present but also about setting the foundations for being able to *take care of oneself* in the future.

By positioning the important, agentic and active role of children within safeguarding and risk society, a growing body of research claims that there tends to be a 'problem of surplus safety' (Wyver et al., 2010) and that the risk today is that there is 'no risk' for children (Bundy et al., 2009). There has been a growth of provisions and processes in order to ensure safety issues leading to the extreme side of overprotection and safety-regulated societies (Sandseter, 2010). This sense of adult control and monitoring of children's interactions and risk avoidance or aversion has rendered lifestyles for children with limited active and physical play, restricted engagement with unfamiliar, unknown environments and only partial contact with nature (Gill, 2007). A possible proposition to reverse this tendency is to take into account and promote children's own risk awareness as active citizens.

The basic argument is not to leave children totally exposed to any sort of hazards, but to allow them opportunities in a structured and appropriate way that would encourage self-care skills, risk appraisal and autonomous decision taking (Christensen and Mikkelsen, 2008). Risk and danger can be pedagogically approached and children can become risk-aware and risk-competent through a gradual taster of educational activities within the 'controlled' environment of the classroom and the broader notion of risk literacy (Nikiforidou et al., 2012). Children need to understand the distinction between the acceptable and unacceptable risk and reach the point where they can realize that *feeling safe* is different from *being safe* (Eichsteller and Holthoff, 2009). They also need to be given time and space to have their opinions, wishes and views heard on what is safe, dangerous, secure and risky. As a matter of fact, allowing children to understand and take risks with an educational goal and incentive is actually a means of safeguarding them.

Summary

This chapter has demonstrated that safeguarding children is a complex and broad issue. This chapter tried to address the issue of safeguarding children and its importance in the EYFS. All settings that care about children have a commitment for children's safety, security and well-being. Whilst there is a requirement in early childhood education and care to protect children from any form of abuse and harm it is essential to be proactive in terms of ensuring that strategies are in place to avoid abuse of children. Central to safeguarding children is their health and well-being, which will be discussed in Chapter 15.

Key points to remember

- The significance of safeguarding and promoting children's welfare is shown by its inclusion in the revised statutory framework for the EYFS (DfE, 2014), which places an obligation and responsibility on settings and the staff who work within them to ensure children's safety and well-being.

- Safeguarding is not limited to child protection as it refers to the child's holistic development as well as prevention of harm, abuse and neglect.

- The four key principles of safeguarding are: protecting children from maltreatment; preventing impairment of children's health or development; ensuring that children grow up in circumstances consistent with the provision of safe and effective care; taking action to enable all children to have the best outcomes in a timely manner.

- Safeguarding is not only about enabling children to be safe at present but also in the future by supporting their development of risk awareness.

> ### Points for discussion
>
> - Why is safeguarding and promoting children's welfare such a current issue?
>
> - What are the challenges a practitioner faces in his/her safeguarding role?
>
> - Would you relate bullying to safeguarding and how would it present itself in settings?

Further reading

Book chapters

Coleman, S. and May-Chahal, C. (2013) 'Understanding child maltreatment', in *Safeguarding Children and Young People*. London: Routledge in association with Community Care. pp.1–16.

Parton, N. (2014) 'The changing politics and practice of child protection and safeguarding in England', in *Thatcher's Grandchildren? Politics and Childhood in the Twenty-First Century*. London: Palgrave Macmillan. pp. 45–68.

Article

Lumsden, E. (2014) 'Changing landscapes in safeguarding babies and young children in England', *Early Child Development and Care*, 184: 9–10, 1347–63.

Useful websites

The Munro Review of Child Protection: Final Report: A Child-Centred System:
www.gov.uk/government/uploads/system/uploads/attachment_data/file/175391/Munro-Review.pdf

Working Together to Safeguard Children (2015):
www.gov.uk/government/uploads/system/uploads/attachment_data/file/419595/Working_Together_to_Safeguard_Children.pdf

Department for Education – The Prevent Duty: Departmental Advice for Schools and Childcare Providers (2015)
https://www.gov.uk/government/uploads/system/uploads/attachment_data/file/439598/prevent-duty-departmental-advice-v6.pdf

References

Adams, J. (2006) *Risk*. London: Taylor & Francis/Routledge.

Ball, S.J. (2013). *Foucault, Power and Education*. New York: Routledge.

Brandon, M., Sidebotham, P., Bailey, S., Belderson, P., Hawley, C., Ellis, C. and Megson, M. (2012) *New Learning from Serious Case Reviews: a two year report for 2009–2011*. Research Report DFE-RR226. London: Department for Education.

Bundy, A.C., Luckett, T., Tranter, P.J., Naughton, G.A., Wyver, S., Spies, G. and Ragen, J. (2009) 'The risk is that there is 'no risk': a simple innovative intervention to increase children's activity levels', *International Journal of Early Years Education*, 17: 33–45.

Cameron, G. and Freymond, N. (2006) 'Understanding international comparisons of child protection, family service and community caring systems of child and family welfare', in G. Cameron and N. Freymond (eds) *Towards Positive Systems of Child and Family Welfare*. Toronto: University of Toronto Press. pp. 3–27.

Christensen, P. and Mikkelsen, M.R. (2008) 'Jumping off and being careful: children's strategies of risk management in everyday life', *Sociology of Health & Illness*, 30 (1): 112–30.

DfE (Department for Education) (2014) *Statutory Framework for the Early Years Foundation Stage: Setting the Standards for Learning, Development and Care for Children Birth to Five*. London: DfE. Available at: www.foundationyears.org.uk/files/2014/07/EYFS_framework_from_1_September_2014__with_clarification_note.pdf (accessed 28 September 2015).

DfE (Department for Education) (2015a) *Keeping Children Safe in Education: Statutory Guidance for Schools and Colleges*. London: DfE.

DfE (Department for Education) (2015b) *Working Together to Safeguard Children: A Guide to Inter-agency Working to Safeguard and Promote the Welfare of Children*. London: DfE.

DfES (Department for Education and Skills) (2003) *Every Child Matters*. London: TSO.

Eichsteller, G. and Holthoff, S. (2009) 'Risk competence – towards a pedagogic conceptualization of risk', *Children Webmag*, 9.

Elfer, P. (2012) *Key Persons in the Early Years: Building Relationships for Quality Provision in Early Years Settings and Primary Schools*. Abingdon: Routledge.

Gill, T. (2007) *No Fear: Growing Up in a Risk Averse Society*. London: Calouste Gulbenkian Foundation.

Hudson, B. (2005) 'Partnership working and the children's services agenda: is it feasible?', *Journal of Integrated Care*, 13 (2): 7–17.

Maslow, A.H. (1943) 'A theory of human motivation', *Psychological Review*, 50: 370–96.

Munro, E. (2011) *The Munro Review of Child Protection: Final Report: A Child-Centred System*. London: TSO.

Nikiforidou, Z. Pange, J. and Chadjipadelis, T. (2012) 'Risk literacy in early childhood education under a lifelong perspective', *Procedia – Social and Behavioral Sciences Procedia*, 46: 4830–4833.

Parton, N. (2011) 'Child protection and safeguarding in England: changing and competing conceptions of risk and their implications for social work', *British Journal of Social Work*, 41 (5): 854–75.

Public Health England (2014) Child obesity and socioeconomic status data factsheet. [Online]. Available at: http://www.noo.org.uk/NOO_pub/key_data (accessed 29 January 2016).

Rawlings, A., Paliokosta, P., Maisey, D., Johnson, J., Capstick, J. and Jones, R. (2014) *A Study to Investigate the Barriers to Learning from Serious Case Reviews and Identify Ways of Overcoming These Barriers*. Research Report DFE- RR340. London: Department for Education.

Sandseter, E.B.H. (2010) 'It tickles in my tummy!' Understanding children's risk-taking in play through reversal theory', *Journal of Early Childhood Research*, 8 (1): 67–88.

Sloth-Nielsen, J. (2014) 'Regional frameworks for safeguarding children: the role of the African Committee of Experts on the Rights and Welfare of the Child', *Social Sciences*, 3: 948–61.

United Nations (1989) *United Nations Convention on the Rights of the Child.* Geneva: Defence International and United Nations Children's Fund. Available at: www.ohchr.org/en/professional interest/pages/crc.aspx.

Weld, N. (2008) 'The three houses tool: building safety and positive change', in M. Calder (ed.), *Contemporary Risk Assessment in Safeguarding Children.* Lyme Regis: Russell House Publishing.

Willow, C. (2009) 'Putting children and their rights at the heart of the safeguarding process', in H. Cleaver, P. Cawson, S. Gorin and S. Walker (eds), *Safeguarding Children. A Shared Responsibility.* Chichester: Wiley–Blackwell. pp. 13–37.

Wyver, S., Tranter, P., Naughton, G., Little, H., Sandseter, E.B.H. and Bundy, A. (2010) 'Ten ways to restrict children's freedom to play: the problem of surplus safety', *Contemporary Issues in Early Childhood*, 11 (3): 263–77.

Want to learn more about this chapter? Visit the companion website at https://study.sagepub.com/EYFS3e for access to free SAGE journal articles and book chapters, weblinks, annotated further readings and more.

15

Children's Health and Well-being

Carolyn Silberfeld

 Chapter overview

The EYFS identifies the importance of children's health, and practitioner responsibility to ensure their health and safety. There is a focus on children's self-care, with an emphasis on children making healthy choices in relation to hygiene, physical exercise and nutrition. In order to support the health needs of young children it is important to place these aspects within a wider context of children's health and well-being. Underpinning children's health and well-being are issues of poverty and inequality because these have the greatest influence, more than any other extraneous factor. Despite the influences of poverty and inequality, however, there is strong evidence to suggest that early interventions and preventive measures such as immunisation, health surveillance and health education make a positive difference (Marmot Review, 2010).

This chapter aims to:

- define children's health and well-being
- discuss the influence of poverty and inequality
- explore health policy and service provision
- explain the work of health professionals and multi-professional practice
- discuss children's participation in decision-making about health needs and health care.

Due to the wealth of information around this area, this chapter is supported by information on the companion website, where factors that influence children's health and well-being will be investigated further. These include:

- mortality and morbidity
- child health screening
- surveillance and immunisation
- children's chronic health conditions
- children's mental health
- children's dental health
- nutrition for young children
- the influence of the media
- the effects of poor nutritional intake.

Defining children's health and well-being

Both health and well-being are complex concepts for which there are a number of well-used definitions. One of the more comprehensive definitions was developed by a World Health Organisation (WHO) working group that discussed the principles of health promotion in 1984. It redefined their original 1948 definition, which had viewed health as an absence of disease, and instead provided the following:

> The extent to which an individual or group is able on one hand to realise aspirations and satisfy needs and on the other hand to change or cope with the environment. Health is, therefore, seen as a resource for everyday life, not the objective of living. It is a positive concept emphasising social and personal resources, as well as physical capacities. (WHO, 1984: 4)

Definitions tend to be contextual to what is being discussed about children's health and well-being by different individuals and organisations. Some of the more interesting definitions are those offered by children, who tend to view health positively, rather than the deficit approach of some adult definitions. A study by Natapoff (1978) showed that children between 6 and 12 years were able to express their ideas on what constituted health; they described it as feeling well and being able to participate in the activities they enjoyed. When children were asked about their views on health in a later study they linked health to lifestyle and a more general sense of well-being (NCB, 2005). In this way health can be seen as a subjective concept, which increases its complexity. In more recent studies (Children's Society, 2012; La Valle et al., 2012), children's views remain similar – rather than seeing health as the absence of ill-health symptoms, they perceive health as feeling good and being able to take part in day-to-day activities. They are able to differentiate mental and physical health and link the importance of feeling good emotionally to being healthy. Physical health is seen as the ability to participate in physical activity, with the health benefits emanating from 'playing, taking part in sports, or having fun' (La Valle et al., 2012: 47).

It is easy to use the term 'well-being' loosely or rhetorically, without clearly defining what is meant. For example, in 2006, the leader of the UK Conservative party (at the time in opposition to the government) made the following statement about well-being in his speech about hopes for the future:

> It's time we admitted that there's more to life than money and it's time we focused not just on GDP, but on GWB – general well-being. Well-being can't be measured by money or traded in markets. It's about the beauty of our surroundings, the quality of our culture and, above all, the strength of our relationships. Improving our society's sense of well-being is, I believe, the central political challenge of our time. (Cameron, 2006)

Well-being thus seems to be a concept that adults can define more easily than children (Counterpoint Research, 2008). This may be because children define being healthy as being well and, in the Good Childhood Inquiry, children viewed health as an essential part of well-being (Children's Society, 2012). According to Statham and Chase, in their overview of evidence about well-being, there is an understanding that it refers to the quality of people's lives.

> It is a dynamic state that is enhanced when people can fulfil their personal and social goals. It is understood both in relation to objective measures, such as household income, educational resources and health status; and subjective indicators such as happiness, perceptions of quality of life and life satisfaction. (2010: 2)

What this clarifies is that well-being is a multi-dimensional concept in which the future of children's lives needs to be considered as well as their present lives, using both subjective and objective dimensions, in relation to children's rights, needs or quality of life. UNICEF (2007) identified six 'dimensions' in children's lives in its exploration of well-being in wealthy countries, such as the UK:

- Material well-being
- Health and safety
- Educational well-being
- Family and peer relationships
- Behaviours and risks
- Subjective well-being

This influential report attempts to put child poverty into perspective using these dimensions. Of concern is that in the overall ranking of the twenty-one countries studied, the UK was placed last for the quality of life indicators (see section below about poverty and inequality). Similarly, in a subsequent comparative report of the 29 most advanced economies (UNICEF, 2013), although the UK was ranked sixteenth, this needs to be seen in the context of a global recession in which other countries were more seriously affected financially. In addition, the dimensions in children's lives used for this report were reduced to five and did not include family and peer relationships (or subjective well-being) – the dimension that children indicated was key to their happiness and well-being (Children's Society, 2006).

Influences of poverty and inequality on children's health and well-being

The health and well-being of children in the UK continues to cause concern (Marmot Review, 2010). During the past 25 years, despite increased prosperity the health of children in the UK is considered to be much poorer than children in other comparable European Countries (BMA Board of Science, 2013). Childhood mortality from all causes remains higher, with, for example, an estimated 2,000 more children dying per year in the UK than Sweden. One of the greatest concerns is that the gap between rich and poor in the UK continues to widen. During the past 15 years, experts in child health and research have consistently argued that this gap will continue to widen unless the causes of poverty are properly addressed and there is greater social and economic equity for children in the UK (e.g. Bardsley and Morgan, 2000; Shaw et al., 2005; Marmot Review, 2010; Child Poverty Action Group, 2012; BMA Board of Science, 2013; Wolfe et al., 2014).

These inequities are most clearly seen through infant mortality statistics, childhood obesity and accidents. Children most adversely affected are looked-after children, children with disabilities or children from black and minority ethnic groups.

> Social and economic inequalities are matters of life and death for children. Countries that spend more on social protection have lower child mortality rates. The messages are stark and crucial. Poverty kills children. Equity saves lives. Social protection is life-saving medicine for the population. (NCB/RCPCH, 2014: 2)

Inequity in access to quality health care for young children has been ongoing with, for example, clear evidence of increased numbers accessing health surveillance programmes in more prosperous geographical areas (Hall and Elliman, 2006). In order to address this social inequality the concept of proportionate universalism has been put forward (Marmot Review, 2010). This is where the scale and intensity of universal services (which should continue to be universal) should be proportionate to the level of disadvantage.

Although children's health and standards of living have improved since the inception of the National Health Service and universal benefits, poverty, deprivation and inequality remains consistent in the UK. Poverty can be viewed as being either absolute or relative. Absolute poverty is measured as there being insufficient resources to meet the needs of child and families, whereas relative poverty is when they lack the resources which others have in the society to which they belong (Townsend, 1979). This is an important differentiation because it recognises that not all societies have the same needs. This concept was further developed by Lansley and Mack (2015), who introduced the concept of 'socially perceived necessities' – necessities of life which people perceived no one in UK society should have to do without. These necessities included adequate housing as well as certain personal and household goods, leisure and social activities. Therefore, poverty is considered to be multi-dimensional and there is global recognition that it cannot be viewed in any society without taking into account political, social and economic processes.

Findings from the Millennium Cohort Study, a multi-disciplinary research project following the lives of around 19,000 children born in the UK in 2000–01, have shown that developmental and health outcomes for children are much more related to social inequalities and material deprivation than social class. The indicators of risk to which children are exposed include parental mental health, physical disability, domestic, substance or alcohol abuse, worklessness, overcrowding, teenage parenthood and financial stress. Only 42% of parents are not exposed to any of these risks, which do not usually tend to occur in isolation of other risks (Sabates and Dex, 2012).

There is also a strong and multi-dimensional relationship between the impact of the recession in 2008 on the UK's national economy and the deterioration of children's health and well-being (UNICEF, 2014). Living in poverty can lead to poor health and housing, poor child health and lower educational attainment. The austerity measures put in place by the Coalition and subsequent Conservative governments since 2010 have negatively impacted mostly on the health and well-being of the poorer and more vulnerable in UK society. Changes in benefit regulations, consistent high unemployment, rising poorly paid insecure employment and insufficient low-cost housing have impacted on those least able to express their voices politically. There has also been a move by the state to require people to take greater responsibility for their lives, both socially and economically (Lansley and Mack, 2015). This can be seen in the following case study, where Sarah feels she has no choice, other than to be independent, even though she may not be accessing the economic and social support to which she is entitled.

Case study

Sarah's family

Robert is 2 years old and lives with his single-parent mother, Sarah, aged 27 years, and his brother, Michael, an asthmatic aged 5 years, on the fifteenth floor of a block of flats. Robert spends his day with his grandmother, a pensioner living alone since the death of her husband last year, on the tenth floor of the same block of flats. Sarah cannot afford other childcare for Robert as she cannot ask for regular hours, due to her employment, and would not always be able to afford to pay the cost of regular childcare. Sarah works on a zero-hours contract for a multi-national chain of food outlets, which usually offers her between 15 and 30 hours per week. She also works on a zero-hours contract for a catering company that usually offers her about 10–20 hours of work per week. Neither employment can offer Sarah regular work, or employment benefits of holiday and sick pay. Sarah does not necessarily work locally as she may have to travel to other branches of the food outlet or geographical distances for the catering company. Although the local benefits office knows her situation, Sarah has had problems and delays accessing the benefits she is entitled to because of the irregular hours of work she is offered. In desperation, she borrowed money from a local money lender when she had her benefits delayed for four weeks. Although this was more than a year ago she is still paying off the debt, which has accrued a lot of interest. Sarah has resorted to food banks when there is no food left for the children but she dislikes asking for charity and feels an inadequate parent when she has to ask for help.

Reflective task

After studying Chapter 11 and familiarising yourself with Bronfenbrenner's Ecological Systems (Bronfenbrenner, 1994), reflect on the case study in relation to the health and well-being of children. Consider the following questions.

- How does the Microsystem, such as the home or EYFS setting, have a direct influence on the children?

- How does the Mesosystem have an influence on the children?

- How does the Exosystem, which does not involve the child directly but which can affect a child such as by parental employment/unemployment, have an influence on the children and Sarah's family?

- How does the Macrosystem, which can include the political, socio-economic and cultural context, influence the children?

- How could you facilitate Sarah's understanding of support services which may be available?

- How effectively could you support the children's health needs whilst they are in your care?

Health policy and service provision

The key UK policy of *Every Child Matters* (DfES, 2003) was followed in 2004 by a national framework for children's services in England which outlined the health provision requirements for children and families for service providers (DH, 2004). The Child Health Programme was introduced, which became the Healthy Child Programme (HCP) (DH, 2009). This programme is intended to be a preventative initiative, tailored to the needs of children and families. In order to achieve improved health outcomes, families are offered screening, immunisation and developmental reviews for their children as well as information to support parents in making healthy choices for themselves and their children. Although the HCP is a universal programme it has to incorporate differing family and health needs depending on circumstances. Central to the programme is the role of health visitors, who have been expected to implement it. Within this programme there is the two-and-a-half-year assessment, usually carried out by health visitors. More recently, there has been a move to integrate the HCP with the Early Years Progress Check in an Integrated Review (see below).

Recent health policy has been heavily influenced by the impact of government reforms that changed the way in which services were delivered (HM Government, 2010). Instead of major funding going to health authorities or Primary Health Trusts, it went instead to Clinical Commissioning Groups (CCGs) who commission hospital and community services in the local areas for which they are responsible. GPs belong to CCGs and are allocated budgets to resource appropriate hospital and community care for their patients. This has had the potential to impact on the services available to children and families as there are always cost implications.

The Marmot Review (2010) was commissioned by the government to develop the most effective evidence-based strategies to reduce health inequalities, including policies that would address the wider determinants of these. The policy recommendations for young children and families were clear: in order to address the inequalities in health there needed to be policy changes that included increased funding for early childhood, priority for interventions that reduced the adverse outcomes of pregnancy and children in their first year of life and routine support for parenting programmes. In 2014 the UK government published a health improvement plan in which they expressed the need to shift the focus from curing illness to sustaining good health and the importance of looking at health holistically, without separating mental, physical and social health (DH, 2014). In the report there were recommendations that included the imperative to meet the needs of those with chronic illnesses, and mental health conditions, whilst continuing with public health expenditure constraints. Surprisingly, there was no mention of the policy recommendations to reduce inequalities in health, outlined in the Marmot Review (2010).

Health professionals and multi-professional practice

The health professionals who work with young children and families are health visitors, school nurses and community children's nurses. Other health professionals include practitioners, family nurse practitioners, paediatricians, physiotherapists, speech and language therapists, learning disability nurses, dieticians and clinical psychologists.

Health visitors are specialist community public health nurses whose aim is to support and empower families with young children. They have broad knowledge of family health and social care issues and child development. They have many roles, which include responsibility for screening, offering advice and guidance to parents and referral to appropriate provision when required. Many health visitors are involved in interventions with young children and families, such as the family nurse practitioner, more about which is written later in this section. Health visitors are supported by mixed skill teams, which include nursery nurses, to deliver what is considered to be an essential public health service. As more is known about the adverse influences of life circumstances on young children's health and brain development, there has been a move by the government, health agencies and local authorities to pledge their support for public health services, such as health visiting, which have been shown to improve outcomes for children and families (NHS England, 2014).

School nurses also have an essential role in supporting and monitoring the health of school-age children. The remit for school nurses has recently been expanded to seventeen areas of health, which include the promotion of good mental health and the emotional well-being of looked-after children.

The Family Nurse Partnership, a home visiting programme, has been offered to first-time young mothers (aged 19 or under) since 2007. Community health professionals, usually health visitors, visit young mothers/parents regularly from early pregnancy until the child is 2 years old. Caseloads are small for the estimated 30,000 families who could benefit from the programme, so there is an additional need for health visitors if the programme is to be carried out comprehensively (Browne and Jackson, 2013). Research has shown the programme to be effective in supporting young parents and reducing risks of health and safety issues, child abuse and neglect, and developmental delay. Dodds (2009) adds a note of caution that the intervention itself may have limited impact if there is no change to the underlying circumstances of poverty and inequality, such as poor housing or insufficient resources to pay for the healthy food, additional childcare or safety equipment. Critics of the intervention are concerned that it is a specialised service that reaches only a small percentage of children who are considered at risk. Additionally, 41% of mothers leave the programme before the children are 2 years old (Browne and Jackson, 2013). Therefore the success of the programmes may be based on the 59% of families that complete the programme. Additionally, it is a costly programme for such a small number of families (Browne and Jackson, 2013). It has been suggested that the criteria for inclusion in the programme be widened to include more children and thus be more cost-effective. It has also been suggested that agencies other than health services should contribute to the funding for this programme because the benefits of the programme could also influence education and social care outcomes. However, it has been recognised that more needs to be done to promote a multi-disciplinary understanding of the benefits of the programme as well as more inter-disciplinary working.

For the past thirty-five years, health visiting and school nursing came under the remit of health authorities. From 2015 they will fall under the remit of the local authority as part of integrated children's service teams, which include social workers, family support practitioners and wider support services for children and families. Although there have been some advantages for practitioners, who have already experienced this integrated way of working, such as improved multi-disciplinary working practices with different professional groups and organisations, there have also been challenges of different working cultures, role boundaries, information sharing and power issues (Richardson-Todd, 2013). Increased multi-disciplinary working is viewed as being beneficial for children and families because it reduces the number of times that children are reviewed and the number of different professionals that families need to engage with.

One such initiative is the Integrated Review implemented in 2015 as one of the recommendations in a government report (DfE/DH, 2012). The Integrated Review will combine the Early Years Progress Check usually carried out by EYPs when children are aged 2 years, and the Healthy Child Programme 2–2½-year health and development review, usually carried out by health professionals. The aims of integrating these two statutory checks are to give a more complete picture of the child's health, learning and development, from both a health and education perspective (Bridgewater Community Healthcare NHS Trust, 2012). Parents will be invited to participate in the review so that their views and concerns are taken into account. It is also seen as a way of combining the professional skills of those working with the child and family to better support children's healthy development. In this way development needs can be identified early and referrals can be made to the appropriate service. Findings in two pilot studies (Blades et al., 2014; Kendall et al., 2014), commissioned by the government, have identified clear benefits and challenges to this approach. The benefits include improved multi-agency working, less duplication and improved information sharing. Challenges included different understanding of child development and the need for referral, when scoring the Ages and Stages Questionnaire (ASQ-3); different data information systems; and differing quality of existing relationships between the different services. There was some confusion as to whether the ASQ-3 was being used as screening for developmental delay or as an assessment tool. Health practitioners were concerned that if the integrated reviews only took place in early childhood settings they would not be able to view children's development and progress in their own social context (home) which may influence outcomes.

Reflective task

- Working in the field of early childhood education and care you will need to collaborate with all the professionals mentioned above. Consider what this means to your practice.

Children's participation in decision-making about health needs and health care

In a review of consultations with children about health service provision, La Valle et al. (2012) found that children had their own opinions and wanted to participate in decision-making about health service and provision. These findings are similar to a similar study by Clavering and McLaughlin (2010), who investigated the ways in which children have been included in health-related studies. Both argue that the involvement of children in health research and health care provision gives them the opportunity to be included in decision-making, which is seen both as respecting children's rights as well as helping to better understand children's viewpoints. A third study (Moore and Kirk, 2010), using similar methodology, reviewed children's participation in decision-making about health care. The review considered several aspects of children's participation. This included whether children actually wanted to participate, to what extent they were given opportunities for participation, what the barriers were to being able to participate, how they were enabled to participate and what advantages and disadvantages there were to children who participated. What they discovered was a lack of evidence of children's participation in decision-making and a lack of clarity regarding the extent to which children are involved in discussions. The decision as to whether children could be included in discussions about health care lay with the health professionals and their interpretations of children's abilities to participate in decision making.

The findings from these reviews are in contrast with studies in which children have participated, such as the State of London's Children (Hood, 2002) and The Good Childhood Inquiry (Children's Society, 2006, 2014), in which children were able to articulate their opinions about different aspects of care and provision. They also had clear ideas as to how their health and well-being could be ameliorated. In my experience, decisions are often taken before discussions and consultation with children take place. If children were invited to participate and offer their views on health care provision, this may present unwanted challenges for health care providers. By keeping control of how and when children participate in decision making, only lip service is paid to children's rights to any involvement in health care and health service provision.

Summary

This chapter attempted to put issues about children's health within a political, social and economic context because, without this, it is impossible to understand present-day implications of health policy and provision for children. Unless the growing poverty and inequality in children's lives is seriously addressed by those who make decisions about children's health and welfare, the health of children will continue to be adversely influenced. Health issues in childhood, such as mental health, nutritional intake and the subsequent chronic ill-health which can develop from these issues, will undoubtedly develop into health issues in later life. These can seriously impact on the health and welfare of the population and future generations of children. Those who work with children need to have an awareness of the influences on child health and well-being in order to understand how they can better support the needs of the children in their care. They also need to understand how difficult it is to ameliorate health issues unless the complexities of the contexts in which children and families live are taken into consideration. Finally, it is up to all those who work with children to support campaigns, such as those of the Children and Young People's Health Outcomes Forum (DH, 2012), who have recommended such achievable ways in which to improve children's health and well-being.

Key points to remember

- Children's health and well-being are complex and broad concepts that can be influenced by social, economical, environmental and personal factors.

- Central to the EYFS is the promotion of healthy children, which is covered under the section of Safeguarding and Welfare Requirements. It is recognised that children's health and well-being has a great impact on children's development.

- Poverty and inequality are key factors for children's health and well-being and early childhood education should be proactive in order to protect children's health and well-being.

Points for discussion

- How can early childhood practitioners help others to understand the complexities of socio-economic inequalities and the effects on child health and well-being?

- After studying the material on the companion website, what are the implications for practitioners of reduced screening in children and the potential reduction in the community health professionals who perform screening and surveillance?

- After studying the companion website material on children's mental health issues, discuss what the implications are for early childhood practitioners of the increased levels of mental health issues in children.

Further reading

Books

Albon, D. and Mukherji, P. (2008) *Food and Health in Early Childhood*. London: Sage.
Burton, M., Pavord, E. and Wiliams, B. (2014) *An Introduction to Child and Adolescent Mental Health*. London: Sage.

Article

Clavering, E.K. and McLaughlin, J. (2010) 'Children's participation in health research: from objects to agents?' *Child: Care, Health and Development*, 36 (5): 603–11.

Useful websites

The Joseph Rowntree Foundation:
https://www.jrf.org.uk

UNICEF:
http://www.unicef.org.uk

Department of Health (Children)
https://www.gov.uk/government/policies/children-s-health

World Health Organisation:
www.who.int/en/

References

Bardsley, M. and Morgan, D. (2000) *Inequalities in Maternal and Early Child Health: Priorities for London. Measuring Inequalities in the Health of Mothers and Children*. Briefing Paper 1. London: Directorate of Public Health, East London & The City Health Authority.
Blades, R., Greene, V. and Wallace, E. (NCB) and Loveless, L. and Mason, P. (ICF GHK) (2014) *Implementation Study: Integrated Review at 2–2½ Years – Integrating the Early Years*

Foundation Stage Progress Check and the Healthy Child Programme Health and Development Review. London: National Children's Bureau & ICF GHK.

BMA Board of Science (2013) *Growing Up in the UK: Ensuring a Healthy Future for Our Children*. London: British Medical Association.

Bridgewater Community Healthcare NHS Trust (2012) *Healthy Child Programme 2 Year Review – A Joint Assessment with Early Practitioners*. London: Department of Health.

Bronfenbrenner, U. (1994) 'Ecological models of human development', In *International Encyclopedia of Education*. Vol 3, 2nd Edn. Oxford: Elsevier.

Browne, K.D. and Jackson, V. (2013) 'Community intervention to prevent child maltreatment in England: evaluating the contribution of the family nurse partnership', *Journal of Public Health,* 35 (3): 447–52.

Cameron, D. (2006) Speech to Google Zeitgeist Europe 2006. www.guardian.co.uk/politics/ 2006/may/22/conservatives.davidcameron (accessed 28 September 2015).

Child Poverty Action Group (2012) *Ending Child Poverty by 2020: Progress Made and Lessons Learned*. London: CPAG.

Children's Society (2006) *The Good Childhood Inquiry: What the Children Told Us*. London: The Children's Society.

Children's Society (2012) *The Good Childhood Report 2012: A Review of Our Children's Well-being*. London: The Children's Society.

Children's Society (2014) *The Good Childhood Final Report*. London: The Children's Society.

Clavering, E.K. and McLaughlin, J. (2010) 'Children's participation in health research: from objects to agents?', *Child: Care, Health and Development*, 36 (5): 603–11.

Counterpoint Research (2008) *Childhood Well-being: Qualitative Research Study*. London: Department for Children, Schools and Families.

DfE (Department for Education)/DH (Department of Health) (2012) *Supporting Families in the Foundation Years*. London: DfE.

DfES (Department for Education and Skills) (2003) *Every Child Matters: Agenda for Change*. Nottingham: DfES Publications.

DH (Department of Health) (2004) *National Service Framework for Children, Young People and Maternity Services*. London: DH.

DH (Department of Health) (2009) *Healthy Child Programme: Pregnancy and the First Five Years of Life*. London: DH.

DH (Department of Health) (2012) *Report Of The Children And Young People's Health Outcomes Forum*. London: Department of Health.

DH (Department of Health) (2014) *Department of Health Improvement Plan: April 2014*. London: DH.

Dodds, A. (2009) 'Families "at risk" and the Family Nurse Partnership: the intrusion of risk into social exclusion policy', *Journal of Social Policy*, 38 (3): 499–514.

Hall, D. and Elliman, D. (2006) *Health for All Children*, 4th edn. Oxford: Oxford University Press.

HM Government (2010). *Healthy Lives, Healthy People: Our Strategy for Public Health in England*. London: Department of Health.

Hood, S. (2002) *The State of London's Children Report*. London: Office of Children's Rights Commissioner for London.

Kendall, S., Nash, A., Braun, A., Bastug, G., Rougeux, E. and Bedford, H. (2014) *Evaluating the Use of a Population Measure of Child Development in the Healthy Child Programme Two Year Review*. London: Policy Research Unit in the Health of Children, Young People and Families UCL Institute of Child Health; and Hertfordshire: Centre for Research in Primary and Community Care, University of Hertfordshire.

Lansley, S. and Mack, J. (2015) *Breadline Britain: The Rise of Mass Poverty*. London: Oneworld Publications.

La Valle, I. and Payne, L. (with Gibb, J. and Jelicic, H.) (2012) *Listening to Children's Views on Health Provision: a Rapid Review of the Evidence*. London: National Children's Bureau.

Marmot Review (2010) *Fair Society, Healthy Lives: Strategic Review of Health Inequalities in England Post-2010*. London: The Marmot Review.

Moore, L. and Kirk, S. (2010) 'A literature review of children's and young people's participation in decisions relating to health care', *Journal of Clinical Nursing*, 19: 2215–25.

Natapoff, J.N. (1978) 'Children's views of health: a developmental study', *American Journal of Public Health*, 68 (10).

NCB (National Children's Bureau)/RCPCH (Royal College of Paediatrics and Child Health) (2014) Press Release 1 May 2014 about their joint new report 'Why children die: death in infants, children and young people in the UK'. London: NCB/RCPCH.

NCB (National Children's Bureau) (2005) *Children's and Young People's Views on Health and Health Services: A Review of the Evidence*. London: NCB.

NHS England (2014). National Health Visiting Service Specification 2014/15. London: NHS England.

Richardson-Todd, B. (2013) 'Integrated working: school nursing in Suffolk', *Education and Health*, 31 (1): 22–5.

Sabates, R. and Dex, S. (2012) *Multiple Risk Factors in Children's Development*. London: Institute of Education (IOE)/Centre for Longitudinal Studies (CLS).

Shaw, M., Smith, G.D. and Dorling, D. (2005) 'Health inequalities and New Labour: how the promises compare with real progress', *British Medical Journal*, 330: 1016–21.

Statham, J. and Chase, E. (2010) *Child Well-being: A Brief Overview*. Briefing Paper 1. London: Childhood Well-being Research Centre.

Townsend, P. (1979) *Poverty in the United Kingdom: A Survey of Household Resources and Standards of Living*. Harmondsworth: Penguin.

UNICEF (United Nations Children's Fund) (2007) *Child Poverty in Perspective: An Overview of Child Well-being in Rich Countries* (Innocenti Report Card 7). Florence: UNICEF Innocenti Research Centre.

UNICEF (United Nations Children's Fund) (2013) *Child Well-being in Rich Countries: A Comparative Overview* (Innocenti Report Card 11). Florence: UNICEF Office of Research.

UNICEF (United Nations Children's Fund) (2014) *Children of the Recession: The Impact of the Economic Crisis on Children's Well-being in Rich Countries* (Innocenti Report Card 12). Florence: UNICEF Office of Research.

WHO (World Health Organisation) (1984) A discussion document on the concept and principles of health promotion. Copenhagen, 29 July 1984. In WHO (2009) *Milestones in Health Promotion: Statements from Global Conferences*. Geneva: WHO. p. 29.

Wolfe, I., MacFarlane, A., Donkin A., Marmot, M., Viner, R., on behalf of the NCB, RCPCH and BACAPH (2014) *Why Children Die: Death in Infants, Children and Young People in the UK: Part A*. London: Royal College of Paediatrics and Child Health.

Want to learn more about this chapter? Visit the companion website at https://study.sagepub.com/EYFS3e for access to free SAGE journal articles and book chapters, weblinks, annotated further readings and more.

16

Inclusion

Alex Owen

 Chapter overview

Inclusion in early childhood acknowledges the rights of *every* child, parent and practitioner to access and participate in high-quality settings where 'diversity is assumed, welcomed and viewed as a rich resource rather than seen as a problem' (Booth et al., 2003: 2). Every child is different – in name, gender, ability, needs, life-experience, culture, home-language, heritage, family background, family experience (to name a few) – and it is this difference which is explored, debated and celebrated, rather than problematised, in truly inclusive settings. In this chapter we shall consider what is understood by the term inclusion and how this foundation of understanding then informs practice within early childhood education and care.

The aim of this chapter is to support the reader to reflect upon their own understandings of difference as it is only when we allow our pre-conceptions to be challenged that our practice can be shaped to truly support every child. With this in mind, it is not the aim of this chapter to prescribe a 'how to' guide for inclusion in the early years, rather to support the reader to explore a number of aspects in relation to inclusive practice.

The chapter aims to help you to:

- reflect upon your own preconceived ideas regarding difference
- consider the role of the practitioner in developing an inclusive culture within the early childhood setting
- explore one domain of exclusion with a view to understanding the underlying, transferable principles of good practice within the Early Years Foundation Stage.

Moving from attendance to inclusion

Inclusion is far more than just a concept concerning the involvement of a child with a particular place at a particular time. It is sometimes thought that as long as all children are able to gather within a certain setting that they are 'included'. 'Inclusion is often seen as simply involving the movement of pupils from special to mainstream contexts, with the implication that they are "included" once they are there' (Ainscow, 1999: 218). However, this negates the importance of recognising each child as an individual with his or her own set of needs, belief system, cultural background, experiences, family situation and more. Ensuring that children are located in the same place just causes them to be 'present', it does not mean that they are 'included' (Corbett, 2001). It is only when the unique needs of each child are authentically recognised within a setting that a child's position moves from attendance to inclusion (Graham and Slee, 2008). Inclusion is thus concerned with overcoming barriers to participation that can be experienced by *any* child (Ainscow, 1999). This is reflected in the Early Years Foundation Stage: 'The EYFS seeks to provide equality of opportunity and anti-discriminatory practice, ensuring that every child is included and supported' (DfE, 2014: 5). Therefore inclusion is far more than just recognising children who have been given a specific diagnostic label or children who have a different ethnic background, for example. Inclusion values all children as unique, precious and worthy of our time, attention and appreciation.

This understanding causes problems in terms of defining inclusion as it does not refer to one specific group of people, one particular characteristic or one distinct experience. Although, in some respects, it might be easier to define inclusion solely in terms of practice it is important initially to take a step back from this to incorporate the subjective, personal and conceptual understanding which originates from each individual. In this respect, we should allow our definition of inclusion to remain organic and evolving as we continually challenge our frameworks of reference in an attempt to become more inclusive (Nutbrown and Clough, 2013). It is only when our world views are challenged and we operate from an understanding that our beliefs and values can evolve and develop that inclusive meaning and practices are advanced.

> Many assumptions about what inclusion means, and looks like, go unchallenged, and make up, bind and constrain our social organisation … If we can re-orientate our attention to the concept of inclusion (by challenging our own preconceptions), we can perhaps move from seeing inclusion as a set of practicalities to seeing it as an attitude of mind and will, for practicalities of inclusion are merely imported remedies that 'compensate' for a 'normal' worldview. (Nutbrown and Clough, 2013: 3)

It is crucial, before we seek to explore the implications of inclusive practice within the early childhood setting, that we take time to understand and question our own attitudes and bias concerning difference so that our worldview is exposed, challenged and potentially broadened. Due to this very nature, therefore, inclusion should be defined personally by probing pre-established norms and will take into account all that makes individuals unique and precious.

Considering this assertion that inclusion is firstly fostered within the individual, authentic inclusive practice cannot be imposed, forced or dictated. It requires genuine, honest dialogue between those who seek to include and those who seek to be included. Through this dialogue both parties must share, struggle, debate and explore to create an appropriate culture where genuine inclusive action is fostered. It is through two-way dialogue, when the experiences, needs and attitudes of children, parents and practitioners meet, that an inclusive culture is created. This inclusive culture allows for the honest exploration of attitudes and beliefs, resulting in the development of practice and authentic inclusive outcomes.

Case study

Karen and Laura's story

I'm a little late today for my weekly 'speech therapy session' in the 'PMLD Class' at Carlton Lodge and I'm feeling a little wobbly having just returned to work after three weeks during which time my mum had died. *'Morning everyone,'* I holler as I enter the hallway of the separate single-storey building on the school site.

One, two, three, four – oh, only four, who's missing? ... Stephen. *'Where's Stephen?'*

'He had a nasty fit just as the minibus arrived so mum kept him off,' called Margaret, the class teacher.

Ian and Jan are clumsily strapping Umang in to his 'standing frame', Diane is 'me-me-ing' as she lies on her back having a stretch on the floor, Margaret is assisting Sonia in having a beaker of thickened orange squash at the table and Karen is, well, where she always is, when I visit the class, curled up on not the most comfortable looking of vinyl-covered armchairs. I quickly whizz around them all almost curtseying a hello as I attempt to meet them at eye-level. I greet Karen last of all, her legs already unfolding from behind her head in anticipation. She lets out a loud *'khhhhh'* as if to say *what time do you call this? 'Oh dear, are you cross with me coz I'm a bit late? Or is it because I've been away for a few weeks?'*

Karen can spend very lengthy spells with her legs crossed behind the back of her head and as such it can take a bit of time to unravel. Strangely the staff employed there have some difficulty with the amount of saliva that Karen produces, hence the plastic chair and sometimes extensive periods sitting curled up in a ball with little interaction. There's been some discussion recently about her taking some medication to reduce the drooling but I've made my feelings clear that we should be asking whose problem it really is.

As Karen's face is gently uncovered I can see that she's grinning widely. Her cheeks are damp and quite red – she looks how I sometimes look when I've just woken up with that creased-looking face which has just emerged from the pillow. I watch her untangling her agile little legs thinking about how much my legs ache when I've sat with them crossed for a while and then I straighten them out – how does she do it? I can't see my feet never mind touch the nape of my neck with them.

'Good morning, did you think I wasn't coming?' 'Khhhhhhhhhh.' 'Ok ok,' I said, 'I'm sorry.'

Karen grabs the side of my shirt and starts hoisting her tiny, nimble body to her feet. I lightly place my arms around her waist so that she doesn't topple over. I sit down on the sticky plastic chair and gently move her legs so that she's leaning against my legs and she's a bit less wobbly.

Karen presses her soggy chin on my forehead – *'Aghhhhhh.'* I place my not so soggy chin on Karen's shoulder – *'Aghhhhhh.'* Karen says, *'Aggghhhhhhhhhhhhhhhhhhhhhhhh.'* I reply, *'Aggghhhhhhhhhhhhhhhhhhhhhhh.'*

It's funny – I have to suffer the underground on my way to work each morning where I loathe the loss of personal space, but it doesn't bother me having that imaginary bubble, which no one should enter, being burst by Karen. She rests her right cheek against my right cheek. *'Mmmmmmmmmmmmmmmmm.'* I reply, *'Mmmmmmmmmmmmmmmmmm.'* *'Are you not going to swing on my hair today?'*

Usually Karen hangs on to both sides of my hair and bounces up and down whilst giving first one *'kchhhh'*, which I repeat, then two, then three. When tired of that game she then usually collapses down on my knee and taps the top of her left leg with the side of her left hand and I repeat the number of times she taps on her right leg. She lightly cups my face and puts her face near my right ear. *'Mmmmmmmmmmmmmmmmmmm.''* I reply, *'Mmmmmmmmmmmmmmmmmmm.'*

(Continued)

(Continued)

She was being unusually gentle today. *'Are you tired? Or hungry? Are you feeling ok?'* Her gentleness is making feel quite emotional. *'Can you tell I'm feeling a bit sad today?'* I ask.

It wasn't easy coming back to work today, indeed my manager had questioned whether I needed to take a bit more time out following the quite unexpected death of my mum. But I can't actually think of a more sensitive person to spend the first part of the day with. I don't have to run through the story of what happened and there's no awkward 'nobody knows what to say' moments with Karen. *'Tsssssssssssssssssss.'* *'Oo that's a new sound. Tsssssssssssssssss.'*

Karen has now slumped down onto my lap and has the right side of her face resting on my right shoulder. I can feel my shirt soaking up her saliva. *'Mmmmmmmmmmmmmmmm.'* *'Mmmmmmmmmmmmmmmm.'* *'I bet you miss your dad don't you?'* Karen had very suddenly lost her father only two months ago. *'Do you know I've just lost my mum? Is that why you're being so gentle?'* *'Tsssssssssssssssss.'* *'Tsssssssssssssss,'* I reply. *'Are we being sad together?'* *'Mmmmmmmmmm.'* *'Mmmmmmmmmm.'*

Karen's twirling some of my hair with her right hand. *'Tsssssssssssssssss.'* *'Mmmmmmmmmm.'*

'Sonia's ready when you are Laura,' the shared moment is broken. *'Oh ok.'* *'I need to go and chat with Sonia now Karen, sorry to have to move on so quickly. Thanks for being so kind and understanding today.'* I carefully lift Karen back into her chair where she immediately slouches down and starts the slow process of moving her feet to behind her head again.

I go over to the speech therapy file on the table and record 'Karen appeared a bit subdued today. New sound – tssssss. Repetition game – only LW copying KR.' I've captured nothing of that moment.

(Waite, 2015)

Reflective task

Reflect on Karen's case study (Waite, 2015) and consider the following questions:

- What can you learn from Karen and Laura?

- How could Karen and Laura's story challenge your attitudes, beliefs and world view?

- What are the potential barriers to inclusion in this practice situation?

- What is the value of reflecting in this way? The story ends, 'I go over to the speech therapy file on the table and record "Karen appeared a bit subdued today. New sound – tsssss. Repetition game – only LW copying KR." I've captured nothing of that moment.' What is recorded in the assessment file is limited to a set of functions – reflect upon the usefulness of this form of record keeping.

- How could the four guiding principles of the EYFS (unique child, positive relationships, enabling environment, children develop and learn in different ways and at different rates) be applied in this practice setting?

Inclusion, therefore, can be understood to involve a genuine celebration of diversity as difference is understood as a key factor that brings a richness of experience to everyone involved. Rather than problematising difference, as so often is the case, the discourse must instead move to developing strategies to enhance increased participation of *all* children as it is understood that difference enriches, rather than erodes, the experience encountered in the early childhood setting (Purdue et al., 2009).

Interpreting policy

Furthering this argument, the rhetoric of policy may be common to a range of early childhood settings; however, it is the individuals involved in the settings who will dictate the level to which reliable inclusive activity truly operates (Ballard, 2003). In addition to this, even before practitioners are presented with policy, the policy itself moves through a number of levels to reach the practice context. As Devarakonda details, 'The policy cascading from global to national, and then to regional to local and then to the early childhood setting will lead to the policy being diluted and perhaps misinterpreted' (2013: 4).

Table 16.1 Examples of global and national legislation and policy

Examples of global legislation and policy		
United Nation Convention on the Rights of the Child	Ratified in the UK 1991	All children have civil, political, economic, social, health and cultural rights
Salamanca Statement and Framework for Action (World Conference on Special Needs Education)	1994	Inclusion of children with SEN and disability should be typical. Adaptations should be made according to children's needs

(Continued)

Table 16.1   (Continued)

Examples of global legislation and policy

United Nation Convention on the Rights of Persons with Disabilities	Ratified in the UK in 2009	Children with disabilities have full access to equality under the law and their rights must be promoted and protected
United Nation Convention on the Rights of Persons with Disabilities	Ratified in the UK in 2009	Children with disabilities have full access to equality under the law and their rights must be promoted and protected

Examples of national legislation and policy

Children Act	2004	A multi-professional approach should be adopted to support children's needs
Equality Act	2010	All children of every race should be treated as equal and practice should not discriminate
Child Poverty Act	2010	By the year 2020 child poverty should be eradicated
Early Years Foundation Stage	Updated 2014	Settings should provide equality of opportunity and anti-discriminatory practice ensuring that every child is included.
Children and Families Act	2014	All children should be included and given the opportunity to participate
Special Educational Needs and Disability Code of Practice	2015	Guidance for the outworking of the Children and Families Act (2014). The needs of all children with SEN must be met

A significant focus of policy and guidance, regarding the issue of inclusion, concentrates purely upon children with special educational needs and disabilities. This narrow view often negates the importance of inclusive practice for all children and operates from a deficit model. Table 16.1 briefly includes some examples of global and national legislation and policy, which have relevance for the practitioner seeking to implement an inclusive agenda within a specific practice setting.

Domains of exclusion

By understanding inclusive practice as the championing of difference within the early childhood setting it is important to appreciate the similarities and differences within strategies for developing inclusive practice, which are promoted by or targeted at particular groups. Thus inclusion involves a move towards full participation of *all* children within a defined setting by appreciating the factors that exclude. Exclusion can be termed as the creation of barriers that prevent children from experiencing full acceptance, participation and learning (Booth and Ainscow, 2011). These barriers can be physical, social, cultural, economic, attitudinal and pedagogical (to name a few) and it is the identification and removal of these barriers that is of importance within an inclusive setting (Purdue et al., 2009).

In relation to this, Nutbrown and Clough (2013) acknowledge that the potential factors for exclusion are unlimited as they are based upon the difference represented within the human race. They provide a list of 'arenas' of inclusion/exclusion (2013: 9), but clearly identify that the list is indicative and incomplete:

Achievement

Age

Challenging behaviour

Disability

Disaffection

Emotional and behavioural difficulty

Employment

Gender

Housing

Language

Mental health

Obesity

Physical impairment

Poverty

Race/ethnicity

Religion

Sexual orientation

Social class

Special Educational Need

The aim of this chapter is not to detail the specifics of all of these domains of exclusion. However, we shall move now to explore one domain with the objective to understand key principles that can be explored by those seeking to authentically adopt inclusive practice within a variety of settings. There is not one set of rules for effective practice that can be applied universally, but rather a set of principles that may have worth when considering inclusion in a variety of early childhood practice contexts (Ainscow, 2000).

> ☁ **Reflective task**
>
> • Consider the inclusion policy, inclusion discourse and inclusive practices in an early childhood setting that you are familiar with. How do they address the various 'arenas of inclusion/exclusion' listed by Nutbrown and Clough (2013)? How has practice evolved to authentically value difference and include *all* children, parents and practitioners?

Child poverty: one domain of exclusion

Issues related to poverty have relevance for many living within the United Kingdom today (Bunyan and Diamond, 2014). There is a significant difference between those who live in poverty and those unaffected and, as this margin of difference continues to grow, the resultant experience of children growing up within the United Kingdom can therefore vary significantly leading to matters of exclusion (Wilkinson and Pickett, 2010). Research has shown that child poverty significantly affects the current experience and future life chances of a child in their early childhood (Field, 2010; Tickell, 2011). Due to these outcomes, it was announced in March 1999 by the Labour government then in power that they intended to halve child poverty by 2010–11 and eradicate it by 2020. This endeavour was signified in the Child Poverty Act (2010) and therefore continues to have relevance for practice today. Despite a range of interventions aimed at enhancing inclusion, the evidence still reveals that the exclusionary issues related to poverty remain a pronounced feature in many children's lives, which has negative implications for their future life chances (Odgers et al., 2012; Ludwig et al., 2013).

Bradshaw and Holmes' research (in Hansen et al., 2010) shows that there are a range of contributing factors, all linked to matters of exclusion, which increase the likelihood of a child being raised within the conditions of poverty.

Table 16.2 Exclusionary factors that increase the likelihood of a child living in poverty

Family background: Single parent under the age of 30 years at child's birth

Race ethnicity: Mother is of Pakistani, Bangladeshi, black or black British ethnicity

Housing: Family does not live in owner-occupied accommodation

Parental education: Mother's educational level is less than lower tertiary level (NVQ Level 3)

Employment: Fewer than two wage-earners in the home

Parenting: Child is parented by a natural mother and a stepfather (compared with married natural parents)

Often these factors combine with other 'arenas' of exclusion (listed above – Nutbrown and Clough, 2013), for example disability or obesity or challenging behaviour, within the context of poverty, to significantly impact upon the young child's present life experience and future life chances.

> Children from low income families in the UK often grow up to be poor adults. However poverty is measured, whether family income, socio-economic status, or educational attainment, poverty blights the life chances of children … [they] are more likely to have preschool conduct and behavioural problems; more likely to experience bullying and take part in risky behaviours as teenagers; less likely to do well at school; less likely to stay on at school after 16; and more likely to grow up to be poor themselves. (Field, 2010: 28)

Research has shown that the variation in development between children who are affected by poverty and children who are unaffected by poverty is revealed as early as 22 months of age due to issues related to exclusion (Whitham, 2012). This then has implications for a child's future in terms of their engagement with opportunities that would support their development. Field (2010) substantiates this notion by providing evidence that young children's future life chances are created and ordained during the first five years of life. Factors, relating to the various domains of exclusion, including for example family background, parental education and childhood experience, are shown to be critical to establishing potential opportunities that would support a child to thrive in the future.

Case study

Foundation Years Project

The assertion of the Foundation Years Project, established by the Foundation Years Trust to make operational the outcomes of Field's (2010) review, was that solely increasing household income did not counter some of the exclusionary factors that impacted upon poor children's future life chances. As Field's review shows, a whole range of exclusionary characteristics linked to, but separate from, a narrow definition of financial poverty determine the future experience of poor children. Examples of these factors include the home learning environment, parental warmth and sensitivity, and parental mental health and well-being. These significant characteristics combine to form a context where a parent's ability to appropriately nurture their child is potentially impeded.

The Foundation Years Project has concentrated its attention upon engaging with a range of interventions aimed at supporting parents living in areas of

(Continued)

(Continued)

economic deprivation. A range of research outcomes validate this emphasis and highlight the importance of external support as a significant resource for parents living in poverty (Kirk, 2003; Attree, 2004; Field, 2010; Tickell, 2011). Building on this, research also points to a lack of engagement with *formal* interventions (Heinrichs et al., 2005), particularly for those living in poverty (Forehand and Kotchik, 2002; Peters et al., 2005).

> The prominence of barriers to attendance and engagement are heightened when parents face a multiplicity of issues such as low income, family discord, disorganised and chaotic lifestyles and/or ill health ... mothers in these circumstances have been found to distrust offers of help and become disinclined to accept the suggestion that a parenting programme might be of assistance. (Whittaker and Cowley, 2012: 142)

Thus, The Foundation Years Project has concentrated some of its attention upon support mechanisms with which parents, who potentially avoid formal support services, may engage – namely the informal social support gained within community-based early childhood groups (for example toddler groups). One of the key aims of these groups is to support parents to counter some of the factors that may have a detrimental impact upon the experience of their child leading to exclusion from the mechanisms that would ultimately support the child's development.

Reflective task

'Inclusion is most importantly seen as putting inclusive values into action. It is a commitment to particular values which accounts for a wish to overcome exclusion and promote participation. If it is not related to deeply held values then the pursuit of inclusion may represent conformity to a prevailing fashion or compliance with instructions from above ... it is possible to divide the framework of values [listed in the Index for Inclusion] further as in Figure 2 [see Table 16.3], by seeing some as emphasising structures, others as concerned with character and the quality of relationships and a third group as concerned with nourishing the human spirit' (Booth and Ainscow. 2011: 21–2).

Table 16.3   Inclusive values (Booth and Ainscow, 2011)

Structures	—	Relationships	—	Spirit
Equality		Respect for diversity		Joy
Rights		Non-violence		Love
Participation		Trust		Hope/optimism
Community		Compassion		Beauty
Sustainability		Honesty		
		Courage		

- How do your values for inclusion compare to this list?

- Which values do you hold but are not listed? Why do you think this is?

- Which values are listed but you do not hold? Why is this?

- How could these values inform your practice?

There is considerable discourse at national and local level concerning early intervention, in relation to the inclusive early childhood agenda, as a significant development in terms of minimising the impact of exclusionary factors upon the experience of the child (Tickell, 2011). Early intervention involves the general approaches and specific policies, related to inclusion, designed to produce benefits for children in their early childhood. This has been shown to be more cost-efficient and more effective than inclusive interventions employed later in life (Allen, 2011). The inference is clear: engaging inclusive interventions within the early childhood setting will support children to develop and thrive, which will have future implications for the child personally and for society corporately.

There are a range of potential barriers to inclusion that children from lower socio-economic situations may face. Many of these barriers are experienced by children facing a range of exclusionary factors and therefore similar challenges may apply in a variety of contexts.

Examples of potential barriers to inclusion faced by children living in poverty

- Low expectation in terms of achievement
- Health and well-being inequality

- Underdeveloped home learning environment
- Parental mental well-being strain
- Limited access to resources
- Labelling of children – for example all 'poor children' will do this/feel this way
- Attitude and prejudice of practitioners

These barriers could be linked to a whole range of the domains of exclusion mentioned previously. Therefore, when considering a response in terms of good practice, it is important to recognise the underlying principles, which this specific domain of exclusion exemplifies, that can be related to a range of situations. These principles clearly relate to the EYFS and have direct relevance for ensuring inclusive practice:

> [E]very child is a **unique child**, who is constantly learning and can be resilient, capable, confident and self-assured … (DfE, 2014; emphasis in original)

This could be achieved by:

- understanding each child has specific learning needs;
- understanding each child has specific interests;
- understanding that each child brings a wealth of experience, culture and understanding to a practice setting;
- celebrating difference with an openness to learn from all children, families and practitioners.

> [C]hildren learn to be strong and independent through **positive relationships** … (DfE, 2014; emphasis in original)

This could be achieved by:

- working with parents and children to understand each child's specific needs;
- forming partnerships with parents to support each child's learning and development;
- working with other professionals to support each child's needs;
- working to build a culture of mutual respect, based on the appreciation of difference;
- encouraging supportive relationships between all children.

> [C]hildren learn and develop in **enabling environments** in which their experiences respond to their individual needs … (DfE, 2014; emphasis in original)

This could be achieved by:

- working to reduce the barriers that exclude therefore enabling equal access and equal participation;
- responding to the experiences and backgrounds of the children involved;

- celebrating, learning from and valuing the difference represented by each child;
- providing learning experiences in response to the difference represented;
- reducing social barriers, for example practitioners' attitudes or preconceived understanding.

> **[C]hildren develop and learn in different ways and at different rates.** The framework covers the education and care of all children in early years provision, including children with special educational needs and disabilities. (DfE, 2014; emphasis in original)

This could be achieved by:

- valuing and nurturing each child individually to support them to achieve their full potential;
- identifying as early as possible any additional needs or exclusionary factors to provide appropriate support strategies;
- seeking to understand each child, rather than purely the label they may have been given (for example 'poor' or 'disabled' or 'ethnic-minority');
- ensuring all settings have designated practitioners, for example a SENCO, responsible for developing coordination of effort;
- ensuring each child has access to a comprehensive and relevant curriculum with a focus initially on the three prime areas.

Summary

Inclusion of all children is fundamental to the Early Years Foundation Stage. As we have seen, inclusion stems from the perceptions and attitudes of everyone involved within an early childhood setting and it is the resultant culture that dictates whether authentic inclusion is truly achieved. Every child has the right to be included and it is the responsibility of the practitioner to ensure that this right is recognised and upheld. Fundamental to this recognition is an understanding of difference that rejects a notion of deficit and, instead, values difference as a necessary component to the enhancement of all early childhood settings. Thus it is within a practice context when all children, parents and practitioners, with their various differences, are valued, respected and celebrated that authentic inclusion can be achieved.

To conclude, it is children who usually model this understanding of inclusion most effectively and it is their example which challenges adults' conscious and subconscious attitudes, motives and practices.

> Children are inclusive and open. Although they do recognise the differences, they are happy to accept these unconditionally. They are, however, influenced by their families, peer group, practitioners and teachers from settings such as early childhood settings and schools ... positive experiences will enable young children to embrace diversity from a young age. (Devarakonda, 2013: vi)

Key points to remember

- Inclusion in early childhood acknowledges the right of *every* child, parent and practitioner to access and participate in high-quality settings.

- Creating an authentically inclusive culture involves exploring, debating and celebrating, rather than problematising, difference.

- The potential domains of exclusion are unlimited as they are based upon the difference represented within the human race.

- When considering a response, in terms of best practice, it is important to recognise the underlying inclusive principles that can be related to a range of early childhood settings:

  - each **child is unique** and their specific needs, interests, culture and life-experience brings a rich and diverse understanding to each practice setting;

  - **positive relationships** between children, parents and practitioners build a culture of mutual respect where each child's needs are recognised and supported;

  - an **enabling environment** is essential for the recognition and removal of barriers that exclude therefore supporting access and participation;

  - **children develop and learn in different ways and at different rates** therefore each child should be valued and nurtured to achieve their full potential.

Points for discussion

- Parents are key partners in developing an authentic inclusive culture within an early childhood setting. How could you develop this crucial relationship to ensure full participation?

- The assertion of this chapter is that difference should be celebrated as a rich resource rather than a troublesome problem. How can early childhood settings authentically celebrate difference?

- The 'Progress report by the ministerial working group on tackling inequalities experienced by Gypsies and Travellers' suggests that 'Gypsies and Travellers experience, and are being held back by, some of the worst outcomes of any group, across a wide range of social indicators ... Studies have reported that

Gypsy and Traveller communities are subjected to hostility and discrimination and in many places lead separate, parallel lives from the wider community' (Department for Communities and Local Government, 2012: 5). Consider the role of the early childhood practitioner and how he/she could develop inclusive practices in response to this situation.

Further reading

Books

Booth, T. and Ainscow, M. (2011) *Index for Inclusion: Developing Learning and Participation in Schools*, 3rd edn. Bristol: Centre for Studies on Inclusive Education. pp. 73–159.
Devarakonda, C. (2013) *Diversity and Inclusion in Early Childhood: An Introduction.* London: Sage.
Nutbrown, C. and Clough, P. with Atherton, F. (2013) *Inclusion in the Early Years*, 2nd edn. London: Sage.

Articles

Macartney, B. and Morton, M. (2013) 'Kinds of participation: teacher and special education perceptions of "inclusion" in early childhood and primary school settings', *International Journal of Inclusive Education*, 17 (8): 776–92.
Nutbrown, C. and Clough, P. (2009) 'Citizenship and inclusion in the early years: understanding and responding to children's perspectives on "belonging"', *International Journal of Early Years Education*, 17 (8): 191–206.

Useful websites

Centre for Studies on Inclusive Education:
http://www.csie.org.uk

Gov.uk:
https://www.gov.uk/search?q=inclusion+and+eyfs+profile

Preschool Learning Alliance:
www.pre-school.org.uk/providers/inclusion

References

Ainscow, M. (1999) *Understanding the Development of Inclusive Schools.* London: Falmer Press.
Ainscow, M. (2000) 'The next step for special education: supporting the development of inclusive practices', *British Journal of Special Education*, 27 (2): 76–80.

Allen, G. (2011) *Early Intervention: The Next Steps*. An Independent Report to Her Majesty's Government. London: Cabinet Office.

Attree, P. (2004) 'Parenting support in the context of poverty: a meta-synthesis of the qualitative evidence', *Journal of Health and Social Care in the Community*, 13 (4): 330–7.

Ballard, K. (2003) 'The analysis of context: some thoughts on teacher education, culture, colonisation and inequality', in T. Booth, S. Nes and M. Stromstad (eds), *Developing Inclusive Teacher Education*. London: Routledge Falmer.

Booth, T. and Ainscow, M. (2011) *Index for Inclusion: Developing Learning and Participation in Schools*, 3rd edn. Bristol: Centre for Studies on Inclusive Education. pp. 73–159.

Booth, T., Nes, K. and Stromstad, M. (eds) (2003) *Developing Inclusive Teacher Education*. London: Routledge Falmer.

Bunyan, P. and Diamond, J. (2014) 'Approaches to reducing poverty and inequality in the UK: a study of civil society initiatives and fairness commissions.' A Report Commissioned by the Webb Memorial Trust for the All Party Parliamentary Group on Poverty.

Corbett, J. (2001) 'Teaching approaches which support inclusive education: a connective pedagogy', *British Journal of Special Education*, 28 (2): 55–9.

Department for Communities and Local Government (2012) Progress Report by the Ministerial Working Group on Tackling Inequalities Experienced by Gypsies and Travellers. London: Crown.

Devarakonda, C. (2013) *Diversity and Inclusion in Early Childhood: An Introduction*. London: Sage Publications. pp. 1–11.

DfE (Department for Education) (2014) *Statutory Framework for the Early Years Foundation Stage: Setting the Standards for Learning, Development and Care for Children from Birth to Five*. London: DfE. Available at: www.foundationyears.org.uk/files/2014/07/EYFS_frame work_from_1_September_2014__with_clarification_note.pdf (accessed 28 September 2015).

Field, F. (2010) *The Foundation Years: Preventing Poor Children Becoming Poor Adults*. Report of the Independent Review on Poverty and Life Chances. London: Cabinet Office.

Forehand, R. and Kotchik, B. (2002) 'Behavioural parent training: current challenges and potential solutions', *Journal of Child and Family Studies*, 11: 377–84.

Graham, L.J. and Slee, R. (2008) 'An illusory interiority: interrogating the discourse/s of inclusion', *Educational Philosophy and Theory*, 40 (2): 277–93.

Hansen, K., Joshi, H. and Dex, S. (2010) *Children of the 21st Century: The First Five Years*. Bristol: Policy Press.

Heinrichs, N., Bertram, H., Kuschel, A. and Hahlweg, K. (2005) 'Parent recruitment and retention in a universal prevention program for child behaviour and emotional problems: barriers to research and program participation', *Prevention Science*, 6: 275–86.

Kirk, R.H. (2003) 'Family support: the role of the Early Years' Centres', *Children and Society*, 17: 85–99.

Ludwig, J., Duncan, G., Gennatian, L., Katz, L., Kessler, R., Kling, J. and Sanbonmatsu, L. (2013) 'Long term neighbourhood effects on low income families: evidence from moving to opportunity', *American Economic Association*, 103 (3): 226–31.

Nutbrown, C. and Clough, P., with Atherton, F. (2013) *Inclusion in the Early Years*, 2nd edn. London: Sage. pp. 6–29.

Odgers, C.L., Caspi, A., Bates, C. J., Sampson, R.J. and Moffit, T.E. (2012) 'Supportive parenting mediates neighborhood socioeconomic disparities in children's antisocial behavior from ages 5 to 12', *Development and Psychopathology*, 24: 705–21.

Peters, S., Calam, R. and Harrington, R. (2005) 'Maternal attributions and expressed emotion as predictors of attendance at parent management training', *Journal of Child Psychology and Psychiatry*, 47: 99–111.

Purdue, K., Gordon-Burns, D., Gunn, A. Madden, B. and Surtees, N. (2009) 'Supporting inclusion in early childhood settings: some possibilities and problems for teacher education', *International Journal of Inclusive Education*, 13 (8): 805–15.

Tickell, C. (2011) *The Early Years: Foundations for Life, Health and Learning*. An Independent Report on the Early Years Foundation Stage to Her Majesty's Government. London: Crown. Available at: www.education.gov.uk/tickellreview (accessed September 2015).

Waite, L. (2015) Unpublished stories from practice.

Whitham, G. (2012) *Child Poverty in 2012: It Shouldn't Happen Here*. London: Save the Children.

Whittaker, K.A. and Cowley, S. (2012) 'An effective programme is not enough: a review of factors associated with poor attendance and engagement with parenting programmes', *Children and Society*, 26: 138–49.

Wilkinson, R. and Pickett, K. (2010) *The Spirit Level: Why Equality Is Better for Everyone*. London: Penguin.

Want to learn more about this chapter? Visit the companion website at https://study.sagepub.com/EYFS3e for access to free SAGE journal articles and book chapters, weblinks, annotated further readings and more.

17

Leadership

Trevor Male and Nyree Nicholson

Chapter overview

The EYFS, both in its former and current modes, offers leadership challenges within early childhood education and care which are profound, but not wholly unique. This chapter will explore those challenges to help identify responses that are appropriate to early childhood settings.

The chapter begins by exploring the complexity of early childhood education and care provision in England in order to identify leadership and management responsibilities within the system. The key role is identified as the formal leader of early childhood settings with more than one employee, whether that be a privately owned company, part of a consortium or a state-maintained institution. Differences between leadership and management are discussed, as is the nature of leadership as a set of social behaviours. This definition, which extends the simple measure of accountability for formal managers, allows for the exploration of shared or collective leadership approaches to creating and sustaining effective learning environments as well as ensuring the safety and welfare of young children. The discussion then moves towards identifying appropriate organisational structures and leadership behaviours that support such ambitions. Issues that are specific to the sector, such as multi-agency working and a heavily gendered workforce, are explored in the context of leadership theories in order to guide practitioners as to their role and possible contribution. The chapter closes with some practical tips as to how it is possible, in early childhood settings, to move beyond the notion of a single accountable executive and towards collective and connective leadership.

This chapter aims to:

- explore issues about leadership in relation to early childhood education, practice and care
- discuss different styles of leadership and reflect on the core values that underpin early childhood education and care
- discuss leadership in early childhood settings in relation to contributing factors that correspond to the shared value system.

The leadership context

The descriptor for state sponsored or private provision for early childhood within England is now commonly referred to as 'early childhood settings', a title that covers all provision from a sole childminder to pre-school group provision. This title tends to disguise, however, the complexity of relationships within the sector that generate significant challenges for those charged with leading and managing such provision. In practice a setting is a place that pre-school children attend on a regular basis and for which there are certain legal, moral and societal expectations. The influences on how the setting is organised and run are multiple which, in turn, present those with responsibility with a wide range of behavioural opportunities. Together these expectations and influences present challenges to all settings, which typically include:

- identification and consolidation of core purpose of provision;
- reconciliation of personal (and institutional) values, ethos and mission with external influences and expectations;
- clarification of leadership and managerial roles and responsibilities;
- adoption of leadership structure, styles and behaviour that match the existing and emerging environment.

The EYFS provides the framework of expectations for early childhood education and care in England, thus heavily influencing the way in which these issues can be addressed and resolved. As can be seen from Chapters 1 and 2, the introduction of EYFS in 2008 was the first time that such a framework had existed. The revised EYFS of 2012 recognised the need for further change and, subsequently has emphasised the need for:

- **quality and consistency** in all early years settings, so that every child makes good progress and no child gets left behind;
- **a secure foundation** through learning and development opportunities which are planned around the needs and interests of each individual child and are assessed and reviewed regularly;
- **partnership** working between practitioners and with parents and/or carers;
- **equality of opportunity** and anti-discriminatory practice, ensuring that every child is included and supported. (Department for Education, 2014: 5; emphasis in original)

As can be deduced from the date of the above citation, the revised EYFS framework was further amended in 2014 and became operational in September of that year. Whilst this did not indicate substantial change in overall policy, there have been two other factors which have the potential to affect the role of leaders and managers in early childhood education and care.

The first is the introduction of childminder agencies, for which there were only 22 trials set up by the government before implementing the new policy (DfE, 2015). The introduction of these agencies has proved to be an emotive issue for home-based practitioners, particularly as at the time of writing there are only four agencies operational nationally, with many individual childminders reported to be against agencies (Goddard, 2015). Whilst the agencies will organise training at a basic level and inspect their own providers it is not clear how the agencies will lead practice beyond this, meaning that leadership in such circumstances thus becomes unclear and distorted. One emerging argument is that the sole childminder will remain autonomous in terms of planning and organising their own provision, rather than being guided by an agency.

The second key issue is changes to the nature of the workforce, including the introduction of Early Years Teacher Status (EYTS) and criteria for Early Years Educators which has changed the original EYFS ambition to place the emphasis for leading learning on those with Early Years Professional Status (EYPS) (see Chapter 5 for further discussion on this issue).

The revised EYFS of 2012 left the emphasis on those leading and managing early childhood settings as having overall responsibility for implementation, whilst having to work within a framework of legislation and other child support agencies. Now there are further potential considerations for this role in terms of the introduction of the new layer of supervisory control (childminder agencies) and changes to the workforce. The emphasis is still on the individual person who has accountability, the formal leader of each setting, but these changes add to the complexity of the role that will be explored in this chapter.

Where does leadership responsibility lie in early childhood education and care?

Leadership differs from management because it is about decision-making, where management is the process by which decisions are enacted. There is still confusion, however, as to who is responsible for decision making in early childhood education and care, as Rodd indicates:

> [...] leadership in the early childhood profession still has to be answered in a way that is meaningful and credible for practitioners [and there is an] apparent vagueness and haziness of what is meant by leadership in early childhood. (Rodd, 2006: 4–5)

Ultimately leadership responsibility in any system will be aligned to those who are formally accountable. Within England, and under present circumstances, the main responsibility falls on the leader/manager of the early childhood setting, despite the fact so many others also have a leadership role. To understand this emphasis requires an understanding of the nature of leadership and, in particular, the difference between formal and informal leadership within social systems.

Case study

Susan's story

Susan is the head of an early childhood setting that had been a maintained nursery before being designated a Children's Centre as part of the Sure Start initiative. Since the transition the pattern of her activity across the year has changed and she now goes into the office at least twice a week during the school holiday period, except when she has her own holiday. This has resulted in fundamental changes to her behaviour; whereas in the past, as the headteacher of the nursery school, such attendance was entirely voluntary, she now feels that she should be present throughout much of the 50 week working year. Interestingly, there has not been any reconsideration of her terms and conditions of service and neither has there been a salary increase. When pressed to say whether her workload had gone up she indicated that changes had been made to the deputy's job that had seen the transference of some duties to the deputy, such as classroom observation and work on curriculum development, which has changed the nature of her own headship. In addition, Susan gets additional support from a SEN worker for the Centre and a community liaison officer who organises and runs parent workshops and adult learning, thus relieving her of tasks that she would have previously done herself.

She perceives the major challenges of leading the Centre to be:

- governance
- funding

(Continued)

(Continued)

- sustainability
- keeping the ideal of the Centre being a community facility
- working to support the parents and children that come.

She considers the focus of attention should be balanced between social welfare and education in early childhood and sees her role as seeking to maintain that balance. It was easy to see how the social welfare agenda could dominate provision, with major policy initiatives such as Every Child Matters being at the forefront of government policy. Clearly, in Susan's opinion, it is impossible to educate children successfully without appropriate social support, but she considers this should be viewed as a means to an end rather than an end in itself. Her conclusion is for heads of Children's Centres to keep driving the learning agenda and to keep families directly involved.

Reflective task

- Reflecting on the case study, try to identify the key contributors to the education and care of young children in a setting known to you and consider who is the most significant figure in decision making.

The formal leader is not only accountable for outcomes and processes, but can also apply sanctions to other members of the organisation. The concept of leadership is much larger than this simple definition, however, and encompasses the way in which the leader is one who modifies the competences, motivation or behaviour of others (Bass, 1981). A good example here is when a Level 3 manager/leader personally known by us stated that she did not see the need to gain further qualifications as she had members of staff who had degrees in early childhood; therefore, her role as a leader was to ensure that the skills of the group were deployed effectively. Leadership can thus be considered as a social interaction and something more than describing the actions of formal leaders. Consequently, in any system most practitioners can be involved in the decision making systems within the setting, meaning there are many potential leaders and many ways in which leadership can be demonstrated.

Much of the literature on leadership confuses this distinction, however, and contributions to the field of leadership in early childhood education and care do not often differ in this respect. Many actors in the field have leadership roles and responsibilities, therefore, with some also having formal accountability. In that regard much of the discourse has been concerned with *headship* more frequently than the broader concept of *leadership*. In other words the contributions are focused on what the formal leader has to do as an individual, rather than what has to be done to create 'the conditions in which all members of the organisation can give their best in a climate of commitment and challenge' (Whitaker, 1993: 74). The institutional leader, in this instance typically the leader/manager of the early childhood setting, consequently has to create the appropriate conditions to support and enhance the key features of the EYFS statutory framework: the learning, development and safeguarding of pre-school children within their setting. To achieve this, the institutional leader (head) has the task of reconciling the expertise and efforts of all other adults also engaged in the support of pre-school children. These other actors range from those with proven expertise (such as those with EYTS, staff holding a recognised qualification as an early childhood practitioner or professionals from other agencies) through unqualified employees and to those with enthusiasm (such as parents or volunteer workers). Leadership in this context, therefore, is headship and will require a set of behaviours and leadership approaches that match the particular context. In this regard, and it has been demonstrated before, 'effective headship is situational and contingent on context and circumstance' (Male, 2006: 3).

Different leadership behaviours are required by others within the system, therefore, with notable contributions to be made by those with professional status, whether they be an employee or a colleague from a related agency. To be successful in this quest the formal leader will need to ensure there are common values that are agreed and shared amongst the early childhood workforce and the community local to the setting (including parents). As has been suggested elsewhere, 'for an organisation or institution to provide an effective service there must be clarity of vision, particularly in regards to core purpose' (Male, 2012: 199). It is imperative, therefore, for the formal leader to establish and sustain a value set that corresponds to the society to be served and for those values to be reflected as the core ethos of the organisation and a framework for decision making (see Figure 17.1).

Figure 17.1 *Establishing the core ethos of an organisation*

Core purpose

The EYFS now provides the statutory framework and also offers non-statutory guidance which provides the minimum standard of acceptable provision, with these two elements becoming the frame of reference for accountability. The institutional leader of each early childhood setting will need to establish those minimum standards and ensure practitioners employed or associated with the setting are sustaining such expectations. Given that many such settings may also have additional expectations (e.g. it may be registered with a childminder agency, have a direct sponsor or be a private profit making institution), there may also be a need to determine difference and diversity in addition to societal expectations. In all instances, however, the legal imperative for formal leaders is to ensure compliance with the statutory framework whilst the moral imperative may be considered as ensuring the provision meets the social and emotional needs of young children within the context of their local community as well as being prepared for school, as it is now a requirement in the EYFS. To that extent, research into the field of leadership in early childhood education and care undertaken by Siraj-Blatchford and Manni (2007) led them to conclude that the focus of leadership within the sector should be on learning:

> We have argued that *contextual literacy*, a commitment to *collaboration* and to the *improvement of children's learning outcomes* should be considered (by definition) to provide fundamental requirements for *leadership for learning*. (2007: 28; emphasis in original)

Leadership for learning is something more, however, than the constructs of learning-centred leadership that grew from the notion of instructional leadership endemic in schools within the USA (see, for example, Southworth, 2002) and include notions of working within the context of the area and the community. This has led us to conclude that the wider elements of leadership are more accurately described in the construct of 'pedagogical leadership', where the focus is on 'the centrality of relationships with others, such as the learners, parents, community and government, and the building of a learning community' (Male and Palaiologou, 2012: 107). In this context the core purpose of the formal leader is to ensure that the efforts of all contributors to the field of children's learning and care are coordinated, with the outcomes matching the statutory elements of EYFS as a bare minimum level of satisfactory provision. Pedagogical leadership lends itself well to the ethos of early childhood, and demonstrates that leadership is not confined simply to those who lead settings, rather than to those who lead practice. MacNeill et al. (2003) suggest that pedagogic leadership is thus not only an alternative to instructional leadership, but extends the concept and demonstrates that everyone involved with caring and educating children has a leadership role (Male and Palaiologou, 2012). Such an approach consequently shifts the focus from leading people to leading practice and encompasses all factors involved in leading children to learning (Van Manen, 1991). This in turn enables practitioners to view themselves in a different light, as leaders of practice, thus aiding self-efficacy. It may also help to change the way that early childhood practitioners are seen in terms of their professional image (as discussed in Chapter 5).

Leadership in early childhood education and care

A key aspect of formal leadership in early childhood education and care, therefore, is the recognition of the potential capability of other actors in the system to make a positive contribution to the setting. As has been discussed previously in this chapter, the workforce comprises a wide range of people, some of whom have advanced qualifications, others with lower level specialist qualifications and other employees. The attempts made by the Children's Workforce Development Council (CWDC) to classify the wide range of qualifications to determine those that are 'full and relevant' (Nutbrown, 2012: 6) have since been supplemented by identification of criteria for Early Years Educators (NCTL, 2013). Legislation now expects that in group settings, the manager (i.e. the formal leader of the setting) and at least half of all other staff must hold full and relevant qualifications. In addition 'the manager should have at least two years' experience of working in an early childhood setting, or have at least two years' other suitable experience, and the provider must ensure there is a named deputy who, in their judgement, is capable and qualified to take charge in the manager's absence' (DfE, 2014: 20). Whilst recognising the potential powerful influence of childminding agencies (if part of a group/consortium) the main actors within the leadership matrix of individual early childhood settings, all of whose efforts need coordinating, are:

- senior leaders and managers
- qualified practitioners
- support staff
- professionals from other related agencies.

To be successful with both the legal and moral imperatives of early childhood education and care, leadership needs to be exhibited throughout the workforce and to be appropriate to situation and context. Leadership in this regard refers to dispositions and opportunities to 'take a lead' on something, or to show initiative (Nutbrown, 2012: 40). Leadership within education and social systems is considered to be 'distributed, differentiated and diverse' in the new century (Southworth, 2006). This is because there are many more people having a leadership role and in early childhood education and care, qualified practitioners and professionals from other agencies. As a consequence we tend to find leadership in early childhood settings to be shared, with the personal accountability of the institutional leader being the key feature that distinguishes them from other members of provision in the sector. That part of the job is unlikely to go away as leaders/managers of early childhood settings have specific responsibilities in law. Operationally, however, the most effective settings are likely to be those where strategic decisions are investigated and determined collectively (Siraj-Blatchford and Manni, 2007).

Case study

Julia's story

Julia is a leader and manager for an early childhood setting operating from a church hall. The setting provides education and care for children from 2½ to 5 years old, also providing government-funded places for children in these ages. The setting is open from 8am until 5pm, working on a sessional basis, although full-time care is provided. The setting is operational during term time only, and Julia is paid for the times the setting is open. Julia has responsibility for running the setting, including staffing, accounting and ensuring the curriculum is followed and the welfare requirements are met, and reporting to the local authority. She also works with the local early childhood teams to access training for both herself and the staff, and to liaise with Quality Improvement Officers. In addition, Julia is also part of the child/adult ratios for the children who attend the setting. Much of the paperwork is taken home and completed during her own time in the evenings and is unpaid. When asked, Julia commented that this is normal practice within early childhood education and care. Julia is completing a Foundation Degree in Childhood Studies in her own time, and at her own expense. Discussions with practitioners studying for a Masters degree have demonstrated Julia's pattern of work is typical of their own experiences. Julia perceives the main challenges to working as a leader to be:

- accountability: is not equal to the pay and recognition received. Julia receives just 10p per hour more as a manager/leader than other practitioners;
- funding and sustainability: the cost to provide childcare is not equal to the funding received from the government, leading to a shortfall in revenue;
- supporting families on a limited budget.

Julia considers the focus should be on the quality service the setting offers to both children and their families, however she increasingly feels pressured due to under-funding. Julia's solution to the current dilemma is to take work home to ensure that the time spent in the setting is effectively used supporting children and their families.

The need for a collective response has led to calls for models of distributed leadership to be central to early childhood settings (Aubrey, 2007; Miller, 2011), although such calls seldom address the necessity to achieve an appropriate balance between leadership and management within settings or to filter influences external to the setting in the quest to provide education and care that is contextually relevant. As has been indicated previously, the key leadership role is the one held by the leader/manager of early childhood setting, whilst others also have significant leadership roles to fulfil. The roles of qualified practitioners (particularly room supervisors) are the most notable within the setting, whilst the knowledge and expertise of professionals external to the setting are also significant. As will be discussed shortly, however, it is with the role of qualified practitioner where operational leadership may be needed if the provision is to be relevant to the needs of all children. In short, therefore, aspects of leadership behaviour need to be exhibited at all levels, but the key role of coordinating all efforts into an effective gestalt of leadership activity lies with the person charged with institutional leadership.

Leadership in the early childhood setting

The most effective settings will be those where internal structures and processes not only successfully support children's learning and provide safeguards relevant to need and context, but also deal more effectively with external influences and initiatives that could affect day-to-day stability.

Internally there are generally some key elements of the organisation that need to be harmonised in order to provide the most effective environment. First, and as indicated above in Figure 17. 1, there must be:

- a clearly defined culture that provides a frame of reference through which possible decisions are explored.

Furthermore, however, there also needs to be:

- a clear grasp of the difference between *leadership* and *management*;
- an effective *senior leadership team*;
- the opportunity and support for *operational leadership*.

As has been stated above, leadership is commonly distinguished from management by means of determination. In other words, leaders make decisions and managers operationalise those decisions. Both terms are verbs, rather than nouns, however, so *leadership and management* are both legitimate activities for all members of an organisation. All settings need effective management systems that can effectively deliver policies and maintain good practice. These become the 'rules' of the organisation, the standard practices that allow for smooth operation on a daily basis. Effective institutional leaders are required, therefore, to establish management systems and practices that fulfil standard operational needs.

There are, of course, a range of leadership responsibilities emerging from the need to respond to different or unusual issues and the challenge for the institutional leader is to recognise that, although they cannot escape their individual accountability, they cannot complete all the leadership tasks that could accompany the job. Others are needed to share the load, and in terms of senior leadership it is the professionally qualified staff within the sector who would normally be identified as prospective senior leaders. Consequently, credence needs to be given to the contribution EYTs and other qualified Early Years Educators can make within the setting. The critical stage of organisational development, however, is to build the capacity of the potential senior leaders so that not only are leadership responsibilities and actions shared, but the members become a *team*. The difference between a group and a team is well documented elsewhere (e.g. Katzenbach and Smith, 1993), but is usually determined as the willingness of members to give up on self-interest in favour of the group. Members of a team tend, therefore, to be prepared to give with no guarantee of getting anything back in return. Conversely members of a working group can be identified as protecting their self-interest at a cost to overall ambition. Teams are generally considered as more desirable and are recognised as creating synergy, where the collective outcome exceeds the sum of individual inputs. A senior leadership team can only operate, however, where there are high levels of trust, in addition to mutual accountability.

The final piece of the internal structure jigsaw is the need for *leadership at the operational level* where individuals are empowered to take decisions that correspond to the shared value system that has been described above as a prerequisite for success. As has been described elsewhere, each practitioner will need to know what their fundamental priority is when the demands of practice present them with conflicting opportunities. The tools they need to determine their priority are the principles for action that are derived from the framework of values. The key issue is that the practitioner has 'the right to respond to the prevailing context, providing they do not contravene the ethical code that has been established for the organisation' (Male, 2012: 205).

Leading the early childhood settings in the wider context

The role of institutional leader in early childhood settings needs to become more team focused, therefore, with individual behaviour moving to the periphery. This model does not deny that institutional leaders still have a major role to play in internal leadership and many modes will have to be adopted according to circumstance (see Figure 17.2).

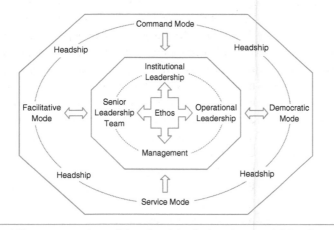

Figure 17.2 *Different modes of leadership behaviour within the organisation*

In this model it can be seen that the institutional manager adopts the headship role needed to sustain the internal structure through appropriate use of leadership style according to capability of their colleagues. Here reference is made to facilitative, demographic, support and command modes, although other contributors to the field of leadership theory have drawn attention to a greater number of styles (e.g. Goleman, 2001). The main point to be made at this stage is that mode (or style) should be appropriate to context and situation. Analysis shows the workforce in early childhood education and care being comprised almost completely of women, with such work being widely seen as low status, low paid and low skilled (Miller, 2011; Nutbrown, 2012). The predominance of women in the workforce has led some commentators to observe that there are distinctive features of leadership in this context that are mainly concerned with feminine attributes and behaviour (Moyles, 2006; Rodd, 2006; Aubrey, 2007; Whalley, 2011). This is too simplistic an analysis, however, and it is more appropriate to recognise that a range of leadership attributes and behaviours are needed at different levels within the system, only some of which are based on traditional feminine leadership styles (see, for example, McDowell Clark and Murray, 2012). It is entirely appropriate, for example, to adopt the 'command' mode in situations where there is little clarity of vision or relevant expertise available; similarly, it would be unwise to adopt a singular approach to decision making where there are professionally qualified and experienced staff with appropriate expertise available for consultation. The principal skill for the institutional leader in this respect is not to employ a pre-determined approach, but to choose a leadership style that is suited to the situation and context.

The key role of the institutional leader in the early childhood setting, however, is more likely to one of managing the boundary and the quest to ensure the needs of children can be met. It has been suggested that the true art of institutional leadership has always been to manage the boundary with the external environment. Selznick (1983), for example, distinguishes institutional leaders from everyday managers by stating that leaders act on the boundary tensions between the core activities of an organization and the wider demands, challenges and opportunities of its environment. This work of boundary spanning involves protecting and supporting critical organizational functions while simultaneously attempting to accommodate external demands. Given the impact of EYFS (which includes the inherent relationships with external agencies), the demands of the local community and the continued emergence of policy initiatives, the institutional leaders needs to be continually scanning the external environment to ensure their setting is remaining on task (see Figure 17.3).

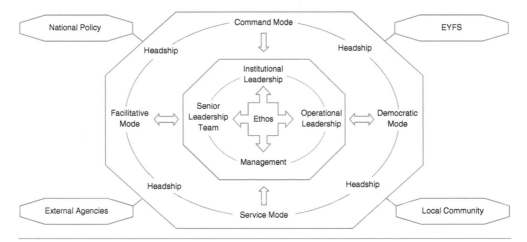

Figure 17.3 *Scanning the external environment*

A critical factor in this management of the 'boundary' is the role played by external agencies, who have a direct influence on the education and well-being of the child, as opposed to those agencies to which the setting is accountable (such as national inspectorates and childminding agencies). Prominent in this regard are those working in health and social services, as well as other educators who have been brought together into local collectives typically labelled 'Children's Services'. The notion of integrated services led to the establishment of a qualification, the National Professional Qualification for Integrated Centre Leadership (NPQICL), which was introduced in 2005 to support the professional development needs of leaders/managers of early childhood settings. As illustrated in her research of 359 practitioners who had been awarded NPQICL, 'working collaboratively and effectively with other professionals requires a higher level of professional sensitivity and commitment' which can present particular challenges and difficulties (Ang, 2012: 296). A key aspect of such challenges is that 'there are many different visions, aims or expectations for early childhood education and care' (Jones, 2008: 18) and this is a field 'dominated by individual beliefs, values and perspectives that can have a strong emotional component' (Rodd, 2006: 110). As a consequence, people from other professions and agencies typically tend to 'view the situation from the perspectives of their own professions' (Miller, 2011: 83).

Bringing it all together

The issue of multi-agency and inter-agency working is the single factor that distinguishes leadership in early childhood education and care from other professions or occupations, therefore, with discussions about 'feminine' leadership approaches for a workforce consisting almost wholly of women being of only marginal consequence in this respect. The centrality of multi-agency support mechanisms widens the responsibility for determining appropriate learning, development and care for young children (the core elements of EYFS) beyond any single institution or individual. Consequently the establishment and maintenance of core values that underpin actions is a task that sits uncomfortably between many actors. Leadership, as has been demonstrated above, is exhibited at a number of levels in any social system, but within early childhood education and care there is this added complex issue of the multi-agency support system.

Summary

This chapter discussed the concept of leadership in relation to EYFS. There has been an increased amount of literature on leadership in early childhood education and care since the first introduction of the EYFS in 2008. The binding factor, however, is the focus on the child and the single accountable position within this system is the leader/manager of the early childhood setting. Whilst that places significant responsibilities on individuals, leadership in early childhood education and care has to be a collective effort, or 'connected effort' as Moyles concludes, that is child-centred. 'Connective leadership' she suggests 'is a new, integrative model of leadership that is vital to early childhood and care [as it provides] the basis of the ways in which practitioners work with children and families' (Moyles, 2006: 4). The starting point for such connected leadership efforts should be a value set that is meaningful not only for early childhood practitioners and the funding agency, but also to the service users and the local community (Male, 2012). Effective leadership in early childhood education and care, therefore, should be concerned with a collective approach that extends the capability of the child beyond the narrow confines of EYFS.

Key points to remember

- There is a difference between formal leadership and other leadership roles within early childhood education and care.

- Formal leaders have to coordinate the collective efforts of all contributors to the education and care of young children.

- The establishment and sustenance of core (and shared) values underpin successful leadership decision making processes.

Points of discussion

- Do you agree that the statutory elements of EYFS are a bare minimum level of satisfactory provision?

- Does the leader/manager of an early childhood setting have the key leadership role in early childhood education and care?

- Think about the contribution each contributor makes to this setting and consider whether this is more focused on children's learning or their safeguarding.

Further reading

Books

Aubrey, C. (2011) *Leading and Managing in the Early Years*, 2nd edn. London: Sage.

Bennett, N., Wise, C., Woods, P. and Harvey, J. (2003) *Distributed Leadership: A Review of the Literature*. Nottingham: National College for School Leadership.

Rodd, J. (2012) *Leadership in Early Childhood*, 4th edn. Maidenhead: Open University Press.

Siraj, I. and Hallett, E. (2014) *Effective and Caring Leadership*. London: Sage.

Article

Davies, G. (2014) 'Graduate leaders in early childhood education and care settings, the practitioner perspective', *Management in Education*, 28 (4): 156–60.

Useful websites

Early Years Matters: *Leadership*:
http://earlyyearsmatters.co.uk/index.php/areas-of-interest/leading-learning/

Early Childhood Australia: 'What does leadership look like in early childhood settings?:
www.earlychildhoodaustralia.org.au/our-publications/every-child-magazine/every-child-index/
    every-child-vol-18-4-2012/leadership-look-like-early-childhood-settings/

Leadership in Early Childhood Education: Cross-Cultural Perspectives:
http://herkules.oulu.fi/isbn9514268539/isbn9514268539.pdf

Ofsted: *Achieving and Maintaining High Quality Early Years Provision: Getting it Right First Time:*
www.gov.uk/government/publications/achieving-and-maintaining-high-quality-early-years-
    provision-getting-it-right-first-time

References

Ang, L. (2012) 'Leading and managing in the early years: a study of the impact of a NCSL pro-gramme on Children's Centre leaders' perceptions of leadership and practice', *Educational Management Administration and Leadership*, 40 (3): 289–304.

Aubrey, C. (2007) *Leading and Managing in the Early Years*. London: Sage.

Bass, B. (ed.) (1981) *Stodgill's Handbook of Leadership*. New York: Free Press.

DfE (Department for Education) (2014) *Statutory Framework for the Early Years Foundation Stage*. London: DfE. Available at: www.foundationyears.org.uk/files/2014/07/EYFS_frame work_from_1_September_2014__with_clarification_note.pdf (accessed 28 September 2015).

DfE (Department for Education) (2015) *Policy Paper 2010–2015 Government Policy: Childcare and Early Education*. Available at: www.gov.uk/government/publications/2010–to-2015–government-policy-childcare-and-early-education/2010–to-2015–government-policy-child care-and-early-education (accessed 17 June 2015).

Goddard, C. (2015) 'Nursery management: childminding strength in numbers', *Nursery World*, 15 March 2015. Available at: www.nurseryworld.co.uk/nursery-world/feature/1150330/nursery-management-childminding-strength (accessed 17 June 2015).

Goleman, D. (2001) *The Emotionally Intelligent Workplace*. San Francisco: Jossey–Bass.

Jones, C. (2008) *Leadership and Management in the Early Years: From Principles to Practice*. Maidenhead: Open University Press.

Katzenbach, J. and Smith, D. (1993) *The Wisdom of Teams: Creating the High Performing Organization*. Maidenhead: McGraw–Hill.

Male, T. (2006) *Being an Effective Headteacher*. London: Paul Chapman Publishing.

Male, T. (2012) 'Ethical leadership in early years settings', in I. Palaiologou (ed.), *Ethical Practice in Early Childhood*. London: Sage.

Male, T. and Palaiologou, I. (2012) 'Learning-centred leadership or pedagogical leadership? An alternative approach to leadership in education contexts', *International Journal of Leadership in Education*, 15 (1): 107–18.

McDowell Clark, R. and Murray, J. (2012) *Reconceptualising Leadership in the Early Years*. Maidenhead: Open University Press.

MacNeill, N., Cavanagh, R. and Silcox, S. (2003) *Beyond Instructional Leadership: Towards Pedagogic Leadership*. Available at: www.learningdomain.com/instructional.beyond.pdf (accessed 17 June 2015).

Miller, L. (2011) *Professionalization, Leadership and Management in the Early Years*. London: Sage.

Moyles, J. (2006) *Effective Leadership and Management in the Early Years*. Maidenhead: Open University Press.

NCTL (National College for Teaching and Leadership) (2013) *Early Years Educator (Level 3): Qualifications Criteria*. Nottingham: NCTL.

Nutbrown, C. (2012) *Foundations for Quality: The Independent Review of Early Education and Childcare Qualifications. Final Report*. Runcorn: Department for Education. Available at: www.gov.uk/government/uploads/system/uploads/attachment_data/file/175463/Nutbrown-Review.pdf (accessed September 2015).

Rodd, J. (2006) *Leadership in Early Childhood*. Maidenhead: Open University Press.

Selznick, P. (1983) *Leadership in Administration: A Sociological Interpretation*. Berkeley, CA: University of California, Berkeley Press.

Siraj-Blatchford, I. and Manni, L. (2007) *Effective Leadership in the Early Years Sector: The ELEYS Study*. London: Institute of Education, University of London.

Southworth, G. (2002) 'Instructional leadership in schools: reflections and empirical evidence', *School Leadership and Management*, 22 (1): 73–91.

Southworth, G. (2006) 'A new flame', *LDR*, 20: 19–21; Nottingham: National College for School Leadership.

Van Manen, M. (1991) *The Tact of Teaching: The Meaning of Pedagogical Thoughtfulness*. Albany, NY: State University of New York Press.

Whalley, M. (2011) *Leading Practice in Early Years Settings*, 2nd edn. Exeter: Learning Matters.

Whitaker, P. (1993) *Managing Change in Schools*. Buckingham: Open University Press.

Want to learn more about this chapter? Visit the companion website at https://study.sagepub.com/EYFS3e for access to free SAGE journal articles and book chapters, weblinks, annotated further readings and more.

18

The Role of Digital Technologies

Lorna Arnott

 Chapter overview

With digital technologies permeating young children's playrooms and homes, theorising around pedagogy with technologies is now widely available (see Plowman and Stephen, 2007; Parette et al., 2010). Yet research still suggests that parents and practitioners are anxious about appropriate technology use and in many cases this results in limited uptake (Zevenbergen, 2007). In order to tackle this issue we need to consider technologies as one element of early childhood and view these resources as tools and resources that can be adapted and integrated in multiple ways. This chapter will unpick this idea to arrive at the conclusion that technologies can be either valuable or a hindrance to children's learning depending upon how they are framed in the experience and positioned in the educational context. The chapter is informed by the understanding that technologies provide 'opportunities' but do not determine children's play (Arnott, 2013).

This chapter aims to:

- introduce the concept of 'technology' in the context of early childhood education
- present an introductory discussion about how perceptions of childhood have evolved in response to the availability of technologies

(Continued)

(Continued)

- position technologies in terms of possibilities and opportunities for children's experiences
- consider how technologies form part of the early childhood landscape and consider their place within the learning environment
- demonstrate that technologies are tools for children, much like traditional early childhood toys.

What are technologies?

In contemporary discussions of digital childhood a range of nuanced terms are used to describe the resources children use as part of everyday life and learning including, but not limited to, 'technologies', 'digital technologies', 'Information and Communication Technologies (ICT)', 'smart toys', 'screen-based media' and 'digital media'. With such fast-paced evolution in technological resources, definitions quickly become erroneous. In its broadest sense, technology could mean the application of scientific knowledge or 'design that meets a need' (Bergen, 2008: 88) and could include common tools such as a pen or a pencil. For most, when considering technologies in contemporary early childhood, however, they are referring to new *digital* technologies that are perceived to be changing childhood.

Research in relation to technologies has evolved through explorations of the desktop computer (Haugland, 1992), to 'electronically enhanced objects', 'clever' robotics (Bergen, 2008) and smart toys (Plowman, 2004) to screen-based media (Neumann and Neumann, 2014) and on to 'internet-enabled' resources (Palaiologou, 2014). Thus definitions of technology include:

- desktop and portable computers, mobile technologies (Edwards, 2013);
- entertainment technologies such as music players and games consoles (McPake et al., 2013);
- 'domestic digital technologies' – the everyday household technologies available to children – as well as digital toys and games (Arnott, 2013; McPake et al., 2013); and
- tablet computers or mobile devices (e.g. Neumann and Neumann, 2014).

These definitions are evolving and already calls for explorations of future technologies are in place, as Livingstone et al. (2015), suggests the need to explore 3D printing and Smart Homes. Irrespective of the definition employed, the central point to note is that whilst technologies are heterogeneous (Bergen, 2008) they are not all the same. Indeed different resources offer different technological affordances (Carr, 2000) and as such may influence children's experiences differently. In order to understand the role of technologies in early childhood, we must therefore consider the range of resources available and explore their affordances and unique properties.

Digital childhood: inevitable change?

As internet access has become ubiquitous, childhood has been transformed (Craft, 2012). Children now live in a 'digitally mediated cultural landscape' (Bird and Edwards, 2014: 2) and are often described as 'The Net Generation' (Tapscott, 2008) or 'Digital Natives' (Prensky, 2001). These perspectives frame the contemporary child as unique in comparison to previous generations, boasting different knowledge, opinions, behaviours and, in some cases, different morals. Learning in the digital age is also perceived to have changed. For example, connectivity afforded by mobile technologies has led to instant access to knowledge and more young people learning through bricolage and trial and error (Kolikant, 2010). Discussions have also emerged around how text messaging is transforming literacy learning (Wood et al., 2013) and we are seeing discussions of changes to creativity (Craft, 2012) and play (Yelland, 2010). As 2014 was the first year that tablet computers overtook televisions as children's first-choice media resource (Livingstone et al., 2015), and because children as young as 3 are now turning to these internet-enabled devices (Palaiologou, 2014), these changes have never been more relevant to early childhood education.

Such change, however, has caused anxiety about whether technologies are detrimental for young children. As a result, perceptions of childhood have become polarised. We are seeing divergent discourses emerging with those fearful of technologies perpetuating the child-at-risk discourse and those excited by technologies embracing the empowering capabilities that technologies can offer (Craft, 2012). That is to say that adults are either viewing children as passive and in need of protection, or active and capable of deciphering messages in media and learning from them (Marsh, 2004). The passive, child-at-risk discourse, in some cases, contradicts sociological perspectives that are now embedded in early childhood education and considers children as active agents in their lives (James et al., 1998). These concerns are also inherently problematic because they are often based on assertions and unsubstantiated evidence (Plowman and McPake, 2013).

There is no question about it, childhood has changed, in part because children (and adults) now live in a digital age. As such, many of the concerns about technology in childhood are born out of romanticisation of childhood (Plowman et al., 2010). Nevertheless, in Western society, technologies are engrained in contemporary work and home lives and so children will encounter these resources as they grow. We live in a socio-cultural world where our knowledge, beliefs and learning are shaped by experience and culture (Tudge, 2008). With this in mind, childhood will also evolve and change, just as society does. With each new generation new knowledge and ways of seeing the world are brought and so future childhood experience will always be different from the generation before. That is not to say that technologies are either good or bad, but rather that they are a central part of children's lives. Since technologies are an active, though not overwhelming, component of children's everyday lives (McPake et al., 2013; Plowman and McPake, 2013) we must focus our attention on how we can support children with these resources.

The acceptance of technologies in children's lives as absolute, and here to stay, means that we are able to move beyond the persistent debate about *whether* children should be using technologies towards *how* children use technologies in early childhood. This question of *how* has not fully been answered – nor do I ever expect it to be – and so I do not intend in this chapter to provide a blueprint for children's early childhood technological experiences. Rather, my aim is to provide some necessary context, based on research evidence, for you to apply to your own practice.

Technologies providing opportunities and possibilities

When planning for effective learning opportunities for children, Claxton and Carr (2004) suggest that we should be striving for *potentiating environment*, i.e. 'those that not only invite the expression of certain dispositions, but actively "stretch" them, and thus develop them' (2004: 91–2). I would argue that, when used effectively, technologies offer this potential. I have eluded to the different discourses in childhood presented in contemporary society and in particular the work of Anna Craft (2012). Her *childhood empowered* position offers an understanding of the great potential of technologies in terms of creating opportunities and possibilities. She draws on her own work and a review of the literature to suggest that technologies not only offer entertainment, but also networking, generation and sharing of content, self-expression, identity experimentation and knowledge-building. In doing so she suggests that the role of educators is to question how technologies can facilitate children's engagement. Similarly, it is also the role of the educator to explore how technologies can facilitate potentiating environments.

In order to explore this further, it is first necessary to view technological resources as positioned within context, something that many studies fail to do. We often see explorations of technology in isolation, whereby the understanding is presented of how children and technologies interact (Ljung-Djärf, 2008). While these studies are very valuable, often a causal link is described between technological activities and children's associated learning. This same position is the one that drives the polarised debate about technology, where the technological resources are held accountable for things like children's troubled childhoods or anti-social behaviours (e.g. Palmer, 2006).

Recent research suggests that technologies form part of a social situation (Marsh, 2010; Plowman et al., 2010) and must be explored as such, rather than as 'singular artefacts' (Edwards, 2013; Livingstone et al., 2015). When explored in this way, technologies become an element of the learning environment rather than the learning context in its own right. In this situation, we are able to see technologies as affording 'opportunities', but not determining the play (Savage, 2011). In terms of Craft's (2012) 'possibility thinking', we can explore how children use technologies to move from considering what is to what might be. By considering the ecological position of technologies in the playroom technologies become one element of a complex matrix of factors, including the physical environment as well as part of the social and cultural context, which shape children's experiences and learning (Arnott, 2013; Savage, 2011). Adopting this ecological stance is the first step towards striving for potentiating environments involving technologies.

The position of technologies in early childhood

Exploring technologies as embedded in context provides a need to understand how adults and children position the resources in early childhood education. Internet-enabled resources, it is argued, open up the world to the child beyond the playroom, classroom or home. The internet offers possibilities for 'learning beyond boundaries, across age phases, harnessing motivation, enabling high participation and nurturing creative possibility thinking [which] are all possible if we are brave enough to acknowledge the potency of childhood and youth and to co-create the future' (Craft, 2012: 183). Craft argues that digital media provide the opportunity for children to be 'agents of change' by engaging in 'playful co-participation' which allows them to make their voices heard. Similarly, interactive resources can act as a mechanism for children to see themselves as co-constructors in the learning (Palaiologou, 2014). Here we see technologies as a key facilitator of the child-centred approach to early childhood education, which is the foundation of our practice.

Despite the potential of technologies, Bers (2012) suggests that these opportunities are not always embraced. She considers how online spaces and technological resources have the potential to be playgrounds – places to explore, take safe risks and play autonomously – but in reality are often turned into playpens – risk-free, narrowly defined spaces with limited room for autonomous exploration. While Bers talks of the design of technological tools in her analogy, similar limitations to children's opportunities with technologies in early childhood pedagogy can be seen. Often technologies are segregated as isolated activities in the early childhood setting; for example, the computer corner, suggesting to the children that computer play is quite separate from other play resources. Plowman and Stephen (2007: 18) suggest that part of the pedagogy of technology includes distal characteristics – 'indirect influences on learning'.

It could be interpreted that the distal characteristic associated with positioning technologies as disjointed from other playroom or classroom practices creates the understanding that technologies are unique resources. In doing so, technologies form the central activity, e.g. playing a computer game, and children adapt to the resource, rather than the resources being adapted to the learning experience.

This is linked to the lack of playful integration of technologies in early childhood settings (Edwards, 2013). As we position technologies as isolated activities, children are not presented with opportunities to integrate the resource into a larger play theme. This could be achieved if we consider what O'Mara and Laidlaw (2011) describe as hybrid play, whereby technologies are integrated as part of traditional pretend play. This is facilitated by a broader definition of technological resources beyond the whiteboard or the computer. For example, mobile phones and toys that simulate adult appliances such as interactive microwaves, for example, allow children to integrate technologies as a prop in the play, rather than being the central activity (Savage, 2011).

Case study

Hybrid play with mobile phones and cash registers in a Chinese restaurant

Three children and one adult are playing in the home corner. In addition to standard home-related toys, a mobile telephone and cash register are also present. In the middle of the space is a medium-sized round table with chairs. Hilary is washing dishes while the adult is sitting at the table observing the play. Intermittently, she moves between washing dishes and pressing the buttons on the cash register. Vanessa also floats around the area, occasionally answering the phone. John appears and informs the adult that they need to wait for 50 minutes and then proceeds to bring her a bowl with food. 'Here you go! Chop sticks as well. What would you like in the cup?' he asks while holding a china cup and pointing to it. She replies 'Irn Bru, please?' John continues the conversation stating, 'Irn Bru – I'll bring you ice cream too.' John reappears and says 'Whoops, I got it wrong this is custard, but this is ice cream.' The adult asks for the bill and John appears with the cash register and says 'Here is your bill' (pretending the cash register is a card reader). She hands him a plastic card and says 'Can I pay by Visa?' He takes the card and swipes it through the card slot. The adult asks 'Is that OK or do you need a PIN?' He repeats 'PIN – yes please' and points at the numbers on the till. The adult enters the PIN, John says 'Thank you' and leaves with the cash register.

Reflective task

- When planning for 'opportunities' with technologies, what elements of your physical and social environment are likely to impact on children's play with technologies? Will this be positive or negative? If the latter, what changes are required to facilitate more creative play experiences for children with technologies?

Here we see technologies being used as part of a pretend play scene, where creativity and imagination are central. This kind of play is particularly still possible with technologies that are framed as open-ended resources. This allows the resources to be transformed by children to meet their play needs. In some cases this involves using the technologies as intended by the manufacturer, but in other cases, when provided with the freedom to explore, technologies can become something else entirely. As Bergen (2008) suggests that play goes from exploratory – to practice – to pretend, it is important to allow this kind of exploration for children with technologies. Bird and Edwards (2014) describe this process as moving from exploratory to innovative as children use technologies as tools to create play experiences.

Case study

Meccano car set becomes doctor's equipment

Leanne is 4 years old and her mother recently had a baby. She had visited her mother in hospital to visit her new baby brother when he was born. Leanne visited us in a local science museum with her mother and we gave her the opportunity to play with a range of motorised and technological toys and resources, one of which was a Meccano Car Set. The resources were presented to Leanne with no introduction, rather they were laid out on a table for her to explore freely. We were available to answer questions if she desired but she did not ask us about the resources. When presented with the range of Meccano pieces designed to construct a remote-controlled car, Leanne immediately transformed the pieces into doctor's equipment. At no point did she use the resources to build a remote-controlled car. Instead, the long panels were eased into her mother's mouth as she used them to examine the back of her mother's throat. Other pieces became a stethoscope or pieces of equipment to test her mother's reflexes. Leanne had clearly developed an interest in medical care, possibly related to her recent visit to hospital to meet her new brother, and she was able to use the resources presented to her to extend this play theme.

Reflective task

- Throughout this chapter we have discussed a broad range of digital technologies and highlighted that these resources are not homogeneous. Reflect on the above case study and an early childhood setting you are familiar with – if someone asked you 'what technologies do you/they have?', what would you answer? Are there more technologies available than you initially thought?

- Starting with the technologies you have listed, consider what 'opportunities' these artefacts provide for children's play and how central the resource is to that process.

While the above examples related to smart toys and resources, internet-enabled resources also offer enormous potential for developing relationships and sharing knowledge with practitioners and children far beyond the school/pre-school walls (Craft, 2012). Figure 18.1 shows a 14-month-old child communicating with her cousin who lives 400 miles away and giving her a kiss goodbye at the end of the conversation. For this child, the screen is not a barrier for affection and communication. She does not communicate any differently from how she would have done if her cousin was standing in front of her; she offers kisses as normal. This recognises children's enormous potential to embrace internet-enabled resources as another medium to interact and offer opportunities to extend the child's network. Already we are seeing this in practice as nurseries are developing a relationship with children from different countries and they share their experiences and ideas over the internet in an attempt to develop and foster global citizenship.

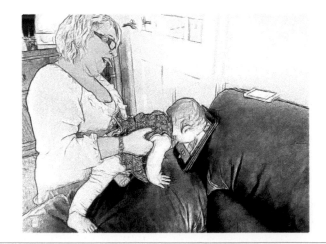

Figure 18.1 *Cyber-cousins*

The link between these examples is positioning the resources in a manner that offers potentiating environments (Claxton and Carr, 2004). Integrating technologies into practice in adaptable ways is only possible if we understand that technologies are another tool for learning.

Summary

Palaiologou (2014: 15) suggests that 'early years pedagogy should cultivate the capacity for learning environments that encourage sharing and communication of ideas using digital technologies and balance children's home digital experiences in navigating their learning environments'. In order to achieve this, technologies must be positioned in a way that facilitates these opportunities. We need to see technologies as integrated into play and not always separately defined activities. A broader definition of technology is required to spot the opportunities for 'hybrid play' and the social and cultural rules around technology use need to reflect those employed for traditional play.

When interviewed about their children's technology use, parents say technologies are just like another toy (Palaiologou, 2014). Taking this approach in practice demystifies the resource and, as Craft (2012) suggests, we need to transform the way adults engage with children and technologies, not because of the affordances of the resource, but because of the educators' own relationship to the resource. In essence it is important to view technologies as a tool within your repertoire for creating potentiating and stimulating learning environments for children. Livingstone et al. (2015) suggest that we need to find creative and educational ways of using digital technologies. This is not new for early years teachers and practitioners and, by recognising technologies as another resource or teaching tool, they can integrate these resources into their practice in line with their already established principles for high-quality early childhood education.

Bergen (2008: 87) suggests that 'the essence of play (at any age) is in its ability to enable players to transform their world through their active engagement, flexible thought, and creative control, using whatever materials are available to them'. I would argue that, with careful consideration, technologies can offer these play experiences. To do so, however, we need to embrace technologies for their potential in early childhood and not shy away from them. We need to recognise that technologies are part of the child's learning landscape and their daily lives and not be fearful of this change. We must give careful consideration to the position of these resources as part of children's experiences and the context within which they are used, just as we do when planning other early childhood activities. Clearly we must offer well-considered experiences, which plan for safe exploration, but do so without limiting the child's potential. We must see our early childhood environments as part of a larger, constantly connected society and community and as such we must involve both children and parents in the design process of how best to use these resources to support children's learning.

Gripton argues that part of supporting child-initiated play and learning is planning for endless possibilities. She argues that 'preparing and enabling endless possibilities is as much about belief and faith as it is about the practicalities' (2013: 18). The same is true for technologies, which should be viewed as another resource in your setting through which you can plan for 'opportunities' (Savage, 2011), 'possibility thinking' (Craft, 2012) and 'endless possibilities' (Gripton, 2013). Balance the risks, but embrace the potential afforded by technologies and utilise them in a manner that suits your practice and children's learning – just as you already do with traditional resources!

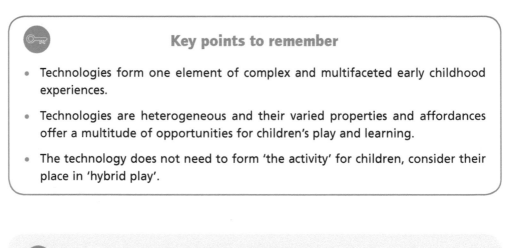

Key points to remember

- Technologies form one element of complex and multifaceted early childhood experiences.

- Technologies are heterogeneous and their varied properties and affordances offer a multitude of opportunities for children's play and learning.

- The technology does not need to form 'the activity' for children, consider their place in 'hybrid play'.

Points for discussion

- What innovative technologies will you incorporate into your practice in the future?

- To what extent do you agree with the perspectives that 'technologies are here to stay' and the focus should be on exploring best practice in using technologies rather than worrying about whether children should be using technologies at all?

- To what degree would you consider virtual social interactions between children across video applications such as Skype to be play?

Further reading

Books

Berson, I.R. and Berson, M.J. (2010) *High-tech Tots: Childhood in a Digital World*. Charlotte, NC: Information Age.

Plowman, L., Stephen, C. and McPake, J. (2010) *Growing Up With Technology: Young Children Learning in a Digital World*. London: Taylor & Francis.

Articles

Craft, A. (2012) 'Childhood in a digital age: creative challenges for educational futures', *London Review of Education*, 10 (2): 173–90.

McPake, J., Plowman, L. and Stephen, C. (2013) 'Pre-school children creating and communicating with digital technologies in the home', *British Journal of Educational Technology*, 44 (3): 421–31.

References

Arnott, L. (2013) 'Are we allowed to blink? Young children's leadership and ownership while mediating interactions around technologies', *International Journal of Early Years Education*, 21 (1): 97–115.

Bergen, D. (2008) 'New technologies in early childhood: partners in play?', in O.N. Saracho and B. Spodek (eds), *Contemporary Perspectives on Science and Technology in Early Childhood Education*. Charlotte, NC: IAP–Information Age. pp. 87–104.

Bers, M.U. (2012) *Designing Digital Experiences for Positive Youth Development: From Playpen to Playground*. New York: Oxford University Press.

Bird, J. and Edwards, S. (2014) 'Children learning to use technologies through play: a digital play framework', *British Journal of Educational Technology*. [epub ahead of print] doi: 10.1111/bjet.12191.

Carr, M. (2000) 'Technological affordance, social practice and learning narratives in an early childhood setting', *International Journal of Technology and Design Education*, 10 (1): 61–80.

Claxton, G. and Carr, M. (2004) 'A framework for teaching learning: the dynamics of disposition', *Early Years*, 24 (1): 87–97.

Craft, A. (2012) 'Childhood in a digital age: creative challenges for educational futures', *London Review of Education*, 10 (2): 173–90.

Edwards, S. (2013) 'Digital play in the early years: a contextual response to the problem of integrating technologies and play-based pedagogies in the early childhood curriculum', *European Early Childhood Education Research Journal*, 21 (2): 199–212.

Gripton, C. (2013) 'Planning for endless possibilities', in A. Woods (ed.), *Child-Initiated Play and Learning: Planning for Possibilities in the Early Years*. London: Taylor & Francis.

Haugland, S.W. (1992) 'The effect of computer software on preschool children's developmental gains', *Journal of Computing in Childhood Education*, 3 (1): 15–30.

James, A., Jenks, C. and Prout, A. (1998) *Theorizing Childhood*: New York: Teachers College Press.

Kolikant, Y.B.-D. (2010) 'Digital natives, better learners? Students' beliefs about how the Internet influenced their ability to learn', *Computers in Human Behavior*, 26 (6): 1384–91.

Livingstone, S., Marsh, J., Plowman, L., Ottovordemgentschenfelde, S. and Fletcher-Watson, B. (2015) *Young Children (0–8) and Digital Technology – UK Report*. Luxenbourg: Publications Office of the European Union.

Ljung-Djärf, A. (2008) 'The owner, the participant and the spectator: positions and positioning in peer activity around the computer in pre-school', *Early Years*, 28 (1): 61–72.

Marsh, J. (2004) 'The techno-literacy practices of young children', *Journal of Early Childhood Research*, 2 (1): 51–66.

Marsh, J. (2010) 'Young children's play in online virtual worlds', *Journal of Early Childhood Research*, 8 (1): 23–39.

McPake, J., Plowman, L. and Stephen, C. (2013) 'Pre-school children creating and communicating with digital technologies in the home', *British Journal of Educational Technology*, 44 (3): 421–31.

Neumann, M. M. and Neumann, D. L. (2014) 'Touch screen tablets and emergent literacy', *Early Childhood Education Journal*, 42 (4): 231–9.

O'Mara, J. and Laidlaw, L. (2011) 'Living in the iWorld: two literacy researchers reflect on the changing texts and literacy practices of childhood', *English Teaching: Practice and Critique*, 10 (4): 149–59.

Palaiologou, I. (2014) 'Children under five and digital technologies: implications for early years pedagogy', *European Early Childhood Education Research Journal*, 1–20.

Palmer, S. (2006) *Toxic Childhood: How the Modern World Is Damaging Our Children and What We Can Do about it*. London: Orion.

Parette, H.P., Quesenberry, A.C. and Blum, C. (2010) 'Missing the boat with technology usage in early childhood settings: a 21st century view of developmentally appropriate practice', *Early Childhood Education Journal*, 37 (5): 335–43.

Plowman, L. (2004) '"Hey, hey, hey! It's time to play." Exploring and mapping children's interactions with "smart" toys', in J. Goldstein, D. Buckingham and G. Brougere (eds), *Toys, Games, and Media*. Mahwah, NJ: Lawrence Erlbaum.

Plowman, L. and McPake, J. (2013) 'Seven myths about young children and technology', *Childhood Education*, 89 (1): 27–33.

Plowman, L., McPake, J. and Stephen, C. (2010) 'The technologisation of childhood? Young children and technology in the home', *Children & Society*, 24 (1): 63–74.

Plowman, L. and Stephen, C. (2007) 'Guided interaction in pre-school settings', *Journal of Computer Assisted Learning*, 23 (1): 14–26.

Plowman, L., Stephen, C. and McPake, J. (2010) *Growing Up With Technology: Young Children Learning in a Digital World*. London: Taylor & Francis.

Prensky, M. (2001) 'Digital natives, digital immigrants part 1', *On the horizon*, 9 (5): 1–6.

Savage, L. (2011) 'Exploring young children's social interactions in technology-rich early years environments.' PhD thesis, University of Stirling, Scotland.

Tapscott, D. (2008) *Grown Up Digital: How the Net Generation is Changing Your World*. New York: McGraw–Hill.

Tudge, J. (2008) *The Everyday Lives of Young Children: Culture, Class, and Child Rearing in Diverse Societies*. Cambridge: Cambridge University Press.

Wood, C., Kemp, N. and Plester, B. (2013) *Text Messaging and Literacy – The Evidence*. London: Taylor & Francis.

Yelland, N. (2010) 'New technologies, playful experiences, and multimodal learning', in I. Berson and M. Berson (eds), *High-Tech Tots: Childhood in a Digital World*. Charlotte, NC: Information Age Publishing. pp. 5–22.

Zevenbergen, R. (2007) 'Digital natives come to preschool: implications for early childhood practice', *Contemporary Issues in Early Childhood*, 8 (1): 19–29.

Want to learn more about this chapter? Visit the companion website at https://study.sagepub.com/EYFS3e for access to free SAGE journal articles and book chapters, weblinks, annotated further readings and more.

PART 4
THE AREAS
OF LEARNING

19

Personal, Social and Emotional Development

John Bennett and Ioanna Palaiologou

Chapter overview

There is little doubt that the early years in a child's life are vitally important for personal, social and emotional development. To be as effective as possible, that development must take place in an environment that is safe, affectionate and encouraging for children: an environment that promotes positive feelings and social skills.

From the moment that children are born they are engaged in interaction with adults, in their growth to becoming both independent and social beings. The early stages of their lives are important for children's acquisition of social and emotional skills that will enhance their personal development and it is also clear that personal, social and emotional development can have a significant impact on academic achievement. The work of significant educational theorists, such as Vygotsky (1986), Piaget (1951) and Bandura (1977), alongside more recent studies into the development of the human brain and how social interaction and experience has an impact on the way in which the brain both works and continues to develop (Davison et al., 2009), confirms the critical role that early personal, social and emotional development has in future personal and academic success.

(Continued)

(Continued)

Personal, social and emotional development tend to be considered together, as they are linked and reinforce one another. This chapter aims to explore children's personal, social and emotional development; it aims to help you understand:

- personal, social and emotional development in early childhood
- the role of the environment in children's personal, social and emotional development.

Personal, social and emotional development in the EYFS

When the EYFS was reviewed in 2010/2011, a request was made as part of the call for evidence which asked what was the most important thing for settings and schools to do in relation to children's learning and development. Eighty-one per cent of the respondents to that request, the highest response, named personal, social and emotional development (PSED) as the most important thing (DfE, 2011). It was no surprise, therefore, that the revised statutory framework stressed the importance of PSED for young children's well-being, not just within the overarching principles it presented, but also as one of the three prime areas of learning and development (DfE, 2014). The subsequent framework maintained this 'crucial' place of PSED (DfE, 2014). The four overarching principles of the framework support each child's PSED (DfE, 2014). This is most evident in the first two principles, those relating to the *unique child* and *positive relationships*. The principle that states that every child is unique cites the characteristics of resilience, capability, confidence and self-assuredness as ideals for children, all of which come through effective provision for PSED. The second principle, stating that 'children learn to be strong and independent through positive relationships' (DfE, 2014: 6), is clearly supported through positive social development.

As has been shown in Chapter 2, at policy level, the personal, social and emotional development of young children continues to be a key issue and a priority in the government's agenda. The strategies of the previous UK governments, such as the National Childcare Strategy, Every Child Matters and the Safeguarding Children policies, aimed to protect children from harm and to promote children's well-being, and the principles embedded within those policies continue to resonate in the latest statutory framework.

The national EYFS guidance identifies the following three elements of PSED, each of which has an associated Early Learning Goal:

- *Self-confidence and self-awareness:* children are confident to try new activities, and say why they like some activities more than others. They are confident to speak in a familiar group, will talk about their ideas and will choose the resources they need for their chosen activities. They say when they do or don't need help.
- *Managing feelings and behaviour:* children talk about how they and others show feelings, talk about their own and others' behaviour, and its consequences, and know that some behaviour is unacceptable. They work as part of a group or class, and understand and follow the rules. They adjust their behaviour to different situations, and take changes of routine in their stride.
- *Making relationships:* children play cooperatively, taking turns with others. They take account of one another's ideas about how to organise their activity. They show sensitivity to others' needs and feelings, and form positive relationships with adults and other children. (DfE, 2014: 11)

Each of these elements is critical to the development of well-rounded, secure children, who feel accepted, both individually and as part of their community, and have the confidence to succeed or fail, knowing they have at least one supportive adult to help guide them.

The importance of PSED, as key aspects of early childhood education and care which should not be underestimated, has been emphasised in many places. The Reggio Emilia pedagogy, for example, focuses on children's well-being and personal development, and expects that activities and the environment are organised around promoting children's well-being. As was discussed in Chapters 1 and 6, a number of theorists have linked pedagogy with children's social relationships (Rubin, 1982; Rubin et al., 1983; Hymel, 1983; Hymel et al., 1990; Howes, 1990, 1992; Dunn, 1993; Elfer et al., 2002). It is a positive factor that the EYFS addresses the key issues of PSED as being equally important as children's learning. However, it can be argued that in pre-set goals and descriptive curriculum approaches such as EYFS, PSED can be seen as measured achievements, rather than as children's journeys towards self-awareness, well-being and building relationships.

Closely allied to the PSED of young children is their moral development, explored by theorists such as Piaget (1932), Kohlberg (1969) and Bandura (1977, 1986) and considered in relation to caring attachment by Gilligan and Wiggins (1987). While this area is not identified explicitly as an area of learning within the EYFS, it is important for all those working with young children to consider how they are supporting children's moral development. This is achieved through how they interact with the children, how they deal with children's behaviour and how they plan activities that allow children to explore right and wrong, through stories and circle time perhaps, which are both covered in this chapter. It is important to realise that young children will act on impulse and on their immediate needs, taking a toy from another child, for example, because they want to play with it. They need to be told why some behaviours are unfair or can hurt others, physically and emotionally. The language of emotions needs to be developed and children need to be guided in basic interactions, such as sharing and turn taking, particularly where resources are limited. Of critical importance is the way in which those who work with young children provide excellent role models with regard to how they behave, particularly towards others. Demonstrating positive social and moral expectations provides children with the examples to follow in their own actions.

The journey made by children on entering the world can be seen as a two-sided process, in which children simultaneously become integrated into their larger community and also develop as distinctive individuals. One side of social development is socialisation and the process by which children acquire the standards, values and knowledge of their community. The other side of social development is personality formation: the process through which children come to have their own unique patterns of feeling, thinking and behaving in a wide range of circumstances.

> In order to effectively and successfully provide for young children's PSED, it is essential for adults working with them to have an understanding of the broad phases that most children go through in those areas, while acknowledging that 'developmental progression from birth to five across the prime and specific areas of learning will follow an individual path. (NCB, 2012: 18)

The assessment of development in these areas, and subsequent actions to meet the needs of the children in developing further, is supported through the non-statutory *Early Years Outcomes* document which offers practitioners 'a guide to making best-fit judgements about whether a child is showing typical development for their age' (DfE, 2013a: 3). The statutory framework, as demonstrated in Chapter 9, includes summative assessment in all prime areas at two stages: The Integrated Review at Age Two and assessment at the end of the EYFS, the EYFS Profile. Both of these summative assessments should reflect children's development and learning and the practitioners should use their own day-to-day observations to complete them and share the information with parents and carers or other services.

As was demonstrated in Chapter 8, observation of children by practitioners, rather than interaction, has increased in early childhood settings in recent years, prompted mainly by a previous assessment system in EYFS, which required judgements to be made against a significant number of criteria. While the assessment system has been slimmed down, the value of observation must still be recognised and it is extremely important that practitioners observe children when they are engaged in social situations, reflecting on their personal, social and emotional development and making decisions about what each child needs to progress in those areas. It is possible to do a considerable amount of that through interaction, but in taking the role of a non-participant observer the practitioner is able to focus purely on identifying features of the development of skills and attitudes that contribute to PSED.

The critical need to ensure the most effective PSED led the last Labour government to develop the SEAD programme (Social and Emotional Aspects of Development) specifically to support those working with young children in their efforts to develop social and emotional skills. The SEAD guidance for practitioners continues to provide a sound basis for work on these aspects (DCSF, 2008). That programme of development and training was aimed at birth to 36 months. The SEAL (Social and Emotional Aspects of Learning) materials, also developed by the previous government, provide similar resources for developing those aspects with children for 30 to 60+ months (DfES, 2005). Practitioners therefore have a wealth of useful support materials available to help ensure that effective PSED takes place.

It is important for practitioners to consider the elements of PSED from theoretical and practical perspectives, to develop the fullest understanding possible of what effective provision is for developing self-confidence and self-awareness, helping children to manage feelings and behaviour and supporting making relationships.

Self-confidence and self-awareness

When babies are born they have a very long way to go before becoming independent. Part of their development can be characterised as a process to differentiate themselves from others and to construct the concept of 'self' (or personal identity).

In the case of developing the self, babies have a gradually increasing awareness of a sense of themselves as distinct and separate entities, clearly differentiated from all other entities (human and non-human) that populate their world. This process of articulation and definition of self begins in early infancy. At first babies do not recognise themselves. For example, when a baby is placed in front of a mirror there is no reaction from them, as they do not recognise that the reflection is of them. At about the age of 18 months babies begin to have a clearer idea that this reflection is a representation of themselves.

The acquisition of the concept of identity is important for children's well-being. Selleck (2001) claims that the parent or carer in a setting plays an important role in this formation of infant identity. That role involves affirming responses, consistent care, ensuring that the child feels special, even when one of many, and acting in a way that builds the confidence of the child at every opportunity.

Adults helping children to develop a personal identity need to be aware that a baby's crying is a form of expressing how they feel (such as discomfort, stress, hunger or tiredness) and at the same time is a way of attempting to communicate with the parent/carer. The adult should respond accordingly, providing an appropriate response (relieving discomfort, stress, hunger or meeting the need for rest).

Social communication, which adults need to be aware of, also develops through the 'social smile'. In the beginning of their lives, a baby's smile is a form of expressing their comfort, as it is related to their biological needs. When their biological needs are covered, they feel comfort, the muscles in their faces relax and they appear to smile. They also appear to smile when the mother strokes and comforts them. At the age of between 6 and 10 weeks, however, infants start to show a clear preference for certain human beings and especially for familiar human faces.

A 'social smile' indicates the progress of babies in differentiating themselves as individual human beings and they respond to the face of another human being by smiling back to them. It is a major developmental stage in babies' lives towards the process of identity formation and towards the acquisition of a repertoire of social skills.

In the sequence of photographs in Figure 19.1 the social smile of a baby is captured. The baby is lying in his cot and an adult is approaching him. The baby looks at the adult's face and soon afterwards his lips form a smile (shown in the last photo) and the expression becomes one of happiness as the smile becomes more intense.

Gradually, when infants become more mobile and explore the world around them (alongside cognitive development), they begin acquiring self-recognition by becoming self-aware, an element central to children's emotional and social lives.

When working with young babies in a setting it is important to offer them opportunities to develop a concept of themselves. Activities such as nursery rhymes combined with physical movement mirrors in which babies explore their reflections, and games such as when adults hide their faces with their hands in front of the baby (peek-a-boo!), are activities that sound simple yet actually help infants in their process of acquiring their concept of self.

Within this development of self-concept, and the understanding of personal identity, the critical areas of self-confidence and self-esteem must be fostered. In early childhood the responses of others, whether they are parents, carers, staff in settings or other children, have an effect on the child's perception of self. All those who have

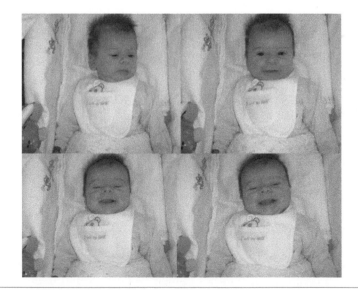

Figure 19.1 *A baby's social smile*

responsibility for the development of young children should ensure that the interactions they have with those children are ones that enable children to feel they are secure and accepted, that they have worth. These affirmations help children to develop a positive self-concept. The adults should engage in activities with the children which build self-confidence, critically through the use of praise and encouragement. The environment must also support this development and it is important that the interactions with other children are monitored and relevant, and appropriate interventions are made when necessary, for example, if another child is likely to cause upset that the child may not be able to cope with personally. Such interventions must be carefully considered because an adult, by always intervening, will not allow the child to gain skills in dealing with difficulties personally or developing resilience to negative social situations.

Managing feelings and behaviour

Attachment

As was discussed in Chapter 11, a dominant and influential theory on the emotional development of children is that proposed by Bowlby (1951, 1960, 1969, 1973, 1980, 1999, 2005) and developed further by Ainsworth (1969, 1979, 1985, 1989), Ainsworth and Bell (1970), Ainsworth and Bowlby (1991), Ainsworth et al. (1971a, 1971b) and Ainsworth et al. (1978) regarding 'attachment'. All these studies proposed that when babies are born they are 'pre-programmed' to form close relationships with the mother/carer. This bond is called attachment. The ideas of Bowlby and Ainsworth have influenced the way mother–child and carer–child relationships are perceived. Bowlby and Ainsworth have each described in detail the stages of attachment and how the formation of the relationship between the mother (or carer) and the baby takes place. They have also discussed the consequences of the separation of the child from the mother or carer.

The *Development Matters* document, created to support assessment and planning for EYFS, clearly stated that staff working with young children must be 'aware of the importance of attachment in relationships' (Early Education/DfE, 2012: 8).

This has considerable implications for early childhood settings. Owing to economic factors, an increasing number of primary carers of children are entering the workforce so more children attend settings from a very young age. In the light of the attachment theory, it is necessary that the EYFS emphasises the importance of the role of the key person in relation to children for smooth transitions of children from home to settings. Prior to joining the setting young children need such emotional warmth as that provided by practitioners when they enter early childhood education and care in order to provide a form of substitute for the attachment, and they also need a continuous and stable relationship with the early childhood practitioners for their personal well-being.

Bowlby claims, 'If a community values its children, it must cherish their parents' 1951: 84). Not only do children form attachment with parents; parents form strong attachments with their children. Consequently, when children join settings, parents can feel guilty for not being with them and may experience anxiety as to whether their children will have an enjoyable time in the setting and make friends. It is essential to support the parents during this process and roles of the key person include continually reconfirming that children are forming stable relationships within the settings and reassuring the family about the care and support being provided.

Making relationships

An important aspect of children's social development is how they form relationships, how they behave during interactions with other children or adults and how they make attempts to become part of the community and the wider social environment.

Children attempt from a very young age to make relationships. For example, small children are interested in the activities of others of a similar age, or they smile at other human beings (familiar faces in particular). Making relationships during early childhood is a major developmental task. It is essential to understand that children's perceptions and criteria for forming relationships differ in many ways from those of adults. Young children choose friends and to make relationships with other individuals on the basis of their pleasurable interactions with them. This does not mean that they are selfish. When children first begin to form relationships they lack abstract thinking, so are unable to conceptualise the meaning of mutual friendships. As they grow older and their cognitive development advances, they evolve into being able to form a more abstract relationship based on mutual consideration and psychological satisfaction.

For example, a child can be a friend with another child during outdoor play time as they have fun riding bikes, running or jumping; when in the class, though, each may be friends with another child as they enjoy playing in the construction area. Phrases such as 'You are not my friend' or 'I do not want to play with you' are common in settings. As Damon (1988) suggested, there are different levels at which children develop their friendships. Damon describes friendships in early childhood as a 'handy playmate', where children choose a friend on the basis that they do together those things each enjoys.

As children grow older and develop their own concept of self, self-awareness and an awareness of others' thoughts and feelings, they are able to form relationships involving mutual trust.

Sociometric status studies have investigated how children form relationships within early childhood settings and have shown that children tend to fall into four major categories (e.g. Rubin, 1982; Rubin et al., 1983; Hymel, 1983; Hymel et al., 1990; Howes and Matheson, 1992; Dunn, 1993; DeRosier et al., 1994; Black and Logan, 1995):

- *Popular* children are liked by their peers. These children are very active, direct or lead activities, make suggestions and structure activities.
- *Rejected* children are those who are actively disliked by and receive many negative comments from their peers. Others do not want to invite them into their play. These 'rejected' children often demonstrate aggressive behaviours, such as hitting, biting, or kicking, none of which helps them.
- *Controversial* children get a large number of positive and negative comments from their peers.
- Finally, *neglected* children are seldom chosen to join in with activities, either positively or negatively. Their peers normally ignore these children, who then find themselves in isolation. Subsequently, neglected children do not participate in activities; they demonstrate isolated behaviour.

The degree of peer acceptance is a powerful predictor of current (as well as later) psychological adjustment. Rejected children, especially, are unhappy, alienated and poorly achieving children with a low sense of self-esteem. Practitioners and parents both view them as having a wide range of emotional and social problems. Research claims that peer rejection during middle childhood is also strongly associated with poor school performance, anti-social behaviour, and delinquency and criminality in adolescence and young adulthood (DeRosier et al., 1994).

With age, children come to develop a number of skills, such as perspective thinking and the ability to understand the viewpoints of others; therefore, they become better at resolving social conflicts and their relationships with others improve. It is important to create activities within which children are offered opportunities to develop all of the necessary social skills and are encouraged to form relationships, for example, taking turns in activities helps children to develop social problem solving skills, while serving one another during snack times helps them to develop a perspective of others.

Case study

Friendships

Kayleigh and Leanne recently joined the nursery class at the same time and appeared to choose to play together all of the time. Each was assigned a different key person.

Initially the girls were always placed in the same group, but over time both key persons identified ways in which the apparently strong bond between the girls was having an impact on their broader interaction and their development of essential

(Continued)

(Continued)

social skills. For example, Kayleigh's key person observed the girls playing with buckets, spades and large jelly moulds in the sand tray. Kayleigh always used the spade, while Leanne held the mould or bucket and when she asked to use the spade, Kayleigh said that was not her 'job'. Whenever another child came to try to join in Kayleigh told him or her it was just for her and her friend. Similarly, Leanne's key person had heard Kayleigh tell another child that she could not play with Leanne, because Leanne was her friend only. Further observations confirmed that Kayleigh dominated and controlled the games she played with Leanne.

Although the practitioners felt that there was no malice in Kayleigh's actions, they decided to make sure that the girls would be placed in separate groups at times, with the result that Leanne gained more independence and confidence and Kayleigh, after some initial difficulties and reassuring words and explanations from her key person, began to share more readily and play happily with others. Over time, although the girls still tended to play together when not in separate groups, they also included others more readily.

Reflective task

- Reflect on the different definitions of social positions of children in the setting (i.e 'popular', 'rejected', 'controversial' and 'neglected') and try to identify which category the children in the case study belong to. How can you help them to form relationships with other children? If you were the key person for these children what strategies would you put in place to enhance their transitions (see Chapter 11), encourage friendships and how would you communicate with the parents (see Chapter 13)?

Play and stories

The role of play in EYFS was explored in Chapter 7, where it was demonstrated how important play is for children's learning and development. This section examines the role of play in relation to children's PSED. When children enter early childhood education and care they begin with non-social activity, and *solitary play* (i.e. unoccupied, onlooker behaviour). They later shift to a form of limited social participation, called *parallel play*, in which a child plays near other children using similar materials, but does not try to interact with or influence their behaviour (Barnes, 1971; Rubin, 1982; Rubin et al., 1983; Dunn, 1993; Smith, 1997).

As children grow older they reach a higher level of social interaction, characterised by two forms of true social interaction: *associative play*, in which children engage in separate activities, although they do interact by exchanging toys and commenting on one another's behaviour, and *cooperative play*, a more advanced type of interaction involving work orientated towards a common goal, such as acting out a make-believe scenario or working on the same product, for example a sand castle or patchwork quilt (Barnes, 1971). All of these types of play co-exist during early childhood, as illustrated in Table 19.1.

Table 19.1   Examples of all types of play in early childhood

Play type	Examples
Non-social activity	**Solitary play**
	A child is sitting alone in the writing corner using the table as a motorway to play with his cars. He plays there for about six minutes
	Parallel play
	Four children are sitting at a table, trying to put together some puzzles. Each child does a different puzzle
	Functional play
	Simple, receptive motor movements with or without objects
Unoccupied	A 3-year-old boy sits for a long time in a chair doing nothing. He was not obviously engaged in anything, but after close observation he is aware of other children and he watches them very carefully
Associative play	**Constructive play**
	Children are sitting on the carpet playing with Lego. They try to make a farm with animals. Each has his or her own pieces, and the children exchange pieces and talk about what animals the farm will include
	Make-believe play
	Two girls are in the dolls' house, pretending that they are friends and that they have invited each other for tea; they talk about their dolls as if these are real babies
Comparative play	Four children are in the yard looking at some lentils that they planted in the morning. Suddenly, they see a tortoise and try to stop it because they think that the tortoise will eat the lentils
Games with rules	Two boys and a girl are in the outdoor area and they want to play in the sandbox area. They make a motorway in order to race their cars. They set two rules: not to damage the motorway by shifting the sand with the cars, and, second, not themselves to step on the sand

Furthermore, although non-social activity eventually declines with age, it is still the most frequent form of behaviour among 3- and 4-year-olds. Even among young children it continues to take up as much as a third of children's free-play time. The occurrence of both solitary and parallel play remains fairly stable between 3 and 6 years of age (Howes and Matheson, 1992).

Make-believe play is developed in parallel with representation. Piaget (1951) believed that through pretending children practise and strengthen newly acquired symbolic schemes. Make-believe play also allows children to become more familiar with social role possibilities, by acting out familiar scenes and highly visible occupations (for example, police officer, doctor or nurse). In this way play provides young children with important insights into links between themselves and society.

Piaget's view of make-believe play as being mere practice of symbolic schemes is now regarded, however, as too limited. More recent research indicates that play not only reflects, but also contributes to children's cognitive and social skills (Nikolopoulou, 1993).

Vygotsky offers a slightly different view of make-believe play. In accordance with his emphasis on social experience and language as vital forces in cognitive development, Vygotsky (1986) granted make-believe play a prominent place within his theory. He regarded it as creating a unique, broadly influential zone of proximal development, during which children advance themselves as they try out a wide variety of challenging skills:

> In play, the child always behaves beyond his average age, above his daily behaviour; in play it is though he were a head taller than himself. As in the focus of a magnifying glass, play contains all developmental tendencies in a condensed form and is itself a major source of development. (Vygotsky, 1978: 102)

During make-believe play, pre-school children act out and respond to one another's pretend feelings. Their play is rich in references to emotional states. Young children also explore and gain control of fear-arousing experiences when, for example, they play the role of a doctor or a dentist, or pretend to be searching for monsters. As a result, they are better able to understand the feelings of others and also to regulate their own. Finally, collectively to create and manage complex narratives, pre-school children must resolve their disputes through negotiation and compromise – skills they develop when they become older (Singer and Singer, 1990; Howes, 1992).

All of the points above highlight the need for those working with children to ensure that opportunities for make-believe play or role-play as it is commonly named, are an integral part of the provision, but also that the setting facilitates child-initiated role-play. Much of this can be achieved by having role-play areas and role-play resources. The areas can be set up to mirror social contexts, such as a shop, a school or a doctor's surgery, or they can simply be spaces where the children can play. The areas could also be set up as settings from stories the children are hearing and sharing, such as the bridge from *The Three Billy Goats*, the wood in *The Gruffalo* or the differing environments in *We're Going on a Bear Hunt*. Resources appropriate to each role-play setting should be added, including props and costumes, as well as toys such as teddies, dolls and puppets. All of these enable the children to role-play social interaction in pretend social spaces, which is essential practice and promotes social development in secure, non-threatening environments. The adult's role in this is very much as the facilitator, but stepping in and playing, also in role, can help to resolve disagreements to support social and emotional development, as well as to model social and emotional responses.

There are strong links between the two prime areas of learning of communication and language, and PSED. The development of talk (which is covered in Chapters 20 and 21) obviously facilitates the building of relationships and the critical ability to communicate feelings in a more refined way, but the strong links between the two areas of learning go further than this.

The importance of stories in the EYFS cannot be underestimated. Stories provide young children with opportunities to explore personality, social situations, interactions, emotions and the broad range of personal, social and emotional experience, from the safety of being a listener. Stories communicate important messages about life and give children opportunities to empathise with the characters. Most children will naturally follow up hearing stories with self-generated activities related to them, engaging in imaginative play, both individually and with others. Adults can support this and also enhance the whole impact of stories through provision of areas to play in, props, puppets, soft toys and costumes. As well as telling stories and giving the children the chance for story-based play, adults should also engage the children in talk about the stories, developing understanding and exploring how characters act and feel. This is one way of helping to develop the language of emotions.

A further method for exploring emotions, which also supports social development, turn taking, and speaking and listening skills, is to introduce the children to circle time (Mosley, 2005). In the context of taking turns going around the circle, questions about feelings can be explored in many different ways, offering children insights into the way in which others feel and the chance to express their own perspectives. When done well, this type of activity can support many aspects of PSED, particularly increasing the children's understanding of emotional language and contributing to their skills in listening to others and identifying the feelings of others.

Case study

Emotional language development through story

Amrit and some of the other children had been listening to a nursery nurse reading the Michael Rosen book *We're Going on a Bear Hunt* (1989). In the story the family do encounter a bear and run away from it. The nursery nurse asked the group

(Continued)

(Continued)

to pretend that they were the children in the family and to say what they were feeling when they found the bear. One of the children responded 'scary', one said 'scared' (a word used a lot in the story) and another said 'fightened' (which the nursery nurse repeats as 'frightened'), but Amrit said that he would feel 'funny'. The nursery nurse asked Amrit why he thought it was funny and he said that 'it isn't funny', but he would 'feel funny'.

Amrit did not yet have the language to fully express his emotions and reverted, therefore, to something he has heard others say, but wasn't entirely appropriate in this situation. Through the responses of the other children and the nursery nurse's repetition of appropriate words, Amrit started to learn the language associated with being scared.

In a later activity, the nursery nurse heard Amrit say that his cat was frightened by a dog in next door's garden. He was beginning to use appropriate language and the nursery nurse planned to consolidate that by using *The Gruffalo* (Donaldson, 1999) as another starting point for further discussion.

Reflective task

- Reflecting on the above case study, how could you use the Gruffalo story further in order to support the PSED of Amrit? What other strategies could you have in place in order to support his emotional language?

Resources and the environment

The quality and quantity of play materials has a major impact upon young children's personal, social and emotional development. In an interesting study, Smith (1997) showed that fights and disruptions increase in settings where children were confined to a relatively small space in which to play and where there were not enough toys to share around.

It is important to make sure that children have access to a variety of toys and play materials. Construction materials, building blocks and puzzles tend to be associated with solitary play, but these are important materials to have available when children decide to engage in solitary activities. As has been demonstrated, all types of play co-exist in children's daily routine within the setting. Children choose what type of play they want to join in according to their needs at that time.

In order to encourage participation from all children, open-ended activities and relatively non-constructed objects (such as using fabrics or instigating face-painting) can facilitate both cooperative and imaginative play. Children will need to use their negotiation, problem solving, communication and listening skills, when participating in these activities, developing and practising these essential abilities.

Using realistic toys such as trucks, dolls, telephones and tea-sets helps children to act out everyday roles and this also promotes role-playing. Role-play requires complex interactions, especially when children try to re-create 'real' events that have happened to them. Additionally, role-play is essential for enabling children to express and articulate their feelings within a safe environment.

Classroom activities need to be adapted in order to increase the participation of all children present. Regular systematic observations of the different areas of the class are required; practitioners need to be prepared to change the organisation of their setting to ensure that children can move around and use all areas to the maximum.

In recent years the use of the outdoor environment has received considerable promotion as part of early childhood education and care. It is essential for PSED that outdoor activities are a planned part of the range of experiences young children have. As was shown in Chapter 12 outdoor play can help promote social interactions, through a broader range of potential cooperative activities, such as sand play and large construction equipment. Some outdoor games and equipment, such as large play equipment that needs space and room for children to move freely, help children to develop respect for their peers by waiting to take turns or, for example, by playing in pairs. Emotional development is supported by the potentially greater freedoms afforded by being outdoors. Children can express their emotions in larger spaces and in louder ways than are often acceptable indoors. They can run and jump and shout and scream, if they wish, expressing pleasure and revelling in the freedom the outdoor environment provides.

The role of the adult in all of these situations is highly important. The adult can help children with activities, or can suggest activities where peer collaboration is required. The adult can monitor interactions among the children, and make sure that all children are encouraged to play with one another.

In a supportive setting or outdoor environment where the social behaviours of children are promoted, and in an environment where children feel safe to express their feelings, the children's developmental journey will be supported effectively.

Reflective task

- If you were introducing circle time in a setting for the first time, how would you go about it? What would you need to do to prepare the children to take part? What environmental factors would you need to consider? What themes would you explore when first implementing this strategy?

Skills of the practitioner

Throughout this chapter reference has been made to how adults can support PSED, but in order to do that effectively practitioners need to have a range of skills and attitudes. Whilst the 2012 review by Cathy Nutbrown had a focus on qualifications, noting that those are the key to the quality of the workforce (Nutbrown, 2012), in order to support effective PSED staff need a range of understanding, skills, qualities and attitudes that go beyond qualifications.

Critically, practitioners need to have empathy with the children. They need to be able to identify children's feelings and be able to understand why they are acting as they are. Alongside empathy, compassion is also critical. In caring for and developing young children genuine and unconditional compassion will help ensure the best early childhood experience. As adults who model good behaviour for young children, practitioners must be constantly aware that the way they behave has an impact on the young children's perceptions of how people behave; practitioners must ensure they do not behave in inappropriate ways that young children will mimic.

The Early Years Teacher Standards (DfE, 2013b) include a number of key expectations of early childhood teachers. A key subheading of Standard 5 is to:

> Demonstrate an awareness of the physical, emotional, social, intellectual development and communication needs of babies and children, and know how to adapt education and care to support children at different stages of development. (2013b: 3)

Other subheadings make it clear that early childhood teachers must know and understand 'how babies and children learn and develop' (Standards 2.2 and 3.1) and about attachment theories (Standard 2.3) as well as how to develop 'children's confidence, social and communication skills through group learning' (Standard 2.6) (2013b: 2) (although this last point fails to acknowledge the importance of one-to-one responses, particularly from adults with very young children). There is a clear expectation that early childhood teachers model 'positive values, attitudes and behaviours expected of children' (Standard 1.3) (2013b: 2). All of these aspects of a good teacher are also relevant to all those who work with young children.

Reflective task

- Choose one of the three elements of EYFS PSED and, using the *Early Years Outcomes* document and observation over time, track one child's progress in that area. Does the development match with what the *Early Years Outcomes* document shows as the developmental journey or are there differences? If there are differences, can you identify the factors that lead to those? (See examples in Chapters 8 and 9 for some help on how to start.)

Summary

This chapter has discussed key aspects of children's development: personal, social and emotional. Although PSED was studied separately here, it is necessary to stress that it is influenced by all aspects of development, such as cognitive development, language and physical development. In the following chapter it will be demonstrated how important PSED is in other aspects of children's development. It is a positive aspect of the EYFS that PSED is a statutory prime area for children's well-being.

Key points to remember

- This chapter looked at the personal, social and emotional development of young children. Although these three aspects of development are studied separately, they are interlinked, and they form the foundation for the other areas of children's cognitive development.

- When working with very young children it is important to understand their relationships with the family and with other children, and how they form relationships in the setting.

- The organisation of the early childhood environment and the materials and resources used play a crucial role in children's personal, social and emotional development.

Points for discussion

- Consider the implications of attachment when you are planning for the arrival of a new child into your setting. What strategies would you use to help with the transition? How would you allocate the key person? How would you plan for involving this child in the setting's daily activities?

- If personal, social and emotional development are not supported by effective planning in a setting, what might the impact of this be?

- How would you encourage a hesitant child to get involved in role-play activities?

Further reading

Books

Broadhead, P., Johnston, J. and Tobbell, C. (2010) *Personal, Social and Emotional Development (Supporting Development in the Early Years Foundation Stage)*. London: Continuum.

Dowling, M. (2014) *Young Children's Personal, Social and Emotional Development*, 4th edn. London: Sage.

Manning-Morton, J. (2014) 'Young children's personal, social and emotional development: foundations of being', in P. Mukherji and L. Dryden (eds), *Foundations of Early Childhood*. London: Sage. pp. 303–19.

Papatheodoropoulou, T. and Moyles, J. (eds) (2009) *Learning Together in the Early Years: Exploring Relational Pedagogy*. London: Routledge.

Sheppy, S. (2009) *Personal, Social and Emotional Development in the Early Years Foundation Stage*. London: David Fulton.

Article

Aubrey, C. and Ward, K. (2013) 'Early years practitioners' views on early personal, social and emotional development', *Emotional and Behavioural Difficulties*, 18 (4): 435–47.

Useful websites

SEAD and SEAL EYFS materials can be accessed here:
www.eriding.net/eyfs/21_respecting_each_other.shtml

TES PSED resources:
https://www.tes.com/teaching-resources/search/personal-social-and-health-education/?&f=categoryRoot%5B%220|3-5%22%5D%5B%223-5%22%5D*&f=categories%5B%220|Personal%2C+social+and+health+education|%22%5D%5B%22Personal%2C+social+and+health+education%22%5D

References

Ainsworth, M.D.S. (1969) 'Object relations, dependency, and attachment: a theoretical review of the infant–mother relationship', *Child Development*, 40: 969–1025.

Ainsworth, M.D.S. (1979) 'Attachment as related to mother–infant interaction', *Advances in the Study of Behaviour*, 9: 2–52.

Ainsworth, M.D.S. (1985) 'Attachments across the life span', *Bulletin of the New York Academy of Medicine*, 61: 792–812.

Ainsworth, M.D.S. (1989) 'Attachment beyond infancy', *American Psychologist*, 44: 709–16.

Ainsworth, M.D.S. and Bell, S.M. (1970) 'Attachment, exploration, and separation: illustrated by the behaviour of one-year-olds in a strange situation', *Child Development*, 41: 49–67.

Ainsworth, M.D.S. and Bowlby, J. (1991) 'An ethological approach to personality development', *American Psychologist*, 46: 333–41.

Ainsworth, M.D.S., Bell, S.M. and Stayton, D.J. (1971a) 'Individual differences in the strange situation behaviour of one-year-olds', in H.R. Schaffer (ed.), *The Origins of Human Social Relations*. New York: Academic Press. pp. 15–71.

Ainsworth, M.D.S., Bell, S.M., Blehar, M.C. and Main, M. (1971b) 'Physical contact: a study of infant responsiveness and its relation to maternal handling'. Paper presented at the biennial meeting of the Society for Research in Child Development, Minneapolis, MN.

Ainsworth, M.D.S., Blehar, M.C., Waters, E. and Wall, S. (1978) *Patterns of Attachment: A Psychological Study of the Strange Situation*. Hillsdale, NJ: Lawrence Erlbaum Associates.

Bandura, A. (1977) *Social Learning Theory*. New York: General Learning Press.

Bandura, A. (1986) *Social Foundations of Thought and Action: A Social Cognitive Theory*. Englewood Cliffs, NJ: Prentice–Hall.

Barnes, K.E. (1971) 'Preschool play norms: a replication', *Developmental Psychology*, 5: 99–103.

Black, B. and Logan, A. (1995) 'Links between communication patterns in mother child, father child, and child peer interactions and children's social status', *Child Development*, 66: 951–65.

Bowlby, J. (1951) *Maternal Care and Mental Health*. Geneva: World Health Organisation Monograph (Serial No. 2).

Bowlby, J. (1960) 'Grief and mourning in infancy and early childhood', *The Psychoanalytic Study of the Child*, 15: 9–52.

Bowlby, J. (1969) *Attachment and Loss, Volume I: Attachment*. London: Hogarth Press.

Bowlby, J. (1973) *Attachment and Loss, Volume 2: Separation: Anger and Anxiety*. (International Psycho-analytical Library No. 95). London: Hogarth Press.

Bowlby, J. (1980) *Attachment and Loss, Volume 3: Loss: Sadness and Depression*. (International Psycho-analytical Library No. 109). London: Hogarth Press.

Bowlby, J. (1999) *Attachment and Loss, Volume I: Attachment*, 2nd edn. New York: Basic Books.

Bowlby, J. (2005) *The Making and Breaking of Affectional Bonds*. London: Routledge Classics.

Damon, W. (1988) *The Moral Child*. New York: Free Press.

Davison, J.D., Sherer, K.R. and Goldsmith, H.H. (2009) *Handbook of Affective Sciences*. New York: Oxford University Press.

DCSF (Department for Children, Schools and Families) (2008) *Social and Emotional Aspects of Development: Guidance for Practitioners Working in the Early Years*. Nottingham: DCSF Publications.

DeRosier, M.E., Gillessen, A.H., Coie, J.D. and Dodge, K.A. (1994) 'Group social context and children's aggressive behavior', *Child Development*, 65: 1068–80.

DfE (Department for Education) (2011) *The Early Years Foundation Stage (EYFS) Review: Report on the Evidence*. London: DfE.

DfE (Department for Education) (2014) *Statutory Framework for the Early Years Foundation Stage: Setting the Standards for Learning, Development and Care for Children from Birth to Five*. London: DfE. Available at: www.foundationyears.org.uk/files/2014/07/EYFS_framework_ from_1_September_2014__with_clarification_note.pdf (accessed 28 September 2015).

DfE (Department for Education) (2013a) *Early Years Outcomes: A Non-Statutory Guide for Practitioners and Inspectors to Help Inform Understanding of Child Development Through the Early Years*. Runcorn: DfE Publications.

DfE (Department for Education) (2013b) *Teachers' Standards (Early Years)*. Runcorn: DfE Publications.

DfE (Department for Education) (2014) *Statutory Framework for the Early Years Foundation Stage: Setting the Standards for Learning, Development and Care for Children from Birth to Five*. London: DfE. Available at: www.foundationyears.org.uk/files/2014/07/EYFS_frame work_from_1_September_2014__with_clarification_note.pdf (accessed 28 September 2015).

DfES (Department for Education and Skills) (2005) *Excellence and Enjoyment: Social and Emotional Aspects of Learning (Guidance)*. Nottingham: DfES Publications.

Donaldson, J. (1999) *The Gruffalo*. London: Macmillan.

Dunn, J. (1993) *Young Children's Close Relationships: Beyond Attachment*. London: Sage.

Early Education/DfE (2012) *Development Matters in the Early Years Foundation Stage (EYFS)*. London: Early Education.

Elfer, P., Goldschmied, E. and Selleck, D. (2002) *Key Persons in Nurseries: Building Relationships for Quality Provision*. London: National Early Years Network.

Gilligan, C. and Wiggins, G. (1987) 'The origins of morality in early childhood relationships', in J. Kagan and S. Lamb (eds), *The Emergence of Morality in Young Children*. Chicago, IL: University of Chicago Press.

Howes, C. (1990) 'Can the age of entry into child care and the quality of child care predict adjustment in kindergarten?', *Developmental Psychology*, 26: 292–303.

Howes, C. (1992) *The Collaborative Construction of Pretend*. Albany, NY: SUNY Press.

Howes, C. and Matheson, C.C. (1992) 'Sequences in the development of competent play with peers: social and social pretended play', *Developmental Psychology*, 28: 961–74.

Hymel, S. (1983) 'Preschool children's peer relations: issues in sociometric assessment', *Merrill-Palmer Quarterly*, 19: 237–60.

Hymel, S., Rubin, K., Rowden, L. and LeMare, L. (1990) 'Children's peer relationships: longitudinal prediction of internalizing and externalizing problems from middle to late childhood', *Child Development*, 61: 2004–21.

Kohlberg, L. (1969) 'Stage and sequence: the cognitive-developmental approach to socialization', in D.A. Goslin (ed.), *Handbook of Socialization Theory and Research*. Chicago, IL: Rand McNally.

Mosley, J. (2005) *Circle Time for Young Children*. London: Bloomsbury.

NCB (2012) *'Know How': The Progress Check at Age Two*. www.gov.uk/government/uploads/system/uploads/attachment_data/file/175311/EYFS_-_know_how_materials.pdf (accessed March 2014).

Nikolopoulou, A. (1993) 'Play, cognitive development, and the social world: Piaget, Vygotsky and beyond', *Human Development*, 36: 1–23.

Nutbrown, C. (2012) *Foundations for Quality: The Independent Review of Early Education and Childcare Qualifications. Final Report*. Runcorn: Department for Education. Available at: www.gov.uk/government/uploads/system/uploads/attachment_data/file/175463/Nutbrown-Review.pdf.

Piaget, J. (1932) *The Moral Judgment of the Child*. New York: The Free Press.

Piaget, J.(1951) *Play, Dreams and Imitation in Childhood*. London: Routledge and Kegan Paul.

Rosen, M. (1989) *We're Going On a Bear Hunt*. London: Walker.

Rubin, K.H., (1982) 'Non-social play in preschoolers: necessarily evil?', *Child Development*, 53: 651–7.

Rubin, K.H., Fein, G.G. and Vandenberg, B. (1983) 'Play', in E.M. Hetherington (ed.), *Handbook of Child Personality and Social Development*, 4th edn. New York: Wiley. pp. 693–744.

Selleck, D. (2001) 'Being under 3 years of age: enhancing quality experiences', in G. Pugh (ed.), *Contemporary Issues in the Early Years*, 3rd edn. London: Paul Chapman Publishing.

Singer, J.L. and Singer, D.C. (1990) *The House of Make Believe*. Cambridge, MA: Harvard University Press.

Smith, P. K. (1997) *Play Fighting and Fighting: How Do They Relate?* Lisbon: ICCP.

Vygotsky, L.S. (1978) *Mind in Society: The Development of Higher Psychological Processes*. London: Harvard University Press.

Vygotsky, L.S. (1986) *Thought and Language*. London and Cambridge, MA: The MIT Press.

Want to learn more about this chapter? Visit the companion website at https://study.sagepub.com/EYFS3e for access to free SAGE journal articles and book chapters, weblinks, annotated further readings and more.

20

Communication and Language

Claire Head

Chapter overview

The Early Years Foundation Stage states that the prime area of communication and language development 'involves giving children opportunities to experience a rich language environment; to develop their confidence and skills in expressing themselves; and to speak and listen in a range of situations' (DfE, 2014: 8).

Communication is a vital human experience that should place children at the heart of their social network from the moment they are born. Learning to communicate in a variety of ways, through non-verbal and verbal means, allows children to explore emotions, develop relationships and begin learning about their world. This process starts within the community of the family.

The range of research evidence that will be explored in this chapter has one common uniting factor: babies and young children are ready to connect and communicate and wait only for encouragement and opportunity from the surrounding world. The 'Face to Face' research project (March 2009–2011), aimed at promoting key messages for effective communication between parents and infants, reminds us that the word 'infant' derives from the Latin *infans* and means 'speechless' (*in* 'not' and *fari* 'to speak'). However, far from being 'speechless', babies and young children find many ways to express themselves and actively seek interaction with others. Indeed, language development and sensitivity to sounds begins before birth as research has shown that babies in the womb can identify the sound of the mother's voice (Karmiloff and Karmiloff-Smith, 2001).

This chapter aims to help you to:

- appreciate that children need the right environment in order to develop effective communication skills – this includes interaction with adults who are genuinely interested in listening to children and in sharing conversations that help children to develop their language for thinking, responding and for expressing feelings
- recognise that early childhood is a critical phase of brain development and the act of communication with the primary care-giver has a decisive influence on how the brain becomes 'wired' for life
- understand that learning a language system is a complex puzzle with interlocking pieces and we need to help children to make use of all their linguistic resources.

Creating connections for communication

Hence, a key consideration for parents of young children *and* early childhood practitioners is how they can positively influence this rich period of potential development from birth to 3 years of age in order to help children to lay secure foundations for lifelong communication. How can adults 'tune in' to the child's voice and encourage children to share their ideas, questions, interests and feelings? Rouse Selleck reminds us that adults need to learn to listen to children: 'Although most infants do not learn to talk until their second year, their voices are there for us to hear from birth' (Rouse Selleck, 1995, cited in David et al., 2003: 80).

In Reggio Emilia (in Northern Italy) the approach to early childhood education founded by Loris Malaguzzi (just after the Second World War) is based on a pedagogy of listening to the child's voice and recognising children can express themselves in many different ways. It is the teacher's task to seek and to hear the voice of the child and to find a way to hear the 'hundred languages of children'.

Similarly, Bruce (2010) encourages adults to share music, rhyme, rhythm and movement with children in order to foster a sense of connection and shared experience. Both these approaches emphasise the primary role that communication and language experience plays as the starting point for immersion in a rich language and literacy context.

The EYFS 2014 indicates that a distinction should be made between the prime aspect – communication and language – and the specific aspect – literacy. The separation of the traditionally interrelated areas of reading and writing (literacy) and speaking and listening skills is prompted by research that highlights the time-sensitive link between early brain development and the acquisition of communication and language skills that 'happen during an optimum window of brain development' and are 'experience expectant' (Tickell, 2011: Annex 8: 98).

Brain development relies on a complex interplay between the genes you have and your interaction with life experiences, which creates neural activity and builds neural connections (for more on brain development, see Chapter 24). Consequently, experiences in early childhood education and care can have a significant impact on the rest of life (Gopnik et al., 2001).

Creating meaning

Effective communication is fundamental to quality of life and learning. In order to become competent language users babies and children need opportunities to rehearse their communication skills in sociable contexts, encouraged by trusted and loving adults who value children's attempts to interact and make connections. The *Birth to Three Matters* framework embraces a positive image of the baby or child as a 'skilful communicator' and emphasises the importance for children of 'making meaning with the familiar people in their lives' (David et al., 2003: 77).

Social interactionist theory about language development hinges on the idea that meaningful interactions with another human are crucial in order to motivate language acquisition. Bruner (1983) points out that the adult–child conversation begins when babies respond sensitively to a mother's facial expressions and the pair take turns in their exchange of utterances in an attempt to reach a shared meaning. Schaffer (1977) highlights the way that this sense of reciprocity is evident when children are feeding and mothers use pauses in sucking to cuddle and talk to their babies. He also noted that mothers and their babies were so attuned to each other that they rarely tried to 'talk' at the same time as they negotiated their interaction in a responsive and warm relationship. Similarly, Trevarthen and Aitken (2001) describe these early interactions as 'protoconversations' as they provide a training ground for the more complex social exchanges that children experience as they mature.

Learning to talk necessitates language acquisition, but this cannot be meaningfully implemented without a growing awareness of social recognition and co-construction of meaning. This flourishes in the warm, regular and playful exchanges in the family home (Bruner, 1986). For example, at 20 months old my niece can certainly make her feelings known with one simple utterance, 'bah!', which is accompanied by a wagging finger when she is seriously displeased or her plans have been thwarted by another family member.

Learning to converse

Children need to learn the rules of interaction and how to sustain the conversation as well as recognising speech and attempting communication. Hart and Risley (1999) emphasise the importance of 'social reciprocity' in this process and describe the way that children successfully communicate when they are able to engage in meaningful exchanges, turn-taking, interpreting and responding in order to maintain the interaction. Responsive adults behave as if they were in a real conversation with the baby and leave gaps for the baby to reply in the form of whole-body movements, hand waving, excited noises or a smile (Trevarthen, 1979). This exchange is a sophisticated and sensitive process that requires inter-subjectivity to be successful as 'learning a language is about co-ordinating what you do with what other people do' (Gopnik et al., 1999: 101). Wells describes this inter-subjectivity established by care-givers as the probable foundation for 'all subsequent communicative development' (1986: 6). This innate ability that mothers seem to have to apportion meaning to their babies' early vocalisations and gestures, random coos and gurgles is more than indulging in baby talk; it is the first stage of scaffolding.

Motherese

However children acquire language, researchers have agreed that there is a common feature present in all languages when care-givers (and older siblings) interact with babies and toddlers, and this is known as 'motherese' or infant-directed speech (Snow and Ferguson, 1977). Motherese is characterised by short, grammatically simple sentences. The adult uses a higher-pitched voice and speaks at a slower pace, using repetitive and exaggerated expression. Most adults seem naturally attuned to this mode of interaction with young children and strengthen the supportive process by placing key words at the end of sentences, drawing attention to these through intonation and expression. Mothers who are in tune with their infants' subtle development instinctively increase the level of complexity in their speech in order to help children take the next step in learning about communication (Henning et al., 2005).

Evidence from research about babies who have not been provided with this early positive experience of interaction indicates that not only is language development affected but also, without the presence of a responsive adult, children's emotional, cognitive and social development is impaired. Goldschmeid and Selleck (1996: 11) describe the way that children discovered in state institutions (in Trieste, Italy, in 1954) had become 'withdrawn, passive and despairing' as they had received adequate 'physical care', but limited 'personal care' and attention, and had consequently given up trying to initiate relationships with others. Babies begin to perceive their own importance in the reflected gaze of their carers and this is a fundamental period in childhood when the sensitive responses of supportive adults can begin to build a child's fundamental sense of self-esteem (Winnicott, 1971).

Language acquisition and development

The way that parents interact with their children plays a pivotal role in language development. The form and frequency of parent interaction has a significant impact on children's vocabulary development, their ability to be articulate *and* it influences emerging literacy skills (Kokkinaki and Kugiumutzakis, 2000). We know from recent research aimed at supporting parents in communicating with their young children that 'talkative parents have talkative children' and that 'early parent talk predicts later language ability' (National Literacy Trust, 2010).

When considering how language develops, theorists are involved in an ongoing debate about the dominance of nature versus nurture. Children are pre-programmed to acquire language and the brain is wired to support this process, particularly from birth to 5 years old (nature). Consequently this predisposition towards language acquisition indicates that nature has designed a clear path for children to follow. Conversely, opposing theorists maintain that the overriding influence on early language development is the language environment in which a child is raised (nurture).

Noam Chomsky (1957, 1965) suggested that all children are born with an inherent ability to acquire language and to decode sounds using their innate language acquisition device (LAD). This helps children to organise language according to appropriate linguistic rules, including using grammatical knowledge to construct new sentences and phrases. Chomsky later defined this as the 'Universal Grammar' (UG) theory, and he uses this inborn ability infants have to explain how they learn phonology and grammar at an early age, despite being exposed to some limited 'degenerate' language models in their environment (e.g. motherese). Critics of this innate theory have argued that environment and, crucially, interaction with others plays a more significant role in language development than Chomsky implies (Vygotsky, 1962; Bruner, 1983). Bruner (1983) felt that the reciprocal relationship between the adult and child involved in conversation was the critical factor in helping children to develop their language and to make meaning from the interaction. He refers to this process as the 'language acquisition support system' (LASS), as it acknowledges that successful interaction relies on the scaffolding that adults, who are in tune with children, are best able to provide and it is this type and level of conversation that helps children to move on a step in learning about language. Similarly, Lev Vygotsky (1896–1934) highlighted the relationship between dialogue (inner speech to self and interpersonal interaction) and cognitive awareness and maintained that: 'language and thought are inseparable' (Vygotsky, 1978).

- Reflect on Bruner's idea of reciprocal relationship between the adult and the child and discuss how successful interactions can be cultivated in an early childhood setting.

Language for thinking

The Ofsted summary report 'The Impact of the Early Years Foundation Stage' in 2011 concluded that 'children's language for thinking was weaker than their language for communication' and attributed this to 'missed opportunities' by practitioners who did not seize the moment to extend children's thinking or did not create time for thinking (2011: 17). Good examples cited by the inspectors included a problem-solving activity devised by one practitioner involving a 'derailed' toy train. 'I wonder who broke the wheel,' the practitioner asked as children arrived in the setting and then engaged them in discussion to explore the situation.

The guidance material that accompanies the EYFS suggests that in order to foster positive relationships adults should create opportunities where children can talk with other children and adults about what they see, hear, think and feel (DfE, 2014). This means making the most of naturally occurring talking points and also planning opportunities for children to be creative, to express their feelings and to solve problems together.

Case study

Hug (based on a sequence of lessons with a mixed age 4–6 class)

One morning the teacher shared the story *Hug* by Jez Alborough (2001) with the children and they talked about how the central character (Bobo the baby monkey) felt when he needed a hug. This was followed up in circle time when the class teacher encouraged the children to think about times when they have needed a hug or given a hug to someone. The teacher used a toy monkey as a puppet to encourage children to extend their vocabulary by modelling words they could use to help express feelings. Repeated readings of the story took place while children

(Continued)

(Continued)

used small hand-held mirrors to look at and describe their own expressions to match each part of the story. The next day when the children arrived at school they discovered that Bobo the toy monkey had got stuck up a tree in the playground and the children spent most of the day talking about how this could have happened, how Bobo must feel and subsequently devising elaborate schemes to get him down!

Figure 20.1   *Toy monkey and Hug story book*

Reflective task

- Reflect on the case study and discuss how early childhood practitioners can create time and opportunities for thinking in the school day. Reflect on activities you have observed that engage children in critical thinking and problem solving activities. Consider how this challenges and encourages children to develop their communication skills.

Talking and learning at home and school

After analysing samples of talk between children and adults in the home and school context, Gordon Wells (Bristol Language Development Project 1984, in Wells, 1986/1990) concluded that the home environment provided richer opportunities for children to engage in genuine and meaningful conversations with adults. Talk at home tended to be led by the child and supportive adults sustained and extended children's interaction, which in turn challenged their emerging linguistic skills. Conversely, at school most of the talk was teacher-directed and children asked fewer questions and conveyed ideas in a simpler manner when responding to their teachers. Wells noted that children who made the most progress in terms of vocabulary learning were those who inter-acted with adults, who 'pick up and extend the meaning expressed in the child's previous utterance' (Wells, 1990: 3). This process requires adults to show genuine interest in children's ideas and conversation and to remember that during this process of developing learning through talk '[c]hildren are active constructors of their own knowledge' (Wells, 1986: 65). Adults need to actively try to help children make con-nections between new knowledge and prior learning by recognising misunderstandings and helping children to make the links through dialogic thinking in order to reach a shared understanding. Edwards and Mercer describe this condition of sympathetic co-construction as 'mutuality of perspective' (1987: 95).

Adults can use a range of strategies to maintain children's interest and attention and to extend interaction, for example recasting, expanding and labelling. This provides a scaffold for children and leads to increased collaborative discussion, particularly in the context of reminiscing about past events and seeking opportunities to use language in a familiar environment.

Case study

The flood

Read the conversation below, which took place one rainy afternoon between a mother (M) and her 4-year-old son (C). Look for evidence of the following:

- context and purpose of the conversation;
- mother following the child's interests and leads;
- introduction of new vocabulary;
- use of 'wh-' questions;
- mother responding by recasting or expanding child's conversational phrases;
- information about causes and effects, objects and actions.

C: So tell me again, Mummy.

M: Tell you about what again?

(Continued)

(Continued)

C: You know, Mummy – the flood! It was horrible!

M: Oh, you mean in our old house.

C: Yeah – when the rain was so much.

M: Well, there was a storm and it rained so much all the water couldn't fit down the drains outside and – [*C interrupts*]

C: It couldn't go to the sea?

M: No, instead some of the water flowed into our house!

C: Did you paddle? [*C laughs*] Where did it comed in – down the chimney?

M: A few raindrops fell down the chimney but most of the water in our house seeped under the back door. Why do you think it seeped in?

C: It sneaked in – yeah, through little holes. It found a way. Is it leaked? Did our house dribble? How did you get it away?

M: It was tricky – can you remember what I told you before about the pump and the special machine?

C: Yeah – the sucker pump and the me-de-fire [de-humidifier].

Reflective task

- During your placement try to observe some spontaneous interactions between children or children and adults. You will need to seek permission from the adult and may decide to record the short conversation that you witness.

- Reflect on the communication you observed. Did the adult demonstrate any 'sign of 'motherese' or change intonation of the voice? How did the child respond? How did both parties maintain the conversation? Was the child trying to communicate his/her experiences, feelings?

Creating a climate for co-construction

The adult's role is crucial if we want children to be active participants in learning and develop language for thinking. The interaction between children and practitioners during some play activities can lead to 'sustained shared thinking' (Siraj-Blatchford et al., 2002). This occurs when the teacher intervenes in the child's learning by asking open-ended questions, which help to extend a child's thinking. Co-construction occurs when adults are able to follow a child's interests and thought process and let the child become a genuine equal in a meaningful experience.

Researching Effective Pedagogy in the Early Years (REPEY) reported on the five-year longitudinal Effective Provision for Pre-school Education (EPPE 1997–2004) Project which investigated the effects of pre-school education and identified the characteristics of effective practice in the early childhood (Siraj-Blatchford et al., 2002). The REPEY research was based on case study evidence collated from 14 'effective' Foundation Stage settings. The following extract from the report illustrates one of the most significant findings:

> The children and practitioners in excellent centres engaged in the highest proportion of sustained shared thinking interactions, suggesting that the excellent settings promote intellectual gains in children through conversations with children in which adult and child co-construct an idea or activity. For the practitioners in the good settings the most commonly used interaction was monitoring, a distinct difference to practitioners in the excellent and in the reception class settings. (Siraj-Blatchford et al., 2002: 51)

One of the key characteristics of effective learning that underpins development across all areas in the EYFS is *creating and thinking critically*. Early childhood practitioners need to create a careful balance between child-led and adult-led learning by providing a wide range of activities that sustain children's interests and promote shared talking and thinking.

Dialogic teaching refers to the enhancement of children's critical thinking and communication skills as they explore ideas and talk together in a purposeful way. Alexander proposes that one of the most effective 'tools' in mediation and 'pedagogical intervention' is 'talk … the most pervasive in its use and powerful in its possibilities' (2008: 2). In the Cambridge Review, Alexander (2008) outlines the many advantages of the dialogic teaching approach, which is about talking to learn and emphasises the 'necessary relationship between how teachers think about their practice and how pupils learn' (2008: 308). One of the key features of dialogic talk is its reciprocal nature, and for this to happen children need time, space and the skills to listen to each other and exchange ideas in a spiral of learning.

The amount of 'talk' and the time given for 'talk' in the classroom often depends on the status and value the class teacher ascribes to talk. Browne suggests that the effectiveness of the practitioner's role when working with young children is related to his/her:

- own understanding of the value of talk;
- attitude to talk;
- organisation for talk;
- own use of language;
- awareness of strategies and activities that encourage speaking and listening. (2009: 11)

Communication difficulties

Teachers are often the adults who first notice when children experience difficulties with communication as a result of early language impairment and need to be ready to support children's specific speech, language and communication needs (SLCN). Without secure oral language skills children experience barriers to learning and attainment in every area across the curriculum is affected (Communication Trust, 2011). Understanding how children acquire language and how this development can be supported is an aspect of teacher training that the Communication Trust is attempting to improve by raising teachers' awareness of the difficulties that the one in ten children with this 'invisible' disability face in school every day.

Kamini Gadhok, the Chief Executive of the Royal College of Speech and Language Therapists, has produced the following definition of speech, language and communication needs (Gadhok, 2007):

- Problems forming sounds and words
- Problems formulating sentences and expressing ideas
- Problems understanding speech and language
- Problems using language socially
- Delays and disorders in the development of speech and language skills

Communication and social and emotional development

Children's communication skills can be developed when playing with peers or siblings, particularly when involved in joint activities, negotiating their role in a game or attempting to resolve conflicts. Adults can encourage this social networking and experimental talk through planning activities that develop emotional literacy and teach children to be good listeners as well as helping them to get their point across.

In Interaction Matters, part of the EPPE project, Siraj-Blatchford (2003) explains that in order for children to move from simply exchanging information into conversing, adults need to help them by:

- explaining what is happening;
- acknowledging feelings – helping children to define the problem;
- suggesting practical solutions to conflict between children.

In Reggio Emilia pre-school teachers encourage children to negotiate, debate differing viewpoints and discuss ideas and feelings with each other as well as with adults. This is how two children responded when asked about children's rights in their setting:

Two friends have the right to argue. It's good for knowing when you're wrong. You can discuss but also argue. It's like hitting someone with your voice. (Two children from the Diana pre-school, ages 5 and 6, in Malaguzzi, 1996: 36)

In order to promote communication and language development in the early childhood setting, these key elements can be considered when trying to create playful contexts for interaction, as in the following examples:

- provide telephones and message pads in role-play areas;
- make use of puppets/persona dolls to model conflict resolution or problem solving;
- invite visitors to talk – children have to seek new words in order to ask questions when motivated by an interested adult;
- introduce games for sharing – for example, 'Teach your teacher and two friends how to play';
- create a musical instrument/sound table – 'Describe the sound to your friend. Does it remind you of anything?';
- set up a cosy corner/meeting area for socialising and news telling;
- install a 'show and tell' table and invite groups of children to discuss significant objects;
- send home mystery bags and encourage children to rehearse their description of the object inside ready to describe the next day at school.

Summary

This chapter discussed communication and language development and aimed to illustrate what is meant when these two terms are used in early childhood education and care. Communication and language development is considered important for children's development and learning, as well as critical when literacy is discussed, as will be shown in Chapter 21. Throughout the chapter it was emphasised that the role of the environment in communication and language development should be rich and stimulating and offer opportunities for children to explore these two key aspects of development in a playful way.

Key points to remember

- Early childhood education and care should provide rich opportunities for children to share ideas, questions and feelings from birth as children do have voices from the moment they are born.

(Continued)

(Continued)

- Learning to communicate requires a meaningful, social environment where all children are valued and feelings are recognised and treated with warmth and respect.

- A number of theoretical perspectives, such as those of Chomsky, Vygotsky and Bruner, have explored the role of adults and the interactions between adults and children and how these interactions can benefit children's communication and language development.

- The partnership between home and the early childhood setting is important for effective development of communication and language skills.

Points for discussion

- Consider a lesson or activity that you plan to introduce to a group of children in EYFS. Discuss ways in which you can introduce and explain new vocabulary and provide opportunities for children to talk and listen together during the session.

- Discuss how you can capture the 'child's voice' to inform observation and assessment records and to ensure that children become accustomed to celebrating and verbalising their learning and sharing their ideas and opinions with supportive adults.

- Robin Alexander outlines five underlying principles of dialogic talk: 'collective, reciprocal, supportive, cumulative and purposeful' (2008: 22). Have you witnessed practitioners engaged in this type of guided talk with children? Discuss the way it can support children's learning.

Further reading

Books

Bruner, J. (1983) *Child's Talk: Learning to Use Language*. Oxford: Oxford University Press.

Evangelou, M., Sylva, K., Kyriacou, M., Wild, M. and Glenny, G. (2009) *Early Years Learning and Development Literature Review*. DCSF Research Report: University of Oxford.

Sylva, K., Melhuish, E., Siraj-Blatchford, I. and Taggart, B. (2004) *The Effective Provision of Pre-School Education (EPPE) Project: Final Report*. London: Department for Education and Skills.

Articles

Henning, A., Strian, T. and Lieven, E.V.M. (2005) 'Maternal speech to infants at 1 and 3 months of age', *Infant Behaviour and Development*, 28: 519–36.

Kokkinaki, T. and Kugiumutzakis, G. (2000) 'Basic aspects of vocal imitation in infant–parent interaction during the first 6 months', *Journal of Reproductive and Infant Psychology*, 18 (3): 173–87.

Useful websites

www.ican.org.uk
www.literacytrust.org.uk
www.talkingpoint.org.uk

References

Alborough, J. (2001) *Hug*. London: Walker Books.

Alexander, R. (2008) *Introducing the Cambridge Primary Review*. Cambridge: University of Cambridge, Faculty of Education.

Browne, A. (2009) *Developing Language and Literacy 3–8*. London: Sage.

Bruce, T. (2010) *Early Childhood: A Guide for Students*, 2nd edn. London: Sage.

Bruner, J. (1986) *Actual Minds, Possible Worlds*. Cambridge, MA: Harvard University Press.

Bruner, J. (1983) *Child's Talk: Learning to Use Language*. Oxford: Oxford University Press.

Communication Trust (2011) *Let's Talk About It: What New Teachers Need to Know About Communication Skills*. London: The Communication Trust.

Chomsky, N. (1957) *Syntactic Structures*. The Hague: Mouton.

Chomsky, N.A. (1965) *Aspects of the Theory of Syntax*. Cambridge, MA: MIT Press.

DfE (Department for Education) (2014) *Statutory Framework for the Early Years Foundation Stage: Setting the Standards for Learning, Development and Care for Children from Birth to Five*. London: DfE. Available at: www.foundationyears.org.uk/files/2014/07/EYFS_framework_from_1_September_2014__with_clarification_note.pdf (accessed 28 September 2015).

David, T., Goouch, K., Powell, S. and Abbott, L. (2003) *Birth to Three Matters: A Review of the Literature*. London: Department for Education and Skills.

Edwards, D. and Mercer, N. (1987) *Common Knowledge: The Development of Understanding in the Classroom*. London: Methuen/Routledge.

Gadhok, K. (2007) 'Speech, language and communication needs – a definition'. National Literacy Trust website. www.literacytrust.org.uk/talk_to_your_baby/news/2528_ Speech_Language_and_communication_needs (accessed July 2012).

Goldschmeid, E. and Selleck, D. (1996) *Communication Between Babies in Their First Year*. London: National Children's Bureau.

Gopnik, A., Meltzoff, A.N. and Kuhl, P.K. (1999) *The Scientist in the Crib: What Early Learning Tells Us About the Mind*. New York: HarperCollins.

Gopnik, A., Sobel, D.M., Schulz, L.E. and Glymour, C. (2001) 'Causal learning mechanisms in very young children: two-, three-, and four-year-olds infer causal relations from patterns of variation and covariation', *Developmental Psychology*, 37 (5): 620–9.

Hart, B. and Risley, T.R. (1999) *The Social World of Children: Learning to Talk*. Baltimore, MD: Paul H. Brookes Publishing Inc.

Henning, A., Strian, T. and Lieven, E.V.M. (2005) 'Maternal speech to infants at 1 and 3 months of age', *Infant Behaviour and Development*, 28: 519–36.

Karmiloff, K. and Karmiloff-Smith, A. (2001) *Pathways to Language: From Fetus to Adolescent*. Cambridge, MA: Harvard University Press.

Kokkinaki, T. and Kugiumutzakis, G. (2000) 'Basic aspects of vocal imitation in infant–parent interaction during the first 6 months', *Journal of Reproductive and Infant Psychology*, 18 (3): 173–87.

Malaguzzi, L. (1996) 'The hundred languages of children', translated by Lella Gandini. Reggio Children, Preschools and Infant–Toddler Centres, Istituzione of the Municipality of Reggio Emilia.

National Literacy Trust (2010) Talk to Your Baby Face to Face Project: Literature Review. www.talktoyourbaby.org.uk (accessed October 2010).

Ofsted (2011) The Impact of the Early Years Foundation Stage. Ofsted document [Online]. Available at www.ofsted.gov.uk/resources/impact_of_early_years_foundation_stage (accessed September 2012).

Schaffer, H.R. (ed.) (1977) *Studies in Mother–Infant Interaction*. London: Academic Press.

Siraj-Blatchford, I., Sylva, K., Muttock, S., Gilden, R. and Bell, D. (2002) *Researching Effective Pedagogy in the Early Years*. London: Department for Education and Skills, Research Report 356.

Siraj-Blatchford, I., Sylva, K., Taggart, B., Sammons, P., Melhuish, E. and Elliot, K. (2003) *The Effective Provision of Pre-school Education (EPPE) Project: Intensive Case Studies of Practice Across the Foundation Stage*. London: Department for Education and Employment/Institute of Education.

Snow, C.E. and Ferguson, C.A. (1977) *Talking to Children*. New York: Cambridge University Press.

Tickell, C. (2011) *The Early Years: Foundations for Life, Health and Learning*. An Independent Report on the Early Years Foundation Stage to Her Majesty's Government. London: Crown. Available at: www.education.gov.uk/tickellreview (accessed July 2012).

Trevarthen, C. (1979) 'Communication and cooperation in early infancy: a description of primary intersubjectivity', in M. Bullowa (ed.), *Before Speech: The Beginning of Interpersonal Communication*. Cambridge: Cambridge University Press.

Trevarthen, C. and Aitken, K.J. (2001) 'Infant intersubjectivity: research, theory and clinical application', *Journal of Child Psychology and Psychiatry*, 42 (1): 3–43.

Vygotsky, L.V. (1962) *Thought and Language*. Cambridge: Cambridge University Press.

Vygotsky, L.S. (1978) *Mind in Society: The Development of Higher Psychological Processes*. London: Harvard University Press.

Wells, C.G. (1986) *The Meaning Makers: Children Learning Language and Using Language to Learn*. Portsmouth, NH: Heinemann Educational.

Wells, G. (1990) *The Meaning Makers: Children Learning Language and Using Language to Learn*. London: Hodder & Stoughton.

Winnicott, D. (1971) *Playing and Reality*. Harmondsworth: Penguin.

Want to learn more about this chapter? Visit the companion website at https://study.sagepub.com/EYFS3e for access to free SAGE journal articles and book chapters, weblinks, annotated further readings and more.

21

Literacy

Claire Head and Ioanna Palaiologou

 Chapter overview

The Early Years Foundation Stage indicates that a distinction will be made between communication and language as a prime aspect and literacy as a specific aspect. The separation of the traditionally interrelated areas of reading and writing (literacy) and speaking and listening skills is prompted by research that highlights the time-sensitive link between early brain development and the acquisition of communication and language skills, as discussed in Chapter 20. Children's literacy skills should not be neglected during this critical period, however, but should be nurtured from birth so that young children are immersed in 'a climate of talk about reading and writing' (Tickell, 2011: 98).

Literacy should be part of a child's development, not isolated from the society and culture in which that child grows up. The process of becoming literate requires collaborative acts of learning as children engage repeatedly in literacy events and experiences.

This chapter aims to help you to:

- appreciate that becoming literate (learning to be a reader and a writer) is a cooperative exploit and needs opportunities for practice in meaningful contexts

(Continued)

(Continued)

- recognise that effective readers pursue understanding and this process requires more than simply decoding the text; it is also about interpretation of the words in context, in order to gain the potential cognitive, social and emotional value literature has to offer
- understand that real writers depend on oral rehearsal before writing; they plan, draft and revise their work, and they need a real purpose and audience for their writing.

Literacy development in early childhood

In early childhood education and care practitioners need to extend the basic notion of literacy to indicate competence that enables literate individuals to function independently and flexibly in a society – a view that underpins the EYFS.

Research and theoretical developments have changed our understanding of young children's movement into literacy. The term 'literacy' relates to both reading and writing and suggests the simultaneous development and mutually reinforcing effects of these two aspects of communication. It is important to remember that children's language acquisition, and consequently their emerging literacy skills, develops at different rates and ages. Ayoub and Fischer (2006) explain that a child's development follows a unique pathway rather than a set linear route and adults need to be sympathetic to this progression when introducing new skills. Macrory (2006) warns against the introduction of formal literacy instruction too early at a stage when children still need to play with language and explore its use in familiar contexts.

Emergent literacy

This refers to the phase when a child is in the process of becoming literate, between approximately aged 6 months and school entry. Marie Clay (1991) introduced this term (in 1966) to describe the growing knowledge and awareness that young children have about print before starting school. Literacy development is seen as emerging from children's oral language development and their initial, often unconventional, attempts at reading (usually based on pictures) and writing (at first, scribbling): hence the term 'emergent literacy' (Holdaway, 1979; Sulzby, 1985, 1989). Within an emergent literacy framework, children's early unconventional attempts at reading and writing are respected as legitimate beginnings of literacy. Clay (1991) emphasises the interrelationship between speaking, listening, reading and writing and the importance of viewing the child as an active, self-motivated learner from an early age who 'creates a network of competences which power subsequent independent literacy learning' (Clay, 1991: 1).

Environmental print

Children are surrounded by print in the environment and this is often the first meaningful print that children recognise in a familiar context. For example, many children today recognise McDonald's food outlets from the two yellow arches that form its logo. Children's print awareness gradually expands and is not limited to learning from the situational context. Their knowledge of print is also enhanced as they are exposed to print in books, magazines, newspapers, letters and other printed materials (Goodman, 1980). These early experiences directly influence children's awareness of print and can thus be considered as steps towards becoming readers.

In this early 'logographic phase' children tend to remember and recognise whole words or shapes rather than attending to individual letters (Frith, 1985). Significant adults at home and school can help children to build on this awareness by talking about the meanings ascribed to the signs and symbols seen in everyday life; for example, children can usually recognise their favourite cereal box at the supermarket. Practitioners in school can provide meaningful print around the classroom and encourage children to engage with it to develop their reading and writing skills. 'Literacy walks' or 'looking for print walks' (in the local environment) are good ways to involve parents and to strengthen links between learning about print inside and outside the classroom.

Literacy learning

Literacy development begins much earlier than previously thought. Teale and Sulzby (1989) suggest that we should no longer speak of reading readiness or pre-reading but, rather, of literacy development. In preference to 'getting a child ready' to learn to read, the emergent literacy perspective emphasises the child's ongoing development. Whitehurst (1998: 23), in an attempt to define emergent literacy, starts with the assumption that 'reading is a developmental continuum starting early in life'. Thus, the definition of emergent literacy is 'a set of skills, knowledge and attitudinal precursors to formal reading and writing and the environment that supports these precursors' (Whitehurst, 1998: 34).

The main competences of emergent literacy include:

- awareness of language
- conventions of print

- emergent writing
- phonological awareness
- graphemes
- phoneme–grapheme correspondence
- attitudes such as interest in interacting with books
- environments such as shared book reading, alphabet play and treasure baskets.

Reading storybooks to young children both at home and in school (Heath, 1983; Neuman and Roskos, 1997), along with opportunities children should have to explore print, words, rhymes and songs, helps children at a very early stage to begin to experiment with a more literate language.

   With increased experience, children begin to focus on the information conveyed in print. They begin by using scribbles and progress through increasingly accurate representations of the relationship between letters and the sounds for which they stand. As children think about how to represent the sounds of words through their writing, they are building skills that will be useful for reading as well. These are the 'foundations for conventional reading and writing and should be celebrated and encouraged at home, in pre-schools, and in the early years of formal schooling' (Searfoss and Readence, 1994: 58).

Literacy from home to school

There are numerous references to the role of the home environment in children's relationship with literature and the influence of early literacy experiences on long-term attainment (Goodman, 1980; Ferreiro and Teberosky, 1983; Hannon, 1995; Neuman, 1992, 1996, 1997 and 1999) has investigated younger children's literacy by examining materials in the home and early childhood settings and opportunities for parent–child storybook reading. Clay concludes that parents' reading proficiency influences conversational interactions with different text types, serving as 'a scaffold' for parent–child interaction. She suggests that parents play a critical role in children's early literacy learning in the context of access to print resources, and opportunities and interaction in storybook reading.

   Research from the Sheffield Raising Early Achievement in Literacy Project (Hannon and Nutbrown, 2003) indicates that promoting family literacy helps to strengthen links between home and school, and improves children's understanding of environmental print, books, early writing and oral language. The project, which began in 1995, focused on pre-school children and suggested that parents/carers could provide a model for their children by adopting three key roles:

- Reading a paper and writing notes/shopping list
- Providing opportunities for children to engage in literacy by making materials available or by drawing children's attention to environmental print
- Providing encouragement and praising achievement

Parents were supported through use of the ORIM framework which highlighted Opportunities, Recognition, Interaction and Models of literacy and showed parents how they could interact with their children by sharing everyday language and literacy events, for example noticing environmental print. The REAL (Raising Early Achievements in Literacy) project outcomes were very positive and reflected a marked improvement in the children's language, literacy and social development. For example, at the end of the first year of the project:

- 78 per cent of children shared books most days compared with 27 per cent in the initial survey;
- 63 per cent of children went on to engage in mark making compared with 17 per cent at the 'start point';
- all the parents reported that they were interacting more with their children and could see more opportunities to help their children learn;
- practitioners felt more confident about working with parents, supporting parents and talking about children's literacy development. (PEAL, 2011)

The links in literacy development between home and school begin when practitioners recognise and value children's pre-school literacy experiences in the community and seek to strengthen this connection by building on familiar literacy practices at school.

Becoming a reader

Children begin to be aware of the fact that to hold a book is to 'read' the pictures. The initial 'literacy event' takes place when a child holds a book and looks at the pictures. Gradually, the child moves from being a 'naïve' reader to being a more 'expert' reader, and learns such things as how to open the book, how to turn the pages, how to pay attention to the text, and so on. Similarly, after these skills have been mastered children start pretending to read or tell stories. This is not simply children's make-believe play, imitating the teacher or the parent who reads a book: it is an actual literacy event.

In order to move on from this role-play reading stage, children need to develop phonological awareness and this begins with the ability to distinguish between different sounds in order to hear sounds that make up words and are meaningful (Williams and Rask, 2003). Phonemic awareness is developed in early childhood settings and at home through the sharing of rhymes and songs and by playing games with language that develop children's oracy skills. As discussed in Chapter 20, the development of communication and language skills, particularly the enrichment of children's vocabulary and their ability to express emotions, is an essential building block for later literacy competence. A number of researchers have established the link between secure phonological awareness and vocabulary development and the way that interaction between these two aspects supports early reading development and later literacy attainment (e.g. Goswami, 2001; Snow, 2006).

Teaching early reading

There is a time-honoured debate about the most effective methods teachers can employ to help children to become readers and contemporary discussion has centred on the teaching of phonics. In 2005, Jim Rose (former HM Chief Inspector) was appointed by the Secretary of State for Education to carry out an independent review of the teaching of early reading, and his report (2006) underpins subsequent policy and practice in primary schools today. The final report made several recommendations about 'best practice' in the 'teaching of early reading and synthetic phonics' (2006: 7). It emphasised the importance of teaching phonics in a discrete, systematic and explicit way beginning during the optimum 'time-sensitive' period reached when most children approach 5 years of age. Advice for teachers was presented in a 'conceptual framework', referred to as the 'Simple View' of reading. This reminds teachers that the aim of reading is to gain meaning from the text and this is dependent on the successful coordination of two elements:

- *Decoding* – reliant on speech sound information: phonology. This requires linking sounds with letters to read words. Rose recommends a 'synthetic phonics' approach which starts with blending letter sounds to read whole words.
- *Comprehension* – relies on broader language skills, including a growing understanding of vocabulary, grammar and an ability to make inferences to discern meaning.

Rose highlighted the prime role that phonics instruction should play in the teaching of early reading, but noted that phonic work should be 'embedded in a broad and rich language curriculum' (2006: 35). In order to support practitioners in providing high-quality phonics instruction the Primary National Strategy (PNS) published *Letters and Sounds* (DCSF, 2007) guidance material. This offered teachers a six-phase phonics programme designed to secure 'fluent word recognition for reading by the end of Key Stage 1' with the acknowledgement that teaching spelling skills would continue beyond 7 years of age (2007: 3). This programme was founded on the principle that 'phonic work should be regarded as an essential body of knowledge, skills and understanding that has to be learned largely through direct instruction' (2007: 10). Learning the skills of blending for reading and segmenting for spelling is a process that requires systematic instruction and then application. This was reiterated in the Tickell Review:

> Becoming literate is culturally constrained and relies on learning a body of knowledge including the alphabetic code (i.e. the teaching of systematic synthetic phonics) in the same way that the learning of mathematics largely relies on securing knowledge and understanding of symbolic representation for number. (Tickell, 2011: 98)

Consequently, this approach to teaching the specific area of literacy can be found in the EYFS: 'Literacy development involves encouraging children to link sounds and letters and to begin to read and write' (DfE, 2014: 8).

What do good readers do?

'Phonics is necessary, but not in itself sufficient, to develop effective and enthusiastic readers' (UKLA, 2008: Section 3). We know that effective readers make use of decoding skills early in the reading process, but teachers also need to keep in mind the longer process that leads to becoming a lifelong reader and the importance of adults sharing their enthusiasm for reading with children and modelling what good readers do.

> Good readers are more than successful print scanners and retrievers of factual experience. They find in books the depth and breadth of human experience. (Meek, 1988: 17)

Through storytelling, discussion surrounding good-quality picture books and shared reading we can help children experience the cognitive, social and emotional value of stepping into the world of a book. Although cumulative, graded and easily decodable reading scheme books build children's confidence and provide opportunities to practise reading skills, they may not provoke the same enthusiasm and interest as immersion in 'real books'. Practitioners need to ensure children's reading diet is not limited by ability and that generating motivation to read remains a priority when planning the literacy curriculum. After decoding her school-reading-scheme book Campbell's 5-year-old granddaughter Alice states, 'Soon I will be able to read real books' (Campbell, 1999: 134). The children in the case study below provide a good example of how imagination, 'real book' knowledge and familiar experiences blend together as children become the storytellers after sharing a range of traditional tales.

Case study

Our version of 'Jack and the Beanstalk' by children and teachers from Childhaven Community Nursery School

We read 'Jack and the Beanstalk' last week and then this week we used masks to retell the story and then add in some extra bits. In our version Jack had a cow called Steeleymoo and two sheep to sell at the market, but he still only got three magic beans for them. After the beans had been thrown out of the window five

(Continued)

(Continued)

butterflies flew into Jack's bedroom to tell him about the beanstalk, which was really huge. Also, when Jack got inside the castle, the Giant was having a cup of tea with Mrs Giant and Batgirl! The Easter Bunny also asked the goose to lay some chocolate eggs, but she said she 'could only make golden ones'. Oh well! At the end of the story Jack and his mum were so happy that they decided to invite the Three Little Pigs for tea – what a busy day it was. I think we might do some more storytelling next week.

Reflective task

- Based on the above case study, reflect on the most successful role-play area you have seen. How did it stimulate literacy activities? How did the practitioner 'feed' it and sustain children's interest?

Becoming a writer

The National Literacy Strategy describes emergent writing as 'mark making with intent' in the guidance given to teachers in *Developing Early Writing* (DfEE, 2001: 166). It is this desire to create intentional marks that highlights a young child's growing understanding that print carries meaning. Adults can encourage a child to talk about his or her writing and its ascribed meaning in order to develop the child's knowledge about both transcriptional and compositional aspects of writing. This is a tricky balance for teachers to achieve, as it is important to encourage and celebrate children's attempts at writing by responding to its content without becoming so focused on the transcription that children are reluctant to try this difficult skill again. Practitioners can foster early writing skills by creating a supportive climate for writing and by using a variety of strategies that encourage children to actively experiment, and 'have a go' at writing.

In his book entitled *Reading with Alice*, which reflects his own granddaughter's development at home and in early childhood settings, Campbell (1999) emphasises the importance of allowing children to emerge as readers and writers. He states that Alice's considerable progression in literacy took place as a result of her active involvement with reading and writing rather than through direct instruction in these skills. He expresses concern that some teachers are relying on worksheets in settings rather than engaging the children in literary activities that capture their interest. Figure 21.1 provides an example of a child (age 6) who was motivated to make her own meaningful marks when she needed to find a way to record complicated dance moves in a sequence that could be repeated and shared with friends.

Figure 21.1 *Example of mark making – symbols for dance moves*

Figure 21.2 *Children's attempts to write*

An important element of the literacy learning process is when children make their first attempts to write as shown in the example in Figure 21.2. Sulzby (1992) suggests that at this age children should be 'encouraged or nudged' and not pushed to start their writing process. When children first spontaneously produce graphic representations, drawing and writing are undifferentiated. When children first experiment with a pencil, what they want to do is to leave their mark everywhere, for instance on a piece of paper or on a wall (Ferreiro and Teberosky, 1983; Morrow, 1992).

Teaching writing

Although children do need to be taught the conventions of writing they also need to learn the context for writing. Children take part as 'active learners' and ideally should be exposed to the delights and challenges involved in the creative process (Graves, 1983). Children can be involved in the compositional aspects as the practitioner scribes: editing, filtering and refining suggestions from the class in a supportive relationship. When appropriate, the practitioner can draw attention to transactional aspects, including spelling, handwriting, punctuation, grammar and layout.

In order to help children understand the textual features of different forms of writing (different genres in varying contexts) practitioners need to discuss the reason and purpose for the writing. Riley and Reedy (2000) suggest that challenging children to answer the following questions when they encounter new text types will provide them with a model for their own writing and a deeper understanding of the way writing is organised in different genres:

- What is it? What is the text for?
- Why do you read it?
- Do we know who wrote it? (Riley and Reedy, 2000: 62)

Providing a real audience as well as spotting a real purpose for children's writing is an essential part of the practitioner's role as this motivates children to take their place in the literate society that surrounds them.

Opportunities to write

Providing opportunities to write is essential, as it will allow young children to appreciate and recognise the links between speech and print. Helen Dutton (1991, cited in Campbell, 2002) describes six main categories of writing that she noticed her children (aged 6) naturally engaged in during role-play:

- letters
- messages

- personal notes
- instructions
- factual descriptions
- stories.

This purposeful writing generated by structural play allows children to develop early writing skills. This can be supported and enhanced by adults who are ready to intervene sensitively to engage in 'teachable moments' that give meaning to children's literacy events (Owocki, 1999: 28).

Creating a rich literate environment

It is important to provide opportunities for children to read and write in different contexts and situations as part of play. Practitioners need to generate talk about classroom and environmental print by encouraging children to understand the purpose of these symbols in meaningful contexts. For example, signs and labels made in response to a real purpose will demonstrate the power that the printed word has to communicate (Figure 21.3).

Figure 21.3 *'Please remember to water this plant every Monday'*

Owocki (1999) advocates the setting up of literacy-enriched play centres in settings and reminds practitioners to evaluate their roles and to ask themselves:

- Do the children read and write during play? Are the materials meaningful?
- What functions does literacy serve in children's play? Are the children exploring a variety of genres and forms of written language?

Figure 21.4 shows a child's annotations on a story map of 'Little Red Riding Hood'. The child felt that the writing was necessary to help other children to play the game and re-enact the story as she intended with the playdough figures.

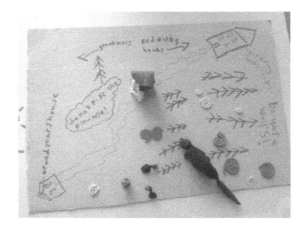

Figure 21.4 *Story map*

Literacy through play

Throughout this book the importance of play within EYFS is emphasised. Once again play maintains an important role in children's literacy development. Neuman (1997) examined settings reflecting literacy-related situations in children's real-world environment. She found that literacy in play might become purposeful in an enriched literacy environment. She also found that literacy becomes part of children's play when literacy activities are in context.

In a study based on research in thirty-five kindergarten classrooms with 5–6-year-old children, Morrow (1992) concluded that many of the settings were not well designed to facilitate literacy behaviours. She observed that few literacy materials were easily available for children to use and practitioners did little to promote authentic literacy activities during play. In order for literacy events to take place during natural play sequences the children need to have literacy materials to hand: 'The inclusion in the play area of literacy materials is a starting point for the encouragement of literacy learning' (Campbell, 2002: 104).

An enriched literacy environment could include:

- pens, paper, books and other printed materials available in every area of the setting;
- environmental print (the home languages of all the children who attend the setting should be on display);
- books – fiction and non-fiction around the room so children can explore different genres in appropriate settings, e.g. a recipe for making porridge alongside 'Goldilocks and the Three Bears' in the role-play area;
- props, puppets, story sacks, dressing up clothes – to stimulate dramatic play;
- sequence cards to retell stories;
- writing area or mark making station;
- post box – to write to characters from stories or friends in other classes;
- calendars – to highlight important events, e.g. children's birthdays, school trips, book day;
- pigeon-holes – to encourage children to write messages to others;
- children's notice board – to celebrate attempts at mark making completed at home and in the setting.

Successful role-play areas naturally stimulate literacy activities; however, practitioners need to continually 'feed' this creativity and to motivate the children to explore print. For example, providing props such as an old telephone and a messages pad can encourage lots of conversation and emergent writing. If the practitioner in that area models taking a telephone message for a child, and reads it aloud to the class, then this could act as the impetus for a flurry of further messages.

Case study

'The Garden Centre' – a teacher recounts

The most successful role-play area I established in my classroom, with the help of the children in my Reception/Year 1 class, was a 'Garden Centre'. The stimulus for this came from a visit to the local garden centre which was owned and managed by one of the parents of a child in my class. Once we returned to school the children were keen to re-create a mini version of this in our classroom and eagerly began

(Continued)

(Continued)

planning its design and listing resources we would need. Here are just some of the activities that germinated from this seed!

- Environmental print – signs, labels, notices
- Growing sunflowers from seeds – linked to our science topic
- Letters – thanking the garden centre staff and asking them technical questions about looking after plants
- Seed-packet designs – children were encouraged to use real seed packets as a model
- Instructions for planting – we devised a class list during shared writing
- Watering plants rota – we found that our plants suffered if they were over-watered and so we had to monitor this
- Measurement of school sunflower competition – we donated one seedling to each class in school with instructions for care and had a special assembly to see whose was the tallest at the end of the term
- Related fiction, e.g. 'Jack and the Beanstalk', and non-fiction, e.g. 'From Seed to Sun-flower' – read during shared reading and made available for the children to re-read
- Price lists – accompanied by a till and 'money' so customers could shop
- Descriptions of flowering plants – art work was accompanied by brief descriptions of each flower; the descriptions were separated from the pictures and children had to match them up again
- 'Guess what this seed will grow into' competitions – related to work on seed dispersal
- Reciting rhymes and songs related to plants
- Stories about talking plants – stimulated by a large painting of two flowers which the children were able to stand behind and poke their heads through (seaside style) and talk in role to each other.

Reflective task

- Consider the range of environmental print and variety of sources that offer potential print encounters for children in the home or setting. Reflect on the way that print helps people to function in everyday life. You could perhaps compare this to your own experience of trying to read print in a foreign language on a visit to another country.

Phonics debate

Although throughout this chapter there is a discussion on how phonics awareness is facilitating the development of literacy, this section aims to introduce the phonics debate – that it has been politicised and it has created much controversy.

Because the government introduced a screening check at the end of Year 1 to identify what phonics children have grasped, in the EYFS there is an emphasis on preparing children for the screening test. Phonics is an important element of teaching young children reading, and in early childhood education and care this can become a playful activity. The use of phonics is a method that helps children learn the correspondences between letters and sounds ('phonemes'), and how to blend the sounds together. The main methods are:

Synthetic phonics – an approach associated with the teaching of reading in which phonemes (sounds) associated with particular graphemes (letters) are pronounced in isolation and blended together (synthesised). For example, children are taught to take a single-syllable word such as *cat* apart into its three letters, pronounce a phoneme for each letter in turn /k, æ, t/, and blend the phonemes together to form a word.

Analytical phonics – an approach associated with the teaching of reading in which the phonemes associated with particular graphemes are not pronounced in isolation. Children identify (analyse) the common phoneme in a set of words in which each word contains the phoneme under study. For example, teacher and pupils discuss how the following words are alike: *pat, park, push* and *pen*.

Analogy phonics – a type of analytic phonics in which children analyse phonic elements according to the phonograms in the word. A phonogram, known in linguistics as a rime, is composed of the vowel and all the sounds that follow it, such as –*ake* in the word cake. Children use these phonograms to learn about 'word families', for example *cake, make, bake, fake*.

Embedded phonics – an approach to the teaching of reading in which phonics forms one part of a whole language programme. Embedded phonics differs from other methods in that the instruction is always in the context of literature rather than in separate lessons, and the skills to be taught are identified opportunistically rather than systematically.

(National Literacy Trust, 2015)

A vast body of research promotes the use of all methods to help children learn to read and write, but currently the government recommends one approach and the debate is focusing of which method of phonics work: analytical or synthetic. In 2005 the House of Commons Education Select Committee called for a larger-scale study of phonics and the debate continued when the government supported the introduction of synthetic phonics. As a result the government commissioned Jim Rose to conduct the independent review which was published in 2006 and promotes the introduction of synthetic phonics as an effective method to teach reading:

> the new Early Years Foundation Stage and the renewed framework should make sure that best practice for beginner readers provides them with a rich curriculum that fosters all four interdependent strands of language: speaking, listening, reading and writing. ... All these skills are drawn upon and promoted by high quality, systematic phonic work. An early start on systematic phonic work is especially important for those children who do not have the advantages of strong support for literacy at home. (Rose, 2006: 31)

There is much scepticism and concern as it appears from government action that evidence-based research on literacy has been silenced and the approach to teaching literacy to young children is becoming a mechanistic approach. Official reports (Rose, 2006; DfES, 2006, 2007; DfE, 2011) not only insist on an approach to teaching literacy to children that places emphasis on Synthetic Phonics, but now also suggest a standard universal test for young children in their literacy levels through the same mechanism. Such an approach runs contrary to what research tells us about literacy acquisition in young children and, in particular, overlooks other understandings about language often referred to as meta-linguistic awareness. Not taking account of such insights appears to be an oversight by the government that militates against effective language and literacy development in young children.

Much research suggests strongly that phonics are important in literacy acquisition, but are not the centre of reading instruction (e.g. Bradley and Bryant, 1983; Anthony et al., 2002; De Cara and Goswami, 2002; Hanley et al., 2004; Hall 2006; Goswami, 2007, 2008a, 2008b, 2010). The government review reduces teaching literacy to what needs transmitting to individual learners and ignores other factors that create a literate environment, as has been explored throughout this chapter, in which children grow up and become competent users of language and literacy. With what is suggested by the National Curriculum on Teaching Literacy (DfE, 2011), there is a fear that literacy learning will be viewed as independent of the central cognitive development of children, leading to curriculum entrenchment and estrangement.

Consequently it is argued that although phonological awareness – the child's ability to detect and manipulate the component sounds that comprise the words (Goswami, 2010) – is central to acquiring literacy, it is not the only aspect of literacy that needs to be considered. In teaching literacy to children, and in particular reading, it is essential to help children understand and conceptualise the correspondence between the orthographic symbols and the phonological sounds that those symbols represent. For many alphabetic languages (letter sound correspondent languages), such as Greek or Italian, this can be achieved by a method which is called synthetic, but in languages like English, phonics need to be taught by more than one psycholinguistic approach:

[r]eading does not consist merely of decoding the written word or language; rather it is preceded by the intertwined with knowledge of the world. Language and reality are dynamically interconnected. The understanding attained by critical reading of a text implies perceiving the relationship between text and context. (Freire and Macedo 1987: 29)

Most research findings conclude that the pedagogy of teaching literacy should not be mechanistic but 'messy', rich in print, and *systematic* teaching to allow children to explore and learn both the nature and the functions of written language. Language must also be considered as a whole process where children's literacy skills are acknowledged and are taken into account in the daily activities. Children are literate when they have competence in communication skills and can function linguistically appropriate to age, functioning effectively in society and its demands. In that sense teaching literacy is not determined by a simplistic approach to phonics knowledge only.

To grow as readers children should develop other understandings about language, often referred to as meta-linguistic awareness. They must, for example, develop a concept of what a word is, both printed and spoken, and to know how it is different from numbers, letters, sounds and sentences. They must learn a number of skills related to reading, such as that in English print is read from left to right and from top to bottom.

For children to develop reading and writing skills they must develop 'the alphabetic principle'. When first introduced to print children often think that the printed word is a concrete representation of an object. Indeed, they need to develop the idea that letters of an alphabet represent sounds. In order to develop an understanding of the alphabetic principle they must become familiar with letter forms and with the idea that spoken words have identifiable sounds in them, referred to as the concept of phonemic awareness. However, English language is a phonologically complex one: for example, children can learn the phoneme 'a' as cat, but what happens with a word such as 'but'?

The Rose Review suggests synthetic phonics as a way of effectively teaching children to read. However, the conception of pedagogy that reduces teaching to a set of recipes for delivering the curriculum into the heads of learners by adopting a mechanistic approach to phonics results only in categorisation and labelling of children. If we assess any group of children according to the amount of phonics they appear to process then automatically we exclude a number of children from literacy. Snow et al. (1998), for example, found that apart from children with genuine neurological disorders, the main body of children facing difficulties in reading are coming from poor socio-economic backgrounds and minority groups.

If every child matters, then policy makers should consider that pedagogy of reading should not be dominated by dogmatic approaches to phonics (Dombey, 2006); inequality in achievement, which is one of the key targets of the government, will not improve and the gap will become bigger. A study conducted in 2003 (Sylva et al., 2003), examining the linguistic and literacy abilities of 3,000 children from entry to pre-school to the end of Key Stage 2, demonstrated that children from privileged backgrounds, whose parents earn more than £67,500 p.a., at age 5 will have reading skills six months in advance of those whose parents are jobless. The emerging issue, therefore, is how this gap can be bridged.

Rigorous research on literacy and the pedagogy of teaching reading and writing argues that *systematic* phonics teaching of a variety of kinds is more likely to result in positive outcomes for children than only one approach to teaching phonics. Despite all the research of phonological awareness, however, the politicians are pushing teaching of synthetic phonics in just one direction and only assessing phonics awareness. Research evidence suggests, however, that children whose homes do not match the school environment will be faced with an intellectual struggle when they are at school, resulting in inequalities and exclusion of children from academic success (e.g. Coles, 2000, 2006; Gee, 2001, 2004; Sylva et al., 2003; Giroux, 2005, 2011).

Reflective task

- The Rose Review (2006) and Letters and Sounds (DCSF, 2007) advocate a multisensory approach to teaching and learning phonic work. Reflect on phonic activities you have seen and consider how multisensory engagement (by touch, sight and sound simultaneously) enhances children's phonic knowledge and skills.

Summary

Although the areas of communication and language and literacy have been explored separately, it is important to say that they are interrelated and communication and language maintains a key role in children's literacy learning. It is essential in early childhood education and care to create an environment to have wealth of opportunities where children are exposed to literacy and explore it through play. Play is central to literacy learning as it enables children to have experiences of literacy.

Key points to remember

- The threads of literacy – reading and writing – are interwoven and build upon a child's early development as a communicator.

- Reading for meaning requires the child to employ decoding skills (converting printed words to spoken words) and linguistic comprehension.

- Literacy-enriched centres and a real audience and purpose for writing can make a difference to a child's literacy behaviour and his/her sense of becoming a writer.

Points for discussion

- As was demonstrated in Chapter 12, many young children now are already more computer-literate in this age of digital literacy (see Marsh et al , 2005). How can practitioners use digital technologies to enhance children's literacy experiences and interactions with multi-modal texts?

- Given that children are surrounded by a host of television icons, videos, toys and related products at home and in society, do we need to incorporate work on these 'texts' into classroom life? Marsh and Hallet (2008) argue that this is essential and practitioners need to ensure children find their culture and lifestyle reflected and provide experiences generated by children's interest and not always guided by adult agendas. Should popular culture be reflected in the classroom?

- Make a list of the available resources in your setting and try to plan activities to create a literacy environment in which you and the children share a story together and create opportunities to explore print (visit the National Literacy Trust website for ideas: www.literacytrust.org.uk/purchase_resources).

Further reading

Books

Bradford, H. (2009) *Communication, Language and Literacy in the Early Years Foundation Stage*. London: David Fulton.

Marsh, J. and Hallet, E. (eds) (2008) *Desirable Literacies: Approaches to Language and Literacy in the Early Years*, 2nd edn. London: Sage.

Riley, J. and Reedy, D. (2000) *Developing Writing for Different Purposes: Teaching About Genre in the Early Years*. London: Paul Chapman Publishing.

Articles

Marsh, J. (2010) 'Young children's play in online virtual worlds', *Journal of Early Childhood Research*, 8: 23–39.

Williams, M. and Rask, H. (2003) 'Literacy through play: how families with able children support their literacy development', *Early Child Development and Care*, 173 (5): 527–33.

Wyse, D. and Goswami, U. (2008) 'Synthetic phonics and the teaching of reading', *British Educational Research Journal*, 34 (6): 691–710.

Useful websites

https://www.gov.uk/government/publications/phonics-screening-check-evaluation-final-report
www.familylearning.org.uk/early_years_foundation_stage.html
www.teachfind.com/national-strategies/best-practice-early-literacy-and-phonics

References

Anthony, J.L., Lonigan, C.J., Burgess, S.R., Driscoll, K., Phillips, B.M. and Cantor, B.C. (2002) 'Structure of preschool phonological sensitivity: overlapping sensitive to rhyme, words, syllables and phonemes', *Journal of Experimental Child Psychology*, 82: 65–92.

Ayoub, C. and Fischer, K. (2006) 'Developmental pathways and intersections among domains of development', in K. McCartney, and. D. Phillips (eds), *Blackwell Handbook of Early Child Development*. Oxford: Blackwell.

Bradley, L. and Bryant, P.E. (1983) 'Categorising sounds and learning to read: a casual connection', *Nature*, 310: 419–21.

Campbell, R. (1999) *Literacy from Home to School: Reading with Alice*. Stoke-on-Trent: Trentham Books.

Campbell, R. (2002) *Reading in the Early Years Handbook*, 2nd edn. Buckingham: Open University Press.

Clay, M.M. (1991) *Becoming Literate: The Construction of Inner Control*. London: Heinemann Educational.

Coles, G. (2000) *Misreading Reading: The Bad Science that Hurts Children*. Portsmouth, NH: Heinemann.

Coles, G. (2006) 'Introduction: Human rights, equality and education', in M. Cole (ed.), *Education, Equality, and Human Rights: Issues of Gender, 'Race' , Sexuality, Disability and Class*, 2nd edn. London: Routledge.

DCSF (Department for Children, School and Families) (2007) *Letters and Sounds: Principles and Practice of High Quality Phonics*. London: DCSF.

De Cara, B. and Goswami, U. (2002) 'Statistical analysis of similarity relations among spoken words: evidence for the special status of rimes', *English Behavioural Research Methods and Instrumentation*, 34 (3): 416–23.

DfE (Department for Education) (2011) *Criteria for Assuring High-Quality Phonic Work*. www.education.gov.uk/schools/teachingandlearning/pedagogy/phonics/a0010240/criteria-for-assuring-high-quality-phonic-work (accessed 10 March 2012).

DfE (Department for Education) (2014) *Statutory Framework for the Early Years Foundation Stage: Setting the Standards for Learning, Development and Care for Children from Birth to Five*. London: DfE. Available at: www.foundationyears.org.uk/files/2014/07/EYFS_frame work_from_1_September_2014__with_clarification_note.pdf (accessed 28 September 2015).

DfEE (Department for Education and Employment) (2001) *Developing Early Writing*. London: DfEE.

DfES (Department for Education and Skills) (2006) *Primary Framework for Literacy and Mathematics: Core Papers Underpinning the Renewal of Guidance for Teaching Literacy and Mathematics*. London: DfES.

DfES (Department for Education and Skills) (2007) *How to Choose an Effective Phonics Programme: Core Criteria and Guidance*. London: DfES.

Dombey, H. (2006) 'Phonics and English orthography', in M. Lewis and S. Ellis (eds), *Phonics: Practice Research and Policy*. London: Paul Chapman and the United Kingdom Literacy Association. pp. 95–104.

Ferreiro, E. and Teberosky, A. (1983) *Literacy Begins Before Schooling*. London: Heinemann Educational.

Freire, P. and Macedo, D. (1987) *Literacy: Reading the Word and the World*. London: Routledge.

Frith, U. (1985) 'Beneath the surface of developmental dyslexia', in K.E. Patterson, J.C. Marshall and M. Coltheart (eds), *Surface Dyslexia*. London: Erlbaum.

Gee, J.P. (2001) 'What is literacy?', in P. Shannon (ed.), *Becoming Political Too: New Readings and Writings on the Politics of Literacy Education*. Portsmouth, NH: Heinemann.

Gee, J.P. (2004) *Situated Language and Learning: A Critique of Traditional Schooling*. Abingdon: Routledge.

Giroux, H.A. (2005) *Schooling and the Struggle for Public Life: Democracy's Promise and Education's Challenge*, Boulder, CO: Paradigm Publishers.

Giroux, H.A. (2011) *On Critical Pedagogy*. London: Continuum.

Goodman, Y. (1980) 'The roots of literacy', in M.P. Douglas (ed.), *Reading: A Humanising Experience*. Claremont: Claremont Graduate School. pp. 42–68.

Goswami, U. (2001) 'Early phonological development and the acquisition of literacy', in S.B. Neuman and D.K. Pickinson (eds), *Handbook of Early Literacy Research*. New York: Guilford Press. p. 111.

Goswami, U. (2007) 'Learning to read across languages: the role of phonics and synthetic phonics', in K. Goouch and A. Lambirth (eds), *Understanding Phonics and the Teaching of Reading: Critical Perspectives*. Maidenhead: Open University Press.

Goswami, U. (2008a) 'Reading dyslexia and the brain', *Educational Research*, 50 (2): 135–48.

Goswami, U. (2008b) *Learning Difficulties: Future Challenges*. London: The Government Office for Science.

Goswami, U. (2010) 'Phonology, reading and reading difficulties', in K. Hall, U. Goswami, C. Harrison, S. Ellis and J. Solder, *Interdisciplinary Perspectives on Learning to Read: Culture, Cognition and Pedagogy*. London: Routledge.

Graves, D.H. (1983) *Writing: Teachers and Children at Work*. Exeter, NH: Heinemann Educational.

Hall, K. (2006) 'How children learn to read and how phonics helps', in M. Lewis and S. Ellis (eds), *Phonics Practice, Research and Policy*. London: UKLA/PLC.

Hanley, R., Masterson, J., Spencer, L. and Evans, D. (2004) 'How long do the effects of learning to read a transparent orthography last? An investigation of the reading skills and reading impairment of Welsh children at 10 years of age', *Quarterly Journal of Experimental Psychology*, 57: 1393–410.

Hannon, P. (1995) *Literacy, Home and School: Research and Practice in Teaching Literacy with Parents*. London: Falmer Press.

Hannon, P. and Nutbrown, C. (2003) 'REAL involvement for parents', *Literacy Today*, September, pp. 24–5.

Heath, S.B. (1983) *Ways with Words*. Cambridge: Cambridge University Press.

Holdaway, D. (1979) *The Foundations of Literacy*. Portsmouth, NH: Heinemann Educational.

Macrory, G. (2006) 'Bilingual language development: what do early years practitioners need to know?', *Early Years*, 26: 159–69.

Marsh, J., Brooks, G., Hughes, L., Roberts. S. and Wright, K., (2005) *Digital beginnings: Young children's use of popular culture, media and new technologies*, funded by BBC worldwide and the Esmee Fairbairn Foundation. Sheffield: Literacy Centre University of Sheffield.

Marsh, J. and Hallet, E. (eds) (2008) *Desirable Literacies: Approaches to Languages and Literacy in the Early Years* (2nd edn). London: Paul Chapman Publishing.

Meek, M. (1988) *How Texts Teach What Readers Learn*. Stroud: Thimble Press.

Morrow, L.M. (1992) *Family Literacy: Connections in Schools and Communities*. Newark, DE: International Reading Association.

National Literacy Trust (2015) 'Phonics – methods of teaching'. [Online] www.literacytrust.org.uk/resources/practical_resources_info/1035_phonics-methods_of_teaching (accessed 12 June 2015).

Neuman, S.B. (1992) 'Is learning from media distinctive? Examining children's inferencing strategies', *American Educational Research Journal*, 29 (1): 119–40.

Neuman, S.B. (1996) 'Children engaging in storybook reading: the influence of access to print resources: opportunities, and parental interaction', *Early Childhood Research Quarterly*, 11: 495–513.

Neuman, S.B. (1997) 'Guiding young children's participation in early literacy development: a family literacy programme for adolescent mothers', *Early Child Development and Care*, 32: 127–8.

Neuman, S.B. (1999) 'Books make a difference: a study of access to literacy', *Reading Research Quarterly*, 34 (3): 286–311.

Neuman, S.B. and Roskos, K. (1997) 'Literacy knowledge in practice: contexts of participation for young writers and readers', *Reading Research Quarterly*, 32 (1): 10–32.

Owocki, G. (1999) *Literacy Through Play*. Portsmouth, NH: Heinemann Educational.

PEAL (Parents, Early Years and Learning) (2011) 'Great first year for REAL'. [Online] www.peal.org.uk/latest_news/news_archive/success_for_real.aspx (accessed 9 May 2012).

Riley, J. and Reedy, D. (2000) *Developing Writing for Different Purposes*. London: Paul Chapman Publishing.

Rose, J. (2006) *Independent Review of the Teaching of Early Reading: Final Report*. Nottingham: DfES Publications. Available at: http://dera.ioe.ac.uk/5551/2/report.pdf (accessed 28 September 2015).

Searfoss, L. and Readence, J. (1994) *Helping Children to Read*. Boston, MA: Allyn and Bacon.

Snow, C., Burns, S. and Griffin, P. (1998) *Preventing Reading Difficulties in Young Children*. Washington, DC: National Academic Press.

Snow, C.E. (2006) 'What counts as literacy in early childhood?', in K. McCartney and D. Phillips (eds), *Blackwell Handbook of Early Childhood Development*. Oxford: Blackwell. pp. 274–94.

Sulzby, E. (1985) 'Kindergarteners as writers and readers', in M. Farr (ed.), *Children's Early Writing Development*. Norwood, NJ: Ablex. pp. 82–126.

Sulzby, E. (1989) 'Forms of writing and rereading example list', in J. Mason (ed.), *Reading and Writing Connections*. Boston, MA: Allyn and Bacon. pp. 51–63.

Sulzby, E. (1992) 'Research directions: transitions from emergent to conventional writing', *Language Arts*, 69: 290–7.

Sylva, K., Melhuish, E., Sammons, P., Siraj-Blatchford, I., Taggart, B. and Elliot, K. (2003) *The Effective Provision of Pre-school Education (EPPE) Project*. London: Institute of Education/ Department for Education and Employment.

Teale, W.H. and Sulzby, E. (1989) 'Literacy acquisition in early childhood: the roles of access and accommodation in storybook reading', in D.A. Wagner (ed.), *The Future of Literacy in a Changing World*. Oxford: Pergamon. pp. 111–30.

Tickell, C. (2011) *The Early Years: Foundations for Life, Health and Learning*. An Independent Report on the Early Years Foundation Stage to Her Majesty's Government, Annex 9. London: Crown. Available at: www education.gov.uk/tickellreview (accessed May 2012).

UKLA (United Kingdom Literacy Association) (2008) Submission to the Review of Best Practice in the Teaching of Early Reading. UKLA International Conference Report.

Whitehurst, G. (1998) 'Relative efficacy of parent and teacher involvement in a shared-reading intervention for pre-school children from low income backgrounds', *Early Childhood Research Quarterly*, 13 (2): 263–90.

Williams, M. and Rask, H. (2003) 'Literacy through play: how families with able children support their literacy development', *Early Child Development and Care*, 173 (5): 527–33.

Mathematics

22

David Needham and Graham Needham

👍 Chapter overview

Without realising it, children develop mathematical knowledge and skills as a social activity and, as they do so, they are equipping themselves for the needs of everyday life. In this way it provides a key role in equipping children for a rapidly changing world (Tipps et al., 2011). This chapter aims to explore why and how children from birth to 5 develop their mathematical abilities as well as why this process should be both developmentally appropriate and meaningful for children (Seefeldt et al., 2012). When children make sense of the world, they have a natural instinct for mathematical education. Daily first-hand experiences with numbers, shapes, space and measurement provides them with a rich diet of meaningful activities that stimulate their curiosity. As they explore and experience play children create, construct and develop their mathematical knowledge. This is simply part of the way in which they experiment and try things that are new for them. Mathematics is, therefore, something that has everyday relevance to the lives of children as they develop meaning from experiences. The chapter then focuses upon how individuals can contextualise and develop simple and practical learning opportunities when working alongside young children to help to develop their mathematical understanding.

This chapter aims to help you:

- consider the key role played by the successful development of numeric reasoning skills
- reflect upon how to develop an appropriate pedagogy for EYFS-aged children to achieve their learning goals within the areas of numeracy and mathematics
- develop an understanding of how young children construct and develop numeric skills
- appreciate how learning opportunities, though play and social interactions, enable children to develop their mathematical knowledge
- recognise factors that influence learning (such as the indoor and outdoor learning environments)
- consider how the existence of home–school links could support children's learning and development of mathematical skills and concepts.

Mathematical reasoning in context

Mathematics reflects how the human mind both perceives and interacts in the world to identify and interpret patterns of life and link them with ideas and thoughts. In this way it is a characteristic of human culture that is carried out every day within our society. This, amongst many others skills we intuitively use, involves logic, reason, calculation, theories, analysis and proof (Courant et al., 1996; Hersh, 1997). It is easy to take for granted the multifarious mathematical skills that help individuals, whatever their age, successfully to survive each day within any context. The processes of telling the time, spending money, mentally budgeting for the week, measuring, making comparisons, interpreting diagrams, reading timetables, undertaking simple calculations, looking at comparative relationships, applying logic and undertaking simple arithmetic are quite literally inculcated into the myriad of daily decisions that people make. These processes, many of which are social (Munn, 1996a), seem almost instinctive as children use their curiosity to learn and develop. Children are natural problem solvers and need to make sense of what they see and what they do. It is a time when children are developing not just their reading skills, but also their mathematical skills. They experiment with what they see, particularly symbols, and this is at the centre of their development (Worthington and Carruthers, 2003). They go on to emphasise that 'our central argument is that children come to make their own sense of abstract symbols through using their own marks and constructing their own meaning' (2003: 70). Munn (1996b) further emphasises this link between literacy and numeracy through symbolic activity. She feels that 'their symbolic activity is related to their understanding of reading and to their identity as a reader' (1996b: 31). In this way, as young children develop, mathematics is just one of the many ways in which they discover who they are and create ways of coping with the world in which they live (Devlin, 2000).

As children develop their symbolic activity and recognition it is more usually in these situations that more sophisticated numeric, reasoning and mathematical skills are required in order to solve a problem or to make a decision. Davis (1984: 1) views problem solving as having a fundamental role in work, social and private lives and he goes on to emphasise that learning about mathematics influences 'how one thinks through the analysis of mathematical problems'.

Children's mathematical experiences are enhanced when they interact with others, including friends, educators and adults, and these may be either adult-initiated or child-initiated (Miller et al., 2010) as children find solutions to everyday problems. For example, parents may do this by talking about problems, questioning children about their approaches to solving them and then getting them to think about how they are going to come up with solutions. This helps them to reason. Often problems can be solved in a variety of different ways and not just through discussion; children also respond to diagrams, pictures, drawing to represent numbers and symbols to make sense of their thoughts. In this way mathematics is a first-hand experience through which they make sense about the world in which they live. As Piaget's work demonstrated, this leads to their construction and use of mathematical knowledge (Piaget and Inhelder, 1969).

Although the use of numeric and mathematical skills to reason and solve problems will be for many individuals largely an unconscious process, it has a key role in everybody's life. Where good decisions are made, it follows that individuals are likely to do the right thing and be happier or more content with the outcomes from such decisions. For this reason children from a very early age need to make sense of numeracy and mathematics as they comprise an evolving life skill, almost like a language, that enables them to face both certain and uncertain situations with greater confidence. According to Nunes and Bryant (1996: 1), 'children need to learn about mathematics in order to understand the world around them'. Doing so helps them to explore, to become rational human beings, to take advantage of the opportunities that surround them and to develop their conceptual abilities to solve problems.

Mathematical skills as lifelong skills

Perhaps the best starting point is to consider what numeric and reasoning skills involve in order to appreciate the extent to which each contributes to problem solving in everyday life. It is frequently felt that as a way of thinking or as a form of language 'mathematics encompasses a wide range of ideas and activities' (Cooke, 2007: 2). As you think about mathematic or numeric skills you probably find that many different thoughts materialise; for example, you may think of some of the more abstract mathematical concepts, such as equations, fractions, algebra, geometry, data handling or even trigonometry. Alternatively, at its very basic level, it is easy to associate numeric skills with counting, measuring, size, patterns, relationships, recognising different shapes or undertaking simple calculations. The Early Years Statutory Framework (DfE, 2014) emphasises that children should recognise and use numbers and quantities in order to count reliably as well as to solve practical problems such as sharing, halving or doubling. This links mathematics and language, so that children understand words such as 'more' and 'less' or 'greater' and 'smaller'. In doing so it implies mathematics is an enabler that contributes to the wider learning and development of young children.

For some children mathematics can seem difficult. There are probably many different kinds of reasons for this. In several ways mathematics is very different from many other curriculum subjects as it has its own signs and symbols and it involves developing an understanding of concepts that require progression in preparation for absorbing other concepts. Even simply the word 'mathematics' has been identified as a barrier, as it can communicate negative perceptions for learners (Skemp, 1989). If children are not confident they may feel challenged by the activities that they face. They may simply get stuck and not be able to think about how to move forward. Such a situation may create anxiety, which makes it more difficult for the learners to become unstuck. Similarly, whereas parents may feel comfortable when reading with children they may feel negative about supporting them in their mathematical development.

These situations are often where the role of the practitioner is so important in being able to identify and recognise that a difficulty exists and then support children, perhaps by providing them with more information or through simplifying or structuring the problem in a way that enables the situation to become a positive learning experience. The irony is that, according to Skemp (1989: 49), 'mathematical thinking is not essentially different from some of the ways in which we use our intelligence in everyday life'.

There is a strong link between how individuals think about mathematics and the pedagogy that might have provided the basis for their learning. For example, learning might take place by rote to include learning how to count from one to ten or by undertaking repetitious activities within the setting. Certainly, children might be able to undertake activities following processes of rote learning, while the real problem is that the learning simply assembles information, and children may not really learn or comprehend what they are doing (Downs, 1998). Learning may simply transform a discipline into an area that depends upon memory rather than real understanding. By contrast, developing numeric and mathematical skills may be used as a way of solving problems so that children make clear connections between what they are learning and how they can use that information to reason, make decisions, or solve problems in everyday life (Cooke, 2007). *Development Matters* (Early Education/DfE, 2012) makes many suggestions about what adults can do as part of developing positive relationships, such as encouraging parents to:

- sing counting songs;
- play games that relate to number order;
- ask questions using mathematical language such as 'how many';
- talk with children about how to work out solutions to simple problems by using fingers or counting aloud;
- discuss with children the methods that they can use to solve problems.

Using the technique of problem solving as a basis for teaching mathematics is grounded in sound educational research. Hiebert et al. (1996: 12) argue that:

> [A]llowing [mathematics] to be problematic means allowing students to wonder what things are, to enquire, to search for solutions, and to resolve incongruities. It means that both curriculum and instruction should begin with problems, dilemmas and questions for students.

They argue that the curriculum should be designed so that instructions can 'problematise' the subject. This means that instead of children simply acquiring the skills and answering questions, they are resolving problems; this builds upon Dewey's (1938) notion of reflective enquiry.

Case study

Gardening

Elliot (2 years and 7 months old) joined the gardening activity. He became responsible for planting some beans. The group responsible for the gardening had to record in a notebook the development of the beans by drawing daily what happened to the beans.

Elliot started the planting with his group, and the practitioner introduced the notebook. The group had to put a symbol for who watered the beans and when, and to draw how the beans developed. Elliot was responsible for counting every day how many beans had grown. Then, with the assistance of the practitioner, the children started to fill in the notebook according to their daily observations. Every day, Elliot's group was asked to spend about five minutes checking on the beans, and then to record their observations in the notebook.

Elliot learned to count from one to four, indicating how many beans had grown, to distinguish between small and big, and also to recognise 'more' or 'less' when he was watering the beans.

Reflective task

- Mathematics is an ongoing journey and it requires lifelong skills. Reflect on your mathematical skills and try to identify what the most important skills are that are required for effective mathematical knowledge.

Developing mathematical knowledge

As young children grow and develop they need to develop strategies enabling them to interact with and make more sense of their own environment and setting. From 0–5 children's learning is a continuum of development whatever the setting they are in. Initially, through this interaction learning takes place before children start their formal schooling. For example, even as early as 6 months old babies are able visually to identify small sets. Babies are also able to identify repetitions and identify size differences. This implies that they have some kind of basis on which they can make quantitative judgements.

There is also an issue concerning the sort of mathematics that children should learn about. Clements et al. (2004: 366) state that 'basic mathematics for preschool children can be organised into two areas: (a) geometric and special skills and (b) numeric and quantitative ideas and skills'. Schaeffer et al. (1974) identified the first three number skills understood by children include 'more', their judgement of relative numbers (which involves recognition that one array has more than another) and their pattern recognition of small numbers. The many different ways in which children learn in the home environment all contribute to the mathematical development of children. For example parents may use:

- Numbers in songs such as 'One, Two, Buckle My Shoe', words in numerical contexts and in everyday situations such as when children do up their buttons.
- Shapes, space and measures as children play with water or sand so that they think about whether something is full, half full or empty or by drawing their attention to the shape of everyday objects such as a placemat or napkin.

Clearly, all of this early learning within the home environment has implications for the requirements of the curriculum once a child attends a nursery or goes to school. As Resnick emphasises:

> [T]here is a constructivist assumption about how mathematics is learned. It is assumed that mathematical knowledge – like all knowledge – is not directly absorbed but is constructed by each individual. This constructivist view is consonant with the theory of Jean Piaget. (Resnick, 1989: 162)

As a result, children bring into their first experience of education a depth of informal mathematical knowledge based upon the strategies that they have developed within their environment. Aubrey points out that:

> [Y]oung children construct their own knowledge and invent their own strategies in everyday situations and through their interactions with the environment. For connections to be made between this knowledge and the formal mathematical knowledge of school, however, analyses of children's strategies, including their errors, must be made, as well as detailed analyses of the mathematical content required to carry out these tasks. (1993: 29)

This has clear ramifications for the role of those who support learning for young children. Furthermore, as Aubrey (1993) emphasises, the competences brought by children into the setting from their own backgrounds may 'pose some challenges to the conventional reception-class curriculum'. She highlights that Reception teachers need to be aware of the mathematical levels and abilities that learners bring into the school, as well as the need to be able to assess the learning that has taken place. Through this understanding of learning, practitioners can build upon the ongoing development of mathematical concepts. The opportunities for parents to support children in developing their mathematical knowledge are endless. This can involve helping children to count real things as they interact with objects. Using fingers to count, pointing to objects, sorting for similarities, identifying patterns, shapes, colours and sizes, looking for differences, playing and keeping scores in a game, looking at angles and figures, using shape sorters and puzzles, setting time limits, looking at parts of a whole are some of the range of other activities that help children to learn about geometry, special sense, number, the concept of time and fractions.

Curiosity

Children are naturally curious and the role of practitioners in supporting children is to foster their curiosity in a way that promulgates their learning. This is because there is a reasoning and logic about mathematics that makes children want to answer questions about themselves and within their environment in order to understand everyday issues that they see or come across (Higgins, 1998). In this sense the term 'the cure for boredom is curiosity; there is no cure for curiosity' attributed to Dorothy Parker, a twentieth-century American author and humourist, might be appropriate as this implies that activities, in this case mathematics, might become a process of discovery initiated by a child as they take ownership of an activity in which they are interested. Curiosity is their desire, therefore, to know about something in a way that motivates them to explore new ideas. Practitioners of mathematics can do this by introducing mathematical elements to daily activities and making activities relevant to real life. For example, everyday discussion about the calendar, days of the week, or simple combinatorics can all be used to develop a child's curiosity. In this sense curiosity is a function of learning as it encourages the learner to ask questions, acquire information and use reasoning, exploring, explaining, generalising, proving, logic and deduction (McInerney and Darmanegara, 2008).

Mathematics is not simply something that children do, based upon an exercise that has been shown to them. It should be something that they talk about and through which they can interact with others as this helps them to ask questions and satisfy their curiosity. Mathematical thinking is something that children develop because they have asked questions that have supported their thoughts. For many years the FunMaths Roadshow, initially developed by Ian Porteous from the University of Liverpool, has provided activities that help children to explore mathematics within their environment in a way that involves discussion, problem solving and interpreting ideas. Making mathematics both challenging and enjoyable is an important element in both encouraging and satisfying a child's curiosity.

Mathematics as a social activity

As has been seen, mathematics is a living subject. It lives because of the need for individuals to deal with numeric issues all around us. As children make sense of the world they begin to understand patterns and seek solutions that help them to explore and deal with everyday issues. For example, Resnick (1989: 162) indicates that: 'infants of about six months can discriminate the numerosity of small sets when these are presented visually. What is more, they can match sets cross-modally, recognising the same quantity where it is presented visually or auditorily.'

According to Schoenfeld (1992: 3), 'mathematics is an inherently social activity'. He also emphasises that as children learn about mathematics the process becomes empowering for the learner. In fact, Vygotsky (1978) mentioned the importance of understanding the social context of learning. Nowhere is the social aspect of learning about mathematics better underlined than the ways in which young children learn through the process of play during early childhood. According to Wood and Attfield (2005: 1), 'early childhood education is underpinned by a strong tradition which regards play as essential for learning and development'. Although not all play is purposeful, playing can contribute to the learning and development of children as they grow. It provides an opportunity for them to be creative and to experiment; such behaviours can have widespread implications for the development of each individual. Many of the activities in which children engage while they play can be used to develop and support learning. As Wood and Attfield emphasise (2005: 13), 'if playing and growing are synonymous with life itself, then lifelong playing can be seen as an important aspect of lifelong learning'.

As will be demonstrated, play is a good opportunity to develop social interactions purposefully with children in a way that provides a context for learning opportunities within the area of mathematics. Well-structured and planned play may provide situations, for example, in which the practitioner can set up a challenging learning environment for the child; it may extend their language and improve their understanding of key areas such as numeracy and mathematics. In doing so, play also provides the opportunity to set up creative and imaginative learning experiences for the child. While these experiences may challenge individuals, they will also satisfy their curiosity and encourage them to ask questions or want to learn more. Play also provides a creative pedagogy through which problem solving can be used as a base for learning.

Contextualised learning opportunities

There are so many different activities and opportunities through which children can interact with adults to develop their mathematical skills that it is just not possible for this chapter to do them all justice. Instead, this section simply highlights a range of contextualised learning opportunities to provide a sample of the sorts of activities in which adults and children can engage.

The context for learning about mathematics may be provided by the home as well as the school. Research shows that both the home and the school have the capability of making key contributions to the development of academic skills at the age of 5 years (Dickinson and Tabors, 1991). Winter et al. (2009) emphasise that children live in two very different worlds. They explain that children learn through their daily activities as they play with members of their family. Although this learning is subtle and hidden from view, it is a key element in learning mathematics. As children are learning in two very different environments, a strong argument can be made that in order to create synergy and make the most of how children learn in such contrasting contexts, home and school should work closely together, so that school can take account of the learning experiences that children bring with them from home (Jones, 1998).

As mathematics involves signs, symbols and elements of progression from one level to another, it often creates barriers for learners and practitioners at home and this can lead to anxiety. In most circumstances, overcoming such barriers simply involves building mathematical confidence. If parents are more involved in supporting children and show that they enjoy it, this can enhance a child's learning experience. Focusing upon reasoning and supporting children through this process is more important than whether an answer is necessarily right or wrong. What this does is get children thinking in a mathematical way irrespective of the solution. In doing this they are building their child's confidence and reasoning skills so that they can then understand and apply concepts. Asking children why they have answered a question in this way and not that way helps children to deepen their understanding and both talk and rationalise about the mathematical process. The following activities may encourage parent/ child synergies within the home environment.

By exploring through interaction children intuitively learn about size and shapes (Price et al., 2003). At a very early stage, simply building a tower with blocks or making a house, having a range of toys with bright colours, or sorting sweets helps them to learn basic mathematical skills. Blocks are particularly useful in introducing children to shapes, sizes and colours. As infants become toddlers, there are many more social opportunities to interact with the child. For example, counting while handing objects over to a toddler, reciting songs that use numbers or using finger-play to reinforce numbers will help them to understand more about the notions of 'more' or 'less', such that they may start to compare numbers. It may also help children to say and use the names of numbers within an appropriate context, and encourage them to start counting objects independently.

Reading books with a mathematical bias helps children to learn literacy skills alongside their development of mathematical terms and concepts in a context that they may enjoy.

Children are naturally curious, which stimulates them to ask many questions. For example, they might want to know how many cars are in the street, or how many people there are on a bus. By answering questions, it is possible to count with them or to provide them with some way of understanding greater, smaller, heavier or lighter. It may also provide an opportunity for them to understand the notion of shapes such as circles or squares or to be able to describe in their own words the shape of something. When slicing up a cake or a pie, for example, it is possible to count each of the pieces out to the child. In a similar vein, when placing objects in front of the child, his or her understanding of adding and subtracting can be developed by adding objects to or taking objects from the pile. Measurement activities may also satisfy curiosity. If the child uses a sand pit or wants to play with water, measuring cups and spoons will enable him or her to understand which containers hold less.

'Story sacks' were initially developed by Neil Griffiths (1998). They provide a creative opportunity to develop materials to stimulate the interest of children and make their stories more 'real'. A story sack is a large cloth bag inside which is placed a children's book and other associated materials related in some way to the story. Items could be counted out, or may involve different shapes and sizes; they can be discussed in relation to the story, in order to make the story come alive. Story sacks provide a fresh approach to enjoying books, and also provide a learning opportunity for the reader and the child to interact using a range of tangible materials in a way that sustains their motivation to read. Materials provide an element of curiosity and at the same time make learning active. By providing materials focused upon numeracy, such as cards, games, activities or lines that promote mathematical development effectively, the story sacks become number sacks to be used to help children to learn key mathematical skills such as counting.

For young children role-play is an imaginative way in which to learn. According to Staub:

[C]hildren role-play extensively in their interaction with other children. By enacting a variety of roles and exchanging roles in interactive situations, children may learn to view events from a variety of points of view. (1971: 806)

Role-playing provides a situation where children can imitate behaviour and act out different situations. The home is a perfect setting for children to engage in role-play. The role of the facilitator is simply to adapt the setting and create a role-play area. For example, the child may help with some cooking and be involved in sorting ingredients; this helps them to learn about more or less, or how to compare the sizes or amount of ingredients. They may have a cooker as a toy or another item that can contribute to the role-playing situation. Role-play might include growing cress or sunflowers, counting plant pots, using money in a retailing role-play, sorting objects such as sweets or shells, weighing ingredients, or developing the notion of time.

Case study

Role-play

A group of 2- to 3-year-old children, after reading the story of Little Red Riding Hood, decided to do a role-play in front of the rest of the group of children. They made a list of the things they would need: a cake and a basket with some food in it. Finally, they decided they would have to choose roles in their play.

First, they chose to prepare the basket with the foods that Little Red Riding Hood was to offer to her grandmother. The children decided to make a cake. They searched for a recipe and they 'wrote the recipe' on a big poster so everyone could see. They had opportunities to explore concepts such as 'more' or 'less', 'big' or 'small' and 'adding'.

They had opportunities to measure the ingredients for the cake, to add or to take away; for example, when they added two glasses of sugar, one glass of water, the flour, and so on. The practitioner decided to focus only on these three concepts during the process of baking the cake and the subsequent activities.

Secondly, the children decided to pack the basket by adding different objects. Again, they had the opportunity to explore the concepts 'big' and 'small', 'more' and 'less', and add how many objects were going into the basket.

Finally, the role-play took place. The children, after preparing Little Red Riding Hood's basket, chose their roles: who would be Little Red Riding Hood, the wolf, the trees, the grandmother, the hunter and the mother. During this activity, derived from a fairy tale, the children had the chance to negotiate roles, responsibilities and plans, and to re-create roles and experiences. The whole project targeted children's problem solving and numeracy while other areas such as language and communication, social development and creativity were also developed.

The practitioner provided opportunities for the children that encouraged them to use the concepts of more/less, and big/small, as well as to count up to five. A number of different materials were used to conceptualise the different concepts and to help the children interact with different materials and objects in order for them to understand the concepts in different contexts. Time was provided for children to initiate discussions from shared experiences.

Reflective task

- Reflect on your own practice or work placement and discuss your role as an early childhood practitioner and how you can interact with children during play situations to provide a context for learning opportunities within the area of mathematics.

Puzzles are good for helping children to develop their spatial skills within a different environment that enables them to achieve a range of purposes (Siraj-Blatchford et al., 2002). As children work with puzzles, they are actually putting bits together and solving problems at first hand. Puzzles help with coordination; children begin to recognise that individual parts all contribute towards a whole. Puzzles help children to understand that by rotating pieces, they can find the way in which each piece fits. Then, piece by piece, the puzzle becomes a whole. A wide range of puzzles designed for different ages of children are available today. They may be 3D puzzles, pegboards, bead threading, as well as puzzles linked to different sounds and made of different materials. In fact it is not difficult to invent a puzzle or mathematical game (Clemson and Clemson, 1994). For example, they could be similar to those in a comic but with an educational content. They might involve:

- quantities
- comparing pictures and objects
- strategies
- songs
- displays.

The indoor and outdoor environments

Young children require an interesting environment with the capability of stimulating their learning and development. The key features of such an environment must be the setting, the materials and the toys available, and any equipment required. While such an environment should prompt a child to explore in a challenging way, it needs to be safe and secure. According to Schroeder (1991: 129): 'the health and well-being of children, in comparison to adults, are often more severely affected by the quality of the physical environment'. An appropriate environment would offer children the opportunity to explore both outdoors and indoors. The children would also need to be supported and supervised by adults.

An indoor play area should be a place where children can be either active or quiet; it should be designed to support their active learning and development. The environment should contain resources and materials that enable children to play and to further their learning at their own pace. The nature of such resources or toys will depend upon the respective age of each child and, of course, their particular phase of development. The items should also be imaginative: natural materials such as shells and pine cones are as enjoyable and instructive as wooden spoons, containers and other simple household equipment; a brief glance at various commercial websites can identify toys such as teaching watches, cash tills with money, blocks and shapes, shopping games, puzzles, number games, electronic maths toys, match-it puzzles, jigsaws, thinking games, wooden toddler toys, manipulative toys and imaginative play sets. The list is almost endless. As Taylor et al. have written, 'toys can be used to promote children's cognitive, physical, motor, language, social and emotional development' (1997: 235).

Any outdoor space should offer children both shade and shelter, and within this area both natural and manufactured resources should be available for play. For example, items could help the child dig, swing, roll, move, stretch, or play with wheeled toys (see Chapter 12). The children can also play in a water area where concepts such as wet, dry, floating, skimming, similarities and differences can be explored. The practitioners, with the help of the children, can create a fish market where children can have opportunities to act such roles as seller or customer, to count money, to think how the fish will be stored, and to count the fish for sale.

In such an environment children need, at their own pace, to make choices about how to explore and learn. Natural materials such as sand, soil, garden snail shells, a slatted tray and cardboard boxes can be very helpful for children's participation in meaningful activities such as those that encourage children to sort, group and sequence play. Resources designed to help their mathematical development might help them to collect, measure, make patterns or build as they play. Swings, seesaws, slides, tents or a climbing house help to support such an environment. The outdoor environment is an enabler for children to be energetic and to exercise while enjoying some concrete experiences. There are a range of outdoor toys designed to help children with the development of their mathematical skills, such as number bean bags, giant inflatable numbers, a numeracy octopus, shape wands, what-is-it boxes and scatter boards, as well as giant puzzles.

Planning for progression

The material in *Development Matters* (Early Education/DfE, 2012) aims to help practitioners to support the learning and development of children with their current needs. In doing so they identify three areas that provide appropriate opportunities to support children in their learning and their development of mathematical skills. Positive relationships emphasise that children should be encouraged to develop mathematical concepts within the context of their own play, particularly in child-centred and child-initiated activities. According to the Mathematical Association (1955: v, vi), 'children developing at their own individual rates, learn through their active response to the experiences that come to them through constructive play, experiment and discussion, [and] children become aware of relationships and develop mental structures which are mathematical in form'.

The second area emphasised by *Development Matters* is that of creating an enabling environment for children. It includes both an outdoor environment in which a physical activity can be used in order to discover about distances, shapes and measurement, as well as an indoor area where children have the chance to learn to count and calculate. Resources are a key feature of both of these environments.

Finally, *Development Matters* links both areas, positive relationships and enabling environments, to the notion of the unique child and the special way in which each and every child reflects the communities and cultures around them. This notion of individuality helps to emphasise that creative elements of mathematical development such as songs, games and imaginative play as well as activities that enable mathematical learning and problem solving to take place, need to be built into daily routines to provide a route for progression.

The importance of home–school links as part of the planning process

The learning and development of young children should be a shared experience among parents and carers as well as early childhood settings. Parents may be concerned about how their children are getting on within the setting while, at the same time, practitioners may want to discuss with parents issues affecting learning. This may not always be easy, particularly for parents who might not be sure about how they could help the educational development of their children. According to Booth and Dunn (1996: 3), 'parents play a critical role in both their children's academic achievement and their children's socio-emotional development'. They identify in their text evidence that illustrates how such a relationship contributes to the success of children within a setting.

Parents or carers may feel that they require information to help them to complement the nature and type of activities engaged in by their child when in the setting. For some (particularly better-educated parents) this may be easier than for parents who were challenged by learning mathematics. The level and strength of participation may depend upon the resources available to parents, the strength of their belief in the need for participating with settings, and attitudes towards education in general.

☁ Reflective task

- After studying Chapters 11 and 13, reflect on your role as practitioner and try to develop a strategy of how you can engage parents in mathematical activities with their children. As was demonstrated in Chapter 18, children have experiences with digital technologies at home; how can you use these experiences to enhance mathematical experiences of children and interaction with parents?

Summary

The *Development Matters* document (Early Education/DfE, 2012) identifies three different areas that help to develop learning in the area of problem solving, reasoning and numeracy. These are:

a   positive relationships, involving the provision of time, space and opportunities for children to explore and develop their learning and understanding;

b   enabling environments, whether indoors or outdoors, which are well resourced to promote and develop learning; and

c   viewing each child uniquely so that learning and development through play and activities are based upon regular daily routines in a way customized to culture and communities.

Mathematics helps children to make sense of and better understand the world around them in their early childhood setting. It enables them simultaneously to develop their conceptual abilities and to solve problems. From the very earliest stage of development babies recognise patterns and make connections. Mathematics can seem difficult for some children because the area has its own language. It is important to develop strategies that help children to develop their mathematical knowledge and problem-solving abilities. As this development is undertaken it must be remembered that learning about mathematics is a social activity. There are a wide variety of ways in which mathematical knowledge can be developed, and this may be within the context of either indoor or outdoor play.

Key points to remember

- Mathematical development of children starts from a very early age and it is important to explore maths in the context of everyday activities and recognise the importance of engaging children in lifelong learning skills.

- Play provides a creative way for children to develop a number of skills related to mathematical development. It is essential to enable creative and imaginative learning experiences for children.

- The importance of an effective home–setting partnership is essential in children's mathematical development.

- Although mathematics has been explored in a separate chapter, it is necessary to emphasise that communication, language and literacy skills are important elements and are interrelated in children's acquisition of mathematical skills and knowledge.

Points for discussion

- Constructed from their individual backgrounds, what are the implications for how early years practitioners organise their strategies for support?

- Based upon your experiences of working with early years children, identify concrete experiences or evidence of situations in which you have observed babies and children constructing mathematical knowledge.

- Think of concrete examples of where the learning of mathematics by children can be set up as a socially mediated activity. How does the social aspect of learning influence the richness of the learning activity? Are there any problems or issues that might arise as part of this social interaction?

Further reading

Books

Cooke, H. (2007) *Mathematics for Primary and Early Years: Developing Subject Knowledge*, 2nd edn. London: Sage.

Carruthers, E. and Worthington, M. (2006) *Children's Mathematics: Making Marks, Making Meanings*, 2nd edn. London: Sage.

Pound, L. (2006) *Supporting Mathematical Development in the Early Years*. Maidenhead: Open University Press.

Tucker, K. (2014) *Mathematics Through Play in the Early Years*, 3rd edn. London: Sage.

Articles

Aubrey, C. (1993) 'An investigation of the mathematical knowledge and competencies which young children bring into school', *British Educational Research Journal*, 19 (1): 27–41.

Carruthers, E. and Worthington, M. (2009) 'Children's mathematical graphics: understanding the key concept', *Primary Mathematics*, 13 (3): (Autumn).

Geary, D.C. (1994) *Children's Mathematical Development: Research and Practical Applications*. Washington, DC: American Psychological Association.

Useful websites

Edhelper:
http://edhelper.com/

Although there are parts of this website that require a subscription, there are a number of free areas with a series of number, shape, colouring, counting and matching activities, attractively presented and really useful for mathematically developing Early Years children.

Apples for the Teacher:
www.apples4theteacher.com/math.html#geometrygames

Describes itself as a 'fun educational website for teachers and kids'. The site links itself to other pages, and has a huge number of downloads and links to puzzles, games and problem solving activities. Activities range from measurement games and money games to those that help learners to make sense of the principles of number.

BBC Learning
www.bbc.co.uk/learning/subjects/maths.shtml

This has a range of short online courses for children centred upon developing their proficiency in mathematics. Either whole units or bits can be downloaded and activities include videos, access to other websites, activities and games.

References

Aubrey, C. (1993) 'An investigation of the mathematical knowledge and competencies which young children bring into school', *British Educational Research Journal*, 19 (1): 27–41.

Booth, A. and Dunn, J. (1996) *Family–School Links: How Do They Affect Educational Outcomes?* Philadelphia: Lawrence Erlbaum Associates.

Clements, D.H., Sarama, J. and DiBiase, A. (2004) *Engaging Young Children in Mathematics*. Philadelphia: Lawrence Erlbaum Associates.

Clemson, D. and Clemson, W. (1994) *Mathematics in the Early Years*. London: Routledge.

Cooke, H. (2007) *Mathematics for Primary and Early Years: Developing Subject Knowledge*, 2nd edn. London: Sage.

Courant, R., Robbins, H. and Stewart, I. (1996) *What Is Mathematics: An Elementary Approach to Ideas and Methods*. New York: Oxford University Press.

Davis, R.B. (1984) *Learning Mathematics: The Cognitive Science Approach to Mathematical Education*. Norwood, NJ: Greenwood.

Devlin, K.J. (2000) *The Language of Mathematics*. New York: Henry Holt.

Dewey, J. (1938) *Logic: The Theory of Enquiry*. New York: Henry Holt.

DfE (Department for Education) (2014) *Statutory Framework for the Early Years Foundation Stage: Setting the Standards for Learning, Development and Care for Children from Birth to Five*. London: DfE. Available at: www.foundationyears.org.uk/files/2014/07/EYFS_frame-work_from_1_September_2014__with_clarification_note.pdf (accessed 28 September 2015).

Dickinson, D.K. and Tabors, P.O. (1991) 'Early literacy: linkages between home, school and literacy achievement at age five', *Journal of Research in Childhood Education*, 6 (1): 30–46.

Downs, S. (1998) 'Technological change and education and training', *Education and Training*, 40 (1): 18–19.

Early Education/DfE (2012) *Development Matters in the Early Years Foundation Stage (EYFS)*. London: Early Education. Available at www.early-education.org.uk (accessed 14 July, 2015).

Griffiths, N. (1998) *Story Sacks*. Video. Bury: Story Sacks Ltd.

Hersh, R. (1997) *What Is Mathematics Really?* New York: Oxford University Press.

Hiebert, H., Carpenter, T.P., Fennema, E., Fuson, K., Human, P., Murray, H., Olivier, A. and Wearne, D. (1996) 'Problem solving as a basis for reform in curriculum and instruction: the case of mathematics', *Educational Researcher*, 25 (4): 12–21.

Higgins, P. M. (1998) *Mathematics for the Curious*, New York: Oxford University Press.

Jones, L. (1998) 'Home and school numeracy experiences for young Somali pupils in Britain', *European Early Childhood Education Research Journal*, 6 (1): 63–72.

Mathematical Association (1955) *The Teaching of Mathematics in Primary Schools*. London: Mathematical Association.

McInerney, D. and Darmanegara, A. (2008) *Teaching and Learning; International Best Practice*. New York: Information Age Publishing.

Miller, L., Cable, C. and Goodliff, G. (2010) *Supporting Children's Learning in the Early Years*, 2nd edn, Abingdon: Routledge.

Munn, P. (1996a) 'Progression in literacy and numeracy in preschool', in M. Hughes (ed.), *Progression in Learning*. Clevedon: Multilingual Matters.

Munn, P. (1996b) 'Assessment of literacy and numeracy acquired before school', in R. Duggan and C.J. Pole (eds), *Reshaping Education in the 1990s: Perspectives on Primary Schooling*. London: Routledge.

Nunes, T. and Bryant, P. (1996) *Children Doing Mathematics*. London: Blackwell.

Piaget, J. and Inhelder, B. (1969) *The Psychology of the Child*. New York: Basic Books.

Price, S., Rogers, Y., Scaife, M., Stanton, D. and Neale, H. (2003) 'Using tangibles to promote novel forms of playful learning', *Interacting with Computers*, 15: 169–85.

Resnick, L.B. (1989) 'Developing mathematical knowledge', *American Psychologist*, 44 (2): 162–9.

Schaeffer, B., Eggleston V.H. and Scott, J.L. (1974) 'Number development in young children', *Cognitive Development*, 5: 357–9.

Schoenfeld, A.H. (1992) 'Learning to think mathematically: problem solving, metacognition, and sense-making in mathematics', in *Handbook for Research on Mathematics Teaching and Learning*. New York: Macmillan.

Schroeder, H.E. (1991) *New Directions in Health Psychology*. Oxford: Taylor & Francis.

Seefeldt, C., Galper, A. and Stevenson-Garcia, J. (2012) *Active Experiences for Active Children: Mathematics*, 3rd edn. London: Pearson.

Siraj-Blatchford, I., Sylva, K., Muttock, S., Gilden, R. and Bell, D. (2002) *Researching Effective Pedagogy in Early Years*. London: HMSO.

Skemp, R.R. (1989) *Mathematics in the Primary School*. London: Routledge.

Staub, E. (1971) 'The use of role playing and induction in children's learning of helping and sharing behaviour', *Child Development*, 42 (3): 805–16.

Taylor, S.I., Morris, V.G. and Rogers, C.S. (1997) 'Toy safety and selection', *Early Childhood Education Journal*, 24 (4): 235–8.

Tipps, S., Johnson, A. and Kennedy, L.M. (2011) *Guiding Children's Learning of Mathematics*, Belmont: Wadsworth.

Vygotsky, I. (1978) *Mind in Society: The Development of Higher Psychological Processes*. Cambridge, MA: Harvard University Press.

Winter, J., Andrews, J., Greenhough, P., Hughes, M., Salway, L. and Yee, W. (2009) *Improving Primary Mathematics: Linking Home and School*. Abingdon: Routledge.

Wood, E. and Attfield, J. (2005) *Play, Learning and the Early Childhood Curriculum*. London: Sage.

Worthington, M. and Carruthers, E. (2003) *Children's Mathematics: Making Marks, Making Meaning*. London: Sage.

Want to learn more about this chapter? Visit the companion website at https://study.sagepub.com/EYFS3e for access to free SAGE journal articles and book chapters, weblinks, annotated further readings and more.

23

Understanding the World

Gary Beauchamp

Chapter overview

The fourth overarching principle of the Early Years Foundation Stage is that children develop and learn in different ways and at different rates. This is true across all areas of learning and development, which are considered equally important and inter-connected. In this context, understanding the world (UW) cannot be considered in isolation from other areas of learning and development when planning. Research has shown that 'the brain will learn from every experienced event, but because cognitive representations are distributed, cumulative learning is crucial. There will be stronger representation of what is common across experience ("prototypical") and weaker representation of what differs' (Goswami and Bryant, 2007: 4). In this situation it is important for practitioners to plan to reinforce key ideas across different areas of learning. In planning these experiences, however, it is essential that key ideas and concepts are presented in a recognisable form in a variety of contexts and formats so that children learn to recognise things which are common (for instance, the concept of a shape, for example of a ladybird, a 2D shape, and in patterns) when presented in different locations and materials, or even in different life forms. As Goswami and Bryant (2007: 4) conclude: 'there will be multiple representations of experience (for example, in motor

(Continued)

(Continued)

cortex and in sensory cortices). This supports multi-sensory approaches to education.' It is here that UW can offer unique and distinctive multi-sensory opportunities both to *introduce* new ideas (which can be reinforced in other areas) and to *reinforce* ideas (as introduced in other areas of learning). The key issue lies in recognising the distinctive opportunities offered by UW in a variety of learning contexts and interactions – including between children and practitioners, among children themselves, and between children and their environment.

This chapter aims to help you:

- develop an understanding of the distinctive features of understanding the world within the context of the EYFS
- develop an understanding of how these features integrate with, and enhance, other areas of learning
- enhance your awareness of the variety of learning perspectives offered by adopting a variety of curricular 'lenses'
- consider the role, and effective use, of information and communication technology (ICT) in learning.

The child: a unique actor in their own social world?

The EYFS acknowledges that 'every child is a unique child'. Nevertheless, although an individual child will learn in different ways and at different rates, what all children have in common is that they will need to develop 'positive relationships' in 'enabling environments'. Hence, it is essential to remember that 'learning in young children is socially mediated. Families, peers and teachers are all important' (Goswami and Bryant, 2007: 20). When the EYFS was reviewed in 2011, this was acknowledged in a call for 'a greater emphasis [to be] given in the EYFS to the role of parents and carers as partners in their children's learning' (Tickell, 2011: 5), resulting in the requirement for 'a strong partnership between practitioners and parents and/or carers' (DfE, 2014: 6) in the current document.

In this situation, although a child is often focused on his or her own world, the role of practitioners is to broaden this focus to help them develop a variety of relationships and partnerships, both within and outside of the setting. As well as providing opportunities to enhance social development, these partnerships should also be considered as vital parts of cognitive development as 'those settings which see cognitive and social development as complementary achieve the best profile in terms of child outcomes' (Siraj-Blatchford et al., 2002: 10). Indeed, there is evidence that enhancing cognitive development can be a catalyst to higher levels of parental involvement. A review of research concluded that 'parental involvement is strongly influenced by the child's level of attainment: the higher the level of attainment, the more parents get involved' (Desforges and Abouchaar, 2003: 4). Although the importance of this partnership will be discussed further in other chapters, it is important to explore here the specific contribution that UW can make due to its requirement to guide children in making sense of 'their physical world and their community through opportunities to explore, observe and find out about people, places, technology and the environment' (DfE, 2014: 8).

It is much easier to enhance professional and personal partnerships within a setting as practitioners have direct access to other professionals and children. Conversely, especially for students on a teaching or other (e.g. observational) placement, it is much harder to develop partnerships with parents and carers as it may seem a higher priority to develop relationships with children. Nevertheless, it is vital that practitioners, and especially students, should not neglect opportunities to develop relationships with families (as mentioned in Chapter 13) and the community (see Chapter 12), even if this appears difficult on a time-limited placement. They should also take chances to understand the family background of the children and the needs of the community whenever possible. Even simple steps, such as being seen by, and making yourself available to talk to, parents at the beginning and the end of each day can be a starting point in achieving this. Further steps can include attending local community events, especially those with no connection to the school – such as a local carnival or village fete – to show your interest in the community.

In trying to develop an understanding of what parents and the community have to offer there should be 'a regular two-way flow of information with parents and/or carers' (DfE, 2014: 29). An essential first step is in seeing the knowledge and expertise of parents (and other members of their families), and indeed the local community, as an asset and as another resource that practitioners can use to enrich the learning experiences they offer to children. This is set in context by the ideas of Perkins (1997: 89), who makes the distinction between the person-solo, 'the person without resources in his or her surround', and the person-plus, 'the person plus [their] surround'. For all practitioners, part of their surroundings (and therefore a resource to be used) are the parents and carers of children in the setting, as well as of others from the local community who may be able to offer specialist knowledge or skills (such as on religion or local history), although normal protocols relating to vetting and health and safety will need to be considered. Overall, we may conclude, as emphasised elsewhere in this book, that the involvement of parents in UW should be viewed as the opportunity it is, rather than a challenge.

Using a subject 'lens' to develop a variety of learning perspectives

Although each aspect of UW will be considered separately below, it is essential that practitioners are aware of how they fit holistically into a child's education. When looking at UW, and indeed other areas of learning, there is always a tension between ensuring subject rigour (for instance, correct science subject knowledge in exploration and investigation) and providing a broader topic-based or thematic curriculum (i.e. in covering a range of 'subjects'). Barnes (2007: 1) points out that 'our experience of the world is cross-curricular. Everything which surrounds us in the physical world can be seen and understood from multiple perspectives.' One of these perspectives may be that of a scientist, geographer or historian and it is here that the challenge begins in framing learning experiences for young children. This does not mean adopting a subject-based approach (this will come soon enough), but adopting a subject methodology or perspective: for example, history (as a body of knowledge) should not be taught as a subject, but an historian's approach to learning may be adopted (see more below). It is suggested that each subject gives a child a unique way of understanding the world and that viewing teaching ideas through, for example, a 'scientific lens' can offer new insights into how to develop effective learning opportunities. Eventually, it may well be that 'this operates at two levels (one for the practitioner thinking of possible approaches to planning, the other for children thinking of ways to approach a problem), but the key idea is that you consider the possible benefits of approaching teaching and learning as, say, a musician or historian' (Beauchamp, 2012: 118–19).

The world, people and community

In essence, the requirement for children to 'explore similarities and differences in relation to places, objects, materials and living things' (DfE, 2014: 12) forms the beginning of scientific enquiry as:

> [t]he child's exploration of the world is the springboard from which the next step is taken, that of more systematic enquiry. Systematic enquiry may be described as 'scientific investigation' in later years. Nevertheless, the first step in any scientific enquiry is exploration, or 'play'. (de Boo, 2000: 1)

This play is not time-scaled; children will often repeat the same activity time and time again. This is not time wasted, as it allows the child to reinforce their understanding of what is happening: for example, every time I tip water from the jug it goes down; every time I put water on the sand it seems to change colour; every time the sun comes out the puddles disappear. Young children need opportunities to explore materials and objects in many different contexts. Modelling clay, for example, can be squashed, made into shapes, joined together with more modelling clay of a different colour and there are still many other properties to be explored: Does it float? Can you paint it? Can it be used to stick things together? Will it mix with other materials? Or does it go hard like pottery clay? A curious child will surely come up with many more enquiries. This example is about exploring just one material, let alone how it works with others. It is therefore essential that practitioners provide opportunities to explore a range of suitable resources (water, different-coloured modelling clay, paint and so on). This open-ended exploration can be a very creative process and Cremin et al. (2015: 406) note that 'Early Years creativity and science education share in common recognition of children's exploratory and investigative engagement, and their consideration of ideas and conceptions'.

Some of these explorations can be anticipated and planned for, while others will be spontaneous and unexpected. Both should be welcomed and encouraged. Indeed, as has been emphasised in Chapters 7 and 8, practitioners learn much from observing the spontaneous explorations of children and considering the extent, if any, to which they are worth replicating in planning for another occasion. Careful observation is the key both to assessment and in considering whether practitioners can help develop children's understanding by building on, and adding progression to, these spontaneous events by providing other resources and settings. Overall, the aim is to provide quality experiences that are meaningful and 'worthy of active involvement. If children are to continue their struggle to make sense of the world, then the world must be worth the struggle' (Fisher, 2002: 15).

One of the key features of active involvement is including children in planning. This is particularly true of exploration and investigation. Most topics can start with a 'brainstorming' by staff and children to ask the questions: 'What do we know already?' and 'What do we want to find out/would we like to learn?' The idea of children's having ownership of the direction of their learning is central, no matter how young the children. Obviously, practitioners need to retain an overview to ensure coverage of relevant skills, and to avoid repetition, but the central message is that they do not always need to follow a predetermined and detailed scheme of work. As one early childhood practitioner interviewed while this chapter was being written put it, with this sort of planning 'You can't just pick it up and run with it'. In addition, ensuring suitable progression in these activities can present challenges. For example, the move away from schemes of work (with pre-defined assessment tasks and progression criteria) means that for each investigation and exploration practitioners need to consider how they are going to assess the outcomes and ensure that adequate challenges are built in to extend children's learning. When considering assessment, the importance of looking at situations through, for example, a 'scientific lens' is crucial, as this may offer unique insights. For instance, the processes of exploration and investigation (including the so-called 'process skills', identified by Harlen [2003] as observing, raising questions, hypothesising, predicting, planning, interpreting and communicating) are in themselves outcomes and are just as important as the end product of the investigation.

To assist practitioners in both teaching and assessment in UW, two skills are central: observation and questioning. Although there is guidance available on observation (see the Further reading section of this chapter) one practitioner interviewed for this chapter noted that there was still a need to 'mould things to what we need to do for our children and it will be different for every school'. The use of questions is a more generic issue and, although good questions can increase the interactivity of teaching, much depends on practitioners developing listening skills (hearing what children actually say, and not what you think they were going to say!). All practitioners should also develop 'a repertoire of strategies to manage critical moments' (Myhill et al., 2006: 117) when children ask questions or make a comment and practitioners need to decide on how best to respond.

Technology

As discussed in Chapter 18, in the current climate of rapid technological change, it is very likely that young children have some understanding of technology, particularly ICT, and a degree of 'tacit knowledge' of computers and electronic toys (Hayes, 2006). They live in an age where ICT is a part of everyday life and many homes have access to the internet. In a review of research into ICT in early childhood in 2008, Aubrey and Dahl suggested that:

> most young children aged from birth to five years are growing up in media-rich digital environments in which they engage actively from a very early age. Family members are positive about this and actively promote the use of new technologies through on-going social-cultural practices of the home. They welcome ICT education outside the home and believe that it should be included in the curriculum from the earliest days. Young children are confident with new technologies and are very willing to explore new gadgets that they have not encountered before. (2008: 4)

More recently, the same authors (Aubrey and Dahl, 2014: 106) undertook a small-scale update study and found that technology use in the home and early childhood settings is 'still dominated by the computer and Internet, television and DVD player, though practitioners are now familiar with and use a wider range of digital technology in the EYFS'.

In addition, children's toys are becoming ever-more sophisticated and children are 'surrounded by products of the information and communication age' (Feasy and Gallear, 2001: 5). Children will need to find out about an ever-increasing range of technology and programmable toys, as well as learning how to use them. In this context, young children's 'openness to explore, or play, with new technologies is something that teachers need to both embrace and facilitate' (Beauchamp, 2012: 6).

This can take place both within and, increasingly with the advent of mobile technologies, outside of the classroom and can take many forms. Even the entry intercom and pelican crossing buttons are practical examples of control technology that could be used during and after a walk around the locality. On this trip children could also be encouraged to look for other uses of ICT as well as other physical features – which can be used when exploring 'people and communities' (see later in this chapter). It may be best to consider ICT as a:

> new tool that could and should be incorporated into existing early-years practice in developmentally appropriate ways, supplementing, not replacing, other important first-hand experiences and interactions and accompanied by quality adult input to help children learn about and through the technology. (O'Hara, 2008: 30)

As children explore ICT resources, all practitioners, parents and children need to consider when it is appropriate to use it and when it is not. In general terms, practitioners make informed choices about how and when to use ICT (if at all) based on the pedagogic demands of a subject and the age of the children concerned (Beauchamp, 2006). With young children the demands of subject teaching do not apply, but the age of the children is central. While practitioners need to consider how to develop children's specific ICT skills (such as moving a mouse), they are also concerned with how it can contribute to the learning environment: what it has to offer that other resources do not. The following features of ICT will influence this:

- *Speed*: making things happen more quickly than by other methods, both for the individual on a device or for the whole group
- *Automation*: making difficult processes happen automatically, e.g. filming and editing video on an iPad
- *Capacity*: the storage and retrieval of large amounts of material, including online and outside of the setting
- *Range*: access to materials in different forms and from a wider range of sources than otherwise possible, including outside of the setting
- *Provisionality*: the facility to change content and then change back (e.g. undo and redo) if necessary, in other words to 'play' with ideas either as an individual or group
- *Interactivity*: in this definition, the ability to respond to user input repeatedly – without getting bored like a person! (Adapted from Kennewell and Beauchamp, 2007)

Some of these features will be more relevant to practitioners as they plan and prepare work (such as the ability to store large amounts of pre-prepared resources); others may be more useful in engaging the children in learning experiences (such as the speed things appear and the range of resources available from, for instance, the internet); others still may be a feature of the learning experience itself (such as interactivity). They are all, however, also open to children as they work with ICT devices. It is necessary, therefore, to consider the role of ICT in early childhood settings and decide how, when and who should use it. To help with this, we should consider the variety of 'roles' that ICT can play, which will help in allocating these to different 'actors' (people in the classroom). Beauchamp has suggested (2011) a categorisation of ICT use, an adaptation of which is shown in Table 23.1.

Table 23.1   The use of ICT

Category of use	End product
a. A ***passive tool*** for interactions: ICT provides a way of completing a practitioner-directed task or a practitioner using ICT to demonstrate or model activity	Practitioner-led demonstration (normally to whole class) or modelling of task with some limited opportunities for pupils to clarify practitioner control of ICT
	Minimal dialogue/discussion about the nature of task
b. The **object** of interaction: ICT provides something to interact about (e.g. video clip or pupil's work) and the practitioner usually provides the structure for interactions	Dialogue/discussion **about** the digital 'object'
c. A **participant** in interaction: ICT 'joins in' the activity (the activity couldn't be done without ICT) and often sets the tasks and provides immediate feedback (such as a game, quiz or simulation)	Completed task – and perhaps discussion to complete task if more than one person
d. An **active tool** for interaction: ICT allows children to communicate and/or build ideas (e.g. email/chat, annotation, mind-mapping) and **learners** usually provide the structure for interactions e.g. by choosing the tool and/or who to interact with – both people and technology	Dialogue/discussion/learning/co-construction of knowledge

Source: Beauchamp, 2011

When planning the use of ICT, these categories should not be considered as something that lasts through the whole session, or even a whole activity, but rather a learning activity could contain all (or indeed none) of these categories, lasting different periods depending on the learning outcome. In making a decision about how and when to use ICT, or technology in general, you are making an important decision about the locus of control in the setting and therefore who has control over the direction of learning, you or the child.

Case study

A class of 4- and 5-year-olds were investigating the creatures that lived in the grounds of the setting. At the start of the session the practitioner used the interactive whiteboard (IWB) to show pictures of some of the creatures they might find and some of the places in the grounds they might look, although they could look anywhere. [*Passive tool for interactions*] The class was split into groups and each group was given an iPad connected to the school wifi – they had used them before so knew how they worked. The groups then went outside with an adult helper and explored the grounds of the setting, taking pictures and videos of what they found. When they returned, the practitioner used Apple TV to mirror one of the iPads on the IWB and the class looked at the creatures they had found. The class talked about these and tried to identify them. [*Object of interactions*] This was repeated with other iPads from different groups. The practitioner then brought up a website on the IWB with an interactive game naming creatures that they had found. The pupils came to the IWB and tapped on the relevant creature and a sound signified if they were right or wrong. [*Participant in interactions*] At the end of the game, there was one creature they could not identify so the practitioner asked the class how they might find out what it was called. Several pupils suggested emailing a picture of the creature to someone who may know, so the whole class discussed what they should write and the practitioner typed it in an email on the IWB in front of them. Having attached the picture, the practitioner then sent the email and the pupils went out for play. In the playtime, the practitioner accessed the email (cunningly sent to themselves!) and sent a reply to the class. When they returned the practitioner opened the email in front of them and read them the reply before moving on to new activities. [*Active tool for interaction*]

Reflective task

- Using the table below (adapted from Beauchamp, 2012), identify how ICT and different subject 'lenses' could be used in planning a UW activity (such as a trip) of your choosing. Add more lenses as appropriate. Ensure you justify your choices by reflecting on the benefits for the children. A start is suggested:

Table 23.2

Lens	ICT resource
The film-maker	☐ Digital camera (still and movie) or iPad
	☐ Digital editing software – e.g. Movie Maker or iMovie
	☐ IWB for showing end product or iPad – with Apple TV to show on IWB
The musician	☐
The poet	☐
The dancer	☐
The artist	☐
The historian	☐
The geographer	☐
The scientist	☐

In planning activities through an ICT 'lens' it may be appropriate to consider which of the categories of ICT use in Table 23.1 practitioners are intending ICT to play. The main consideration when using ICT is that children are required to 'select and use technology for particular purposes' (DfE, 2014: 12). The key question should perhaps always be: is this use of ICT supporting learning, or is it just an end in itself? If it is the latter, don't use it!

People and communities – past and present events

It is always difficult for young children to understand the past when they cannot conceive that it directly affects them. Cooper (2002: 18) cites Marbeau's argument that 'history at first is the historicisation of a child's own existence' and contends that children 'build continuity into their existence by reciting it to others (and to themselves)'. This reflects a view of history which is based on evidence or an experience, and which is interpreted and then retold to others in a variety of forms (such as written or oral stories, photographs, movies or through art or song) – both separately and combined. To do this effectively, a cross-fertilisation with other areas of the EYFS is necessary, as well as within UW – such as activities in exploring and investigating, which may allow children to notice the effects of change over time (for example, when growing plants).

The key starting point for children is that they find out about past and present events relevant to *their own lives or those of their families*. There are many ways in which they can tell their own stories (including the use of ICT above), and much can be learned about diversity and culture in the process. It is necessary, however, to record a note of caution here as the very fact that these stories are so personal means that they should be handled with care – see 'Reflective tasks' below. If any details emerge that cause concern practitioners should remember that if you have any concerns about a child's safety or welfare you should follow the relevant procedure within the setting as 'If providers have concerns about children's safety or welfare, they must notify agencies with statutory responsibilities without delay.' (DfE, 2014: 17).

When planning activities within this aspect of UW, practitioners need to be aware of the historical processes of enquiry (the historical lens) so that appropriate foundations are laid for subject work as children grow older. Again, we are not considering teaching knowledge of the subject (historical 'facts', such as the year of a particular battle), but considering what skills need to be developed to allow children to become effective historians later in their school life. The following are suggested as processes of enquiry that are appropriate for historians:

- Searching for evidence
- Examining the evidence
- Recording of accounts
- Summarising historical narrative or argument (Turner-Bisset, 2005)

You may well notice that these have much in common with processes in other areas that have already been identified. In considering 'time' activities, the importance of skilful questioning becomes most apparent as you untangle what happened first – often relating events to personal milestones, such as, 'Was this before or after you came into my class?' It should be self-evident that to develop the enquiring skills above, practitioners need to use open-ended questions that encourage children to seek their own answers to questions (both individually and with others), as well as other questions that focus their attention on important details and processes. When planning learning activities, it is always helpful to consider how to develop the processes outlined above and how adequate progression in each can be ensured.

Some examples of relevant progression might be in:

- children's use of language (for example, 'yesterday', 'tomorrow' or 'next week' leading to 'past', 'now' and 'then') – 'learning about the past involves learning vocabulary which is to some extent specific to the history' (Cooper, 2002: 16);
- moving from considering events that affect themselves to those that affect others;
- the ability to sequence ever-longer and more complicated series of events.

People and communities – families, communities and traditions

Work in this area is fundamentally about developing concepts of 'space' and 'place' (Palmer and Birch, 2004) and the position of families, communities and traditions within it. This development will be based on children's existing awareness of the world around them and their place in it; children are 'young geographers with a world inside their head' (Smeaton, 2001: 15). These worlds may, however, vary tremendously based on the experience, or lack of it, children have already had before they come into an early childhood setting. In order both to broaden experience and to provide common ground (both literally and metaphorically), it is common for UW themes to begin with a trip. This could be in the local area or further afield, and the stimulus provides a focus for planning subsequent work – using the brainstorming approach with children, as discussed above ('What do you know already? What do you want to know?'). A shared experience of a new place can provide the basis for an open discussion without any loyalties to street, town or even country influencing views. It also ensures that all children have the same level of exposure to the location – for example, in a study of 'On the farm' it is important to determine whether all of the children have indeed been to a farm and experienced the sights (and smells!). In planning such trips it is important to remember that children's experience will be varied and we cannot take equality of previous experience for granted, even in the area around you, especially in view of the large catchment areas of some settings (for more detail on using areas outside the classroom see Chapter 12).

> ### ☁ Reflective task
>
> Central to the EYFS is the safeguarding of children (see Chapter 14 for more information). In exploring the world around children, in designing and making tools, both inside and outside the setting, there will be times when you need to consider the safety of children as they discover things through using their senses.
>
> - Can you identify any particular situations or types of activity you need to consider in order to keep children safe when planning UW?

One idea for using any area (including inside the setting) is to consider how it can be made 'strangely familiar' (Barnes and Shirley, 2007). This means encouraging the children to explore and express the unique features of the place by representing it through a range of curricular areas, specifically the arts such as poetry, painting and music. In this approach practitioners are again looking at the area of learning though a variety of 'lenses' (for instance, the musician, the film-maker or the dancer) to see how children can be engaged in their own learning, by presenting them with alternative perspectives and new challenges. The role of the practitioner is to act as a facilitator and pass control to the children, as well as providing relevant resources to choose from. In presenting their views of the local area (including their likes and dislikes) children can use sounds, shapes and materials collected from around the area, using video images, still photos (digital and paper), stories, dances, songs, art shows and even sculpture. Such an approach also naturally leads on to, or better still incorporates, an exploration of the communities that make up the area. The end result can be shared with a variety of audiences (including the community) using traditional means (paintings), ICT (websites, slide shows and movies) and live performances (music, drama and dance).

In exploring communities, as we have already mentioned above, the knowledge of families, and key figures within the community, can also be very valuable, as these can often provide first-hand experience and life stories of growing up in, or moving into, the area and different communities. These stories may, however, be deeply personal and revealing, so it is important to allow time for discussion with visitors on what they will be saying before they meet with the children.

> ### ☁ Reflective task
>
> In this chapter there was a warning about how children could reveal personal details in some of the activities. In addition, it was stressed how important it was to know what visiting family or community members may say if talking to the children.

- Consider how you would deal with each of these situations in the following scenarios. Remember to keep the interests of the child at the heart of your reflection but also be very aware of the safeguarding requirements outlined in the EYFS:

  ○ A child is telling their own life story to other children and reveals they had seen their parents killed in front of them before they moved to the country they are now in.

  ○ When you invite a member of the community to come and talk to the children, they tell you that they intend to talk about an issue you consider inappropriate.

  ○ Despite telling you they wouldn't, the person talks about it anyway when they speak to the class.

Summary

Overall, we have seen that understanding the world has unique opportunities in its own right, as well as being inter-connected with other areas of learning and development. The activities that children undertake should contribute to forming effective relationships with others, both within and outside of the setting and the family, including the local community. The singular nature of UW also helps to build foundations for later work in the areas, especially science, geography, history and technology. As stated above, however, this does not mean starting these subjects early, but using their subject 'lenses' to view activities to ensure their specific perspectives are taken into account. By doing this, practitioners are providing unique opportunities for 'igniting children's curiosity and enthusiasm for learning, and for building their capacity to learn, form relationships and thrive' (DfE, 2014: 4).

Key points to remember

- Understanding the world (UW) is a learning area of the EYFS where practitioners can help children develop a set of skills to help them explore the world around them and also in laying the foundation for later work in science, history, geography or technology.

- For young children to develop skills, learning could be viewed through a variety of subject 'lenses' as each of these offers a unique insight into the world. The way these skills are developed depends on good practice, such as the use of questioning and careful, systematic observation.

(Continued)

(Continued)

- UW can become the area in settings where a number of different, creative activities can be hosted.
- UW can be met both within and outside of the setting, using mobile technology if appropriate.

Points for discussion

- Can you identify the unique features, opportunities and approaches provided by UW that do not arise in other areas of learning?
- Is it ever appropriate to use ICT (such as an interactive whiteboard or iPad) in place of 'real' objects, such as plants and creatures? If so, when and why? If not, what do the real objects offer that ICT cannot?
- Can you see young children using ICT to explore the outdoor environment and how?

Further reading

Books

Beauchamp, G. (2012) 'ICT in the early years', in *ICT in the Primary School: From Pedagogy to Practice*. London: Pearson.

Price, H. (ed.) (2008) *The Really Useful Book of ICT in the Early Years*. London: Routledge.

Article

Cremin, T., Glauert, E., Craft, A., Compton, A. and Stylianidou, F. (2015) 'Creative Little Scientists: exploring pedagogical synergies between inquiry-based and creative approaches in Early Years science', *Education 3–13: International Journal of Primary, Elementary and Early Years Education*, 43 (4): 404–19.

Useful websites

Homerton Early Years Centre provides a wide range of resources for planning and using ICT within the early years:
http://homerton.cambs.sch.uk/information-for-practitioners/ict-in-the-early-years/

References

Aubrey, C. and Dahl, S. (2008) *Parents as Partners in Education*. Coventry: Creative Partnerships.

Aubrey, C. and Dahl, S. (2014) 'The confidence and competence in information and communication technologies of practitioners. Parents and young children in the Early Years Foundation Stage', *Early Years*, 34 (1): 94–108.

Barnes, J. (2007) *Cross-curricular Learning 3–14*. London: Paul Chapman Publishing.

Barnes, J. and Shirley, I. (2007) 'Strangely familiar: cross-curricular and creative thinking in teacher education', *Improving Schools*, 10 (2): 162–79.

Beauchamp, G. (2006) 'New technologies and "New teaching": a process of evolution?', in R. Webb (ed.), *Changing Teaching and Learning in the Primary School*. Maidenhead: Open University Press. pp. 81–91.

Beauchamp, G. (2011) 'Interactivity and ICT in the primary school: categories of learner interactions with and without ICT', *Technology, Pedagogy and Education*, 20 (2): 175–90.

Beauchamp, G. (2012) *ICT in the Primary School: From Pedagogy to Practice*. London: Pearson.

Cooper, H. (2002) *History in the Early Years*, 2nd edn. London: Routledge Falmer.

Cremin, T., Glauert, E., Craft, A., Compton, A. and Stylianidou, F. (2015) 'Creative Little Scientists: exploring pedagogical synergies between inquiry-based and creative approaches in Early Years science', *Education 3–13: International Journal of Primary, Elementary and Early Years Education*, 43 (4): 404–19.

de Boo, M. (2000) *Science 3–6: Laying the Foundations in the Early Years*. Hatfield: ASE.

Desforges, C. and Abouchaar, A. (2003) *The Impact of Parental Involvement, Parental Support and Family Education on Pupil Achievement and Adjustment: A Literature Review*. Research Report No. RR 433. Norwich: HMSO.

DfE (Department for Education) (2014) *Statutory Framework for the Early Years Foundation Stage: Setting the Standards for Learning, Development and Care for Children from Birth to Five*. London: DfE. Available at: www.foundationyears.org.uk/files/2014/07/EYFS_framework_from_1_September_2014__with_clarification_note.pdf (accessed 28 September 2015).

Feasey, R. and Gallear, B. (2001) *Primary Science and ICT*. Hatfield: ASE.

Fisher, J. (2002) *Starting from the Child: Teaching and Learning from 3 to 8*, 2nd edn. Maidenhead: Open University Press.

Goswami, U. and Bryant, P. (2007) *Children's Cognitive Development and Learning* (Primary Review Research Survey 2/1a). Cambridge: University of Cambridge Faculty of Education.

Harlen, W. (2003) *The Teaching of Science in Primary School*, 3rd edn. London: David Fulton.

Hayes, M. (2006) 'What do the children have to say?', in M. Hayes and D. Whitebread (eds), *ICT in the Early Years*. Maidenhead: Open University Press.

Kennewell, S. and Beauchamp, G. (2007) 'The features of interactive whiteboards and their influence on learning', *Learning, Media and Technology*, 32 (3): 227–41.

Myhill, D., Jones, S. and Hopper, R. (2006) *Talking, Listening, Learning: Effective Talk in the Primary Classroom*. Maidenhead: Open University Press.

O'Hara, M. (2008) 'Young children, learning and ICT: a case study in the UK maintained sector', *Technology, Pedagogy and Education*, 17 (1): 29–40.

Palmer, J. and Birch, J. (2004) *Geography in the Early Years*, 2nd edn. London: Routledge Falmer.

Perkins, D.N. (1997) 'Person-plus: a distributed view of thinking and learning', in G. Salomon (ed.), *Distributed Cognitions: Psychological and Educational Considerations*. Cambridge: Cambridge University Press. pp. 88–110.

Siraj-Blatchford, I., Sylva, K., Muttock, S., Gilden, R. and Bell, D. (2002) *Researching Effective Pedagogy in the Early Years*. Research Report No. RR 356. Norwich: TSO.

Smeaton, M. (2001) 'Questioning geography', in R. Carter (ed.), *Handbook of Primary Geography*. Sheffield: Geographical Association. pp. 15–17.

Tickell, C. (2011) *The Early Years: Foundations for Life, Health and Learning.* An Independent Report on the Early Years Foundation Stage to Her Majesty's Government. London: Crown. Available at: www.education.gov.uk/tickellreview (accessed July 2012).

Turner-Bisset, R. (2005) *Creative Teaching: History in the Primary Classroom.* London: David Fulton.

Want to learn more about this chapter? Visit the companion website at https://study.sagepub.com/EYFS3e for access to free SAGE journal articles and book chapters, weblinks, annotated further readings and more.

24

Physical Development

Ioanna Palaiologou

 Chapter overview

One of the most important characteristics in a child's life is the physical activity that takes place during their early childhood. Bruner (1983: 121) emphasised the importance of physical activity in young children and claimed that the physical activities of a child are part of their 'culture of childhood'. A number of theorists that have been explored throughout this book have discussed in detail the importance of the physical aspects of a child's life. Piaget, for example, states that children start their development from a sensory motor stage where they acquire sensory schemata. Currently, the importance of physical literacy is being discussed more than ever, as is the integration of physical activity into curricular approaches as an essential aspect of children's overall, and therefore holistic, development (Parry, 1998; Bailey, 1999; Talbot, 1999; Almond, 2000).

The Early Years Foundation Stage (EYFS) sets the physical development of children as one of the prime areas of learning and development. Aspects of physical development are stated as being moving and handling, and health and self-care (DfE, 2014: 8).

This chapter aims to help you to understand:

- the importance of the physical and biological development of children
- the impact of physical development on children's health and well-being
- how physical development can be enhanced in early years settings.

Physical and biological growth

When children are born, they display a number of skills crucial to their survival. In the first few months of infants' lives reflexes play an important role in physical development; they help infants to build social relationships, essential to all other aspects of their development. Infants' reflexes, such as breathing, sucking, swallowing and blinking, help babies and parents to establish interactions. When babies grasp a parent's fingers, for example, parents respond and encourage these behaviours, and this is the start of an intimate relationship.

Around the age of 6 months babies begin losing these reflexes. Gradually, as the brain matures, the reflexes become voluntary control behaviours. This is a complex developmental task. For example, initially babies suck the bottle or the mother's breast as an automatic reflex, yet at around the age of 6 months they are able to combine their vision with arm movement and eventually reach for the bottle or the mother's breast by themselves.

One of the aspects in the physical development of children, as stated in the EYFS, is that of movement. The motor development of children is divided between 'gross' and 'fine' motor development. 'Gross' motor development refers to all spatial movements used by children to manoeuvre around their environment, such as crawling, sitting, walking and, eventually, running, jumping and climbing. 'Fine' motor development concerns all of the smaller and more intricate movements, such as grasping, building a tower with cubes, putting objects into boxes, drawing and writing.

During their early years children are undergoing rapid physical development. There are changes in the size and proportions of the body with both skeletal and hormonal growth. During this period children display tireless physical activity, thus it is essential for children to be provided with the space in which to move freely and safely as well as with activities to encourage their developing movements. Hale (1994), among other researchers (Parry, 1998; Bailey, 1999; Talbot, 1999; Almond, 2000; Doherty and Bailey, 2003), emphasises the importance of an enriched and stimulating environment that helps children to engage with physical activity, because an active, supportive environment makes children feel comfortable and leads to their learning.

Children learn constantly by moving. They touch, feel, smell, move around and have fun 'translating movements into spoken language' in a variety of contexts (Hopper et al., 2000: 1). Physical activity is the best way for children to experience the world around them, practising skills, gaining in confidence by achieving, and making explorations through motor play such as running, walking, jumping, climbing, catching or throwing.

Much of children's play is characterised by movement and it is impossible to keep young children from running or to force them to sit down for long periods of time. When children are given opportunities to move around freely at home or in early childhood settings they engage in constant motor play. Activities such as songs with movements, role-playing involving movement, climbing, jumping and balancing are among the favourite activities in early childhood settings. All of their play is characterised by constant movement.

Brain growth

Essential to physical development is the development of the brain. The brain regulates all areas of development. As has been shown in Chapter 6, neuroscientific evidence has an impact on pedagogy, and has helped us to understand the importance of brain growth in all aspects of children's learning and development.

The first years of a child's life are very important for brain development. A baby's brain develops at an astonishing rate in the first three years, such that by the age of 3 years a child's brain is as complex as it will ever be (Shore, 1997). The brain comprises billions of nerve cells (neurons) designed to send and retrieve information across organs and muscles. An important process in the growth of the brain is the development of synapses. All of the billions of neurons are rapidly connected to each other in the first years of life.

As can be seen in Figure 24.1, during the first six years there is a rapid development of synapses in the human brain. The number of new synapses decreases as children enter adolescence, however, and then adulthood. Babies acquire more synapses than they will need. After the age of 3 years some connections are lost. For example, a typical 18-year-old has lost half of the synapses acquired in early childhood. Synapses in the brain that are unused disappear. It is inevitable that an individual wonders why we could do certain things when we were children that we cannot do now as adults. Shore (1997) argues that synapses are eliminated if they are not used, which has implications for the continuation of a stimulating environment. For example, if children fail to continue being physically active, they will become less interested in physical activity and it is less likely to become part of their adult lives. Kimm et al. (2002) found that by the age of 15 one in five English girls exercise for no more than sixty minutes a week. In Western societies teenagers spend more than five hours a day watching television, at computer screens and playing video games (Hardman and Stensel, 2003).

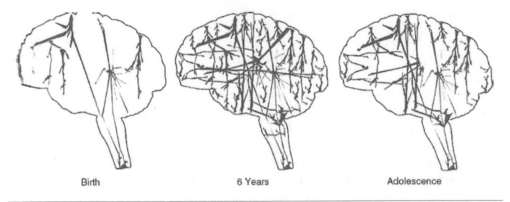

Birth   6 Years   Adolescence

Figure 24.1   *The development of synapses in early childhood (after Chugani, 1997)*

Growing up in urban apartment buildings, with fewer opportunities for physical development, movement and activity, may create a loss of those synapses responsible for physical activity. It is crucial that physical activity be promoted from a very early age; there is emphasis on continuing children's physical activity for their progression.

As illustrated in Figure 24.1, the first six years of a child's life are important for brain development. This period is considered as 'prime time' for neuron growth. Shore (1997: 26) suggests that the primary responsibility of parents and care providers is 'day to day care of young children's brains'. The care of the brain is accomplished through the creating of a stimulating environment. Early stimulation is important for helping children to achieve their developmental potential and for promoting infant brain growth. Providing a number of opportunities for physical and cognitive development will enhance the formation of synapses in the brain, then the continuation of stimulation will prevent the loss of these synapses.

The study of brain growth has given researchers an understanding of many aspects of children's development. Chapters 11 and 19, for example, discussed the importance of 'attachment' during early childhood. It is known that infants under stress, or infants who suffer from anxiety, are more likely to produce a hormone called cortisol (Hertsgaard et al., 1995; Nachmias et al., 1996). When this hormone is produced, the brain is threatened and reduces the synapses, leaving neurons vulnerable to damage. Gunnar (2001) found that when infants form secure relationships with their parents and their carers, the levels of cortisol are kept low. A warm and secure environment with parents and with other care-givers – an environment where the children are playing happily with stimulation – helps positively towards the physical development of their brain.

Studies into the development of the brain have offered an extensive knowledge and understanding of children's development, not only as regards the physical development of children, but other aspects, such as language (as shown in Chapter 20), numeracy (Chapter 22) and creativity (Chapter 25). Knowing about rapid brain growth in the infancy of a child helps early childhood practitioners to create environments where children are stimulated and their development promoted.

Cultural influences on children's physical development

Although children's physical development follows similar patterns and stages across the world, cross-cultural research demonstrates how the respective environment contributes to motor development. In a study conducted by Dennis (1960), babies in Iranian orphanages were observed. These babies were deprived and Dennis observed that they were spending a lot of time lying in cots with no toys available to them. After several observations he found that these babies delayed movement until they were 2 years of age. When they finally moved, the experience of constantly lying on their backs led them to remain in a sitting position, rather than crawling as children normally do.

In a later study, Hopkins and Westra (1988) studied babies around the world and found that in some cultures there is an emphasis on children starting to move from an early stage. They found that in Western India, for example, the parents have a routine in which they exercise their babies daily. From the first months, parents exercise their babies by stretching each arm while suspending the baby, or holding the baby upside down by the ankles. However much these routines may surprise us, Hopkins and Westra found through interviewing the mothers that it is embedded in their culture for them to help their babies to grow physically strong, healthy and attractive.

In Kenya, Kipsigi parents deliberately teach children motor skills. In the first few months babies are rolled in blankets to keep them upright then seated in holes dug into the ground. Walking is promoted by frequently bouncing babies on their feet (Super, 1981). It was observed that these babies walk earlier than do babies in economically more developed societies.

Levels of physical activity vary by culture. A study of Puerto Rican and Euro-American mothers revealed that children's physical activities were rated more highly by Puerto Rican mothers, while the Euro-American mothers characterised physical activity as undesirable (Harwood et al., 1995).

When working with children from different cultural backgrounds, it is important to understand cultural differences. As it is important to work in partnership with parents, their values and beliefs need to be understood and channels of communication need to be developed, so the parents will feel comfortable with the level of their children's physical activity in the early childhood setting.

In the modern Western world there is a trend to emphasise academic development of children, whereas there is far less emphasis on physical activity. Children are supported and encouraged when they try to be physically active during early childhood, but this is limited later when formal schooling is starting and the focus on the children's academic progress is more intense.

It is noticed that there is a lack of physical activity among children when they grow older. The World Health Organisation (1999) states: 'in many developed countries, less than one third of young children and people are sufficiently active to benefit their present and future health'. It is a positive point that the EYFS clearly views physical activity of children as being important for children's development, a foundation on which children can build confidence and acquire habits leading to a healthy lifestyle. The EYFS (DfE, 2014) identifies physical development as a prime area for children's learning and development, and the two key aspects are: moving and handling, and health and self-care. The Integrated Review at Age Two aims to assess children's physical development as a means of early identification of 'any areas where the child's progress is less than expected' (DfE, 2014: 10). The age 2 integrated review can become an indicator of any areas of concern that the child 'may have developmental delay' (DfE, 2014: 10) and strategies can be put in place in order that children can be offered opportunities to be physically active, both indoors and outdoors, as a significant factor in brain muscle fibre development as well as their overall physical development.

Health and well-being

Within the EYFS, central to physical development is helping children to learn what healthy living is and to sustain attitudes towards healthy living. Chapter 15 explored the medical approach and requirements for what constitutes a healthy child. In this section we focus on health and physical development. As discussed above, children are physically active during early childhood, but they do not sustain this level of activity as they grow older. Hardman and Stensel (2003) state that three modern trends – obesity, physical inactivity and an ageing population – are the main 'diseases' of the twenty-first century and highlight the importance of physical activity.

As mentioned in Chapter 15, obesity has increased rapidly over the past two decades. More and more children are overweight. There are a number of factors involved in the increase of obesity, such as eating habits, poor nutrition and lack of physical activity. A number of researchers, however, link obesity with physical inactivity rather than with overeating (Prentice and Jebb, 1995; Baur, 2002; Kimm et al., 2002). Given that most children are brought up in urban settings with a lack of space in which to move around, children tend to adopt alternative ways to play, such as with computer and video games. It is important to create opportunities for young children to be able to be physically active. The activities around physical development should appeal to children and be enjoyable for them. Contextualised activities, such as catching and throwing in games situations, or more complex activities such as singing, dancing and swimming (where movements by children are required), promote their physical development.

Doherty and Bailey (2003) suggest that activities designed to promote physical development within early childhood settings should be characterised first and foremost by enjoyment. Children should want to take part in these activities and have fun. Such activities should be continued throughout the curriculum and not only during early childhood. By promoting physical activities across all ages a 'firm foundation base of movement experience' (DCSF, 2008) is established from a very young age.

Doherty and Bailey (2003) also suggest that children should, on a daily basis, become involved in physical activities if the aim is to develop physical activity as a lifelong habit for health and well-being. Children should have the freedom to choose the activities and the materials, according to their personal interests and physical skills.

Children's physical development and brain growth are important in order to sustain good health and well-being in children's lives. Young children should acquire habits of healthy living from an early age. There are many factors influencing a child's health and well-being, such as nutrition, emotional health, the structure of the family and the structure of their communities, which combine to contribute to children's physical, biological, mental and sexual health.

The physical activities of children help them to sustain a healthy lifestyle. In their study, Biddle et al. (1998: 4–5) highlight the benefits of physical activity. They claim that physical activity leads to psychological well-being, the increase of self-esteem, contributes to children's moral and social development, and prevents obesity, chronic disease and risk factors. Thus, it is essential that children in their daily routine are provided with opportunities to be physically active, that they have adults who are supportive and who facilitate children to move and, of course, most importantly, that children are given time to be physically active and to be able to play within early childhood.

Whitehead extends this idea by introducing the concept of 'physically literate' children. He claims that children who are physically active, become physically literate:

> The characteristics of a physically literate individual are that the person moves with poise, economy and confidence, in a wide variety of physically challenging situations. In addition the individual is perceptive in 'reading' all aspects of the physical environment, anticipating movement needs or possibilities and responding appropriately to these with intelligence and imagination. Physical literacy requires a holistic engagement that encompasses physical capacities embedded in perception, experience, memory, anticipation and decision making. (2000: 10)

Whitehead emphasises the importance of a challenging environment where children are offered opportunities to move in a way that stimulates them and where, at the same time, they can experience enjoyment. He also suggests that physical activities are linked with other areas of development. For example, when children are having a dance activity or play in the water area, they are not only physically active but they are engaged in a number of cognitive activities such as language development ('let's put our hands up', 'let's move around in a circle', 'let's move in a line') or problem solving activities ('let's throw objects in the water that float or objects in the water that sink'). Central to this is the creation of an environment that promotes physical activities.

The role of the environment

Before exploring the role of the environment in children's physical development it is important to understand what a 'healthy environment' means. Nutbeam (1998: 362) characterises a healthy environment as 'a place or social context in which people engage in daily activities, in which environmental, organizational and personal factors interact to affect health and well-being'.

A healthy environment has many forms and is influenced by cultural values and practices. In some families, for example, the home environment is redesigned and furniture is moved so children can move freely and have space to play; in other families children have rules about what they may touch and where they can go to play. It is not necessarily the case that one situation is 'wrong' and the other is 'right'. Physical activity and the space around children are related to the families' values. In the second situation it could be argued that in this way children learn about rules, learn about what is right and what is not, learn about safety from a very young age, and learn about their limitations.

A classic study conducted by Levine (1996) showed the diversity of strategies used in the world to provide healthy and safe environments for children. He observed different tribes and different cultures around the world and he offers a case from Kenya. In Kenya, babies and young children spent a lot of time outdoors as mothers were involved in their daily chores. Leaving young children outdoors without supervision seemed to hold many risks, as they could burn themselves in cooking fires, fall off cliffs or into lakes, or suffer snakebite. He found, however, that the parents in one village studied protected their children by carrying them on their backs and allowed them to be outdoors, without supervision, only when they were old enough to understand rules and the dangers around them.

Cultural aspects have an impact on physical development in terms of choosing outdoor or indoor environments. In the following case studies from three different curricular approaches, it can be seen how the indoor and outdoor environments are used to promote children's physical development.

Case study

Arts to promote physical development: example from Reggio Emilia

In the Reggio Emilia approach the artistic development of children is central. Gandini (1997) describes activities such as drawing, painting, sculpting and singing as fundamental methods for children's learning, at the same time as they enhance the physical development of children (i.e. gross motor development and fine motor development). Gandini describes the arts as essential not only to children's cognitive development, but as a major part of children's physical development.

The arts can help children more with their personal, social and creative development. Children, after a visit to a museum or gallery, can use materials to express themselves and experiment with water, painting, sculpting, etc., and all these activities require sophisticated and complex movements. Consequently, their physical development is shaped in a contextualised environment. Children's movements are viewed as creative; there are no constraints in time and space, and children can take as much time or space as they need in which to express themselves.

Physical development in a Te Whāriki class

The Te Whāriki curriculum has been introduced in New Zealand's early childhood settings. Emphasising multiculturalism and allowing children the freedom to choose materials and activities, it promotes children's having ownership of their own learning. This curriculum approach views children as 'competent and confident learners and communicators, healthy in mind, body and spirit, secure in their sense of belonging and in the knowledge that they make a valued contribution to society' (Ministry of Education, 1996).

A Te Whāriki class, similarly to the EYFS, is underpinned by five goals: well-being, belonging, contribution, communication and exploration. In a Te Whāriki class children move freely between indoors and outdoors, and choose which materials to play with. In the sand area they can make castles, whereas in another area they can make solid objects, such as chairs, using a number of tools that develop their fine motor skills.

Figure 24.2 *Children playing outdoors: practising balancing*

(Continued)

(Continued)

Figure 24.3 *Practising climbing*

Outdoors, children are offered opportunities to practise climbing, running and jumping, either individually or in small groups. The Te Whāriki outdoors environment is rich in real objects and thus encourages and motivates children to engage in physical activity through play (see Figures 24.2 to 24.5). They create tunnels from car tyres for children to crawl through, swings and water points, where they can 'splash about'.

Inside the class, singing is accompanied by physical movement, such as children imitating waves by using their bodies and their hands. The children have the opportunity to move constantly and to use a number of materials. In a corner of the room there are clothes for dressing up, and this way the children's motor skills are developed.

Physical exploration of different materials meets one of the main principles in the Te Whāriki approach: Kotahitanga ('holistic development'), where the child is viewed as a 'whole'. It is emphasised that the child learns in a holistic way by taking into consideration not only the child's physical, social, emotional and cognitive development, but also the cultural context and the spiritual aspects of the children's environment.

Figure 24.4   *Children running outdoors*

Reflective tasks

- Consider an early childhood setting you are familiar with and reflect on the daily activities. Are children engaged physically (fine or gross motor skills)?

- More than ever, emphasis is placed on health and healthy environments. In your view what is a healthy environment and how can you promote that in your setting?

- Reflect on the case studies and think how indoors and outdoors are used in an early childhood setting within the EYFS.

Summary

This chapter discussed the importance of physical development for children's holistic development. Children's play is characterised by movement, and it should be encouraged. The physical activity of children is important to all aspects of their learning. Additionally, brain growth in early childhood is rapid. The formation of synapses between neurons is happening far more rapidly in the first few years of a child's life than later. This has implications when an environment is created for young children. Children's concepts of healthy living and well-being are strongly related to the enjoyment of physical movement. If adults want children to acquire healthy living styles then physical activity has to become a lifelong habit. Only when they are pleasurable will children wish to carry out physical activities.

Key points to remember

- Physical development of children is a prime area of the EYFS and the two important key elements are moving and handling, and health and self-care. More than ever, emphasis is placed on children's physical activity as a way of children acquiring healthy habits.

- Physical development is influenced by a number of factors, such as culture and the social and economic context in which children are growing.

- Early childhood education and care should offer numerous opportunities to children to enhance their physical development. Opportunities for physical development should be embedded in the daily life and activities of the early childhood setting and it should underpin all the activities, as was demonstrated in the case studies.

Points for discussion

- Look at the plan in Figure 24.6. Consider that this is the room you have been given in which to work with 2-year-old children. How are you going to design the environment so that you can promote children's physical development? In your new design you need to consider whether there is sufficient space for children to move around, what equipment you will have, and how you will redesign and resource your room. Do children have access to outdoor areas so they can move in and out?

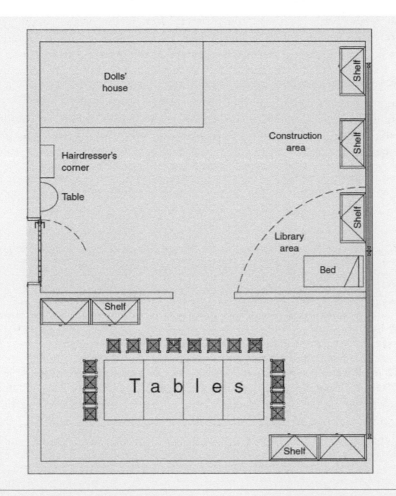

Figure 24.5 *Floor plan of a nursery*

- Bilton (2003: 38) suggests that when organising work in the outdoor environment the following should be considered:

  o layout of the environment

  o the amount of space available

  o the use of fixed equipment

(Continued)

(Continued)

- o the weather element
- o the need for storage.

Can you think of any other aspects when you organise activity in the outdoor environment? What activities can you plan that will offer appropriate physical challenges to children?

- After studying Chapter 12, compare a Reggio Emilia, a Te Whāriki, a Forest school and an early childhood setting within the EYFS. Where do they differ and where are they similar in promoting the physical movement of children?

Further reading

Archer, C. and Siraj, I. (2015) *Encouraging Physical Development Through Movement Play*. London: Sage.

Bilton, H. (2010) *Outdoor Learning in the Early Years*. London: Routledge.

Knight, S. (2011) *Forest School for All*. London: Sage.

Nurse, A. (2009) *Physical Development in the Early Years Foundation Stage*. London: David Fulton.

Warden, C. (2015) *Learning with Nature*. London: Sage.

Useful websites

Forest Schools:
www.forestschools.com/index.php

Institute of Outdoor Learning (IOL):
www.outdoor-learning.org

Outdoor play in Europe: this is the official website of the European Institute of Outdoor Adventure Education and Experiential Learning (EOE):
www.eoe-network.org

References

Almond, L. (2000) 'Physical education and primary schools', in P.R. Bailey and T.M. Macfadyen (eds), *Teaching Physical Education 5–11*. London: Continuum.

Bailey, P.R. (1999) 'Play, health and physical development', in T. David (ed.), *Young Children Learning*. London: Paul Chapman Publishing.

Baur, L.A. (2002) 'Child and adolescent obesity in the 21st century: an Australian perspective', *Asia Pacific Journal of Clinical Nutrition*, 11: 524–8.

Biddle, S., Cavill, N. and Sallis, J. (1998) 'Policy framework for young people and health-enhancing physical activity', in S. Biddle, J. Sallis and N. Cavill (eds), *Young and Active? Young People and Health Enhancing Physical Activity: Evidence and Implications*. London: Health Education Authority.

Bilton, H. (2003) *Outdoor Play in the Early Years*, 2nd edn. London: David Fulton.

Bruner, J. (1983) *Child's Talk: Learning to Use Language*. Oxford: Oxford University Press.

Chugani, H.T. (1997) 'Neuroimaging of developmental nonlinearity and developmental pathologies', in R.W. Thatcher, G.R. Lyon, R. Rumsey and N. Krasnegor (eds), *Developmental Neuroimaging: Mapping the Development of Brain and Behaviour*. San Diego, CA: Academic Press.

DCSF (Department for Children, Schools and Families) (2008) *The Early Years Foundation Stage: Setting the Standards for Learning, Development and Care for Children from Birth to Five*. Nottingham: DCSF Publications.

Dennis, W. (1960) 'The effects of cradling practices upon the onset of walking in Hopi children', *Journal of Genetic Psychology*, 56: 77–86.

DfE (Department for Education) (2014) *Statutory Framework for the Early Years Foundation Stage: Setting the Standards for Learning, Development and case for Children from Birth to Five*. London: DfE. Available at: www.foundationyears.org.uk/files/2014/07/EYFS_framework_from_1_September_2014__with_clarification_note.pdf (accessed 28 September 2015).

Doherty, J. and Bailey, R. (2003) *Supporting Physical Development and Physical Education in the Early Years*. Buckingham: Open University Press.

Gandini, L. (1997) 'The Reggio Emilia story: history and organization', in J. Hendrick (ed.), *First Steps Towards Teaching the Reggio Emilia Way*. Englewood Cliffs, NJ: Merrill/Prentice–Hill.

Gunnar, M.R. (2001) *Quality of Care and Buffering Stress Psychology: Its Potential for Protecting the Developing Human Brain*. Minneapolis, MN: University of Minnesota Institute of Child Development.

Hale, J. (1994) *Unbank the Fire: Visions for the Education of African American Children*. Baltimore, MD: Johns Hopkins University Press.

Hardman, A. and Stensel, D. (2003) *Physical Activity and Health*. London: Routledge.

Harwood, R.L., Miller, J.G. and Irizarry, N.L. (1995) *Culture and Attachment: Perceptions of the Child in Context*. New York: Guilford Press.

Hertsgaard, L., Gunnar, M., Erickson, M.F. and Nachmias, M. (1995) 'Adrenocortical responses to the strange situation in infants with disorganized, disoriented attachment relationships', *Child Development*, 66: 1100–6.

Hopkins, B. and Westra, T. (1988) 'Maternal handling and motor development: an intracultural study', *Genetic, Social and General Psychology Monographs*, 14: 377–420.

Hopper, B., Grey, J. and Maude, T. (2000) *Teaching Physical Education in the Primary School*. London: Routledge Falmer.

Kimm, S.Y.S., Glynn, N.W., Barton, B.A., Kronsberg, S.S., Daniels, S.R., Crawford, P.B., Sabry, Z.I. and Liu, K. (2002) 'Decline in physical activity in black girls and white girls during adolescence', *New England Journal of Medicine*, 347: 709–15.

Levine, R.A. (1996) *Child Care and Culture Lessons from Africa*. Cambridge: Cambridge University Press.

Ministry of Education (New Zealand) (1996) *Te Whāriki. He Whāriki Matauranga mo nga Mokopuna O Aotearoa. Early Childhood Education*. Learning Media. www.minedu.govt.nz/web/downloadable/dl3567_v1/whariki.pdf (accessed December 2008).

Nachmias, M., Gunnar, M., Mangelsdorf, S., Parritz, R.H. and Buss, K. (1996) 'Behavioral inhabitation and stress reactivity: the moderating role of attachment security', *Child Development*, 67: 508–22.

Nutbeam, D. (1998) 'Evaluating health promotion – progress, problems and solutions', *Health Promotion International*, 13: 27–43.

Parry, J. (1998) 'The justification for physical education', in K. Green and K. Hardman (eds), *Physical Education: A Reader*. Aachen: Meyer & Meyer.

Prentice, A.M. and Jebb, S.A. (1995) 'Obesity in Britain: gluttony or sloth?', *British Medical Journal*, 311: 437–9.

Shore, N. (1997) *Rethinking the Brain: New Insights into Early Development*. New York: Families and Work Institute.

Super, C.M. (1981) 'Behavioural development in infancy', in R.H. Monroe, R.L. Monroe and B.B. Whiting (eds), *Handbook of Cross Cultural Human Development*. New York: Garland.

Talbot, M. (1999) 'The case for physical education'. Paper presented at the World Summit on Physical Education, Berlin, November.

Whitehead, M. (2000) 'The concept of physical literacy'. Paper presented to the HEI Conference, 'Meeting Standards and Achieving Excellence. Teaching PE in the 21st Century', Liverpool John Moores University, 11 June.

World Health Organisation (1999) 'Health Promotion, Active Living: The Challenge Ahead'. [Online] www.who.int (accessed September 2008).

Want to learn more about this chapter? Visit the companion website at https://study.sagepub.com/EYFS3e for access to free SAGE journal articles and book chapters, weblinks, annotated further readings and more.

25

Expressive Arts and Design

Nick Owen, Laura Grindley and Michiko Fujii

 Chapter overview

Although the EYFS (DfE, 2014) replaced the creative development area of learning with the expressive arts and design prime area, with emphasis on exploring and using media and materials, and being imaginative, it is still important to creativity for children to engage in arts, music, movement, dance and role-play. It is stated in the EYFS:

> Expressive arts and design involves enabling children to explore and play with a wide range of media and materials, as well as providing opportunities and encouragement for sharing their thoughts, ideas and feelings through a variety of activities in art, music, movement, dance, role-play, and design and technology. (DfE 2014: 8)

In this chapter, however, it is viewed that expressive arts and design is only one aspect of creativity. Arts is an important element of creativity, thus the focus will be to discuss creativity as an important element of children's intellectual, emotional, social and cognitive development.

This chapter aims to show that 'being creative' in early childhood settings is a rich, extensive and common form of human expression and explores how we can promote creative practice. A particular model of expressive arts activities will be

(Continued)

(Continued)

highlighted – the Midas Touch Creative Learning Project – to identify the mindset and skills necessary to optimise children's creative learning experiences.

The activities that will be discussed will reflect the principle that creative practice is not a domain exclusive to arts practice and the importance of collaboration will be stressed. It is suggested that instead of interpreting creativity solely as an attribute of individuals, creativity arises from the gravitational pull of relationships; it is thus a situational and contextual phenomenon, as opposed to an individual or psycho-logical one. Collaboration stresses the need for the co-intentional imaginations of adults and children to embrace, together, attitudes of improvisation, keeping an eye open for the off-chance, taking the occasional, unassessed risk and accepting the generation of and pleasure in 'mess'.

This chapter aims to help you to:

- understand that creative practice can be developed in all areas of early childhood settings and is not exclusive to arts practice
- undertake activities that form the basis in a setting of an action research project, which aims to address a 'creativity challenge'
- appreciate the contextual factors that have informed the development of contemporary creative practice in settings.

Developing creative practice: what's all the fuss about?

The notion of developing children's creativity has never been far off the political agenda in recent years. The educational establishment has frequently been required by politicians to come up with more and better methods to make sure not only that children are more creative, but that creativity is part of the daily routine, especially within the early childhood environment.

More jobs, more wealth, more growth, more prosperity: the drive towards creative nirvana is fuelled by the political expediency of economic growth, an element clearly identified in the 1999 NACCCE report on creativity and cultural education, *All Our Futures*. That report produced an almost canonical definition of creativity – 'imaginative activity fashioned so as to produce outcomes that are both original and of value' (Robinson, 1999: 30) and subsequently many educationalists have applied themselves in recent years to thinking how to get more creative bang for the always-limited educational buck. Do we achieve it by amending learning outcomes, rewriting the

Foundation Stage curriculum, training practitioners to be more creative and building new Children's Centres? Or do we do it by being completely child-centred in our outlook – an outlook that privileges the ideas of the children over the ideas of adults, one that interprets all children's views and attitudes as the sacrosanct voice of the pure, unadulterated human being and witnesses the holy grail of creativity in the play and expression of very young children, for whom the world is a perpetual mystery? How can we promote creative development without stifling it?

Ironically, there are two easy routes to stifling creativity in young children.

- *Route One*: say 'no' to everything they suggest, muse on, play with and are curious about. Be sure to block initiative, stifle unacceptable behaviour and generate fear about the consequences of their actions. Worry them about their appearance, their status in other people's eyes, and what their attitudes and behaviour might rather say about *you* than it might about *them.*
- *Route Two*: say 'yes' to everything they suggest, muse on, play with and are curious about. Be sure they understand there are no such things as boundaries of any sort, that all kinds of behaviour in any circumstances are completely acceptable. Encourage them to think that all of their ideas are perfect and require no further modification from any other source at all. Offer free, unconditional, unending praise for any kind of behaviour and have an unending supply of house points for every time they do something you deem creative.

Creativity development in early childhood settings – if it is to encourage and challenge children's experiences of creativity – needs to inhabit a place, however, somewhere in between the extremes set out by those two approaches and steps can be taken to ensure that a child stands the best possible chance of undertaking and completing the creative development journey. Making a child 'more creative' is not as tangible as letting their hair grow longer or passing an examination; it is about offering time and space to understand and experience the processes involved – which need personal qualities of application, struggle and testing, alongside the social qualities of cooperation, collaboration and mutual criticism. To accomplish all of that needs the presence of an element far more important than a paintbrush, a guitar or a pair of ballet shoes, it needs *you* – another human being.

Creative relationships

Understanding creativity has been introduced into many settings in recent years through Anna Cutler's work on the Four-Phase Stepped Progression model of creative learning. This model suggests what we might look for when it comes to encouraging our children's creativity and approaches to learning. These are simply entitled *Input, Doing, Showing* and *Reflecting* (see Figure 25.1).

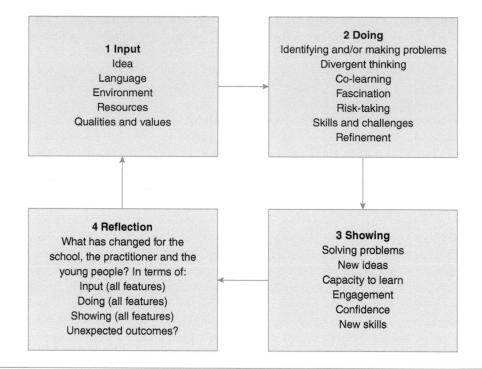

Figure 25.1 *A four-phase stepped progression model of creative learning (Cutler, 2005)*

Cutler (2005) lists seven features required for creative learning within the Doing phase of the model: the ability to identify and/or to make problems, the ability to think divergently (opening the mind to new, surprising, unusual and perhaps uncomfortable ideas), attributes such as being open to experiences of fascination and curiosity, the ability to take risks, to play with and to suggest. These would occur in a climate marked by an absence of fear and in which children find pleasure in their endeavours for their own sake, as opposed to an anxious educational agenda that might be hovering over their shoulders. Briefly, the key questions characterising these seven features can be summarised as follows:

Identifying problems: Does this project seek to challenge any issues? What kinds of problems might the project bring up and will these be an important part of the experience for everyone? How will such issues be handled?

Divergent thinking: How does the project offer different and original ways of thinking, different perspectives and opportunities for the novel use of the imagination? What unusual elements or ideas can be put together, and how can people try them out?

Co-learning: How do practitioners work with children and staff in a situation where all participants are learning something new together, or where practitioners are learning with the children from doing things together?

Fascination: How is this generated by the activity? Is it sustained beyond the project hours?

Risk-taking: Is the project able to offer something beyond the comfort zone of the individuals concerned? Is the project offering opportunities for risk-taking in practice?

Skills and challenges: Does the programme or project effectively use the skills of those involved and stretch them? Or are they kept within what they can do (and so risk boredom) or thrown in the deep end without the resources to get themselves out (and so risk fear)?

Refinement: How does the activity allow for practice, repetition and fine tuning?

While this is a significant description of the climate needed to bring forth creative practice, Cutler's work also makes it clear that creativity is not solely a feature of individuals alone: it is a shared, constructed and collaborative experience. It makes more sense to talk of 'our' rather than 'my' or 'your' creativity, for instance, so when it comes to our own thoughts about how we make our own children more creative, and how to prevent their creativity being stifled, then starting with ourselves – and how we are creative *with* our children (not *on* them or *to* them or *at* them) – is indeed an excellent place to start.

Towards creative relationships: constructing pedagogies for creative practice

Craft (2002) envisages creative practice as something of which all individuals are capable: a function such as breathing or digestion, which we carry out unconsciously and automatically in order to get us through our daily lives. Creativity is not the exclusive preserve of the rich, famous, artistic genius, but is a phenomenon that we all share, irrespective of age, class, gender, race, ability or impairment. It is a frighteningly democratic and democratising process and thus might, one would think, be an easy enough matter to identify when '*little-c creativity*' or '*possibility thinking*' (as Craft, 2002, refers to it) is present:

> Little-c creativity … focuses on the resourcefulness and agency of ordinary people … it refers to an ability to route find, successfully charting new courses through everyday challenges … It involves being imaginative, being original/innovative, stepping at times outside of convention, going beyond the obvious, being self-aware of all of this in taking active, conscious, and intentional action in the world. It is not, necessarily, linked to a product outcome. (Craft, 2002: 56)

Were it such a simple matter to identify the subconscious, automatic – and perhaps invisible – nature of creativity, however, there would be no need for chapters like this or the myriad texts attempting to explain how creativity can be encouraged.

What is offered here is a methodology of how creative practice within early childhood settings can be developed from the most unlikeliest of sources: mess, scrap and rubbish (as demonstrated in the Midas project below).

Creative learning through recycling: the Midas Touch Project, St Helens

The Midas Touch Project was set up as a four-week pilot in March 2010 in St Helens, Merseyside, funded by the Find Your Talent programme, a national pilot scheme to encourage children and young people to participate in cultural activities, both in and out of settings.

Midas Touch was a transformative learning programme for very young children and their families and carers that aimed to enhance their sense of awe and wonder in their everyday lives. Using recycled, 'ordinary' objects as tools of play, work and learning, the Midas Touch programme aimed to uncover the unusual within the usual, the strange in the familiar, and the beauty within the unsuspecting. It relied on the metamorphosis of recycled, discarded and apparently worthless objects, their incorporation into challenging learning experiences and the documentation of children's learning for its affects and effects.

The Midas Touch Project was based on the *Remida* approaches of Reggio Emilia in Italy, where an early childhood practitioner (pedagogue Laura Grindley) and an artist (atelierista Michiko Fujii) worked collaboratively to enhance children's learning and promote the idea that waste materials can be resources. The team also wanted to adapt some key principles from the Reggio Emilia approach. These were:

- Children must have some control over the direction of their learning.
- Children must be able to learn through experiences of touching, moving, listening, seeing and hearing.
- Children have a relationship with other children and with material items in the world that children must be allowed to explore.
- Children must have endless ways and opportunities to express themselves.

Another vital factor within the project was the role of the adult, whether that be a practitioner or a parent/carer. The role of the adult within Midas Touch was to be the listener, the observer and a compass. Children were able to explore their interests through processes that did not necessarily lead to an end product. The adult could observe and listen to their children's interests, views and opinions and act as a compass by guiding their learning through appropriate questions, which would not impose their own views and opinions, but extend the child's learning. The project provided an opportunity for the practitioner and the child to go on a learning journey together which led to the opportunity to engage in sustained shared thinking. This led to a better understanding of the children in their care by making clear their interests, opinions and schemas of play, which in turn would help to better support a child's learning.

Planning, reflection and documentation were essential elements of the four-week pilot project. These elements are very important in the EYFS requirements. Each week involved suggesting a loose theme relating to the objects used: plastics, wood and metal, natural materials, and blacks and whites. The majority of the planning was emergent and reflective, looking at observations and reflections from the previous week. This meant that materials were introduced to extend learning and interests, such as a variety of mark making media and real tools. Children's learning was observed and documented in such ways as taking photographs, recording videos and making written observations. This documentation was used to enhance learning opportunities while at the Midas Touch Project, but also made into books and wall displays to share with children, parents/carers, practitioners and the community.

Case study

Midas Touch case study: The Gunpowder Plot

Along with three other Reception class children, five nursery children and two teachers, Adam and Levi attended several Midas Touch sessions. During Session One, Adam and Levi were particularly keen to explore the Midas Touch environment. We laid out an assortment of plastic objects which the two boys searched through extensively, tipping and emptying different containers and spreading all the objects they could find onto the floor. It seemed that they were not used to this amount of freedom and wanted to explore everything that the space had to offer.

The following week, however, we shifted the focus slightly by introducing wood and metal objects and tools in addition to the smaller plastic objects. Upon their return, Adam and Levi were drawn to a box of bike parts and began to think about different ways to attach or join the metal parts together. They discovered a box containing real tools, such as a hammer and pliers. It was clear that they were particularly keen to use these tools, having never had the opportunity to use them before. They continued to use these throughout the rest of the project. In particular,

(Continued)

(Continued)

they were drawn to the hammer which they would share and interact with in a number of ways. The hammer became a tool for construction, role-play, mark making and noise making.

Adam and Levi returned to the work area that they had been exploring the previous week. Taking turns, they picked up a hammer and began to bash it against the wooden sleepers and planks, listening to the different sounds they made. Michiko had brought some charcoal and mark making tools out for some of the other children and Adam picked up a piece of willow charcoal. He found a piece of tree bark and began to blacken it with the charcoal. He and Levi then proceeded to smash pieces of charcoal with the hammer and the piece of tree bark.

Michiko suggested that they move into the back space so that they could have more room and Adam asked if he could have more charcoal. He and Levi hammered away in their work area. They listened to the noises, explored the marks and then realised that the charcoal released a kind of dust as it was hit by the hammer.

'I've found smoke!' Adam exclaimed. 'It's gunpowder!' He then said to Michiko, 'You brought gunpowder ... let's make some more!' The two boys continued to hammer away throughout the session and then took turns to clean up the mess, which they actually seemed to really enjoy.

Our identified EYFS focus for each session was as described by the Reception teacher:

> I loved the approach. I believe it's how children should learn in an ideal world – exploring their own ideas. We are there to scaffold that learning. (Reception teacher)

Laura, Michiko and the Reception teacher worked together over the four-week project to allow Adam and Levi to explore the space and materials in a way that they were not used to normally. The teacher identified a number of potential risks or hazards within the space, but despite this she recognised the benefits of allowing the boys to explore freely. Laura, Michiko and the teacher brushed aside any preconceived ideas or judgements about the boys and engaged with them equally at their level throughout the four sessions.

Despite her fears, the teacher trusted Michiko and Laura to work with Adam and Levi. Laura and Michiko took the teacher's approval as an unspoken sign of trust and support, which encouraged them to support Adam and Levi's development even further. All three wanted the boys to have an experience that would enhance their confidence, communication and creativity as well as working towards achieving the identified EYFS goals.

What got in the way?

Although 'The Gunpowder Plot' was a one-off observation of creative play, when creating similar experiences it is likely there will be constraints that stand in the way. It seems that we now live in a risk-averse society where we are stopping children from experiencing and exploring due to our fear of risk. Letting children experience things first-hand, however, not only satisfies their curiosity but allows them to risk-assess for themselves.

Consumerism and curriculum also play a part in holding back these kinds of experiences for children. In early childhood settings we are often left with very little time for truly open-ended play and give children less opportunity to explore with open-ended resources. It seems that we are all too ready to open an educational catalogue and buy shiny, bright new toys and prescriptive resources that unintentionally limit children's creativity.

> If our ultimate goal is to ensure that children grow up as engaged, self-confident, responsible, and resilient individuals who feel they have some control over their destinies and are alive to the consequences of their actions, childhood needs to include frequent, unregulated, self-directed contact with people and places beyond the immediate spheres of family and school, and the chance to learn from their mistakes. (Gill, 2008)

Overcoming obstacles

After the end of the first session, Laura and Michiko recognised that Adam and Levi had had a lot of fun tipping and piling materials onto the floor. They decided to introduce different tools in the second session as a way of encouraging the boys to focus their attention in a way that was more constructive. As the theme for Session Two was wood and metal, the idea of introducing tools fitted in nicely.

(Continued)

(Continued)

Figure 25.2 *Children exploring a variety of objects*

Sure enough, the boys were drawn to certain real tools as they began to investigate a corner where different metal and wooden parts were laid out. This interest was recognised by Laura, Michiko and the teacher and, rather than preventing Adam and Levi from exploring their interests further, the three adults sat by the two boys and supported them as they pursued their interest over the four weeks. The Midas Touch space became an 'enabling environment' where a mutual level of trust was agreed between adults and children. Materials were organised throughout different parts of the project space to encourage different types of activity for different needs and interests.

Outcomes

After the Midas Touch project had finished, we returned to the school a few months later to catch up with Adam, Levi and the teacher. We brought our book of photos and learning journeys and spent some time talking about our experiences with the hammer, the real tools, the charcoal and the scary gunpowder!

The teacher discussed her perceptions of the project and also showed photographs which demonstrated ways she had tried to extend the approach back in school. For Levi and Adam it was a chance to revisit the experience by looking at photos and talking about what we had done.

Adam, on working with wood and real tools:

I was making ... church, drawing on it and then putting it on and banging it and then it goes everywhere. That's what I did with the charcoal. Levi did the same as me. He let me have the hammer, didn't he? And we swapped. The teacher took pictures. When I banged it [the charcoal] it went everywhere ... gunpowder. And I cleaned up.

On what was important to him:

The hammer.

The teacher, on noticing outcomes:

Levi's dad is absolutely beaming and he's just asked me at the door [after the reunion with the two boys], 'How did it go? Did he enjoy himself?' His dad came on numerous occasions and said what a difference it's made to him, they've seen the difference at home. He seems much more confident.

On the future:

The nursery teacher and I both know the principles of early education and we agree with them 100 per cent. But putting them into a school setting when you've got your constraints, we find it difficult. So for us to actually come in [to the Midas Touch] and operate in that system, it was lovely. So we've decided we are going to definitely try and, within the boundaries, adopt those principles ... your way.

Reflective tasks

- One of the conflicts that practitioners report is that an overemphasis on the creative nature of learning conflicts with the requirements to raise standards. But are they to be mutually exclusive? Does your setting perceive a conflict between a

(Continued)

(Continued)

creative curriculum and a standards-raising agenda? And what reasons are given, if any, for this conflict?

- How are recycled materials used in your setting for creative learning purposes? Can you identify how you might use those resources to better inform your practice? How would you go about documenting the learning that arises from this type of work?

- The open-ended approach to learning demonstrated by the Midas Touch Project has several risks associated with it. How does your setting respond to risk? Is it one where more time is spent on creating new learning opportunities or on cutting costs? Does your management team spend more time during meetings generating new ideas or discussing performance metrics? What might constitute a risk-tolerant or risk-averse culture in your setting?

Summary

This chapter has addressed the complexities of trying to approach creativity. Our views about creativity are often influenced by our personal experiences and attitudes towards creative practice. It is important in order to meet the EYFS prime area of expressive arts and design to develop a theoretical understanding of creativity when we plan activities to promote creativity in early childhood education and care. As has been demonstrated with the other prime areas of development identified in the EYFS, creativity can be a solitary activity, yet a social activity at one and the same time. It is argued that when creativity is seen as a social activity with play as a tool then children are able to produce outcomes that are beyond adults' expectations.

Key points to remember

- 'Being creative' is a rich and extensive concept and it requires the encouragement and challenge of children's experiences of creativity.

- Early childhood settings should create opportunities for children to be able to explore different materials and ideas, and to be able to engage in self-expression so that they have the best possible chance to embark upon a creative development journey.

- Creativity is a social activity and as such it is a shared, constructed and collaborative experience.

Points for discussion

- What are your personal experiences and perceptions of, and attitudes towards, creativity? Considering the example of Cutler's work, can you remember whether you were given opportunities to explore creativity in a shared, constructed and collaborative way?

- Within the statutory framework for the EYFS, creativity is not explicitly referred to as one of the specific areas in which providers must support children. Why do you think this is?

- How do staff and parents in your setting accept the importance of 'mess'? What sources of 'mess' or 'scrap' are used in your setting and what role do you think they have in promoting creative learning?

Further reading

Abbott L. and Nutbrown, C. (2001) *Experiencing Reggio Emilia: Implications for Pre-school Provision*. Buckingham: Open University Press.
Bruce, T. (2011) *Cultivating Creativity in Babies, Toddlers and Young Children*, 2nd edn. London: Hodder and Stoughton.
Sefton-Green, J. (2008) *Creative Learning*. London: Creative Partnerships.

Articles

Sternberg, R.J., Kaufman, J.C., and Pretz, J.E. (2004) 'A propulsion model of creative leadership', *Creativity and Innovation Management*, 13 (3): 145–53.

Useful websites

Creative Partnerships, national creative learning programme: www.creative-partnerships.com

Sightlines, the national agency for Reggio Emilia schools: www.sightlines-initiative.com

References

Craft, A. (2002) *Creativity and Early Years Education: A Lifewide Foundation*. London/New York: Continuum.
Cutler, A. (2005) *Signposting Creative Learning*. Kent: Creative Partnerships.

Daniels, H. (2001) *Vygotsky and Pedagogy*. London: Routledge.

DfE (Department of Education) (2014) *Statutory Framework for the Early Years Foundation Stage: Setting the Standards for Learning, Development and Care for Children from Birth to Five*. London: DfE.

Gill, T. (2008) 'No fear – growing up in a risk averse society', *Children, Youth and Environments*, 18 (1).

Okri, B. (1997) 'Newton's child', in *A Way of Being Free*. London: Phoenix.

Robinson, K. (1999) *All Our Futures: Creativity, Culture and Education*. London: National Advisory Committee on Creative and Cultural Education.

Stern, D. (1985) *The Interpersonal World of the Infant*. New York: Basic Books.

Sternberg R.J., Kaufman J.C. and Pretz J.E. (2004) 'A propulsion model of creative leadership', *Creativity and Innovation Management*, 13 (3): 145–53.

Trevarthen, C. (1993) 'The self born in intersubjectivity: the psychology of an infant communicating', in U. Neisser (ed.), *The Perceived Self*. Cambridge: Cambridge University Press.

Vygotsky, L.S. (1978) *Mind in Society: The Development of Higher Psychological Processes*. Cambridge, MA: Harvard University Press.

Woolf, F. and Belloli, J. (2005) *Reflect and Review: The Arts and Creativity in Early Years*. London: Arts Council of England.

Wright, B. (2001–2002) Review of D. Trotter, *Cooking with Mud: The Idea of Mess in Nineteenth-century Art and Fiction*, Oxford: Oxford University Press. 2000. In: *Nineteenth-Century French Studies*, 30 (1 and 2): 179–82.

Index